D0929579

cE

Robert M. Stern is Professor of
Economics at the University of Michigan.
He has served as consultant for the
United Nations Conference on Trade and
Development and for the Bureau of
Economic Affairs of the U.S. Office of
International Trade. He has written two
other books, *Foreign Trade and Economic
Growth in Italy* and *Quantitative
International Economics* (with Edward E.
Leamer), and his writings have appeared
internationally in major professional
journals.

THE BALANCE OF PAYMENTS
THEORY AND ECONOMIC POLICY

THE BALANCE OF PAYMENTS

THEORY AND ECONOMIC POLICY

Robert M. Stern

University of Michigan

MACMILLAN

ABOUT THE AUTHOR

Robert M. Stern is Professor of Economics at the University of Michigan. He has served as consultant for the United Nations Conference on Trade and Development and for the Bureau of Economic Affairs of the Office of International Trade of the U.S. State Department. He has written two other books, *Foreign Trade and Economic Growth in Italy* and *Quantitative International Economics* (with Edward E. Leamer) and his writings have appeared internationally in major professional economic journals.

© Robert M. Stern 1973

00116650 2

All rights reserved. No part of this publication may be reproduced or transmitted, in any form or by any means, without permission.

First published in the United States 1973
First published in the United Kingdom 1973

Published by
THE MACMILLAN PRESS LTD
London and Basingstoke
Associated companies in New York Dublin
Melbourne Johannesburg and Madras

SBN 333 14145 8

Printed in the United States by
Ber-Glad Service, Inc.
Arlington Heights, Illinois

To Lucetta

Foreword

The purpose of the Aldine Treatises in Modern Economics is to enable authorities in a particular field of economics, and experts on a particular problem, to make their knowledge available to others in the form they find easiest and most convenient. Our intention is to free them from an insistence on complete coverage of a conventionally defined subject, which deters many leading economists from writing a book instead of a series of articles or induces them to suppress originality for the sake of orthodoxy, and from an obligation to produce a standard number of pages, which encourages the submergence of judgment of relevance in a pudding of irrelevant detail. The Aldine Treatises seek to encourage good economists to say what they want to say to their fellow economists, in as little or as much space as they consider necessary to the purpose.

The theory of the balance of payments, what determines it and how it may be influenced by governmental economic policies, was two decades or so ago a subject of little interest to American economists. The United States appeared to have an impregnably strong balance-of-payments position, and the only important issue appeared to be how to manage U.S. aid, trade, and foreign investment policies so as to avoid imposing too much strain on foreign countries. But the position has changed rapidly, and for the past fifteen years the United States has had a balance-of-payments deficit which it has tried with repeated lack of success to remedy by one policy device after another—culminating in the so-called "dollar crisis" of August 15, 1971 and its resolution (at least temporarily) by the "Smithsonian agreement" of December 18, 1971. The difficulties the United States administration has experienced strongly suggests that there is a lack of understanding of basic principles at the highest policy-making levels, and a corresponding need for a book that brings together these principles as they have evolved through the empirical and theoretical research of a host of scholars in many different countries, directed not at the policy-makers but at the economists who sooner or later will have either to make policy decisions or to understand and interpret policies determined by others.

During the same period, there has been a rapid development of the theory of the balance of payments, in terms of both its theoretical structure and the problems with which it has been concerned.

With respect to structure, the 1930s produced the "elasticity approach" to devaluation, an approach which explicitly or implicitly assumed the existence of unemployed resources that could absorb the multiplier effects of de-valuation-induced changes in the demand for domestic output. That approach proved extremely unsatisfactory in the postwar-two situation of general inflationary pressure, and provoked the production of the rival "absorption approach." The synthesis of the two was found in the recognition that to achieve the two targets of internal balance (full employment, assumed to be non-inflationary) and external balance (equilibrium in the balance of pay-ments) a nation needed two policy instruments—one to adjust aggregate demand to aggregate supply capacity, another to allocate demand between domestic and foreign goods so as to match total (foreign and domestic) demand for domestic goods with supply capacity—though these had to be employed in tandem. The former instrument was identified with fiscal and monetary demand-management policy, the latter with exchange rate policy. Subsequently, with the growing reluctance of nations to resort to exchange rate adjustment, there has emerged the theory of the fiscal-monetary mix, according to which fiscal and monetary policy operate differentially on the capital account of the balance of payments, so that even with a fixed exchange rate a nation can achieve its two policy objectives by mixing fiscal expansion (or constraint) and monetary contraction (or expansion) in the right pro-portions.

With respect to problems, theoretical attention has come to be focused once again on the relation between spot and forward exchange rates and the associated question of private speculation; on the case for floating exchange rates as a solution to the problems of the fixed rate system; and on a whole range of issues involved in the reformation of the present international monetary system. In addition, some economists have begun to question the "elasticities approach" inherited from the 1930s and to explore the monetary implications of the reserve flows associated with balance-of-payments disequilibria.

The author of this Treatise, Robert M. Stern, is eminently qualified to survey this burgeoning literature and to relate it to current problems in the area of the balance of payments and international monetary reform. He is one of a very small group of American economists who have devoted themselves to the field of international economics—he took his graduate training at Columbia University—and he is distinguished by his capacity to roam freely over the three major branches of the field: the pure theory of international trade, the theory of the international monetary system, and techniques and applications of empirical research on international trade and monetary problems. In this book, the emphasis is on the analysis of the international monetary system; but that analysis is enriched by Professor Stern's familiarity with the field as a whole, and his sense of the relevance of material from the cognate branches to the problem of the balance of payments. He does not attempt to provide simple answers to immediately pressing problems. Instead, he seeks to marshall the relevant principles and frameworks of analysis that the student (at whatever level) will need to understand these problems, into a coherent and consistent account of the state and main propositions of contemporary balance-of-payments theory. I believe that he has done this with consummate scholarship and care, and that the resulting volume amply satisfies the standards that the Aldine Treatises were intended to meet.

HARRY G. JOHNSON

Preface

This book is an outgrowth of the material prepared for a beginning graduate course in international finance that I taught at Michigan for a number of years during the 1960's. It is not merely a transcription of notes, however, since in writing it I found it necessary to reread much of the basic literature and to rethink many issues on which I was unclear. It was my original intention to cover in one book the important theoretical, empirical, and policy issues in international finance. However, the empirical issues were too detailed and complex for inclusion here and were therefore treated separately in Chapters 2–5 of the book, *Quantitative International Economics*, co-authored by Edward E. Leamer and myself (1970). It was also not possible in the present book to examine international financial markets and institutions in great detail. Ample references on these matters have been supplied accordingly.

The fact that the international monetary system has been in a state of turmoil since the late 1960s has made this an exciting book to write. Yet it has also been frustrating, especially since the pace of events was so rapid at times that I feared that some chapters would become prematurely obsolete. If the book was ever to be finished, it was obviously impossible to remain completely current and, in late 1971, to be clairvoyant about the course of events. In any case, much of the theoretical material presented is independent of current events, although some of the issues may recede in importance as conditions change. The concluding chapter dealing with problems of the international monetary system proved particularly difficult to write since some assumptions had to be made about how in fact the system might evolve. Because of the uncertainties involved regarding exchange rates and reserve assets in late 1971, the options for changing the system were discussed in general terms only.

In preparing a work of this scope, one incurs numerous intellectual debts. My greatest ones are to my former graduate students at Michigan, in particular Edward E. Leamer, Jay H. Levin, Johan A. Lybeck, John E. Morton, and J. David Richardson. All of them, together with many others in my graduate course and research seminar, supplied invaluable assistance, collaboration, and critical comments on drafts of the individual chapters. I am extremely grateful to Harry G. Johnson, editor of this series, for his painstaking reading of the entire manuscript. His detailed and incisive comments were of great value in tightening up and clarifying the presentation in many places. I benefited immeasurably from the many useful comments and insights supplied by J. David Richardson and Warren L. Smith, who also read the entire manuscript. Finally, several colleagues and friends read and commented upon individual chapters, and I am grateful to them. They include: Jean-Paul Abraham, William R. Allen, James M. Arrowsmith, Max Corden, Alan V. Deardorff, Gunter Dufey, Robert S. Holbrook, Norman C. Miller, Bernard E. Munk, Martin F. J. Prachowny, Don E. Roper, Ian G. Stewart, and Wolfgang F. Stolper. Richard W. Kopcke and Peter Hooper assisted me in checking numerous details and compiling the indexes.

I would like to express my gratitude to the National Science Foundation for supporting research in international economics at Michigan under grants GS–943, 2010, and 3073. The released time that they provided made it possible for me to direct this research in conjunction with the preparation of this book.

I owe special thanks to Patricia G. Rapley for her consummate skill, patience, and good humor in typing the various drafts of the manuscript. The illustrations were prepared by Leslie R. Thurston.

This book is dedicated to my wife, Lucetta. She saw it and me through the most trying periods, including those when there may have been some confusion about my labor of love.

ROBERT M. STERN

Contents

THE BALANCE OF PAYMENTS
THEORY AND ECONOMIC POLICY

1

Balance-of-Payments Concepts and
Measurement

Our concern in the present chapter is the arrangement and interpretation of balance-of-payments information for purposes of economic analysis and policy assessment. Balance-of-payments accounting is illustrated briefly in the appendix to this chapter. Those interested in greater detail, especially on matters related to accounting, are advised to consult specialized sources.[1]

Balance-of-Payments Concepts

It is appropriate to begin by a definition: *the balance of payments is a summary statement of all economic transactions between the residents of one country and the rest of the world, covering some given period of time.*

Like many definitions, this one requires clarification, especially with respect to the coverage and valuation of economic transactions and the criteria for determining residency. The coverage of economic transactions refers to both commercial trade dealings and noncommercial transfers, which may or may not be effected through the foreign exchange markets and which may not be satisfactorily recorded because of inadequacies in the system of data collection. Particularly difficult questions of valuation are posed by noncommercial transactions and by transactions that take place between domestic and foreign-based units of individual corporations. The determination of residency should ordinarily not be difficult, but even here questions may arise concerning the treatment of overseas military forces and embassies, corporate subsidiaries, and international organizations.[2]

1. See, for example, International Monetary Fund (1961) and Powelson (1955, Chaps. 21–22).
2. For some illustrations and further discussion of these matters of coverage, valuation, and residency with respect to the United States balance-of-payments accounts, see the Bernstein Report, Review Committee for Balance of Payments Statistics (1965, pp. 23–97) and Cooper (1966, pp. 380–83).

1

Transactions are recorded in principle on a double-entry bookkeeping basis. Each transaction entered in the accounts as a credit must have a corresponding debit and vice versa. The distributions commonly made in classifying the various accounts can be seen from the schematic balance of payments represented in Table 1.1 and from the illustrative transactions recorded in the appendix to this chapter. There are many possible inter-relationships among the various items shown in Table 1.1 that arise from the complexities of the market and nonmarket transactions typically recorded for an individual nation. Thus, the receipts and payments arising from merchandise and service exports and imports shown in the current account may have their counterpart debits or credits recorded in one or more of the remaining accounts.[3] The balance of payments must accordingly be looked at as a whole rather than in terms of its individual parts.

It follows from double-entry bookkeeping that the balance of payments must always balance: total debits equal total credits. When we speak therefore of a positive or negative balance or a surplus or deficit, we evidently have in mind some particular group or classification of accounts. For example, a positive balance of trade refers to an excess of merchandise exports over merchandise imports (item 1) and vice versa for a negative balance of trade. Similarly, a current–account surplus or deficit refers to the difference between receipts and payments coming from exports and imports of merchandise and services (items 1–5). As such, it represents the net contribution of foreign trade to national income and expenditure. The balances on current account and on unilateral transfers are frequently added together.[4] This balance of items 1–7 constitutes a measure of net foreign investment.[5]

The nation's long-term foreign investments, which are assumed to have a maturity in excess of one year, are recorded in item 8. These consist generally of direct investment in tangible physical assets of business firms and of portfolio investment in securities of various kinds. Item 8 may also include private short-term capital movements with maturity of less than one year, which represents changes in foreign- or domestic-currency working balances intended to facilitate the financing of regular commercial transactions or to take advantage of international differences in interest rates. There is some controversy, however, as to whether private short-term capital movements should be recorded in whole or in part in item 9 rather than in item 8. The argument for recording these movements in item 9 is that they may in large part be transitory in nature, and further, that they cannot be distinguished

---

3. For some examples, see illustrative transactions (1)–(8) in the appendix to this chapter.

4. As noted below, the balance on current account and unilateral transfers is labeled as the "balance on current account" in the official U.S. balance-of-payments tables.

5. Note further, as in illustrative transaction (15) in the appendix to this chapter, that the receipt of the allocation of Special Drawing Rights can be considered as a unilateral transfer and will thus be included as a part of net foreign investment. See also footnote 13 below.

readily from official short-term capital transactions. We shall discuss these matters more fully later in this chapter. Assume for now that all the private short-term capital transactions are recorded in item 8.

This means that items 9 and 10 in Table 1.1 represent the "balancing" or "settlement" items in the balance of payments. These items are applicable in a system in which exchange rates are fixed by virtue of the nation's monetary authority standing ready to buy and sell foreign exchange in order to keep the exchange rate at some given level or within a specified range. These official transactions may take the form of increases or decreases in short-term capital assets or liabilities or an inflow or outflow of gold or other international monetary reserves. The size of the balancing items can be interpreted consequently as a measure of the foreign exchange authority's transactions undertaken to maintain exchange-rate stability. This suggests that if we wish in this context to speak of the balance of payments being in "equilibrium," the sum of the balancing items should be equal to zero. There should, in other words, be no net movement of official short-term capital and of gold and other international reserves. This will be the case when the total debits and credits in items 1–8, commonly referred to as the items "above the line," are equal. If the total debits and credits above the line are not equal, we can then speak of a positive or negative balance, or more commonly of a balance-of-payments surplus or deficit. This surplus or deficit will be reflected "below the line" with opposite sign in the balancing items 9 and 10.[6] Since the sum of these balancing items follows directly from the difference in totals of items 1–8, it should be clear that the cause of a surplus or deficit cannot be inferred directly from particular items above the line.

The transactions recorded in Table 1.1 are sometimes interpreted according to whether they are "autonomous" or "accommodating" in character. Transactions are considered autonomous insofar as they may be assumed to have been undertaken in response to commercial incentives or political considerations that are given independently of the state of the overall balance of payments or of particular accounts. Thus, items 1–8 in Table 1.1 might be treated as autonomous. Accommodating transactions arise accordingly out of the need to fill the gap between total autonomous debits and credits. The filling of the gap by a nation's foreign exchange authority, as recorded in items 9 and 10, can therefore be considered as accommodating in nature.

---

6. If we were to assume a flexible rather than a fixed exchange-rate system, there would not be any surplus or deficit in the balance of payments except perhaps in a transitional sense. That is, the excess of credits over debits or vice versa would cause the exchange rate to vary. This would bring about changes in items 1–8 until equality of receipts and payments was attained.

Note also that we have assumed all transactions to be correctly recorded. Since in actuality credits and debits may not be matched exactly because of reporting inadequacies, there will be a need for an "errors and omissions" item above the line. This item may be substantial especially in cases where short-term capital movements are imperfectly recorded.

TABLE 1.1

Schematic Balance of Payments

	Debits (−)	*Credits* (+)
A. *Current account*		
1. Merchandise	(−)	(+)
2. Transportation	(−)	(+)
3. Tourist expenditures	(−)	(+)
4. Investment income; fees and royalties; other services	(−)	(+)
5. Military and other government expenditures	(−)	(+)
Total, 1–5	(−)	(+)
B. *Unilateral transfers*		
6. Private remittances	(−)	(+)
7. Government transfers	(−)	(+)
Total, 1–7	(−)	(+)
C. *Capital account [increase in assets or reduction in liabilities* (−)]		
8. Foreign investment; direct and portfolio	(−)	(+)
Total, 1–8ᵃ	(−)	(+)
D. *Balancing items [increase in assets or reduction in liabilities* (−)]		
9. Short-term official capital movements		
10. Gold and other international reserve movements		
Total, 1–10	(−) equals (+)	

ᵃ The difference in totals (+) or (−) of items 1–8 "above the line" measures the balance-of-payments surplus or deficit which will be reflected in the balancing items recorded "below the line" in items 9 and 10.

Our discussion of the balance of payments has focused on the transactions recorded for some given period in the past and the resultant deficit or surplus. We have thus been considering an ex post conception of what has been called the "actual" balance-of-payments deficit or surplus.[7] It is also possible to conceive of the balance of payments in an ex ante sense of transactions that would be carried out in given market conditions. The criterion of balance-of-payments "equilibrium" in this ex ante sense is again no net movement of short-term capital and of gold and other international reserves, but the qualification must be added that this equilibrium be sustainable for the given market period. This corresponds to what Machlup (1950) has called the "market" balance of payments.[8]

7. This is the terminology used by Meade (1951, p. 15).
8. According to Machlup (1950; 1964, p. 70): "A dollar deficit in a country's market balance of payments may be tentatively defined as an excess of dollar amounts effectively demanded at the given exchange rate by would-be purchasers (who are not restricted by specially adopted or discretionary government control measures) over the dollar amounts supplied at that exchange rate by would-be sellers (who are not motivated by a desire to support the exchange rate)."

It is instructive to compare Machlup's market balance with another ex ante concept, the "true" or "potential" balance, which is identified with Nurkse (1945) and Meade (1951). Both Nurkse and Meade posited that equilibrium should be defined subject to two conditions: (1) given some reference point in the past, the authorities have not imposed additional trade or payments restrictions in order to reach equilibrium; and (2) equilibrium is not attained unless there is a simultaneous attainment of full employment without price inflation. What is noteworthy about these conditions, as Johnson (1951) and Machlup (1950) have emphasized, is that they result in a definition of equilibrium that depends on political value judgments concerning the use of restrictions and the desirable level of employment. Prohibiting the use of restrictions overlooks their possible welfare benefits under certain circumstances and creates a perhaps unwarranted bias in favor of general price adjustments as a means of restoring equilibrium. This latter "ideological" point applies also to the full-employment condition, which as Machlup (1950; 1964, p. 124) has noted, amounts to "infusing a political philosophy or programme into the concept of equilibrium."

This is not to say that value judgments have no place in economic analysis. The point is that these judgments should not be used in defining analytical concepts, but rather should furnish criteria in evaluating the workings of particular measures of economic policy. The Nurkse-Meade equilibrium concept might thus be more properly labelled as the "full-employment balance."[9] This would then make it a variant of what Machlup (1950; 1964, p. 78) has called the "programme balance," which reflects the desires of the authorities to achieve certain specified national goals such as full employment or some particular rate of economic growth.

The question of specifying balance-of-payments equilibrium subject to the aforementioned conditions is not merely terminological in nature. For once it is granted that the authorities will carry our various policies to achieve certain national goals,[10] it may no longer be possible to retain the aforementioned distinction between autonomous and accommodating transactions and therefore to talk unambiguously about a certain sized surplus or deficit in the balance of payments. There is a continuous interaction between transactions and changes in policies. Transactions may be undertaken as a consequence of particular changes in policy at home and abroad. And by the same token, changes in policy may be introduced in order to offset the effects of particular transactions that may contribute to balance-of-payments

9. Cf. Machlup (1950; 1964, p. 126). To be more realistic, we might conceive of alternative full-employment balances subject to given tradeoffs between price inflation and unemployment as embodied in a modified Phillips curve. See Smith (1970, pp. 366–68 and 381–83) for a treatment of the modified Phillips curve.
10. We shall have more to say about the use of domestic monetary and fiscal policies for the attainment of external and internal equilibrium in the following chapters, particularly Chapter 10.

disequilibrium. There is, in other words, a shifting of cause and effect that makes it difficult to distinguish autonomous from accommodating transactions, and vice versa. The consequence is that full-employment balance-of-payments equilibrium cannot be determined precisely in an ex ante sense.

There is no unambiguous way in an actual, ex post statement of the balance of payments for any given time period to separate the autonomous from the accommodating items. It is possible, of course, to arrange the balance-of-payments accounts in a variety of manners for purposes of analysis. But it should remain clear that insofar as any arrangement hinges on imputing specific motivations of an autonomous or accommodating nature to particular classes of transactions, it is bound to involve some degree of arbitrariness.

In most countries great importance has not been attached to different possible arrangements of the balance of payments. In the United States, however, and to a lesser extent in the United Kingdom, these matters have provoked extended discussion and controversy. This has been the case especially in view of the change in the U.S. balance-of-payments position after 1958 and the special role that the dollar plays in financing world trade and in serving as a reserve currency. We turn next, therefore, to the major issues involved in the various alternative measurements of the U.S. balance of payments.

Alternative Measurements of the U.S. Balance of Payments

The schematic balance of payments in Table 1.1 was intentionally over-simplified in order to focus attention on the differences in various concepts. It would thus be expected that the actual balance of payments for a given country would normally contain a greater amount of detail particularly in the capital account and in the balancing items. Some flavor of such detail can be had from Table 1.2, which indicates the three main groupings of accounts that are presently (1971) in use by the U.S.,[11] and from the illustrative transactions recorded and summarized in the appendix to this chapter. The actual balances corresponding to Table 1.2 are shown with minor modification for 1968–71 in Table 1.3. It is evident in reading down these tables that the two balances differ according to whether particular accounts are placed below or above the line.

The balance on goods and services indicated in Table 1.3 is equal to net exports in the U.S. national income and product accounts. It corresponds to items 1–5 in Table 1.1. The balance on current account in Table 1.3 is equal

---

11. See the source of Table 1.2 for an extended discussion of the merits and drawbacks of the different groupings.

TABLE 1.2

Three Kinds of Summary Groupings of U.S. International Transactions

---

I. Using concept of "balance on current account and long-term capital"

Goods and services

Remittances, pensions, and other transfers

U.S. Government grants, capital flows, nonscheduled repayments of U.S. Government assets, U.S. Government nonliquid liabilities to other than foreign official reserve agencies

Long-term private capital flows, U.S. and foreign
  Direct investments abroad and in the U.S.
  Foreign securities and U.S. securities other than Treasury issues
  Other (bank and nonbank)

Balance on Current Account and Long-Term Capital

II. Using concept of "net liquidity"

Balance on current account and long-term capital
Nonliquid short-term private capital flows, U.S. and foreign
  Claims reported by U.S. banks and nonbanks
  Liabilities reported by U.S. nonbanks
Allocation of Special Drawing Rights (SDR's)
Errors and omissions, net

Net Liquidity Balance

III. Using concept of "official reserve transactions"

Net liquidity balance
Liquid private capital flows, net
  Liquid claims reported by U.S. banks and nonbanks
  Liquid liabilities to foreign commercial banks, international and regional organizations, and other foreigners

---

Official Reserve Transactions Balance

Financed by changes in:
  Nonliquid liabilities to foreign official agencies reported by U.S. Government and U.S. banks
  Liquid liabilities to foreign official agencies
  U.S. official reserve assets, net
    Gold, SDR's, convertible currencies, and gold tranche position in IMF

SOURCE: Adapted from U.S. Department of Commerce, Office of Business Economics, *Survey of Current Business,* 51 (June 1971), 30.

to net foreign investment in the U.S. national income and product accounts. It corresponds to items 1–7 in Table 1.1.

The rationale of the "balance on current account and long-term capital" is to distinguish those items above the line that are essentially more stable

TABLE 1.3

The U.S. Balance of Payments, 1968–71
(Billions of Dollars)

(Credits +; debits −)	1968	1969	1970	1971
1. Goods	+0.6	+0.7	+2.1	−2.9
2. Services	+1.9	+1.3	+1.5	+3.6
Balance on goods and services[a]	+2.5	+2.0	+3.6	+0.7
3. Personal and U.S. Government transfers	−2.9	−2.9	−3.2	−3.5
Balance on current account[b]	−0.4	−0.9	+0.4	−2.8
4. U.S. Government capital flows, unscheduled repayments, and nonliquid liabilities	−2.2	−1.9	−2.0	−2.4
5. Long-term private capital flows, U.S. and foreign	+1.2	−0.1	−1.5	−4.1
Balance on current account and long-term capital	−1.3	−2.9	−3.0	−9.3
6. Nonliquid short-term private capital flows, U.S. and foreign	+0.2	−0.6	−0.5	−2.5
7. Allocation of SDR's	—	—	+0.9	+0.7
8. Errors and omissions	−0.5	−2.6	−1.1	−10.9
Net liquidity balance	−1.6	−6.1	−3.9	−22.0
9. Liquid private claims (increase in assets −)	−0.6	+0.1	+0.3	−1.1
10. Liquid private liabilities (increase in liabilities +)	+3.8	+8.7	−6.2	−6.7
Official reserve transactions balance	+1.6	+2.7	−9.8	−29.8
11. Financed by changes in (increase in liabilities +; increase in assets −)				
a. Nonliquid liabilities to foreign official agencies	+2.3	−1.0	−0.3	−0.2
b. Liquid liabilities to foreign official agencies	−3.1	−0.5	+7.6	+27.6
c. U.S. official reserve assets	−0.9	−1.2	+2.5	+2.4

[a] Equal to net exports of goods and services in national income and product accounts.
[b] Equal to net foreign investment in national income and product accounts. Corresponds to balance on current account and unilateral transfers (items 1–7) in Table 1.1.
SOURCE: Same as Table 1.2 and later issues.

over time and that evolve regularly and predictably from underlying commercial and political considerations.[12] The items below the line are supposed, in contrast, to be more volatile and transitory. Separation of these latter items has been further justified by Lary (1963, pp. 142–54), for example, on

12. This balance on current account and long-term capital is practically the same as the balance on "basic" transactions that was used in official U.S. balance-of-payments tables during the 1950's and early 1960's and in the U.K. until the late 1960's. The main difference is the inclusion now above the line of nonscheduled repayments of U.S. Government assets and nonliquid liabilities to other than foreign official reserve agencies.

the grounds that they are particularly sensitive to changes in monetary policy. However, as Johnson (1964, pp. 15–18) and Kindleberger (1969b, pp. 880–81) have noted, there are several difficulties with this arrangement. It is by no means clear that merchandise, services, unilateral transfers, and long-term capital transactions are necessarily stable and slowly growing as compared, say, to certain types of short-term capital movements designed to build up working balances. It may also be misleading to draw too fine a distinction between long-term and short-term capital. The reason is that relatively large flows of short-term capital may lurk in the direct- and portfolio-investment totals, while short-term credits may in effect be long-term in nature if they are repeatedly renewed. The special financial transactions on U.S. Government account may, furthermore, be sporadic rather than regular in occurrence. Finally, it cannot be said that the transactions above and below the line respond to different sets of forces. Thus, many of the basic transactions above the line will be highly sensitive to monetary policy especially when the object is to influence domestic activity and the foreign balance.

The "net liquidity balance" indicated in Table 1.3 is designed to measure the change in the U.S. liquidity position, which is composed of the net changes in liquid liabilities to private foreigners, nonliquid and liquid liabilities to foreign official agencies, and U.S. official reserve assets. The point of this measure is to focus attention on the ability of the U.S. authorities to act in defense of the exchange value of the dollar. The liabilities in question consist of the claims held in the U.S. by private and official foreigners in the form of demand deposits, time deposits, money-market paper, and U.S. Government short-term securities, bonds and notes. The official reserve assets consist of the nation's stock of monetary gold, Special Drawing Rights (SDR's),[13] convertible currencies, and the gold-tranche position in the International Monetary Fund.[14]

13. SDR's are international reserve assets whose creation was authorized by amendment to the Articles of Agreement of the International Monetary Fund (IMF). SDR's are to be allocated under this amendment to member countries in proportion to their IMF quotas. Allocations of $3,414, $2,949, and $2,952 million were made on January 1, 1970, 1971, and 1972, respectively. The U.S. shares of these allocations were $867, $717, and $710 million. The totals for subsequent years will be determined by Fund members in the light of world liquidity needs. More will be said about this below.

Since an SDR allocation adds to U.S. reserves (and to those of other participating countries) and there is no corresponding increase in liabilities, both the net liquidity balance and the official reserve transactions balance are favorably affected. U.S. holdings of SDR's can also change through purchases from or sales to other countries for balance-of-payments purposes. The aforementioned balances will not be affected, however, since the change in SDR holdings will be exactly offset by the change in liquid liabilities to foreign official agencies.

14. Drawings from the Fund can be made automatically for the country's gold-tranche position, which is normally equal to the member's quota minus the Fund holding of its currency. Further drawings are limited to amounts that will not cause the Fund holdings of the member's currency to increase by more than 25 percent in any 12-month period nor to exceed 200 percent of its quota. Additional details can be found in any monthly issue of the IMF, *International Financial Statistics*.

The "net" liquidity balance is a definite improvement over the "gross" liquidity balance that had been reported in the official U.S. balance-of-payments accounts during the 1950's and 1960's.[15] The gross liquidity balance drew a somewhat artificial distinction between the transactions of private U.S. residents, which were recorded above the line, and those of private foreigners, which were recorded below the line. The rationale for this procedure was that the assets being accumulated abroad by private U.S. residents were not readily available to the U.S. authorities for use in protecting the dollar in the event of a sudden increase in the foreign official demand for gold caused by a large-scale liquidation of foreign-owned dollar claims. Whether or not the U.S. authorities were in fact powerless to effect such a repatriation of U.S. owned short-term assets abroad is an empirical question, however. But more important, the gross liquidity concept failed to take into account the far greater threat that would be created if foreign-official dollar claims were enlarged significantly as a result of an increase in the demand for foreign assets by private U.S. residents who decided for some reason to liquidate assets of all kinds held in the U.S. An additional drawback of the gross liquidity balance was in the handling of special financial transactions that shifted funds of foreign official agencies from liquid to presumably nonliquid categories. This type of window dressing improved the gross liquidity balance, but worsened it when the transaction was subsequently reversed.

However, the net liquidity balance is not without its problems. It will be noted, first, that net errors and omissions are recorded above the line. To the extent that this represents unrecorded outflows of U.S. short-term funds to the Eurodollar market especially,[16] U.S. claims on foreigners will be understated and the net liquidity deficit therefore overstated. A second difficulty is in distinguishing liquid from nonliquid claims and liabilities. This is in part a problem of information since adequate data are not available on all the various forms in which the claims are held and particularly on the motivations—whether short- or long-term—of the holders of the claims. A sizable part of the U.S. bank liabilities to foreigners may also be nonliquid insofar as they include custody liabilities for customers and compensating balances held against loans to foreigners.

The balance on "official reserve transactions" recorded in Table 1.3 is essentially the same as the balance on "official settlements" recommended in the (Bernstein) report of the Review Committee for Balance of Payments

15. See Lederer (1963) for an extended discussion and defense of the gross liquidity balance.
16. The Eurodollar market, which is centered primarily in London, is one in which commercial banks accept interest-bearing deposits denominated in foreign currencies, mainly dollars, and then relend these funds in the same or some other currency. For a description and analysis of this market, see Einzig (1965), Clendenning (1970), Little (1969), and the annual reports of the Bank for International Settlements (BIS). See the appendix to this chapter for some illustrative transactions involving the Eurodollar market.

Statistics (1965).[17] In contrast to the net liquidity balance, the balance on official reserve transactions records below the line only the changes in U.S. liabilities to foreign official reserve agencies and changes in U.S. official reserve assets. That this change in arrangements can yield strikingly different results is evident in Table 1.3. Thus, in 1969, the net liquidity balance showed a $6.1 billion *deficit* and the balance on official reserve transactions a $2.7 billion *surplus*. In 1970, the net liquidity *deficit* was $3.9 billion and the official reserve transactions *deficit* was $9.8 billion. The deficits for 1971 were $22.0 and $29.8 billion, respectively.[18]

The purpose of the balance on official reserve transactions, in the Review Committee's words (1965, pp. 109–10), is "to measure the gap between the normal supply of and demand for foreign exchange—a gap which the monetary authorities here and abroad, must fill by adding to, or drawing down, their reserve assets if exchange rates are to be held stable.... The size of these transactions in international reserves provides the best available measure of the market intervention that has been necessary, of the gaps that have had to be filled, and hence of payment disequilibrium."

Cooper (1966, pp. 387–89) has pointed out two important difficulties with the concept of the balance on official reserve transactions. The first has to do with whether the "normal supply of and demand for foreign exchange" can be determined precisely. In recommending that U.S. liquid liabilities to private foreigners be recorded above the line, the assumption is that these balances are held exclusively to finance ordinary commercial transactions. This may not be the case, however, insofar as changes in these balances may frequently be the result of responses by commercial banks to changes in policies designed by the U.S. and foreign monetary authorities to influence conditions domestically and in the foreign exchange market. Thus, for example, foreign central banks, by means of domestic interest-rate and forward-market exchange policies, can induce their commercial banks to hold dollars the central banks themselves would otherwise have had to hold. The balance on official reserve transactions can therefore be subjected to changes that are transitory rather than normal. The net liquidity balance would in contrast not be affected by these shufflings of U.S. claims.

The second difficulty noted by Cooper is that the balance on official reserve transactions may not be a reliable and exact measure of the foreign exchange "gaps that have had to be filled." The reason is that the disequilibrium notion of gaps to be filled is ex ante in character and cannot therefore be observed. We have noted in our earlier discussion of autonomous

17. The main difference is that prepayments to the U.S. on government debt and advance payments for future military sales are recorded above the line rather than below as recommended in the Report. For a brief discussion of the issues involved in handling prepayments, see Cooper (1966, p. 388).

18. Substantial differences exist as well in some earlier years in the 1960's. Details can be found in the periodic reports on the U.S. balance of payments published regularly in the U.S. Department of Commerce, *Survey of Current Business*.

and accommodating transactions that there is a continuous interaction between changes in policies and international transactions of all kinds. It is therefore not possible in the ex post sense to distinguish precisely settlement items from other items in the balance of payments. In other words, as Cooper put it (1966, p. 389): "The 'gap to be filled' is thus a variable one, depending on economic policies at home and abroad."[19]

It is evident that the concepts of the net liquidity and official reserve transactions balances have important drawbacks. These drawbacks stem mainly from the fact that we are dealing with variations merely in an accounting framework of ex post phenomena, whereas we would like ideally an analytical framework that would correspond to ex ante theoretical considerations. What it comes down to is that one should not use any particular concept blindly. Rather, an attempt should be made, with full realization of the conceptual problems involved, to specify alternative foreign exchange gaps as targets for purposes of economic policy.

Thus, if it is believed that the balance on official reserve transactions is a reasonable reflection of autonomous and policy factors, we might strive to attain a policy goal of a zero balance on official reserve transactions,[20] subject to the attainment of certain other specified norms such as full employment without inflation and without increased restrictions on trade and payments.[21] In principle, at least, the authorities would seek to evaluate periodically the realization of their external and internal objectives and then in this light to implement changes in policies designed to accomplish their objectives in a subsequent period. This is not to say that the implementation of proper policies is easy to achieve in actuality. Moreover, there may be certain additional complexities that affect policy making in the case of the U.S. in particular.

These additional complexities arise from the special role played by the dollar internationally in connection with the financing of world trade and in the use of the dollar as a reserve currency. Thus, if we assume that foreign

19. One further difficulty may be mentioned that has developed in connection with the "recycling" of official dollar holdings through the Eurodollar market and back to the U.S. What this involves is one central bank transferring funds to the Eurodollar market. These funds are lent to a private foreigner who converts them into domestic currency via a second central bank, and the second central bank places them back in a U.S. bank. The official reserve transactions balance will not be affected by this chain of events. But the dollar holdings of the central banks combined will be greater, which could lead to increased foreign-exchange-market pressures. See illustrative transaction (14) in the appendix to this chapter for the case in point.

20. A similar goal of zero balance would not be appropriate using the net liquidity concept in view of the important role that dollar holdings play in private international financial transactions. That is, if private foreign dollar holdings were not permitted to expand by means of a net liquidity deficit, there would be a drain upon officially held dollar reserve assets, with the possible consequence of a serious deflationary impact.

21. Again, rather than speaking in terms of full employment without inflation, the norms might refer to alternative degrees of unemployment and inflation in the sense of the Phillips curve.

dollar holdings will continue to expand to serve both trade financing and reserve purposes, the desirability of a zero balance on official reserve transactions may be subject to question. It does not follow of course that the liquidity balance should furnish the appropriate policy criterion. Rather what might be sought is a concept that would measure the provision to the rest of the world of dollar balances and monetary reserve assets by the U.S. in its capacity as a world banker and supplier of international reserve currency. We might call this concept the "net contribution to world liquidity."[22]

Shifting attention from the official reserve transactions and net liquidity balances to a different concept of this kind would clearly require important changes in the way we think about the U.S. balance of payments. Up to this point it has been assumed that all capital flows have a counterpart in the movement of real goods and services. This ignores the substantial amount of international trade in financial claims. Trade in claims may have no real counterpart. It may be highly responsive nevertheless to international economic differences in cost and demand and in credit availability, which are associated with national capital markets of varying efficiency and breadth and with variations in taste with respect to liquidity and asset-portfolio balance.

The point is that the U.S. is at one and the same time a major source of international capital for the financing of trade and a financial intermediary that provides facilities whereby money and financial claims of varying maturity can be exchanged. Thus, when the U.S. is referred to as "lending long" and "borrowing short," there are both capital-market efficiency and asset-portfolio factors involved. Once this is granted, conventional measures of balance-of-payments equilibrium can no longer be applied with clear meaning. This is especially the case since the criterion of equilibrium now cannot be specified as a zero balance, but rather must reflect some net contribution to world liquidity. The amount of this net contribution will be determined by the interplay of the forces underlying the expansion, stability, and pattern of international trade and financial transactions.[23]

The major question that all of this raises is the extent to which the dollar will continue to be used as an international reserve currency. If SDR's or some other new international reserve unit were completely to replace the dollar and agreement were reached on planned expansion of world liquidity, the proper goal of policy would be a balance-of-payments surplus as measured by the desired accretion of the country's reserves that was consistent with the attainment of its internal policy goals. But suppose, as seems likely, that SDR's and the dollar are to exist side by side for official reserve purposes. In such an event, if pressures were strongly exerted on the U.S. to reduce

22. The discussion in this and the succeeding two paragraphs draws upon ideas that have been developed especially by Kindleberger (1965), Despres *et al.* (1966), and Salant (1969).

23. The determination of optimal world liquidity will be discussed at length in Chapter 12.

sharply or to eliminate altogether its balance-of-payments deficit without compensating allowance for the growth of other international reserves, the resulting squeeze on world liquidity could have important deflationary implications for the world as a whole.

Conclusion

We have focused on various concepts of balance-of-payments equilibrium. It was suggested that an ex ante concept of balance-of-payments equilibrium may not be easily determined because of the continuous interplay between the implementation of economic policies and the carrying out of international transactions of all kinds. It may therefore be difficult to distinguish satisfactorily between autonomous and accommodating transactions and to assume some given magnitude of balance-of-payments disequilibrium for purposes of maintaining exchange-rate stability. While recognizing the importance of these reservations, we shall proceed nevertheless in much of what follows on the assumption that the conventional distinction between autonomous and accommodating items can be maintained. This assumption will serve conveniently for many purposes and will be relaxed wherever relevant.

We also had occasion to discuss briefly in the context of the U.S. balance of payments the issues involved in attempting to measure the balance on current account and long-term capital, the net liquidity balance, and the official reserve transactions balance. The question was also raised as to whether, in the light of the special role of dollar balances in financing world trade and serving as an official reserve currency, it might not be preferable to use an altogether different concept that would focus on the net contribution of the U.S. to world liquidity.

Appendix: Balance-of-Payments Accounting

In order to clarify the nature of balance-of-payments accounting and the measurement of various balances, it may be useful to consider the illustrative transactions for the U.S. that are listed below.[1] The debits and credits corresponding to each transaction have been entered with their identifying number in parentheses in the appropriate balance-of-payments accounts listed in Table 1.A.1. The recording of debits and credits in the current account and unilateral transfers should not create any particular difficulty. It should be noted that in the capital account and balancing items increases in assets are indicated by $(-)$ and reductions by $(+)$ while increases in liabilities are indicated by $(+)$ and reductions by $(-)$. Since the balance-

---

1. The organization of this appendix was suggested by Ingram's (1966, pp. 51–62) treatment of this subject. See also Fieleke (1971a).

TABLE 1.A.1

Illustrative Balance-of-Payments Transactions for the U.S.

		Debits (−)	Credits (+)
A. Goods and services			
			$500,000 (1)
1. Merchandise		$425,000 (2)	100,000 (8)
			150,000 (10)
2. Shipping		43,000 (3)	
3. Tourist expenditures		30,000 (5)	
4. Banking and insurance		2,000 (4)	
5. Dividends and interest			75,000 (6)
	Total, 1–5	500,000	825,000
B. Unilateral transfers			
6. Private remittances		10,000 (7)	
7. Government transfers		100,000 (8)	
	Total, 1–7	610,000	825,000
C. Capital account [increase in assets (−)]			
8a. Long-term foreign investment		200,000 (9)	
		150,000 (10)	
	Total, 1–8a	960,000	825,000
8b. Allocation of SDR's			100,000 (15)
8c. Short-term capital movements:			
U.S.		500,000 (1)	10,000 (7)
private		75,000 (6)	
		100,000 (13)	
8d. Short-term capital movements:			425,000 (2)
foreign		50,000 (11)	43,000 (3)
private			2,000 (4)
			30,000 (5)
			100,000 (13)
			50,000 (14)
D. Balancing items [increase in assets (−)]			
9. Short-term capital movements:			200,000 (9)
foreign		75,000 (12)	50,000 (11)
official		50,000 (14)	90,000 (16)
10. Gold and SDR movements		100,000 (15)	75,000 (12)
		90,000 (16)	
	Total, 1–10	$2,000,000	$2,000,000

of-payments accounts are kept on a double-entry basis, the total debits and credits in the table must be equal.

The various balances discussed in Chapter 1 have been computed in Table 1.A.2. It is evident that when foreign-official reserves held in the U.S. are switched to the Eurodollar market, the official reserve transactions balance

TABLE 1.A.2

Various Illustrative Balances in the U.S. Balance of Payments

		Thousands of Dollars
1. Merchandise	+325	
2–5. Services		
A. *Balance on goods and services*		+325
6–7. Unilateral transfers	−110	
B. *Balance on current account*		+215
8a. Long-term capital: private	−350	
C. *Balance on current account and long-term capital*		−135
8b. Allocation of SDR's	+100	
D. *Net liquidity balance*		−35
8c. Short-term capital: U.S. private	−665	
8d. Short-term capital: foreign private	+600	
E. *Official reserve transactions balance*		−100
9. Short-term capital: foreign official	+215	
10. Change in gold stock and SDR's		−115

will worsen. This balance will be unchanged, however, if the official holdings are recycled back to the U.S. The allocation of SDR's to the U.S. by the IMF will improve both balances, whereas sales and purchases of SDR's by foreign official institutions will be offsetting balancing items.

ILLUSTRATIVE TRANSACTIONS

(1) A German manufacturer purchases $500,000 of electrical machinery from an American manufacturer; payment is made by creating a mark deposit in Frankfurt in favor of an American bank.

(2) American firms import $425,000 of bananas from Ecuador, paying with dollar checks on New York banks.

(3) A freight charge of $43,000 is incurred by the American firms on the preceding import of bananas; payment is made to a Panamanian shipping line with dollar checks on New York banks.

(4) An insurance charge of $2,000 is incurred by the American firms on the preceding import of bananas; payment is made to a British insurance company with dollar checks on New York banks.

(5) American tourists traveling in Italy spend $30,000. They obtain the necessary Italian lire by cashing traveler's checks at Italian banks. These banks, in turn, added these checks to their dollar balances in New York.

(6) American corporations receive $75,000 in dividends and interest from their overseas investment in France. Payment is made by increasing franc deposits of these corporations in Paris.

(7) Americans contribute $10,000 for the restoration of Italian art; payment is made by drawing down lire deposits held in Rome by an American bank.

(8) The U.S. Government donates $100,000 of wheat to India.

(9) The Government of Belgium sells a $200,000 issue of 25-year bonds in the New York capital market and adds the dollar proceeds to its official foreign exchange reserves held in New York banks.

(10) American corporations export $150,000 of machinery to expand their branch operations in Japan.

(11) German banks transfer $50,000 of deposits held in New York to the German Central Bank in exchange for mark balances in Frankfurt.

(12) The Bank of France purchases $75,000 of gold from the U.S. Treasury, paying with a check on its dollar deposits held in New York.

(13) American corporations transfer $100,000 of deposits held in New York to banks in the Eurodollar market in London.[2]

(14) The Bank of Italy transfers $50,000 of its official reserve holdings in New York banks to banks in the Eurodollar market in London.[3]

(15) The U.S. receives an allocation of $100,000 in SDR's from the IMF.

(16) The Japanese Central Bank increases its official dollar holdings in New York by $90,000 in exchange for a like amount of SDR's.

2. If these banks then arrange interbank transfers with other Eurobanks and/or lending takes place to private foreigners, the U.S. balance of payments will not be affected so long as these balances remain within the Eurodollar market and are not "repatriated" to the U.S. There will similarly be no effect on the U.S. balance of payments if U.S. banks borrow existing Eurodollars from their foreign branches or other Eurobanks, except perhaps for a transfer of U.S. liquid liabilities from one foreigner to another. This assumes again no repatriation of Eurodollar balances to the U.S. See Little (1969, pp. 18–21) for further details.

3. Suppose that the Eurobanks then loan these funds to a private foreigner, who in turn converts them into domestic currency via his central bank, and the latter deposits them in a New York bank. There will be no net effect on the official reserve transactions balance since the transactions of the two central banks cancel each other. However, the dollar holdings of the first central bank are unchanged and those of the second central bank increased so that this recycling could conceivably increase the foreign exchange-market pressures on the dollar.

2

The Foreign Exchange Market

Given the existence of separate national currencies, there is an evident need for the conversion of domestic into foreign exchange when goods and services are traded internationally and when international capital transactions of all kinds occur. A basic justification of a foreign exchange market is therefore to permit the conversion and transfer of funds between nations in the most efficient way possible. Since there are many international transactions that do not require immediate settlement, a foreign exchange market must function also to facilitate the implementation of contractual arrangements for extension of credit and subsequent payments for the obligations involved. To the extent that exchange rates may vary through time and it is desired to avoid losses through unfavorable movements in the rates, this will involve the provision of facilities in the foreign exchange market for hedging against exchange risks. The major functions of the foreign exchange market can thus be characterized in terms of both space and time dimensions.

A foreign exchange rate is measured typically as the number of units of a given currency that exchange for a unit of some other currency. A separate exchange rate, say for the U.S. dollar, will thus exist with respect to each of the existing independent national currencies. And in turn there will be rates for these national currencies vis-a-vis one another. In a free market without government intervention, these rates will be determined by competitive forces on the demand and supply sides, with arbitrage serving to keep cross rates in line for particular currencies vis-a-vis others. Where exchange rates are fixed by gold export and import points as under the gold standard or by official exchange-market intervention as in the present-day system, these demand and supply forces will still be operative, although within a relatively much narrower range.

Exchange rates are most commonly quoted at any given point in time for immediate purchase and sale—the so-called spot rate, and for future purchase and sale—the so-called forward rate. A major objective of this chapter will be to examine how these rates are determined under alternative exchange-

18

market conditions. We shall proceed first to derive the demand and supply schedules of foreign exchange in order to have a common set of tools for purposes of analysis. We shall then focus on the determination of the spot rate under conditions of the free market, the gold standard, and the present-day system of the adjustable peg. We shall look thereafter at the joint determination of the spot and forward rates under the aforementioned conditions.

Derivation of the Demand and Supply Schedules of Foreign Exchange

Our objective here will be to derive hypothetical demand and supply schedules of foreign exchange and then determine the equilibrium rate of exchange under free market conditions. To simplify the discussion, assume that there are only two countries, say America and England, composed of producers and consumers that buy and sell goods and services competitively between them. Prices are assumed to be perfectly flexible in both directions and resources are fully employed at all times. Assume further that neither government intervenes explicitly in the foreign exchange market, and that, for the time being, there are no capital transactions. We abstract, finally, from the forward market by assuming that all transactions involve immediate payment or receipt.

We begin by noting in Figure 2.1 how America's import-demand, D_m^a, and export-supply, S_x^a, schedules for given goods are derived in terms of the horizontal distance between the home-demand, D_h^a, and home-supply, S_h^a, schedules below and above the equilibrium price P at which no trade will occur. What is noteworthy from Figure 2.1 is that when there is home consumption and production as well as imports or exports of a good, the import-demand schedule will be more highly elastic than the home-demand schedule and the export-supply schedule more elastic than the home-supply schedule.[1] This is because at prices below P, imports will be stimulated by increasing home consumption and reducing home production. At prices above P, exports will be stimulated by reducing home consumption and increasing home production. Figure 2.1 suggests, therefore, especially in countries with substantial home consumption and production of foreign traded goods, the likelihood that import-demand and export-supply schedules may in fact be relatively elastic. These elasticities will vary empirically of course for different goods and countries.

Once the import-demand and export-supply schedules for individual goods are obtained, we can combine them into aggregative schedules of import demand and export supply. Abstracting from the index-number problems entailed in aggregation, we shall treat the import-demand and export-supply schedules in Figure 2.1 as if they were aggregative schedules and posit further that such schedules can be derived for England. In Figure 2.2, we

---

1. The relationship involving these elasticities is demonstrated formally in the appendix to this chapter.

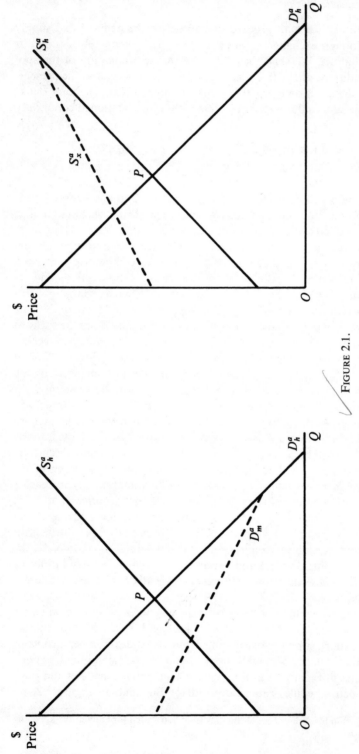

FIGURE 2.1.

Derivation of the Import-Demand and Export-Supply Schedules

The import-demand schedule, D_m^a, in the left-hand figure and the export-supply schedule, S_x^a, in the right-hand figure are derived in terms of the horizontal distance between the home-demand, D_h^a, and home-supply, S_h^a, schedules. When there is home consumption and production, the import-demand schedule and the export-supply schedule more elastic than the home-supply schedule.

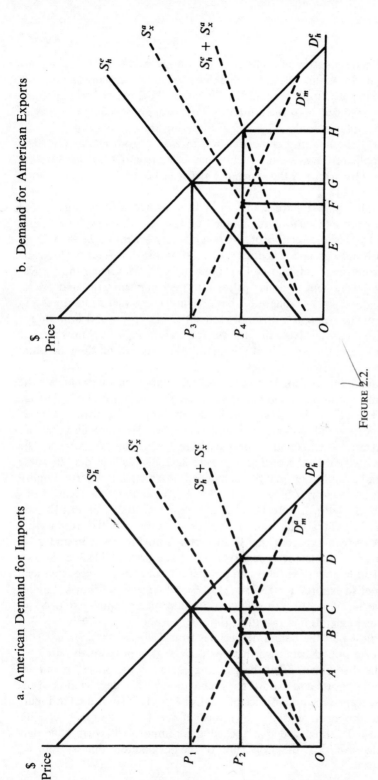

FIGURE 2.2.

Determination of Home Demand, Supply, and Imports in Two Countries

In the left-hand figure, adding the English export-supply schedule, S_x^e, to the American home-supply schedule, S_h^a, equilibrium price and quantity are OP_2 and OD. American imports are OB, which is the difference between home demand and home supply, $OD - OA$.

In the right-hand figure, adding S_x^a to S_h^e, the equilibrium price and quantity are OP_4 and OH, and English imports are OF.

indicate the determination of home demand, supply, and imports in America and England. In Figure 2.2a, which refers to the American demand for imports, the export-supply schedule for England, S_x^e, converted from pounds into dollars, is added onto the American home-supply schedule in order to get a total-supply schedule, $S_h^a + S_x^e$. Comparing the equilibrium positions at P_1 and P_2, the quantity demanded has increased from OC to OD. The quantity supplied from home production has fallen from OC to OA. Imports are equal to OB, which is the difference between home demand and home supply, $OD - OA$.

Correspondingly in Figure 2.2b, which is measured also in dollars, the equilibrium price and quantity demanded of American exports by England is depicted by the intersection of the total-supply schedule, $S_h^e + S_x^a$, and the English home-demand schedule. The relationships in Figure 2.2 can be presented from the standpoint of England simply by converting the vertical axes from measurement in dollar prices into measurement in pound prices. This gives us two pairs of diagrams that are shown together in Figure 2.3 in terms only of the demand and supply schedules of exports and imports for the respective countries. Note that the vertical axes in Figure 2.3 now refer to dollar or pound prices per unit of the quantities measured on the horizontal axes.

Let us assume that the solid-line demand and supply schedules indicate the initial equilibrium imports and exports corresponding to a rate of exchange equal to $3 = £1. It should be noted that the upper and lower parts of Figure 2.3 correspond as far as the solid-line schedules are concerned, but that the price axes measured in pounds have been adjusted to reflect the assumed exchange rate. According to Figure 2.3a, and as is evident in Table 2.1, the initial equilibrium-quantity demanded of American imports (English exports) is 92.6 at a price of $32.8, or $3,037. The pound equivalent of this can be seen in Figure 2.3c to be 92.6 at a price of £10.93, or £1,012 (i.e., $3,037 × £1/$3). In similar fashion we can read the initial equilibrium values of American exports (English imports) from Figures 2.3b and 2.3d. Thus the quantity of American exports is 199.1 at a price of $24.3, or $4,839. The equivalent in pounds is 199.1 at a price of £8.1 or £1,613. Since American imports (English exports) are $3,037 (£1,613) and American exports (English imports) are $4,839 (£1,613), it is evident that, at the exchange rate of $3 = £1, America (England) has an export (import) surplus.

Suppose now that the pound depreciates from $3 = £1 to $2 = £1. That is, instead of a pound being worth three dollars, it is now worth only two. What will be the impact, other things being equal, on the prices, quantities, and values of imports and exports for each country? The depreciation of the pound will cheapen the dollar price of English exports, as indicated in Figure 2.3a by the proportional shift downward of the English supply schedule from S_x^e to $S_x^{e'}$. The English demand schedule for imports will correspondingly be shifted downward by the proportion of the devaluation, that is, from D_m^e

to $D_m^{e'}$ in Figure 2.3b. The dollar price and value of English imports have evidently fallen in Figure 2.3b, which will be the case unless England's import demand were perfectly inelastic. The dollar price of English exports has fallen in Figure 2.3a, which will be the case unless England's export-supply schedule were perfectly inelastic. The dollar value of English exports has apparently risen because D_m^a has been drawn with an elasticity of greater than one. Should this elasticity have been unity or less than unity, the dollar value of

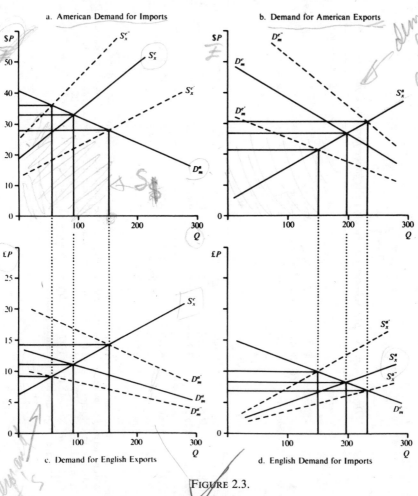

FIGURE 2.3.

Demand and Supply Schedules of Exports and Imports for Two Countries

The solid-line schedules refer to an exchange rate of $3 = £1. Variations in the exchange rate are shown by the proportional shifts in the relevant schedules. The demand and supply of dollars and pounds at different exchange rates are measured by the areas of the rectangles inscribed under the relevant schedules.

TABLE 2.1

Demand and Supply Schedules of Foreign Exchange for Two Countries

	U.S. Imports						U.K. Imports			
Exchange Rate $ per £	$ Price	Quantity	$ Value (U.K. Supply of $)	£ Value (U.S. Demand for £)	Exchange Rate £ per $	£ Price	Quantity	£ Value (U.S. Supply of £)	$ Value (U.K. Demand for $)
(1)	(2)	(3)	(4) = (2) × (3)	(5) = (4) × 1/(1)	(6)	(7)	(8)	(9) = (7) × (8)	(10) = (9) × 1/(6)
$4.00	$36.0	55.2	$1,987	£ 497	£0.25	£ 6.9	232.7	£1,606	$6,424
3.00	32.8	92.6	3,037	1,012	0.33	8.1	199.1	1,613	4,839
2.40	30.0	125.2	3,756	1,565	0.417	9.0	173.9	1,565	3,756
2.00	27.7	152.0	4,210	2,105	0.50	9.8	151.5	1,485	2,970
1.00	19.0	253.5	4,816	4,816	1.00	12.3	81.5	1,002	1,002
0.50	11.6	339.7	3,941	7,882	2.00	14.2	28.3	402	201

NOTE: The multiplications are inexact due to rounding. The dollar and pound values in columns (4) and (5) and the pound and dollar values in columns (9) and (10) were derived from the assumed proportional shifts in the relevant demand and supply schedules. The exchange rates implied by these shifts are indicated in columns (1) and (6). The shifts were made with reference to the schedules shown in solid lines which were drawn according to the following equations: $D_m^a = 475 - 11.66P^\$$ and $S_x^\$ = -125 + 20P^£$ in Figures 2.3a and 2.3c; and $S_x^a = -42.11 + 10P^\$$ and $D_m^a = 425.89 - 28P^£$ in Figures 2.3b and 2.3d. Note that $P^\$$ and $P^£$ refer, respectively, to prices in terms of dollars and pounds and £1 = r.

English exports would have been unchanged or would have fallen. It may be noted further that the dollar prices of English exports and imports have declined proportionately less than the exchange-rate depreciation.

This depreciation can also be depicted in the lower part of Figure 2.3 in terms of pounds. America's import demand in Figure 2.3c shifts upward to $D_m^{a'}$. America's export supply shifts upward to $S_x^{a'}$, indicating the increase in the pound price of American export goods. The pound price and value of English exports have increased in Figure 2.3c, which will be the case unless D_m^a were perfectly inelastic. The pound price of English imports has risen in Figure 2.3d, which will be the case unless D_m^e were perfectly elastic. The pound value of English imports has fallen because D_m^e has been drawn with an elasticity greater than one. Should this elasticity have been unity or less than unity, the pound value of English imports would have been unchanged or would have risen.

It we compare the schedules in the upper and lower parts of Figure 2.3, they appear no longer to be identical as in the case of the solid-line schedules. The reason is that we have not adjusted the price axes measured in pounds to reflect the new exchange rate of $2 = £1. We can nevertheless determine from Figure 2.3 the new equilibrium values that correspond to this exchange rate. The numerical values are given in Table 2.1, where it can be seen that America (England) now has an import (export) surplus. As will be noted shortly, there must evidently be an exchange rate between $3 = £1 and $2 = £1 at which exports and imports are equal.

The effects of an appreciation of the pound vis-a-vis the dollar can be determined along the lines just indicated by the upward shifts of S_x^e and D_m^e and the corresponding downward shifts of D_m^a and S_x^a that have been drawn in Figure 2.3 according to an exchange rate of $4 = £1. This suggests that by varying the rate of exchange between the two currencies as in Figure 2.3, it is possible to derive the demand and supply schedules of dollars in terms of pounds and of pounds in terms of dollars and thus to determine the equilibrium rate of exchange. Taking S_x^e in Figure 2.3a, assume the pound to appreciate or depreciate with respect to the dollar by shifting this schedule proportionately up and down with respect to D_m^a. We can then obtain the English supply schedule for dollars by determining the areas of the rectangles under the various intersections that correspond to the particular rate of exchange of pounds in terms of dollars. In the range where D_m^a is elastic, the English supply of dollars will be increasing with the depreciation of the pound. Where the elasticity of D_m^a is equal to unity, there will be no change in the English supply of dollars, i.e., the supply schedule will be vertical. In the inelastic portion of D_m^a, the English supply of dollars will be negatively inclined for a depreciation of the pound. These results can be seen more clearly in Figure 2.4b, where $S_{\$}^e$ is nearly perfectly inelastic between £0.50 and £1.00 per dollar and negatively inclined thereafter.

It should be evident from the foregoing discussion that once $S_{\pounds}^e$ has been determined, we have automatically determined America's demand for pounds. This can be seen from Figure 2.3c in which D_m^a has been shifted up and down with respect to S_x^e to indicate the effects of depreciation and appreciation of the pound by measuring the areas of the rectangles corresponding to different exchange rates. The relevant schedule, $D_{\pounds}^a$, is plotted in Figure 2.4a. It may be noted that given S_x^e, $D_{\pounds}^a$ will be more elastic the more elastic is D_m^a. Correspondingly, given an elastic D_m^a, $D_{\pounds}^a$ will be more elastic the greater the elasticity of S_x^e. If D_m^a is inelastic, $D_{\pounds}^a$ will be more elastic the more inelastic is S_x^e.[2]

Since $D_{\pounds}^a$ is equivalent to $S_{\$}^e$, it is further evident that one schedule can be derived from the other and vice versa. Thus, point A on $D_{\pounds}^a$, which indicates that, at an exchange rate of \$4 per pound, the amount demanded will be equal to £497, corresponding to point A on $S_{\$}^e$ at an exchange rate of £0.25 per dollar. Points B, C, and D on $D_{\pounds}^a$ likewise correspond to the ones similarly marked on $S_{\$}^e$. In the absence of the numerical results in Table 2.1, each of these points on $S_{\$}^e$ could be obtained from points along $D_{\pounds}^a$ in Figure 2.4a by plotting horizontally the areas of the rectangles under $D_{\pounds}^a$, which are equal to the amount of dollars offered for each particular amount of pounds, and plotting vertically the exchange rate in pounds per dollar, which corresponds to each particular amount of dollars. By this same line of reasoning, $S_{\$}^e$ could be transformed into $D_{\pounds}^a$ and $D_{\$}^e$ into $S_{\pounds}^a$.[3]

The Spot Rate under Free Market Conditions

Once we have derived the demand and supply schedules for pounds and dollars as shown in Figure 2.4, we can determine the equilibrium rate of exchange. Under the conditions assumed, this rate will be \$2.40 = £1, as in Figure 2.4a, which is shown equivalently in terms of the reciprocal in Figure 2.4b as about £0.417 = \$1. Each country's balance of payments is in equilibrium at these rates.

At rates of exchange below \$2.40 per pound it is evident that there will be an excess demand for pounds and an equivalent excess supply of dollars at rates above £0.417 per dollar. This is because English exports have

2. The relationship between the elasticities of the demand and supply schedules of goods and the demand and supply schedules of foreign exchange is demonstrated formally in the appendix to this chapter. It may be worth noting at this point that in the example developed in the text the demand and supply schedules of foreign exchange reflect the varying demand and supply elasticities of goods. Perfectly elastic supply schedules of goods are sometimes assumed for purposes of simplification, in which case the import demand and foreign exchange demand schedules have identical elasticities. On this last point, see for example, Allen and Allen (1959, pp. 273–78) and Sohmen (1969, pp. 3–4).

3. Machlup (1939; 1964, p. 9) has remarked with reference to the relations described in this paragraph: "This sounds complicated—yet every sophomore ought to be able to do it, or he has never grasped the meaning of supply and demand curves." These relations are also treated in the references cited in the preceding footnote and in Haberler (1949).

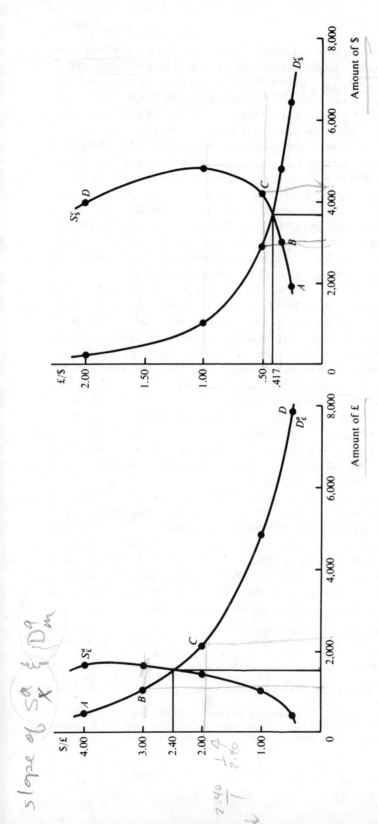

FIGURE 2.4.

Demand and Supply Schedules of Pounds and Dollars

The demand and supply schedules can be obtained from the areas inscribed under the relevant schedules in Figure 2.3 at different exchange rates. Points A, B, C, D correspond in the two figures above. If $D_£^a$ were given as in Figure 2.4a, $S_^{a} could be obtained as in 2.4b by plotting the number of pounds converted into dollars and the inverse of the exchange rate. The equilibrium exchange rate noted above is $2.40 = £1, or $1 = £0.417.

become relatively cheaper to America and American exports relatively more expensive to England. The dollar-exchange rate would thus be bid up and its reciprocal pound exchange rate would fall until equilibrium was restored. Correspondingly, at rates above $2.40 per pound there will be an excess supply of pounds and an equivalent excess demand for dollars at rates below £0.417 per dollar. This is because English exports have become relatively more expensive to America and American exports relatively cheaper to England. The dollar-exchange rate would thus fall and its reciprocal pound-exchange rate would be bid up until equilibrium was restored. Since the exchange rates shown are presumed to reflect market forces only, any shift in the underlying import-demand or export-supply schedules, due to such factors as changes in income, tastes, technology, etc., will cause the relevant demand and supply schedules of foreign exchange to shift. The rate of exchange will thus be affected and there will be a new equilibrium in the balance of payments corresponding to the new exchange rate.

We may note that the equilibrium illustrations just given would be valid even if the intersections occurred on the negatively inclined, i.e., backward bending, portion of the relevant supply schedule. The equilibrium is stable when both schedules are negatively inclined, given that the supply schedule is steeper than the demand schedule, or in terms of elasticities that the elasticity of demand is greater than the elasticity of supply. These considerations can perhaps be seen more clearly in Figure 2.5, where only the negatively inclined portions of the supply schedules are shown. In Figure 2.5a, where $D_£$ is less steep than $S_£$, r_1 is a stable equilibrium-exchange rate. Should the rate be set temporarily at r_2 or r_3, forces will be set into motion to restore the rate to r_1. If, as in Figure 2.5b, $S_£$ is less steep than $D_£$, r'_1 will be an unstable rate. Should the rate happen to move to r'_2 or r'_3, there will be a continuous movement away from rather than towards r'_1.[4]

The question is, however, whether there will exist stable equilibria at some point above and below r'_1. That is, will there not be some price for imports in the two countries at which the demand becomes elastic? If this is not the case, it means that the demand for foreign exchange will remain inelastic in the face of a continually appreciating exchange rate. This implies that a country might devote a larger and larger portion of its income to imports as their prices rise even to the point of spending everything on imports. Such a situation is of course conceivable but is not very probable.[5]

4. Stability and instability are being conceived here in the sense of Walras rather than of Marshall. That is, with Walrasian stability if ex ante supply falls short of demand or vice versa, the price will rise or fall to equilibrium. This type of adjustment is presumably most typical of the foreign exchange market. Marshallian stability is based in contrast on the adjustment of output to reach equilibrium, and the conditions for stability are exactly opposite to those of Walras. The differences in these stability concepts are discussed more completely in Allen (1956, pp. 19–23).

5. Johnson (1958b; 1968, p. 384) has noted that exchange instability "implies that the country's output is in a sense a 'Giffen case' in world consumption; and that the market for at least one of the commodities it produces is in unstable equilibrium."

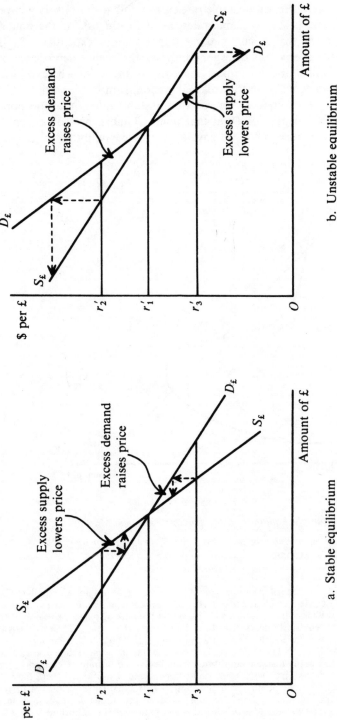

FIGURE 2.5.

Stable and Unstable Equilibrium in the Foreign Exchange Market

With negatively sloped demand and supply schedules, the foreign exchange market will be stable so long as the supply schedule is more steeply sloped than the demand schedule. The rate r_1 is stable in Figure 2.5a, whereas r_1' in 2.5b is unstable.

Thus, to the extent that an unstable rate exists at all, it most likely will be bounded above and below by stable rates, as in Figure 2.6. As the pound appreciates vis-a-vis the dollar, making imports more expensive, $D_£$ is assumed to become elastic. Correspondingly, as the pound depreciates, it means that the dollar price of imports may rise to the point where $D_$$ will become elastic and $S_£$ will turn towards and eventually meet the vertical axis. Point A in Figure 2.6 therefore represents an unstable rate in that the slope of $S_£$ is less steep than that of $D_£$ at that point. B and C are consequently points of stable equilibrium.[6] If we have an unstable equilibrium at A, any

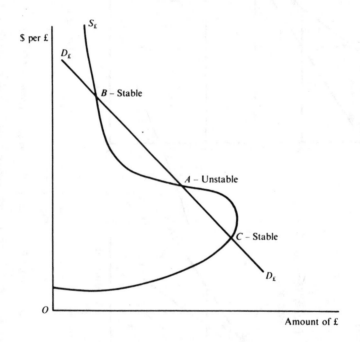

FIGURE 2.6.

Multiple Equilibria in the Foreign Exchange Market

A is an unstable equilibrium since $S_£$ is less steep than $D_£$. A is bounded by points of stable equilibrium at B and C.

6. The classic discussion of multiple equilibria is to be found in Marshall (1923, Appendix J) in the context of his treatment of reciprocal demand or offer curves. It is of interest to note that Bhagwati and Johnson (1960, pp. 89–93) have disputed the Marshallian contention of stable equilibria necessarily bounding an unstable region. Their analysis is useful because it brings out clearly the assumptions on which Marshallian offer curves are based. Sohmen (1969, pp. 10–11) has shown, however, that the Bhagwati-Johnson argument can be interpreted to imply a stable equilibrium rate below the unstable region, but that this rate will be negative and therefore of limited economic significance. There may be some question in any event about the applicability of Marshallian offer curves to the foreign exchange market since these curves are based on real rather than on monetary considerations and refer to situations of general rather than partial equilibrium.

change in the exchange rate will bring about a new equilibrium at either *B* or *C*.

While the question of foreign exchange-market instability is interesting theoretically, how likely is it that instability will in fact occur? There are two important reasons for presuming that such an occurrence will be unlikely. First, we noted in connection with Figure 2.1 that the import-demand and export-supply schedules for many goods that enter foreign trade are likely to be much more highly elastic than the total home-demand and supply schedules. Thus, in a given instance, imports into a country may be stimulated by lower prices not only because of increased home consumption, but also because of the reduction of competing home supply. This will be the case especially when we are considering one country vis-a-vis the rest of the world.[7] Second, as prices change, the dividing line among exports, imports, and domestic goods will be altered. An increase in foreign prices, for example, might encourage new exports and discourage certain types of imports. A decrease in foreign prices might accordingly discourage existing exports and encourage new imports.[8] The existence of competing supply and potentially tradable goods thus creates a strong presumption for the supply schedule of foreign exchange to be positively sloped and relatively elastic.[9]

We shall return to many of these matters below in Chapters 3–5, when the price approach to balance-of-payments adjustment will be discussed more fully. Thus, unless otherwise stated, it shall be assumed that the supply schedule of foreign exchange is positively sloped in the relevant range and that consequently the foreign exchange market can be presumed to be characterized by stable equilibrium.

The Spot Rate under the Gold Standard

We turn now to exchange-rate determination under the gold standard. The major characteristics of the gold standard can be summed up in terms of the so-called rules of the game. These rules involve a mixture of strictly legal requirements together with certain specified institutional practices that must be followed by the central monetary authorities if this standard is to be operated successfully. *The first rule is that in each country the appropriate*

7. Thus, as Machlup (1939; 1964, p. 14) has stated, "the elasticity of supply of foreign exchange will be higher, the higher the elasticity of supply of foreign products which compete in the foreign market for our exports. . . . It is this factor which may be decisive in making the elasticity of supply of foreign exchange a positive value . . . in cases where the foreign demand for the articles which we export happens to possess an elasticity smaller than unity." This proposition is demonstrated formally in the appendix to this chapter.

8. All of this may take time of course, which is equivalent to saying that long-run elasticities will be greater than short-run elasticities.

9. The main exceptions here will thus be countries that are highly specialized and have a dominant market position in their export goods and that cannot easily substitute home produced goods for imports. See Haberler (1949, pp. 207–10) for a discussion of the points made in this and the preceding paragraphs.

authority must establish once and for all the gold value of its national currency.[10]
This can be done by establishing a specified gold content for the currency
unit, for example, 1/20 of an ounce of gold being worth $1. The actual
currency in circulation would consist either of gold coins whose dollar value
reflected their gold content or notes that could always be exchanged in
certain specified amounts for their equivalent in gold. The former would
correspond to a gold-specie standard and the latter to a gold-bullion standard.
These are to be distinguished from a gold-exchange standard in which the
central monetary authority undertakes to buy and sell at predetermined rates
in terms of its own currency the notes of some other country which is operating a gold-specie or gold-bullion standard.[11]

Thus, for example, England might declare that 5/20 of an ounce of gold
would be worth £1. Since the gold value of the pound would then be five
times that of the dollar, the exchange rate between the currencies would be
$5 per £1, or £0.20 per $1. The result would be the same under a gold-
exchange standard simply if England undertook always to buy and sell
dollars at the rates indicated. Given these relationships, what would happen,
say, if there was an excess demand for pounds? Would the exchange rate be
driven higher than $5 per £1? The answer would appear to be no, since at any
higher rate it would pay to buy gold in America for shipment to and sale in
England. This would evidently require that there be free movement of gold
out of and into the countries maintaining a gold standard. *The freedom of
such movement constitutes the second rule of the game.*

It is obvious that the shipment of gold is by no means costless. There may
be a small cost involved in melting down the gold or in purchasing it from the
monetary authority. Further, some costs will be incurred in the shipment of
the gold to cover the actual transportation, insurance against loss, and the
interest foregone while the shipment is in transit. An additional slight charge
might be made, finally, in the receiving country for conversion of the gold into
coin or for the issuance of currency. If these costs amounted, say, to $0.05
per $5, it means that it would be economical to settle a payment by a gold
shipment only if the rate of exchange were above $5.05 per £1 or below
$4.95 per £1. In order to spare businessmen from the need to make their own
arrangements, specialized dealers in foreign exchange and gold can be assumed to offer their services in effecting the various kinds of transactions.
That is, an excess demand for pounds that would tend to drive the exchange
rate above $5.05 per £1 would motivate the gold arbitrageurs to purchase
gold with dollars and export it to England for conversion into pounds. An
excess demand for dollars that would tend to drive the exchange rate below

10. As Meade (1951, p. 178) has pointed out, the basis of the standard need not
necessarily be gold. It could be any other commodity or group of commodities, or even
some specially created international monetary unit to be held by countries for their reserve
purposes.
    11. *Ibid.*, p. 179.

$4.95 per £1 would correspondingly lead gold arbitrageurs to purchase gold with pounds and ship it to America for conversion into dollars.

Such transactions could be completed more or less at constant costs per unit of shipment. This means that the supply and demand for foreign exchange will be perfectly elastic at the gold-export and import points noted.[12] This assumes of course that the mint-parity rates in terms of gold in the countries concerned will be kept unchanged. It is evident under these conditions that the dollar price of pounds cannot rise much above the gold-export point or fall much below the gold-import point. Consequently, the businessman is virtually assured of never having to pay more than $5.05 per £1 or receive less than $4.95 per £1.

The foregoing discussion may be clarified by Figure 2.7.[13] Assuming first that the demand and supply of foreign exchange arise only from current-account transactions, the intersection of the $D_{£}^{a}$ and $S_{£}^{a}$ schedules gives an equilibrium rate of exchange of OQ and an equilibrium amount of £ of OM. The corresponding equilibrium in terms of dollars is the area of the rectangle, $OQPM$. The initial balance-of-payments receipts and payments can thus be written in terms of pounds as $OM = OM$ and in terms of dollars as $OQPM = OQPM$. Assume now that there is a switch from domestic expenditure to expenditure for foreign investment purposes. Abstracting from the real impact this switch may have, there will be an increase in the demand for pounds, which has the effect of shifting $D_{£}^{a}$ to $D_{£}^{a'}$. Under free market conditions, the exchange rate would rise from OQ to OT. Such a rate could not persist under the gold standard, however, because at OA, which is the exchange rate corresponding to the gold-export point, the supply of pounds is perfectly elastic as a consequence of the gold-arbitrage movement described above. Thus, in the new equilibrium, the amount of pounds supplied is OH from current-account receipts and HF from the export of gold. It will be noted that the increase in the dollar price of pounds from OQ to OA has resulted in a reduction in the demand for pounds for current-account purposes from OM to OG and an increase in supply from OM to OH. These changes reflect of course the fact that American imports in terms of pounds are relatively more costly and exports relatively cheaper. The balance-of-payments receipts and payments in terms of pounds are $OH + HF = OG + GF$ and in terms of dollars, $OAEH + HECF = OADG + GDCF$.

The foregoing situation is one of balance-of-payments disequilibrium in the sense that there has been an accommodating movement of gold equal to HF, which has kept the exchange rate from rising above the gold-export point, OA. This gold movement is of further interest because it is a measure in the present context of the further adjustment required in the current

12. There may in fact be some variability in these transactions costs so that the gold-export and import points will not be completely fixed.

13. This figure and the ensuing discussion have been adapted from Machlup (1939; 1964, pp. 27–34).

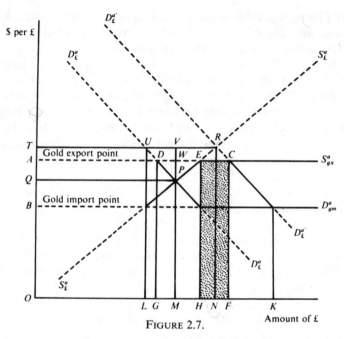

FIGURE 2.7.

The Spot Rate under the Gold Standard

*The initial equilibrium rate of exchange is OQ. With an
increase in the demand for pounds, the rate will move to
the gold-export point and HF will constitute gold exports.
The movement of gold will have an impact on the stock of
money and upon money income so that the demand and
supply schedules will be shifted to the left and right until
the gold movement has ceased.*

account in order to complete the remaining portion of the capital transfer.
*The nature of this further adjustment involves the third rule of the game of the
gold standard, which is that the persistent movement of gold must be permitted
to influence the domestic money supply in each country.* The implication of this
third rule for the country losing gold is that the decline in the money supply
will bring about a decline in money income, while the opposite will be the
case for the country receiving gold. The demand and supply schedules for
pounds will thus be shifted to the left and right respectively, in Figure 2.7,
until the gold movement has ceased altogether. At this point, the amount of
pounds demanded for current-account and capital-export purposes will be
equal to the amount supplied from current-account receipts. The equilibrium
in terms of dollars for the country gaining gold will reflect the corresponding
shifts in the demand and supply schedules for dollars.

The third rule of the game thus requires that the monetary authorities will not take any offsetting action with respect to the gold movement. But just exactly what the precise effect will be on the money supply in each country will depend upon the type of banking-reserve rules followed. A simple arithmetic example may help to illustrate this point. Assume that we have a banking system consisting only of a single bank, in which the required reserve ratio of gold to liabilities outstanding is equal to one-half. Further assume that the amount of cash held by the public is given. Suppose the initial situation to be as follows:

Banking System

Assets		Liabilities	
Gold	50	Deposits	50
Domestic assets	50	Notes in circulation	50
Total	100	Total	100

Thus, the money supply is initially equal to 100 and it is backed by a gold reserve of 50. Imagine then that this country experiences a gold inflow equal to 25. The position of the banking system will then be:

Assets		Liabilities	
Gold	75	Deposits	75
Domestic assets	50	Notes in circulation	50
Total	125	Total	125

It will be evident that the money supply has been expanded from 100 to 125. The reserve ratio is now three-fifths, which exceeds the legal requirement. Domestic credit can therefore be expanded from 75 to 100. The result is that the money supply would be further increased to 150, which would lower the reserve ratio to the required level of one-half. The final position would be:

Assets		Liabilities	
Gold	75	Deposits	100
Domestic assets	75	Notes in circulation	50
Total	150	Total	150

More realistically, the banking system would consist of private commercial banks and a central bank that was responsible for regulating the domestic money supply especially via changes in the central bank discount rate and by open market operations. In our example, with gold flowing in, the monetary authority could lower the discount rate. By reducing the cost of commercial bank borrowing from the central bank, the intended effect would be to lower market-interest rates. The monetary authority could also purchase securities in the open market with the same interest-rate objective in mind. In the case of the country losing gold, the central bank could increase the discount rate or engage in open market sales of securities in order to prevent domestic credit from expanding and to cause market-interest rates to rise. These interest-rate changes may be important not only because they will affect money income and prices, but also because they may create an incentive for the movement of short-term capital from surplus to deficit countries.

In order to be assured that changes in money income and prices will occur when there are changes in the money supply, it is necessary that *in each country on the gold standard there must be wage and therefore price flexibility*. Such flexibility is the basis for the mechanism of adjustment to operate in our classical-type world in which there is competition in product and factor markets and resources are fully employed. Thus, in terms of our example, the inflow of gold and the consequent expansion of the money supply will create an excess demand for labor, which will cause money wage rates to rise. As wage rates rise, the forces of competition will induce a rise in the prices of the surplus country's goods. There will presumably be opposite effects on money wages and prices in the deficit country. Given the rise in the prices of the surplus country's products and the reduction in the prices of the products of the deficit country, there will be a shift of demand in both countries onto the relatively cheaper products of the deficit country and a corresponding reallocation of resources in the two countries. The balance of payments will therefore adjust as imports rise relative to exports in the surplus country and the converse takes place in the deficit country. There is a presumption in this process of adjustment, it may be noted, that because of the fall in export prices relative to import prices the country losing gold will undergo a worsening in its net barter terms of trade.

In summary, the determination and maintenance of the spot rate of exchange under the gold standard depends upon the adherence to certain rules of the game that provide for the specification of the gold value of each national currency, free movement of gold, and automatic effects of such movements on the domestic money supply. The balance-of-payments mechanism of adjustment functions by virtue of the changes in relative prices and interest rates brought about in response to gold movements, with imports and exports and international short-term capital flows being affected until balance-of-payments equilibrium is restored and the gold movements cease. The gold standard thus involves a system of exchange rates fixed at certain limits and a mechanism of adjustment for attainment of internal and external balance.

Insofar as changes in relative prices provide the basis for adjustment, the gold-standard and freely fluctuating exchange-rate systems are similar in principle. The systems differ, however, in that, with fluctuating rates, relative real prices are adjusted by exchange-rate changes, whereas, under the gold standard, changes in the level of money prices are the focus for adjustment.

The gold standard will not function effectively, therefore, if the rules of the game become inoperative and if internal price flexibility is thwarted especially in the downward direction. In such an event, a country losing gold might undergo unemployment and not merely a reduction in its money income as we have posited.

The international monetary system operated on the gold standard for about four decades prior to World War I and apparently functioned effectively on the whole during this time. However, as will be noted in Chapter 4 below, the rules of the game were by no means followed to the letter since the authorities often refrained from deliberate monetary expansion or contraction in response to changes in their monetary reserves. The gold standard was suspended during World War I, and following a period of freely fluctuating exchange rates from 1919–26, it was restored in most countries. But this restoration lacked a solid foundation insofar as the reestablishment of prewar exchange rates resulted in the over- and undervaluation of important currencies with respect to their free-market-equilibrium levels. Moreover, the authorities in many countries were reluctant to expose their economies to purposeful deflation or inflation in order to correct balance-of-payments disequilibria because of the possibly adverse domestic consequences such policies might have.

In any case, with the severe decline in incomes and the financial chaos of the Great Depression, the balance-of-payments strains became so acute that most countries were forced to abandon the gold standard during the 1930's. Great Britain and the other countries tied to sterling led the way with devaluation in 1931. They were followed subsequently in 1934 by the United States and the other dollar countries and thereafter by the remaining countries of commercial consequence. Besides overt devaluations, trade and payments restrictions of all kinds were commonplace during the 1930's as many countries sought to stimulate domestic employment and offset contractionary influences from abroad. Many of these devaluations and restrictions were not of lasting significance for individual countries especially to the extent that they served merely to cancel the actions of other countries. Thus, by the end of the 1930's, while the various devaluations had served to raise the price of gold and consequently to increase international liquidity, the pattern of exchange rates did not differ greatly from what it was a decade earlier. However, there was most certainly a retrogression with respect to the earlier period in view of the restrictions that had been widely adopted.

The Spot Rate under the Adjustable Peg

Out of the experience of the interwar period there evolved the present-day system of pegged-but-adjustable exchange rates. This system is similar to the gold standard with respect to the determination and maintenance of exchange-rate limits. But there are also important differences: gold does not move freely today; the monetary authorities in many countries consciously seek, for domestic employment reasons, to offset rather than to reinforce the effects of international monetary movements; and under certain circumstances the exchange-rate limits may be changed. The present-day system is thus akin to the gold standard, but lacks its automaticity and certainty.

Instead of gold-export and import points, all countries today, except the U.S., have exchange-rate limits or intervention points at which the monetary authorities will buy or sell foreign exchange in order to keep the exchange rate at or within the specified limits. Such intervention was already widely practiced during the interwar period and became institutionalized in the postwar exchange-rate system through the establishment of the International Monetary Fund in 1946. According to the original Fund Agreement, the U.S. dollar was given a fixed parity in terms of gold at $35 an ounce. All other member countries were permitted, with some qualifications, to substitute dealings in dollars for gold dealings and thus fix the par value of their currency with respect to the dollar and to keep their currency stable vis-a-vis the dollar. Prewar exchange rates were adopted for par-value purposes for many important currencies, and provision was made for dollars held by official monetary institutions to be converted freely into gold at the official selling price of $35 an ounce. Stability was defined as 1 percent on either side of parity according to Article 4, Section 3 of the Agreement. Countries were free to stabilize their rate within a range of less than 1 percent, which many in fact chose to do.

The original Fund Agreement remained operative until August 15, 1971 when the U.S. acted unilaterally to suspend dollar convertibility and thereby exert pressure for a realignment of exchange rates. This realignment was effected on December 18, 1971, with the acceptance by the major industrialized countries of the so-called Smithsonian Agreement. Under the Smithsonian Agreement, the dollar was devalued in terms of gold by raising the official price of gold from $35 to $38 an ounce. Convertibility was not restored at this time, however. Currency revaluations against the dollar were also undertaken by the major industrialized countries. It was further decided to widen the margins for supporting exchange rates to $2\frac{1}{4}$ percent on either side of parity.[14]

Exchange-rate stabilization is thus carried out today by national central banks or their designated agents mainly through the buying and selling of dollars, although nothing prevents dealing in other currencies if the stabilizing effect in terms of dollars is the same. If their exchange rate appreciates in terms of dollars, central banks will purchase dollars in the foreign exchange market in order to keep the rate from moving above the established limit. They will correspondingly sell dollars out of their accumulated reserves, or convert gold or SDR's for the same purpose, in order to keep their exchange

14. Details of the Smithsonian Agreement are contained in IMF, *International Financial News Survey,* Vol. XXIII, No. 50, Dec. 22-30, 1971, p. 419.

rate from moving below the lower limit. If their own reserves are inadequate, they may arrange to borrow additional reserves for stabilization purposes from the IMF and other international and national sources.[15]

Figure 2.8 may be helpful in illustrating the nature of stabilization operations.[16] The situation depicted is the same as Figure 2.7, except that the gold-export and import points have been redesignated as the upper and lower limits. These limits indicate where the demand and supply schedules of the exchange stabilization fund became perfectly elastic. As before, the equilibrium exchange rate is OQ and the equilibrium amounts of pounds and dollars,

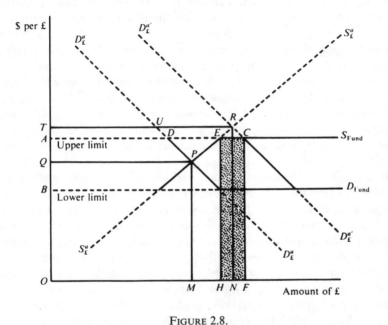

FIGURE 2.8.

The Spot Rate under the Adjustable Peg

The initial equilibrium rate of exchange is OQ. With an increase in the demand for pounds, the rate will move to the upper support point. The authorities will sell HF pounds in exchange for HECF dollars. Any further adjustment domestically will depend upon the discretion of the authorities in the light of their objectives for internal and external balance.

15. Swap arrangements among central banks in the advanced industrialized countries have contributed importantly to foreign exchange-market stability at various times since the mid-1960's. For details, see the semiannual reports published in the U.S., *Federal Reserve Bulletin.*

16. See Machlup (1939; 1964, p. 34–39) for a more extensive discussion of the operations of exchange-stabilization funds.

OM and *OQPM*. With an increase in the demand for pounds, the exchange rate would be bid up under free market conditions from *OQ* to *OT*. The U.K. authorities will intervene at *OA*, however, by selling an amount of *HF* pounds in exchange for *HECF* dollars. The reduction in the demand for pounds and the increase in the supply of pounds due to the change in the exchange rate are the same as before. The balance of payments will also be the same, except that *HF* pounds or *HECF* dollars will be recorded as a short-term capital movement. The need for the authorities to sell dollars in exchange for pounds can be worked out analogously from Figure 2.8 by positing intersections of the schedules below the lower limit indicated.

The present-day system differs further from the gold standard in that the par value about which the exchange-rate limits are set may be altered in accordance with the Articles of Agreement of the IMF, if there is a "fundamental disequilibrium" in the balance of payments. What this refers to essentially is a disequilibrium that is structural or long-term rather than temporary in nature and thus a condition that will not be reversed easily and quickly by market forces or domestic policy measures.[17] The continued accumulation or depletion of international monetary reserves under these circumstances would not be warranted. It might be justified, therefore, to appreciate or depreciate the exchange rate as a means of restoring balance-of-payments equilibrium.

Since it will often be difficult in fact to determine when a disequilibrium is temporary or fundamental, considerable uncertainty may at times be attached to existing exchange-rate limits. This is a very different situation as compared to the gold standard under which it was virtually unthinkable to alter the mint-parity rate of exchange. Changes in expectations about the permanence of the existing exchange rate may thus give rise to substantial international capital flows in today's adjustable peg system. The exchange rates maintained in today's system may frequently be over- or undervalued with reference to the free-market-equilibrium rate discussed earlier. This should be obvious in terms of the possible intersections of the demand and supply schedules of foreign exchange in Figure 2.8 outside of the upper and lower limits shown. Yet, as will be noted in our later discussion, this matter is often confused because of a tendency to conceive of a pegged official rate as an equilibrium rate. International capital movements are thus sometimes misconstrued as being disequilibrating in nature when in fact the official rate may overvalue or undervalue the currency in question in relation to the free-market-equilibrium rate.

The foregoing discussion has perhaps overstressed the potential flexibility of the adjustable-peg system. The fact is that the advanced industrial countries, which account for the bulk of world trade and payments, altered their exchange rates only at relatively infrequent intervals between 1950 and the late

17. The provision in the Articles of Agreement of the IMF regarding changes in par values is contained in Article IV, Section 5(a).

1960's. Since the late 1960's and particularly during 1969–71, the frequency of exchange-rate adjustment has increased markedly, although some of the countries concerned were often reluctant to carry out the changes.[18] For some time then, the present system seemed de facto to be evolving into a fixed-rate system without, however, making provision for an effectively functioning balance-of-payments adjustment mechanism.

Another related and important development not consciously sought was the predominant role that the dollar and to a lesser extent the pound sterling came to play as reserve currencies in the postwar period. Efforts by both the U.S. and U.K. to maintain exchange-rate stability vis-a-vis one another and with respect to the other major currencies came under speculative pressures at various times during the 1960's. Devising new measures to meet these responsibilities often required considerable ingenuity on the part of the policy makers and brought forth some important new developments in the theory of economic policy. These and the foregoing are matters that we shall have occasion to elaborate on in subsequent chapters.

The Spot and Forward Rates under Free Market Conditions

We have assumed thus far that all transactions were confined to the spot market. This is an oversimplification since in actuality there are many transactions involving future receipts and payments in foreign exchange. It will become clear shortly that since the spot and forward exchange markets are connected directly through the operations of the various transactors, the determination of spot and forward rates must be considered jointly. As in our discussion of the spot rate under free market conditions, we shall assume that we have only two countries that produce and trade competitively and that the governments do not intervene in the foreign exchange market. The possibility of exchange-market instability will be ruled out by assuming the demand and supply schedules of foreign exchange to have their conventional slopes.

---

18. The major European currencies were devalued by varying proportions in 1948–49. The most notable developments in the 1950's were the adoption of a flexible exchange-rate system by Canada in 1950 and devaluations by France in 1957 and 1958 prior to the formation of the European Common Market. There were relatively small appreciations of the German and Dutch exchange rates in 1961. The Canadian rate was pegged officially in 1962. The next major exchange-rate changes took place in 1967 with the devaluation of sterling by the U.K. and a number of other countries tied to sterling. France, together with the members of the franc zone, devalued again in the summer of 1969, and, after a temporary float of a few weeks, Germany appreciated that fall. Canada again instituted a flexible rate system in June 1970. Finally, in the spring and summer of 1971, under the pressure of a substantial buildup of official dollar balances and the suspension by the U.S. of gold convertibility, many of the industrialized countries were forced to appreciate their currencies via floating rates or movement to a new par value. As noted above, a new pattern of exchange rates received official sanction in late 1971 under the Smithsonian Agreement.

In analyzing the joint determination of spot and forward rates, it is common to view the various transactors in terms of the activities they carry on in the foreign exchange market. The typical activities are short-term in character and involve interest arbitrage, speculation, and commercial trade. Long-term portfolio and direct investment activities are also carried out via the foreign exchange market, but we shall subsume these activities under the spot market on the assumption that they are not influenced by forward exchange-market considerations.

Viewing foreign exchange-market transactions solely in terms of activities can be misleading because it obscures the motivations influencing the behavior of the various transactors. Ideally, we would like to separate the different groups of transactors—nonfinancial corporations; commercial banks; other institutional investors; government and official institutions; and households—according to the behavioral characteristics that they have in common.[19] Some progress has been made in this regard by assuming that certain transactors engage in activities on the basis of return and risk considerations in the context of a model of portfolio adjustment. The portfolio view seems applicable particularly in analyzing investment behavior with respect to the purchase and sale of domestic and foreign securities. Also, some aspects of the financing of commercial trade that partake of interest arbitrage can be analyzed in a portfolio framework. In what follows, we shall have occasion to draw upon the insights offered by portfolio analysis, but we eschew the development and presentation of a formal portfolio model.[20]

INTEREST ARBITRAGE

The object of interest arbitrage is to allocate funds between financial centers in order to realize the highest possible rate of return subject to the least possible risk. Suppose, for example, abstracting from risk, that the interest rate on 90-day government securities is 2 percent per annum in America and 4 percent per annum in England. There would be an incentive under these circumstances for individuals and institutions holding short-term assets in America to liquidate these assets and transfer the proceeds for investment in England at the higher rate of interest. Such a transfer would necessitate a purchase of pounds in exchange for dollars in the spot market at the going exchange rate, say $2.40 per pound.

Suppose accordingly that an investor in America sells domestic government securities in the amount of $2,400. At a spot rate of $2.40 and abstracting from transaction costs, he could purchase the equivalent of £1,000 for investment in England. This investment would on maturity yield £1,010 (i.e., £1,000 $[1 + 0.04/4]$). If at this time the investor wished to repatriate his funds to America, he would sell the pound proceeds of his investment in

19. For some preliminary suggestions along these lines, see Leamer and Stern (1972).
20. See Levin (1970a) for a comprehensive theoretical analysis of portfolio selection in the context of the foreign exchange market. The discussion in Leamer and Stern (1970, esp. pp. 78–90) draws heavily upon Levin's work.

exchange for dollars in the spot market at whatever the exchange rate happened to be. If the rate were $2.40, as it was 90 days earlier, the sale of £1,010 would yield $2,424, which is greater than the $2,412 (i.e., $2,400 [1 + 0.02/4]) that would have been realized if the funds had remained invested in America.

The difficulty is, however, that the spot rate of exchange 90 days hence may be different from the $2.40 rate at which the original conversion was made. If the rate turned out for example to be $2.35, the sale of £1,010 would yield $2,373.50. The investor would thus have incurred a loss in investment abroad as compared to having left the funds in America. Alternatively, if the rate happened to be $2.45, the sale of £1,010 would yield $2,474.50, which would provide a return in addition to the interest earned in England.

Suppose the investor wished to avoid a possible foreign exchange loss in converting the proceeds of his investment upon maturity or was not attracted by the possibility of making a gain on top of the added interest by converting at a more favorable exchange rate. He could then enter into a forward contract to sell the pound proceeds of his investment at the currently quoted 90-day rate for forward exchange. The greater return from investing at short term in England could thus be assured by obtaining "forward cover" for the subsequent conversion of the proceeds. A transaction of this kind is thus called *covered interest arbitrage*.

Assuming interest rates to be determined exogenously, the foregoing example suggests that interest arbitrage is profitable provided that the difference in interest rates is not offset by the discount on forward exchange. Thus, with the given interest differential and a spot rate of $2.40, interest arbitrage would be profitable at $2.40 or $2.45. Arbitrage would be unprofitable, however, with a forward rate of $2.35, as noted, because of the implied loss on the sale of forward pounds. It follows therefore that there will be no incentive for arbitrage if the added interest earnings are just offset by the loss from forward exchange conversion. This is the so-called condition of interest parity.

Let us examine this concept of interest parity somewhat more precisely as follows:[21]

r_s = the current spot rate of exchange; the dollar price of one pound delivered today.

r_f = the current 90-day forward rate of exchange; the dollar price today of one pound to be delivered in 90 days.

$p = (r_f - r_s)/r_s$, the forward premium or discount expressed as a percent of the spot rate of exchange.

i_a = the American 90-day interest rate.

i_e = the English 90-day interest rate.

---

21. The discussion of interest parity has been based on Sohmen (1966; 1969), Spraos (1959), and Tsiang (1959b).

direction of interest arbitrage is opposite to that of commercial trade

Thus, $1 invested in America for 90 days would become $1(1 + i_a)$. If converted into pounds at the spot rate of exchange and invested in England, this would yield $1(1 + i_e)/r_s$. If this latter amount were converted back into dollars at the presently quoted 90-day forward rate, it would become $1 \cdot r_f (1 + i_e)/r_s$. Short-term funds would therefore move from America to England if:

$$\frac{r_f(1 + i_e)}{r_s} > (1 + i_a). \qquad (2.1)$$

Alternatively, funds would move from England to America if:

$$(1 + i_e) < \frac{r_s(1 + i_a)}{r_f}. \qquad (2.2)$$

The equilibrium condition of interest parity will be obtained when:

$$\frac{r_f(1 + i_e)}{r_s} = (1 + i_a). \qquad (2.3)$$

Expressing r_f/r_s as $1 + p$, where p is the forward premium if positive and the forward discount if negative, equation (2.3) can be written as:

$$(1 + p)(1 + i_e) = (1 + i_a). \qquad (2.4)$$

Since both p and i_e are generally small decimals, their product may be considered to be of the second order of smalls. In this case, equation (2.4) reduces to:

$$\boxed{p = i_a - i_e,} \qquad (2.5)$$

which is the conventional formulation of the equilibrium condition for interest parity. As will become clear shortly, interest parity will be established by efforts to buy pounds spot and sell forward (or vice versa) providing arbitrage funds are perfectly elastic in supply. Note also from equation (2.5) that if the interest rate in England is greater than in America, forward pounds will be at a discount in terms of dollars and correspondingly the forward dollar will be at a premium in terms of pounds. The opposite will be the case if the interest rate is higher in America than in England.

SPECULATION

Speculation may be characterized as the deliberate assumption of a net open position in foreign exchange. This position will be based upon the difference between the rate currently quoted on forward exchange for some specified time period and the spot rate that is expected to prevail when this time period has elapsed. The speculator may assume a long position, which means an excess of uncovered foreign exchange claims over liabilities, or a short position, which is an excess of uncovered foreign exchange liabilities over claims. Speculation can occur in the spot market as well as in the forward market. However, we shall confine our attention mainly to the latter operations since they are much more significant and since, as will be noted below, speculation in spot exchange can be treated essentially as a form of interest arbitrage.

If he believes that the future spot rate, say 90 days hence, will be higher than the current 90-day forward rate, the "bull" speculator will take a long position by purchasing forward exchange. The speculator hopes to profit by this deliberate assumption of risk by selling spot exchange 90 days hence at a rate higher than what he paid initially. If he believes that the future spot rate will be less than the current forward rate, the "bear" speculator will take a short position by selling forward exchange in anticipation of a future spot purchase at a rate lower than the one contracted earlier.

Thus, if we suppose that a speculator buys forward sterling at $2.40 per pound, he must sell at a higher rate in the future, say $2.41, in order to make a profit. Alternatively, if he sells forward sterling at $2.40, he must buy at a lower rate in the future, say $2.39, to make a profit. The speculator will obviously suffer a loss if the future spot rate turns out to be less than $2.40 in case he has a long position and if the future spot rate exceeds $2.40 in the event of a short position.

It was mentioned above that speculation could be carried out in the spot as well as in the forward market. There is a difference in these transactions, however, in that spot-market speculation requires access to funds whereas forward speculation does not, except to the extent that banks may impose margin requirements on such transactions. What is important for analytical purposes, however, is that speculation in spot exchange can be treated as a form of (uncovered) interest arbitrage. That is, when a speculator buys spot exchange rather than forward exchange, his expected profits will depend not only on the present and expected future spot rate, but also upon the difference between the domestic and foreign rate of interest. In effect then, a speculator who purchases uncovered spot exchange will implicitly undertake a forward sale matched by an implicit forward purchase of equal amount. The speculator can thus be looked upon in this way as buying forward exchange from himself in anticipation of an expected future spot rate that will be higher than the current forward rate.[22]

COMMERCIAL TRADE

When commercial transactions between countries require future receipt and payment of foreign currency, importers and exporters may wish to guard against whatever foreign exchange risk may arise. In this regard, the importer

22. To illustrate, suppose that an investor transfers $1 through the spot market to obtain a foreign security worth $1/r_s$ pounds. This transaction is equivalent to a $1 transfer through the spot market covered in the forward market by the sale of forward pounds equal to $(1/r_s)(1 + i_e)$ combined with a speculative purchase of $(1/r_s)(1 + i_e)$ pounds. Spot-market speculation will be undertaken therefore only if both the covered arbitrage and the forward speculative transactions are expected to be profitable.

can pay for the merchandise immediately or buy the foreign currency forward and pay the exporter in 90 days.[23] The method of payment chosen will depend upon the same factors as in the case of interest arbitrage: domestic and foreign interest rates and spot and forward exchange rates. The type of transaction at issue is thus termed appropriately *trade arbitrage.*

Assume that there is no time required for the shipment of goods between countries and that the importers are able to forecast sales with perfect accuracy. In this case, there is no need for inventory since the importers will arrange to have the goods delivered on precisely the same day as they are sold. The American importer is assumed to face a perfectly elastic supply of English exports at a price of £P_m for payment on delivery. If he can obtain the goods on credit from the English exporter, he will owe £$P_m(1 + i_e)$ in 90 days. If immediate payment is made via the spot market, the cost of the goods to the American importer will be $\$P_m r_s$. Alternatively, if forward covering is chosen, the American exporter will have to pay $\$P_m(1 + i_e)r_f$ in 90 days. The present value of the future commitment is $\$P_m(1 + i_e)r_f/(1 + i_a)$. Assuming competition, the importers will then choose the least costly method of financing, which can be seen to depend upon domestic and foreign interest rates and spot and forward exchange rates. The American importer will thus choose spot covering if:

$$P_m r_s < \frac{P_m(1 + i_e)r_f}{(1 + i_a)}$$

or alternatively

$$r_s(1 + i_a) < \frac{r_f(1 + i_e)}{r_s},$$

which turns out to be the condition expressed in equation (2.1). It is evident therefore that if the covered interest differential favors England, this means from the American importer's standpoint that *covered borrowing costs* are higher in England than at home. The American importer will then finance his trade domestically and make immediate payment via the spot market. If the sign of the trade-arbitrage condition were reversed, the American importer would change his method of covering and the location of his trade financing.[24]

23. As Levin (1970a, pp. 26–27) notes, in the case of immediate payment, the importer may borrow domestic currency and sell it in the spot market to pay the exporter. The payment will be effected through the importer's bank and the correspondent bank abroad. In the case of future payment, the exporter can discount the commercial bill with his bank if he requires immediate payment.

24. The foregoing discussion and that which follows is based on Levin (1970a, pp. 27–28 and 34). For a discussion of trade credit used to finance inventories of the traded goods, see Leamer and Stern (1970, p. 90; 1972). The conditions for financing inventories parallel those for trade arbitrage, but the decision involves the determination of the return to inventories rather than the return to arbitrage.

Suppose now that we consider the financing of American exports from the English importer's standpoint. If the English importer pays for the goods immediately via the spot market, the cost to him is $£P/r_s$, whereas if he buys the goods on credit, he will owe $\$P(1 + i_a)$ in 90 days. If the English importer covers forward, he will pay in 90 days in order to honor his forward contract an amount $£P(1 + i_a)/r_f$, the present value of which is $£P(1 + i_a)/r_f(1 + i_e)$. The English importer will thus choose spot covering if:

$$\frac{P}{r_s} < \frac{P(1 + i_a)}{r_f(1 + i_e)}$$

or alternatively

$$(1 + i_e) < \frac{r_s(1 + i_a)}{r_f},$$

which turns out to be the condition expressed in equation (2.2). This says that American exports (English imports) will be financed through the spot market only when the covered interest differential favors America. This is just the opposite of the condition just noted for the spot covering of American imports (English exports). It follows, therefore, with perfect capital markets that American imports and exports will be financed in the same country. Moreover, in view of the arbitrage condition, if American imports are financed through the spot market, American exports will be financed through the forward market, and vice versa.

Commercial traders may also engage in speculation in the manner described earlier. The expected profits from speculative activity should be treated separately from the trade financing decision, however, since traders presumably are primarily concerned with the profits from their trading activity.

SPOT AND FORWARD EXCHANGE-MARKET EQUILIBRIUM

Having discussed the three main types of transactions—interest arbitrage, speculation, and commercial trade—that are undertaken in the foreign exchange market, let us examine the determination of spot and forward exchange rates. Consider Figure 2.9 in which it is assumed that arbitrage demand and supply are infinitely elastic. The demand and supply schedules of spot and forward exchange involving commercial transactions are indicated by $D_£^a$ and $S_£^a$. As we have just noted, the profitability of importing and exporting will be influenced by the domestic and foreign interest rates and the spot and forward exchange rates. The demand and supply schedules of foreign exchange will thus embody these factors in addition to the ones reflected in the underlying commodity schedules discussed earlier in connection with the spot market. $D_£^a$ and $S_£^a$ have been drawn so as to insure stability.

We assume that speculation is confined to the forward market and is thus unaffected by changes in the spot rate. In the forward market, there will be

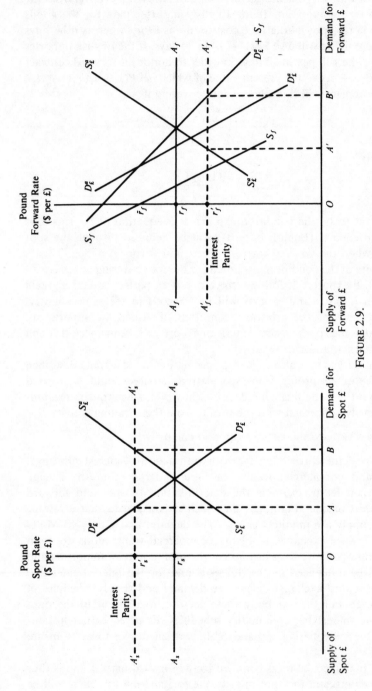

FIGURE 2.9.

*Spot and Forward Market Equilibrium under Free Market Conditions
with Infinitely Elastic Covered Interest Arbitrage*

Assume interest rates to be equal and that the spot and forward rates coincide. If the English interest rate is increased, arbitrageurs will demand spot pounds and sell forward pounds until the discount on forward pounds equals the interest differential. At the point where interest parity is assumed to hold, the spot rate will be r'_s and the forward rate, r'_f.

some forward rate, $\bar{r}_f$, at which there will be no speculation insofar as this rate coincides with the expected future spot rate. At this point, the speculative schedule will cut the vertical axis. If we can rule out the case of elastic expectations according to which the expected future rate would be adjusted upward or downward whenever the current forward rate rose or fell, speculative demand (or supply) can be taken as a decreasing (increasing) function of the current forward rate. Thus, the higher the current forward rate in excess of the rate at which speculation would be zero, the greater will be the speculative sales of forward exchange on the expectation that these sales can be covered at an actual lower spot rate in the future. The lower the current forward rate relative to the zero speculation point, the greater will be the speculative purchases of forward exchange in anticipation of a higher actual spot rate in the future. Speculative positions will not be undertaken without limit in view of the fact that expectations concerning the future spot rate are not held with complete confidence. The speculative schedule will thus be of finite rather than infinite elasticity. This schedule is indicated in Figure 2.9 as S_f, and it has been added to the commercial demand schedule for forward exchange to obtain the combined schedule, $D_{£}^a + S_f$.

Assuming interest rates to be equal in America and England and that the spot and forward rates coincide at r_s and r_f, the spot arbitrage schedule is designated in Figure 2.9 as A_s and the forward arbitrage schedule as A_f. There is no interest arbitrage under these conditions in accordance with the interest-parity condition noted above in equation (2.5). Suppose now that there is an increase in the English interest rate, with the American interest rate unchanged. Interest arbitrageuers will consequently be motivated to purchase pounds in the spot market in exchange for dollars and simultaneously to sell forward the pound proceeds of their investment in exchange for dollars. This will guarantee their profit by eliminating the risk of exchange-rate fluctuation. In terms of Figure 2.9, the change in the English interest rate will cause the arbitrage schedule to shift upward in the spot market from A_s to A_s' and downward in the forward market from A_f to A_f' to the position where interest parity is attained. This is depicted in Figure 2.9 at the new equilibrium spot and forward rates, r_s' and r_f' where the discount on forward sterling, $(r_f' - r_s')/r_s'$, is assumed to be equal to the given 90-day interest differential, $i_a - i_e$.[25]

In balance-of-payments terms, in the new equilibrium the amount of spot pounds demanded is OA for current-account purposes and AB represents the short-term capital movement for interest-arbitrage purposes. The amount of spot pounds supplied from current-account receipts is OB. In the forward market the demand for forward pounds for current-account and speculative purposes, OB', will be matched by the forward receipts from commercial

25. Note that if the movement of funds were to cause the interest rates to change, interest parity could be achieved in this way as well as by means of an increased discount on forward pounds.

trade, OA', and the forward sales of interest arbitrageurs, $A'B'$. Assuming that the interest earnings represent only a small fraction of the amount of pounds sold forward, the spot purchases and simultaneous forward sales of pounds are seen to be equal, i.e., $AB = A'B'$. Thus, when arbitrage funds are in perfectly elastic supply and domestic and foreign interest rates diverge, covered interest arbitrage links the determination of exchange rates in the spot and forward markets.

The interest-parity condition that governs interest arbitrage is as a matter of fact much less precise than implied by our discussion so far. For example, it may be difficult to specify exactly what the short-term rate of interest should be for purposes of analysis. There are many such rates for the various kinds of money-market instruments, different maturities, and classes of investors and borrowers. Also, the arbitrage incentive may have to exceed a certain minimum in order to make the transaction worthwhile. The minimum most commonly suggested prior to World War II was 1/2 percent per annum,[26] while in the postwar period it appears that arbitrage may be undertaken for as little as 1/10 or 1/32 percent per annum.[27] However, in addition to these institutional factors, there are some important economic reasons suggested by portfolio-balance considerations that make it unlikely that the arbitrage schedule will be infinitely elastic.[28]

The first reason is that there may be increasing opportunity costs of arbitrage relative to other uses of funds. This is a question of avoiding the possible inconvenience and loss of liquidity in tying up excessive amounts of short-term liquid assets in arbitrage transactions. Secondly, there may exist differential default risks on domestic and foreign assets, particularly if governments intervene in the foreign exchange market. Third, according to portfolio-balance theory, there are gains to be made from the diversification of asset portfolios in terms of lowering the aggregate risk of the portfolio. This may be the case even when foreign assets are more risky than domestic assets.[29] After some point, however, there may be diminishing returns to diversification so that arbitrage funds may become limited. Finally, foreign assets may not be perfectly substitutable for comparable domestic assets in the event of the need for premature repatriation of funds prior to maturity. This is especially the case if forward markets for particular maturity points are relatively thin and would thus generate somewhat higher than usual costs for early liquidation of foreign asset holdings.

26. This was first pointed out by Keynes (1923, p. 128).
27. See Einzig (1961, esp. pp. 50, 167, 169–70, and 201–02). Branson (1969b) has estimated that the minimum differential for both U.S.-U.K. arbitrage and U.S.-Canadian arbitrage was 0.18 percent per annum in the early 1960's.
28. See Officer and Willett (1970). The following paragraph is based upon their work.
29. The reduction in aggregate riskiness comes about because of the low covariations in returns for the various types of assets. For a formal discussion, see Levin (1970a). See Grubel (1968) and Levy and Sarnat (1970) for empirical analyses of international portfolio diversification.

While some of the factors just mentioned arise from market imperfections and the inadequate functioning of the balance-of-payments mechanism especially under the adjustable-peg system, others would be operative even under free market conditions so as to make the arbitrage schedule less than infinitely elastic. Thus, in Figure 2.10, the arbitrage schedules, A_s and A_f, have been drawn with finite elasticity.[30] It will be noted that we have retained the assumption of initial interest equality in the two countries and that $r_s = r_f$. The amounts of arbitrage supply and demand in the two markets are indicated along A_s and A_f to the left and right of the vertical axes at r_s and r_f, where the arbitrage movement will be zero.

Thus, with interest rates equal and the forward rate given at r_f, for spot rates below r_s there will be a premium on forward pounds and consequently an interest-arbitrage incentive in favor of England. The demand for spot pounds would thus be increased along A_s. For spot rates above r_s there will be a discount on forward pounds, an arbitrage incentive favoring America, and hence an increase in the supply of spot pounds along A_s. With interest rates equal and the spot rate given at r_s, for forward rates below (above) r_f, there will be a discount (premium) on forward pounds, an arbitrage incentive favoring America (England), and an increase in the demand (supply) for forward pounds along A_f. Equilibrium requires that the arbitrage demand (supply) in each market be equal to the excess supply (demand) from all other transactions, from which it follows that spot arbitrage demand (supply) will equal forward arbitrage supply (demand).[31]

An assumed increase in the English interest rate with the American rate unchanged would evidently cause A_s to shift upward and A_f to shift downward in Figure 2.10. If A_s and A_f were infinitely elastic as in Figure 2.9 and the interest-parity-equilibrium spot and forward rates were r_s' and r_f', the arbitrage purchase of spot pounds would be AB and the sale of forward pounds $A'B'$. It should be evident, however, from Figure 2.10 that if A_s and A_f shifted to

30. It will be noted that the arbitrage schedules in Figure 2.10 have been drawn without any reference to the aforementioned minimum percent per annum return that might be necessary to make arbitrage worthwhile. The schedules could be altered easily to take this into account by introducing a range above and below r_s and r_f where arbitrage would not be undertaken. The schedules could also be made relatively more inelastic beyond some point in the supply and demand quadrants to reflect the limitations on the generation of additional arbitrage funds. See Reading (1960, esp. pp. 307–11), Auten (1963), Grubel (1966, pp. 18–20), and Branson (1969b, pp. 1029–31) for constructions of the arbitrage schedule that embody these refinements.

31. Note that we are abstracting from interest earnings. We are also presuming that arbitrage takes place only in the direction indicated by the covered interest differential. In Levin's portfolio-selection model (1970a) of the foreign exchange market, where returns and risk are taken explicitly into account, arbitrage may occur in both directions simultaneously. Note also that in Levin's model the financing of commercial trade is allocated between the spot and forward markets in accordance with the trade-arbitrage conditions stated in our earlier discussion. Thus, if the covered interest differential favored England, American imports would be covered in the spot market and exports in the forward market. The interested reader may wish to adapt Figure 2.10 to take these various factors into account.

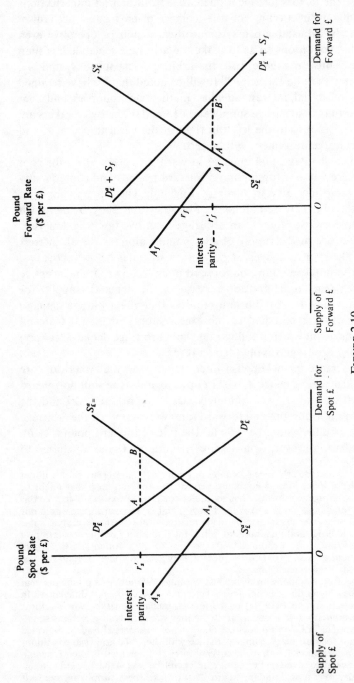

FIGURE 2.10.

Spot and Forward Market Equilibrium under Free Market Conditions with Finitely Elastic Covered Interest Arbitrage

Assume interest rates to be equal and that the spot and forward rates coincide. If the English interest rate is increased, the spot arbitrage schedule will be shifted upward and the forward schedule downward. The new equilibrium will be below r'_s and above r'_f so that the arbitrage movement will be less than $AB = A'B'$. The interest-parity condition will not hold in this case.

positions where they intersected the axes at r'_s and r'_f, this could not be an equilibrium result. This is because at these rates the arbitrage movement would be zero while there would be an excess supply of spot pounds and an excess demand for forward pounds.

The equilibrium-arbitrage movement in Figure 2.10 will therefore be less than AB. Correspondingly, the equilibrium spot rate will not be as high as r'_s and the equilibrium forward rate not so low as r'_f. It is unfortunately not possible to indicate graphically in Figure 2.10 precisely what the new equilibrium will be. This is because the arbitrage schedule in each market is drawn subject to a given exchange rate in the other market. Since both the spot and forward exchange rates will be altered simultaneously when the English interest rate is increased, the new arbitrage schedules cannot be depicted.[32]

The conclusion to be drawn from Figure 2.10 is that the interest-parity condition as outlined earlier must be amended in order to allow for limitations on the supply of arbitrage funds. Once these limitations are recognized, it need not be expected that arbitrage movements will take place on a scale that results in a forward discount or premium that more or less offsets the given interest differential. The interest-parity condition may therefore not be an altogether reliable indicator of arbitrage incentives and equilibrium unless the arbitrage schedules are infinitely elastic, which may well not be the case.

This concludes our analysis of spot and forward exchange-rate determination under free market conditions. We have focused particularly on the role played by interest arbitrage in linking the spot and forward markets and thus in determining the spot and forward rates of exchange. The analysis has of course been greatly simplified. This has been the case especially with regard to the separation of the transactions into interest arbitrage, speculation, and commercial trade. It may well be that the actual transactors carry on more than one of these activities at any given time. We have also not dwelt in detail on the institutional factors and the portfolio risks and constraints that might in actuality limit the availability of funds for arbitrage purposes. Finally, we have not considered forward market transactions for periods shorter or longer than 90 days.[33] Our leaving aside these various refinements is not to deny, however, their factual importance in given circumstances.

---

32. See Leamer (1968) for a graphical exposition that attempts to deal with this question of simultaneity by positing that the arbitrage schedule is made an approximate function of the absolute difference between the forward and spot rates. The problem of simultaneity might also be dealt with by assuming the spot rate to be pegged by the authorities. This would fix the position of the forward arbitrage schedules. Such an assumption is not appropriate, however, for the analysis of exchange-rate determination under free market conditions, although it may be legitimate for the gold-standard and adjustable-peg conditions to be examined below.

33. See Grubel (1966) and Sohmen (1966, esp. pp. 36–40) for an analysis of the structure of exchange rates for different time periods. Leland (1971) contains a portfolio analysis of forward speculation with multiple forward exchange markets.

The Spot and Forward Rates under the Gold Standard

It was shown in our earlier discussion that the spot rate under the gold standard could fluctuate only within the limits established by the gold-export and import points. The same is true for the forward rate. This means that interest arbitrage cannot cause the spot and forward rates to diverge by more than the specified limits. We shall see that as a consequence there are substantial opportunities for completely riskless and profitable speculative transactions in the forward exchange market. This can be illustrated by Figure 2.11 in which the exchange-rate fluctuations in both the spot and forward markets are confined to within the gold-export and import points. Figure 2.11 is thus different from Figure 2.10 in that the demand and supply schedules of spot and forward exchange become perfectly elastic at the exchange-rate limits. Any excess demand or supply of spot exchange will be furnished by importers and exporters of gold. In the forward market, speculative transactions will furnish the excess demand or supply. Thus, at the gold-export point speculators will sell unlimited amounts of forward exchange. They will be able to cover these sales subsequently at least at this same exchange rate or at a lower rate in which case they will make a profit. Speculators will buy unlimited amounts of forward exchange at the gold-import point since they will be able to sell at least at this same rate or at a higher one.

The demand and supply schedules of spot and forward exchange for transactions other than arbitrage have been drawn in Figure 2.11 to intersect at the gold-export point in each market. Equal interest rates and equal spot and forward rates are assumed initially. If the rate of interest were now increased in England and the American rate were unchanged, there would be an increase in the demand for spot pounds and in the supply of forward pounds for arbitrage purposes. If the arbitrage schedules were infinitely elastic in Figure 2.11, the amount of the arbitrage movement would be indeterminate so long as the interest differential was maintained. But suppose the schedules have finite elasticity as A_s and A_f in Figure 2.11.

The increase in the English interest rate will initially cause A_s to shift upward to A_s' and A_f to shift downward to A_f'. While the spot rate would rise in a free market, our gold-standard assumptions in Figure 2.11 assure that this rate will remain fixed at the gold-export point. The forward rate will fall below the gold-export point, however, due to the increase in the supply of forward pounds. This means that the spot arbitrage schedule cannot remain at A_s' and that it will shift downward to A_s''. The equilibrium arbitrage movement will thus be AB purchases of spot pounds, which will be matched by $A'B'$ sales of forward pounds. The spot arbitrage purchases will be supplied entirely from the export of gold, and the forward arbitrage sales taken up by

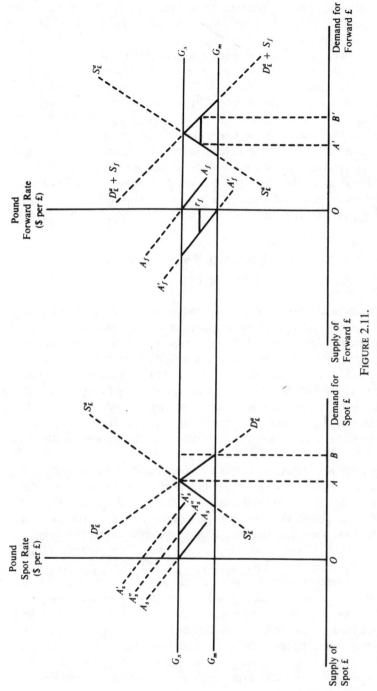

FIGURE 2.11.

Spot and Forward Market Equilibrium under the Gold Standard

Assume interest rates to be equal and that the spot and forward rates coincide at the gold-export point. An increase in the English interest rate will cause the arbitrage schedules to shift to A'_s and A'_f. The movement along A'_f will cause a shift to A''_s. In equilibrium, the arbitrage movement will be $AB = A'B'$, with the spot purchases being supplied by gold exports. The gold movement will then engender further adjustment in response to changes in interest rates and prices.

the increased demand of commercial traders and speculators. The equilibrium spot rate will remain, as noted, at the gold-export point and the equilibrium forward rate will be r_f.

The new equilibrium indicated in Figure 2.11 is unlikely to be sustained, however, because internal monetary and price adjustments will take place in each country in keeping with the gold-standard rules of the game as a consequence of the loss and receipt of gold. Thus, in Figure 2.11, there will be upward pressure on the rate of interest in the country losing gold and downward pressure in the other country. The arbitrage incentive will therefore be reduced. In addition, the reduction in relative prices of goods and services in the country losing gold will have a favorable impact on the trade balance. The combined effects of the interest and price changes may be sufficient to stem the outflow of gold and to cause a downward movement in the spot rate below the gold-export point.

The Spot and Forward Rates under the Adjustable Peg

We have already indicated the essential similarities and differences in the determination of the spot rate of exchange under the gold standard as compared to the present-day system of the adjustable peg. It was mentioned in particular that the IMF member countries are obliged to keep their currencies stable within narrow limits vis-à-vis the U.S. dollar by purchasing or selling dollars, or converting gold or SDR's for this purpose, in the foreign exchange market. These limits are not altogether certain at times, however, particularly when it is thought that a country's balance of payments may be in fundamental disequilibrium and that the exchange rate may consequently be altered.

This latter point is of especial significance since countries are not obligated under present-day circumstances to maintain their forward exchange rates within specified limits. It is possible, therefore, that when a country's spot exchange rate is in doubt, this will give rise to forward market transactions that will in turn exert considerable pressures on the spot market that may be difficult to withstand. Thus, if we have a situation of an expected future devaluation, speculators will sell the currency forward in the hope of covering their sales subsequently at a lower rate of exchange, thereby making a profit by the difference in rates. By creating a discount on forward exchange, the speculative transactions may create an incentive for outward arbitrage. Since this will lead to spot sales of the domestic currency in exchange for foreign currency, the exchange-stabilization authorities may have to intervene in the market in order to keep the spot rate from falling below the lower limit. Such intervention, if substantial, could result in a severe depletion of the country's foreign exchange reserves.

In analyzing the behavior of the forward rate under the adjustable peg, it is necessary therefore to distinguish "normal" from "speculative" periods. Thus, in normal periods, fluctuations in the forward rate will be confined to within the established upper and lower exchange-rate limits since there are no expectations that these limits will be altered. The analysis of the spot and forward markets under these circumstances is exactly the same as in our preceding discussion of the gold standard. That is, the speculative supply and demand schedule of forward exchange will be perfectly elastic at the upper and lower limits. The amount of interest arbitrage would be determined in a similar manner as in Figure 2.11, and there would be no risks whatever involved in uncovered purchases of forward exchange at the lower limit and sales at the upper limit.

The speculative period case can be analyzed with the aid of Figure 2.12. Assume that interest rates in both countries are the same and that spot and forward rates are equal initially. The spot and forward market-demand and supply schedules are labeled as in our earlier discussion. It will be noted that in the spot market these schedules are perfectly elastic at the upper and lower exchange-rate limits where the foreign exchange authorities will intervene to keep the limits from being breached. The distinguishing characteristic of the speculative case is, however, that these limits might possibly be changed by means of a devaluation or appreciation of the exchange rate. Since the authorities are not obligated to support the forward rate, this rate is free to move outside of the specified limits and will do so depending especially upon speculative anticipations concerning the future spot rate. Hence in the speculative case the combined commercial trade and speculative schedule, $D_£^a + S_f$, will not be perfectly elastic at the forward rate limits as in the normal case.

Suppose that the spot and forward rates had been at the lower limit for some time and that this led speculators to believe that a devaluation might occur. Assume then that the combined commercial trade and speculative schedule shifts to the left to $D_£^a + S_f'$ as speculators sell forward pounds in the amount of CD, hoping subsequently to fulfill their forward obligations at the devalued rate. As a consequence of these speculative forward sales, the forward rate would be depressed below the lower limit to r_f, and an arbitrage incentive would be created in favor of America.

Assuming interest rates in the two countries still to be equal, the decline in the forward rate will cause the spot arbitrage schedule to shift to the left from A_s to A_s' by the amount of AB, which represents the arbitrage sales of spot pounds. Under free market conditions this would depress the spot rate below the lower support limit. The foreign exchange authorities will therefore have to absorb this sale of spot pounds by selling dollars in order to keep the spot rate at its lower limit. Arbitrageurs will cover their spot sales of pounds by a simultaneous forward purchase, moving along A_f, of $A'B'$ pounds. The equilibrium spot exchange rate will be r_f'.

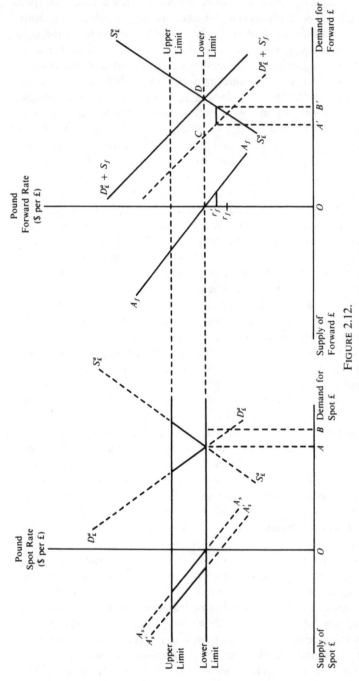

FIGURE 2.12.

Spot and Forward Market Equilibrium under the
Adjustable Peg in a Speculative Period

Assuming a speculative attack on the pound in the forward market indicated by the shift to $D_£^a + S_f'$, the forward rate will decline to r_f and the spot arbitrage schedule will shift to A_s'. The arbitrage movement will be $AB = A'B'$ and the equilibrium forward rate, r_f'. The authorities would have to purchase forward pounds equal to CD to prevent the arbitrage incentive that would otherwise occur with the speculative attack.

Thus, in the speculative case represented in Figure 2.12, the expectation of a devaluation gives rise to speculative forward sales, which create a discount on forward sterling and an incentive for arbitrage. The pressure on the forward market due to speculative sales is shifted consequently to the spot market as interest arbitrageurs are led to sell spot sterling. With the spot rate already assumed to be at the lower limit, there will be a drain on foreign exchange reserves as the authorities strive to support this rate. It is obvious that this support can continue only up to the point of exhaustion of the foreign exchange reserves or when it is decided that these reserves cannot be further depleted below some given level. At such a juncture, the authorities may be forced to institute corrective action.

It is unlikely of course that the authorities will stand idly by until a crisis is at hand. They might, for example, raise the rate of interest in order to affect the direction of the arbitrage movement. Their success here would depend importantly on the reaction of speculators. If it were widely believed that stability would be restored, speculative forward selling might cease. Otherwise, forward selling might increase further, thus widening the discount on forward pounds and causing even greater pressure on the spot market due to increased arbitrage sales of spot pounds.

It is also possible for the authorities to intervene in the forward market by purchasing forward pounds. Thus, assume as before that in Figure 2.12 the combined commercial trade and speculative schedule in the forward market shifts downward to $D_£^a + S_f'$. The intersection of this schedule with the lower exchange-rate limit indicates that at this rate forward sales by speculators of CD would have to be matched by forward purchases by the authorities of the same amount in order to keep the forward rate the same as in the initial equilibrium. The success of this policy will also depend upon how speculators react. If confidence is restored in the exchange-rate limits, the threat to the nation's foreign exchange reserves can be averted because there will be no interest-arbitrage incentive.

But if there is a continuing underlying weakness in the balance of payments, forward exchange intervention may provide only temporary relief. Moreover, in the event that a devaluation actually occurs, the authorities will suffer a loss in fulfilling their forward commitments to speculators. That is, speculators will profit at the expense of the authorities according to the difference between the rate at which the speculative forward sales were made and the lower devalued rate at which the speculators actually discharge their commitments.

Forward market intervention has other implications besides those we have mentioned. The most important is that official management of the forward rate may give the authorities leeway in establishing interest-rate policies in order to accomplish certain given domestic objectives. For example, the authorities may decide for domestic stabilization purposes that the rate of interest should be relatively higher or lower. If interest rates elsewhere are unchanged, an arbitrage incentive will be created. The authorities can avoid this, however, by purchasing or selling forward exchange up to the point where the forward discount or premium will offset the interest differential. A further implication of forward-market intervention is that the authorities may set the rate of interest and buy or sell forward exchange in order to attract or repel arbitrage movements as a means of augmenting or reducing their foreign exchange reserves. We shall have occasion to discuss these various ramifications of forward exchange policies in greater detail in Chapter 5.

Before concluding this section, a few words are in order regarding "leads" and "lags" in commercial payments that may arise whenever a devaluation is expected to occur. It was mentioned in our earlier discussion that when commercial traders are motivated to switch the location of their trade financing from one center to another, they are acting in effect as interest arbitrageurs. This is because their decision will depend upon the existing interest rates and upon the spot and forward exchange rates. It was also mentioned that the activities of commercial traders who assumed uncovered forward commitments could be analyzed in the same way as speculators. Thus, in Figure 2.12, the speculative schedule could be interpreted to cover both types of activities.

Leads and lags refer to the acceleration of payments in foreign currency in connection especially with exports. Payments will be accelerated in order to avoid being caught with foreign currency obligations and they will be delayed in the hope of obtaining a more favorable exchange rate in the event of a devaluation. In our example in Figure 2.12, the creation of a forward discount on pounds will make it cheaper to finance trade in England than in America. Suppose we have an American importer who had financed his trade in America and discharged his pound obligation immediately in the spot market to avoid an exchange risk. It may now pay him to switch his financing to England and contrive to owe pounds. This will evidently result in a delay of foreign exchange receipts to England. If an English importer were similarly motivated to finance his trade in England and to discharge his foreign currency obligation immediately, there would be a speed-up of English foreign exchange payments.

The combined effect of leads and lags may thus be to create a drain on the nation's reserve position as a consequence of the arbitrage considerations that determine where it is cheapest to finance trade and that affect the timing of payments and receipts of foreign exchange. Leads and lags are consequently somewhat different than pure speculation in that their form will vary depending upon arbitrage incentives. Pure speculation on the other hand can be said to be confined entirely to the forward market where it is focused on the difference between the current forward rate and the expected future spot rate.

If we wished to represent our example of leads and lags in terms of Figure

2.12, we could imagine that in the spot market the demand and supply schedules of spot pounds shifted respectively to the left and to the right. The authorities would then be forced to absorb the excess supply of pounds by selling dollars in order to keep the spot rate at its lower limit. This drain on reserves would thus augment the arbitrage-induced drain indicated in Figure 2.12. There would be no additional impact on the forward market in our example, although it is quite conceivable in other arbitrage-induced circumstances that commercial traders could assume speculative positions in forward sterling.

Conclusion

This chapter has been devoted to an analysis of the spot and forward foreign exchange markets under alternative exchange-rate systems. We first derived the basic tools of analysis in terms of the demand and supply schedules of foreign exchange in a two-country world and thereafter analyzed the determination of the spot rate of exchange under free market conditions. This rate was shown to be stable so long as the demand and supply schedules of foreign exchange have their conventional slopes. While the actual slopes of the schedules depend on empirical considerations, it was argued that there were important reasons for presuming that the schedules would most likely be relatively elastic. We next considered the determination of the spot rate under gold-standard conditions. The gold-export and import points were seen to establish the upper and lower limits for the spot rate, and the demand and supply schedules of foreign exchange were perfectly elastic at these limits. If gold movements occurred, the balance of payments would adjust in response to changes in relative prices and interest rates as the monetary authorities contracted or expanded the money supply and therefore the level of money income. Our analysis of the spot market was concluded by examining the present-day system of the adjustable peg. This system is similar to the gold standard insofar as the determination and maintenance of the exchange-rate limits are concerned, but different in that gold does not move freely today as it once did, countries commonly give more weight to domestic employment and income goals than they give to the balance of payments, and under certain conditions the exchange-rate limits may be altered.

After considering the spot market, we examined the joint determination of the spot and forward rates under the different exchange-rate systems. Three types of foreign exchange-market activities were analyzed: interest arbitrage, speculation, and commercial trade. It was shown how covered interest arbitrage linked the spot and forward markets in terms of the interest-parity condition when the arbitrage schedule was infinitely elastic and less than infinitely elastic. Under gold-standard conditions, the forward and spot rates were seen to be fixed at the gold-export and import points, and speculative demand and supply in the forward market was infinitely elastic at the gold points. If gold movements occurred, the spot and forward markets would adjust in the same manner as outlined for the spot market alone. The analysis of the spot and forward markets under conditions of the adjustable peg was seen to be basically the same as under the gold standard in normal periods when there was no question about the maintenance of the upper or lower exchange-rate support limits. But in periods when the maintenance of these limits was in doubt, as for example in case of an impending devaluation, a country might suffer reserve losses due to arbitrage outflows in response to the forward discount created by speculative sales in the forward market. If the balance-of-payments difficulties were temporary in nature, forward intervention by the authorities might be justified to counteract the speculative impact. Some further implications of forward intervention were mentioned regarding policies designed to affect the level of reserves and to achieve purely domestic objectives. Finally, leads and lags in commercial payments were discussed briefly, and the manner in which they might create pressure on exchange reserves was indicated.

Appendix

1. *Relation of the price elasticity of import demand and export supply to the price elasticity of home demand and supply.*[1] Assume a situation as in Figure 2.1 in which a country has home consumption and home production and will export or import the good in question if the price is above or below P. Holding income and other things constant, let the home-demand and supply schedules be:

$$Q_d = F_1(P) \tag{2.A.1}$$

$$Q_s = F_2(P). \tag{2.A.2}$$

The demand schedule for imports will be the difference between these equations:

$$Q_m = Q_d - Q_s = F_1(P) - F_2(P). \tag{2.A.3}$$

The price elasticity of demand for imports, η_m, will be:

$$\eta_m = \frac{dQ_m}{dP}\frac{P}{Q_m} = \frac{P}{Q_m}\left(\frac{dF_1}{dP} - \frac{dF_2}{dP}\right). \tag{2.A.4}$$

Since $dF_1/dP = \eta_d(Q_d/P)$, and $dF_2/dP = e_s(Q_s/P)$, where η_d and e_s refer respectively to the elasticity of demand and supply, we can write (2.A.4) as:

$$\eta_m = \frac{P}{Q_m}\left(\eta_d \frac{Q_d}{P} - e_s \frac{Q_s}{P}\right) = \frac{Q_d}{Q_m}\eta_d - \frac{Q_s}{Q_m}e_s. \tag{2.A.5}$$

The sign of η_d will be negative and that of e_s positive. If the quantity supplied domestically were equal, say, to three times the quantity imported, it

---

1. The derivation in this section and the one following is based on Orcutt (1950, p. 127). See also Yeager (1966, pp. 139–41).

follows from the identity, $Q_d = Q_m + Q_s$, that home demand would be four times the quantity imported. If η_d and e_s were equal respectively to -1 and $+1$, the price elasticity of demand for imports would be: $\eta_m = 4\eta_d - 3e_s = -7$.

It follows from (2.A.1) and (2.A.2) that the export-supply schedule will be:

$$Q_x = Q_s - Q_d = F_2(P) - F_1(P). \qquad (2.A.6)$$

Using the same line of reasoning as in (2.A.4), the price elasticity of supply for exports, e_x, will be:

$$e_x = \frac{Q_s}{Q_x} e_s - \frac{Q_d}{Q_x} \eta_d. \qquad (2.A.7)$$

It may be noted from (2.A.5) that even if we assumed η_d to be zero, import demand could be relatively elastic. By the same token it should be evident from (2.A.7) that export supply could be relatively elastic even if home supply were perfectly inelastic. These propositions may also be demonstrated in Figure 2.1 by drawing the home-demand and home-supply schedule vertically through P and then deriving the import-demand or export-supply schedules.

2. *Relation of the price elasticity of demand for the exports of an individual country to world demand and the supply of competing exporters.* This relation can be demonstrated in the same manner as the one in the preceding section. The world demand schedule for some homogeneous product and the supply schedule of competing exporters is:

$$Q_w = F_1(P) \qquad (2.A.8)$$

$$Q_c = F_2(P). \qquad (2.A.9)$$

The demand schedule for the exports of an individual country is the difference between these equations:

$$Q_x = Q_w - Q_c = F_1(P) - F_2(P). \qquad (2.A.10)$$

The price elasticity of demand for the individual country's exports, η_x, will be:

$$\eta_x = \frac{dQ_x}{dP} \frac{P}{Q_x} = \frac{P}{Q_x} \left(\frac{dF_1}{dP} - \frac{dF_2}{dP} \right),$$

or

$$\eta_x = \frac{Q_w}{Q_x} \eta_w - \frac{Q_c}{Q_x} e_c, \qquad (2.A.11)$$

where η_w and e_c refer, respectively, to the price elasticity of world demand and the price elasticity of supply of competing exporters. If η_w and e_c were equal to -1 and $+1$, respectively, and the world market were shared equally between the competing exporters and the individual country, the price elasticity of demand for the latter's exports would be: $\eta_x = 2\eta_w - 1e_s = -3$. It may be noted from this example that even if world demand were perfectly inelastic (i.e., $\eta_w = 0$), η_x would still be equal to -1. It should also be clear that η_x will be larger for a given country, the smaller are its exports in relation to those of competing suppliers.

3. *Relation of the price elasticity of demand and supply of exports and imports to the elasticity of demand and supply of foreign exchange.*[2] Assume a two-country world, as in Figure 2.3, in which exports and imports each refer to one single homogeneous commodity. Also, money incomes and other factors are to be held constant in each country when the rate of exchange is varied. Let us confine our attention to the current account and assume the demand and supply of foreign exchange to be equal in initial equilibrium.

Let p_{fx} and p_{fm} denote the dollar (foreign currency) prices of exports and imports initially and X and M the quantities of exports and imports. The trade balance, B_f, will thus be:

$$B_f \equiv p_{fx}X - p_{fm}M. \tag{2.A.12}$$

The supply of dollars is represented by $p_{fx}X$ and the demand by $p_{fm}M$. Noting changes by the prefix Δ, the change in the trade balance, ΔB_f, as a consequence of a depreciation of the pound (home currency) can be expressed to a linear approximation as:

$$\Delta B_f \equiv (p_{fx}\,\Delta X + X\,\Delta p_{fx}) - (p_{fm}\,\Delta M + M\,\Delta p_{fm}). \tag{2.A.13}$$

If we indicate the initial values of exports and imports in dollars as V_{fx} and V_{fm}, we can write (2.A.13) rearranged in the form of relatives as:

$$\Delta B_f \equiv V_{fx}\left(\frac{\Delta X}{X} + \frac{\Delta p_{fx}}{p_{fx}}\right) + V_{fm}\left(-\frac{\Delta M}{M} - \frac{\Delta p_{fm}}{p_{fm}}\right). \tag{2.A.14}$$

The elasticities of demand and supply of exports and imports are defined below, with additional notations p_{hx} and p_{hm} referring to the domestic (home currency) prices of exports and imports:

$$e_x \equiv \frac{\Delta X}{X}\bigg/\frac{\Delta p_{hx}}{p_{hx}} \qquad \text{Home export-supply elasticity} \tag{2.A.15}$$

$$\eta_x \equiv -\frac{\Delta X}{X}\bigg/\frac{\Delta p_{fx}}{p_{fx}} \qquad \text{Foreign export-demand elasticity} \tag{2.A.16}$$

$$e_m \equiv \frac{\Delta M}{M}\bigg/\frac{\Delta p_{fm}}{p_{fm}} \qquad \text{Foreign import-supply elasticity} \tag{2.A.17}$$

$$\eta_m \equiv -\frac{\Delta M}{M}\bigg/\frac{\Delta p_{hm}}{p_{hm}} \qquad \text{Home import-demand elasticity} \tag{2.A.18}$$

2. The derivation in this section is based primarily on Alexander (1959, esp. pp. 37–39). See also Haberler (1949, pp. 200–07), Kindleberger (1968, pp. 569–77), J. Robinson (1947b, pp. 90–92), Vanek (1962, pp. 68–72), and Yeager (1966, pp. 136–39 and 158–60).

Since foreign-currency and home-currency prices are equated by means of the exchange rate, r, we can write:

$$p_{fm} = p_{hm}r. \tag{2.A.19}$$

If we assume the home currency to be depreciated by some proportion, k, so that the home currency is worth $r(1 - k)$ units of foreign currency, the corresponding changes in prices can be written as:

$$p_{fm} + \Delta p_{fm} = (p_{hm} + \Delta p_{hm})r(1 - k). \tag{2.A.20}$$

Since $p_{fm} = p_{hm}r$, (2.A.20) can be written as:

$$\Delta p_{fm} = (p_{hm} + \Delta p_{hm})r(1 - k) - p_{hm}r$$

$$\Delta p_{fm} = p_{hm}r - p_{hm}rk + \Delta p_{hm}r - \Delta p_{hm}kr - p_{hm}r$$

$$\Delta p_{fm} = -p_{hm}rk + \Delta p_{hm}r - \Delta p_{hm}kr.$$

If we divide by p_{fm} on the left and $p_{hm}r$ on the right, we get:

$$\frac{\Delta p_{fm}}{p_{fm}} = -k + \frac{\Delta p_{hm}}{p_{hm}}(1 - k). \tag{2.A.21}$$

In a similar manner we can obtain:

$$\frac{\Delta p_{fx}}{p_{fx}} = -k + \frac{\Delta p_{hx}}{p_{hx}}(1 - k). \tag{2.A.22}$$

By combining (2.A.21)–(2.A.22) and (2.A.15)–(2.A.18), the relative changes in export and import quantities and prices in (2.A.14) can be expressed in terms of the elasticities and k, the devaluation proportion. Thus, for example from (2.A.15) we can write:

$$\frac{\Delta X}{X} = e_x \frac{\Delta p_{hx}}{p_{hx}},$$

or using (2.A.22):

$$\frac{\Delta X}{X} = \frac{e_x \left(\dfrac{\Delta p_{fx}}{p_{fx}} + k \right)}{1 - k},$$

or using (2.A.16):

$$\frac{\Delta X}{X} = e_x \frac{\left(-\dfrac{\Delta X}{X} \right)}{(1 - k)\eta_x} + e_x \frac{k}{(1 - k)}$$

$$\frac{\Delta X}{X} = \frac{e_x \dfrac{k}{1 - k}}{1 + \dfrac{e_x}{(1 - k)\eta_x}}$$

$$\frac{\Delta X}{X} = \frac{ke_x\eta_x}{e_x + \eta_x(1 - k)}. \tag{2.A.23}$$

In a similar manner we can obtain:

$$\frac{\Delta p_{fx}}{p_{fx}} = - \frac{ke_x}{e_x + \eta_x(1 - k)} \qquad (2.\text{A}'.24)$$

$$\frac{\Delta M}{M} = - \frac{ke_m \eta_m}{\eta_m + e_m(1 - k)} \qquad (2.\text{A}.25)$$

$$\frac{\Delta p_{fm}}{p_{fm}} = - \frac{k\eta_m}{\eta_m + e_m(1 - k)}. \qquad (2.\text{A}.26)$$

Substituting (2.A.23)–(2.A.26) into (2.A.14), we can obtain the formula for the change in the trade balance in foreign currency in terms of the elasticities of demand and supply of exports and imports:

$$\Delta B_f = k \left[V_{fx} \frac{e_x(\eta_x - 1)}{e_x + \eta_x(1 - k)} + V_{fm} \frac{\eta_m(e_m + 1)}{\eta_m + e_m(1 - k)} \right].$$
$$(2.\text{A}.27)$$

The formula in terms of domestic currency can be obtained in a similar manner. It is evident from (2.A.27) that all of the elasticities enter positively into the expression. The conventionally negative demand elasticities can be taken therefore in terms of their absolute value disregarding sign.

On the assumption that k is small and $V_{fx} = V_{fm}$, the expressions within the brackets that represent, respectively, the elasticity of supply and demand for foreign exchange, e_f and η_f, are:[3]

$$\frac{e_x(\eta_x - 1)}{e_x + \eta_x} + \frac{\eta_m(e_m + 1)}{\eta_m + e_m} = e_f + \eta_f. \qquad (2.\text{A}.28)$$

The general condition for foreign exchange-market stability, in the sense that a depreciation of the exchange rate will improve the trade balance (i.e., ΔB_f will be positive), is that the expression in (2.A.28) be greater than zero. Thus, with a devaluation of a given proportion, the change in the amount of foreign exchange supplied will be determined by $e_f \cdot V_{fx}$ and in the amount demanded by $\eta_f \cdot V_{fm}$. When both of these elasticities are relatively high, the foreign balance will increase as the consequence of larger export receipts

---

3. The elasticity of supply and demand for the domestic currency, e_h and η_h, are:

$$\frac{e_m(1 - \eta_m)}{\eta_m + e_m} + \frac{\eta_x(e_x + 1)}{e_x + \eta_x} = e_h + \eta_h. \qquad (2.\text{A}'.28)$$

Note that the supply of domestic currency constitutes the demand for foreign currency and the demand for domestic currency constitutes the supply of foreign currency. It follows from (2.A.28) and (2.A'.28) that:

$$e_h + \eta_f = 1 \qquad \text{and} \qquad \eta_h + e_f = 1.$$

and smaller import payments. In the event that depreciation causes export receipts to decline, the foreign balance could nevertheless increase due to an even greater decline in import payments. This is the case illustrated in Figure 2.5a where $\eta_f > e_f$.

The general condition for stability is to be distinguished from the Marshall-Lerner condition, which is based upon the assumption of infinite supply elasticities of exports and imports. This can be seen by rewriting (2.A.28):

$$\frac{\eta_x - 1}{1 + (\eta_x/e_x)} + \frac{\eta_m[1 + (1/e_m)]}{(\eta_m/e_m) + 1} . \qquad (2.A.29)$$

Thus, if the supply elasticities are assumed to be infinite, (2.A.29) reduces to the familiar Marshall-Lerner condition:[4]

$$\eta_x + \eta_m - 1,$$

which says that the trade balance will be improved if the sum of the export- and import-demand elasticities is greater than one. It will be noted that the Marshall-Lerner condition is a sufficient rather than a necessary condition for stability. That is, even if the demand elasticities sum to less than one, it can be seen from (2.A.29) that the situation may nevertheless be stable if the export and import-supply elasticities are sufficiently small.

4. *Relation of exchange-rate variation to the terms of trade.*[5] We make the same assumptions as in the section preceding. It will be recalled from Figure 2.3a and 2.3c that a change in the exchange rate is represented by shifting the supply function of imports and the demand function for exports, thereby inducing a change in the home price of imports, p_{hm}, and in the home price of exports, p_{hx}. The effect on the net barter (or commodity) terms of trade, $T = p_{hx}/p_{hm}$, will depend upon the price elasticities of the supply and demand functions for imports and exports.

4. With infinite supply elasticities, we have:

$$\eta_m = \eta_f \quad \text{and} \quad \eta_x = \eta_h.$$

The Marshall-Lerner condition can thus be written:

$$\eta_f + \eta_h > 1.$$

Noting that $\eta_h = 1 - e_f$, we get:

$$\eta_f - e_f > 0$$

or

$$\eta_f > e_f,$$

which is the condition for foreign exchange-market stability noted in our discussion in the text.

5. I am indebted to Edward E. Leamer for working out the details to be presented here. See Yeager (1966, pp. 168–69) for an alternative derivation.

Let us consider the following constant-elasticity functions and their associated elasticities:[6]

$$\text{Home export supply} \quad = p_{hx}^{e_x}; \qquad e_x = \left.\frac{\Delta X}{X}\right/\frac{\Delta p_{hx}}{p_{hx}} \qquad (2.A.30)$$

$$\text{Foreign export demand} = p_{fx}^{-\eta_x}; \quad -\eta_x = \left.\frac{\Delta X}{X}\right/\frac{\Delta p_{fx}}{p_{fx}} \qquad (2.A.31)$$

$$\text{Foreign import supply} \quad = p_{fm}^{e_m}; \qquad e_m = \left.\frac{\Delta M}{M}\right/\frac{\Delta p_{fm}}{p_{fm}} \qquad (2.A.32)$$

$$\text{Home import demand} \quad = p_{hm}^{-\eta_m}; \quad -\eta_m = \left.\frac{\Delta M}{M}\right/\frac{\Delta p_{hm}}{p_{hm}} \qquad (2.A.33)$$

Note that all the elasticities have been defined to be positive. Also, since foreign-currency and home-currency prices are equated by means of the exchange rate, r, we can write:

$$p_{fx} = r p_{hx} \qquad (2.A.34)$$

$$p_{fm} = r p_{hm}. \qquad (2.A.35)$$

Setting supply equal to demand in equations (2.A.30) and (2.A.31) and in equations (2.A.32) and (2.A.33) and taking note of equations (2.A.34) and (2.A.35), we have

$$p_{hx}^{e_x} = p_{fx}^{-\eta_x} = (r p_{hx})^{-\eta_x} \qquad (2.A.36)$$

$$p_{fm}^{e_m} = (r p_{hm})^{e_m} = p_{hm}^{-\eta_m}. \qquad (2.A.37)$$

Equation (2.A.36) can be solved as follows from p_{hx}:

$$p_{hx}^{e_m} = r^{-\eta_x} p_{hx}^{-\eta_x}$$

$$p_{hx}^{e_x} p_{hx}^{\eta_x} = r^{-\eta_x} p_{hx}^{-\eta_x} p_{hx}^{\eta_x}$$

$$p_{hx}^{(e_x + \eta_x)} = r^{-\eta_x}$$

$$p_{hx} = r^{-\eta_x/(e_x + \eta_x)}. \qquad (2.A.38)$$

In a similar manner we can solve equation (2.A.37) to obtain p_{hm}:

$$p_{hm} = r^{e_m/(-e_m - \eta_m)}. \qquad (2.A.39)$$

Recalling from above the definition of the terms of trade and substituting equations (2.A.38) and (2.A.39), we obtain:

$$T = p_{hx}/p_{hm}$$

$$T = r^{[(-\eta_x)/(e_x + \eta_x) + (e_m)/(e_m + \eta_m)]}$$

$$T = r^{[(e_x e_m - \eta_x \eta_m)/(e_x + \eta_x)(e_m + \eta_m)]}. \qquad (2.A.40)$$

6. Since we are dealing with very small exchange-rate variations, the demand and supply schedules of exports and imports can be approximated reasonably by a suitable constant-elasticity function. For a more general derivation, see Vanek (1962, pp. 76–79).

Since our object is to determine the manner in which the terms of trade vary with the rate of exchange, we can differentiate equation (2.A.40) to obtain:

$$\frac{dT}{dr} = \frac{e_x e_m - \eta_x \eta_m}{(e_x + \eta_x)(e_m + \eta_m)} r^{[(e_x e_m - \eta_x \eta_m)/(e_x + \eta_x)(e_m + \eta_m)] - 1}. \qquad (2.A.41)$$

Since the exchange rate, r, is positive, r raised to any power will also be positive. Moreover, since e_x, η_x, e_m, and η_m are all positive, the denominator in (2.A.41), $(e_x + \eta_x)(e_m + \eta_m)$, will be positive. The relation (2.A.41) is then greater or less than zero depending on the sign of $(e_x e_m - \eta_x \eta_m)$. This can be expressed as:

$$\left(\frac{dT}{dr} \gtrless 0\right) \equiv (e_x e_m - \eta_x \eta_m \gtrless 0) \equiv (e_x e_m \gtrless \eta_x \eta_m) \qquad (2.A.42)$$

In other words, the terms of trade will improve or worsen as the exchange rate increases (i.e., depreciates) depending upon whether the product of the elasticities of supply of exports and imports, $e_x e_m$, is greater or less than the product of the elasticities of demand for exports and imports, $\eta_x \eta_m$.[7]

---

7. This is essentially the same condition set out in J. Robinson (1947a, p. 400). Additional treatment of the terms-of-trade effects of exchange-rate variations is to be found below, especially in Chapters 5 and 7.

3

Balance-of-Payments Adjustment Under Freely Fluctuating Exchange Rates

While focusing so far primarily on balance-of-payments concepts and exchange-rate determination, we nevertheless have made frequent reference to the mechanism of balance-of-payments adjustment and policies to attain balance-of-payments equilibrium. We shall examine these latter topics in greater detail in the present chapter for the system in which exchange rates are freely fluctuating. The gold-standard and adjustable-peg systems will be treated in the following two chapters. Our objectives will be to uncover the important forces in the adjustment process that work more or less automatically and to indicate the governmental actions that may be necessary when the automatic adjustment forces are in themselves incomplete.

It should be clear from our discussion of the three main types of exchange-rate systems that the adjustment mechanism is manifested by the changes in imports and exports and in short-term capital movements that occur in response to automatic or policy-determined changes in relative prices and interest rates. The magnitude of the changes in trade will depend, as already noted, upon the elasticities of home and foreign demand and supply of exports and imports. The amount of short-term capital flows will hinge especially upon the return and risk factors that affect interest arbitrage, speculation, and the financing of commercial trade via the foreign exchange market.

The Mechanism of Adjustment with Freely Fluctuating Exchange Rates

When exchange rates are freely fluctuating, the mechanism of adjustment can be illustrated simply by means of the diagrammatic analysis employed in the preceding chapter to illustrate the relation between the demand and supply schedules of imports and exports of goods and services and the

70

demand and supply schedules of foreign exchange. Thus, in Figure 2.4 we saw that the equilibrium exchange rate was $2.40 per pound (or £0.417 per dollar). If this rate were displaced temporarily to $2.00 per pound (£0.50 per dollar), there would be an excess demand for pounds and an equivalent excess supply of dollars. America would thus have an incipient balance-of-payments deficit and England a corresponding incipient surplus.

This same situation is also depicted in Figure 2.3. Comparing the areas of the rectangles bounded by the solid lines in the top and bottom parts of this figure reveals the incipient deficit and surplus conditions of the respective countries. Since an exchange rate of $2 per pound is a disequilibrium rate, the pound will have to appreciate vis-à-vis the dollar in order for the foreign exchange market to be cleared. This means that American imports from England will become relatively more expensive and English imports from America relatively cheaper. The appreciation of the pound (depreciation of the dollar) will be represented by shifts of the schedules in Figure 2.3 so that the areas of the rectangles for exports and imports are equal in the respective currencies. This will occur with schedule shifts (not drawn) that correspond to an equilibrium exchange rate of $2.40 per pound (£0.417 per dollar), as is shown in Figure 2.4.

It should be clear from our discussion that under a system of freely fluctuating exchange rates the process of balance-of-payments adjustment works automatically through the changes which occur in imports and exports in response to changes in relative prices associated with exchange-rate variations. Thus, a balance-of-payments deficit or surplus can exist only in an incipient sense in view of the automatic equilibrating forces always at work. These forces are, of course, part and parcel of the competitive market-equilibrium adjustments that will occur in the respective countries in accordance with our assumptions. We know from the theory of comparative advantage that under competitive conditions free international trade will result in an optimal allocation of resources for the world as a whole. A system of freely fluctuating exchange rates is to be looked upon, therefore, as the monetary counterpart of a system of free international trade. The essence of the argument in support of freely fluctuating exchange rates is to be understood accordingly in terms of optimal resource allocation. As will become clear shortly, our criterion of optimality is to be interpreted with respect to the present-day system of the adjustable peg in which government intervention often results in the misallocation of resources.

We have already noted that the process of adjustment may be aided significantly by short-term capital movements as well as by changes in the balance of trade. Suppose, for example, that we have a country with an incipient balance-of-payments deficit on account of domestic inflation and that the rate of interest is increased by tightening monetary policy in order to curb domestic expenditure. Assuming interest parity initially, the increase in the rate of interest will result in an arbitrage-induced inflow of short-term capital that will help to adjust the balance of payments. Since under the assumed conditions there will be a tendency for the exchange rate to depreciate, adjustment will occur also through changes in the country's balance of trade. But it may be noted that since creation of an inward arbitrage incentive means an increase in the demand for the nation's currency, this will offset to some extent the exchange-rate depreciation required for adjustment via the trade balance alone.[1]

Speculative short-term capital movements may have a stabilizing effect similar to that just described. That is, if a country's exchange rate has depreciated, say, because of domestic inflation and the authorities take corrective measures to remove the inflation, speculators may decide to purchase the currency in anticipation of its policy-induced appreciation. The rate might, therefore, fall less than would be the case if speculation were absent. Since speculation may consequently reduce exchange-rate variability, speculators can be looked upon accordingly as performing a socially useful function.

It should be clear from our discussion that the beneficial effects of speculation will be realized when speculators are well informed about the potential course of exchange-rate movements. Such a state of affairs can exist so long as the authorities act promptly and decisively to maintain full employment and price stability. It is possible, however, as Meade (1951, pp. 222–23) has indicated, that speculative anticipations may be mistaken in that speculation may occur in the wrong direction or take place on too large a scale. That is to say, speculators may expect the rate to go one way whereas in fact it goes the other way, or they may expect the rate to move more in a given direction than is justified by underlying foreign exchange-market conditions. Speculative behavior may, under these circumstances, intensify rather than ease balance-of-payments adjustments.

If misinformed speculation is in fact a real possibility, it would then become necessary for the authorities to move funds in a direction that will counteract the speculative movement. This would require the authorities to anticipate the future development of exchange rates more accurately than speculators are able to do. While it is not possible to determine the likelihood of misinformed speculation, it would appear that this likelihood would be smaller the more successful the authorities are in devising policies for attainment of the goals of full employment and price stability and in moderating, therefore, the extent of exchange-rate fluctuation. What is important to stress is that unrestricted interest arbitrage and speculative short-term

1. The analysis in this paragraph is applicable similarly in the case of a country with an incipient balance-of-payments surplus caused by domestic deflation. That is, the combination of exchange-rate appreciation and a lower rate of interest will serve to curb both the deflation and the incipient surplus in the balance of payments. In the case of inflation and incipient surplus, a higher rate of interest will be combined with exchange-rate appreciation. With deflation and incipient deficit, a lower rate of interest will be combined with exchange-rate depreciation.

capital movements will, under ordinary circumstances, reinforce rather than frustrate the attainment of the aforementioned policy goals.

An additional important feature of freely fluctuating exchange rates is that they permit individual nations to follow relatively independent monetary and fiscal policies for purposes of domestic stabilization and growth. Given the desire to pursue independent national goals, it would appear that some type of system of exchange-rate variability will in fact be required. Thus, if one country decides for domestic purposes to adopt a low or high rate of interest relative to other nations, and capital is less than perfectly mobile internationally, it can do so without undue concern for external balance since its exchange rate can be relied upon to vary automatically to help achieve this end. This presumes, of course, that individual nations do not wantonly expose themselves to deliberate inflation or deflation domestically and that they do not seek to improve their economic position at the expense of other nations. If neither of these presumptions is valid in actuality, then it may not be surprising, under the circumstances, if a system of freely fluctuating exchange rates gives the appearance of being ineffective. What is important to realize in such instances, however, is that the source of the difficulty lies in the nature of the policies being followed rather than in the system per se of freely fluctuating exchange rates. The efficacy of freely fluctuating exchange rates can be said to depend fundamentally, therefore, upon the successful implementation of monetary and fiscal policies for domestic stabilization purposes.

Assuming that the objectives of policy are sustained full employment, with stable domestic prices, it is important to inquire about the degree to which exchange rates may in fact fluctuate and the theoretical conditions that must prevail in order for the foreign exchange market to be stable. Both of these points can be dealt with, as we already have seen, in terms of the relative elasticities of demand and supply schedules of foreign exchange and of the underlying demand and supply schedules of imports and exports of goods and services. It should be evident from Figures 2.3 and 2.4 that the more highly elastic are the latter schedules, the more highly elastic will be the former schedules,[2] and, hence, the smaller the extent to which the exchange rate will fluctuate within any given range of demand and supply variations. This is a matter of some consequence because the smaller the degree to which the exchange rate fluctuates, in response to particular disturbances, the less important for a country of given size will be fluctuations in its terms of trade in the process of adjustment.[3]

As far as foreign exchange-market instability is concerned, we saw that this might arise in the event of inelastic demands for imports and exports that

2. The relation between these elasticities is demonstrated formally in the appendix to Chapter 2.

3. See the appendix to Chapter 2 for a formal demonstration of the relation between exchange-rate variations and the terms of trade.

would result in negatively inclined supply schedules of foreign exchange that were less steep than the relevant demand schedules (see Figure 2.5b above). It was mentioned earlier that the likelihood of instability occurring was an empirical question, although there were grounds for presuming that this likelihood would be relatively small. That is, the demand and supply schedules of imports and exports will be relatively elastic especially when goods that enter foreign trade are produced and consumed in substantial amounts domestically and there exist many potential export and import-competing goods that will enter foreign trade as relative prices are changed.

Our discussion suggests that attitudes towards a system of freely fluctuating exchange rates will depend upon the importance attached to the goal of achieving optimal resource allocation for the world as a whole and for individual countries. Attitudes will also be colored significantly by the interpretation of the actual experiences of individual countries with freely fluctuating rates. Since the choice of an exchange-rate system is a matter of great consequence for economic welfare, it would appear worthwhile to concentrate attention on some of the theoretical issues that have been raised in the preceding discussion, look briefly at some important examples of experiences with freely fluctuating rates, and consider, finally, the conditions for an effective and efficient functioning of a world-wide system of freely fluctuating rates.

The major theoretical issues we shall examine with respect to a system of freely fluctuating exchange rates are: (1) whether exchange risks significantly deter international trade and investment; (2) whether speculation stabilizes or destabilizes exchange-rate movements; (3) whether balance-of-payments adjustment costs may be higher than if exchange rates were fixed; (4) whether countries will engage in exchange-rate manipulation; and (5) whether exchange depreciation may lead to inflation. The significant experiences with freely fluctuating exchange rates to be discussed are those of the major Western European countries, the U.K. and France in particular, from 1919–26 and of Canada from 1950–62.

Costs of International Transactions[4]

In our earlier discussion of exchange-rate determination, it was noted that whenever there was a future receipt or payment of foreign currency at issue in connection with commercial trade, the trader could arrange his financing by a spot or forward market transaction in accordance with interest-arbitrage relationships. This would enable him to fix the exchange rate at which the foreign currency conversion would be made when the obligation became due, thereby avoiding the risk of the exchange rate moving unfavorably towards

4. See Machlup (1970), Sohmen (1969, pp. 83–84 and 107–11), and Yeager (1966, pp. 209–32) for more extended treatment of the issues to be presented in this section.

him (or foregoing an exchange profit) in the interim. It is often contended that this type of transaction will impose a cost on the trader that will be especially large under conditions of exchange-rate flexibility and that there will be a consequent deterrent to international trade. The cost involved is supposedly measured in terms of the difference between the spot and forward exchange rates, that is, the discount or premium on forward exchange. There are two sources of confusion on this issue that are worth noting.

The first is the improper analogy drawn between the futures market for foreign exchange and for commodities and the role played by speculators as risk bearers. There are indeed commodity futures markets that consistently reflect forward discounts. In such circumstances, traders will incur hedging costs, which can be looked upon as the payment to speculators for the risk undergone by their assumption of forward positions opposite to those of traders. It is by no means the case, however, that forward foreign exchange markets consistently reflect a forward discount for a given country's currency. Moreover, currencies cannot all have forward discounts in any event. The point is that there are ordinarily substantial numbers of both buyers and sellers operating in the forward market in connection with commercial trade, and that currencies can reflect forward premiums or discounts. The counterpart transaction of forward covering need not be looked upon therefore in terms of a payment for risk bearing since both parties involved may be engaged in commercial trade without any exchange risk whatever. This is not to say of course that speculation has no impact on the forward rate. But what must be recognized is that speculators do not profit from a difference between spot and forward rates at some given time, but from the difference between the forward rate now and the actual spot rate in the future.

The second point of confusion arises from the failure to distinguish the attributes of the different exchange-rate systems from each other. The issue here is whether forward covering would be materially more expensive under freely fluctuating as compared to fixed rates of exchange. This will depend on the extent of exchange-rate variability, the relative ease or difficulty with which commercial traders adapt to price fluctuations, and whether our basis for comparison is the gold standard or the adjustable peg.

The extent of exchange-rate variability is, as we have noted, a question of how the demand and supply of foreign exchange for commercial purposes and for the movement of short-term capital respond in terms of the elasticities of the schedules and the magnitude of the underlying real changes that cause the schedules to shift. Given the factors just mentioned, exchange-rate variability will be influenced also by the success of the authorities in promoting domestic stability. It is quite possible that the foreign exchange-market facilities for some countries would be "thin" in the sense that these currencies are not used widely and are, therefore, comparatively less desirable for carrying out arbitrage and speculative operations. The costs of covering might under these circumstances be considerable when the currency was at a sizable forward discount. This is not to say, however, that covering costs would always be large since, as noted, presumably the currency would at times exhibit a forward premium as well as a discount. But should these costs prove to be a deterrent to trade, it is always possible for traders to rely on relatively more stable currencies for financing purposes. Moreover, if we could relax somewhat our assumption concerning government intervention, the authorities might take steps intermittently to buy and sell foreign exchange in order to make the exchange market function more effectively and with greater stability.

For reasons that may derive from the use of domestic currency as legal tender at an absolutely fixed rate in all parts of a single nation, the inference is often drawn that a fixed exchange rate is clearly desirable for international transactions because it eliminates uncertainty. This is not correct necessarily for, under a gold standard, there may still be uncertainty with regard to the internal price adjustments required to keep the exchange rate fixed. Moreover, there is no reason why, with fluctuating exchange rates, traders cannot learn to deal with uncertainty by covering on the forward exchange market in precisely the same way that they cover domestically on a large scale in futures markets for many kinds of primary commodities that are in fact often susceptible to relatively wide fluctuations in price. There need not be, in other words, anything sacrosanct about an exchange rate since it represents a price (of foreign exchange) just like the price of anything else. Since we know that commodity markets function efficiently on a very large scale, there appears to be no intrinsic reason why the foreign exchange market could not function similarly. This may be the case especially since the relevant elasticities of demand and supply in the foreign exchange market will be significantly greater than in particular commodity markets, which means that exchange-rate fluctuations would likely be small in comparison to fluctuations in commodity prices.

Under the gold standard where both spot and forward exchange rates are fixed at the gold points, the costs of covering cannot of course exceed the difference between these points. The same is true under a system of pegged exchange rates so long as the upper and lower limits are not in doubt. When these limits are in doubt, however, it is possible in the absence of official forward-market intervention that very sizable forward discounts can appear that will make covering relatively expensive. This will be the case particularly if the official pegs are supported by restrictive measures of various kinds that are designed to suppress the demand for spot foreign exchange. The effects of adjustable-peg measures should thus not be confused with the operation of a freely fluctuating exchange-rate system. This is especially the case since the adjustable-peg measures may result in shifting the burden of adjustment to other international transactions and in the process significantly deterring and even distorting international trade by causing resources to be misallocated.

Consideration of the cost of covering under fluctuating exchange rates leads logically to the question of the impact such rates may have upon long-term foreign lending and borrowing. The contention is that long-term foreign investment may subject lenders or borrowers to an exchange risk that cannot be covered satisfactorily by forward transactions. While it may be true that forward markets may not exist or function effectively at present for relatively long maturities, this does not mean that such facilities could not be developed should the occasion arise. It is likely, moreover, to the extent that a country's domestic prices diverge from those elsewhere, that any losses to long-term investors from exchange depreciation will tend to be balanced by increased earnings and interest rates in terms of domestic currency.

If asked to choose, commercial traders and foreign investors would be in favor of eliminating all future exchange risk. It might be thought that this could be accomplished under a gold standard, but this ignores the uncertainty that would be created with regard to internal price adjustments to keep the gold standard operative. The point is that uncertainty will exist under both fixed and fluctuating rates, although in a different form in the respective systems. The gold standard is thus not to be preferred a priori because it will minimize the costs of international transactions. In any event, the issue is really between fluctuating rates and pegged rates. We have mentioned the frequent resort under pegged rates to restrictive measures for supporting the rates plus the fact that the pegs are subject at times to possibly substantial changes by official action. It may well be, therefore, that pegged rates deter international trade and investment as much if not more than fluctuating rates would.

Stabilizing and Destabilizing Speculation[5]

It was stated earlier that in an environment of domestic economic stability when speculators were well informed, speculative activities would be socially beneficial insofar as they resulted in a reduction of exchange-rate variability and helped to ease the balance-of-payments adjustment process. It is nevertheless widely believed today especially in official government circles that freely fluctuating exchange rates are synonymous with unstable rates because of the perverse effects that may result from speculation. Since it is this issue perhaps more than any other that has kept freely fluctuating exchange rates in disrepute, the effects of speculation deserve careful examination.

We should first make clear that stability or instability in the present context is to be understood in terms of the dynamic factors associated with exchange-rate expectations and the consequent behavior of speculators. We may

5. I am indebted to Edward E. Leamer for his assistance in clarifying some of the mathematical details involved in this section and for the preparation of Figures 3.1-3.6 below. Sohmen (1969, pp. 59–74) and Yeager (1966, pp. 189–208) also treat the issues to be discussed.

conceive of speculation dynamically as involving two separate questions. The first is whether speculative demand or supply is stable in itself in the sense that changes due to some outside force tend to be damped rather than to feed cumulatively one upon the other.[6] The second question is whether speculation tends to modify or intensify exchange-rate variations that would occur if speculation were not present. It is with the second question that we shall be mainly concerned.

Let us assume that interest rates at home and abroad are the same for all maturities and that there are no transaction costs and impediments to international transfers. Since the spot and forward rates will be equal in such circumstances, we can refer to the rate of exchange irrespective of the maturity involved. Speculation would thus involve taking an open position in forward foreign exchange without our having to specify the time period. This is of course an oversimplification since we are abstracting from the general portfolio considerations of return and risk from all activities, including speculation itself, that will influence speculative behavior.[7]

Suppose that, in the absence of speculation, the exchange rate will follow a sinewave pattern over time such as the one shown in Figure 3.1. We assume that this real nonspeculative cycle arises from demand and supply factors that interact systematically in a regular periodic manner. At any point in time the prevailing exchange rate is determined by the usual intersection of the static demand and supply schedules of foreign exchange, as in Figure 2.4. The time path depicted in Figure 3.1 thus implies that either the demand schedule or the supply schedule, or both, have cyclical movements.[8] Spec-

6. See Tsiang (1958, esp. pp. 399–413) for an analysis of the stability properties of speculative demand.

7. Thus, we are assuming that we can isolate speculative activity from the returns and risks associated with interest arbitrage and commercial trade.

8. It may be noted that a cyclical time path can be described mathematically in several ways. The most straightforward of these is to specify a functional form such as a sine or cosine that is cyclical. Thus, consider the equation:

$$p(t) = -\alpha \sin (\omega t) + \beta$$

in which the amplitude is equal to 2α since the sine will vary from -1 to $+1$. With the period of the sine being equal to 360°, the length of a full period is 360°/ω. The frequency, which is the number of cycles per time period, is $\omega/360°$. β refers to the mean price. An alternative to the foregoing equation is to specify difference or differential equations that have cyclical solutions. Whatever form is chosen, there will be several possible demand and supply schedules underlying that form. Thus, for example, we might have the following demand schedule:

$$Q_d = \beta - 1/2\,p$$

and the following supply schedule subject to cyclical movement:

$$Q_s = \alpha \sin (\omega t) + 1/2\,p$$

In equilibrium, these latter two equations will imply the first one shown:
$$Q_d = Q_s$$
$$\beta - 1/2\,p = \alpha \sin (\omega t) + 1/2\,p$$
$$p = -\alpha \sin (\omega t) + \beta$$

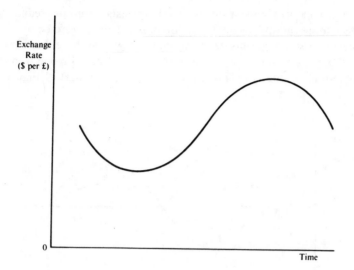

FIGURE 3.1.

Exchange-Rate Variation
in a Real Nonspeculative Cycle

The time path depicted implies that the underlying
demand or supply schedules (or both) of foreign exchange
have cyclical movements.

ulative buying can be depicted in terms of Figure 2.4 as moving the demand schedule to the right or the supply schedule to the left. The rise in the exchange rate ($ per £) will have the effect of inducing a reduction in the nonspeculative demand and an increase in the nonspeculative supply of foreign exchange. The excess supply in this instance will be purchased by the speculators. Equilibrium will be described in any time period by the nonspeculative excess demand, E_t, plus the speculative excess demand, E_{st}, being equal to zero:

$$E_t + E_{st} = 0. \tag{3.1}$$

It will be evident from our discussion that we consider nonspeculators to buy and sell foreign exchange in response to the current prevailing exchange-rate level and not in response to past exchange rates or trends in rates. This rules out the possibility that nonspeculators will behave as speculators. In such an event, for any time period in which net speculative activity is zero, the cyclical movements of price, as noted in Figure 3.1, can result only from real demand and supply forces.

In our analysis, speculators will buy foreign exchange when the rate is relatively low and expected to rise and to sell foreign exchange when the rate is relatively high and expected to fall. Speculative buying will thus induce exchange-rate increases and speculative selling, exchange-rate reductions. With perfect foresight and zero transaction costs, if there were competition among speculators, the profits from speculation would be eliminated by entry into the market. As a consequence, there would be no scope whatever for exchange-rate fluctuation. This can be seen in the top part of Figure 3.2

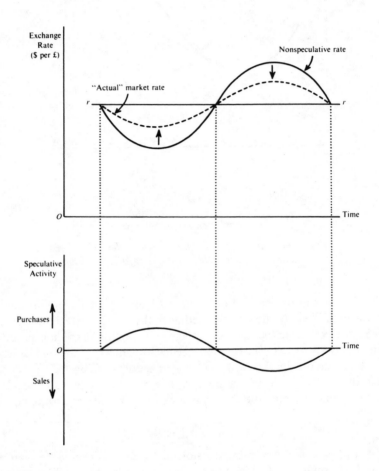

FIGURE 3.2.

Stabilizing Influence of Speculation on Exchange-
Rate Variations in a Real Nonspeculative Cycle

Assuming perfect foresight and zero transaction costs,
perfectly competitive speculation will result in perfect ex-
change-rate stability at rr. With one monopolistic speculator
seeking to maximize profits, the exchange-rate path will
be intermediate between the path without speculation and the
path of perfect stability.

where the effects of perfectly competitive speculation will result in a constant rate of exchange, *rr*. Alternatively, if we assumed one monopolistic speculator, maximization of profits will result in an exchange-rate path, indicated by the dashed line in Figure 3.2, that is intermediate between the paths in the absence of speculation (solid line) and with perfect stability, *rr*.[9] It is evident that along this intermediate path the exchange rate will be lower than the real nonspeculative rate when foreign exchange is being sold and higher when being purchased.[10]

Suppose now that we relax especially our assumption of perfect foresight. Competitive speculation will not result under these circumstances in perfect exchange-rate stability. Then if we can assume that speculators concentrate their activities at peaks and troughs in the movement of the nonspeculative rate, it can be shown that speculators will make maximum profits and in the process reduce the amplitude of exchange-rate variations.[11] It is in view of the foregoing considerations that Friedman (1953, p. 175) has remarked: "People who argue that speculation is generally destabilizing seldom realize that this is largely equivalent to saying that speculators lose money, since speculation can be destabilizing in general only if speculators on the average sell when the currency is low in price and buy when it is high."[12] Friedman's remark is noteworthy in that it has provoked an interesting controversy as to whether profitable speculation is necessarily stabilizing. In this regard, Baumol (1957) in particular has attempted to demonstrate by means of counterexamples that this need not be the case.

9. See Sohmen (1969, esp. pp. 63–65) for details.

10. The two parts of Figure 3.2 relate to each other on the assumption that the volume of speculative activity can be determined by the difference between the exchange rates with and without speculation. This assumption is valid when nonspeculative demand is linearly related to price. The greatest differences between the rates are to be found accordingly at the peak and trough of the real cycle, which is also where maximum speculation will occur.

11. See Telser (1959, pp. 297–99) for a formal proof of this statement. It is perhaps worth mentioning here that if speculators as a whole make profits and stabilize the exchange rate, this is not accomplished necessarily at the expense of nonspeculators. Thus, as Telser has emphasized (pp. 296–97), we are not concerned here with a zero-sum game:

> Such an implication [a zero-sum game] holds only if the population of traders remained the same and their total wealth is constant. However, if traders enter or leave the market or if their total wealth changes, the game is not really zero-sum. Consider the following example. Trader *A* sells some amount of the commodity to *B* and then has zero commitments (leaves the market). If the price should subsequently rise, permitting *B* to realize a profit when he sells the commodity to a third party, trader *A* has not *realized* a loss thereby, although he has *foregone* a profit. If the total wealth of the participants in the market has changed, then *B* has not profited at the expense of the others.

12. He adds, however, in a footnote:

> A warning is perhaps in order that this is a simplified generalization on a complex problem. A full analysis encounters difficulties in separating 'speculative' from other transactions, defining precisely and satisfactorily 'destabilizing speculation,' and taking account of the effects of the mere existence of a system of flexible rates as contrasted with the effects of actual speculative transactions under such a system.

Baumol's first counterexample involved nonspeculators who respond not only to the exchange-rate level, as we have assumed above, but also to the exchange-rate movement in the last two periods.[13] This situation is depicted in Figure 3.3. The time path which the exchange rate would assume in the absence of the trend-responsive part of the nonspeculative demand is indicated in the top part of Figure 3.3 by a horizontal line. What makes the rate move cyclically in Figure 3.3 is the assumption that nonspeculators

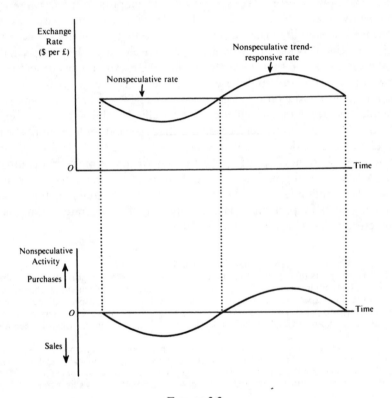

FIGURE 3.3.

*Exchange-Rate Variation with Nonspeculative
Trend Responsiveness*

*In Baumol's first counterexample, nonspeculators are
assumed to respond to the exchange-rate trend. This leads
them to buy foreign exchange when the exchange rate is high
and to sell when the rate is low.*

13. Baumol's discussion runs in terms of the price of some given commodity. Since we are dealing with the price of foreign exchange, our reference will be to the exchange rate.

respond to the exchange-rate trend.[14] It is evident from Figure 3.3 that the response pattern of nonspeculators leads them to buy foreign exchange when the exchange rate is high and to sell when the rate is low. It is this rather peculiar activity which is seized upon and exploited by Baumol's speculators.

It was assumed earlier that maximum speculative activity would occur at the peaks and troughs of the exchange-rate cycle. The implication was that by attempting to forecast these turning points and concentrating their activity accordingly, speculators would earn maximum profits and stabilize the exchange rate. Baumol's speculators are assumed in contrast to sell foreign exchange after the peak-rate movement has been passed and to buy after the upturn has begun. This is because speculators are believed capable of identifying turning points only after the exchange-rate trend has been clearly established. Speculators, therefore, "give up any chance to skim off the cream but hope in return significantly to reduce their risks."[15] Their activity will be profitable since they will be selling at higher prices than they are buying. But, at the same time, they may exert a destabilizing influence through the acceleration of both upward and downward rate movements. This is because sales are made when the rate is falling and purchases when the rate is rising. Speculation may, therefore, be profitable but yet on balance turn out to be destabilizing with respect to exchange-rate movements.

The possible effect that speculation may have in increasing both the frequency and amplitude of exchange-rate movements can be seen in Figure 3.4. The solid line in the top part of Figure 3.4 represents the nonspeculative cycle, which as noted stems from the response of nonspeculators to exchange-rate trends, while the dashed line reflects the "actual" movement of the rate as a consequence of both nonspeculative and speculative activity. It is evident that the "actual" cycle exhibits greater frequency and amplitude as compared to the nonspeculative cycle.[16]

Because we have assumed the nonspeculative excess demand to be linear in terms of the exchange rate, we can adjust our units so that a speculative purchase or sale of one unit of foreign exchange induces an increase or reduction of one unit in the exchange rate. This permits us to show separately in the second and third parts of Figure 3.4 the trend-responsive activity of the nonspeculators and the activity of the speculators. The algebraic sum of these two types of activity will equal the actual exchange-rate cycle shown in the top part of the figure. It can be seen that the maximum speculative activity is concentrated one period after the trough and peak in the actual cycle. Figure 3.4 should make it clear that the profits made by the speculators from buying low and selling high arise from the activity of the nonspeculators who

14. See Baumol (1957, pp. 264–65) for a representation of the nonspeculative excess-demand function and of the time path that the exchange rate will follow in this case.
15. *Ibid.*, p. 263.
16. The speculative behavior specified in Baumol's first counterexample always increases the frequency of fluctuation. According to the initial conditions assumed, this behavior may or may not increase the amplitude as well. *Ibid.*, p. 267.

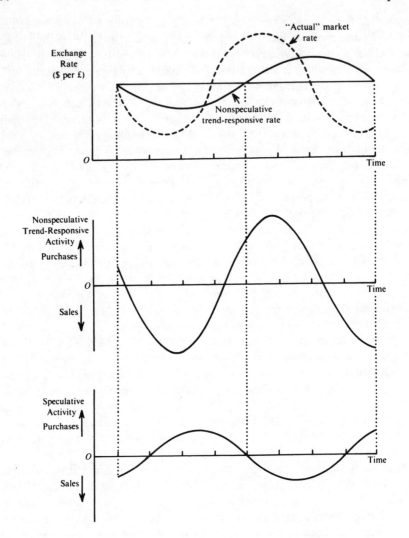

FIGURE 3.4.

*Destabilizing Influence of Speculation on Exchange-
Rate Variations with a Nonspeculative
Trend-Responsive Cycle*

*The algebraic sum of the nonspeculative and speculative
activity equals the actual exchange-rate cycle shown in the
top part of the figure. Speculative activity exaggerates the
trend-responsive behavior of nonspeculators. Speculative
profits arise from the activity of nonspeculators, who buy
high and sell low.*

buy high and sell low. It should also be clear from Figure 3.4 that speculative activity in this case exaggerates the trend-responsive behavior assumed on the part of nonspeculators. Strictly speaking, therefore, the destabilizing effect in this example is the consequence of nonspeculative behavior. In other words, this effect is not due in itself to the behavior of speculators who concentrate their activity after the troughs and peaks have passed.

Baumol was aware of his special assumption concerning nonspeculative activity and that if he assumed nonspeculators to respond only to the exchange rate level, profitable speculation would necessarily be stabilizing. He proceeded in this light, therefore, to offer a second counterexample. This was based upon a real nonspeculative cycle without nonspeculative trend-responsiveness, but with a speculative excess-demand function that "demonstrated its destabilizing ability by knocking the system from its position of delicate constant amplitude balance into a time path of explosive fluctuation."[17] The effects of speculation in Baumol's second counterexample are depicted in Figure 3.5. The solid line in the top part of Figure 3.5 represents the real nonspeculative cyclical exchange-rate movement in the absence of speculation, and the dashed line the "actual" movement as a consequence of speculation. It is evident that the actual movement becomes explosive once the rate moves outside the rates circumscribed by the real nonspeculative cycle. The forces making for this explosive movement can be seen from the speculative behavior indicated in the second, third, and fourth parts of Figure 3.5.

This behavior can be divided into two parts in terms of the speculative excess demand (E_{st}), which is given by:

$$E_{st} = U(\bar{r} - r) + W \frac{dr}{dt}, \qquad U, W > 0 \qquad (3.2)$$

where U and W are constants, $\bar{r}$ is the mean exchange rate, r is the actual exchange rate, and dr/dt is the rate of change in the actual exchange rate. Equation (3.2) says that speculators will concentrate their buying when exchange rates are simultaneously low ($r < \bar{r}$) and rising ($dr/dt > 0$).[18] Thus, in Figure 3.5, the two parts of speculative excess demand have been drawn to yield algebraically the volume of net speculative activity, which in turn is represented in comparable units by the difference between the real and actual exchange-rate movements. Even though it is implied from the first term of the speculative-excess-demand function that speculators will be selling foreign exchange so long as $r > \bar{r}$, the effect of speculative purchases with rising rates reflected in the second term becomes so powerful that the net result is to cause the actual exchange rate to move upward in an explosive manner.[19]

17. *Ibid.*, p. 269.
18. *Ibid.*, p. 268.
19. *Ibid.*, pp. 268–69, the mathematical details of this argument are given.

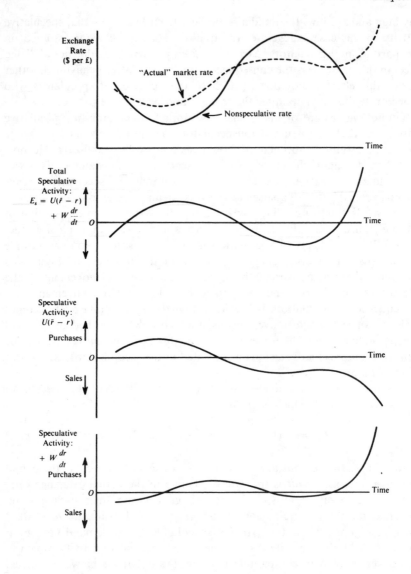

IGURE 3.5.

*Explosive Influence of Speculation on Exchange-
Rate Variations in a Real Nonspeculative Cycle*

*In Baumol's second counterexample, the effect of speculative
purchases with rising rates becomes so powerful that the
actual exchange rate is moved upward explosively.*

Speculative activity thus appears in Baumol's second counterexample to be destabilizing. The question now is whether this type of speculation can be profitable. We may note that within the time confines of the real non-speculative cycle shown, speculation is both profitable and stabilizing.[20] It would appear that speculators are making profits in the subsequently explosive range of the exchange-rate movement since in a rising market the value of their holdings will continually increase. The point is, however, that these are "paper" profits only. Should the speculators as a group seek to "cash in" their profits by selling foreign exchange, the exchange rate would surely collapse to the mean level or possibly even lower. Baumol's second counterexample is unacceptable, therefore, because it implies that the exchange rate rises indefinitely while speculators accumulate foreign exchange indefinitely.[21] Although in such an instance speculation can be shown to be destabilizing, it will in all likelihood not be profitable once the speculative bubble is burst.[22]

It should be clear from our discussion that disagreement concerning the stabilizing or destabilizing effects of speculation on the exchange rate stems from the nature of the different assumptions made about the behavior of nonspeculators and speculators. In terms of theory, the response only to exchange-rate levels on the part of nonspeculators together with profit-maximizing behavior on the part of speculators should be sufficient to reduce the amplitude of exchange-rate fluctuations.[23] This will be especially the

20. Baumol is thus in error when he states, *ibid.,* p. 270, that: "In the short run, the time path may still be approximately cyclical and the previous arguments [of the first counterexample] apply." See also Kemp (1963, p. 186) who apparently has accepted Baumol's reasoning on this score.
21. See Telser (1959, pp. 300–01) for a proof of this property and for some brief remarks on the economic implications of Baumol's second counterexample.
22. Baumol's second counterexample may nevertheless be of interest since it demonstrates that speculative behavior which is both profitable and stabilizing for a short time can turn out eventually to be unprofitable and destabilizing. We might therefore imagine an evolutionary process in which speculators made profits for a while, the market exploded, and the speculators were wiped out. A new group of speculators might then be induced to enter the market, to make profits for a while, only to be wiped out in turn, and so on.
23. Indeed, Telser (1959, p. 299) shows that speculative profits need only be positive and not necessarily at a maximum to stabilize the exchange rate, and further that even if speculators suffer losses, they may still stabilize the exchange rate. Farrell (1966) has sought to analyze the basic proposition that profitability implies stabilization by an approach that avoids assumptions about speculative behavior. He concluded that linearity of the nonspeculative-excess-demand function was both a necessary and sufficient condition for the basic proposition to be valid, although the introduction of transactions costs made this condition unnecessary and less stringently sufficient. In view, however, of the temporal interdependence found frequently in actual market situations, he was led to the final conclusion that specific behavioral assumptions about speculation might be required after all in investigating particular markets.
Kemp (1963) has developed an example of profitable but destabilizing speculation, which is based upon a perverse nonspeculative demand curve characterized by multiple equilibria. While such an example is possible, its occurrence is rather implausible except in cases where the nonspeculative demand for foreign exchange is highly inelastic. Obst (1967) has examined the conditions required for profitable speculation to be stabilizing

Continued on p. 88

case the more successful the authorities are in promoting domestic stability. For under these circumstances speculative anticipations concerning future exchange-rate movements can be formed with more certainty than would otherwise be possible.

But even though there may be a strong theoretical presumption that speculation will reduce exchange-rate variability, there is still the question of whether in fact this can be observed to be true. Thus, it is interesting to note that Baumol (1959, p. 301) apparently accepted Telser's criticism of his second counterexample but was adamant as far as his first counterexample was concerned.[24] Baumol's argument (1959, p. 302) was that in many actual market situations in which perfect hedges were impossible, nonspeculators would in their own interest consider the trend of exchange rates as well as the level. Whether he is correct on this score would seem to be more a question of fact than of theory. But his contention does point up the difficulty mentioned by Friedman (see footnote 12) of "separating 'speculative' from other transactions."[25]

In his original article Baumol (1957, p. 270) made the further interesting observation that:[26]

> Governments or the central banking systems can, at nearly zero cost, expand their currencies at will, and frequently they do not resist that temptation.... This means ... that there is little reason to expect any consistent pattern of cyclical price movements on these exchanges. Rather, the time path can plausibly be expected to be erratic, responding to the political developments in the countries involved.

---

when there is a trend in the movement of exchange rates and speculation minimizes the squared deviations from the trend line rather than with respect to the mean exchange rate as in Telser's analysis (1959, p. 296). Canterbery (1971) has developed a formal mathematical model of the foreign exchange market in which speculation is related to differences in expected and actual rates of change in the exchange rate. He concludes that speculation will be stabilizing under free market conditions.

We may note finally that Stein (1961) has presented an example of profitable but destabilizing speculation in which speculators profit from an official devaluation as the consequence of the depletion of official foreign exchange reserves in attempting to counteract the initial speculative attack on the currency. This example is more relevant, however, to an adjustable-peg system than to a system of freely fluctuating rates such as we have been discussing.

24. According to Kemp (1963, p. 186), however, Baumol has stated in correspondence that he sticks by both of his counterexamples.

25. Friedman (1953, p. 175) also mentioned the possibility that speculation might be destabilizing if professional speculators on the average made money while a changing body of amateurs regularly lost larger sums. Glahe (1966) has developed a model in which he shows that the exchange rate will be stabilized if both professional and amateurs do well, but that if one group does well and the other does not, the rate may or may not be stabilized depending upon net profits.

26. Baumol attributes his view to an argument by Viner (1956) that maintains that the equilibrating forces that characterize commodity markets cannot be relied upon in the foreign exchange market. The reason is that the cost of money creation is practically nil and governments may frequently resort to the printing presses for expenditure purposes.

Again, whether or not Baumol is right on this matter is primarily an empirical question. But what would be important to emphasize in any event is that with a system of freely fluctuating exchange rates, if government stabilization policies were erratic, it would not be too surprising to observe that the time path of exchange-rate movements was also erratic. The destabilizer in such circumstances would, therefore, be the government authorities themselves rather than the foreign exchange-market speculators.[27] This also suggests, of course, that if speculative forces are or threaten to become destabilizing, the authorities have it within their power to resist these forces by offsetting sales or purchases of foreign exchange.

In conclusion, there would appear to be a strong presumption that speculation will help to reduce exchange-rate variability. Whether or not this presumption is borne out in practice can be determined only by examining actual experiences with freely fluctuating exchange rates.[28] This we shall do presently.

Factor Mobility and Adjustment Costs

It should be evident from our earlier discussion that balance-of-payments adjustment in a system of freely fluctuating exchange rates assumes productive factors to be mobile domestically. This is necessary in order that

---

Also, since currency per se has no direct utility to consumers and does not enter in any form into the production process, it may be subject to limitless fluctuation vis-à-vis other currencies. The conclusion is, therefore, that the time path of exchange rates is essentially erratic in its response basically to politically determined forces.

Viner's view seems to be derived in large measure from a situation of hyperinflation when indeed speculative anticipations concerning the exchange rate may be very pessimistic and speculation may dominate the foreign exchange market. However, under conditions of domestic price stability or relatively mild inflation, there would be close links between the goods and foreign exchange markets and reason to believe that these markets would be stable even with the presence of speculation.

27. This is in essence the conclusion reached by Tsiang (1958, p. 413) in his analysis of the stability of foreign exchange speculation under floating rates.

28. There have been some studies of speculation in markets for commodity futures that may have some relevance in evaluating the issues raised in our discussion. Thus, Houthakker (1957) examined speculative transactions in grain and cotton futures in the U.S. for selected periods before and after World War II. He concluded on the basis of profits earned that large "professional" speculators exercised considerable skill in forecasting prices in these markets. Using the same data as Houthakker for cotton futures, Aliber (1964) has purported to show that profitable speculation may have amplified spot price movements and therefore was destabilizing particularly in the vicinity of peaks in spot prices. Aliber's findings may be subject to question, however, as Yamey (1966, p. 207) pointed out, because of "the difficulty of estimating the course prices would have taken in the absence of the speculation in question." Yamey went on to add: "Information about turning points in an observed price series can give no guidance as to the timing, frequency, and amplitude of fluctuations in a price series relating to a different situation from which the speculative activities have been excluded hypothetically." For additional studies of the price effects of speculation in organized commodity markets, see the papers especially by Cootner, Rockwell, Telser, and Gray published in *Food Research Institute Studies* (1967).

production for export and for the home market can be expanded or contracted in the process of adjustment without creating unemployment. While
it is convenient to assume that there is domestic mobility, this assumption
nevertheless raises some issues that merit further discussion. Among the most
important of these issues are: (1) the nature of exchange-rate changes and
their effect upon production and employment in different industries; (2)
differences between intra- and inter-regional mobility; and (3) the relative
size of the export, import-competing, and domestic-goods sectors.

The first issue is significant in considering whether freely fluctuating
exchange rates may lead to economically wasteful shifts of resources among
industries. Suppose, for example, in response to a depreciation of the exchange
rate that there is an expansion of production and employment in the export
and import-competing industries. If subsequently the exchange rate appreciates, resources would then be shifted away from the foreign sector to the
domestic sector. If the exchange rate were to swing widely over time, resources
might be shifted constantly back and forth among industries. Assuming these
shifts to be substantial and admitting the possibility that factor markets may
sometimes function imperfectly, the economic costs of the adjustment could
be considered socially wasteful in comparison to a situation in which the
exchange rate was fixed. This assumes, of course, that owners of productive
factors are incapable of forming a view of the long-run average exchange rate
and of adjusting their behavior accordingly. Moreover, if speculation does
in fact stabilize the exchange rate on the basis of our earlier argument, there
may be less incentive for resource movements. Finally, variations in domestic
prices under fixed exchange rates may motivate resource movements just as
much as exchange-rate variations may. In any event, this issue cannot be
resolved by theoretical argument alone since there are important empirical
considerations involved.

Mundell (1961) especially has pointed out in connection with the second
issue mentioned that if, within a given nation, there is intraregional but not
interregional mobility of factors, a system of freely fluctuating exchange rates
may not be optimal from the standpoint of the nation as a whole. Thus,
suppose that we have a nation composed of two regions, *A* and *B*, factors are
mobile within but not between regions, and there is full employment. Now
assume that there is a shift in foreign demand away from region *A*'s goods
and no change in the foreign demand for region *B*'s goods. The restoration
of balance-of-payments equilibrium will clearly require an exchange-rate
depreciation unless the domestic demand in the two regions for *A*'s goods
can be assumed to increase entirely at the expense of imports from abroad.

Since we have assumed factors to be immobile between regions, the
exchange-rate depreciation is likely to create inflationary pressure in region
B because of the increase in the foreign demand for *B*'s goods and in *B*'s
demand for import substitutes. At the same time, resources will be reallo-
cated in region *A* in order to expand the production of other export goods

and import substitutes. If there happened to be any market imperfections present in *A* that interfered with this reallocation of resources, *A* might experience temporary unemployment. In the end, the system of freely fluctuating exchange rates will operate of course to restore balance-of-payments equilibrium for the nation as a whole. But it should be evident that the costs of adjustment in terms of unemployment and inflation may be distributed unevenly between regions in the process.

This is not to say that it would be better under the assumed circumstances to have a fixed exchange rate and to use domestic monetary and fiscal policy to sustain the level of employment. For even here it may be difficult to avoid unemployment in region *A* and inflation in region *B*. The point is, therefore, that neither a freely fluctuating nor a fixed rate of exchange is really appropriate for the nation in question. Rather, it might be preferable to treat the two regions as separate entities, each with its own currency that would fluctuate vis-à-vis the other and with the rest of the world. Thus, in our example, equilibrium would be restored by a depreciation of *A*'s exchange rate vis-à-vis *B* and the rest of the world. The appreciation of *B*'s exchange rate would spare it from the inflationary pressures noted above while presumably the depreciation of *A*'s rate would minimize any unemployment difficulties.

This issue of intraregional versus interregional factor mobility is of great interest because it turns out to have important implications for a system of freely fluctuating exchange rates based on individual national currencies. Thus, as Mundell has noted (1961, p. 661):

> If factor mobility is high internally and low internationally a system of flexible rates might work effectively enough. But if regions cut across national boundaries or if countries are multiregional then the argument for flexible exchange rates is only valid if currencies are reorganized on a regional basis.[29]

The conclusion is, therefore, that fixed exchange rates would work best for regions wherein factors were mobile and freely fluctuating rates for regions between which factors were immobile.[30]

In contrast to Mundell's emphasis on geographic factor mobility among regions, McKinnon (1963) has suggested that optimum currency areas should be distinguished according to the relative importance of tradable goods—exportables and importables—and nontradable goods that are too costly to move internationally. He has stressed also the importance of

---

29. This is not to say, of course, that currency reorganization could be effected unless there were important political changes. Thus, as Mundell points out (1961, p. 661): "The concept of an optimum currency area therefore has direct practical applicability only in areas where political organization is in a state of flux, such as in ex-colonial areas and in Western Europe."

30. This suggests with regard to individual nations according to Mundell (1961, p. 664) that "if factors are mobile across national boundaries then a flexible exchange system becomes unnecessary, and may even be positively harmful. . . ."

maintaining a stable internal price level in order to insure that the nation may possess a currency that is stable in value and, therefore, can be relied upon for both exchange and liquidity purposes.

Thus, suppose we have a nation in which tradable goods comprise a large proportion of domestic consumption and production, resources are fully employed, and the exchange rate is permitted to fluctuate freely. If now there were an increase domestically in the demand for importables, this would cause the exchange rate to depreciate. The point of the consequent changes in relative prices is to encourage the domestic production of exportables and importables and to discourage the domestic consumption of exportables and importables from abroad. A question arises, however, concerning the effectiveness of these changes in restoring balance-of-payments equilibrium because of the effects they may have upon price stability in the nontradable goods sector.

That is, given full-employment conditions, would it not be more effective if the exchange rate were fixed and expenditure-reducing policies were instituted? For in such a case these policies might restore equilibrium more readily by releasing export goods formerly consumed at home, directly reducing importables from abroad, and encouraging the consumption of domestically produced importables. Since the nontradable goods sector is assumed to be relatively small, expenditure reduction might, therefore, affect it less than would be the case if resources were to be squeezed from it by relative price changes alone. This would be reinforced to the extent that factors were immobile between the nontradable and tradable goods sectors.

The preceding example suggests accordingly that a system of freely fluctuating exchange rates might work best in situations where tradable goods were of much less importance than nontradable goods. Changes in relative prices as a consequence of exchange-rate variations would have the greatest impact on the tradable goods sector. If in contrast we had a fixed exchange rate and used a policy of expenditure reduction, the comparatively larger nontradable goods sector would feel the greatest impact of the changes in policy. In this case, as McKinnon (1963, p. 720) put it, "we would have permitted the tail (tradable goods) to wag the dog (non-tradable goods) . . . ." Since such a policy could not be carried out without significant internal price changes, the value of the domestic currency would be impaired especially for liquidity purposes.

It should be clear from McKinnon's analysis that a nation's industrial structure comprised of tradable and nontradable goods is the key variable in determining the desirability of an exchange-rate system. In this sense he takes (1963, pp. 724–25) the existing degree of factor immobility to be given as a "painful fact of economic life which has to be overcome as efficiently as possible." This is not to say, however, that the considerations of geographic factor mobility emphasized by Mundell are of no consequence, for, as McKinnon notes (p. 724), the degrees of geographic and industrial factor mobility are often closely related. Thus, the Mundell and McKinnon analyses may possibly, although not necessarily, lead to the same conclusion. In any event, these analyses are valuable insofar as they call attention to considerations of factor mobility and economic structure that have previously for the most part been assumed away or overlooked, but which are of interest and importance in evaluating alternative exchange-rate systems.[31]

Exchange-Rate Intervention

An important question in a system of freely fluctuating exchange rates is whether individual countries may seek to manipulate the exchange rate for national purposes at the expense of other countries. Thus, to take some examples: (1) a country with presumably inadequate international monetary reserves may depreciate its exchange rate to improve its reserve position; (2) faced with domestic unemployment, a country may depreciate in order to stimulate its economy; and (3) a country may depreciate in order to increase its rate of economic growth.

We have stressed that a system of freely fluctuating exchange rates is likely to work best when countries implement domestic policies to promote full employment and price stability and when they do not interfere materially with international trade and investment. Now it is conceivable that a country with presumably inadequate reserves may undertake to improve its reserve position. The issue is, however, whether it will be motivated to do so and if it can succeed without retaliation from other countries. If a country is experiencing unemployment, there may be some circumstances, as in the case where there is simultaneously an incipient deficit in the balance of payments, when exchange-rate depreciation alone can work to restore internal-external balance. This may be a beggar-my-neighbor policy, however, if the result is simply to export the country's unemployment. The point is that domestic expansionary measures and exchange-rate depreciation can work in combination to achieve the desired objectives. One is not a substitute for the other necessarily. When it comes to increasing the rate of economic growth, a country can adopt whatever monetary-fiscal mix it believes appropriate and the exchange rate can be left free to equilibrate as the international trade and investment implications of the policies are manifested through the foreign exchange market. Exchange-rate depreciation can of course be a stimulant to growth, but, as just mentioned, it should not be looked upon separately from domestic policies.

In order to minimize the incentive for exchange-rate manipulation, it is thus important that countries agree upon the desirability of consistently pursuing

31. For more recent contributions attempting to clarify how such matters as differences in economic structure among regions and the range of policy objectives and tools affect the choice of an exchange-rate system, see Snider (1967), Kenen (1969), Grubel (1970), and Willett and Tower (1970).

domestic policies to attain full employment and price stability. If this pursuit is hampered by constraints on domestic policies, the incentive to resort to exchange-rate changes will be increased. It cannot be expected in these circumstances that a system of freely fluctuating exchange rates will operate effectively. And for that matter, no alternative system is likely to function any better.

Exchange Depreciation as a Cause of Inflation

We have noted in our previous discussion McKinnon's suggestion that freely fluctuating exchange rates might produce undesirable effects upon domestic price stability when the nontradable goods sector was small relative to the tradable goods sector. It is of interest to consider this point of domestic price stability further in light of the assertion sometimes made that exchange depreciation may lead to domestic inflation. The assertion is that inflation will occur as a result of increased import prices, a higher cost of living, demands for higher wages, and, therefore, higher domestic prices in the event wages are generally increased. Inflation will thus offset the relative price changes produced by the initial depreciation in the exchange rate. There may as a consequence be a further depreciation that will have the effect of causing the wage-price spiral to continue its upward movement. We will have, in other words, a continuing situation of "cost-push" inflation.

Although McKinnon was not concerned directly with the possibility of cost-push inflation, his analysis is nevertheless suggestive of it in the case in which tradable goods predominated and a fluctuating rate led to domestic price instability through the resource pressures resulting from variations in the rate. While we may grant the possible occurrence of cost-push inflation via exchange depreciation, it does not follow necessarily that fluctuating exchange rates per se are to be held responsible for this state of affairs. Thus, as Friedman (1953, p. 181) has noted:

> The rise in prices of foreign goods may add to the always plentiful list of excuses for wage increases; it does not in and of itself provide the economic conditions for a wage rise—or, at any rate, for a wage rise without unemployment. A general wage rise—or a general rise in domestic prices—becomes possible only if the monetary authorities create the additional money to finance the higher level of prices. But if the monetary authorities are ready to do so to validate any rise in particular prices or wages, then the situation is fundamentally unstable without a change in the exchange rate, since a wage rise for any other excuse would lead to similar consequences.

While Friedman's remarks apparently abstract from the possibility of cost-push inflation and thus perhaps oversimplify the dynamics of the inter-relationships between changes in prices and wages, they nevertheless call attention to the role that domestic policy plays with regard to the encouragement or restraint of inflation. The cogency of his remarks may thus be better appreciated after we have examined some actual experiences that countries have had with fluctuating rates. We will see, particularly in the case of France from 1919–26, that the impetus for internal inflation and consequent exchange depreciation was primarily of domestic origin due to the absence of effective control by the authorities over the rate of monetary expansion.

European Experiences with Freely Fluctuating Exchange Rates after World War I

Reference has been made to the essentially empirical nature of many of the issues involved in analyzing a system of freely fluctuating exchange rates. It is important, therefore, to review briefly some of the modern experiences with these rates.[32] The European experiences after World War I are of especial interest because they served to color in a negative manner much of the later thinking and official attitudes towards freely fluctuating rates during the interwar period and the early post-World War II years. The Canadian experience with free exchange rates during 1950–62, which we shall examine in the next section, is also significant because of its influence upon contemporary thought and attitudes.

With the great need in Europe after World War I for imports of capital equipment, raw materials, and foodstuffs, many countries were faced with sizable import surpluses which had somehow to be financed. Since foreign credits were insufficient given the magnitudes of the imports involved and since substantial inflation had taken place in Europe during the war, the prewar-parity exchange rates could no longer be maintained. Many countries were forced, therefore, to resort to exchange depreciation for balance-of-payments purposes beginning in 1919. Some indication of the forces at work is given in Table 3.1. It can be seen that while U.S. wholesale prices doubled compared to prewar, prices for the European countries shown increased much more. The dollar-exchange rates of the Belgian and French francs in 1919 were about one-third below their 1913 parity while the pound sterling had depreciated about 10 percent. The Dutch guilder and Swiss franc were close to parity in 1919 as these currencies had remained relatively strong during the war because of the nonbelligerent status of the two countries.[33]

32. See Yeager (1969) for a review of the Austrian and Russian experiences with fluctuating exchange rates in the late nineteenth century. It is noteworthy also that the U.S. dollar was on a fluctuating basis from 1872–79 without suffering disastrous consequences.

33. The dollar exchange rates for this period for other countries in Europe and those elsewhere can be found in Board of Governors of the Federal Reserve System (1943, pp. 662–82). For references to some of the major works dealing with the exchange-rate experiences of the European countries, see Aliber (1962, esp. p. 172).

TABLE 3.1

Wholesale Price Indexes and Exchange Rates in the United States and Selected European Countries, 1919–27[a]

(Annual Averages, 1913 or 1914 = 100)

	1919	1920	1921	1922	1923	1924	1925	1926	1927
United States									
Wholesale prices	199	221	140	139	144	141	148	143	137
Belgium									
Wholesale prices	n.a.	n.a.	n.a.	367	497	573	558	744	847
Exchange rate	67	38	39	40	27	24	25	18[b]	15
France									
Wholesale prices	364	520	352	334	428	499	561	718	630
Exchange rate	71	36	39	43	32	27	25	17[c]	20
Netherlands									
Wholesale prices	304	292	182	160	151	156	155	145	148
Exchange rate	98	86	84	96	97	95	100	100	100
Switzerland									
Wholesale prices	n.a.	n.a.	196	168	180	176	161	148	147
Exchange rate	99	88	90	99	94	95	100	100	100
United Kingdom									
Wholesale prices	258	307	197	159	159	166	159	148	141
Exchange rate	91	75	79	91	94	91	100	100	100

n.a. Not available.

[a] Exchange rates are expressed in U.S. cents per unit of foreign currency and taken as a percentage of the rate in 1913.

[b] Rate stabilized in November 1926.

[c] Rate stabilized in December 1926.

SOURCES: Aliber (1962, p. 184) for wholesale price indexes and Board of Governors of the Federal Reserve System (1943) for exchange rates.

It can be seen that in the first postwar boom in 1919–20 prices increased substantially both in Europe and in the U.S. In an effort to cope with this inflation the U.S. authorities instituted a policy of monetary restraint. This affected not only domestic credit expansion but foreign lending as well. In particular the flow of trade credit to Europe was reduced. Caught in a squeeze, therefore, between rising prices and reduced credit availability, the European currencies noted in Table 3.1 depreciated sharply vis-à-vis the dollar in 1920, with the declines in the Belgian and French francs being especially marked. Prices fell substantially with the collapse of the boom and in 1921–22 the currencies in question tended to appreciate.[34] After this time, however, there were substantial price increases and currency depreciations

34. The movements described were typical of other countries in Europe except for those (e.g., Austria, Germany, and Poland) in which uncontrolled increases in domestic prices resulted in hyperinflation.

in the cases of Belgium and France in contrast to the relative stability in the Netherlands, Switzerland, and the U.K. Since it would take us too far afield to examine each country's experience in detail, we may profitably confine our attention to the two most important countries noted, the U.K. and France, and look in particular at the nature and effects of speculation in the respective currencies.[35]

Since direct information on speculative holdings is not available, it is necessary to seek indirect measures of the extent and effects of speculative behavior. One approach is to compare the actual exchange rate with some hypothetical rate while another is to examine the relationship between changes in spot and forward exchange rates. In the first case, the hypothetical exchange rate can be calculated by comparing price movements between countries relative to some base period for the exchange rate and the price indexes used. This gives a so-called purchasing-power-parity exchange rate that is designed to reflect the differences in relative prices that govern the movement internationally of goods and services.[36] Should the actual rate (expressed on a comparable base period) show a sustained divergence within a short time from the purchasing-power-parity rate, this is assumed to be indicative of speculative pressures that may be destabilizing. Alternatively, speculative pressures may be assumed to exist when there is a widening of the forward premium or narrowing of the forward discount when the exchange rate is appreciating and the opposite when it is depreciating.

The analysis of the British experience by Tsiang (1959a, pp. 250–56) using deviations of actual exchange rates from purchasing-power-parity rates and Aliber (1962, pp. 188–98) using both techniques mentioned revealed some instances of speculative pressures on sterling especially during 1919–21, the years of immediate postwar scarcity, rapid inflation, and recession.[37] By

35. See Aliber (1962, pp. 291–338) for a discussion of the experiences during this period of Belgium, the Netherlands, and Switzerland and Tsiang (1959a, pp. 256–59) for a discussion of Norway.

36. The problems with purchasing-power-parity calculations are legionary. They involve such considerations as whether to use wholesale or retail prices, different methods of weighting the indexes, the assumption of unchanged reciprocal demand and supply conditions, and comparable variations in income levels in the countries involved. These calculations may nevertheless be of some value in analyzing speculative pressures over short periods of time, provided of course that we do not interpret literally the rates calculated as being equilibrium rates of exchange. We shall have occasion to treat these matters more fully in Chapter 5 when we discuss devaluation in a system of pegged exchange rates.

37. The authors differ somewhat in their dating of the speculative disturbances. Tsiang (1959a, p. 25) identified two periods of disturbance on the basis of wholesale price indexes: a sharp depreciation of sterling from November 1919 to February 1920 and a rapid appreciation from December 1920 to May 1921. Similar calculations by Aliber (1962, p. 195) led him to identify the summer of 1920 and the first six months of 1921 as periods in which "speculative purchases of sterling must have tended to increase the extent of overvaluation." It would appear on the basis of Aliber's graph (1962, p. 197) showing the actual exchange rate and the purchasing-power-parity rate that his dating of the first disturbance is not correct. That is, the two rates practically coincided in the summer of 1920.

98   *Chapter 3*

1922, however, when some semblance of price stability had been attained, the authorities were then faced with the choice either to adopt measures to restore sterling to its prewar parity or to attempt to reduce unemployment, which at that time was in excess of 15 percent of the labor force.[38] On the one hand, parity could not be restored without appreciating the pound and, therefore, increasing unemployment especially in the export industries. On the other hand, domestic expansionary measures could not be undertaken without depreciating the pound. It would thus appear in retrospect that the authorities were caught on the horns of a dilemma.

But since the government had announced after the war its intention as an objective of national policy to restore the pound to its prewar parity, once price stability was attained beginning in 1922, this objective became a dominant factor in shaping speculative anticipations concerning the exchange rate. This was evidenced in the more or less continuous premium on forward sterling after 1921 despite some official vacillation with regard to domestic policy goals and a certain amount of domestic political disturbances. When the Government announced in early 1924 that it fully intended to restore the pound to its prewar parity, the only question remaining was when this would be accomplished. The date chosen was April 30, 1925; sterling was at this time stabilized at its prewar rate of $4.86.

If we can omit the immediate postwar years in which conditions in the domestic economy and foreign exchange market were unsettled and concentrate instead on the more or less "normal" period from 1922 to the restoration of parity in 1925, it is noteworthy as Tsiang (1959a, p. 256) has pointed out that "... the exchange rate of the pound was ... definitely more stable not only than domestic wholesale prices but also than the purchasing power parity of sterling in terms of the U.S. dollar. The relative stability of the exchange rate implies that, over the periods concerned, speculative activities on the exchange market were mainly in a stabilizing direction."[39]

38. Aliber (1962, p. 189); this period is also discussed briefly in Stein (1962, pp. 45–48).
39. Aliber's test of speculative pressure based upon an increase in the forward premium as sterling appreciated led him to identify the period from October 1924 to January 1925 as one of speculative disturbance (1962, pp. 196–98):

> In late 1924 and early 1925, speculation forced sterling toward its prewar parity before the underlying price and cost situation warranted stabilization at this level. . . . Speculators were able to force the hand of the authorities because the authorities had proposed the return to the prewar parity as their objective, but were unable or unwilling to take the measures to accomplish this.

Aliber suggests earlier (p. 194), however, that this instance of speculative behavior "may be a feature of the adjustment from one level of the spot rate to another." It would seem that this is really the point since the authorities had made their intention clear with regard to the exchange rate. The speculators can hardly be blamed for helping to ratify this intention, which in retrospect was probably ill-advised in any case because of the social costs entailed in terms of continuing unemployment.
See Stein (1962, pp. 48–55) for some statistical support that sterling speculation was generally profitable from 1921–25. His analysis led him to conclude (p. 55) that: "History fails to prove that the free sterling dollar market was a chaotic market where the activities of professional risk-bearers were irrational." The conclusion that sterling speculation was mostly stabilizing was reached also by Stolper (1948).

Turning now to the French experience, we have already noted the very substantial domestic inflation and depreciation of the franc that occurred in the immediate postwar years. Both Tsiang (1959a, pp. 259–60) and Aliber (1962, p. 206) found during these years large deviations between the actual and purchasing-power-parity exchange rates, which was testimony to the important role of speculation against the franc. The reason that the franc was unusually vulnerable at this time can be traced in large measure according to Tsiang (1959a, pp. 259–61) to the ineffectiveness of French monetary policy. That is, the authorities were unable or unwilling to raise the official discount rate because they wished to avoid increasing the interest costs on the re-financing of Government debt. This meant essentially that they were pegging the market rate of interest.[40]

Prices were relatively stable in France during most of 1921 and the first half of 1922. After this time, however, they increased substantially and depreciation of the franc was renewed. These price and exchange-rate movements reflected the underlying forces mentioned in the preceding paragraph together with a series of political disturbances abroad and at home connected with such factors as disagreements over German reparations, the French occupation of the Ruhr in January 1923, the collapse of the German mark in the summer of 1923, and crises of confidence in the French Government itself.[41] Each of these shocks caused the franc to weaken continuously in 1922–23, and from the end of 1923 to mid-March 1924 there was a particularly heavy assault that was stemmed only after the Government intervened with the aid of foreign loans and a substantial tax increase.[42]

The restoration of confidence in the franc proved, however, to be short lived in the wake of French involvement in hostilities in Morocco, legislative opposition to tax increases, falsification of the balance sheet of the Bank of France in an attempt to circumvent limitations on Bank advances to the

---

40. Thus, as Tsiang (1959a, pp. 260–61) stated:

. . . because of the existence of a large amount of floating debt consisting chiefly of *bons de la défense nationale,* which were issued constantly on tap at fixed rates of interest and a large proportion of which was continuously maturing, the discount rate of the central bank had become very ineffective in regulating market short-term rates of interest in France. For if there was any stringency in the supply of credit, the public and the commercial banks could always obtain additional supplies of money simply by refusing to reinvest the proceeds of maturing short-term Treasury bills. The Government was then forced to borrow from the Bank of France to meet the net withdrawal of funds from government short-term bills by the public or commercial banks.

This in effect implied that the market rates of interest were pegged to a large extent by the Government, and that the Bank of France was quite powerless to regulate the market rates by manipulating its own discount rate.

41. Aliber (1962, p. 199) and Tsiang (1959a, pp. 262–63).

42. The reasons and source of the speculative attack on the franc at the end of 1923 are not clear. Aliber (1962, p. 200) and Tsiang (1959a, p. 262) mention that it became known in November 1923 that the French Treasury would be unable to honor its commitment to reduce its annual borrowings from the Bank of France as specified by law. Aliber also makes reference to accounts which alleged that the attack may have begun in Amsterdam or Vienna "as the financial manipulators who had profited so well from their machinations . . . looked elsewhere for profits."

Treasury, and a Government proposal for a capital levy designed to reduce the amount of Government securities in the hands of the public. The situation kept deteriorating as successive Governments were unable to cope with the continuing inflation and the disarray in the foreign exchange market in 1925–26. Finally in the summer of 1926 the Poincaré government came into power on the strength of a strong program of domestic reform designed to increase taxes significantly and to stabilize the exchange value of the franc. Confidence in the franc and in government securities was restored consequently, The franc was stabilized at the end of 1926 at a rate which was about 20 percent of its prewar parity.

It should be evident from our discussion that the foreign exchange crises in France in 1924 and in 1925–26 were manifestations of ineffectual government policies, which made it virtually impossible to maintain restraint on domestic monetary expansion.[43] Thus, as Tsiang (1959a, pp. 271–73) concluded, France would have courted disaster at this time whether its exchange rate was pegged or freely fluctuating:[44]

> ... the instability of the French franc from 1923 to 1926 was the result of an extremely elastic money supply, which would have caused great instability in the economy whether the exchange rate was freely fluctuating or controlled. It therefore should not be regarded as evidence that a freely fluctuating exchange rate can, as a general rule, be expected to lead to cumulative depreciation through self-aggravating speculative capital movements regardless of the elasticity of the money supply and the flexibility of the interest rate.

While there is admittedly always some danger of interpreting historical events with preconceived notions, it seems reasonable to conclude that the European experiences with freely fluctuating exchange rates during 1919–26

43. Tsiang (1959a, p. 271) has noted in this connection that:
   Even if dealings in foreign exchange had been under the strictest possible control, the political disturbances that had shaken public confidence in government securities in the early part of 1925 would still have been able to induce the French public to shift their capital from short-term *bons* to such assets as real estate, commodities, or industrial shares. The public's refusal to renew their holdings of short-term *bons* at constant interest rates would automatically have drawn additional money into circulation, and prices of all commodities and all assets whose values and yield could be expected to rise with the general price level, would have been driven up. The general rise in prices would have provided a further incentive to shift capital from fixed interest securities, which in turn would have drawn more money into circulation.

44. Aliber (1962, esp. pp. 209–10 and 218; 1970) has argued that foreign exchange speculation was the driving force in France's inflation from 1923 onward. This was because of the cost-push effect that exchange-rate depreciation had on the domestic price level through increased prices of imports. He concluded therefore (p. 219) that in the French case speculation provided "its own justification." Aliber's conclusion may be questioned on the grounds that rather than focusing on the impact of speculation, it would seem more appropriate to inquire into the reasons why speculation continued. These reasons lay in the basic unsoundness of France's domestic finances. It may be true, of course, that speculation made it more difficult for the authorities to bring the situation under control. But the fact remains that for some time the authorities tied their own hands by virtue of inflexible fiscal and debt-management policies. How else would we expect speculators to have behaved under such circumstances?

do not by any means constitute grounds for rejecting such a system.[45] In retrospect, it would appear that no exchange-rate system could have functioned altogether smoothly at this time in view of the unsettled conditions after the war and the difficulties that most countries had in maintaining domestic economic stability. The British experience of this period is noteworthy chiefly because it illustrated that an exchange rate which is to be pegged at an inappropriately overvalued level may result in substantial domestic unemployment. The French experience showed in contrast that in the absence of effective domestic monetary restraint it cannot be expected that exchange-rate fluctuations will be confined to relatively narrow bounds.[46]

There were certain isolated experiences with freely fluctuating exchange rates in Europe and elsewhere during the 1930's. But since these were years in which unemployment was substantial and international trade and payments greatly impeded, such experiences may not be very revealing. It is of interest accordingly to look for more recent examples in the period since World War II. There is only one major case to consider here. This is Canada, the world's fifth largest trading nation, which maintained a system of freely fluctuating exchange rates during the period from 1950 to 1962.

The Canadian Experience with Freely Fluctuating Exchange Rates, 1950–62

During World War II Canada maintained a rate of exchange of $0.909 (U.S.) to the Canadian dollar. Since this rate was apparently undervalued, there was a substantial capital inflow after the war into Canada from the U.S. especially and a consequent sharp rise in Canadian official reserve holdings. The Canadian authorities responded to this potentially inflationary situation by revaluing the dollar to parity with the U.S. dollar in mid-1946. Shortly thereafter, however, Canada found itself in balance-of-payments difficulties as a result of large increases in imports due to pent-up demand from wartime, a reduction and reversal of capital flows, and the accumulation of inconvertible balances with the U.K. and continental Europe. Thus, Canadian official reserves fell from $1,667 million (U.S.) in May 1946 to $480 million in November 1947.[47] This time the authorities responded not by devaluing

45. Issue can be taken therefore with Nurkse's well known conclusion in his study of the interwar period (1944, pp. 210–11) that freely fluctuating exchanges are "apt to intensify any initial disequilibrium" because speculative movements will be self-inflammatory. The difficulty with Nurkse's conclusion is that he placed greatest emphasis on the symptoms (speculation) rather than the underlying roots of the problem (an elastic credit supply). Thus, the point of our discussion has been that once proper recognition is given to the role of monetary expansion in fostering inflation, we have found the key in evaluating a system of freely fluctuating exchange rates. A somewhat more acid criticism of Nurkse's conclusion is to be found in Friedman (1953, p. 176).

46. For conclusions on the experiences of other European countries, see the references cited above in footnote 35.

47. These figures were cited by Yeager (1966, p. 423).

but by introducing import restrictions, curbs on foreign travel, domestic excise taxes on consumer goods, and arranging a loan of $300 million with the United States Export-Import Bank.[48]

Canada's reserves increased substantially during 1948 and then levelled off in the first three quarters of 1949. In September 1949 when there were devaluations of all the major world currencies vis-à-vis the U.S. dollar, Canada joined in with a 10 percent devaluation to ward off potentially unfavorable pressures on its balance-of-payments position. Official reserves began to climb shortly thereafter as capital inflows increased in response to an apparent belief that the Canadian dollar was again undervalued and would be appreciated as was the case in 1946. The reserves increased from $1,117 million (U.S.) at the end of 1949 to $1,255 at the end of June 1950. With the outbreak of the Korean War in June, it became clear that Canada's primary exports would be in great demand and that a revaluation of the exchange rate might, therefore, be all the more likely. Within three months, Canadian reserves jumped to $1,790 million.[49]

The Canadian authorities tried to combat the inflationary implications of the capital inflow by massive open-market operations. But since they were not altogether successful and the capital inflow showed no signs of abating, something more decisive had to be done. The authorities were deterred from revaluing again because of incipient weaknesses in the current account. They were reluctant, moreover, to resort to direct capital controls because of possibly undesirable long-run effects on foreign investment and borrowing. The decision was therefore made to free the exchange rate at the end of September 1950. Thus begun an experiment with a fluctuating exchange-rate system which lasted until May 1961. Steps were taken after this time to drive the Canadian dollar to a discount, and in May 1962 the exchange rate was pegged officially.

The extent of the annual average exchange-rate movement is indicated in line 1 of Table 3.2. Once the rate was freed, it appreciated from the former official peg of $0.909 (U.S.) per Canadian dollar in September 1950 to an average of $0.949 for October. It then appreciated further in 1952 to reach a premium in terms of the U.S. dollar. This premium persisted until May 1961, with the exchange rate ranging in the interim from $1.014 in 1955 to $1.043 in 1957.[50] It can be seen from line 2 of Table 3.2 that Canadian official

48. The exchange crisis of 1947–48 is examined in some detail by Wonnacott (1965, esp. pp. 52–58).

49. The monthly increases were $65 million in July, $184 million in August, and $285 million in September according to figures cited by Yeager (1966, p. 424).

50. The monthly average range from March 1952 to May 1961 was between $1.000 in November 1955 and $1.055 in August 1957 and October 1959 according to data recorded in McLeod (1965, p. 52). The spread between the highest and lowest monthly average rates within years ranged from a low of $0.020 in 1954 to a high of $0.045 in 1952, *ibid.* See Yeager (1966, pp. 425–26) for some additional calculations of various ranges of fluctuations, all of which were relatively small.

TABLE 3.2
Canada: Selected Economic Data, 1950–62

	1950	1951	1952	1953	1954	1955	1956	1957	1958	1959	1960	1961	1962
1. Spot exchange rate in U.S. dollars (annual average)	0.920[a]	0.950	1.022	1.017	1.027	1.014	1.016	1.043	1.030	1.042	1.031	0.987	0.936[b]
2. Canadian official reserves (millions of U.S. dollars, end of period)	1,845	1,901	1,938	1,902	2,029	1,985	2,035	1,926	2,038	2,029	1,989	2,276	2,547
3. Volume of Canadian exports (1950 = 100)	100.0	109.7	122.2	120.8	116.7	126.4	137.5	138.9	138.9	143.1	150.0	162.5	168.1
4. Volume of Canadian imports (1950 = 100)	100.0	112.1	125.8	137.9	128.8	147.0	171.2	165.2	151.5	168.2	165.2	169.7	175.8
5. Long-term capital inflow (millions of Canadian dollars)	613	637	450	608	550	361	1,275	1,229	1,012	1,100	900	910	668
6. Short-term capital movements (millions of Canadian dollars)	443	−64	−577	−203	6	293	124	60	182	290	304	301	415
7. Real GNP (1950 = 100)	100.0	106.2	114.7	119.1	115.6	125.6	136.4	138.1	139.7	144.5	148.0	151.8	162.0
8. Percentage of labor force unemployed	3.6	2.4	2.9	3.0	4.6	4.4	3.4	4.6	7.0	6.0	7.0	7.1	5.9
9. Wholesale prices (1950 = 100)	100.0	112.9	106.5	104.3	102.2	103.2	106.5	107.5	107.5	108.6	108.6	109.7	112.9
10. Cost of living (1950 = 100)	100.0	111.0	113.4	112.2	113.4	113.4	114.6	118.3	122.0	123.2	124.4	125.6	126.8
11. Treasury bill rate	0.55	0.80	1.08	1.69	1.44	1.56	2.90	3.78	2.29	4.81	3.32	2.83	4.00
12. Government bond yield	2.78	3.24	3.59	3.68	3.14	3.07	3.60	4.19	4.22	5.14	5.26	5.08	5.09

[a] Rate pegged officially at $0.909 from January through September.
[b] Rate pegged officially at $0.925 in May.

SOURCES: Lines 1, 5, and 6 from McLeod (1965, pp. 52–54); lines 2–4 and 9–12 from International Monetary Fund, *International Financial Statistics*; lines 7 and 8 from Bank of Canada, *Statistical Summary: Supplement* (annual).

reserves showed only minor changes between 1950 and 1960. From this it can be inferred that there was some intervention by the foreign exchange authorities during the period, but not on a scale large enough to make them a dominant and continuing force in the market. Fluctuations in the Canadian dollar thus occurred mainly in response to variations in private commercial transactions.[51]

Data on the volume of Canada's merchandise exports and imports are recorded in lines 3 and 4 of Table 3.2. It is noteworthy that the greatest increases occurred from 1950–56, and that from 1956–60 exports increased only slightly while imports receded noticeably from their 1956 high. Whether Canada's foreign trade during the 1950's would have been greater than it actually was if the exchange rate had been pegged rather than fluctuating is a difficult question to answer because we do not know what domestic policies would have been followed under a pegged rate. In any event, if we take into account the relatively small degree of exchange-rate fluctuation that characterized both the spot and forward markets together with the existence of well developed facilities for forward covering, it seems rather unlikely that exchange risks as such offered any serious impediment to Canada's trade. Thus, the slowdown in trade noted after 1956 can be attributed mainly to the slackening of economic growth at home and abroad, in the U.S. especially. The exchange-rate premium at this time no doubt reinforced the relative stagnation of exports. But what should be noted is that since the premium was associated with a substantial capital inflow, Canada's lag in foreign trade cannot be attributed per se to fluctuations in the exchange rate.

Long-term capital inflows into Canada are shown in line 5 of Table 3.2. It is especially noteworthy that there was a great upsurge in foreign investment in Canada during the period of fluctuating rates, particularly from 1956–59. This upsurge was stimulated in great part by important natural resource developments in Canada and the rapid growth generally of the economy. It seems doubtful that exchange-rate movements appreciably affected these long-term flows, except maybe from the standpoint of their timing.

Turning now to short-term capital movements, which are recorded in line 6 of Table 3.2, we would like to determine whether such movements tended on

51. According to Yeager (1966, p. 426), the average monthly change in Canadian official reserves during the period from the end of October 1950 to the end of December 1960 was $21 million (U.S.), which was less than 5 percent of the monthly current-account credits or debits. Detailed examination of the Canadian Exchange Fund policy revealed that they tended to increase official reserves when the exchange rate was appreciating and to draw down reserves when the rate was depreciating in 100 out of the 123 months of the period in question. Fund intervention did not persist, however, once the trend of exchange-rate movement had become clearly established. Thus, as Yeager concluded (1966, p. 427), during the period the authorities "apparently avoided determining the rate and limited themselves to trying to moderate minor short-run wobbles." This is essentially the conclusion that a number of other investigators have reached, as noted *ibid*. For further support, see Mellish (1968).

balance to aggravate or moderate exchange-rate fluctuations. In our earlier discussion of the British and French experiences with fluctuating rates, cumulative deviations of the exchange rate from purchasing-power parity were considered prima facie to be indicative of disequilibrating speculation. The Canadian case is noteworthy in comparison to these earlier experiences insofar as fluctuations in the Canadian dollar were relatively small. Moreover, the major instances of serious exchange crises occurred only at the beginning and end rather than during the decade of fluctuating rates. Having said this, it does not follow necessarily that short-term capital movements were in fact always stabilizing. Rather what the data seem to show on the basis of a number of different investigations is that such movements were by and large, but not always, stabilizing.[52] If we accept this conclusion (that speculation was generally stabilizing) in consideration with the aforementioned absence of exchange crises, the Canadian experience can be interpreted to the effect that, provided the underlying situation is basically sound, fears of speculative domination of the foreign exchange market can be greatly exaggerated.

We have already indicated that Canada abandoned its fluctuating-rate system de facto in 1961 and de jure the following year. Just what went wrong? It is evident from the data on real gross national product (GNP) and the unemployment rate recorded in lines 7–8 of Table 3.2 that there was a pronounced slackening of economic growth in Canada after 1956. Thus, from 1956–60, real GNP increased only by 8.5 percent and unemployment rose from 4.6 to 7.0 percent of the labor force. On the external side, it was mentioned above that there was a marked slowdown in foreign demand. This was especially true in the case of the U.S. which accounted at this time for nearly 60 percent of Canadian merchandise exports. It was also mentioned that the premium on the Canadian dollar may have contributed to some extent to Canada's export lag.

In the face of low growth in income and substantial unemployment after 1956, one would have expected the authorities to have eased monetary conditions through credit expansion and lower interest rates. Unfortunately, just the opposite was done for reasons which even at that time were difficult to comprehend.[53] Thus, the Governor of the Bank of Canada instituted a

---

52. The relationship examined in these studies was between exchange-rate changes and short-term capital flows, using monthly and quarterly data. The criterion for flows to be stabilizing was, that appreciation (+) of the Canadian dollar would be negatively associated with net short-term capital outflows (−) and depreciation (−) positively associated with inflows (+). For the methodology utilized and the detailed results, see the discussion and references cited especially in Yeager (1966, pp. 427–30). For more recent studies of exchange-rate variations during this period, see Pippenger (1967), Poole (1967a, 1967b), Hawkins (1968), Caves and Reuber (1971), and Dunn (1971). See Officer (1968) for a comprehensive econometric analysis of Canadian economic performance during the period of fluctuating rates.

53. For an authoritative account of the events and policies of the period from 1958–62, see Wonnacott (1965, esp. pp. 203–61). Much of what follows is based on Wonnacott's work. See also Yeager (1966, pp. 432–38), Caves and Reuber (1971), and Dunn (1971).

policy of tight money ostensibly to stem inflation and to promote balance on current account with the aim of reducing the capital inflow. On top of this the Government decided through the Conversion Loan of 1958 to lengthen the maturity of 40 percent of the total outstanding national debt. Given the weakness of the financial markets at that time and the slowdown in growth, the timing of this decision was inopportune, to say the least. In effect then, a policy of tight money and high interest rates was imposed on the Canadian economy at a time when unemployment was at a postwar high and there was no real threat of serious inflation. Lines 7–12 of Table 3.2 sum up the major elements of this situation.

The continued pursuit of tight money in the face of low growth and high unemployment carried the Bank of Canada on a collision course with the Government. Matters were brought to a head at the end of May 1961 when the Government took the unprecedented step of demanding the resignation of Mr. Coyne, the Governor of the Bank of Canada.[54] This was followed in June by the presentation of the Government Budget message in which it was announced that steps would be taken to stimulate expansion directly by lowering interest rates and in the process to depress the exchange rate by discouraging capital inflows. It was also announced at that time that the Canadian dollar was to be depreciated to a "significant discount" by means of official Exchange Fund intervention. This signalled the end de facto of Canada's fluctuating exchange rate. In response to the changes in interest rates and the announced change concerning exchange-rate policy, the Canadian dollar depreciated nearly five cents within a short period of time to reach a discount vis-à-vis the U.S. dollar of more than three cents.

The exchange rate was sustained at about a three-cent discount until late 1961 when it came under renewed downward pressure. In order to prevent the rate from falling below $0.95 (U.S.), the authorities intervened heavily in the foreign exchange market in the first part of 1962 by selling $461 million (U.S.) of their official reserves in the four-month period from January to April.[55] Despite this sizable intervention, however, the authorities refrained from making a public commitment to a $0.95 (U.S.) exchange rate and from adopting domestic policies that were aimed directly at sustaining such a rate. Speculative pressures against the Canadian dollar continued unabated therefore. Faced with the prospect of a further drain on their foreign exchange reserves, the Government announced as of May 2, 1962 that it would henceforth peg the exchange rate at $0.925 in accordance with IMF principles.

However, even this action did not suffice to forestall speculation against the dollar and there was a further decline in official reserves in May. The situation became even more uneasy with the approaching general elections in June and the prospect of a minority government. Thus, according to Wonnacott

54. His resignation took effect on July 12, 1961 after special legislation was introduced for the purpose. See Wonnacott (1965, p. 239).
55. *Ibid.*, p. 256.

(1965, pp. 257–58), official reserves fell from $1,472.8 million (U.S.) on June 1 to $1,215.4 million on June 22 (four days after the elections), while official forward commitments rose from $85.6 million (U.S.) to $329.0 million during this period. To prevent things from deteriorating further, the Government quickly instituted a set of drastic measures. Among these were sharp reductions in Government spending, an increase in the discount rate to 6 percent, increased bank-reserve requirements, temporary surcharges on imports, receipt of stabilization loans totalling $650 million (U.S.) from the U.S., U.K., and the IMF, and arrangement of a $400 million line of credit from the U.S. Export-Import Bank. These measures proved sufficient to bring immediate relief from existing pressures on the dollar. Canada thereafter maintained an official rate of $0.925 for about 8 years, until the spring of 1970, when it began to experience substantial increases in reserves. It was subsequently decided to free the rate beginning in June, and thus a new episode of Canadian experimentation with fluctuating exchange rates was set into motion.

There would seem in retrospect to be little room for disagreement over the facts that fluctuating rates in Canada during the 1950's displayed none of the signs of excessive exchange risk, perverse speculation, and resource waste that have frequently in the past been attributed to such rates. With the slowing down in growth and the increase in unemployment, a policy of credit expansion and lower interest rates would have stimulated the economy directly and mitigated the exchange-rate appreciation that had occurred. Canada's return to a pegged rate in 1962 should not, therefore, be taken as an acknowledgement of the failure of a system of fluctuating rates to work effectively.[56] The point rather is that no exchange-rate system will function properly if inappropriate domestic policies are pursued and if official intervention in the foreign exchange market creates doubts about the expected future course of exchange-rate movements. Given this historical judgment, it will be interesting to see the outcome of Canada's most recent venture with fluctuating rates.

Conditions for an Effective System of Exchange-Rate Flexibility

As an aid in rounding out the discussion, it is convenient to take note of the conditions that Mundell (1961, p. 663) has outlined for a system of freely fluctuating exchange rates to work effectively and efficiently in the world economy:

> ... For this to be possible it must be demonstrated that: (1) an international price system based on flexible exchange rates is dynamically stable after taking

---

56. See Marsh (1969; 1970) for an exceptionally forceful statement criticizing Canada's return to a pegged rate.

speculative demands into account; (2) the exchange rate changes necessary to eliminate normal disturbances to dynamic equilibrium are not so large as to cause violent and reversible shifts between export and import competing industries (this is not ruled out by stability); (3) the risks created by variable exchange rates can be covered at reasonable costs in the forward markets; (4) central banks will refrain from monopolistic speculation; (5) monetary discipline will be maintained by the unfavorable political consequences of continuing depreciation, as it is to some extent maintained today by threats to levels of foreign exchange reserves; (6) reasonable protection of debtors and creditors can be assured to maintain an increasing flow of long-term capital movements; and (7) wages and profits are not tied to a price index in which import goods are heavily weighted.

We have attempted to show with reference to Mundell's seven points that there are no compelling reasons in theory why a system of freely fluctuating exchange rates could not function effectively and efficiently. Our review of the two major twentieth century experiences with fluctuating rates tends on the whole to support this conclusion. It would be an exaggeration to claim that a system of fluctuating rates would be a panacea for every nation's internal and external adjustment problems. But if our standard of comparison is with the present-day system of the adjustable peg, it might very well be that fluctuating rates would provide a better functioning mechanism for dealing with adjustment problems in a wide variety of circumstances in individual nations.[57]

In contemplating a world-wide system of fluctuating exchange rates, it should be pointed out that not all rates need to fluctuate. As Mundell (1968, p. 195) has noted: "Only $n - 1$ independent balance-of-payments instruments are needed in an n-country world because equilibrium in the balances of $n - 1$ countries implies equilibrium in the balance of the nth country." The problem here, which Mundell has labelled the *redundancy problem*, is to decide what country will be the nth country. It is most likely that if the present-day system were changed to one of freely fluctuating rates, the nth country would be the U.S. in view of the obvious need for a currency to serve as a numeraire and vehicle for international trade and investment. Thus, we could contemplate a system in which the currencies of individual countries or groups might fluctuate vis-à-vis the dollar as the authorities in the various countries sought to achieve their domestic objectives by what they considered to be an appropriate mix of monetary and fiscal measures. The U.S. would have to be especially concerned to maintain domestic stability in order to assure stability in the world price level and pattern of exchange rates.

Our earlier discussion of optimum currency areas suggests criteria for individual countries or groups of countries in choosing a particular exchange-rate system. We have a number of cases in point of individual important

57. In making this statement, we are abstracting from political considerations that may in fact be important in maintaining the status quo of pegged exchange rates. For further elaboration, see Johnson (1970b, esp. p. 92) and Lanyi (1969, esp. pp. 21–34).

countries adopting a fluctuating rate, beginning with Canada in 1950 and again in 1970 and becoming more widespread in Western Europe in the spring and summer of 1971 with the buildup of official dollar balances and the decision taken by the U.S. to sever the link between the dollar and gold. Group choices can be illustrated by the decision of the Common Market members to attempt, beginning in 1971, to narrow the range of fluctuation among their currencies as a step towards currency unification. It is conceivable that if the exchange rates can be fixed among these countries, they might permit the rate to fluctuate vis-à-vis the rest of the world. Thus, we could have a world situation in which some countries' rates were fixed and others fluctuating,[58] though always remembering the point just noted concerning the *n*th country's rate.

Conclusion

We have seen in this chapter how the mechanism of balance-of-payments adjustment operates with fluctuating exchange rates via changes in exports and imports and international capital movements. Many arguments have been levied in opposition to a system of freely fluctuating exchange rates. But it is not always made clear that the reference criteria for evaluating freely fluctuating exchange rates should distinguish between a system of fixed as opposed to adjustably pegged exchange rates. In considering the various theoretical allegations against fluctuating rates, the following conclusions were reached: (1) the contention that costs of international transactions would be increased stemmed from an improper analogy between speculative risk bearing in commodity futures markets and the activities of traders and speculators in the forward exchange market; (2) models of destabilizing speculation were based on some rather special and not always plausible behavioral assumptions; (3) the presence of interregional factor immobility and a domestic sector that was small relative to the foreign sector might militate against exchange-rate flexibility; (4) whether countries would attempt to manipulate the exchange rate for national gain depends upon the possibility of retaliation and the freedom from constraints on the use of domestic policies to achieve national stabilization objectives; and (5) continued exchange depreciation can lead to inflation only if the authorities engage in continual monetary expansion.

We also saw that negative attitudes toward freely fluctuating rates stemmed from misconceptions of historical experiences. The allegedly unfavorable experience in Europe from 1919–26 was in large measure attributable to ineffective restraint over credit expansion, particularly in the case of France. Canada's experience during the 1950's showed that a system of fluctuating

---

58. Smaller countries with relatively large tradable goods sectors might be motivated to fix their exchange rate to the dollar or some other currency that was reasonably stable.

exchange rates could be operated with a minimum of friction and disturbances so long as appropriate domestic stabilization policies were followed.
The demise of the system occurred in Canada when contractionary domestic
policies were followed during a period of recession and substantial unemployment.

Even though official opinion has been unfavorable to fluctuating exchange
rates, many important countries have nevertheless decided or been forced
by events in recent years to opt out of the pegged-rate system. Even if such
defections were to become less common, we nevertheless still would have a
useful yardstick for evaluating the existing state and future development of
the international monetary system.

4

Balance-of-Payments Adjustment
Under the Gold Standard

It will be recalled from our earlier discussion that the gold standard is a system in which the rates of exchange are determined by the legally established mint-parity relationships of individual currencies in terms of gold. Exchange rates are not completely fixed by such relationships, however, because of transactions costs involved in the buying and selling of gold. Rather, the rates are constrained at the gold-export and import points, but can vary freely within the relatively narrow confines of these points. It will be recalled further that, in the idealized version of the gold standard, the domestic money supply was supposed to respond passively to the inflow or outflow of gold, and that monetary policy was supposed to reinforce the effects of gold movements on the money supply, depending upon the extant banking-reserve rules. Finally for adjustment to occur, wages, prices, and the rate of interest were assumed to respond to the monetary changes with the result that the balance of trade and the flow of international short-term capital would be altered until gold flows ceased and balance-of-payments equilibrium was restored.

The Mechanism of Adjustment under the
Gold Standard

In discussing the mechanism of adjustment under the gold standard, let us refer back to the disequilibrium situation depicted earlier in Figure 2.7 in our discussion of exchange-rate determination. It will be recalled that given the initial equilibrium indicated at P, and assuming an increase in the demand for pounds represented by the shift from $D_£^a$ to $D_£^{a'}$, with an implied exchange rate of OT it would be cheaper to obtain pounds by means of exporting gold. The new equilibrium will be at C, where $D_£^{a'}$ and the supply schedule, which is now perfectly elastic, intersect at the gold-export point. The outflow of gold is equal to *HF* in pounds, or *HECF* in dollars. It is presumed that in the country exporting gold there will be a reduction in the money supply and, as prices decline domestically, in the level of money income. The demand and supply schedules of pounds will consequently be shifted to the left and right respectively until the gold movement has stopped and the balance of payments restored to equilibrium. This new equilibrium will be located below the gold-export point where the new schedules (not drawn) intersect. The opposite pattern of adjustment is presumed to occur for the country receiving gold.[1]

The foregoing account of the mechanism of adjustment is how the gold standard was designed to function in principle. As we move further away from the historical period, roughly 1870–1914, in which the gold standard could be said to have been operative, there is a tendency to idealize its functioning rather than to consider exactly how it did work at the time. It is worthwhile therefore to look briefly at the gold standard's functioning historically in order to remove any misconceptions about its supposed simplicity and automaticity. This will enable us subsequently to deal with the issue of whether the gold standard could be operated effectively under present-day circumstances in which great emphasis is placed in the industrialized countries especially upon the attainment of full employment domestically without undue inflation. Since fixed exchange rates under the gold standard derive their special characteristics from the nature of the metallic currency reserve, it is of interest to consider more generally the case that can be made for a fixed exchange-rate system of a fiduciary character. This we shall do in the final section of this chapter.

Historical Evaluation of the Gold Standard

It is not our intention here to discuss in detail the actual operation of the pre-1914 gold standard.[2] Rather, we shall focus on the system's most salient features, relying in particular upon some important recent studies that have sought to reevaluate the system. For convenience in exposition we shall pattern our discussion according to a number of interrelated points that Triffin (1964) has emphasized in his historical reappraisal. These are as follows:

1. In the major trading countries, individually and as a group, there was a pronounced tendency for imports and exports to move in a parallel fashion

---

1. This account of the adjustment mechanism under the gold standard is very much oversimplified. In particular, we have not spelled out the relationships between the demand for goods and for money and between national income and expenditure that make the system operative and lead to equilibrium when a disturbance occurs. For more complete treatment of these issues, see especially Chacholiades (1971).
2. Many excellent references are cited especially in Bloomfield (1959).

in the pre-1914 period This implied a relatively close cyclical phasing of economic activity, which meant that countries did not get too far out of line vis-à-vis one another and that sizable balance-of-payments disturbances were avoided

2. Related to the first point is the fact that prices in the major trading countries moved generally in a parallel rather than in a divergent fashion. There was not much evidence, in other words, of divergent price movements as the consequence of the inflow or outflow of gold. This suggests that changes in relative prices may have been substantially less important than the idealized version of the gold-standard mechanism of adjustment would lead us to believe.

3. The comparatively small divergent movements in prices meant, furthermore, that money wages in the major trading countries moved in a generally parallel fashion. There were few instances of significant and long-lasting reductions in money wages during the period.

4. The central banks in the major trading countries frequently neutralized changes in their international assets by offsetting changes in their domestic portfolio. The rules of the game were thus violated on a broad scale since the impact of inflows or outflows of gold and foreign exchange on the domestic money supply was frequently negated rather than reinforced.[3]

5. The reliance upon changes in the central-bank discount rate as the chief instrument of monetary policy for purposes of maintaining exchange stability was relatively more common in the case of Great Britain than in the other major trading countries. Great Britain may have been in an especially favorable position, moreover, because of the widespread use of sterling in the financing of international trade and because of Britain's relative importance as an importer of foodstuffs and raw materials.

Great Britain was, of course, the predominant international financial center during the gold-standard period. A substantial proportion of world trade was thus financed in terms of sterling and as a consequence sizable sterling balances were held in London. It is interesting that prior to 1914 the Bank of England's gold reserves were a very small fraction, on the order of 5 percent, of the aggregate liabilities of the banking system. Yet, as Bloomfield has noted (1959, p. 2), "at no time during the period . . . were the continuing

---

3. That is, according to the rules of the game, central-bank policy was supposed to result in the expansion of domestic assets when international assets rose and the contraction of domestic assets when international assets declined, the exact amount of the changes depending upon the banking-reserve rules followed. In comparing the year-to-year changes in both types of assets for eleven countries during all or part of the 1880–1913 period, Bloomfield (1959, pp. 48–50) found that the two components of assets moved in the opposite direction rather than in the same direction for 60 percent of the observations. This percentage proved to be identical to the one calculated by Nurkse (1944) in his study of the interwar experience. Bloomfield thus concluded (1959, p. 50) that "central banks in general played the rules of the game just as badly before 1914 as they did thereafter!" For a comment on the propriety of the test employed by Nurkse and Bloomfield, see Triffin (1964, p. 5).

stability and convertibility of sterling, or indeed the currencies of other leading gold standard countries, ever seriously questioned." The fact that Britain could get along with such small reserves is indicative of the reliance that had to be placed upon discount-rate changes and the apparent success of these changes in affecting short-term capital movements that served to relieve pressure on the British balance of payments.

What is important about the observation just made is the implication that changes in central-bank discount rates and market rates of interest played a crucial role in the attainment in Great Britain especially not only of external stability but internal stability as well. Since Great Britain was the single largest trading nation at this time, its policies thus imparted substantial stability in general to much of the rest of the world. The successful implementation of discount-rate policy in Britain and in the other major trading countries meant that domestic expenditure, particularly investment, was sufficiently responsive to changes in the cost and availability of credit so that resources could be adapted and output switched readily between the home and foreign sectors without undue deflationary effect. Discount-rate policy meant also that interest-rate considerations had an important effect upon short-term capital movements in connection with interest arbitrage and the financing of commercial trade. Since, as noted, the gold points in the major trading countries were rarely, if ever, subject to doubt, forward speculation could have been undertaken often with little or no risk of loss. It appears in retrospect therefore that one primary reason why the gold-standard mechanism of adjustment worked so effectively in the short-run was because of the sensitivity of domestic expenditure and short-term capital movements to changes in monetary conditions.[4]

All of this is not to say that the discount rate was the only instrument employed during this period, and that what occurred in Great Britain was typical of what occurred elsewhere. France, for example, according to Bloomfield (1959, p. 31), relied relatively more on variations in its reserves to deal with imbalances than it did upon discount-rate changes. Moreover, as Bloomfield (1959, pp. 52–59) has further pointed out, the major central banks resorted on numerous occasions, particularly in the later phases of

---

4. Note, however, the following comment by Bloomfield (1963, pp. 90–91):

Unquestionably, short-term interest-rate differentials and exchange-rate fluctuations within the gold points played a dominant role in directing the flow of private short-term funds between gold-standard countries, even if the degree of mobility of the funds so motivated has sometimes been exaggerated. But by no means all private short-term capital movements can be explained in these simple terms. Preferences, based on institutional arrangements or long-standing banking connections, as to foreign lenders or as to markets in which to place short-term funds; the availability of credit as contrasted with its cost; the requirements of external debt service; the changing needs for maintaining working balances in given centers; considerations of bank liquidity; all these and other factors exerted an influence on the volume and direction of short-term capital flows that may at times have over-shadowed interest-rate and exchange-rate factors.

the operation of the gold standard, to the manipulation of gold points, foreign exchange-market intervention, special borrowings from foreign commercial banks or foreign governments, and exchange control and discrimination in order to maintain exchange stability. In view of the experiences of other countries, particularly France, Germany, and the U.S. where relatively large foreign balances were held and important international lending was carried on during the period, Bloomfield (1963, p. 93) concluded that the assertion that the world was really on a "sterling-exchange standard" prior to 1914 is an evident oversimplification.

The comparative ease with which Great Britain and most of the other major trading countries maintained external stability should not be taken to mean that the "rest of the world" experienced no difficulties in this respect. As a matter of fact, many less developed, primary-producing countries outside of the British Empire were faced frequently with considerable difficulties under the gold standard, especially when the foreign demand for their exports fell off and when capital inflows were interrupted because of the tightening of credit conditions in Britain and elsewhere. There were some countries such as Spain and a number of those in Latin America that were either never on the pre-1914 gold standard but instead had fluctuating exchange rates, or that were forced off of it at times when they could not maintain exchange-rate stability. Moreover, because Britain imported sizable amounts of foodstuffs and raw materials, the primary-producing countries were susceptible at times to price reductions in their exports during periods of credit stringency in Britain. To the extent that Britain's terms of trade improved because of the fall in import prices, there was a favorable effect on the British balance of payments. It would thus appear that the interruption of exports from and of capital inflows into the primary-producing countries frequently created problems of balance-of-payments adjustment that many countries could not readily solve.[5] The gold standard can be said therefore to have been more suitable for the economic structure and functioning of Great Britain and the other major trading countries than for the comparatively less developed countries that relied heavily upon the production of primary commodities.

6. The preoccupation in the idealized version of the gold standard with adjustment via the current account diverted attention away from the role played by long-term international capital movements from Western Europe in financing sizable and lasting import surpluses in the borrowing countries. It has been estimated that in 1913 the long-term foreign investments of the major countries of Western Europe totalled about $40.5 billion and of the U.S. about $3.5 billion. Great Britain ($18 billion), France ($9 billion) and Germany ($5.8 billion) were the largest overseas investors. The geographical

---

5. See Ford (1960) for a discussion of the special adjustment problems faced by the primary-producing countries and a qualification of the view that in general the gold standard imposed an undue share of the burden of adjustment on these countries.

distribution of the total amount of $44 billion was estimated as follows: Europe, $12 billion; U.S., $6.8 billion; Latin America, $8.5 billion; Asia, $6.0 billion; Africa, $4.7 billion; Canada, $3.7 billion; and Australia and New Zealand, $2.3 billion.[6]

Great Britain's role as a capital exporter was of long standing during the nineteenth century, which meant that it traditionally ran a surplus on current account. Interestingly enough, Britain's balance on merchandise trade became increasingly in deficit during the gold-standard period. The inflow of investment income into Britain grew to such an extent, however, that the financing of the trade deficit posed no problems of consequence. British foreign lending, especially during the period 1906–13, was truly something amazing to behold. An annual average of $850 million was lent during these years. In 1911–13 alone, the level exceeded a billion dollars annually, which at that time was equal to about a third of British exports and 10 percent of its net national income.[7]

What is noteworthy about these overseas investments is that they were executed so rapidly and without greatly disturbing balance-of-payments effects in terms of exchange-rate pressures and gold flows. Indeed, the relative ease with which this transfer process was carried out was puzzling to contemporary observers at that time who were unable to explain their observations in terms of the traditional specie-flow analysis.[8] It appears in retrospect

---

6. These figures, which are cited in Triffin (1964, p. 7), were taken by him from United Nations (1949, p. 2).

7. These estimates by Triffin (1964, p. 7) were derived by him from Imlah (1958, pp. 70–75). Yeager (1966, p. 256) has noted in this context that:

> By World War I an estimated one-third of all accumulated British wealth had taken the form of private foreign investment. Adjusted to the size of the American economy in 1955, this would mean something like $300 or $400 billion, as against an actual figure of about $25 billion. In the four decades preceding World War I, about 40 percent of British savings was invested overseas. Corresponding figures for America in the 1950's would have amounted to a capital outflow upwards of $20 billion a year, as contrasted with a net private outflow of some $1 to $3 billion.

It is true of course that the conditions affecting foreign investment were quite different in the 1950's as compared to the pre-1914 period. The figures cited provide nevertheless an interesting comparison that serves to illustrate the predominant role that Great Britain played in the international financial system before World War I. For additional commentary along similar lines, see Ford (1965) and Brown (1965).

8. Thus, as Taussig (1927, pp. 239–40) remarked:

> The point which is less familiar in connexion with the theory of the subject, or at all events is not commonly considered, is the closeness and rapidity with which the varying balance of payments has found its expression in the varying balance of trade. . . . The process which our theory contemplates . . . can hardly be expected to take place smoothly and quickly. Yet, no signs of disturbance are to be observed such as the theoretical analysis previses, and some recurring phenomena are of a kind not contemplated by theory at all. It must be confessed that here we have phenomena not fully understood. . . .

It is interesting to note that with the application in the 1940's of Keynesian models of income determination to the analysis of international capital movements, it became

that in the pre-1914 period in Great Britain especially, home and foreign investment tended to move inversely.[9] The real counterpart to the overseas lending was thus made up of goods that were available for export because of the damping down of home demand. Sizable variations in Britain's current account could occur therefore as expenditure on British goods alternated relatively between the home and foreign markets in response to changing investment incentives. The net result was to lend comparative stability to the British economy prior to 1914.

The process just described did not of course work perfectly in the short run. When short-run imbalances did occur, as Ford (1964, p. 27) especially has noted, it was "here the task for Bank Rate became more important, and its influence on international short-term capital movements became crucial." Except for 1881–86, Ford (1964, pp. 28–29) observed that during the 1870–1914 period there was a close positive association involving current-account improvements, boom conditions, and a higher Bank Rate.[10] This association is to be explained by the export-induced boom that led to a deterioration of the Bank of England's reserve ratio. This deterioration was due to the increase in the domestic transactions demand for money relative to the gold stock. Moreover, at these times the given structure of interest rates was conducive to British overseas lending and to the financing of trade in London. It was necessary under such circumstances accordingly for the Bank Rate to be increased in order to reduce domestic expenditures and effect a short-term capital inflow.

International investment was of great importance from the standpoint of many borrowing countries for it enabled them to finance the acquisition of additional resources from abroad that served to enhance their economic growth. Coupled with these sizable foreign borrowings, there were rising trends for exports particularly from the rapidly developing countries that were important producers of temperate-zone foodstuffs and raw materials.[11]

---

fashionable to attribute the smoothness of the adjustment under the gold standard to the induced changes in imports which followed from increases in income due to autonomous changes in exports. However, as will be clear from our discussion of the income approach in Chapter 6 below and as Sohmen (1969, p. 79) points out:

> ... the income adjustment in the country experiencing the export surplus presupposes the existence of unemployment. With literally full employment, real income cannot rise and the adjustment cannot be due to income effects. ... A more serious criticism concerns the speed of adjustment with which the foreign trade multiplier is supposed to work [as compared to changes in prices]. ... The real clue to the smooth balance-of-payments adjustment under the gold standard must be sought ... [in] ... the effects of changes in interest rates on real absorption out of a given real national income.

9. See, for example, Ford (1960, pp. 68–69).
10. This association was measured on the basis of absolute deviations from 9-year moving averages.
11. These countries are frequently referred to as the "regions of recent settlement." Included are the U.S., Canada, Argentina, Southern Brazil, South Africa, Australia, and New Zealand.

As a consequence, these countries were spared from serious balance-of-payments pressures during most of the pre-1914 gold-standard period. As mentioned earlier, however, this was not the case for many of the less developed countries elsewhere that were dependent upon exports of primary products.

In summary, what was remarkable under the gold standard was the broad synchronization of fluctuations in economic activity in the major trading countries and the comparative absence in these countries of serious disturbances to internal and external stability. As Triffin has pointed out (1964, pp. 10–11), there was a:

> ... harmonization of national monetary and credit policies [that] depended far less on *ex post* corrective action, requiring an extreme flexibility, downward as well as upward, of national price and wage levels, than on the *ex ante* avoidance of substantial disparities in cost competitiveness and in the monetary policies which would allow them to develop.
>
> As long as stable exchange rates were maintained, national *export* prices remained strongly bound together among all competing countries, by the mere existence of an international market not broken down by any large or frequent changes in trade or exchange restrictions. Under these conditions, national price and wage levels also remained closely linked together internationally, even in the face of divergent rates of monetary and credit expansion, as import and export competition constituted a powerful brake on the emergence of any large disparity between internal and external price and cost levels.
>
> Inflationary pressures could not be contained within the domestic market, but spilled out *directly*, to a considerable extent, into balance-of-payments deficits rather than into uncontrolled rises of internal prices, costs, and wage levels. These deficits led, in turn, to corresponding monetary transfers from the domestic banking system to foreign banks, weakening the cash position of domestic banks and their ability to pursue expansionary credit policies leading to persistent deficits for the economy and persistent cash drains for the banks. (Banks in the surplus countries would be simultaneously subject to opposite pressures, which would also contribute to the harmonization of credit policies around levels conducive to the re-equilibration of the overall balance of payments.)

The interesting question that emerges from Triffin's remarks is whether there was some ironclad discipline inherent in the gold standard that made this system function so effectively. It is true of course that the monetary authorities were preoccupied with maintaining currency convertibility and exchange-rate stability. This should not divert our attention, however, from the profound economic changes that were manifested between 1870 and 1914 in the "clustering and spread of technological discoveries and innovations in production, transportation, etc., by the vast migrations from old to new settlement areas, and—last but not least—by the preparation, waging and aftermath of wars."[12]

12. Triffin (1964, p. 14).

Monetary and banking developments clearly played an important role in facilitating economic growth during the period of the gold standard. The dimensions of this role are to be measured not so much by the increases that occurred in gold circulation, but rather by the credit expansion that took place. Thus, as Triffin has noted (1964, p. 15):

> Increases in credit money—paper currency and demand deposits—accounted, in the major and more developed countries, for two-thirds or more of total monetary expansion after the middle of the nineteenth century, and more than 90 percent from 1873 to 1913. . . . .
>
> These facts can hardly be reconciled with the supposed *automaticity* still ascribed by many writers—particularly in Europe—to the so-called nineteenth century gold standard. The reconciliation of high rates of economic growth with exchange-rate and gold-price stability was made possible indeed by the rapid growth and proper management of bank money.[13]

The Ill-Fated Restoration of the Gold Standard After World War I

Reference was made in the preceding chapter to the inflationary experiences of the major trading countries during and immediately after World War I that made it impossible to maintain convertibility and the system of exchange rates that had existed prior to 1914. The prewar gold standard thus gave way to a system of freely fluctuating exchange rates in most of these countries from 1919–26. Many who observed the chaos in the domestic and inter-national financial markets in Europe at this time concluded that the European experiences with freely fluctuating exchange rates were disastrous.[14] How-ever, as pointed out in the preceding chapter, it was not the exchange-rate system per se that was at fault. Rather, it was the inability of the monetary authorities to exercise effective restraint upon domestic credit expansion that was at the root of things. It was not surprising in the absence of such restraint that speculation occurred frequently against particular European currencies.

13. Triffin (1964, p. 19) points out further that during the period a substantial amount of the existing gold and silver currency in circulation and of the newly mined gold was absorbed in central bank reserves: "The proportion of monetary gold and silver stocks absorbed in centralized monetary reserves rose from about 10 percent in 1848 to 16 percent in 1872, 41 percent in 1892, and 51 percent in 1913."

14. Thus, Triffin concluded (1964, p. 21):

> Freely fluctuating rates failed signally . . . to restore a competitive price and cost pattern among the major trading nations, to induce the adoption of monetary policies compatible with even a moderate degree of stability in prices and exchange rates, and to bring about any sort of tenable equilibrium in the world's balance-of-payments pattern.

Fixed exchange rates and currency convertibility were reinstituted in most countries in the mid-1920's. However, the system proved to be very short-lived because it rested upon disequilibrium exchange rates and an inadequate reserve base. That is, the restoration of the pound to its prewar parity was inappropriate for Great Britain because of the inflation that had occurred.[15] Sterling was pegged therefore at too high a level. This was accomplished, as we have already noted, by means of a policy of domestic deflation that resulted in substantial unemployment. By the same token, some of the other European currencies were undervalued relative to the pound. In such cases, exports and domestic activity were stimulated.

The restoration of the reserve base in the 1920's was accomplished in the countries with undervalued currencies by means of the currency devaluations that they carried out, foreign borrowings, the generation of balance-of-payments surpluses, and the repatriation of funds particularly from Great Britain. Britain faced serious difficulties in increasing its reserves because of its unfavorable domestic conditions and overvalued exchange rate and the outflow of funds to the continent. In an attempt to keep their existing reserves from being depleted, the British sought to have other countries hold sterling balances in place of gold. The base on which this gold-exchange standard rested was comparatively small, however, in view of Britain's reserve position.[16] Indeed following the onset of the Great Depression in 1929 and some banking failures in continental European countries that were holding sterling balances, there occurred a run on the pound. Britain was forced to suspend gold payments and the pound was devalued in September 1931. The international monetary system ceased to function effectively thereafter as other devaluations took place and various restrictions were placed upon international payments and trade.

The attempted reconstitution of the pre-1914 gold standard in the interwar period thus ended in failure because too little account was taken of the important structural changes that had occurred particularly in Great Britain. The pattern of exchange rates that emerged was inappropriate and could not be sustained. Moreover, the system rested on a relatively narrow gold base and the loss of confidence in sterling was enough to render the system a fatal blow.

15. See Moggridge (1969) and Reddaway (1970) for accounts of British policy during this period based on official documents that were hitherto unavailable to public scrutiny.

16. According to Triffin (1964, p. 23): "Central-bank reserves of foreign exchange rose from about $700 million in 1913 to more than $3 billion in 1928, of which some $2½ billion —i.e., three to four times the total gold reserves of England—may be estimated to have been held in sterling, legally convertible into gold on demand or on very short notice." As just noted, foreign balances were already being held in some countries prior to 1914 so that a gold-exchange standard could be said to have existed then. See Lindert (1969) for additional details on this matter and for discussion of other aspects of the role of key currencies prior to World War I.

The Feasibility of the Pre-1914 Gold Standard
Under Present-Day Conditions

Given the rather special historical circumstances that characterized the operation of the gold standard prior to 1914 and the ill-fated attempts to reinstitute this system during the interwar period, it is of interest to consider briefly the conditions that would have to obtain today for such a system to be implemented successfully. Perhaps most important is that it would be necessary to have a substantial and continually expanding stock of gold for monetary-reserve purposes so that balance-of-payments disturbances could be handled without undue pressure on exchange rates and serious impact on domestic stability. The maintenance of external convertibility would become the primary policy goal in this system, and domestic stabilization policies would be oriented towards this end. This means that countries would be forced to institute corrective measures domestically whenever their presumably limited monetary reserves were in danger of depletion.

How likely is it that these conditions would be met under present-day circumstances? We have noted in Chapter 2 that, since World War II the world's stock of gold used for monetary-reserve purposes has been inadequate in size, and that it has been necessary accordingly to rely primarily on the U.S. dollar, to a lesser extent the pound sterling, and most recently the creation of Special Drawing Rights to supplement gold. A movement now from today's gold-exchange standard to a true gold standard would most probably require an increase in the price of gold in order to effect an enlargement of the value of the existing gold stock, bring about dishoarding, and encourage new supplies. Merely increasing monetary reserves is no guarantee, however, that the system would succeed unless all countries had enough reserves for exchange-stabilization purposes and oriented their domestic stabilization policies towards the maintenance of external convertibility.

It is perhaps on this latter score more than any other that the greatest difficulties might be experienced in instituting a gold-standard system today. That is, the orientation of domestic stabilization policies towards external convertibility would probably conflict at times with the attainment of internal stability. This would be particularly the case if prices and wages were relatively inflexible on the downward side. A deflationary domestic policy adopted for balance-of-payments purposes under such circumstances might result in a level of unemployment that would be considered socially intolerable. By the same token, a country with a balance-of-payments surplus would experience inflationary pressures domestically as its reserves increased. The major question concerning the gold standard is therefore whether countries would willingly expose themselves more than they are already doing under the present adjustable-peg system to domestic instability in order to maintain stable rates of exchange. We have already seen that, strictly speaking, the rules of the game were seriously violated before 1914, and that attempts to restore the gold standard in the interwar period were marked by failure. Could we expect anything different in this day and age?[17]

The Case for Fixed Exchange Rates

Thus far we have focused on the historical aspects and contemporary implications of the gold standard. Let us now consider more generally the case to be made in favor of fixed exchange rates. In order to avoid the complications of a gold-based currency, we shall assume a fixed exchange-rate system that is fiduciary in character. It will be recalled from our earlier discussion of the optimum-currency domain that importance was attached to national currencies being stable in value and useful therefore for exchange and liquidity purposes. These are matters worth pursuing further because they are of central importance in a system of fixed exchange rates. We shall thus consider first the advantages that a unified currency confers upon individual nations and then seek to determine whether these advantages can be obtained on a world scale by means of a system of fixed exchange rates.

According to Johnson (1963, p. 112), the advantages of a unified national currency are: (1) a measure of value and standard for deferred payments in common use by and familiar to all; (2) a medium of exchange acceptable everywhere in the economy and with a minimum of transactions costs; (3) a store of value that varies only in response to changes in the general level of prices. These advantages will be best realized when the goods and factor markets function competitively so that money tends to have the same purchasing power in all parts of the economy. It does not follow, however, as our discussion of optimum-currency domains made clear, that a unified national currency will be appropriate for all regions within a country. Johnson (1963, p. 114) has pointed out that unless the country's monetary system is managed skillfully, individual regions may suffer. This is particularly the case if a national monetary policy is adopted without regard to differential regional impacts. As we have seen, regions are sometimes subject to wage and price inflexibilities and factor immobility, and are consequently vulnerable to changes in national policy. This has made it necessary, particularly in the advanced countries, to introduce special financial measures to assist certain production activities and to effect redistributions of income towards regions in which factor movements are constrained.

A worldwide system of fixed exchange rates is supposed to secure the advantages noted for a unified currency. Johnson (1963, pp. 114–17) has observed, however, that these advantages are by no means easily transferred

17. See Rueff (1964) for a view that takes issue with the one taken here.

from a nation to the world as a whole. First of all, competition may be imperfect among the national market areas covered by the fixed exchange-rate system, and it may be difficult to establish a supranational authority that can furnish the special incentives and effect the redistribution of income in favor of nations that may suffer from membership in the system. Secondly, in comparison to a uniform currency that is used widely and accepted everywhere, a system of fixed rates may not provide the same convenience because of conversion costs and uncertainties regarding the fixity of the rates. Third and most important is that the nature of monetary reserves will differ in the two alternative systems.

That is, within a nation a bank must maintain strict convertibility between its monetary liabilities and the money used for reserve purposes. This does not hold necessarily between nations, however, particularly if exchange rates are adjustably pegged as today rather than completely fixed. Thus, in the present-day system, any nation can alter by means of devaluation or appreciation of its exchange rate the relationship between its national money and the money used for international reserves. Moreover, national monetary reserves are created in individual nations with domestic stabilization and growth objectives in mind. This is difficult to accomplish internationally, however, unless nations can agree on worldwide stabilization and growth objectives and the creation and allocation of reserves consistent with these objectives.

Our discussion thus suggests, following Johnson (1963, pp. 118–19), that to obtain the advantages of a unified currency on an international scale with fixed exchange rates, there be a minimum of barriers to the free movement internationally of goods and productive factors. Furthermore, exchange rates must be fixed once and for all so that national and international moneys coincide and have identical purchasing power everywhere. Finally, there must be international agreement and cooperation in promoting short-run stability in the system and assuring a growth in reserves that is commensurate with a rapid expansion of world trade and production.

Conclusion

We first set forth in this chapter the nature of the balance-of-payments mechanism of adjustment under the gold standard in its idealized form and then proceeded to discuss the actual functioning of the gold standard in the period from 1870–1914. This brief historical survey revealed a number of important differences between the idealized version and observed operation of the gold standard. In short, the gold standard was in actuality far more complex and functioned much less automatically than the idealized version of it implies. The special historical circumstances of economic growth in the pre-1914 period also cannot be overlooked. We had occasion thereafter to examine the abortive attempts to reinstitute the gold standard during the interwar period, and to consider the implications of adapting the present-day international financial system along gold-standard lines. The important question here was whether countries would willingly expose themselves to domestic instability in order to maintain exchange-rate stability. We stepped finally outside of the gold standard and examined in more general terms the case to be made for a system of fixed exchange rates and the special conditions that would have to be met for such a system to function effectively.

Having treated the major considerations involved in freely fluctuating and fixed exchange-rate systems, we can turn in the next chapter to the present-day system of the adjustable peg. The issue here is whether the present-day system represents the better or the worse of both possible exchange-rate worlds.

5

Balance-of-Payments Adjustment Under Pegged Exchange Rates

It was pointed out in our previous discussion that the present-day system of pegged-but-adjustable exchange rates was designed to incorporate some of the automaticity of adjustment and certainty of the gold standard together with some of the flexibility of a system of freely fluctuating exchange rates. The automaticity of adjustment was supposed to be achieved through variations in money income and interest rates in deficit and surplus countries in response to changes in international reserves. Exchange rates were to be pegged within relatively narrow limits presumably to minimize the disruption of international trade and capital flows on account of exchange-rate uncertainty. In the event that a country's balance of payments reflected a "fundamental disequilibrium" due to the occurrence of some structural change, adjustment could be sought by means of changing the exchange rate in an orderly fashion after consultation with the IMF. In this way, the domestic economy might be given more time to effect whatever adjustment was required for balance-of-payments purposes.

We have already mentioned in Chapter 2 that, during the nearly two decades following the 1948–49 devaluations, exchange rates in the industrialized countries especially were altered only on a few occasions. It thus appeared for some time that the issues involved in exchange-rate adjustment were becoming academic in character. However, there has been renewed interest in this subject especially since the sterling devaluation of November 1967 and other developments culminating in the currency appreciations and floating rates adopted by several major industrialized countries in the spring and summer of 1971 in response to the buildup of official dollar balances and the U.S. suspension of gold convertibility.[1]

1. Up-to-date details on exchange-rate adjustments and other policies affecting exchange rates can be found in the monthly issues of the IMF, *International Financial Statistics* and in the IMF, *Annual Reports on Exchange Restrictions*. Useful retrospective surveys are provided by deVries (1969a) for the period 1945–65 and Davis (1969) for 1946–68.

In the present chapter we shall review the major theoretical issues relating to the adjustment process under pegged exchange rates. After some general discussion of this process, we shall examine the effects of exchange-rate adjustment on a country's balance of trade and terms of trade, and the institutional and policy considerations that are relevant for devaluation to be effective. We shall then investigate possible norms for exchange-rate adjustment, concentrating particularly on the correction of a "fundamental disequilibrium" in a country's balance of payments and the use of purchasing-power-parity calculations as a guide in selecting equilibrium exchange rates. This section will also include a brief discussion of the empirical measurement of the import and export-demand elasticities that are relevant in estimating the likely outcome of a devaluation. Our final section will be devoted to an evaluation of the pegged-rate system in relation both to freely fluctuating exchange rates and the gold standard.

The Mechanism of Adjustment under the Adjustable Peg

In what follows, we shall maintain the assumptions made earlier that goods and services are produced and consumed competitively, that import and export relationships can be expressed in aggregative form, and that the authorities maintain full employment by means of domestic stabilization policies.

It will be recalled from our discussion in Chapter 2 that in the present-day system the currencies of the countries belonging to the IMF are defined in terms of gold, which establishes a set of exchange parities among them. The original IMF Agreement provided that the U.S. would buy and sell gold at $35 an ounce, while other IMF member countries were obligated to maintain their exchange rates vis-à-vis the dollar within 1 percent on either side of parity. In late 1971, under the Smithsonian Agreement, the official price of gold was raised to $38 per ounce and the exchange-support margins were widened to $2\frac{1}{4}$ percent around parity. With the exchange rates of the other member countries pegged vis-à-vis the dollar and the dollar directly linked to gold, there is a presumptive indirect link between these other countries' currencies and gold.[2] This link is also presumed with respect to Special

2. It should be noted that on March 18, 1968 a two-tier gold market was created when the major industrial nations agreed to stop supplying the private gold market from official reserves at the price of $35 an ounce. This decision was taken as an aftermath of the purchases of about $3 billion of gold by private interests in late 1967 and early 1968 in the hope that the official price of gold would be increased. Since the U.S. had been the residual supplier of gold to the private market in London, the acceleration of private purchases threatened to deplete the U.S. gold stock. At the same time, the prospective creation and allocation of Special Drawing Rights (SDR's) suggested that the existing stock of gold in official hands could be made to serve adequately for official reserve purposes.

Following the segmentation of the market, the price of gold in the private market went as high as $43.82 an ounce in March 1969 and subsided thereafter, falling slightly below

Drawing Rights (SDR's) that have been allocated annually to IMF member countries for reserve purposes since January 1970. Thus, the international monetary reserves of IMF members other than the U.S. are presently held mainly in the form of gold, dollars, and SDR's. In addition to its stock of gold and SDR's, the U.S. holds varying amounts of foreign currencies which it sometimes uses for exchange-market stabilization purposes.

The nature of exchange-rate pegging by the authorities has already been described in connection with Figure 2.8. Thus, if a country's exchange rate shows signs of moving above or below the official limits, the exchange authorities will buy or sell dollars to keep the rate within the specified limits. They will ordinarily use their holdings of gold, SDR's, and dollars for this purpose. But if their reserves are inadequate, they may borrow additional reserves from the IMF and other national and international sources for exchange-stabilization purposes. In this practice of exchange-rate support, there is a basic similarity in the gold-standard and pegged-rate systems. Where the two systems differ conceptually, however, although not necessarily in terms of the way they have been operated in practice, is in the adjustment process.

That is, in the idealized version of the gold standard, the authorities were supposed to reinforce gold inflows or outflows by policies of monetary expansion or contraction. The pegged-rate system carries no such presumption. Rather, it is taken for granted that the authorities may take action to offset the impact of international monetary movements in order to maintain domestic stability. One should not of course make too much of the conceptual differences on this account, for we know that it was quite common under the gold standard for the authorities to take offsetting actions, although they did not necessarily have in mind explicit domestic stabilization goals.

The gold-standard and pegged-rate systems converge, however, when a country finds that it can no longer finance a balance-of-payments deficit or, because of a surplus can no longer continue to absorb additions to its international reserves. In such circumstances the country will be forced to take steps to contract or expand money income, thereby reducing or increasing domestic expenditure. The changes that are brought about in relative prices and interest rates will ordinarily serve to restore equilibrium in the

---

the official \$35 level in early 1970. This easing of pressure on the price of gold raised the issue, particularly with respect to South Africa, of what policy the major industrial countries and the IMF should follow if the price were to fall below \$35 an ounce. It was decided at the end of 1969 that South Africa could sell gold to the Fund to meet its foreign exchange needs when the private market price fell to \$35 an ounce or lower and when, regardless of price, the sales to the private market and the Fund were in total below these needs.

It may be noted, finally, that the U.S. suspended convertibility of dollars into gold on August 15, 1971, pending a realignment of exchange rates. However, even with the new pattern of rates following the Smithsonian Agreement, the U.S. declined to restore convertibility.

For an account of official policies towards gold and the developments in the private gold market, see the annual reports of the IMF. We shall have more to say on the role of gold in the international monetary system in our concluding chapter.

balance of payments. If, however, the source of the disequilibrium lies in some structural change that has taken place, the domestic deflationary or inflationary implications of a gold-standard type of adjustment can be mitigated by exchange-rate devaluation or appreciation. This possibility of altering the exchange rate thus distinguishes the present-day system from the gold standard in which exchange-rate variations were in effect ruled out at least as far as the major industrialized countries were concerned.

Exchange-Rate Adjustment

In our discussion of freely fluctuating exchange rates, we saw that balance-of-payments adjustment took place in response to the changes in the relative prices of exports and imports brought about by the change in the exchange rate. The very same analysis can be applied in the present context. Thus, as in our previous illustrations, suppose we have two countries, America and England, and that we confine our attention to trade in goods and services between these countries. In the case of freely fluctuating exchange rates, we saw that, in terms of comparative statics, an incipient balance-of-payments deficit for America (surplus for England) was eliminated by a depreciation of the dollar (appreciation of the pound). This meant that American imports from England became relatively more expensive and English imports from America relatively cheaper. American imports (English exports) were reduced consequently and American exports (English imports) increased. Balance-of-payments equilibrium was attained when each country's exports and imports were equal in value. This occurred in our example at an exchange rate of $2.40 to the pound.

THE MARSHALL-LERNER CONDITION

The effects of exchange-rate changes were also treated at length in our earlier discussion of the foreign exchange market in Chapter 2. One of the important questions of concern there was the stability of this market. In the Appendix to Chapter 2, we derived formally the general condition for foreign exchange-market stability in terms of the price elasticities of demand and supply for imports and exports.[3] Using this general condition, it was possible to derive

---

3. On the assumption that the devaluation proportion was small and trade was balanced initially, this condition in terms of foreign currency (dollars) was that:

$$\Delta B_f = V_{fx} \frac{e_x(\eta_x - 1)}{e_x + \eta_x} + V_{fm} \frac{\eta_m(e_m + 1)}{\eta_m + e_m} > 0,$$

where ΔB_f was the change in the trade balance; V_{fx} and V_{fm}, the foreign currency values of exports and imports; e_x, the home export-supply elasticity, η_x, the foreign export-demand elasticity; e_m, the foreign import-supply elasticity, and η_m, the home import-demand elasticity. It will be noted that the conventionally negative demand elasticities have been defined so as to enter positively into this expression.

as a special case the Marshall-Lerner condition that is commonly used in the two-country analysis of a devaluation.

The Marshall-Lerner condition is based upon the same assumptions mentioned earlier of competition, one homogeneous (aggregative) export good and one import good, and the maintenance of full employment. Assuming in addition that the elasticities of supply of exports and imports are infinite and trade is balanced initially, this condition states that a devaluation will improve the trade balance if the sum of the foreign elasticity of demand for exports and the home elasticity of demand for imports is greater than unity.[4] That is, if:

$$\eta_x + \eta_m > 1, \tag{5.1}$$

where η_x and η_m refer respectively to the elasticities of demand for exports and imports.

A diagrammatic illustration may be useful in order further to clarify the Marshall-Lerner condition. Thus in Figure 5.1 we have plotted the demand and supply schedules for our two countries. Figure 5.1 is similar to Figure 2.3 except that the supply schedules are infinitely elastic and it is assumed that trade is balanced initially. Suppose now that England were to devalue the pound, say by 25 percent, which would cheapen English goods to America in terms of dollars (foreign currency) and make American goods more expensive to England in terms of pounds (home currency). The English export-supply schedule is thus shifted in terms of dollar prices in Figure 5.1a from S_x^e to $S_x^{e'}$ and the American export-supply schedule in terms of pound prices in Figure 5.1d from S_x^a to $S_x^{a'}$. The equivalent effects of these shifts in supply schedules can be seen in Figure 5.1c where the American import-demand schedule is shifted in terms of pound prices from D_m^a to $D_m^{a'}$ and in Figure 5.1b where the English import-demand schedule is shifted in terms of dollar prices from D_m^e to $D_m^{e'}$.

It will be evident from Figure 5.1 that in the new equilibrium position following the devaluation, there has been an increase in the dollar proceeds of English exports (American imports) from OP_1AQ_1 to OP_2BQ_2 and a reduction by England in its dollar expenditures on imports (American exports) from OP_1EQ_3 to OP_1FQ_4. The net effect is an increase in England's

---

4. Rewriting the expression in footnote 3, we have

$$\Delta B_f = V_{fx} \frac{\eta_x - 1}{1 + \eta_x/e_x} + V_{fm} \frac{\eta_m(1 + 1/e_m)}{\eta_m/e_m + 1} > 0.$$

Assuming infinite supply elasticities, $e_x = e_m = \infty$, and $V_{fx}/V_{fm} = 1$, the foregoing expression reduces to:

$$\Delta B_f = \eta_x + \eta_m > 1,$$

which is the Marshall-Lerner condition. As we have already noted in the Appendix to Chapter 2, the Marshall-Lerner condition is a sufficient but not a necessary condition for improvement of the trade balance.

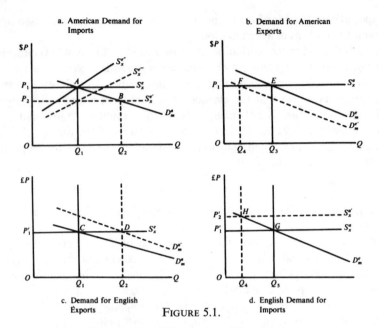

a. American Demand for
Imports

b. Demand for American
Exports

c. Demand for English
Exports

FIGURE 5.1.

d. English Demand for
Imports

*Diagrammatic Illustration of Devaluation
with Infinite Supply Elasticities*

*With trade balanced initially and assuming infinite supply
elasticities, a devaluation by England will increase its
exports in terms of dollars from OP_1AQ_1 to OP_2BQ_2
and reduce imports from OP_1EQ_3 to OP_1FQ_4. England's
trade balance will thus be improved with devaluation in this
case and in general so long as the sum of the elasticities of
demand is greater than one.*

trade balance measured in dollars. We could also measure the increase in
England's trade balance in terms of pounds in the lower part of Figure 5.1.
Taking the new exchange rate into account, the new trade balance in pounds
can be converted into the aforementioned dollar equivalent.[5] The currency
in which the trade balance is to be measured is therefore immaterial in the
present instance.[6] The demand schedules in Figure 5.1 are clearly highly

5. Note that the initial demand and supply schedules in Figure 5.1 are drawn on the
assumption of some specified exchange rate so that the dollar and pound prices on the
vertical axes are proportional. When the exchange rate is altered, as pointed out in Chapter
2, the top and bottom graphs cannot be directly compared unless the price axes are
appropriately redefined.

6. This is not the case, however, if trade is assumed to be unbalanced initially. Suppose,
for example, that imports exceed exports in value initially. The Marshall-Lerner condition
in terms of foreign currency will then be:

$$\Delta B_f = \eta_x + \frac{V_{fm}}{V_{fx}}\,\eta_m > 1.$$

elastic in the ranges indicated.[7] Thus, in this instance the Marshall-Lerner condition for an improvement in the trade balance is easily satisfied.[8]

If, on the other hand, the demand schedules in terms of dollars were relatively inelastic as in Figure 5.2, the Marshall-Lerner condition would not be satisfied, in which case a devaluation would worsen rather than improve the trade balance.[9] That is, a devaluation would result in a decline in English dollar-export proceeds from OP_1AQ_1 to OP_2BQ_2 in Figure 5.2, which would more than offset the small reduction in England's dollar expenditure on imports from OP_1EQ_3 to OP_1FQ_4.

Suppose now that we drop the assumption of infinite supply elasticities.[10] If, say, the demand for English exports were relatively elastic, as is the case for D_m^a in Figure 5.1a, the increase in England's dollar-export proceeds due to a devaluation would be greater the more highly elastic is the English export-supply schedule. That is, with the initial equilibrium at P_1 and Q_1 in Figure 5.1a, there will be a much greater increase in export proceeds with the shift from S_x^e to $S_x^{e'}$ than from $S_x^{e''}$ to $S_x^{e'''}$. Alternatively, if the demand for English exports were relatively inelastic, as is the case for D_m^a in Figure 5.2a, the smaller the elasticity of the English export-supply schedule the better. That is, in Figure 5.2a, England's export proceeds will decline with a

---

If V_{fm}/V_{fx} exceeds unity, it is evident that the trade balance in foreign currency could be improved even if the sum of the elasticities were less than or equal to unity. In such an event, the Marshall-Lerner condition would become sufficient. But this is not to say that the trade balance need be improved in terms of home currency. The condition here is that:

$$\Delta B_h = \frac{V_{hx}}{V_{hm}} \eta_x + \eta_m > 1,$$

where ΔB_h is the change in the trade balance in home currency and V_{hx} and V_{hm} refer, respectively, to the home-currency value of exports and imports.

An arithmetic example of the foregoing point is given in Case II of Table 5.A.1 in the Appendix to this chapter. The significance of this case stems from the possibility of a deficit country improving its trade balance in foreign currency, which is what matters, even when faced with relatively low demand elasticities. The fact that the deficit may worsen in home currency is in itself not of great moment since further adjustment is likely to be required to eliminate the deficit completely. A position will thus soon be reached where the trade balance is improved in both currencies.

7. The demand schedules in question are those indicated in Figure 5.1a, which is measured in dollar prices, and Figure 5.1d, which is measured in pound prices. Since all of our expressions for the change in the trade balance are measured either in dollars (foreign currency) or pounds (home currency), we evidently have to convert one of the relations in question into the same terms as the other. See the Appendix to Chapter 2 for additional details.

8. Some illustrative examples of the Marshall-Lerner condition with various assumed values for the demand elasticities are given in Case I of Table 5.A.1 in the Appendix to this chapter.

9. If the sum of the elasticities were less than one, the correct policy would be one of appreciation rather than devaluation.

10. As noted in the Appendix to this chapter, it may also be instructive to introduce a third country in order to bring out more clearly the importance of the supply side in the analysis of a devaluation.

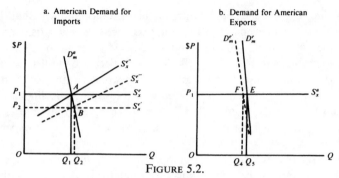

FIGURE 5.2.

*Diagrammatic Illustration of Devaluation with
Inelastic Demand and Finite Supply Elasticities*

*With trade balanced initially and assuming inelastic demand
and infinitely elastic supply schedules, a devaluation by
England will worsen its trade balance. Given an inelastic
demand for English exports, a devaluation by England will
result in a smaller decline in export proceeds the more
inelastic the export-supply schedule.*

devaluation, but the decline will be less with the relatively more inelastic supply schedule, $S_x^{e''}$, than with S_x^e. The overall effect of the devaluation must of course take English imports into account as well. But the same rules of thumb apply, as just noted.[11]

DEVALUATION AND THE NET BARTER (OR COMMODITY) TERMS OF TRADE

We have seen that devaluation brings about changes in relative prices that will cause a shift of expenditures towards the devaluing country's exports and away from its imports. Since these relative price changes may affect the devaluing country's real income, they deserve examination in their own right. The effects in question can be analyzed via the changes that occur in the

11. Given relatively small demand elasticities, it is possible that a devaluation may result in an improvement of the trade balance if the supply elasticities are small enough. This possibility, which can be discerned from the expression noted above in footnote 3, is illustrated in Case III of Table 5.A.1 in the Appendix to this chapter on the assumption that the demand elasticities are each equal to one half and the supply elasticities are each equal to unity. Thus, in an instance when both the demand and supply elasticities are relatively low, the Marshall-Lerner condition for an improvement in the trade balance becomes sufficient.

Case III in Table 5.A.1 is also interesting because it shows how the foreign currency and home prices of exports and imports change with varying demand elasticities when the supply elasticities are assumed to be unity. That is, the supply price of exports is seen to rise as the assumed demand elasticities increase while the supply price of imports is seen to be reduced. It might be instructive if the reader were to work out these various examples diagrammatically.

devaluing country's net barter (or commodity) terms of trade, that is, the changes in the price of exports vis-à-vis imports.

This relation of exchange-rate variation to the terms of trade has already been treated formally in the Appendix to Chapter 2. We saw there that the net barter (or commodity) terms of trade, $T = p_{hx}/p_{hm}$,[12] depended upon the price elasticities of the supply and demand functions for imports and exports. The condition derived was that the terms of trade will improve or worsen with a devaluation depending upon whether the product of the elasticities of supply of exports and imports, $e_x e_m$, is greater or less than the product of the elasticities of demand for exports and imports, $\eta_x \eta_m$. That is:

$$T \text{ will worsen if } e_x e_m > \eta_x \eta_m$$

or

(5.2)

$$T \text{ will improve if } e_x e_m < \eta_x \eta_m.$$

The implications of changes in the terms of trade can be seen by noting that in equilibrium with initial balance where exports and imports are equal in value in home currency, we have:

$$p_{hx} q_x = p_{hm} q_m,$$

or

$$T = \frac{p_{hx}}{p_{hm}} = \frac{q_m}{q_x}. \tag{5.3}$$

Assuming infinite supply elasticities and the sum of the demand elasticities equal to unity, a devaluation will leave the balance of trade unchanged but will result in worsened terms of trade. This is evident from Figure 5.1c and 5.1d since, with a devaluation, p_{hx} will be unchanged while p_{hm} will rise by the extent of the devaluation. In effect then, the country will be giving up a larger volume of domestic produce in exchange for a smaller volume of imports.[13] It is in this sense therefore that we can interpret devaluation as possibly leading to a reduction in real income on account of worsened terms of trade.

When supply is less than infinitely elastic, the effect on the terms of trade will of course depend on the magnitudes of the supply and demand elasticities. Some of the possible outcomes with respect to both the terms of trade and the balance of trade are listed in Table 5.1. The first case in which all the relevant elasticities are assumed to be high is the most favorable from the standpoint of the trade balance and one in which the terms of trade may deteriorate only moderately or improve. The trade balance will be less favorably affected in case 2 as compared to case 1, although the terms of trade will improve if the

---

12. The price of exports and imports refer here to measurement in home currency. The terms of trade can also be measured of course in foreign currency prices.

13. The reasoning is the same in terms of foreign currency, only then the price of exports in foreign currency will fall by the extent of the devaluation while the foreign currency price of imports will remain unchanged.

TABLE 5.1

Summary of the Effects of a Devaluation on the Net Barter Terms of Trade and Balance of Trade

Demand Elasticities	Supply Elasticities	Effect on	
		Net Barter Terms of Trade	Balance of Trade
		In relation to initial balance:	
1. Both high and sum > 1	Both high	Moderate worsening or improvement[a]	Improvement
2. Both high and sum > 1	Both low	Improvement[b]	Improvement
3. Both low and sum < 1	Both high	Worsening	Worsening
4. Both low and sum < 1	Both low	Improvement[b]	Improvement[b]

[a] Depends on whether the product of the supply elasticities is greater or less than the product of the demand elasticities.
[b] If supply elasticities are sufficiently small in relation to the demand elasticities.
SOURCE: Adapted from Meade (1951, pp. 246–47).

supply elasticities are sufficiently low. The third case is the most unfavorable, given that the sum of the demand elasticities is less than unity and supply elasticities are high. The fourth case is unusual in that the trade balance will be improved even though the sum of the demand elasticities is less than unity. This improvement stems from the assumption that the supply elasticities are sufficiently small relative to the demand elasticities. In this event the terms-of-trade effect will also be favorable.

Since the magnitudes of the demand and supply elasticities will vary in particular empirical circumstances, there is no a priori way of telling which way the net barter (or commodity) terms of trade will move with a de-valuation.[14] There is a further consideration, moreover, which is especially relevant for devaluation in the case of pegged exchange rates. This involves whether the net barter (or commodity) terms of trade is the proper criterion for evaluating the effects of a devaluation upon real income. The issue here is whether devaluation will have a favorable effect on the productivity of domestic resources. When this is the case, as we shall now see, devaluation will result in an increase in real income. What we need then is a measure of

14. See Machlup (1956; 1964, pp. 195–97) for a representative sampling of the differences in views that have been expressed in the literature concerning the terms-of-trade effects of a devaluation.

the single factoral terms of trade which takes productivity changes into account.

DEVALUATION AND THE SINGLE FACTORAL TERMS OF TRADE

Conceptually the single factoral terms of trade, T_f, measures the change in the "import-buying power" of a unit of domestic resources. T_f is calculated by adjusting the net barter terms of trade, p_{hx}/p_{hm}, for changes in the productivity of resources employed in the export industries. Measuring these changes in productivity in terms of the changes in $(O/I)_x$, which is an index of output per unit of input in the export industries, we have:

$$T_f = \frac{p_{hx}}{p_{hm}} \left(\frac{O}{I}\right)_x. \tag{5.4}$$

Thus, for example, if devaluation resulted in an increase in import prices in domestic currency and export prices were unchanged, the net barter terms of trade would show a deterioration. But if in the process of devaluation, resources were shifted domestically from relatively lower productivity sectors to the more highly productive export sector, the improvement in productivity might more than offset the decline in the net barter terms of trade.[15] The net effect might then be an improvement in real income.[16]

The circumstances under which this might occur have been noted by Machlup (1956; 1964, p. 211) as follows:

A reallocation of resources effected by currency devaluation and resulting in increased production of import substitutes and/or export goods can involve a net increase in national product

15. Machlup (1956; 1964, pp. 200–01) has suggested in this light that:

One may formulate a general rule for the kinds of changes or events for which the commodity terms of trade are useful tools in the analysis of effects upon a nation's income. Changes or events that take place *abroad* and alter the relative prices of exports and imports, regardless of any subsequent substitutions in the use of products and resources within the nation, will increase or reduce its income initially by an amount which is calculable with the aid of the commodity terms of trade. Subsequent adjustments in the use of products and resources will increase the initial gain or reduce the initial loss. On the other hand, changes or events taking place *within* the economy and causing changes in productivity *together* with changes in the commodity terms of trade—the extent of change in one depending on the extent of change in the other—will increase or reduce income not even approximately or initially calculable with the aid of the commodity terms of trade. [Italics in original.]

16. Machlup notes (1956; 1964, p. 211) that: "The resource reallocation induced by the changes in relative prices that result from devaluation does not have to involve an increase in exports. It may equally well be domestic production of import substitutes that is given a lift, and all sorts of additional substitutions in production, investment, and consumption may be engendered." It is noteworthy that since the benefits of resource reallocation may stem from increased production of import substitutes as well as from exports, the single factoral terms of trade, as defined above, may not capture all the relevant changes. It may be more appropriate therefore to analyze the effects of a devaluation upon the price level generally in the devaluing country in order to assess the change in real income. See Sohmen (1969, pp. 175–77) for an analysis of these effects in terms of Laspeyres and Paasche index-number inequalities.

(a) If the exchange-rate adjustment permits the abolition of direct controls and quantitative restrictions which had created (or increased) disproportions in the marginal productivities of productive services and/or discrepancies between private and social costs and benefits;

(b) if such disproportions or discrepancies due to price inflexibilities, resource immobilities, and restrictions or serious imperfections of competition are reduced in consequence of the exchange-rate adjustment;

(c) if the improvement in the trade balance checks or stops a loss (i.e., an unintended realization) of foreign assets and thus conserves them for future use with a presumably greater value for consumer welfare and/or production potential.[17]

Machlup was fully aware that there is no guarantee that these reallocation benefits will necessarily be realized. As he stated (1956; 1964, p. 211): "Thus one has to establish in each particular situation that the resource allocation before devaluation is not an optimal one—owing to certain defects or restrictions in the operation of the markets—and can be improved through an adjustment of the exchange rate."[18] There is nevertheless a strong presumption that these benefits may be realized in many instances since under present-day conditions devaluation is undertaken only as a last resort after various restrictions have been imposed in order to conserve international reserves. What the foregoing argument signifies therefore is that a worsening of the net barter (or commodity) terms of trade may be a precondition to an increase in real income especially when devaluation replaces restrictions and there are benefits arising from resource reallocation.[19, 20]

17. As Machlup notes (1956; 1964, p. 212), if domestic residents were voluntarily exchanging foreign assets or incurring liabilities in exchange for goods, this cannot be considered as worsening economic welfare. While this is correct in static terms, the issue must be looked at dynamically and may involve a distinction between private and social returns. That is, under pegged exchange rates, a country cannot run down its international reserves without limit even though the satisfaction of private interests would dictate a continuing imbalance of payments. The authorities might then be justified to intervene on social grounds if a better intertemporal allocation of resources could be obtained.

18. We are abstracting here from the imposition of restrictions, such as the optimum tariff, that may enable a country to improve its welfare position. More will be said on this in a later chapter.

19. There is an important practical problem of measurement here, which Sohmen (1969, pp. 175–77) has noted, arising from the fact that most countries use some modified form of Laspeyres price index with base weights from some previous period. Because devaluation may cause certain prices quoted in domestic currency to rise, the official price indexes may show an increase. But these indexes may well fail to take account of the shifts in production and consumption that occur if resources are used more efficiently and if the removal of trade restrictions results in a shift in the import mix to goods not previously imported. If these favorable changes are obscured because of measurement difficulties and there happens to exist strong pressures for wage increases to offset the higher recorded (Laspeyres) prices, the effects of the devaluation can be undone if the authorities succumb to these pressures and adjust the money supply accordingly.

20. It is noteworthy that the framework of analyzing a devaluation has been conceived by writers such as Haberler (1953) and Smith (1954) as involving a "primary burden" due to the reduction in domestic expenditure required to correct a trade imbalance and a "secondary burden" that may result from worsened net barter terms of trade. The possibility

INSTITUTIONAL AND POLICY CONSIDERATIONS FOR AN EFFECTIVE
DEVALUATION

In discussing balance-of-payments adjustment under freely fluctuating
exchange rates and the gold standard, we drew attention to the main considerations necessary for such adjustment to work effectively. Much of this
discussion is relevant in a pegged-rate system. In particular, the effectiveness
of exchange-rate variations will be enhanced by: (1) flexibility of real wages;
(2) sharing of adjustment between deficit and surplus countries; (3) adequate
international monetary reserves; (4) relatively low barriers to international
trade; and (5) absence of fixed money debts.[21]

The significance of flexibility of real wages derives from the possibility
of adverse movement in the devaluing country's net barter (or commodity)
terms of trade uncompensated by favorable resource reallocation effects.
With less than infinitely elastic supply schedules, devaluation will result in
increases in prices measured in domestic currency of both exports and
imports. Insofar as the latter increases may predominate, the terms of trade
will be adverse and real income will fall. This reduction in real income must
be tolerated if the devaluation is to be effective. For if the authorities were
to acquiesce in an expansion of money wages to compensate for the fall in
real income, the effect of the devaluation would be negated. It may be
important therefore to keep any deterioration in the terms of trade to a
minimum to insure that a devaluation will "stick." How successful an
individual country is in this regard may depend importantly upon the other
factors mentioned above which we may now consider.

To share the adjustment between deficit and surplus countries means that
the surplus countries will undertake exchange appreciation jointly with
devaluation by the deficit countries vis-à-vis the rest of the world.[22] The
extent of devaluation and possible adverse movements in the terms of trade
of the deficit countries may be reduced in this way. This requires cooperative
action on the part of deficit and surplus countries. Should cooperation prove
difficult to obtain, the deficit countries will be forced to bear most of the
adjustment.

---

of a beneficial effect from resource reallocation suggests that this framework may be
misleading. Thus, if a country is in balance-of-payments deficit, a reduction in total
domestic expenditure is inevitable so long as its international reserves are limited. Some
of the decline in expenditure may be offset, however, by favorable resource reallocation
effects. See Machlup (1956; 1964, pp. 213–17) for additional comments. See also Krueger
(1969, pp. 13–14) for a discussion of the resource reallocation effects of a devaluation when
exchange controls are liberalized or removed altogether.

21. These conditions are discussed in detail in Meade (1951, pp. 201–17) in a more
general context. See Cooper (1971) for an analysis of devaluation with special reference to
the problems faced by less developed countries.

22. For a theoretical analysis of the division of the burden of adjustment between
countries, see Mundell (1968, pp. 187–98). He shows that adjustment should be divided in
inverse proportion to the sizes of the countries involved. Thus, the larger the country, the
smaller the proportion of the adjustment it should assume.

International monetary reserves are designed to be used in a system of pegged exchange rates mainly to smooth out the pressures that develop in the foreign exchange market due to balance-of-payments deficits and surpluses. The greater the availability of reserves to a deficit country especially, the longer will be the period of time over which the balance-of-payments adjustment can be spread. This will be particularly important if wages and prices were relatively inflexible on the downward side. In such an event, rapid adjustment might cause unemployment to increase significantly in the short run.[23] Reserves may also be useful in the context of a devaluation particularly if there are significant time lags in the response of exports and imports to the changes in relative prices.

The international price mechanism will work more effectively the lower the barriers to international trade. Thus, the success of a devaluation will depend importantly upon the relative ease with which shifts in demand may take place among the products of different countries. If the nondevaluing countries follow highly restrictive commercial policies or adopt measures to counteract the changes that occur in relative prices, the devaluing country will be frustrated in its attempt to improve its trade balance.

The incurrence of debts fixed in foreign currency is potentially burdensome for a country contemplating devaluation since its import demand for the servicing of such debt has an elasticity equal to zero. That is, no matter how its exchange rate may be changed, it will still have to pay a fixed amount in foreign currency. If the debt were to be serviced in domestic currency, however, the import-demand elasticity would be equal to unity. In this case, the devaluing country would be transferring an amount in its own currency that would have a constant purchasing power over its goods in terms of the foreign currency equivalent. It is therefore most favorable from the standpoint of the devaluing country to have a minimum of fixed money debts to be serviced in foreign currency.

It should be clear from our discussion that the success of a devaluation cannot be taken for granted. It is vitally important that the authorities in the devaluing country do not introduce measures that increase money wages and prices and thus prevent balance-of-payments adjustment from occurring.

---

23. The view that it is desirable to slow down the process of adjustment has been questioned by Friedman in particular in the context of the role that private speculation may play in smoothing exchange-rate fluctuations. As he states (1953; 1968, pp. 435–36), this view:

> ... derives, I believe, from an implicit tendency to regard any slowing-down of the adjustment process as an improvement; that is, implicitly to regard no adjustment at all or an indefinitely prolonged one as the ideal. This is the counterpart of the tendency to believe that internal monetary policy can and should avoid all internal adjustments in the level of income. And both, I suspect, are a manifestation of the urge for security that is so outstanding a feature of the modern world and that is itself a major source of insecurity by promoting measures that reduce the adaptability of our economic systems to change without eliminating the changes themselves.

If such restraint is exercised and the other factors mentioned are operative, the likelihood of a successful devaluation will be significantly enhanced.

Norms for Exchange-Rate Adjustment

EXCHANGE-RATE ADJUSTMENT TO CORRECT A "FUNDAMENTAL DISEQUILIBRIUM"

Having described how exchange-rate adjustment works and the conditions for its success, let us consider now the circumstances when its use may be appropriate in the pegged-rate system. The issue here is whether the disequilibrium in a country's balance of payments is transient or cyclical as opposed to being structural in character. If the disequilibrium is transient or cyclical, this means that the events causing the disequilibrium either will not recur or that they will tend to reverse themselves in time. A country in these circumstances is supposed to use its international monetary reserves as a buffer when its balance of payments is in deficit or surplus. This presumes of course that a deficit country has sufficient reserves for this purpose. If this is not the case, other policies such as import restriction or domestic deflation may become necessary. It is also conceivable that a country might be forced to consider seriously devaluation as an alternative.

The IMF was, as we have seen, designed to provide additional reserves to countries in temporary balance-of-payments difficulties and avoid thereby the need for these countries to resort to more drastic policies. Devaluation was looked upon accordingly in the IMF framework as a means of correcting a "fundamental disequilibrium" in a country's balance of payments. Thus, it was stated in the Articles of Agreement of the Fund, Article IV, Section 5, that:[24]

> (a) A member shall not propose a change in the par value of its currency except to correct a fundamental disequilibrium.
>
> (b) A change in the par value of a member's currency may be made only on the proposal of the member and only after consultation with the Fund.
>
> (c) When a change is proposed, the Fund shall first take into account the changes, if any, which have already taken place in the initial par value of the member's currency.... If the proposed change, together with all previous changes, whether increases or decreases,
>
>> (i) does not exceed ten percent of the initial par value, the Fund shall raise no objection;
>>
>> (ii) does not exceed a further ten percent of the initial par value, the Fund may either concur or object, but shall declare its attitude within seventy-two hours if the member so requests;
>>
>> (iii) is not within (i) or (ii) above, the Fund may either concur or object, but shall be entitled to a longer period in which to declare its attitude.

24. See International Monetary Fund (1969, Vol. III, p. 190).

This part of the Fund Agreement represented the desire of member countries to protect themselves against the widespread and competitive devaluations that had occurred in the 1930's. The intention therefore was to condone devaluation so long as it was carried out in an orderly fashion. There was a difficulty with all of this, however, since the meaning of a fundamental disequilibrium was nowhere specified in the Agreement. This was a matter for concern because this part of the Agreement could not be made operational so long as the criteria for Fund approval of a devaluation remained unclear.

One of the early and most notable attempts to furnish some clearcut criteria was that made by Nurkse (1945; 1949, p. 5) who stated that: "The only satisfactory way of defining the equilibrium rate of exchange is to define it as that rate which, over a certain period of time, keeps the balance of payments in equilibrium." A disequilibrium rate of exchange thus meant that a country would be experiencing a continuing net increase or decrease in its international reserves.[25] In order to give content to the foregoing definition, a number of points needed clarification: (1) how long a time period was envisaged before a disequilibrium was to be judged fundamental; (2) how disequilibrium was to be measured; and (3) whether there were any special qualifications to be taken into account.

Nurkse suggested on the first point (1945; 1949, p. 6) that: "If . . . a country's external accounts, at a given rate of exchange, attain an even balance over a period of five to ten years, then that exchange rate would be regarded as an equilibrium rate." This period would be long enough to cover a whole business cycle. In cases where cyclical movements were not pronounced, a somewhat shorter period of two or three years was the recommended standard. We have already mentioned that disequilibrium was to be measured by the net change in a country's international reserves. In this regard, all short-term capital movements that took place in response to such policy actions as a change in the discount rate were considered by Nurkse to fulfill the same function as a country's international reserves. Such movements were to be treated therefore as offsets to the country's reserves. In addition, short-term capital movements motivated by abnormal factors such as political disturbances were to be excluded from the standard to be used in defining equilibrium. Finally, Nurkse stressed that balance-of-payments equilibrium should not be attained by virtue of specially imposed restrictions on trade and payments or by a policy of domestic deflation leading to underemployment.

---

25. A qualification might be noted here to take into account a country's share in the growth of total world reserves. This has been mentioned by Bernstein (1958, p. 133) and also by Fleming (1968a, p. 7) who has stated that: "A country should be deemed to be in balance-of-payments deficit if it is . . . losing reserves on a larger scale, or gaining them on a smaller scale, than corresponds to its share in world reserve growth. . . ."

Nurkse's criteria for determining the existence of a fundamental disequilibrium were of course colored by the international monetary experience of the interwar period. His conception of the time period reflected the "major" type of business cycle that was five-to-ten years in length. His suggested exclusion of short-term capital movements from the balance-of-payments proper (i.e., the items "above the line") was based on the sizable amount of capital flight and "hot money" movements that occurred in the 1930's especially. And his qualifications concerning changes in domestic policy were influenced in particular by Great Britain's deflationary policies of 1925–30 and the widely instituted policies of exchange controls in many countries during the 1930's.

If we look at the way the international monetary system has evolved since 1946, it is evident that Nurkse's criteria for a fundamental disequilibrium require some reinterpretation. That is, the fluctuations in business activity in the major industrialized countries especially have been relatively minor and the downturns in particular of comparatively short duration. Moreover, with the return to currency convertibility in 1958, there have been very substantial movements of short-term capital. These movements have occurred for a variety of reasons involving the financing of an ever expanding level of world trade, interest arbitrage, and the expectation of exchange-rate changes. Finally, we may note that the growing use of the U.S. dollar especially as a vehicle and reserve currency in the postwar period has raised the question of whether the concept of a fundamental disequilibrium is applicable to a country like the U.S.

In view of these various considerations, suppose we were to put ourselves in the position today of a central bank or IMF official faced with the need to decide whether or not a fundamental disequilibrium existed in any particular country's balance of payments. Clearly we would have to make some judgment concerning the size and time duration of the disequilibrium as measured by the net changes in the country's international reserves. Thus, for example, we would want to assess whether a deficit, say, is temporary or cyclical since in such a case it would be most desirable to employ existing or borrowed reserves until conditions reversed themselves. This will evidently require an analysis of the present economic conditions as well as some type of forecast of future conditions in the country in question as well as in its major trading partners. There is much at stake here since foreign exchange resources may be depleted if what was thought to be a cyclical movement in the balance of payments turned out to be a trend.

In trying to distinguish the forces at work, it may be of interest to consider the suggestion made by Bernstein (1958) that balance-of-payments problems can be classified into three main types stemming from: (1) current inflation; (2) price and cost disparity; and (3) structural maladjustments. In a fully employed economy, a balance-of-payments deficit is equal by definition to an excess of aggregate expenditure over aggregate output. A deficit will have emerged under these circumstances as the consequence of excessive credit expansion, which by raising money income and expenditure, will worsen the trade balance. The impact will be felt in terms both of increased imports and reduced exports and will be larger the more elastic the country's domestic demand and supply schedules with respect to the goods and services involved.[26]

Bernstein related the cases of price-cost disparity and structural maladjustment to a situation in which a country was experiencing a balance-of-payments deficit together with underemployment. The price-cost disparity may well be due to inflation that reduces the competitiveness of exports and increases the competition of imports with domestic production to the point where unemployment results. Structural maladjustment refers to particular industries that may have been adversely affected by more rapid technological change abroad than at home or by changes in tastes.

Supposing that one of the three factors mentioned is judged to be responsible for the country's balance-of-payments difficulties, what are the implications as far as devaluation is concerned? With respect to inflation, it is obvious that its source must be removed by monetary contraction if devaluation is to succeed. Assuming that there is underemployment, a devaluation might correct existing price-cost disparities so as to permit expansion of the export and import-competing industries and an improvement in the trade balance. Devaluation will be helpful in correcting structural maladjustments insofar as resources are shifted to alternative uses in response to the changes in relative prices. It may well be, however, that additional incentives will be required to help shift resources and to encourage investment to raise efficiency and foster new lines of activity.

The situation will of course be complicated if the foregoing factors cannot be separately identified and if, as may well be the case, they are present more or less in combination. Thus, as Machlup (1958, p. 139) has noted, Bernstein's distinctions between the major types of balance-of-payments problems may lack analytical clarity and are therefore difficult to utilize in formulating specific policy remedies. This is not to deny of course the need to resolve a balance-of-payments problem, for as Machlup (*ibid.*) further stated in this regard: "What we need is an analysis of comparative costs and advantages of alternative measures, taking for granted that everything will hurt somewhere."

Thus, so long as we continue to operate within the pegged-rate system, there remains a need to determine whether there exists a fundamental disequilibrium and, if so, what should be done about it. It should not be too

26. This can be seen with reference to Figure 2.1 above, where inflation will have the effect of shifting the domestic demand schedule up to the right and the domestic supply schedule up to the left. The import-demand and export-supply schedules will be shifted accordingly in these same directions.

difficult to obtain a reasonably objective measurement of disequilibrium by examining the behavior of a country's international reserves over time.[27] What should be done in terms of policy must in the final analysis rest on judgments about the sources of the disequilibrium. But we should bear in mind, as Fleming (1968, p. 20) has noted, that this is more than a matter of relating "prescriptions to presumed causes of disequilibrium," since the various causes may "be merely ways of defining the situation in terms of the remedy that is required . . . ."

PURCHASING-POWER-PARITY AS A GUIDE IN SELECTING
EXCHANGE RATES

It should be clear from our discussion that a judgment concerning the existence of a fundamental disequilibrium in a country's balance of payments is equivalent to judging the appropriateness of the country's rate of exchange. It is of interest for this reason to consider whether there may be any reliable statistical indication of the degree to which a currency may be overvalued or undervalued in relation to its "true" equilibrium level. One possible indication that has been discussed at great length at various times in the past utilizes the comparison of the actual exchange rate with a rate based upon calculations of purchasing-power-parity (PPP).

There are essentially two versions of the PPP doctrine that we shall discuss. These are what Balassa (1964c, p. 584) has called the "absolute" and "relative" interpretations. According to the "absolute" interpretation, the rate of exchange between two countries will be determined by the quotient of their general price levels. Since the general price level in a country is representative of the purchasing power of money, the quotient will be a measure of the PPP of one country's currency vis-à-vis the other. Under conditions of relatively free and substantial mutual trade, it is held that the actual rate of exchange cannot deviate significantly from the PPP rate.

In principle, the calculation of PPP on the basis of the absolute interpretation requires taking a common basket of goods with a standard system of weighting for the individual countries. Information of this kind is rarely available in practice, however. It is necessary rather to use weights that reflect the actual consumption expenditures in each country. But this creates an immediate difficulty since the price structures of countries will diverge because of different resource endowments. Since consumption will be directed in each country towards goods with relatively lower prices, the weights in terms of the relative expenditure components will vary from

27. It may be worth repeating here that a fundamental disequilibrium can exist even though payments and receipts are in balance if such balance has been obtained by increased restrictions on trade and payments or resort to domestic deflation. The test of whether a fundamental disequilibrium did exist in fact under these circumstances would be to lift the restrictions or expand the domestic economy and see if a persistent balance-of-payments deficit materialized.

country to country. Thus, the purchasing power of a country's currency will be different depending upon whether its consumption pattern or another country's is used for weighting purposes. What is done commonly in such circumstances is to take a geometric mean of the PPP's based on the weights of the respective countries.

The question then is whether such calculations provide any insight into what the equilibrium exchange rates should be. We may consider, for example, the data in Table 5.2 which lists for 1960 in terms of U.S. dollars the official exchange rates, calculations of PPP's based on different weights and the geometric mean in relation to the official exchange rate, and per capita incomes for the major industrial countries. What is noteworthy is that the PPP's as a percentage of the official rates are all below 100 percent rather than being distributed on either side of 100 percent. The explanation of this lies in the fact that services have been included in the consumption basket. Since the prices of services will be higher in countries with higher levels of productivity and therefore higher wages, there will tend to be a positive correlation between the PPP's as a percentage of the official exchange rates and the level of per capita income. This is borne out by comparing the last two columns of Table 5.2.

It thus appears that PPP calculations based upon general price levels do not adequately reflect equilibrium exchange rates because of the inclusion of nontraded items that vary in price systematically with different levels of income. Suppose therefore that we were to include only the prices of internationally traded goods in our calculations in order to focus more directly on what should determine equilibrium exchange rates. There is a difficulty here, however, for in theory the prices of internationally traded goods will be equated in the respective trading countries via the exchange rate, allowance being made for costs of transportation and market imperfections.[28] Now it is possible that to the extent markets do not function perfectly, there may be a divergence between national price levels aside from that noted in the case of nontraded goods. It is doubtful, however, whether such a divergence would provide a precise indication of the degree to which a particular currency was overvalued or undervalued at a given point in time.

Let us consider now the "relative" interpretation of the PPP doctrine. According to this interpretation, if we take a period in the past when equilibrium exchange rates were assumed to prevail, changes in the relative prices

28. Thus, as Metzler has noted (1947; 1959, pp. 291–92):

   To clarify this point, suppose that Canada is an exporter of . . . a product, *Z*, to the United Kingdom. If the exchange rate between Canada and the United Kingdom is $4 = £1, and if the British price of *Z* is one-fourth pound per unit, the Canadian price will necessarily be $1.00, since Canada is an exporter of *Z*, and its price is governed by the world price.

   If the indexes used to calculate PPP were heavily weighted with internationally traded goods, the effect would then be to justify whatever the exchange rate happened to be.

TABLE 5.2
Purchasing-Power-Parities for Gross National Product in 1960
(National Currency per U.S. Dollar)

Country	Currency Unit (1)	Official Exchange Rate (2)	At U.S. Quantity Weights (3)	At National Quantity Weights (4)	Geometric Mean of Columns (3) and (4) (5)	Purchasing Power Parity as a Percentage of Exchange Rate $100 \times (5) \div (2)$ (6)	Income Per Capita (7)
United States	Dollar	1	1	1	1	100.0	2051
Canada	Dollar	0.996	*	*	0.921	92.8	1550
Belgium	Franc	50.0	44.4	36.5	40.2	80.4	1273
France	Franc	4.903	4.47	3.23	3.80	77.4	1152
Germany	Mark	4.171	3.86	2.73	3.25	77.9	1200
Italy	Lira	620.6	574	330	435	70.1	704
Netherlands	Florin	3.770	2.96	2.13	2.51	66.6	1166
United Kingdom	Pound	0.357	0.338	0.225	0.294	82.4	1212
Denmark	Krona	6.906	6.06	4.70	5.34	77.4	1269
Norway	Krona	7.143	6.81	4.84	5.74	80.4	1186
Sweden	Krona	5.180	*	*	4.66	90.0	1307
Japan	Yen	359.6	*	*	225	62.6	507

* Not separately calculated.
SOURCE: Balassa (1964c, p. 588).

of individual nations would be indicative of the adjustments to be made in exchange rates. Thus, for example, assume we have an initial period in which the balance of payments was in equilibrium and the exchange rate between the dollar and the pound was $4.50 = £1.[29] Now assume that because of some disturbance such as a war, there is a uniform doubling of prices in the U.S. and a tripling of prices in the U.K. Since the internal purchasing power of the dollar has dropped to one-half and the pound to one-third of its former value, the new exchange rate should be $3.00 = £1 in order to produce balanced trade. That is:

$$\frac{\$4.50}{£1} \cdot \frac{p^{US}}{p^{UK}} = \frac{\$4.50}{£1} \cdot \frac{2.00}{3.00} = \frac{\$3.00}{£1} \,.$$

The relative interpretation of PPP evidently follows directly from a quantity-theory-of-money relationship. Thus, at full employment, increases in the money supply are assumed to result in proportionate increases in prices. If the price changes are uniform and there have been no changes in tastes or economic structure, both countries will continue to trade in volume terms that are identical to the base period.[30] The exchange rate would then be changed as in our example.

There are a number of possible reasons why a PPP rate calculated on the basis of the relative interpretation may differ significantly from the equilibrium rate of exchange. Among the most obvious of these reasons are the following: (1) if there is a disequilibrium rate in the base period, the PPP rate that takes the relative price changes into account will perpetuate the original disequilibrium; (2) in the event a disequilibrium rate in the base period is due to underemployment, it is possible, depending on the degree of underemployment, that subsequent changes in the level of income could affect the exchange rate without necessarily affecting relative prices significantly; (3) if international capital movements were required, say, for reparations or foreign aid purposes, after the base period, they would result in an exchange rate different from PPP; and (4) the occurrence of changes in taste and productivity may have caused nonuniform changes in relative prices that may not be revealed simply by comparing changes in general price levels.

29. This example has been taken from Metzler (1947; 1959, p. 288).
30. Thus, according to Metzler (1947; 1959, p. 288):

. . . suppose in the above example that an American product, X, before the war sold for $1.50, while a British product, Y, sold for £1. At the old exchange rate, American purchasers of Y would have had to pay $4.50 per unit, and the price per unit in the United States would thus have been three times the price of a unit of the American product, X. We may assume, now, that as a result of the war inflation the cost of production and the price of each commodity, in the currency of the selling country, rises according to the general price rise. In other words, the selling price of X, the American product, is doubled while the price of Y, the British product, is tripled; the new price of X is $3.00, and the new price of Y is £3. At the parity exchange rate of $3 = £1, the American price of the British product is thus $9. Once again, therefore, the unit price of the British product, in dollars, is three times the unit price of the American product.

This last point in particular raises the same problems of weighting in index-number construction and the interpretation of sectoral price changes of traded and nontraded goods already mentioned in discussing the absolute interpretation of PPP. Thus, Balassa has shown in this regard (1964c, pp. 593–95) that productivity and prices changed differentially by sector in the major industrial countries in the course of the 1950's in a manner similar to what was suggested in his calculations recorded above in Table 5.2 based on the absolute interpretation of PPP. The conclusion therefore is that comparisons of changes in general price indexes according to the relative interpretation of PPP will provide misleading indications of what exchange rates should be. And again the difficulties cannot be resolved by using price comparisons that are heavily weighted with internationally traded goods because of the tendency towards equality in the prices of these goods among the various trading countries.[31]

Our discussion of the usefulness of PPP calculations in determining equilibrium exchange rates has been rather negative on the whole.[32] As we have already mentioned, such gross comparisons may conceivably show signs of currency overvaluation or undervaluation when markets function imperfectly. It is also conceivable that currency misalignments will be revealed by PPP calculations especially during periods of rapid inflation when the assumption of uniform price changes is most valid. The point is, however, that PPP calculations are very likely to miss the essence of the balance-of-payments problems of many countries that stem from changes in relative prices under more normal conditions. The choice of an exchange rate under these conditions should be made therefore mainly on the basis of elasticity considerations involving the country's export and import-competing in-dustries and in view of these considerations, the desired change that is to be effected in the country's trade balance. This suggests consequently that it will be more fruitful for purposes of policy to seek out information in dis-aggregated form relating to the elasticities of the relevant producing sectors than trying to obtain more refined calculations of PPP.[33]

---

31. To get around this difficulty, the suggestion has been made to substitute data on unit costs of production for price data. The suggestion is based on the grounds that costs of production adjust much less quickly than do prices and that costs are more likely to measure permanent changes in monetary values in contrast to prices that will reflect transitory inflation. Unfortunately, indexes of cost are beset with such problems as which firms are to be covered and how variations in output should be handled. But perhaps of even greater importance is that information of this kind is practically unavailable in most countries.

32. See Gailliot (1970) for some calculations of PPP for the major industrialized countries for the period spanning 1900–04 and 1963–67 that purport to demonstrate the usefulness of PPP as an indication of *long-run* equilibrium exchange rates. For additional skeptical comment concerning PPP, see Samuelson (1964).

33. This conclusion is similar in spirit but different in substance than that reached by Yeager (1958) in his attempted rehabilitation of PPP. Yeager's intention was to show the connection between changes in domestic prices and exchange rates and consequent

Continued on p. 148

THE EMPIRICAL MEASUREMENT OF IMPORT AND
EXPORT-DEMAND ELASTICITIES[34]

In seeking norms for exchange-rate adjustment, it is obviously important
to have information on the demand elasticities relating to a country's imports
and exports in order to determine how a devaluation may affect the trade
balance. These elasticities can be estimated statistically by means of multiple
regression analysis of the demand functions in question. To illustrate, the
simplest demand function for imports can be written:

$$M = f(Y/p_Y, p_M/p_Y), \tag{5.5}$$

which says that the quantity of imports, M, is a function of the level of real
income, Y/p_Y, and the price of imports relative to domestic goods, p_M/p_Y.[35]

In order to fit statistically a relationship such as equation (5.5), a particular
functional form must be chosen. The most common forms are linear as in
equation (5.6) and log-linear as in equation (5.7):

$$M = a + b(Y/p_Y) + c(p_M/p_Y) + u \tag{5.6}$$

$$\log M = a_1 + b_1 \log (Y/p_Y) + c_1 \log (p_M/p_Y) + u. \tag{5.7}$$

In equation (5.6), a is the constant term in the regression, b is the marginal
propensity to import with respect to income, c is the import coefficient of
relative prices, and u is an error term that is assumed to be uncorrelated with
the explanatory variables.[36] In the linear form the income and price elasticities of demand will depend upon the levels of these variables. For this reason
the log-linear form in equation (5.7) is often used, in which case the income
and price elasticities will now be measured by b_1 and c_1.[37]

What is of interest for our present discussion is that during the 1940's
especially a substantial number of estimates were made of income and price
elasticities of demand for imports and exports of individual countries covering
the interwar period. Most of these estimates were based upon some variant
of equations (5.6) and (5.7). What is particularly noteworthy is that the price

---

adjustment in the balance of payments. He was concerned in particular with how the
theory of PPP can be used to elucidate the existence of relatively high elasticities in
international trade, in which case the existence of unstable equilibrium in the foreign
exchange market was unlikely. In this respect his analysis is similar to the one presented
earlier in Chapter 2. There is some question, however, about whether Yeager's statistical
results provide really strong support for PPP calculations. See Balassa (1964c, esp. pp.
591–92) for additional comments.

34. A more extensive treatment of these issues is given especially in Chapter 2 of Leamer
and Stern (1970).

35. The demand for exports can be similarly represented with the income and relative
price terms appropriately defined.

36. This is an assumed property of least squares regression.

37. These elasticities are constrained to be constant by virtue of the log-linear form in
contrast to the variable elasticities that may be calculated using the linear form. These
latter elasticities are commonly evaluated at the means of the relevant variables.

elasticities measured were commonly substantially less than unity. The obvious policy implication for a country contemplating devaluation was therefore that this might tend to worsen rather than improve its trade balance. Such "elasticity pessimism" gave rise consequently to serious consideration of policies other than changes in relative prices for the purpose of correcting an imbalance of trade.

The contention that the international price mechanism could not be relied upon for adjustment purposes was of course unacceptable to those who believed on a priori grounds that foreign trade elasticities were relatively high. But it remained for Orcutt (1950) to demonstrate in a path-breaking article that the calculated price elasticities were in any case open to serious question. This was because the statistical method and data employed tended to bias the measured price elasticities in a downward direction towards zero. While the thrust of Orcutt's criticisms at that time was to question the usefulness of the traditional analysis in measuring demand elasticities,[38] the discussion did not end there since it turned out upon further scrutiny that a number of Orcutt's points were less damaging to the use of the traditional procedures than first appeared.

Thus, as Leamer and Stern (1970, pp. 34–35) have discussed, Orcutt's criticisms can be met in part by estimating equations (5.6) and (5.7) for countries that are relatively small and using observations drawn from time periods when demand was relatively stable. Meaningful results may also be obtained by using data specifications that avoid lumping together commodities with widely varying elasticities and by making explicit allowance for lags in the adjustment process. These conclusions seem to be borne out, it may be noted, in a number of studies using data for the period following World War II.[39] That is, price elasticities have been calculated that are in reasonable accord with a priori expectations. These elasticities appear in many instances to be sufficiently great so that if devaluation were undertaken, it would be virtually certain to bring about an improvement in the devaluing country's balance of trade. This is provided of course that monetary expansion in the devaluing country does not negate the effect of the devaluation and that other countries do not take offsetting actions. It seems quite reasonable therefore to be an "elasticity optimist" these days on the basis of empirically estimated price elasticities.

An Evaluation of the Pegged-Rate System

We have already intimated that the intention of having the pegged-rate system combine the best features of the gold-standard and freely fluctuating

38. The reasons Orcutt gave why this might be the case involve some technical statistical considerations of traditional least-squares multiple regression analysis. For details, see Leamer and Stern (1970, esp. pp. 29–35).

39. See Leamer and Stern (1970, esp. pp. 51–55) for detailed references.

exchange-rate systems has not been realized. The reason has been due mainly to lack of a satisfactory mechanism of adjustment in the pegged-rate system. That is, countries have been reluctant to rely upon variations in domestic expenditures and prices for adjustment purposes because of the desire to maintain full employment and price stability. Yet at the same time they have refrained from altering exchange rates apparently for fear of adverse terms-of-trade effects and the possible unsettling of the foreign exchange markets. Since the functioning of the pegged-rate system may appear to avoid rather than expedite adjustment, it might be more fitting to characterize this system, as Mundell (1968) has suggested, as the "international disequilibrium system."

Perhaps the chief point of criticism of pegged exchange rates is that their maintenance may result in a dimunition of economic welfare. This might not be a serious matter so long as the divergence between the pegged and "true" equilibrium-exchange rates and imbalances of trade in goods and services were relatively small. However, in cases where the rates were pegged above and below the equilibrium rate from period to period and trade deficits and surpluses realized, the intertemporal effects on consumption and on the price of imports might have adverse effects on economic welfare.[40] Moreover, as Sohmen (1961, p. 118) has pointed out, a small divergence between the pegged and equilibrium rates may not be tolerable for international capital movements:

> It is hardly proper to separate capital movements from a market which the ease and speed of transfer make so notoriously volatile. Speculative activity is bound to aggravate the disequilibrium if a pegged rate is just slightly out of line. Once holders of liquid funds realize that the administered rate overstates the long-run equilibrium value of a currency, and if they have reason to believe that the authorities are unwilling to impose the hardships of deflationary action merely to improve its rating on the exchanges—a very reasonable hypothesis in many instances—they can rest assured that the currency will not appreciate in the foreseeable future. Rational behavior dictates a transfer of funds abroad; the result is large-scale capital outflow if capital movements are free.

To the extent that a country's exchange rate may in fact be overvalued and the authorities persist nevertheless in trying to maintain it, their foreign exchange reserves are bound to be depleted.[41] The greater the loss of reserves,

40. For analyses of the welfare costs of exchange-rate stabilization using a two-period model, see especially Hause (1966) and Johnson (1966b).

41. In our discussion in Chapter 2, we noted that an argument could be made in favor of counterspeculation by the authorities in the forward market to forestall a loss of reserves as a consequence of a speculative attack in circumstances when the exchange rate was not out of line. If devaluation were imminent, counterspeculation would expose the authorities to a capital loss on their forward commitments. Aliber (1963, 1967a) has noted, however, that this capital loss might be smaller than if the authorities were to sell reserves during the period of the speculative attack and then have to repurchase them at the devalued rate. While such an outcome is plausible, Levin (1970a, p. 62) has pointed out that Aliber's argument is incomplete because it overlooks other current-account effects and may involve distributive effects that differ depending on which action the authorities follow.

the greater will be the apprehension concerning the likelihood that devaluation may occur. Under these circumstances bear speculation and leads in payments and lags in receipts will tend to increase pressure on reserves, thus enhancing the likelihood of devaluation. While one would think that the authorities would wish to alter the par value of their currency when it is patently overvalued, this has often not been the case. Sohmen (1961, p. 119) has explained their reluctance as follows:

> Irrational motives play their part. Devaluation may be seen as a disturbing reflection on a country's honor and its international standing, or the monetary authority may regard it as an embarrassing admission of failure in its task of safeguarding stability of prices and incomes.

So long as devaluation is looked upon as a measure to be taken only in desperation and so long as adjustment policies are avoided domestically, it will be necessary for a country to resort to restrictions on trade and capital movements in order to prevent its international monetary reserves from vanishing altogether. The imposition of such restrictions will very likely lead to a misallocation of resources domestically and a consequent reduction in economic welfare.[42] It is this effect on welfare, it will be recalled, that figured in our earlier discussion of the beneficial effects of resource reallocation as a consequence of a devaluation accompanied by removal of restrictions on trade and payments. The most basic criticism of the pegged-rate system rests therefore on efficiency grounds. The point is that under competitive conditions if domestic policy were aimed at attaining the stability of prices and incomes and the exchange rate were free to vary, it would be possible to avoid the welfare-reducing intertemporal distortions, encouragement of speculation, and the undesirable effects of resource misallocation resulting from exchange-rate pegging and from restrictions imposed on balance-of-payments grounds.

It will be evident from our discussion that under the pegged-rate system the independent use of monetary policy for domestic purposes is seriously circumscribed. Thus, for example, a country experiencing a balance-of-payments deficit and actual or incipient unemployment may be unable to follow a policy of domestic expansion by means of lowering interest rates because of the short-term capital outflow that may occur.[43] By the same

42. It is conceivable that a country might seek to make the "best" of its balance-of-payments restrictions by exercising its monopoly power in order to improve its terms of trade in accordance with the optimum-tariff argument. We will discuss this argument in a subsequent chapter dealing with the use of commercial policy for balance-of-payments purposes. Suffice it to say at this point that it is probably not too common for a country to be able in fact to identify what its optimum tariff should be, much less succeed in exploiting its monopoly position for any length of time.

43. It may be possible, however, to deal with this kind of situation by following an expansionary fiscal policy for employment purposes and at the same time a higher interest-rate policy for the balance of payments. This procedure of "assigning" policies to particular targets raises a number of questions which we shall have occasion to discuss at length in Chapter 10.

token, countries may be particularly vulnerable under the pegged-rate system to variations in foreign interest rates. This will be the case especially when fluctuations in economic activity are not synchronized internationally. The pegged-rate system can only work effectively therefore so long as there is substantial cooperation and coordination of domestic economic policies by the major trading countries.[44]

An additional point of criticism of the pegged-rate system, which Sohmen (1961, pp. 119–20) in particular has emphasized, concerns the risks and uncertainty that this system imposes upon international trade and investment:

> The disturbances caused by the discrete changes characteristic of the 'adjustable peg' are considerably more serious than those provoked by the smooth, day-to-day fluctuations in a system of fluctuating rates. Even though changes occur less frequently, they are bound to be much larger, and the exact time of their incidence must necessarily remain secret. The degree to which exporters, importers, and international lenders can protect themselves from large windfall losses owing to sudden and drastic exchange-rate adjustment depends on their dexterity in outguessing the forced lies of ministers of finance and chancellors of the exchequer.... It is a moot question whether these factors do not frequently impose more uncertainty and bothersome impediments on their [international traders and investors] operations than the most erratic of exchange fluctuations.

The foregoing argument is especially relevant to those less developed countries with overvalued exchange rates maintained by comprehensive restrictions affecting international trade and payments. Such restrictions may impede significantly the international flow of private capital to these countries, particularly if they involve limitations on the foreign transfer of interest and dividends. These countries might be better served therefore by an exchange-rate system that obviated the necessity of exchange restrictions.[45]

A final point of criticism worth mentioning is that the need for international monetary reserves is greatly increased under the pegged-rate system in comparison to other systems because of the lack of an efficient balance-of-payments adjustment mechanism. That is, the longer the period during which balance-of-payments deficits are financed without adjustment occurring, the greater will be the reserves required. It will be necessary furthermore to establish institutions, both national and international, to carry out the international financial policies involving the provision and use of international reserves for balance-of-payments purposes.

44. The effects of policy coordination and the lack thereof in attaining national policy objectives will also be treated later.
45. This argument should not be construed as a pacacea for the foreign exchange and savings problems of the less developed countries because there may be many other factors that impede private international capital flows. One such factor may be the economic and political stability of these countries. A good illustration of how important stability may be is provided by the Canadian experience with freely fluctuating exchange rates during the 1950's that was discussed in Chapter 3. As we noted there, long-term capital inflows were very substantial at that time.

In contrast to the pegged-rate system the need for reserves under the gold standard would be less so long as exchange parities remained fixed and balance-of-payments adjustment was achieved by variations in domestic prices and money income. As far as freely fluctuating exchange rates are concerned, there would be no need whatever for official international reserves unless the authorities engaged at times in smoothing exchange-rate fluctuations. It would be possible with freely fluctuating exchange rates therefore to seek more productive uses for the resources presently engaged in the production of international monetary reserves and in the administration and operation of national and international agencies concerned with the balance of payments.

Having reviewed the chief criticisms of the pegged-rate system, it seems fitting to ask whether there are any points that can be made in favor of this system. One such point sometimes made is that the pegged-rate system helps to maintain comparative stability in exchange risks affecting international trade and investment. We have already had occasion to question this, however, in view of the great uncertainty that pervades the foreign exchange markets especially during times of balance-of-payments crises under the pegged-rate system. This particular claim might be applicable to the gold standard, although as we have seen, the uncertainty may take a different form in terms of the variations in domestic prices required to keep the exchange rate fixed. It is probably stretching things therefore to claim that the pegged-rate system in fact minimizes exchange risks.

It has also been mentioned in defense of pegged rates that the loss of international monetary reserves in financing a balance-of-payments deficit focuses the attention of the authorities on the need for domestic policy actions designed to eliminate the deficit. But this is another argument that is difficult to accept since there is no reason why, under a system of freely fluctuating exchange rates, the authorities would not be motivated to change their domestic policies in response to continued depreciation of the exchange rate.

We may mention, in addition, Triffin's view that the pegged-rate system is advantageous because errors of national policy may be cushioned through the balance of payments by means of central bank intervention in stabilizing the exchange rate, and, further, that risks associated with differential rates of national monetary expansion may be spread among countries. This view stems from Triffin's judgment that speculation exaggerates exchange-rate variability and that there would be a "devaluation bias" in a system of free rates because of upward wage flexibility and downward wage rigidity.[46]

46. Thus, he states (1960, pp. 82–83):

Under convertibility conditions, an excessive rate of credit expansion, particularly in a small country, may spill out very quickly into balance of payments deficits, long in advance of any substantial price increases, these being held down anyway by the

Continued on p. 154

While this point about wage flexibility may have some validity, the general argument is faulty, as Sohmen (1961, p. 127) has pointed out, since it attributes the devaluation bias to exchange-rate variability per se rather than to the domestic monetary conditions that give rise to this variability.

It might be argued finally that despite its many drawbacks, the pegged-rate system might not be so bad after all. This is especially the case when we take into account the fact that this system has been in operation during a period since World War II when world production and trade have expanded greatly. Moreover, whatever interruptions that may have occurred in this expansion from the standpoint of individual countries could be considered to stem primarily from events in the countries themselves rather than specifically from the pegged-rate system. This line of argument can be questioned, of course, on the grounds that it is misleading to claim that the system has in fact been operated so successfully. This is especially the case when account is taken of the massive support operations required from time to time for particular currencies in periods of balance-of-payments crisis, the numerous ad hoc control measures that have been adopted for external purposes by individual countries, the panoply of cooperative arrangements developed to promote foreign exchange-market stability, and the inability of the system to withstand the inflationary pressures emanating from the U.S. since the late 1960's.

Granted all of the foregoing, it is important to emphasize that whatever one's views on the pegged-rate system, the fact remains that there are strong forces in official circles, both nationally and internationally, making for continued commitment to this system. This commitment stems, on the one hand, from an unwillingness of these countries to accept the domestic adjustment policies required by the gold standard, and on the other hand it reflects distrust of a world-wide system of freely fluctuating exchange rates for fear of the chaotic conditions that might result in the foreign exchange markets due especially to disequilibrating speculation.

---

competition of imports from abroad. The depreciation of the national currency under the free interplay of market supply and demand would, however, stimulate increases in import prices which would, in turn, affect internal price, cost and wage levels in general. Speculation would accelerate and amplify these disequilibrating movements without, of and by itself, correcting the internal financial policies which lie at the root of the balance-of-payments deficits. If, however, such policies were continued indefinitely, the accelerated currency depreciation and price rises could hardly fail either to end in a currency collapse, or, more probably, to induce the authorities to resort to stringent trade and exchange restrictions, bringing to an end the flexible exchange rates experiment. If, on the other hand, the authorities decide, instead, to arrest their inflationary rates of monetary and credit expansion, price and wages rigidities will make it difficult to reverse the intervening cost increases. The new 'equilibrium' exchange rates, even in the absence of renewed inflationary forces, will be lower than would have been the case if exchange flexibility and speculation had not previously driven exchange rates, import prices, and overall wage and cost levels further than they would have gone under a system of pegged exchange rates.

It should be obvious from our discussion that so long as countries attempt to follow divergent national policies subject to limitations on their international monetary reserves, some degree of exchange-rate variability will be required. By the same token, permanently fixed exchange rates will necessitate a high degree of policy coordination among countries and perhaps ultimately common policies. Neither system can be operated effectively of course unless the authorities are willing to take prompt and decisive measures to maintain the stability of domestic prices and incomes. The statement just made is well illustrated by the difficulties that the major industrialized countries have experienced especially since the late 1960's when the U.S. began to generate significant inflation domestically that was in turn transmitted abroad via deficits in the U.S. balance of payments. The buildup of dollar liabilities held by foreign central banks occurred in connection with their exchange-stabilization activities and served at the same time to increase domestic inflationary pressures. Thus, it was in large part to ease these pressures that we witnessed exchange-rate changes in Canada and Western Europe in 1970–71 coupled with much discussion of the need for policies to control short-term capital movements. When the U.S. suspended gold convertibility in August 1971, many countries opted to let their exchange rate float rather than continue absorbing substantial amounts of dollars.

The point is therefore that the adjustable-peg system does not correspond fully to either the fixed or freely fluctuating exchange-rate alternatives. As a consequence, constraints have frequently been imposed particularly on monetary and exchange-rate policy, thus making it more difficult for countries to attain their domestic economic goals. As a consequence, the pegged-rate system has resulted in greater reliance upon selective and ad hoc measures for promoting external equilibrium than would otherwise be the case.

It is the cost of these measures in terms of reductions in economic welfare that is at issue in evaluating the pegged-rate system. Policy makers in most countries have apparently judged this cost to be low relative to other exchange-rate systems. The basis for such a judgment is by no means clear, however, when countries follow divergent national policies, for it is extremely difficult in such circumstances to maintain pegged exchange rates without imposing at times restrictions on trade and payments.

Logic dictates therefore that serious consideration be given to improving today's balance-of-payments mechanism of adjustment by permitting exchange rates to vary freely in response to foreign exchange-market conditions. This would be most desirable, as indicated in our earlier discussion of optimum currency areas, in cases where the foreign sector is relatively small in relation to the rest of the economy and resources are relatively immobile vis-à-vis other countries. Moreover, given the role of the U.S. dollar in the international monetary system, it means in all likelihood that other currencies would fluctuate vis-à-vis the dollar and the U.S. would follow an essentially passive balance-of-payments policy.

Conclusion

We have sought in this chapter to provide insight into the issues of balance-of-payments adjustment in the present-day system of pegged exchange rates. Our discussion has focused primarily on the issues arising in exchange-rate adjustment, with reference especially to the Marshall-Lerner condition and how the balance of trade and terms of trade would be affected. Attention was given particularly to the possible benefits of resource reallocation that might be realized by the lifting of trade and payments restrictions when devaluation was undertaken. We had occasion thereafter to treat some of the important institutional and policy considerations involved in the success of a devaluation, with the emphasis here on the avoidance of monetary expansion by the authorities.

After treating exchange-rate adjustment in the abstract, we considered at length the IMF concept of devaluation in order to correct a fundamental disequilibrium in the balance of payments. The choice of policies to correct a disequilibrium was seen in large part to be a matter of judgment concerning the sources of the disequilibrium. We discussed the use of purchasing-power-parity calculations as a guide to exchange-rate adjustments and concluded that these calculations were unlikely to be a valid indication for such adjustments. It thus appeared most desirable to approach this question in conventional elasticity terms. In reviewing the empirical questions at issue and on the basis of studies using postwar data, it seemed reasonable to be an elasticity optimist as far as devaluation was concerned.

Our final task in this chapter was to evaluate the present-day system of pegged exchange rates. The chief objection to this system was that the maintenance of disequilibrium exchange rates, which is often accomplished by imposing restrictions on trade and payments, will reduce economic welfare. We had difficulty in making any unambiguous claims on behalf of the present system. Yet it may be that despite its obvious faults, this system has functioned reasonably well considering the relatively great expansion that has occurred in world trade and payments since World War II. This conclusion may be correct, but it rests on a judgment that the welfare costs of the present system have been smaller than would have been the case if exchange rates were truly fixed or freely fluctuating. Our analysis suggests that this judgment may be open to serious question.

Appendix

1. *Arithmetic examples of the effect of a devaluation upon the trade balance measured in foreign and domestic currency.* Three examples of a hypothetical 10 percent devaluation by England vis-à-vis America are presented in Table

5.A.1. The initial exchange rate is taken to be unity. It is assumed in Case I that trade is initially balanced and that elasticities of supply of exports and imports are infinite. The effects of the devaluation on English exports (American imports) and English imports (American exports) and the English trade balance are then calculated with different assumptions concerning the elasticities of demand for exports and imports. Thus, following devaluation, the price of English exports in foreign currency falls to $0.90 and the price of English imports in foreign currency is unchanged. In terms of domestic currency, the price of English exports is unchanged and the price of English imports rises to £1.10 after devaluation.

TABLE 5.A.1

The Effect of a Devaluation on the Trade Balance Measured in Foreign and Domestic Currency

	English Exports (American Imports)			English Imports (American Exports)			English Trade Balance
	Price	Quantity	Value	Price	Quantity	Value	
Case I—							
Initial balance,							
$e_x = e_m = \infty$							
Foreign Currency							
1. Before devaluation	$1.00	100	$100	$1.00	100	$100	$ 0
2. After 10% devaluation							
a. $\eta_x = \eta_m = 0$	0.90	100	90	1.00	100	100	−10
b. $\eta_x = \eta_m = 1/2$	0.90	105	95	1.00	95	95	0
c. $\eta_x = \eta_m = 1$	0.90	110	99	1.00	90	90	9
d. $\eta_x = \eta_m = 2$	0.90	120	108	1.00	80	80	28
Home Currency							
1. Before devaluation	£1.00	100	£100	£1.00	100	£100	£ 0
2. After 10% devaluation							
a. $\eta_x = \eta_m = 0$	1.00	100	100	1.10	100	110	−10
b. $\eta_x = \eta_m = 1/2$	1.00	105	105	1.10	95	105	0
c. $\eta_x = \eta_m = 1$	1.00	110	110	1.10	90	99	11
d. $\eta_x = \eta_m = 2$	1.00	120	120	1.10	80	88	32
Case II—							
Initial deficit,							
$e_x = e_m = \infty$							
Foreign currency							
1. Before devaluation	$1.00	100	$100	$1.00	200	$200	−$100
2. After 10% devaluation							
a. $\eta_x = \eta_m = 1/2$	0.90	105	95	1.00	190	190	−95
Home Currency							
1. Before devaluation	£1.00	100	£100	£1.00	200	£200	−£100
2. After 10% devaluation							
a. $\eta_x = \eta_m = 1/2$	1.00	105	105	1.10	190	209	−104

TABLE 5.A.1 (*Continued*)

	English Exports (American Imports)			English Imports (American Exports)			English Trade Balance
	Price	Quantity	Value	Price	Quantity	Value	
Case III—							
Initial balance,							
$e_x = e_m = 1$*							
Foreign currency							
1. Before devaluation	$1.00	100	$100	$1.00	100	$100	$ 0
2. After 10% devaluation							
a. $\eta_x = \eta_m = 0$	0.90	100	90	1.00	100	100	−10
b. $\eta_x = \eta_m = 1/2$	0.93	103	96	0.97	97	94	2
c. $\eta_x = \eta_m = 1$	0.95	105	100	0.95	95	90	10
d. $\eta_x = \eta_m = 2$	0.97	107	104	0.93	93	86	18
Home Currency							
1. Before devaluation	£1.00	100	£100	£1.00	100	£100	£ 0
2. After 10% devaluation							
a. $\eta_x = \eta_m = 0$	1.00	100	100	1.10	100	110	−10
b. $\eta_x = \eta_m = 1/2$	1.03	103	106	1.07	97	104	2
c. $\eta_x = \eta_m = 1$	1.05	105	110	1.05	95	100	10
d. $\eta_x = \eta_m = 2$	1.07	107	114	1.03	93	96	18

e_x = home elasticity of supply of exports; e_m = foreign elasticity of supply of imports; η_x = foreign elasticity of demand for exports; and η_m = home elasticity of demand for imports.

* The relation between the percentage change in the exchange rate and the change in prices indicated can be illustrated as follows. Assume the following demand and supply functions which have constant elasticities equal to unity: $q_d = p_\$^{-1}$ and $q_s = rp_\$^1$, where q_d refers to the quantity demanded, say of exports by America, $p_\$$ is the dollar price, q_s is the quantity supplied, and r is the exchange rate. In equilibrium, $q_s = q_d$, or $rp_\$^1 = p_\$^{-1}$. Solving for r, we have $r = p_\$^{-2}$. Differentiating this expression gives $dr = 2p_\$^{-3} dp_\$$, which in percentage form yields $dr/r = (-2p_\$^{-3}/p_\$^{-2}) dp_\$ = -2dp_\$/p_\$$. Solving for the percentage change in price, we have $dp_\$/p_\$ = 1/2 \ dr/r$. Thus if the devaluation is 10 percent, the change in the dollar price will be 5 percent, as is shown in line (2c) of Case III in terms of foreign currency. The other examples follow accordingly.

NOTE: The multiplications may be inexact due to rounding.

The changes in quantities demanded of English exports and imports are indicated with different assumptions about the elasticities of demand. Thus, when $\eta_x = \eta_m = 0$, both exports and imports are unchanged. But since the foreign currency price of English exports has fallen, the trade balance is worsened. This worsening of the trade balance is also evident in home currency since the home-currency price of English imports has risen. When $\eta_x = \eta_m = 1/2$, exports rise to 105 and imports are reduced to 95. When the price changes are taken into account, it is evident that the trade balance remains unchanged. The trade balance measured in both foreign and home currencies can be seen to increase as the sum of the assumed demand elasticities grows larger in relation to unity. This is of course what the Marshall-Lerner condition tells us.

In Case II, we assume an initial balance-of-payments deficit for England. Thus, according to the Marshall-Lerner condition, we can write the change in the trade balance in foreign currency, ΔB_f, as:

$$\Delta B_f = \eta_x + \frac{V_{fm}}{V_{fx}} \eta_m > 1,$$

where V_{fm} and V_{fx} refer to the value in foreign currency of imports and exports respectively. If $\eta_x = \eta_m = 1/2$ and $V_{fm}/V_{fx} = 2$, then it is clear that the trade balance will be improved in terms of foreign currency even though the sum of the demand elasticities is only equal to unity. By the same token, if the change in the trade balance is measured in home currency, η_x must be weighted by V_{hx}/V_{hm}, in which case it follows in this example that the trade balance will worsen in home currency. From the standpoint of a deficit country, it is the deficit in foreign currency that matters. Presumably further changes in domestic prices and money income will occur in the deficit country until the trade balance is improved in both foreign and home currency.[1]

In Case III, it was assumed that trade is initially balanced and the elasticities of supply of exports and imports are equal to unity. With upward sloping supply schedules, prices will not be changed by the full proportion of the devaluation, except when the demand elasticities equal zero. The relation between the devaluation proportion and the calculated price changes is given in the footnote to Table 5.A.1. It will be observed in line 2b of Case III that the trade balance is improved even when the sum of the demand elasticities is equal to unity.

2. *Devaluation in a three-country world.*[2] Our purpose here will be to examine briefly the effect of a devaluation in a world consisting of three countries, A, B, and C, on the assumption that A and B export homogeneous goods to C. To simplify the discussion, let us assume that C's currency is the dollar, all prices are dollar prices, and A and B do not trade with each other. We shall concentrate our attention upon the effects of a devaluation by A on its exports on the assumption that B does not devalue simultaneously. The effects to be illustrated can be noted in Figure 5.A.1, in which A and B are assumed to have identical export-supply schedules, S_A, S_B, and share the market equally between them. The initial-equilibrium price and quantity are OP_1 and OQ_2. Each country exports a quantity equal to OQ_1, and earns an amount thereby equal to $OQ_1 \times OP_1$.

1. For a formal analysis and discussion of the Case II type of situation, see especially Kindleberger (1968, pp. 570–74), Meade (1951, p. 72), J. Robinson (1947b, p. 94), and Hirschman (1949).
2. This discussion is based on Zupnick and Stern (1964, pp. 1–8).

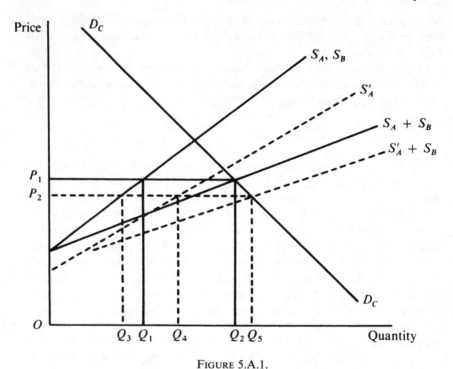

FIGURE 5.A.1.

Devaluation in a Three-Country World

The initial-equilibrium price and quantity are OP_1 and OQ_2, with each country exporting OQ_1. If A devalues, the new equilibrium price and quantity become OP_2 and OQ_5. The increase in A's exports from OQ_1 to OQ_4 consists of the increase in the quantity demanded by $C(Q_2Q_5)$ and the reduced exports from $B(Q_3Q_1)$.

Assume now a devaluation by A, which shifts its export-supply schedule from S_A to S'_A. Assuming B does not devalue, its export-supply schedule is unaffected and the aggregate export-supply schedule is thus represented by $S'_A + S_B$. The new equilibrium price and quantity are OP_2 and OQ_5. As a result of the devaluation the volume of A's exports to C increases from OQ_1 to OQ_4, while the volume of B's exports is reduced from OQ_1 to OQ_3. In a two-country model the increase in A's exports consequent upon a devaluation is determined exclusively by C's elasticity of demand. It is evident, however, that in the present three-country model, the elasticity of C's demand is but one of the factors influencing the increase in the volume of A's exports. The elasticities of A's and B's export-supply schedule are other determinants of this increase. The smaller the elasticity of A's export-supply schedule, all other things equal, the smaller will be the increase in the volume of exports following a devaluation. On the other hand, the greater the elasticity of B's export-supply schedule the greater will be the increase in the volume of A's exports following a devaluation.

The conclusion that the expansion in the volume of A's exports is affected by the supply elasticities of the exporting countries as well as by the importing country's elasticity of demand suggests that the value of A's exports can increase following a devaluation even though C's demand is inelastic. In fact, provided the elasticity of B's export-supply schedule is sufficiently high, the value of A's exports can increase even if C's demand has zero elasticity.

The preceding discussion was predicated on the assumption that B does not devalue simultaneously with A. If B were to devalue, the increase in the volume of A's exports would of course be less than if A devalued alone. It may be of interest accordingly to analyze the likelihood of B devaluing simultaneously with A. This will depend, among other things, especially upon the impact of a devaluation by A on B's balance of payments and terms of trade.[3]

3. A treatment of the various considerations involved here as well as an extension of the analysis to cover the cases of A and B exporting to C nonhomogeneous, albeit substitutable goods and complementary, goods are to be found in Zupnick and Stern (1964, pp. 6–11).

6

The Income Approach to
Balance-of-Payments Adjustment

Our analysis of the balance-of-payments adjustment mechanism has been focused thus far primarily upon the changes in exports and imports that occur in response to automatic or policy-determined changes in relative prices under conditions of full employment of resources. In this full employment context, the price or elasticities approach has the apparent merit of being relatively simple. This simplicity may be deceptive, however, since the home and foreign demand and supply elasticities in question are basically partial in nature and therefore may be subject to change during the process of adjustment. This will be especially the case when the level of real income is permitted to vary. Thus, in itself, the price approach to balance-of-payments adjustment may not suffice. We need as well an approach in which variations in real national income play an important role in the adjustment process. The development and application of the Keynesian theory of national income determination to open economies has furnished us with such an approach. Since both income and prices may be subject to variation in the process of adjustment, the need is evident for both an income approach and a price approach to analyze this process. These approaches are therefore not in conflict, although as we shall see, there may be grounds in certain situations for preferring one or the other.

National Income and Expenditure in Closed and Open Economies[1]

We begin our discussion of the income approach to balance-of-payments adjustment by indicating how foreign trade is represented in a country's national income accounts. By a country's national income, we mean the

1. For a more extended discussion of many of the points mentioned in this section, see Meade (1951, pp. 29–39), Tsiang (1950, pp. 254–61), and Smith (1970).

income received by the different factors of production from the production and sale of goods and services that these factors produce. National income may thus be measured at factor cost in terms of the total earnings of the productive factors. Alternatively, it may be measured at market prices in terms of the expenditures upon the goods and services that these factors produce. In a closed economy, for any given time period, the total national income and expenditure (GNP) should thus be identical, with allowance being made for depreciation and indirect taxes and subsidies. This identity is represented schematically in Table 6.1.

TABLE 6.1

National Income and National Expenditure in a Closed Economy

National Income		National Expenditure	
1. Wages and salaries	xxx	8. Private consumption	xxx
2. Rent	xxx	9. Gross private investment	xxx
3. Interest	xxx	10. Government expenditure on	
4. Profit	xxx	goods and services	xxx
5. National income at factor prices	xxx		
6. Add indirect taxes and deduct			
subsidies	xxx		
7. National income at market		11. Gross national expenditure at	
prices ($= 11$)	xxx	market prices ($= 7$)	xxx

From Table 6.1, we can write:

$$Y = C + I + G, \tag{6.1}$$

where Y is national income, C is private consumption expenditure, I is gross-private-investment expenditure, and G is government expenditure on goods and services. Since the disposition of all private income will involve consumption, saving, or payment of taxes to the government, we have:

$$Y = C + S + T, \tag{6.2}$$

where S is gross private saving and T is total tax proceeds (plus the income of government-owned factors). Setting the right-hand sides of (6.1) and (6.2) equal to each other and transposing terms, we obtain:

$$I = S + (T - G), \tag{6.3}$$

which is the equilibrium condition for a closed economy. If there were no government activity, the equilibrium condition would be:

$$I = S. \tag{6.4}$$

Suppose now that we consider an open economy in which there will be exports and imports of goods and services. Since the foreign demand for our country's exports generates factor earnings in precisely the same manner as other forms of expenditure upon home-produced goods and services, the value of the country's exports must be added to the expenditure total in item 11 of Table 6.1 in order to maintain the equality between national income and expenditure. In contrast, expenditure upon imports, which would now be reflected in items 8–10 together with expenditure on domestically produced goods, generates factor earnings in other countries. This expenditure on imports must consequently be deducted from the expenditure total in item 11 if national income and expenditure are to be equal.

In order to differentiate the closed and open economies, let us relabel item 11 in Table 6.1 as *domestic absorption* at market prices and interpret it to include expenditure on both home-produced goods and imports. We must accordingly now conceive of item 7, national income at market prices, as including the factor costs of total home production that is sold both domestically and exported. In order to achieve equality between national income and expenditure at market prices, it is necessary to deduct imports and add exports to domestic absorption. This is indicated in Table 6.2, where item 11c, national expenditure on home-produced goods is equal to item 7, national income.[2] The center of focus in an open economy in the sense both of economic accounting and analysis is thus on the relations between domestic and foreign expenditure and the level of national income.

TABLE 6.2

National Income and National Expenditure in an Open Economy

National Income		National Expenditure	
1–6. (Same as Table 6.1)	xxx	11. "Domestic absorption" at market prices	xxx
		11a. Deduct imports	−xxx
		11b. Add exports	xxx
7. National income at market prices (= 11c)	xxx	11c. National expenditure on home-produced goods at market prices (= 7)	xxx

2. It will be evident from Table 6.2 that if a given country's exports, X, of goods and services are greater than, less than, or equal to its imports, M, net national income, Y, will be greater than, less than, or equal to its domestic absorption, A. We can thus write:

$$X - M \equiv Y - A,$$

where $X - M$ is the export or import surplus on goods and services. This identity, which was first given prominence by Alexander (1952, pp. 265–66), is of fundamental importance since it focuses attention on the fact that foreign trade enables a country's expenditures to be more or less than what is produced at home. We shall examine the foreign trade and domestic policy implications of the income-absorption identity in the next chapter.

Since in an open economy, national income and expenditure (GNP) are equal, we can write:

$$Y = C + I + G + X - M, \qquad (6.5)$$

where C, I, and G now include expenditure on both domestically produced and imported goods and services, and X and M refer to exports and imports of goods and services. Suppose that in addition to foreign trade we have unilateral transfers that are made between countries in the form of private remittances and donations of various kinds. The disposition of private income will then be:

$$Y = C + S + T + U, \qquad (6.6)$$

where C is as just defined, S is saving, T is taxes, and U represents the net amount of unilateral transfers to foreigners.

Equating the right-hand sides of (6.5) and (6.6) and transposing terms, we have

$$I + (X - M - U) = S + (T - G). \qquad (6.7)$$

It will be evident that $(X - M - U)$ is equal to the balance on current account and net unilateral transfers. It will be recalled from Chapter 1 that this is equal to the balance of foreign lending, which we may designate as I_f. We may thus write:

$$I + I_f = S + (T - G), \qquad (6.8)$$

which is the equilibrium condition for an open economy.

The manner in which the balance of payments fits into the equilibrium relation between income and expenditure can be seen from the preceding paragraph. That is, the effect of the balance of payments on income enters via the amount of the surplus or deficit on current account plus net unilateral transfers, which as noted is by definition equal to the balance on capital account. As far as equilibrium income and expenditure are concerned therefore, international capital transactions do not matter in themselves since such transactions result merely in a change in the asset and liability positions of domestic residents. Because the balance of payments must balance, it will suffice for national income purposes to be concerned only with the balance on current account plus net unilateral transfers.

If we can again assume there is no government activity and, further, that unilateral transfers can be ignored, we can write the equilibrium condition for an open economy using equation (6.7), with some rearrangement of terms, as:

$$I + X = S + M. \qquad (6.9)$$

This may be compared to the closed economy equilibrium noted in equation (6.4), $I = S$.

With the foregoing definitional relations in mind, we can now consider the question of the determination of national income in an open economy. We shall continue with the simplification that there is no government activity. This will permit us to focus on equations (6.4) and (6.9) in terms of the forces making for expansion or contraction of national income. Thus, for example, if investment and exports are treated *ex ante* and saving and imports are as determined by current income, the forces can be summarized as follows:

Closed Economy	Open Economy	Effect on National Income
$I > S$	$I + X > S + M$	Expansion
$I = S$	$I + X = S + M$	Equilibrium
$I < S$	$I + X < S + M$	Contraction

Thus, in the absence of foreign trade and assuming no government activity, the economy will expand, remain stable, or contract depending upon whether *ex ante* investment is greater than, equal to, or less than saving as determined by current income. In an open economy, there will be expansion, stability, or contraction depending upon whether *ex ante* investment plus exports is greater than, equal to, or less than saving plus imports as determined by current income.

National Income Determination in an Open Economy[3]

We have so far not made a sharp distinction between measurements of national income and expenditure in monetary and in real terms. The forces just summarized making for expansion or contraction of national income will operate by effecting changes in both real output (income) and in prices. Our present concern will be primarily with the changes in real output.

We assume therefore that all prices, including wage rates and interest rates, are constant as output is varied. Real income and money income will move consequently in a completely parallel manner. We are assuming in other words that there are unemployed productive factors, constant returns in production, and constant factor prices. The monetary authorities are assumed to supply and withdraw money from the economy in sufficient amounts so that interest rates are kept perfectly fixed. Output can be varied therefore without any effect upon the price level until full employment is reached. We shall abstract for present purposes from all forms of government demand for goods and services and from all matters of taxation. The exchange rate is assumed completely fixed as the authorities accumulate or decumulate

3. Among some of the most noteworthy contributions that deal at length with the subject matter of this section are the following: Holzman and Zellner (1958, esp. pp. 73–87); Kindleberger (1968, Ch. 16); Machlup (1943); Meade (1951, esp. Ch. IV–VII and pp. 125–48); Metzler (1942b); Nurkse (1952); Polak and Haberler (1947); Smith (1970, Ch. 22); Stolper (1947); Tsiang (1950, esp. pp. 261–88); and Vanek (1962, Ch. 7).

official reserves without limit. All secondary effects of reserve movements on the level of money income are to be ignored. Finally, we shall concentrate solely on trade in goods and services.

Recalling the income-expenditure equality in equation (6.5):

$$Y = C + I + X - M,$$

note that C is to be interpreted as total consumption expenditure on goods and services, both domestically produced and imported. The same would be true for investment expenditure and for exports, but in order to simplify the analysis we shall assume that imports consist solely of consumption-type products, none of which are used as inputs for investment purposes and the production of exports. We thus can conceive of the total consumption function, expressed in linear form for purposes of simplicity, as:

$$C = cY + C_a, \tag{6.10}$$

consisting of the consumption function for domestic goods and services and for imports:

$$C_d = c_d Y + C_{ad} \tag{6.10a}$$

$$M = mY + M_a. \tag{6.10b}$$

The interpretation of these functions follows along the same well known lines as in a closed economy. That is, we can speak of the marginal propensity to consume domestic goods and services (c_d) and to import (m) and the average propensities:

$$c_d = \frac{\Delta C_d}{\Delta Y} \quad \text{and} \quad m = \frac{\Delta M}{\Delta Y}$$

$$APC = \frac{C_d}{Y} \quad \text{and} \quad APM = \frac{M}{Y}.$$

The marginal propensities are assumed to be constant for all changes in income while the average propensities will vary depending on the level of income. The relationship between the marginal and average propensities can be seen from the import functions shown in the three separate graphs in Figure 6.1.[4] The marginal propensity to import is indicated in each instance by the slope of line M. The average propensity to import for any given level of income can be approximated by the slope of a ray from the origin to the relevant point on the import schedule. It can be seen from the slopes of these rays that in (a), APM_1 is greater than, in (b) less than, and in (c) equal to APM_2. By comparing the slopes of these rays with the slope of the import

4. The illustration could apply just as well to the consumption function for domestic goods.

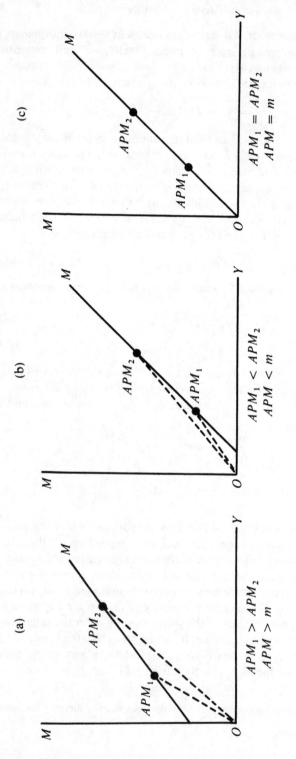

FIGURE 6.1.

Relation Between the Average and Marginal Propensity to Import

By comparing the slopes of the rays from the origin with the slope of the import schedule, it can be determined that the average propensity will be greater than, less than, or equal to the marginal propensity.

schedule, we can also see in the three cases, respectively, that the average propensity is greater than, less than, and equal to the marginal propensity. Note finally that the intercept is positive, negative, and zero according to the different positions of the import schedule.

It is worth reiterating that the import function is conceived in real terms. It shows how the expenditure on imports varies with changes in real national income. Should there occur changes in foreign or domestic prices, tastes, commercial policy, transportation costs, income distribution, etc., there will be a shift in the schedule rather than a movement along it. Suppose that the import function does shift due to a change in one of the factors just mentioned. How may this affect the consumption function for domestic goods and services? This will depend upon the degree of substitutability between imports and domestic goods and how any change in imports will affect domestic saving. Let us, for the time being at least, assume that imports are perfect substitutes for domestic goods. Thus, an autonomous increase or reduction in the demand for imports will be at the expense of or in favor of domestic consumption. Total consumption will be unchanged under these circumstances. But, as we shall note shortly, an autonomous increase in imports, other things equal, will cause national income to fall, and an autonomous decrease in imports will cause national income to rise.

The magnitude of the marginal propensity to import is assumed to lie between 0 and 1. We thus rule out the possibility of inferior goods. This would arise if expenditure on imports fell with increases in income. We also rule out the instability that would occur if expenditure on imports was greater than the related change in income. Limiting the marginal propensity to import in this way is unlikely, except in unusual or temporary circumstances, to do great violence to reality. The actual size of the marginal propensity to import will of course vary from country to country, depending especially upon the nature of the goods demanded and whether they can be obtained more cheaply abroad than at home. The average propensity to import will also differ widely among countries. It will depend upon the economic size of the country and the degree to which its overall needs can be satisfied domestically.[5]

Another way of looking at the relation between imports and income is in terms of the income elasticity of demand for imports, *YEM*. This is equal to the percentage change in imports divided by the percentage change in income that caused the change in imports and can be represented as:

$$YEM = \frac{\Delta M}{M} \div \frac{\Delta Y}{Y} .$$

5. Some of the problems in estimating import-demand functions statistically were mentioned in Chapter 5. See Leamer and Stern (1970, Ch. 2) for detailed discussion and references.

With some rearrangement, this can be seen to be equal to the marginal divided by the average propensity to import:

$$YEM = \frac{\Delta M}{\Delta Y} \div \frac{M}{Y}.$$

Thus, if income rose by 5 percent and imports by 10 percent, YEM would equal 2. This same result would be obtained if the marginal propensity to import was twice the average.

EQUILIBRIUM INCOME AND THE FOREIGN TRADE MULTIPLIER
WITH AN AUTONOMOUS CHANGE IN EXPORTS

Let us assume that both domestic investment and exports are autonomous and thus constant at all levels of income, and for the time being that our country is small enough so that we need not take into account the effects of variations in its income upon income in the rest of the world. We assume in other words that there are no foreign repercussions. Substituting equation (6.10) into (6.5), the equilibrium solution for an open economy will be:

$$Y = cY + C_a + I + X - mY - M_a$$

$$Y = \frac{C_a + I + X - M_a}{1 - c + m}. \tag{6.11}$$

Note that the consumption function, $cY + C_a$, refers to total consumption of domestic goods and services plus imports. Since expenditure on imports creates income abroad rather than at home, the import function has been written with negative signs. The coefficient c refers to the total marginal propensity to consume so that $c = c_d + m$; $1 - c$ is therefore equal to the marginal propensity to save, s.

Let us first examine the determination of the level of national income on the assumption that saving and domestic investment are always equal to zero. Since under these circumstances all income received will be spent on the consumption of domestic goods and services plus imports, c will be equal to unity and there will be no autonomous consumption. Equilibrium national income is therefore:

$$Y = cY + X - mY.$$

Since $c = 1$, we have:

$$Y = Y + X - mY = \frac{X}{m}.$$

This result is depicted in Figure 6.2, where consumption is broken down into domestic goods and services and imports. The consumption function for domestic goods and services is shown by line C_d which emanates from the origin because autonomous consumption is zero in this case. The import function is shown by line M and is the vertical distance between the 45° line

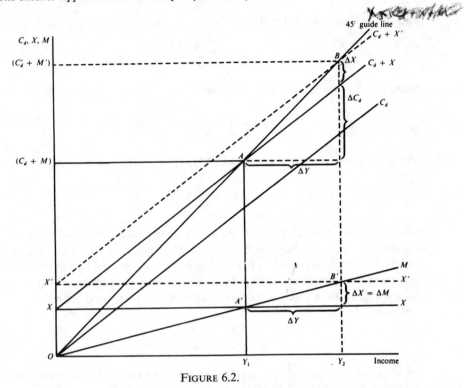

FIGURE 6.2.

*Equilibrium in an Open Economy
with Zero Saving and Investment*

*The initial equilibrium level of income is Y_1, where $C_d + X$ intersects
the 45° line at A and M and X intersect at A'. With an autonomous
increase in exports from X to X', the new equilibrium income will be
Y_2 and there will be balanced trade.*

and C_d. Assuming exports to be given autonomously at level X and adding
this amount vertically to C_d to get $C_d + X$, the equilibrium position will be
determined by the intersection of $C_d + X$ with the 45° line at point A, which
corresponds to equilibrium income of Y_1. The equilibrium is also indicated
by the intersection of the import and export schedules at A', at which point
the balance of trade is zero.

Assume now an autonomous increase in exports from X to X', which will
result in a corresponding shift from $C_d + X$ to $C_d + X'$. The new equilibrium
will be at B and B', which corresponds to the higher level of income Y_2. If we
compare the change in income, ΔY, with the autonomous increase in exports,
ΔX, the foreign trade multiplier effect is clear. That is, in initial equilibrium:

$$Y_1 = \frac{X}{m},$$

and the new equilibrium will be:

$$Y_2 = \frac{X'}{m}.$$

Subtracting these expressions, we have:

$$Y_2 - Y_1 = \frac{X'}{m} - \frac{X}{m}.$$

Taking $\Delta Y = Y_2 - Y_1$ and $\Delta X = X' - X$, we have:

$$\Delta Y = \frac{1}{m} \Delta X.$$

The change in income will thus be equal to the multiplier, $1/m$, times the multiplicand, which is here the change in autonomous exports. The numerical value of the multiplier will be the change in income divided by the change in exports which caused the change in income. The foreign trade multiplier for an autonomous change in exports, with zero saving and investment, is therefore

$$\frac{\Delta Y}{\Delta X} = \frac{1}{m}, \tag{6.12}$$

which is unity divided by the marginal propensity to import. This result could also have been obtained by differentiating equation (6.11) with respect to X and setting $c = 1$.

We have noted that at Y_1 the balance of trade is zero since $X = M$. The increase in exports from X to X' will increase income and produce initially a trade surplus. With increased income, there will be an increase in domestic consumption and imports as determined by the marginal propensities. The increase in domestic consumption will cause production and therefore income to rise further. Domestic consumption and imports will thus continue to rise until the new equilibrium level of income is obtained. It will be noted that as imports increase with rising income the initial trade surplus will be continually eroded until trade equilibrium is again restored at the higher level of income. Thus, our illustration shows that when trade equilibrium is disturbed by an autonomous change in exports, there is a mechanism of adjustment that will work automatically to restore equilibrium. In the present example when saving and investment are zero, the balance of trade is seen to be adjusted fully in the new equilibrium.

Let us now assume that saving is positive and that domestic investment is given autonomously at some level. The initial equilibrium, given as in equation (6.11) above, is depicted in Figure 6.3. The consumption function for domestic goods is indicated by C_d and the import function by M. As shown in the bottom of the graph, domestic investment is given autonomously

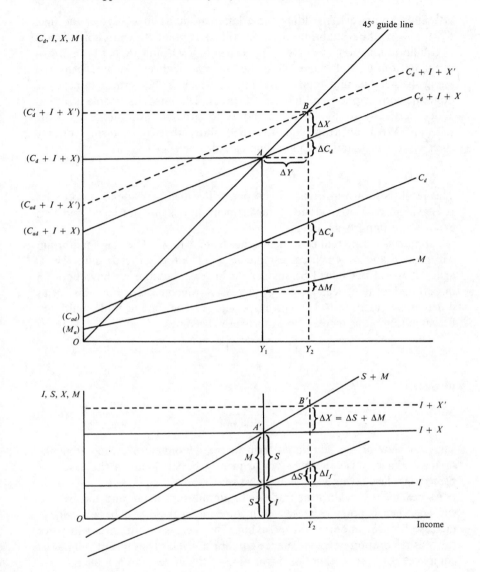

FIGURE 6.3.

Equilibrium in an Open Economy with Saving and Investment

*The initial equilibrium level of income is Y_1, where $C_d + I + X$ intersects
the 45° line at A and $S + M$ and $I + X$ intersect at A'. With an autonomous
increase in exports from X to X', the new equilibrium income will be Y_2 and
there will be a trade surplus equal to $\Delta X - \Delta M = \Delta I_f$.*

at I and exports at X. Adding these latter amounts to C_d to get the line, $C_d + I + X$, the equilibrium position will be at point A, which corresponds to equilibrium national income of Y_1. The saving schedule, S, has been drawn in the bottom part of the graph as the difference between income measured along the 45° line and total consumption, which is the vertical sum of the domestic consumption and import schedules. The import schedule has been added vertically to the saving schedule to produce a combined $S + M$ schedule. We know from equation (6.9) above that in an open economy such as we are assuming, equilibrium can also be expressed as:

$$I + X = S + M.$$

This result is shown in Figure 6.3 at point A' which corresponds also to Y_1. It is evident at Y_1 that domestic investment and saving are equal and that exports and imports are equal.

Suppose as before that exports increase from X to X'. The new equilibrium will be at B and B' which correspond to Y_2. The foreign trade multiplier is again at work, but it will be smaller in this case because we have both an import and a saving leakage out of increases in income. To show this, let us differentiate equation (6.11) with respect to X. The foreign trade multiplier for an autonomous increase in exports now becomes:

$$\frac{dY}{dX} = \frac{1}{1 - c + m},$$

or since $1 - c = s$

$$\frac{dY}{dX} = \frac{1}{s + m}. \tag{6.13}$$

Thus, in view of the additional term in the denominator representing the saving leakage, this multiplier will evidently be less than in the case just preceding when saving was taken to be zero.

As before, the balance of trade is in equilibrium at Y_1 and moves into surplus when exports increase. As income rises, there will be an induced increase both in imports and in saving. The increase in imports will work towards restoration of trade-balance equilibrium. This restoration will not be complete, however, because of the portion of the increase in income that has leaked into saving. At Y_2, therefore, there will be a trade surplus of the amount $\Delta X - \Delta M$, which is by definition equal to the change in foreign investment, ΔI_f. This is shown in Figure 6.3 by the excess of saving over net domestic investment at equilibrium income Y_2. Given the assumptions of our model, the trade surplus realized in the new equilibrium will be "permanent" in the sense that there will be no automatic forces working towards its removal.

The illustrations of the foreign trade multiplier presented thus far are simple extensions of the multiplier in a closed economy. Although we have focused on the effects of an autonomous change in exports upon national income and the trade balance, we could just as well have assumed autonomous changes to occur in imports or in any of the other major components of expenditure. The analysis of the effects upon income and the trade balance would be carried out in the same way.

The condition for stability of equilibrium in an open economy is also the same as in a closed economy. That is, so long as the leakages out of income are positive so that the marginal propensity to consume domestic goods and services is less than one, we shall have stable equilibrium. Otherwise, the equilibrium will be unstable.[6]

We have assumed thus far that the country represented by our model is relatively small and therefore that we could ignore the repercussions of changes in foreign trade and income upon other countries. Let us now alter this assumption by introducing a second country explicitly into the analysis and proceed to examine the workings of foreign repercussions in terms of the foreign trade multiplier. This will enable us to see how income fluctuations are transmitted from country to country via changes in exports and imports.

THE FOREIGN TRADE MULTIPLIER WITH FOREIGN REPERCUSSIONS

We know from equation (6.11) above that with domestic investment and exports assumed to be autonomous, the equilibrium solution for an open economy, which we may call country 1 (written without subscripts), is:

$$Y = cY + C + I + X - mY - M. \qquad (6.14)$$

If we now introduce a second country which we call country 2 (written with subscripts), its equilibrium solution is:

$$Y_2 = c_2 Y_2 + C_2 + I_2 + X_2 - m_2 Y_2 - M_2. \qquad (6.15)$$

It should be obvious in a two-country model that one country's exports are the other country's imports. That is:

$$X = m_2 Y_2 + M_2 \qquad (6.16)$$

$$X_2 = mY + M. \qquad (6.17)$$

Taking these export and import relationships into account, equations (6.14) and (6.15) can be written after some rearrangement as:

$$Y = \frac{C + I + m_2 Y_2 + M_2 - M}{(1 - c + m)} \qquad (6.18)$$

$$Y_2 = \frac{C_2 + I_2 + mY + M - M_2}{(1 - c_2 + m_2)}. \qquad (6.19)$$

The income of each country can thus be seen to depend in part on the income-induced and autonomous imports of the other country.

6. See Smith (1970, pp. 141–44) for a good illustration of the stability of equilibrium.

Substituting the expression for Y_2 in equation (6.18) and solving for Y, we have:

$$Y = \frac{(1 - c_2 + m_2)(C + I + M_2 - M) + m_2(C_2 + I_2 + M - M_2)}{(1 - c + m)(1 - c_2 + m_2) - mm_2}.$$

(6.20)

A comparable expression could be obtained for Y_2 by substituting the expression for Y in equation (6.19). In order to obtain the multiplier for a change in autonomous exports, we can differentiate the expression for Y in equation (6.20) with respect to M_2. All of the other autonomous terms in the expression will accordingly drop out and we will have:

$$\frac{dY}{dM_2} = \frac{dY}{dX} = \frac{(1 - c_2 + m_2) - m_2}{(1 - c + m)(1 - c_2 + m_2) - mm_2}.$$

(6.21)

Taking note of the fact that $1 - c = s$ and $1 - c_2 = s_2$, we have:

$$\frac{dY}{dX} = \frac{s_2}{(s + m)(s_2 + m_2) - mm_2}$$

$$= \frac{s_2}{ss_2 + ms_2 + m_2s}.$$

Dividing numerator and denominator by s_2 gives us the multiplier for country 1 that we are seeking:

$$\frac{dY}{dX} = \frac{1}{s + m + m_2(s/s_2)}.$$

(6.22)

The multiplier formula for country 2 will be the same as in equation (6.22), with appropriate changes being made in the subscripts. This is not to say, however, that the numerical value of the multiplier will be the same for each country. Such equality will be attained only if the marginal propensities to save are identical.

The autonomous export multiplier in equation (6.22) will be smaller than the one derived in equation (6.13) because of the foreign repercussion term that appears in the denominator. The reasoning behind this is that the autonomous increase in country 2's imports (1's exports) will cause income in country 2 to fall as imports are substituted for domestic goods. This fall in income will in turn induce a decline in country 2's imports according to its marginal propensity to import. Since country 2's imports are 1's exports, the effect will be to dampen the rise in 1's income. From country 2's standpoint, the fall in its income will be dampened somewhat by an increase in exports to country 1 that is induced by the rise in 1's income.

As far as the balance of trade is concerned, the initial effect will be to create a surplus for country 1 and a deficit for country 2. As just mentioned, the increase in 1's income will bring about an increase in its imports from 2, while the reduction in 2's income will result in a decline in 1's exports to 2. Country 1's trade surplus and 2's deficit will thus be reduced by these income-induced changes in trade. The adjustment will not be complete, however, so long as the marginal propensity to save is positive in each country.

The expression in equation (6.20) can be used to derive multipliers for changes in the other autonomous elements shown as well as in exports. Let us for example derive for country 1 the multiplier for a change in autonomous investment by differentiating the expression with respect to I. This result is:

$$\frac{dY}{dI} = \frac{(1 - c_2 + m_2)}{(1 - c + m)(1 - c_2 + m_2) - mm_2}. \tag{6.23}$$

Since $1 - c = s$ and $1 - c_2 = s_2$, and taking note of the fact that the denominator is the same as before, we have:

$$\frac{dY}{dI} = \frac{s_2 + m_2}{ss_2 + ms_2 + m_2 s}.$$

Dividing numerator and denominator by s_2, we obtain:

$$\frac{dY}{dI} = \frac{1 + m_2/s_2}{s + m + m_2(s/s_2)}. \tag{6.24}$$

It will be noted that this multiplier will be larger than in the case of a change in autonomous exports because of the added term in the numerator. The foreign repercussion effect will now be working to augment the rise in income rather than to diminish it as before. That is, the increase in investment in country 1 will have a multiplier effect in increasing 1's income, which will in turn lead to an increase in 1's imports from 2. Country 2's income will thus rise and so will its imports from 1. The increase in 1's exports will accordingly increase its income. This process will continue until equilibrium is attained at a higher level of income in both countries. Assuming that we started in equilibrium, the end result of the increase in 1's investment will be most likely to leave it with a trade deficit and 2 with a corresponding surplus.

In order to clarify the foregoing discussion, it may be useful to analyze the foreign trade multiplier by graphic methods. We may also be able in this way to illustrate some of the points that have been made regarding the stability and instability characteristics of our model.

GRAPHIC REPRESENTATION OF THE MULTIPLIER
WITH FOREIGN REPERCUSSIONS[7]

The Keynesian 45° diagram that was used previously for the graphic exposition of the multiplier without foreign repercussions cannot be readily adapted to handle a situation in which such repercussions are present. The

7. This section follows closely the treatment developed by R. Robinson (1952). Other graphic analyses of the foreign trade multiplier can be found in Black (1957) and Johnson (1953a).

reason for this, as already noted, is that each country's income will be determined in part by its exports to the other country. We can see this more clearly by rewriting equations (6.14) and (6.15) as follows:

$$Y = c_d Y + C_d + I + m_2 Y_2 + M_2 \tag{6.25}$$

$$Y_2 = c_{2d} Y_2 + C_{2d} + I_2 + mY + M. \tag{6.26}$$

The first two terms in each equation represent the propensity to consume domestic goods and services; c_d and c_{2d} are the marginal propensities to consume and C_d and C_{2d} are autonomous consumption. I and I_2 refer as before to autonomous domestic investment. The final two terms refer to exports and are represented by the propensity to import of the other country.

Once we assign specific values to the autonomous items and the various marginal propensities, we have two linear equations in two unknowns, Y and Y_2. The two equations can be plotted graphically in linear form and a solution reached for the equilibrium values of Y and Y_2 that satisfy these equations. To show this, let us focus on equation (6.25), which can be written:

$$Y = \frac{C_d + I + m_2 Y_2 + M_2}{(1 - c_d)}. \tag{6.27}$$

This equation can be rearranged in the following manner:

$$Y = \underset{(1)}{(C_d + I)} + \underset{(2)}{\frac{c_d}{1 - c_d}(C_d + I)} + \underset{(3)}{(m_2 Y_2 + M_2)} + \underset{(4)}{\frac{c_d}{1 - c_d}(m_2 Y_2 + M_2)}.$$

$$\tag{6.28}$$

Y can thus be seen to be composed of: (1) the sum of autonomous home consumption and investment; (2) consumption induced by the income generated in component (1); (3) earnings from exports; and (4) consumption induced by the earnings from exports.[8] These components are indicated in Figure 6.4a in a cumulative fashion,[9] the total of which is labeled as $Y(Y_2)$ to indicate the interdependence involved between the incomes of the two countries. Once we specify a value of Y_2, we can obtain the equilibrium value

8. As R. Robinson (1952, p. 549) has noted, the full domestic multiplier effect in equation (6.28) is equal to the sum of the respective autonomous and induced consumption components, that is, (1) + (2) and (3) + (4). The domestic multiplier is $1/(1 - c_d)$ rather than $c_d/(1 - c_d)$. That is, adding components (1) and (2), or (3) and (4), we get:

$$(C_d + I) + \frac{c_d}{1 - c_d}(C_d + I) = \frac{1}{1 - c_d}(C_d + I).$$

9. Presentation of the components in this fashion assumes that all the domestic multiplier effects upon income are worked out first and that all changes in imports take place subsequently. This assumption will do for our static analysis but not for a dynamic analysis in which consumption of domestic goods and imports would change jointly in response to changes in income.

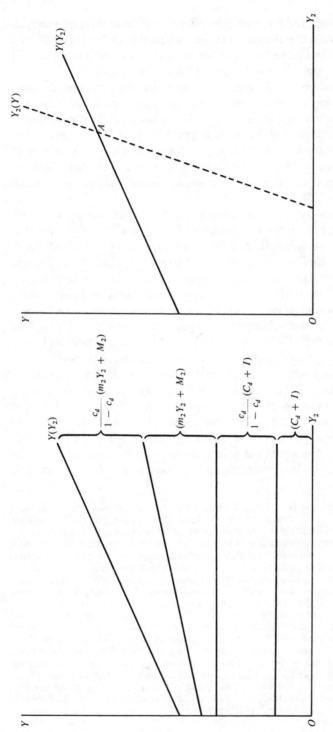

FIGURE 6.4.

Equilibrium National Income in a Two-Country World

a. Income in Country 1 as a Function of Income in Country 2

The components of $Y(Y_2)$ are shown cumulatively, assuming that the domestic multiplier effects are worked out first and the changes in imports occur subsequently.

b. Equilibrium Income in Countries 1 and 2

$Y_2(Y)$ is conceived in the same manner as $Y(Y_2)$. Equilibrium income in the two countries is indicated at point A.

of Y that will embody the full multiplier effects. The function for country 2, $Y_2(Y)$, can be conceived in the same manner as equation (6.28). It is indicated by the dashed line in Figure 6.4b together with $Y(Y_2)$. Equilibrium national income in the two countries will be at point A in Figure 6.4b.[10]

A glance at equations (6.25) and (6.26) will reveal that given fixed values for the marginal propensities to consume and to import, the national income, say, in country 1 could be increased by a rise in autonomous consumption, investment, or exports as well as by an increase in income in country 2 that would be transmitted back to 1 via $m_2 Y_2$. Two examples of the effects of such shifts are given in Figure 6.5 to correspond to the multiplier effects we examined earlier in connection with changes in autonomous investment and in exports.

Let us consider first the case shown in Figure 6.5a of an increase in autonomous investment in country 1. In order to focus more clearly on this case we have drawn in an enlarged form only the portions of $Y(Y_2)$ and $Y_2(Y)$ around the initial equilibrium at point A. In terms of equation (6.28) and Figure 6.4a, the increase in autonomous investment would be represented by an upward shift of the segment, $C_d + I$, plus the domestic multiplier effects that this increase would produce, depending on the magnitude of $c_d/(1 - c_d)$. The combined effects of the foregoing changes in Y are shown in Figure 6.5a by the upward shift to $Y'(Y_2)$ in the amount AB. The increase in Y will, however, lead to increased imports from country 2 and accordingly to an increase in Y_2 by an amount $m \Delta Y$ times the internal multiplier in country 2. This is shown by BC. And as Y_2 rises so will country 2's imports rise, with a consequent feedback upon Y. The new equilibrium will be at point F. It is evident that the total multiplier effect for country 1 will be equal to AG and that BG of this total will represent the foreign repercussions as just noted. As for country 2, the multiplier effect on its income resulting from the change in autonomous investment in country 1 is equal to GF. The increase

10. This equilibrium will be stable so long as both schedules are positively sloped and the slope of $Y_2(Y)$ is greater than that of $Y(Y_2)$. These slope requirements will be satisfied given that: (1) the various marginal propensities can be taken as positive; (2) the marginal propensities to consume domestic goods and services are less than unity; and (3) both countries are "stable in isolation." Taking all marginal propensities to be positive means ruling out the possibility of inferior goods, which seems reasonable since we are dealing with aggregates. If the marginal propensity to consume domestic goods and services is greater than one, the geometric series that underlies the multiplier expansionary process will fail to converge and the equilibrium will be unstable.

For both countries to be stable in isolation, the sum of their respective marginal propensities to consume domestic goods and to import must be less than one. Both countries must, in other words, have positive marginal propensities to save. This condition is not absolutely necessary, however, since it is possible for a stable equilibrium to be attained when one (but not both) of the countries is unstable in isolation (i.e., the marginal propensities to consume and import add up to more than one). This last case will be examined below in our discussion of the balance-of-payments effects of autonomous changes in expenditure. For additional details on stability conditions, see R. Robinson (1952, esp. pp. 551–53) and Metzler (1942b, p. 97).

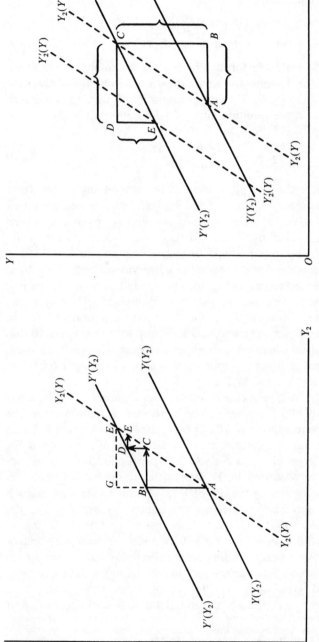

FIGURE 6.5.

The Multiplier with Foreign Repercussions

a. *Increase in Autonomous Investment in Country 1*

The initial equilibrium is at A. An autonomous increase in investment in country 1 will increase 1's income by $AB + BG$ (the foreign repercussion) and 2's income by GF. The new equilibrium is at F.

b. *Increase in Autonomous Exports from Country 1 to Country 2*

The initial equilibrium is at A. An autonomous increase in country 1's exports increases 1's income by $BC - DE$ and reduces 2's income by $DC - AB$. The new equilibrium is at E.

in investment in country 1 can thus be seen to have raised income in both countries.

In terms of our previous formulas, the multiplier for country 1 will correspond to equation (6.24):

$$\frac{dY}{dI} = \frac{1 + m_2/s_2}{s + m + m_2(s/s_2)}.$$

In order to obtain the multiplier formula in this case for country 2, we would need an expression for Y_2 that was comparable to the one for Y that was noted earlier in equation (6.20). If this expression for Y_2 were then differentiated with respect to I, the resulting multiplier for country 2 in the present case would be:

$$\frac{dY_2}{dI} = \frac{m}{ss_2 + ms_2 + m_2 s}. \qquad (6.29)$$

Let us now consider the case of an increase in autonomous exports from country 1 to 2 that is shown in Figure 6.5b. We start in initial equilibrium at point A. It will be recalled from our earlier discussion that imports have been assumed to be perfect substitutes for domestic goods. This means that a rise in country 2's propensity to import will be matched by an equivalent fall in its propensity to consume domestic goods and services. Country 2's total consumption will be unchanged, but its income will fall by an amount equal to the fall in consumption times the domestic multiplier, $1/(1 - c_{2d})$. The autonomous increase in country 1's exports will have a multiplier effect in increasing its income, which in turn will cause its imports (2's exports) to rise. However, since 2's income has fallen, its imports (1's exports) will be reduced. These income-induced changes in imports and exports will dampen the fall in country 2's income and the rise in 1's.

The outcome of the foregoing case is indicated in Figure 6.5b by the intersection of $Y'(Y_2)$ and $Y_2'(Y)$ at point E. The increase in Y resulting from the autonomous increase in exports is BC. This is offset by an amount DE that represents the effect transmitted to Y as the consequence of the autonomous decline in domestic expenditure in country 2. The net effect on Y is accordingly $BC - DE$. The reduction in Y_2 due to the autonomous increase in imports is CD. This is offset by the rise in Y_2 of AB due to the increase in Y resulting from the autonomous increase in country 1's exports. The net effect on Y_2 is therefore $DC - AB$. It follows that when both the Y and Y_2 functions shift, the full multiplier effect will embody the domestic effect of the autonomous change in expenditure plus the effect that will be transmitted from the other country as a consequence of the autonomous change there.[11]

Having examined graphically the impact of autonomous changes in expenditure upon income in the two countries, let us now consider the impact

11. The generalized foreign-trade-multiplier formulas for this case and the one just discussed are presented in R. Robinson (1952, pp. 555–57).

of such changes on the balance of trade. This can be accomplished by means of the same diagram that we have been using. It will be recalled from equation (6.18) and Figure 6.4a that one of the components of $Y(Y_2)$ was exports from country 1 to 2 that were represented by 2's propensity to import, $m_2 Y_2 + M_2$. Country 1's exports are indicated accordingly by the line $X(Y_2)$ that has been drawn in the bottom part of Figure 6.6a. In order to compare country 1's imports, $mY + M$, directly with its exports, it is necessary to obtain an expression for these imports in terms of Y_2 rather than Y. This can be done by substituting the expression for Y in equation (6.27) above in 1's import function, $mY + M$, in order to obtain an expression for 1's imports as a function of Y_2.[12] This is shown in Figure 6.6a by the line $M(Y_2)$.

The vertical distance between $X(Y_2)$ and $M(Y_2)$ indicates country 1's trade balance. This will be favorable when exports are greater than imports and unfavorable when the opposite is the case. Should there occur an autonomous increase in expenditure in country 2 so that $Y_2(Y)$ is shifted to the right, it is evident in such an instance that country 1's trade balance will be improved.

Suppose we examine now the case in which country 1 is assumed to be unstable in isolation. This will be when the sum of its marginal propensity to consume domestic goods and services plus its marginal propensity to import is greater than one (i.e., $c_d + m > 1$). This possibility might arise if we were to assume that investment was responsive to changes in income rather than being strictly autonomous. The presence of such induced investment could be handled by defining the marginal propensity to consume to include investment as well as consumption goods. In such an event, country 2's marginal propensity to spend on domestic goods and imports could exceed one.[13] What this means now is that if autonomous expenditure were to increase in country 2, the effect would be to worsen rather than to improve country 1's trade balance.

This case is illustrated in Figure 6.6b. It is evident that the slope of $M(Y_2)$ is now greater than that of $X(Y_2)$ and that the schedules do not intersect in

12. This expression for country 1's imports is:

$$M(Y_2) = M + \frac{m}{1 - c_d} (C_d + I + M_2) + \frac{m}{1 - c_d} m_2 Y_2.$$

The slope of country 1's export function, m_2, will be greater than that of its import function, $mm_2/1 - c_d$, so long as country 1 is stable in isolation. This will require that $c_d + m < 1$. Subtracting c_d from both sides of the inequality gives us $m < 1 - c_d$; dividing both sides by $(1 - c_d)$, we have $m/(1 - c_d) < 1$. When this expression is multiplied by m_2, the resulting product will yield a slope of the import function less than m_2.

13. Note that a marginal propensity to spend greater than one, which is the criterion for a country to be unstable in isolation, does not mean that this country is internally unstable. This latter condition would exist if the marginal propensity to consume domestic goods and services were greater than one. We have ruled out this possibility since the relevant income schedule would then have a negative slope and equilibrium income would be unstable.

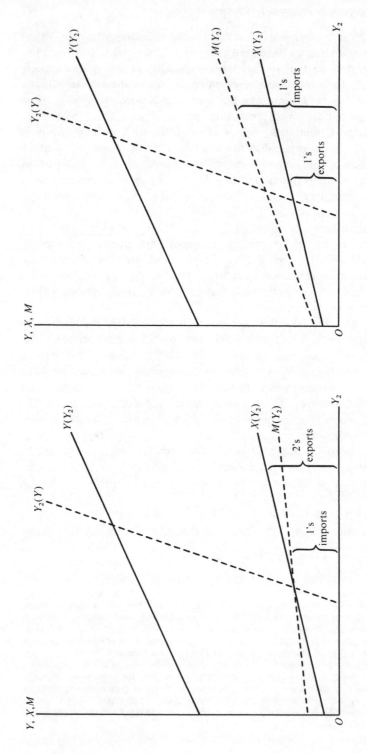

FIGURE 6.6.

Equilibrium National Income and the Balance of Trade in a Two-Country World

| *a. Both Countries Stable in Isolation* | *b. Country 1 Unstable in Isolation* |

A rightward shift of $Y_2(Y)$ improves country 1's trade balance.   *A rightward shift of $Y_2(Y)$ worsens country 1's trade balance.*

this quadrant.[14] It thus appears from Figure 6.6b that regardless of the level of its income, country 1 will always experience an import surplus and as $Y_2(Y)$ shifts to the right due to an autonomous increase in expenditure in 2, this import surplus will tend to worsen. The likelihood of obtaining such a result stems, as we have noted, from the introduction into the analysis of induced investment.[15]

This presupposes that the propensity to invest is a reasonably stable function. Machlup (1943; 1965, p. 22) and R. Robinson (1952, p. 562) especially have taken issue with such a presupposition, however. They have argued that since investment decisions are subjective in nature, depending upon businessmen's expectations regarding the future, the propensity to invest may be difficult to determine. This is of course a question of fact that must be investigated before we can pass judgment on the results that follow from the inclusion of induced investment in the theoretical analysis. It should also be remembered that we have been abstracting from government activity. If we were to take into account the leakage in income due to government taxation, the likelihood of countries being stable in isolation might be enhanced. In such a case, the favorable trade-balance effects on country 1 of an increase in autonomous expenditure in country 2 would constitute a reasonable expectation.

RECAPITULATION OF THE VARIOUS FOREIGN TRADE MULTIPLIERS

It may be useful at this point to recapitulate the various multipliers that have been derived and illustrated in the preceding two-country model. This is done in Table 6.3. It is evident that the multipliers for a change in a country's exports or imports are the same except for the sign that is indicative of the direction in which income will be changed. The multipliers for a change in investment depend on the country in which the change was initiated. These

14. That the slope of $M(Y_2)$ will now be greater than that of $X(Y_2)$ can be shown by the same line of reasoning as in footnote 12 above. If country 1 is unstable in isolation, $c_d + m > 1$. Subtracting c_d from both sides of the inequality, we have $m > (1 - c_d)$; dividing both sides by $(1 - c_d)$ gives us $m/(1 - c_d) > 1$. Since this last expression is greater than one, multiplying it by m_2 will therefore result in a slope of the import function greater than m_2, which is the slope of the export function.

The intercept of $M(Y_2)$ lies above that of $X(Y_2)$ in Figure 6.6b because all elements of autonomous expenditure have been taken as positive. That this assumption will result in a higher intercept for $M(Y_2)$ can be seen from the equation in footnote 12 and from the point made in the preceding paragraph that in the present case, $m/(1 - c_d) > 1$. If, on the other hand, negative autonomous expenditure elements were permitted, the two schedules might cross in the quadrant shown. R. Robinson (1952, pp. 563–64) has argued that such a result is not economically meaningful. Such an argument is not necessarily valid, however, because whether an autonomous expenditure element is positive or negative in an analysis of this kind is more a question of mathematical convenience rather than economic meaningfulness.

15. It is worth noting that induced investment must be distinguished from investment due to accelerator effects, which are more properly considered in a dynamic setting and can be studied within the framework of multiplier-accelerator models.

TABLE 6.3

Various Foreign Trade Multipliers in a Two-Country Model

Initiating Cause	Multipliers	
	Country 1	Country 2
1. Autonomous increase in country 1's exports (2's imports)[a]	$\dfrac{dY}{dX} = \dfrac{1}{s + m + m_2(s/s_2)}$	$\dfrac{dY_2}{dM_2} = -\dfrac{1}{s_2 + m_2 + m(s_2/s)}$
2. Autonomous increase in country 1's imports (2's exports)	$\dfrac{dY}{dM} = -\dfrac{1}{s + m + m_2(s/s_2)}$	$\dfrac{dY_2}{dX_2} = \dfrac{1}{s_2 + m_2 + m(s_2/s)}$
3. Autonomous increase in country 1's investment	$\dfrac{dY}{dI} = \dfrac{1 + m_2/s_2}{s + m + m_2(s/s_2)}$	$\dfrac{dY_2}{dI} = \dfrac{m}{ss_2 + ms_2 + m_2 s}$
4. Autonomous increase in country 2's investment	$\dfrac{dY}{dI_2} = \dfrac{m_2}{ss_2 + ms_2 + m_2 s}$	$\dfrac{dY_2}{dI_2} = \dfrac{1 + m/s}{s_2 + m_2 + m(s_2/s)}$

[a] With foreign repercussions absent, the foreign trade multipliers would be:

$$\frac{dY}{dX} = \frac{1}{s+m} \quad \text{and} \quad \frac{dY_2}{dM_2} = -\frac{1}{s_2+m_2}.$$

SOURCE: Adapted from equations (6.18)–(6.20).

latter multipliers are all positive with respect to the direction of income change.

It is also of interest to note how the trade balance will be affected in each case. The trade balance for country 1 is: $B = X - M = M_2 - M$, or in terms of changes:

$$\Delta B = \Delta M_2 - \Delta M.$$

Since $\Delta M_2 = m_2 \, \Delta Y_2$ and $\Delta M = m \, \Delta Y$, we have:

$$\Delta B = m_2 \, \Delta Y_2 - m \, \Delta Y. \tag{6.30}$$

The change in income from some particular autonomous change in exports (imports) or domestic investment can be read from the multiplier formulas in Table 6.3. Making the appropriate substitutions in equation (6.30) and adding or subtracting any autonomous change in exports (imports), the effects on country 1's trade balance can be determined. These are shown in Table 6.4. The change in country 2's trade balance, ΔB_2, is, of course, the same as the change in country 1's trade balance, but with opposite sign. It is evident that country 1's trade balance will be affected favorably by an autonomous increase in exports and conversely for imports. An autonomous increase in country 1's investment will worsen its trade balance and conversely if investment increases in country 2.

TABLE 6.4

Various Trade-Balance Changes in a Two-Country Model

Initiating Cause	Change in Country 1's Trade Balance
1. Autonomous increase in country 1's exports (2's imports)	$\Delta B = \dfrac{s}{s + m + m_2(s/s_2)} \Delta X$
2. Autonomous increase in country 1's imports (2's exports)	$\Delta B = -\dfrac{s}{s + m + m_2(s/s_2)} \Delta M$
3. Autonomous increase in country 1's investment	$\Delta B = -\dfrac{ms_2}{ss_2 + sm_2 + ms_2} \Delta I$
4. Autonomous increase in country 2's investment	$\Delta B = \dfrac{sm_2}{ss_2 + sm_2 + ms_2} \Delta I_2$

SOURCE: Adapted from equation (6.30) and the multipliers recorded in Table 6.3.

The foregoing relationships are illustrated in the appendix to this chapter in terms of arithmetic examples of the income and balance-of-trade effects of an autonomous increase in country 1's exports and an autonomous increase in country 1's net domestic investment. A dynamic model is used in order to illustrate the workings of the foreign-trade-multiplier process of adjustment.

SOME REFINEMENTS IN FOREIGN-TRADE-MULTIPLIER ANALYSIS

A number of explicit and implicit assumptions that have been made thus far in our discussion of the foreign trade multiplier are deserving of clarification. Among the most important are the following: (1) all expenditures on exports are income creating; (2) imports are perfect substitutes for domestic goods and services; (3) imports consist only of consumption goods; and (4) there are only two countries, 1 and 2.

Insofar as exports include goods produced in previous periods, income may not be increased unless inventories are replenished. Also, some sales may be on capital account, in which case the exporter's asset portfolio, rather than his income, may be affected. For many nations it may be important to note that their exports contain a significant amount of imports. This can arise from transshipments as well as from the processing and fabricating of imported materials that are embodied in exported goods. It may be noted finally that some types of receipts, such as investment income and unilateral transfers, do not give rise to further income creation until they have been spent. But not all such receipts will be spent domestically; some part may be saved and there may be a substantial import component as, for example, in the receipt of transfers in kind.[16]

16. The main points developed in this paragraph and the three following ones have been drawn primarily from the work of Holzman and Zellner (1958, pp. 73–87).

As far as our analysis is concerned, the import content of exports does not pose a serious problem since imports will be included with a negative sign in the multiplicand. In the case of the other items mentioned, however, it may be necessary to adjust the multiplicand for a change in export receipts according to the proportion of this change that is income creating. If we call this proportion, t, then the effect on national income of an autonomous change in exports, assuming no foreign repercussions,[17] would be:

$$\Delta Y = \Delta X \frac{t}{s + m}. \tag{6.31}$$

If all export receipts were income creating, t would be equal to unity, and the multiplier effect would be the same as in our earlier discussion in connection with equation (6.13). But if t is less than one, the multiplier in equation (6.31) will clearly be smaller than before.

The assumption of perfect substitutability between imports and domestically produced goods and services was seen to mean that any autonomous change in imports would be matched by an equal but opposite shift in the propensity to consume domestic goods and services. Total consumption would therefore remain unchanged. It is possible, however, that some part or even all of the change in imports may be at the expense of saving, in which case national income may be affected not at all or only by the proportion of imports that affects domestic consumption. Thus, if we call p, the proportion of imports that substitutes for domestic consumption, the effect on national income of an autonomous change in imports, in the absence of foreign repercussions, would be:

$$\Delta Y = \Delta M \frac{p}{s + m}. \tag{6.32}$$

If imports and domestic goods were perfect substitutes, p would be equal to one and the effect on income would be the same as in our previous discussion. But if changes in imports were financed completely out of saving, p would be equal to zero and there would be no effect on income. Imperfect substitutability would consequently yield a value of p between zero and one and the multiplier effect would have to be adjusted as indicated in equation (6.32).

The foregoing considerations are of interest in analyzing the effects on national income of equal changes in exports and imports. According to the traditional formulation of equilibrium in an open economy noted earlier in equation (6.11), we have:

$$Y = \frac{C_a + I + X - M_a}{1 - c + m}.$$

If the autonomous changes in consumption and domestic investment, ΔC_a

17. The effects of foreign repercussions are treated, *ibid.* pp. 86–7, in terms of the expression derived earlier in connection with equations (6.20) and (6.21).

and ΔI, are zero and if exports and imports change by an identical amount, there will be no effect whatever on national income, as the following expression will reveal:

$$\Delta Y = \frac{\Delta X - \Delta M_a}{1 - c + m} = 0. \qquad (6.33)$$

In other words, the balanced trade multiplier will be equal to zero. Suppose, however, that we take into account the possibilities that not all expenditure on exports will be income creating and that imports are imperfect substitutes for domestic goods and services. Equation (6.33) therefore becomes:

$$\Delta Y = \frac{t \, \Delta X - p \, \Delta M_a}{1 - c + m}. \qquad (6.34)$$

The multiplier effect will evidently be zero if $t = p$, greater than one if $t - p > 1 - c + m$, less than one if $t - p < 1 - c + m$, and negative if $t < p$. The outcome of a balance change in trade and by implication of an unbalanced change in trade may therefore be indeterminate unless we know the values of t and p. Knowledge of these values is of course an empirical rather than a strictly theoretical question.

It will be recalled that our analysis was confined to imports of consumer goods alone, and that we assumed investment to be autonomously determined. This latter assumption was relaxed somewhat with respect to changes in investment due to changes in the level of income. We saw that induced investment could be handled by redefining the propensity to consume as a propensity to spend that would embrace both induced consumption and induced investment.[18] It was but a short step from here to consideration of unstable situations arising from the possibility of the marginal propensity to spend being greater than one. Since our analysis was carried out mainly in terms of comparative statics, we were not concerned with accelerator effects of investment responses to the rate of change in income. Such responses could be treated in an open economy by means of the same type of multiplier-accelerator models that have been developed for closed economy conditions. Thus, we could conceive of a "foreign trade accelerator" in terms of the changes in investment brought about by the effects of export expansion or contraction upon income.[19]

The important point about multiplier-accelerator models is the different types of fluctuations in income that may be produced depending upon the parameters chosen for change.[20] While it would take us too far afield to

18. See Johnson (1956; 1968, p. 156) for a further extension in which the marginal propensities are defined to include induced expenditures by government and purchases of intermediate goods used in production.

19. The question of the foreign trade accelerator was in part the subject of an exchange between Bloomfield (1949) and Kindleberger (1949). It has also been treated briefly by R. Robinson (1952, p. 561) and more extensively and formally by Brems (1956).

20. See, for example, the discussion by Smith (1970, pp. 178–82).

consider these matters here, our analysis would presume that increases in exports that increase income through multiplier-accelerator effects will cause the balance of trade to adjust much more rapidly and fully than if only multiplier effects were present. Indeed, it is possible, as our discussion of stability and instability in isolation suggests, that an initial increase in a country's exports may well lead to a worsening rather than an improvement in its trade balance. This is not the only possibility, however, for if the increase in investment were to result in increased productivity and lower relative prices, the balance of trade might improve rather than deteriorate. As we will note in later discussion in Chapter 11, this productivity effect on investment is one of the main points of emphasis in the so-called export-led models of economic growth.

We focused on a two-country model primarily for the purpose of bringing out the essentials of the foreign-trade-multiplier relationships. There are many instances in international economic analysis when it is convenient to treat the second country, so to speak, as the rest of the world and therefore to deal meaningfully with a two-country framework. Such a convention cannot be adopted, however, in the case of foreign-trade-multiplier analysis. If we group countries rather than treat them separately, the marginal propensity to import for the group will not be representative of that for each country since a part of what was international trade will now become intranational trade. The marginal propensity to import will also vary depending upon the combinations of countries chosen. Finally, the grouping of countries would obscure the differential impacts that individual countries would experience in actuality according to the relative significance of their trade relationships with the one country that was singled out for purposes of analysis.[21] In the hope that most of the important points about the foreign trade multiplier have been grasped within the confines of a two-country model, it may suffice simply to note that there have been a number of efforts made using algebraic methods to generalize the analysis to the case of *n*-countries.[22]

The International Transmission of Fluctuations in Income

It should be clear from our discussion that the theory of income determination for an open economy offers us at one and the same time a framework for analyzing the international transmission of fluctuations in economic activity and of the mechanism of adjustment in the balance of trade. Thus, we saw that an expansion or contraction of autonomous expenditure originating in a given country will be propagated abroad by means of the effects that

21. See Machlup (1943; 1965, esp. pp. 90–92) for an elaboration of the foregoing discussion.
22. See especially Johnson (1958, pp. 196–99) and the references cited therein.

changes in income will have upon imports. If, say, there is a domestic investment boom, there will be a spillover to other countries as the given country's
imports rise with increased income. This "leakage" into imports, while it
serves to limit the increase in income at home, is what serves to transmit the
process of expansion abroad. If the given country is small relative to the rest
of the world, a boom caused by an increase in domestic investment will have
comparatively little impact abroad. How long the boom will persist in such
an instance before a substantial trade deficit occurs will depend on the size
of the country's marginal propensity to import (as well as domestic price
changes).

If, on the other hand, the given country is relatively large, as in the case
say of the U.S. or of a regional grouping such as the European Common
Market, a domestic boom may quickly spill over to other countries. The relative strength of this spillover will depend again on the marginal propensity
to import in the given country with respect to its trading partners. One
should not lose sight of the fact, of course, that even if the marginal propensity to import is small, the spillover effect can nevertheless be significant
if absolute changes in income are substantial as they would be in a country
like the U.S. Whether the given country will in turn be stimulated further
through the effects of foreign repercussions will depend upon the increase in
income in countries abroad and the size of the marginal propensity to import.
The transmission process just described is applicable, it should be noted, to
the international spread of a recession as well as to a boom originating in a
given country.

In contrast to the propagation effects of domestic booms and recessions,
there are some types of autonomous changes that will have a favorable
effect upon income in a given country and an unfavorable effect abroad. Such
a possibility might arise, for example, in the event of devaluation of the given
country's currency, a tariff reduction abroad, or a spontaneous change in
consumer preferences as between domestically produced goods and imports.
These types of changes can be studied equally well with the aid of our
analysis. The implications for world income are somewhat different, however,
as compared to the transmission of booms and recessions since income
changes in different countries may cancel out rather than be reinforced.[23]

---

23. To illustrate, we can write the change in income for the world as a whole, ΔY_w, as:

$$\Delta Y_w = \Delta Y + \Delta Y_2.$$

If country 1's exports are increased for one of the reasons mentioned, the effect on world
income can be found by substituting the values of ΔY and ΔY_2 given in case 1 of Table
6.3. This yields, with some rearrangement:

$$\Delta Y_w = \frac{s_2 - s}{ss_2 + sm_2 + ms_2} \Delta X.$$

Thus, total world income will rise or fall depending upon which country has the higher
marginal propensity to save.

Our analysis has obvious implications for economic policy with respect especially to the attainment of internal and external balance. This is the case insofar as full employment and external balance are not looked upon today as a state of affairs that will occur naturally in the course of time, but rather as goals that must be sought consciously with the assistance of policies of various kinds. It is clear from our analysis that a given country's income can be increased either by monetary and fiscal measures to expand domestic consumption, investment, and government expenditure or by measures to expand exports or reduce imports. The trouble in using foreign trade measures to stimulate income is the danger of reducing income abroad. Domestic monetary and fiscal expansionary measures might be preferable therefore insofar as income will tend to be increased both at home and abroad. It is possible, of course, that the balance of trade will be affected unfavorably by these domestic measures. However, as will be pointed out in Chapter 10 below, the measures can conceivably be differentiated in terms of their impact to attain both internal and external balance.

Price Effects in Income Determination and Balance-of-Trade Adjustment

We have assumed prices to be constant in our analysis in order to focus attention on movements in real income. This has meant that output in real terms could be expanded, at least until full employment was attained. This situation is depicted in Figure 6.7 in which the rate of change in the general level of prices is measured vertically and real income horizontally. Starting at some assumed price level, p_o, income, pY, will expand along a horizontal path until full employment is reached at Y_f. Any further expansion beyond Y_f will result only in increases in the price level since there is no possibility of further expanding real output. This implies that the monetary authorities will continue to increase the money supply in order to keep the interest rate fixed even though the result is purely inflationary.

In actuality, prices may begin to rise long before full employment income is reached. One possible reason for this is the occurrence of production bottlenecks insofar as resources may not be available in unlimited supply and there may be decreasing rather than constant returns in production. But perhaps of greater importance, especially in industrialized countries, is the presence of market power stemming from labor union pressures and the existence of structural imbalances in the labor market that result in money wage increases that exceed increases in average labor productivity. Empirically speaking, as shown by Phillips (1958) and others, these wage pressures are apparently inversely related to the level of unemployment. When faced with higher wage costs, employers seek to raise product prices. To the extent that this process becomes economy-wide, price inflation can occur therefore

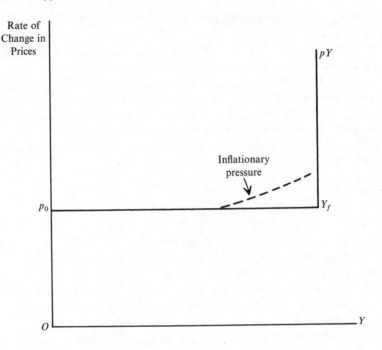

FIGURE 6.7.

Price Effects of a Multiplier-Induced Expansion

Assuming unemployed factors and constant returns in production, real output will expand along a horizontal path until full employment is reached. Alternatively, inflationary pressure may be felt before full employment is reached due to resource limitations and decreasing returns in production or to labor-market influences leading to higher money wages in excess of productivity.

even with unemployed resources. This inverse relationship between the rate of change in prices and the level of unemployment is embodied in what has been called the "modified" Phillips curve.[24]

The realization of inflationary pressures is illustrated in Figure 6.7 by the dashed line. At full employment (i.e., zero unemployment), there is as before purely a rise in prices. Once we permit changes in both prices and real output to occur, it is clear that money income, pY, and real income, Y, need not move in a parallel fashion. This creates problems in measuring real income changes, but we shall assume that satisfactory price deflators for money income can be devised for this purpose. A conceptual problem also arises, however, in that if prices and real output move together and are mutually

24. A good discussion of "market-power" inflation and the analytical and empirical underpinnings of the Phillips curve is to be found in Smith (1970, esp. pp. 350–71).

reinforcing, there is some question about whether or not our propensities will remain stable.

As far as the balance of trade is concerned, the implication of changes in prices as income expands is to introduce an additional factor in the process of adjustment. Thus suppose that there is an autonomous increase in country 1's exports. This will have a multiplier effect on income that gives rise to induced imports. If prices rise in addition, imports may increase even more and exports may decline, the precise changes depending upon the elasticities of home and foreign demand and supply. The effect on the balance of trade, assuming we start in equilibrium, can be seen as follows:

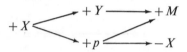

That is, a surplus will be created initially by the autonomous increase in exports. Equilibrium will tend to be restored by the increase in imports and decline in exports that result from the rise in income and prices. It is conceivable, depending upon the size of the marginal propensity to import and the relevant price elasticities, that the initial balance-of-trade surplus might be turned into a deficit.

In the event of an autonomous increase in domestic expenditure, say domestic investment, the effect of price increases will be to worsen the balance of trade even more than otherwise. Again assuming initial equilibrium, this can be seen as follows:

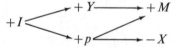

Thus, in the case of an autonomous increase in exports, equilibrium in the balance of trade may be restored more readily if both income and prices change, whereas with an autonomous increase in domestic investment the balance-of-trade deterioration may be worsened.

No allowance has been made explicitly in the foregoing examples for income and price changes abroad. If imports are perfect substitutes for domestic goods, an autonomous increase in imports will lower income and therefore imports. If prices also decline, the initial balance-of-trade deficit may be more readily adjusted as imports are further reduced and exports increased. In the case of an autonomous increase in investment, the effect may be to increase both income and prices abroad, which may help somewhat to restore equilibrium. Thus, from the standpoint of country 2, the effects may appear as follows:

(1) Autonomous increase in 2's imports (1's exports)

$$+M_2 \begin{cases} -Y_2 \longrightarrow -M_2 \\ -p_2 \longrightarrow +X_2 \end{cases}$$

(2) Autonomous increase in investment in 1

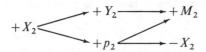

The foregoing discussion raises the important question of the kind of economy and economic environment in which the income approach may be most applicable. This will depend in large measure upon the existence of underutilized resources and the degree to which these resources can be mobilized in the short run in order to increase output without affecting prices significantly. The conditions of the 1930's in the advanced industrialized countries perhaps come the closest to the assumptions we have relied upon for the most part in this chapter. It is clear, however, that in the period since World War II underemployment in the advanced countries has been nowhere as severe as before the War and in many cases the control of inflation has posed a much more serious problem. This suggests that the income approach tells us only part of the story and, depending on the nature of the forces affecting prices, it may not be the most important part in seeking to analyze the actual experiences of many advanced countries.

When we consider the situations of less developed countries that rely importantly on primary commodities in their domestic production and export trade, the point just made acquires even greater significance. That is, it is very common in such countries for supply conditions in the production of both home goods and exports to be relatively inelastic. Home demand for many goods may also be relatively inelastic. In such cases an autonomous increase in exports might result in substantial domestic price increases. It may also be the case that the marginal propensity to import may be relatively high in many countries because of the unavailability of import substitutes. It would not be surprising under these conditions to expect the increase in imports to be substantial. Autonomous increases in expenditure in less developed countries may therefore have only a fairly limited impact on real income. There may be some question consequently about the meaningfulness of applying the income approach to such countries.

The Role of Money in Income Determination and Balance-of-Trade Adjustment

The monetary authorities have been assumed in our analysis to vary the money supply in order to keep the rate of interest from changing. This means that as income rises, the money supply must also rise to keep pace with the increase in the demand for money for transactions purposes in a way that will not affect the rate of interest. This type of policy has been referred to by Tsiang (1961; 1968, p. 401) as "Keynesian neutral monetary policy." It underlies explicitly or implicitly most analyses of income determination. The

Keynesian neutral policy is to be distinguished from what Tsiang has called "orthodox neutral monetary policy," which refers to a policy of holding the money supply constant while permitting interest rates to vary freely.

In focusing attention on the relationships between income and expenditure, there may be a tendency to take for granted or perhaps even overlook the role of money. Yet this role may have a direct bearing upon these relationships. Thus, we saw in Figure 6.7 that under the assumption of constant prices and interest rates, real income would expand until full employment was reached, at which point any further increases would be only in money income as prices would shoot upwards. This process of income expansion followed by a rise in prices is, as we have noted, dependent upon an expansion of the money supply in accordance with a Keynesian neutral monetary policy. It should be obvious, however, that such a policy makes no sense once full employment is reached. Rather it would be desirable under these conditions to institute an orthodox neutral monetary policy in order to avoid inflation. In case prices begin to rise before full employment is reached, as in Figure 6.7, the orthodox policy might have to be implemented sooner.

The role of money and credit creation takes on special significance once it is realized that a positive or negative trade balance has to be conceived in money rather than in real terms. The reason for this lies in the nature of international transactions that may give rise to changes in foreign assets and liabilities. Thus, as we have seen in our earlier discussion of the balance of payments, the counterpart of a positive or negative current-account balance is to be found in the capital account in terms of an increase or decrease in foreign assets or liabilities. Since foreign assets or liabilities cannot be treated in other than money terms, the difference between exports and imports of goods and services must perforce be treated in the same way.

In terms of the policy problem of dealing with the balance of payments, it is therefore necessary to emphasize the essentially monetary nature of the problem and to devise policies that take the supply of money and credit (as well as fiscal policy) explicitly into account. This is not to conclude that for policy purposes we will be unable to utilize the income-expenditure analysis that has been framed for the most part in real terms. Rather, the point is that we must be clear on the monetary assumptions made in such analysis in order to be able to evaluate alternative policies. We shall have occasion to treat these issues at greater length in our discussion in the next chapter and in Chapter 10 dealing with policies for internal and external balance.

Conclusion

In developing the income approach to balance-of-payments adjustment, we saw that the distinction between a closed and open economy in terms of accounting definitions and equilibrium relations was that exports had to be added to and imports deducted from domestic absorption in order for national income and expenditure to be equal. In the absence of government activity and ignoring unilateral transfers, national income will expand, remain stable, or contract depending upon whether domestic investment plus exports was greater than, equal to, or less than saving plus imports.

National income determination in an open economy was analyzed using a traditional Keynesian model. The foreign trade multiplier for an autonomous change in exports, assuming no foreign repercussions, was seen to be equal to the reciprocal of the sum of the marginal propensities to save and import. Using a two-country model and taking foreign repercussions into account yielded a smaller multiplier than just noted because a repercussion term appeared in the denominator of the multiplier expression. Multipliers were also derived for an autonomous increase in domestic investment. In this case, the foreign repercussion effect added to the increase in income. Autonomous changes in exports, imports, and domestic investment were thus seen to be transmitted from one country to the other in terms of the changes in foreign trade induced by income changes. These changes in trade served in turn to help equilibrate or worsen the trade balance, depending upon the initiating cause of the change in income.

After treating some refinements to foreign-trade-multiplier analysis, we had occasion to examine how variations in prices affected income determination and the trade balance. If prices rose as full employment was approached, money and real income would diverge. Price increases would also serve to equilibrate the trade balance more quickly in the event of an autonomous increase in exports and worsen the trade balance even more in the event of an autonomous increase in investment. We had occasion finally to examine the monetary assumptions of the model, in particular that the authorities varied the money supply in order to keep interest rates fixed. The implication was that the trade balance had to be conceived in money rather than in real terms in order to take into account how monetary variations were manifested in changes in foreign assets and liabilities.

Appendix: The Dynamic Multiplier Process Involving Two Countries

This appendix is designed to show by means of arithmetic examples the nature of the dynamic multiplier process involving two countries. We shall retain all of the assumptions made earlier concerning the constancy of prices, wages, the rate of interest, and the rate of exchange. The dynamic model used is based on an output lag of one period. Lags in expenditure and earnings are ignored. Two cases will be presented: an autonomous increase in exports from country 1 to country 2 and an autonomous increase in investment in country 1.

AUTONOMOUS INCREASE IN EXPORTS FROM COUNTRY 1 TO COUNTRY 2

Consider the following two-country model:

Country 1	Country 2
(6.A.1) $Y = (C_{t-1}) + (I_{t-1})$ $+ (X_{t-1})$	(6.A.1′) $Y_2 = (C_{t-1})_2 + (I_{t-1})_2$ $+ (X_{t-1})_2$
(6.A.2) $C = 0.6(Y_t) + 5$	(6.A.2′) $C_2 = 0.6(Y_t)_2 + 10$
(6.A.3) $I = 20$	(6.A.3′) $I_2 = 15$
(6.A.4) $X = 0.2(Y_t)_2 + 35$	(6.A.4′) $X_2 = 0.3(Y_t) + 5$
(6.A.5) $X = M_2$	(6.A.5′) $X_2 = M$

Equations (6.A.1) and (6.A.1′) define national income in any period as the sum of the previous period consumption of domestic goods and services, domestic investment, and exports. Equations (6.A.2) and (6.A.2′) are the consumption functions for domestic goods and services. Investment is assumed wholly autonomous according to equations (6.A.3) and (6.A.3′). Each country's exports are shown according to equations (6.A.4) and (6.A.5) and (6.A.4′) and (6.A.5′) to correspond to the propensity to import of the other country. Equilibrium national income in each country (ignoring the time subscripts) will be initially:

$$Y = 0.6Y + 5 + 20 + 0.2Y_2 + 35$$

$$Y_2 = 0.6Y_2 + 10 + 15 + 0.3Y + 5.$$

Solving for Y in terms of Y_2 and Y_2 in terms of Y, we have:

$$Y = \frac{60 + 0.2Y_2}{0.4} \qquad\qquad Y_2 = \frac{30 + 0.3Y}{0.4}.$$

Substituting the expression for Y_2 into that for Y, we obtain:

$$Y = \frac{60}{0.4} + \frac{0.2}{0.4}\left(\frac{30 + 0.3Y}{0.4}\right) = 300.$$

When the equilibrium value of 300 for Y is substituted in the expression for Y_2, we see also that in equilibrium:

$$Y_2 = 300.$$

The original equilibrium values for national income and its components are shown for each country in the first column of Table 6.A.1. It will be noted that initially investment and saving, S, are equal and that exports equal imports.

TABLE 6.A.1

The Dynamic Multiplier Process Involving Two Countries: Autonomous Increase in Exports from Country 1 to 2

Variable	How Calculated	Original Equilibrium	1	2	3	4	5	6	7	8	9	10	∞ New Equilibrium
	Country 1													
Y	$(C_{t-1}) + (I_{t-1}) + (X_{t-1})$	300	300	310	314	315.8	316.76	317.37	317.82	318.17	318.46	318.7	320
C	$.6(Y_t) + 5$	185	185	191	193.4	194.48	195.06	195.42	195.69	195.9	196.08	196.22	197
I	Autonomous	20	20	20	20	20	20	20	20	20	20	20	20
X	$.2(Y_t)_2 + 35 + (10)$	95	105	103	102.4	102.28	102.32	102.4	102.48	102.56	102.62	102.68	103
M	$.3(Y_t) + 5$	95	95	98	99.2	99.74	100.03	100.21	100.35	100.45	100.54	100.61	101
S	$(Y_t) - (C_t) - (M_t)$	20	20	21	21.4	21.58	21.68	21.74	21.78	21.82	21.85	21.87	22
ΔS	Cumulative	—	0	1	1.4	1.58	1.68	1.74	1.78	1.82	1.85	1.87	2
$\Delta(X - M)$	Cumulative	—	10	5	3.2	2.54	2.29	2.18	2.13	2.11	2.09	2.07	2
$\Delta(Y_t)$	Cumulative	—	0	10	14	15.8	16.76	17.37	17.82	18.17	18.46	18.7	20
$\Delta(Y_t)/\Delta X$	Cumulative	—	0	1	1.4	1.58	1.67	1.74	1.78	1.82	1.85	1.87	2
	Country 2													
Y_2	$(C_{t-1})_2 + (I_{t-1})_2 + (X_{t-1})_2$	300	300	290	287	286.4	286.58	286.98	287.4	287.78	288.12	288.41	290
C_2	$.6(Y_t)_2 + 10 - (10)$	190	180	174	172.2	171.84	171.95	172.19	172.44	172.67	172.87	173.05	174
I_2	Autonomous	15	15	15	15	15	15	15	15	15	15	15	15
X_2	$.3(Y_t) + 5$	95	95	98	99.2	99.74	100.03	100.21	100.35	100.45	100.54	100.61	101
M_2	$.2(Y_t)_2 + 35 (+10)$	95	105	103	102.4	102.28	102.32	102.4	102.48	102.56	102.62	102.68	103
S_2	$(Y_t)_2 - (C_t)_2 - (M_t)_2$	15	15	13	12.4	12.28	12.32	12.4	12.48	12.56	12.62	12.68	13
ΔS_2	Cumulative	—	0	-2	-2.6	-2.72	-2.68	-2.6	-2.52	-2.44	-2.38	-2.32	-2
$\Delta(X_2 - M_2)$	Cumulative	—	-10	-5	-3.2	-2.54	-2.29	-2.18	-2.13	-2.11	-2.09	-2.07	-2
$\Delta(Y_t)_2$	Cumulative	—	-10	-10	-13	-13.6	-13.42	-13.02	-12.6	-12.22	-11.88	-11.59	-10
$\Delta(Y_t)_2/\Delta M_2$	Cumulative	—	0	-1	-1.3	-1.36	-1.34	-1.3	-1.26	-1.22	-1.19	-1.16	-1

Suppose now in period 1 that there is an autonomous increase in imports of 10 in country 2 at the expense of its consumption of domestic goods and services. This will result in the following changes in the model:

Country 1

(6.A.4a) $X = M_2 = 0.2(Y_t)_2 + 35 + 10$

Country 2

(6.A.4'a) $C_2 = 0.6(Y_t)_2 + 10 - 10.$

Assuming that the new level of 1's exports (2's imports) is attained instantaneouly without disinvestment, it can be seen in period 1 that country 1 will have an export surplus $\Delta(X - M)$ and 2 an import surplus $\Delta(X_2 - M_2)$ equal to 10. The increase in 1's income, ΔY, from 300 in period 1 to 310 in period 2 is reflected in increased consumption (185 to 191), imports (95 to 98) and saving (20 to 21). The reduction in 2's income, ΔY_2, from 300 to 290 results in decreased consumption (180 to 174), imports (105 to 103), and saving (15 to 13). The changes noted in 1's imports (2's exports) and 2's imports (1's exports) will offset in part the autonomous changes that occurred and thus serve to reduce 1's export surplus (2's import surplus) from 10 to 5 between period 1 and 2. This can be seen more clearly as follows:

Effects on Trade Balance

Period 1	Country 1	Country 2
Autonomous change	$+X = \quad 10$	$+M_2 = -10$
Period 2		
Induced changes	$+M = -3$	$+X_2 = \quad 3$
	$-X = -2$	$-M_2 = \quad 2$
Change in trade balance	$\Delta(X - M) = \quad 5$	$\Delta(X_2 - M_2) = -5$

Income in period 3, which is equal to the sum of domestic consumption, investment, and exports in period 2, is seen to rise to 314 in country 1 and fall to 287 in 2. Domestic consumption, imports, and saving therefore rise in 1 and fall in 2. The foreign repercussion effect can again be seen to be operative as 1's imports (2's exports) rise and 2's imports (1's exports) fall. These changes will serve further to reduce 1's trade surplus (2's deficit) to 3.2 in period 3.

Income in 1 will continue to increase and after the passage of an infinite number of periods will settle down to its new equilibrium value of 320, which is 20 greater than in the original equilibrium. The new equilibrium value of domestic consumption in country 1 will be 197, while exports and imports will be 103 and 101, respectively. Country 1 thus will have a permanent export surplus equal to 2, which is seen to be equal to the increase in saving, ΔS.[1] As income increases, the truncated multipliers can be observed also to increase until the full multiplier of 2 is attained in the new equilibrium.[2] We could of course have anticipated this result by calculating the static foreign trade multiplier for an autonomous change in country 1's exports:

$$\frac{\Delta Y}{\Delta X} = \frac{1}{s + m + m_2(s/s_2)} = \frac{1}{0.1 + 0.3 + 0.2(0.1/0.2)} = 2.$$

The new equilibrium value for income in country 2 is 290 and for domestic consumption, 174. Country 2's equilibrium exports (1's imports) are 101 and its imports (1's exports) are 103, yielding a permanent trade deficit which is evidently equal to the decline in saving, ΔS_2. Country 2's income shows a wave-like movement in the process of adjustment, falling from periods 1 to 4 and rising thereafter. This movement arises because the increase in income in 1 exceeds the decline in 2. As a consequence, the income-induced increase in 1's imports (2's exports) will become large enough to compensate for the induced decline in 2's income.[3] The equilibrium multiplier for 2 is seen to be equal to -1. That is:

$$\frac{\Delta Y_2}{\Delta M_2} = - \frac{1}{s_2 + m_2 + m(s_2/s)} = - \frac{1}{0.2 + 0.2 + 0.3(0.2/0.1)} = -1.$$

AUTONOMOUS INCREASE IN INVESTMENT IN COUNTRY 1

Using exactly the same model as in Table 6.A.1, let us assume, as indicated in Table 6.A.2, that there is an autonomous increase in investment of 10 in country 1 in period 1. Country 1's income in period 2 will thus be 310, its

1. Thus, country 1's trade balance in the new equilibrium can be expressed as

$$\Delta(X - M) = s\,\Delta Y.$$

Taking note of the fact that the change in 1's income can be expressed in terms of the multiplier formula noted in Table 6.4 for an autonomous increase in 1's exports, we can write:

$$\Delta(X - M) = \frac{s}{s + m + m_2(s/s_2)}\,\Delta X.$$

Dividing numerator and denominator by s, we obtain the expression for 1's ultimate trade surplus (2's ultimate trade deficit)

$$\Delta(X - M) = \frac{1}{1 + (m/s) + (m_2/s_2)}\,\Delta X = \frac{1}{1 + (.3/.1) + (.2/.2)}\,10 = 2.$$

See Machlup (1943; 1965, pp. 86–87) for further discussion of the above relations.
2. For the derivation of the multiplier as a function of time in a model such as we are using, see Machlup (1943; 1965, pp. 219–23).
3. See Machlup (1943; 1965, esp. pp. 83–84) for a discussion of waves in the sequence of income changes.

TABLE 6.A.2

The Dynamic Multiplier Process Involving Two Countries: Autonomous Increase in Investment in Country 1

Variable	How Calculated	Original Equilibrium	\[1\]	\[2\]	\[3\]	\[4\]	\[5\]	\[6\]	\[7\]	\[8\]	\[9\]	\[10\]	∞ New Equilibrium
Country 1													
Y	$(C_{t-1}) + (I_{t-1}) + (X_{t-1})$	300	300	310	316	320.2	323.44	326.07	328.25	330.08	331.62	332.92	340
C	$.6(Y_t) + 5$	185	185	191	194.6	197.12	199.06	200.64	201.95	203.05	203.97	204.75	209
I	Autonomous	20	30	30	30	30	30	30	30	30	30	30	30
X	$.2(Y_t)_2 + 35$	95	95	95	95.6	96.3	97	97.61	98.13	98.57	98.95	99.27	101
M	$.3(Y_t) + 5$	95	95	98	99.8	101.06	102.03	102.82	103.47	104.02	104.49	104.88	107
S	$(Y_t) - (C_t) - (M_t)$	20	20	21	21.6	22.02	22.34	22.61	22.82	23.01	23.16	23.29	24
ΔS	Cumulative	—	0	1	1.6	2.02	2.34	2.61	2.82	3.01	3.16	3.29	4
$\Delta(X - M)$	Cumulative	—	0	-3	-4.2	-4.74	-5.03	-5.21	-5.35	-5.45	-5.54	-5.61	-6
$\Delta(Y_t)$	Cumulative	—	0	10	16	20.2	23.44	26.07	28.25	30.08	31.62	32.92	40
$\Delta(Y_t)/\Delta I$	Cumulative	—	0	1	1.6	2.02	2.34	2.61	2.83	3.01	3.16	3.29	4
Country 2													
Y_2	$(C_{t-1})_2 + (I_{t-1})_2 + (X_{t-1})_2$	300	300	300	303	306.6	310.02	313.04	315.65	317.86	319.74	321.33	330
C_2	$.6(Y_t)_2 + 10$	190	190	190	191.8	193.96	196.01	197.83	199.39	200.72	201.84	202.8	208
I_2	Autonomous	15	15	15	15	15	15	15	15	15	15	15	15
X_2	$.3(Y_t) + 5$	95	95	98	99.8	101.06	102.03	102.82	103.47	104.02	104.49	104.88	107
M_2	$.2(Y_t)_2 + 35$	95	95	95	95.6	96.3	97	97.61	98.13	98.57	98.95	99.27	101
S_2	$(Y_t)_2 - (C_t)_2 - (M_t)_2$	15	15	15	15.6	16.32	17	17.61	18.13	18.57	18.95	19.27	21
ΔS_2	Cumulative	—	0	0	0.6	1.32	2	2.61	3.13	3.57	3.95	4.27	6
$\Delta(X_2 - M_2)$	Cumulative	—	0	3	4.2	4.74	5.03	5.21	5.35	5.45	5.54	5.61	6
$\Delta(Y_t)_2$	Cumulative	—	0	0	3	6.6	10.02	13.04	15.65	17.86	19.74	21.33	30
$\Delta(Y_t)_2/\Delta I$	Cumulative	—	0	0	0.3	0.66	1.0	1.3	1.56	1.79	1.97	2.13	3

consumption 191, imports 98, and saving 21. Assuming that the increase in 1's imports (2's exports) is attained instantaneously without disinvestment in 2, it is evident that country 1 will have a trade deficit in period 2 equal to -3 and country 2 will have a corresponding surplus.

With the increase in domestic consumption in country 1 in period 2, the higher level of investment, and unchanged exports, 1's income in period 3 will be 316. This can be seen to result in increased domestic consumption, imports, and saving in country 1. Since 2's income in period 3 will also be larger because its exports increased in the preceding period, it will also experience higher consumption, imports, and saving in period 3. Since the imports of both countries have risen, the foreign repercussion effect will serve to reinforce the rise in income in the two countries. As 1's income rises, its imports will increase. This worsening of 1's trade balance will be offset to some extent, however, by the increase in its exports induced by the increase in 2's income.

In the new equilibrium, 1's income will be 340 and its trade balance will be -6,[4] which is equal to the difference between investment and saving. Since with an increase in investment of 10, income in 1 increased by 40, the multiplier is equal to 4, that is

$$\frac{\Delta Y}{\Delta I} = \frac{1 + m_2/s_2}{s + m + m_2(s/s_2)} = \frac{1 + 0.2/0.2}{0.1 + 0.3 + 0.2(0.1/0.2)} = 4.$$

Country 2's new equilibrium income is 330, which is 30 above the original equilibrium value. This corresponds to a multiplier of 3 for the increase in investment in country 1:

$$\frac{\Delta Y_2}{\Delta I} = \frac{m}{(s + m)(s_2 + m_2) - mm_2} = \frac{0.3}{(0.4)(0.4) - 0.06} = 3.$$

4. Country 1's trade deficit (2's surplus) can be derived with the use of the foreign-trade-multiplier formulas noted in Table 6.3 for an autonomous change in investment in 1. That is, the change in income in the two countries will be:

$$\Delta Y = \frac{1 + m_2/s_2}{s + m + m_2(s/s_2)} \Delta I$$

$$\Delta Y_2 = \frac{m}{ss_2 + ms_2 + m_2s} \Delta I.$$

The change in country 1's exports and imports between the original and new equilibrium positions will be equal respectively to $m_2 \Delta Y_2$ and $m \Delta Y$. Multiplying the equation for ΔY by m and the equation for ΔY_2 by m_2 and subtracting these equations, country 1's ultimate trade deficit (2's surplus) will be:

$$m_2 \Delta Y_2 - m\Delta Y = \frac{-s_2 m}{(s + m)(s_2 + m_2) - mm_2} \Delta I$$

$$= 10 \frac{-(.2)(.3)}{(.4)(.4) - .06} = -6.$$

Ibid., esp. pp. 180–82, are given some additional points concerning the foregoing relations.

7

The Price and Income Approaches to Balance-of-Payments Adjustment

Our discussion in Chapters 3–5 of the reliance upon variations in relative prices for purposes of balance-of-payments adjustment was predicated generally on the maintenance of a full employment level of output (income), whereas prices were assumed for the most part to remain unchanged in our discussion in Chapter 6 of the effects on the balance of payments of variations in the level of output. In actuality, income and prices change together so that we need to combine our two approaches. Unfortunately, this is rather difficult to do in a formal manner because of the complexity of the relationships. We shall nevertheless go part of the way and hope that our analysis does not do too much violence to reality.

We set out first, therefore, using a formal model, to analyze the effects of a devaluation when the level of output is permitted to change, and in this regard to indicate the conditions under which the devaluing country's trade balance may be improved. The objective here is to incorporate variations in relative prices and changes in the level of output into a single analysis. We shall then delve a bit further into the analysis of a devaluation in the context of the income-absorption framework that was first suggested by Alexander (1952) as an alternative to the traditional approach based on variations in relative prices. We shall have occasion here to consider the relative merits of the two approaches for purposes of analysis. We examine, finally, the implications suggested by our discussion with regard to balance-of-payments analysis and policy.

The Effects of Devaluation upon National Income and the Balance of Trade[1]

The analysis of devaluation to be presented is to be carried out under conditions that permit outputs to change. This will be in contrast to our earlier

1. I am indebted to Jay H. Levin and especially to J. David Richardson for working out and simplifying the mathematical details of the model presented in this section and for clarifying a number of points in the discussion.

discussion when outputs were assumed to remain unchanged at their full employment level. We shall deal with two cases. In the first, stabilization policies in the rest of the world are assumed to negate the effects of the devaluation on foreign output. In other words, foreign repercussion effects are prevented from occurring by virtue of the policy maintenance of foreign real output. In the second case, devaluation is allowed to run its course abroad and foreign repercussion effects are explicitly taken into account.

In order to keep the analysis manageable, we shall stay within the framework of our two-country, two-goods model that has been the basis of our earlier discussion. Constant costs are assumed. This means that the supply of output in each country is perfectly elastic with respect to price. That is domestic currency prices do not change. Each country is assumed to be stable in isolation.[2] It is presumed furthermore that the monetary authorities at home and abroad peg the interest rate. We shall have occasion subsequently to consider how the relaxing of some of these assumptions affects our conclusions. We shall abstract throughout from changes in the long-term capital account.

The following notation will be used:

B = Trade (current-account) balance measured in country 1's currency

X = Country 1's export volume

M = Country 1's import volume

D = National expenditure in country 1

Y = Gross national product in country 1

D_2 = National expenditure in country 2

Y_2 = Gross national product in country 2

r = Rate of exchange (in units of domestic currency per unit of foreign currency)

p = Price of country 1's output

p_2 = Price of country 2's output

p^i = Price index in country 1

p_2^i = Price index in country 2

$a = \dfrac{rp_2 M}{D}$ = Proportion of national expenditure in country 1 spent on imports

$a_2 = \dfrac{pX/r}{D_2}$ = Proportion of national expenditure in country 2 spent on imports.

2. In the context of equation (7.3) below, stability in isolation means that the partial derivative of real expenditure with respect to real income is less than one.

FOREIGN REPERCUSSION EFFECTS ABSENT

The model to be used for purposes of analysis is as follows, with the signs of the derivatives indicated as $+$ or $-$:

$$\text{(Definition)} \qquad B = pX - rp_2 M \qquad\qquad (7.1)$$

$$\text{(Equilibrium condition)} \qquad Y = D + B \qquad\qquad (7.2)$$

$$\text{(Behavioral equation)} \qquad \frac{D}{p^i} = D\left(\overset{+}{\frac{Y}{p^i}}\right) \qquad\qquad (7.3)$$

$$\text{(Definition)} \qquad p^i = arp_2 + (1 - a)p \qquad\qquad (7.4)$$

$$\text{(Behavioral equations)} \qquad \begin{cases} M = M(\overset{+}{Y}, \overset{+}{p}, r\overset{-}{p}_2) & (7.5) \\[2mm] X = X\left(\overset{+}{Y}_2, \overset{+}{\frac{p}{r}}, \overset{+}{p}_2\right) & (7.6) \end{cases}$$

As noted, the domestic currency price of domestic output in country 1 and the foreign currency price of output in country 2 are assumed constant. For convenience, these prices have been set equal to unity. Units of currency are assumed to be similarly chosen in order to make the initial exchange rate equal to unity. Equation (7.1) defines country 1's trade (current-account) balance in domestic currency. Equation (7.2) is the equilibrium condition for country 1. Equation (7.3) states that real national expenditure (consumption plus investment) in country 1 depends upon real national income. Real variables are represented as nominal variables divided by the price index, which is defined in equation (7.4) as a weighted average of foreign and domestic prices. The weights are the proportion of expenditure spent on foreign and domestic goods, respectively. Equation (7.5) assumes that the volume of imports depends upon national income and all prices, and will be homogeneous of degree zero if there is no money illusion. Equation (7.6) is analogous to (7.5).[3]

Differentiating totally the foregoing model and making use of the assumption that prices are initially equal to unity, we have:

$$dB = dX - dM - M\,dr \qquad\qquad (7.1')$$

$$dY = dD + dB \qquad\qquad (7.2')$$

3. We shall abstract in what follows from the possibility that exchange-rate variations may affect the propensities to consume domestic goods and to import. This is in contrast to such writers as Laursen and Metzler (1950) and Johnson (1956), who argue that the marginal effects on consumption and saving and on imports will be different for increases in real output as compared to changes in the terms of trade due to exchange-rate variations. We shall examine these differences in marginal effects in our treatment of the transfer problem in the next chapter. However, in our subsequent discussion in Chapter 10 of policies for internal and external balance, we shall revert to the treatment adopted in the present chapter.

$$dD = (1 - s) \, dY + [D - (1 - s)Y] \, dp^i \qquad (7.3')$$

$$dp^i = a \, dr \qquad (7.4')$$

$$dM = m \, dY + M\eta_m \, dr \qquad (7.5')$$

$$dX = X\eta_x \, dr \qquad (7.6')$$

where $(1 - s) = \partial(D/p^i)/\partial(Y/p^i)$;[4] $m = \partial M/\partial Y$, which is the marginal propensity to import; η_m is the elasticity of demand in country 1 for imports; and η_x is the elasticity of demand in country 2 for country 1's exports.[5]

To find the effect of a devaluation on the trade balance, we are interested in the value attached to dB/dr. To determine this, first substitute from (7.5') and (7.6') into (7.1'):

$$dB = (X\eta_x - M\eta_m - M) \, dr - m \, dY. \qquad (7.7)$$

Then, to find an expression for dY, substitute (7.4') into (7.3') and substitute the result into (7.2') to obtain:

$$dY = (1 - s) \, dY + [D - (1 - s)Y] \, a \, dr + dB.$$

To simplify the exposition, let us assume that trade is balanced $(B = 0)$, in which case we know from equation (7.2) that $Y = D$. Recalling that $a = rp_2 M/D = M/D$, then $[D - (1 - s)Y]a = sM$, and we have:

$$dY = (1 - s) \, dY + sM \, dr + dB$$

or[6]

$$dY = M \, dr + \frac{dB}{s} . \qquad (7.8)$$

4. In Chapter 6, s referred to the marginal propensity to save. Here it will be the "marginal propensity not to spend," or in Alexander's terminology (1959) the "marginal propensity to hoard." The derivation of equation (7.3') proceeds as follows:

$$d\left(\frac{D}{p^i}\right) = (1 - s)d\left(\frac{Y}{p^i}\right).$$

Remembering that prices have been set equal to unity, we have:

$$dD - Ddp^i = (1 - s)(dY - Ydp^i)$$

from which we obtain (7.3').

5. Note that since $\eta_m \equiv (r/M)(\partial M/\partial r)$, it follows that $\partial M/\partial r \equiv (M/r)(r/M)(\partial M/\partial r) \equiv (M/r)\eta_m$. Since we have set $r = 1$, the second term in (7.5') has been written as $M\eta_m \, dr$. The elasticities are taken in the model to be negative, η_m, and positive, η_x, respectively. Equation (7.4') should be interpreted to the effect that the domestic price index changes proportionally with the exchange rate, depending upon how much expenditure goes for foreign goods. In deriving (7.4'), note again that prices are assumed equal to unity and to be unchanged.

6. In order to determine how income changes with a devaluation, we can rewrite equation (7.8) as:

$$\frac{dY}{dr} = M + \frac{1}{s}\left(\frac{dB}{dr}\right).$$

Continued on p. 208

Substituting (7.8) back into (7.7), we obtain a relation strictly in terms of dB and dr:

$$dB = (X\eta_x - M\eta_m - M)\, dr - m\left(M\, dr + \frac{dB}{s}\right)$$

or

$$\frac{dB}{dr} = \left(\frac{s}{s+m}\right)[X\eta_x - M\eta_m - (1+m)M]. \tag{7.9}$$

It is interesting that the first term in equation (7.9) is the multiplier, dB/dX, that is (see Table 6.4 above), the change in the balance of payments with respect to an autonomous change in exports without foreign repercussions. The question now is to determine the condition under which a devaluation will improve the trade balance, that is $dB/dr > 0$. Looking at the second term in (7.9), if trade is initially balanced ($X = M$), this term will be greater than unity only if

$$\eta_x - \eta_m > 1 + m, \tag{7.10}$$

which says that devaluation will improve the trade balance if the sum of the elasticities is greater than one plus the marginal propensity to import in the devaluing country. This condition is more stringent than the Marshall-Lerner condition derived earlier in Chapters 2 and 5, under the assumption of unchanged income, to the effect that devaluation will improve the trade balance so long as the sum of the elasticities is greater than one. The difference stems from the fact that in equation (7.3) there is a direct effect of price

---

Money income will thus increase with a devaluation as long as the devaluation is successful, that is, $dB/dr > 0$. In the event that $dB/dr = 0$, money income will rise since $dY/dr = M$, but real income will be unchanged. If the trade balance improves, real income will go up and conversely if the trade balance deteriorates with a devaluation. To see this, note that:

$$\frac{d(Y/p^i)}{dr} = \frac{dY}{dr} - Y\frac{dp^i}{dr},$$

assuming prices are equal to unity. We can substitute for dp^i/dr from (7.4') and for dY/dr from (7.8) to obtain:

$$\frac{d(Y/p^i)}{dr} = M + \frac{1}{s}\left(\frac{dB}{dr}\right) - Ya.$$

Since $a = rp_2 M/D$ and if trade is balanced, $Y = D$. It follows therefore that since $Ya = M$, we have:

$$\frac{d(Y/p^i)}{dr} = \frac{1}{s}\left(\frac{dB}{dr}\right)$$

and the foregoing statements concerning the behavior of real income in relation to dB/dr will hold.

changes, *ceteris paribus*, upon expenditures. This is sometimes referred to as the "terms-of-trade" effect on expenditures.[7]

FOREIGN REPERCUSSION EFFECTS PRESENT

Certain additions must be made to the foregoing model when foreign repercussion effects are admitted. These are as follows:

$$Y_2 = D_2 - \frac{B}{r} \tag{7.11}$$

$$\frac{D_2}{p_2^i} = D_2 \left(\overset{+}{\frac{Y_2}{p_2^i}} \right) \tag{7.12}$$

$$p_2^i = a_2 \left(\frac{p}{r} \right) + (1 - a_2) p_2. \tag{7.13}$$

These equations, which refer to country 2, are analogous to equations (7.2), (7.3), and (7.4) above. The full differentiated model is now:

$$dB = dX - dM - M\, dr \tag{7.1'}$$

$$dY = dD + dB \tag{7.2'}$$

$$dD = (1 - s)\, dY + [D - (1 - s)Y]\, dp^i \tag{7.3'}$$

$$dp^i = a\, dr \tag{7.4'}$$

$$dM = m\, dY + M\eta_m\, dr \tag{7.5'}$$

$$dX = m_2\, dY_2 + X\eta_x\, dr \tag{7.6''}$$

$$dY_2 = dD_2 - dB + B \tag{7.11'}$$

$$dD_2 = (1 - s_2)\, dY_2 + [D_2 - (1 - s_2)Y_2]\, dp_2^i \tag{7.12'}$$

$$dp_2^i = -a_2\, dr \tag{7.13'}$$

where s, m, η_m, and η_x are as already defined; $m_2 = \partial X / \partial Y_2$, which is country 2's marginal propensity to import; and $(1 - s_2) = \partial (D_2/p_2^i) / \partial (Y_2/p_2^i)$.

This system can be solved for dB/dr in the same way as before. First

7. It would appear from equation (7.10) that, given stability in isolation, the more stringent condition on the sum of the elasticities of demand is both necessary and sufficient for the trade balance to improve. For earlier analyses that reach this conclusion, see Harberger (1950), Johnson (1956), Jones (1960), and Tsiang (1961). Recently, however, the generality of this conclusion has been questioned, especially when a monetary sector is explicitly considered. Using general equilibrium models, Hahn (1959) and Negishi (1968) emphasize the role of gross substitutability among all goods in determining the necessary and sufficient conditions for trade-balance improvement. Negishi (1968, p. 226) questions in particular the common interpretation of the various elasticities conditions as "stability" conditions for the foreign exchange market. See Krueger (1969, pp. 10–11) and Negishi (1968, pp. 218–20) for additional discussion.

substitute from (7.5') and (7.6'') into (7.1') to obtain an equation analogous to (7.7), only with an additional term, $m_2 \, dY_2$:

$$dB = (X\eta_x - M\eta_m - M) \, dr - m \, dY + m_2 \, dY_2. \qquad (7.14)$$

Then, to find expressions for dY and dY_2, substitute (7.4') and (7.3') into (7.2') as before and (7.13') and (7.12') into (7.11'). Again assuming that trade is initially balanced ($B = 0$) so that $Y = D$ and $Y_2 = D_2$ and recalling the definitions of a, a_2, s, and s_2, we obtain equation (7.8) as above for country 1 and an analogous equation for country 2:

$$dY = M \, dr + \frac{dB}{s} \qquad (7.8)$$

$$dY_2 = -X \, dr - \frac{dB}{s_2}. \qquad (7.15)$$

Substituting (7.8) and (7.15) back into (7.14) above, we have:

$$dB = (X\eta_x - M\eta_m - M) \, dr - m\left(M \, dr + \frac{dB}{s}\right) + m_2\left(-X \, dr - \frac{dB}{s_2}\right)$$

or

$$\frac{dB}{dr} = \left[\frac{s}{s + m + m_2(s/s_2)}\right][X\eta_x - M\eta_m - (1 + m)M - m_2X]. \qquad (7.16)$$

It will be noted that the first term in equation (7.16) is the multiplier, dB/dX, that was obtained in Table 6.4, Chapter 6, for an autonomous change in exports with foreign repercussions taken into account. The impact of a devaluation on the trade balance can now be determined by evaluating the second term in equation (7.16). If trade is balanced initially ($X = M$), this term will be greater than unity only if

$$\eta_x - \eta_m > 1 + m + m_2. \qquad (7.17)$$

That is, the sum of the elasticities must be greater than one plus the sum of the marginal propensities to import in order for a devaluation to improve the trade balance. We again see that when income-induced changes in trade are taken into account, the condition for a successful devaluation is more stringent than the simple Marshall-Lerner condition.[8]

RELAXING THE CONSTANT COST AND INTEREST-RATE ASSUMPTIONS

It is possible to make the foregoing model more general by permitting prices to vary directly with output. As shown in the appendix to this chapter, the

8. The analysis is changed somewhat when one or both countries are unstable in isolation. For details, see Tsiang (1961; 1968, pp. 404–05).

inclusion in the model of rising prices does not affect the critical values of the elasticities of demand required for a devaluation to improve the balance of trade, as long as we can assume that the terms of trade deteriorate. In this case, however, a devaluation will result in a smaller absolute improvement in the balance of trade than in the case of constant domestic prices just examined. This result will hold both when foreign repercussions are ignored and when they are considered. Moreover, if the terms of trade do not deteriorate, it can be shown that the balance of trade actually becomes more negative when the more stringent conditions hold as in equations (7.10) and (7.17). Put differently, taking these latter conditions for granted, a successful devaluation necessarily implies a deterioration in the terms of trade.

It is also possible to take interest-rate considerations into account in terms of the demand for money in the two countries. We shall refrain from doing so on a formal basis and instead shall indicate qualitatively how the results of the model would be affected.[9] We noted in Chapter 6 that the pegging of the rate of interest by maintaining an infinitely elastic supply of money and credit at the going rate was a standard feature of Keynesian models of national income determination. This kind of monetary policy, which Tsiang (1961; 1968, p. 401) has called "Keynesian neutral monetary policy," may be acceptable in dealing with underemployment conditions. But it has drastic implications for exchange-rate stability once resources are literally fully employed. When this point is reached, the elasticity of supply of domestic output becomes zero, with the consequence that devaluation would have no effect whatever on the balance of trade. If we add to this the possibilities of market-power inflation with the approach to full employment and speculative capital movements in anticipation of a change in the exchange rate, the instability would be heightened. A policy of continuous monetary expansion under such conditions would thus be disastrous for exchange-rate stability.[10]

In contrast, what Tsiang (1961; 1968, p. 401) called "orthodox neutral monetary policy" can play an important stabilizing role in the foreign exchange market. This will be because of the interest-rate variations that will occur when there is a devaluation and the money supply is kept unchanged.[11] What will happen then is that there will be a reduction in aggregate expenditure as the rate of interest rises with a devaluation at full employment

9. For a formal treatment, see Tsiang (1961; 1968, pp. 404–10) and Richardson (1971a).

10. This is what Tsiang claims to have been the case in France during the period in the 1920's when the franc was freely fluctuating. See our earlier discussion in Chapter 3 for additional details.

11. Tsiang points out (1961; 1968, p. 408) that there will be stability at full employment in these circumstances even if the marginal propensity to spend were equal to or greater than unity. The interest rate will also respond to changes in fiscal policy when the supply of money is unchanged. We shall have occasion later in this chapter and at greater length in Chapter 10 to analyze changes in both monetary and fiscal policies in the attainment of internal and external balance.

insofar as individuals and firms strive to maintain the real value of their money-cash balances. Evidently then, monetary factors play a crucial role in terms of the way in which adjustments in relative prices and income and expenditures work together in determining the effect of a devaluation.

This focus on the role of monetary factors in the adjustment process is a direct outgrowth of the development, originating with Alexander (1952), of the income-absorption approach to the analysis of a devaluation. It is worthwhile examining this approach especially since Alexander contended that it was superior to the traditional elasticities approach that we have already treated at length.

The Income-Absorption and Elasticity Approaches
to the Analysis of a Devaluation

We have seen in the traditional approach to the analysis of a devaluation under conditions of full employment that the effect on the balance of trade depended principally upon the home and foreign elasticities of the demand and supply of imports and exports. That is, when relative prices change due to a devaluation, the elasticities will tell us something about the substitution effects that will occur. What our previous discussion in this chapter has made clear, however, is that in addition to the substitution effects there may be income effects as well. Thus, to the extent that the elasticities in question reflect both income and substitution effects, they must be considered as "total" rather than partial elasticities.

The question then is how important changes in income will be. The smaller such changes, the more closely will the elasticities approximate the pure substitution effects. However, under conditions of underemployment when variations in income may be substantial, the meaningfulness of price elasticities is open to doubt because the demand and supply schedules in question will be shifted around a good deal as real output changes. It was for this reason that Alexander (1952) suggested that an approach based upon aggregate income and expenditure considerations was to be preferred to the elasticities approach.[12]

12. Thus, according to Alexander (1952; 1968, p. 360):

Partial elasticities measure the effect of a change of price on the quantity supplied or demanded when all other things remain equal. Total elasticities relevant to a devaluation measure the corresponding relationship when the other things have changed that are likely to change as a result of the devaluation. Accordingly, a total elasticity does not measure the direct effects of price changes on quantity, but the covariation of price and quantity as the whole economic system seeks a new equilibrium. . . . Therefore the total elasticities appropriate for the analysis of the effects of a devaluation depend on the behavior of the whole economic system, and the statement that the effect of a devaluation depends on the elasticities boils down to the statement that it depends on how the economic system behaves.

The starting point in Alexander's analysis is to be found in the income-expenditure identity noted in the preceding chapter:

$$Y \equiv C + I + G + X - M,$$

where Y is national income, C is private consumption expenditure (including imports), I is private investment expenditure, G is government expenditure on goods and services, and X and M are exports and imports of goods and services. All measurement is supposed to be in real terms, and no autonomous capital movements are to be permitted. This equation can be shortened by combining the $C + I + G$ expenditure terms into a single term, A, representing absorption (i.e., total domestic expenditure) and the $X - M$ terms can be represented by B, the trade balance. Thus we have:

$$Y \equiv A + B, \tag{7.18}$$

which says that national income equals absorption plus the trade balance, or alternatively:

$$B \equiv Y - A, \tag{7.19}$$

which says simply that the trade balance is the difference between income and absorption.

According to Alexander, a devaluation could affect the trade balance in two ways by: (1) the change in income and the income-induced change in absorption that would result, and (2) the direct change in absorption. In his original analysis (1952; 1968, pp. 362–70), he considered several different effects that devaluation might have upon income and absorption. Since relative price changes were presumably absent from the model, the income-absorption effects were the focus of the adjustment process. This struck some observers, Machlup in particular (1955), as strange since the response to relative price changes was considered to be the essence of the adjustment process set into motion by a devaluation. While it would take us too far afield to discuss in detail all Machlup's criticisms of Alexander, some of these criticisms are especially noteworthy because they call attention to the crucial role that monetary considerations play in the analysis.

The income-expenditure identity and equations (7.18) and (7.19) based upon it were presumed by Alexander to hold both in real and money terms. While this equivalence is possible in a closed economy, Machlup pointed out (1955; 1964, p. 185) that this cannot be the case in an open economy. That is, while it makes sense to think of exports and imports separately in real terms, the difference between exports and imports can only be conceived in money terms. Thus, a change in a country's trade balance corresponds in money terms to a change in foreign debts or claims. A surplus or deficit on trade or current account is essentially then a *monetary* rather than a real phenomenon.

Once the monetary nature of a payments imbalance has been recognized, some important policy implications follow with regard to correcting the imbalance. Machlup noted here (1955; 1964, pp. 188–90) the role that official reserves play in financing a payments deficit under pegged exchange rates. The point he emphasized was that once the authorities stopped financing the deficit by selling reserves, the deficit would disappear automatically via exchange-rate depreciation. He went on further to point out that a negative trade balance can persist only if there is a continued dishoarding of idle cash balances or an expansion of bank credit made possible by the authorities. Otherwise the negative trade balance could not continue. Thus, assumptions concerning the supply of money were held by Machlup to be of crucial importance in the analysis of a devaluation.[13]

It will be recalled that Alexander criticized the price approach on the grounds that the relevant total elasticities were neither given nor knowable. Machlup's response (1955; 1964, pp. 191–92) was that the same argument applied even more to the marginal propensity to spend, since it could not be expected to be stable over time. He stated (1955; 1964, p. 192):

> From the point of view of changeability in the very process the outcome of which they help determine, the spending propensities are less reliable than the price elasticities. And from the point of view of malleability through public policy, one probably should regard the price elasticities as the tougher factors to deal with, and the spending propensities more subject to the influence of (monetary and fiscal) policy—which means in the last analysis not given propensities but chosen policies will determine the outcome.

In the light of all the foregoing considerations, Machlup concluded (1955; 1964, p. 194) that aggregate spending and propensities were by themselves not sufficient to do the job that Alexander had assigned to them. Rather, both the price and the income-absorption approaches were needed to analyze the effects of a devaluation.

The question then is that if both sets of tools are needed, how should we proceed in employing them? One possible procedure is the one adopted in our earlier discussion in this chapter. We showed in equations (7.9) and (7.16) that the effects of a devaluation on the trade balance could be analyzed by means of an expression containing terms for a foreign trade multiplier and a more stringent Marshall-Lerner sum-of-the-elasticities condition. This result was obtained, however, only because we had assumed constant costs

---

13. In Machlup's words (1955; 1964, pp. 190–91):

If the chief purpose of devaluing a country's currency is to remove or reduce a deficit in its balance of international payments, consistency implies a policy of monetary restraint. For, by and large, devaluation achieves its purpose by effectively reducing the foreign value of the domestic money supply and of the volume of domestic spending. A monetary policy which allows domestic spending to increase subsequently and regain its previous (presumably excessive) foreign value is clearly inconsistent with the purpose of the devaluation.

in each country. Once we permit prices (and interest rates) to vary with increases in output, as Tsiang (1961; 1968, pp. 389–90) has noted,

> ...the multiplier effect of the initial change in the trade balance will bring about further changes in relative prices, and hence further substitution between imports and domestically produced goods in both countries. Thus if the conventional elasticities solution is treated as a sort of multiplicand, to which a multiplier (or a damping coefficient) is to be applied to obtain the final effect, then the multiplier itself should again involve the relevant elasticities that are in the multiplicand. There can be no neat dichotomy of the final effect of a devaluation into a part that consists of the elasticities solution and another that consists of the multiplier (or absorption solution). The total effect of a devaluation must be analyzed in a comprehensive system in which changes in incomes, prices and outputs are all taken into consideration.

Models such as Tsiang's (1961) and the ones developed in the appendix to this chapter bear witness to the complexities quickly encountered in trying to develop a more comprehensive system incorporating changes in incomes, prices, and outputs.[14] Rather than pursue the formal analysis any further, therefore, it may be fruitful at this point to examine some of the policy implications that our previous discussion suggests.

Policy Implications of the Income-Absorption Approach[15]

We have already noted that a deficit in a country's balance of payments can persist only so long as: (1) domestic residents ran down their cash balances in exchange for foreign currency provided by the monetary authority from its international reserves; or (2) the monetary authority engaged in credit creation to replenish the cash holdings of its residents by means of open market operations or relending of domestic currency received. In the first instance, the deficit would be self-correcting when residents felt it no longer desirable to continue reducing their cash balances and took steps in response to rising interest rates and tightened credit conditions to restore their cash balances to a higher level. This presumes, however, that the monetary authority has sufficient international reserves to finance the deficit until the corrective forces take effect. The removal of the deficit in the second instance requires clearly that the monetary authority cease expanding credit.

14. It is of interest to note that, subsequent to his original article and criticisms by Machlup and others, Alexander (1959) attempted a synthesis of the elasticities and absorption approaches. While his synthesis contains many useful insights, it is subject to Tsiang's criticism that it is not valid to dichotomize the analysis of a devaluation, when prices vary, into a relative price effect and a multiplier effect.

15. The seminal article on this subject is by Johnson (1958b; 1968). Much of what follows is based upon his discussion.

In analyzing the decisions that may have led to a deficit, Johnson has suggested that a distinction be made between "stock" and "flow" balance-of-payments deficits.[16] He pointed out (1958b; 1968, p. 379) that inasmuch as a stock decision involved a "once-for-all change in the composition of a given aggregate of capital assets, a 'stock' deficit must be a temporary affair; and itself implies no deterioration (but rather the reverse) in the country's economic position and prospects." A flow deficit, in contrast, may not be a temporary affair and, further, may be indicative of a deterioration in the country's economic position.

Since a stock deficit is temporary in character, the monetary authority need not be concerned unduly so long as their international reserves are sufficient to finance the deficit brought about by the change in asset composition. Some policy action may be required to deal with the deficit, however, in case reserves are not adequate. In such an event, according to Johnson, the authorities will have to decide whether to restrict credit, devalue, or impose controls over international trade or payments. The effects of credit restriction and devaluation upon the holdings of stocks of imported goods or foreign securities are meant to be achieved through the market mechanism. These effects could be overshadowed, however, by changes in expectations that may result in larger rather than smaller stock holdings. Given such circumstances, an argument can be made in favor of direct control measures. All of this presumes in the first place of course that international reserves were insufficient, which suggests that steps should be taken to deal with this state of affairs if indeed it is the root of the difficulties.

We have already noted that a flow deficit will not be self-correcting so long as the monetary authority continues to create credit. In considering alternative policies to deal with flow deficits, it is useful to cast the discussion in terms of the already familiar identity of the trade balance and the difference between national income and absorption (i.e., expenditure): $B \equiv Y - A$. Ruling out the growth complications arising from consideration of long-term capital movements, this identity suggests that the correction of a balance-of-payments deficit requires making real output, Y, equal to real expenditures, A. In other

16. Thus, he stated (1958b; 1968, p. 379):

Two sorts of aggregate decision leading to a balance-of-payments deficit may be distinguished in principle, corresponding to the distinction drawn in monetary theory between 'stock' decisions and 'flow' decisions: a (stock) decision to alter the composition of the community's assets by substituting other assets for domestic money, and a (flow) decision to spend currently in excess of current receipts. Since both real goods and securities are alternative assets to domestic money, and current expenditure may consist in the purchase of either goods or securities, the balance-of-payments deficit resulting from either type of aggregate decision may show itself on either current or capital account. That is, a current account deficit may reflect either a community decision to shift out of cash balances into stocks of goods, or a decision to use goods in excess of the community's current rate of production, while a capital account deficit may reflect either a decision to shift out of domestic money into securities or a decision to lend in excess of the current rate of saving.

words, the deficit can be corrected by policies whose initial impact is designed to increase output or to reduce expenditures.

As Johnson has pointed out (1958b; 1968, p. 382), the distinction just made can be looked at in another way:

> Since output is governed by the demand for it, a change in output can only be brought about by a change in the demand for it; a policy of increasing domestic output can only be effected by operating on expenditure (either foreign or domestic) on that output. Given the level of expenditure, this in turn involves a switch of expenditure (by residents and foreigners) from foreign output to domestic output. The distinction between output-increasing and expenditure-decreasing policies, which rests on the *effects* of the policies, may therefore be replaced by a distinction between expenditure-switching and expenditure-reducing policies, which rests on the *method* by which the effects are achieved.

Expenditure-reducing policies can be implemented, according to Johnson (1958b; 1968, pp. 382–83), through several means, including credit restriction, budgetary policy, and direct controls. This method of dealing with a deficit will be unattractive, however, if a deficit is coupled with recession because the recession may be made worse. There is also a question of how large a proportion of the expenditure reduction will fall on domestically produced goods. The different policy measures may vary in this regard so that the choice of measures will depend upon whether there are inflationary or deflationary forces present. It may be mentioned, finally, that to the extent that expenditure-reducing policies result in price deflation domestically, some degree of expenditure switching may occur.

Johnson has noted (1958b; 1968, p. 383) that there are two main types of expenditure-switching policies: devaluation (including domestic price deflation), which is a general type of policy measure, and trade controls (including tariffs, subsidies, and quantitative restrictions), which are selective in nature. Both types of policies are aimed at switching expenditure away from foreign goods and towards home goods. The success of these policies will thus depend on switching demand in the correct direction and also on the ability of the economy to supply the output which is necessary to meet the added demand.

It will be recognized that the question of switching demand in the correct direction depends upon the relevant demand elasticities for exports and imports being sufficiently high so as to insure an improvement in the trade balance. As for the supply of additional output that is required, different considerations will apply depending on the level of employment. Thus, if there are underemployed resources, the additional output needed can of course be obtained by increasing domestic production. Expenditure-switching will thus have favorable effects upon income and employment under these circumstances. When there is full employment, however, the requisite output can be had only by effecting a reduction in expenditure either directly by policy or as a result of the inflationary effects that will be induced by the switch policy. As Johnson has noted (1958b; 1968, p. 385), it is the explicit recognition of this last point that one might consider to be the most significant contribution of the absorption approach.

This can be simply illustrated. Suppose we have a country in balance-of-payments deficit under inflationary circumstances. If, say, a devaluation were undertaken without any other change in policy, expenditures would be switched towards home goods. The result would be a worsening of the inflation. Now it is possible that inflation may work to reduce aggregate expenditure through one or more of the direct absorption effects posited by Alexander in his original analysis. Thus, for example, assuming an inflexible money supply, an increase in the domestic price level would reduce the real value of the cash balances of money-holders. Individuals and firms would then be motivated to restore the real value of their cash balances by reducing their expenditures and selling some of their assets. The sale of assets would cause the rate of interest to rise, which might in turn reduce expenditures. While it is possible that foreign investors would be attracted by the reduction in asset prices, we have ruled out such capital movements by assumption. The cash-balance effect would thus operate directly through the reduction of expenditures and indirectly through increases in the rate of interest. Another example of a direct absorption effect that might result from an increase in the price level due to devaluation is a redistribution of income at the expense of fixed income recipients and wage earners and in favor of firms and government in the form of higher profits and taxes. The net effect on absorption and the trade balance would of course depend upon the difference between the marginal propensities to spend of those disfavored and bene-fited by the income redistribution. What is noteworthy here, as Johnson pointed out (1958b; 1968, p. 386), is that these absorption effects depend upon monetary and aggregate expenditure considerations rather than upon elasticity factors.[17]

17. This is not to say, however, that these matters are mutually exclusive and that the absorption and elasticity approaches are in conflict. Rather, the opposite is the case, for as Michaely has demonstrated (1960, p. 146), under conditions of full employment:

> . . . an increase in the ratio of international to domestic prices, which is essential for a decrease in the import surplus according to the relative-prices approach, can take place if and only if there is a decrease of absorption, and a decrease of absorption can occur only if there is an increase in the general price level. Hence the two approaches to the analysis of devaluation must lead to the same conclusions.

See Yeager (1970) for a fuller reconciliation of the two approaches. Krueger (1971) has developed a model incorporating home goods and money in the analysis of exchange-rate adjustment. She shows that a trade deficit can be eliminated only by reducing the excess supply of money *and* lowering the relative price of home goods.

In Chapter 11 below, we shall have occasion to examine more explicitly the balance-of-payments implications that money has in the context of economic growth. Johnson (1971b) presents a monetary framework for balance-of-payments theory that suggests some new departures that go beyond the elasticities and absorption approaches.

It is unlikely, however, that the monetary authority would seek to achieve balance-of-payments adjustment via the inflation process. Certainly it would be much simpler and more direct to couple the expenditure-switching policy with a policy of expenditure reduction. Attention would have to be given of course to designing an expenditure-reducing policy that would have its greatest impact in releasing goods for export and cutting down on imports as opposed to cutting down the demand for nontraded goods. In the latter case, it would be necessary for resources to be shifted to the production of exports and imports substitutes, which may be difficult without incurring some unemployment if factors cannot be easily moved. It would thus appear in this case as well as the one discussed in the preceding paragraph that elasticity considerations may be subordinate to the factors at issue in deciding upon the impact of an expenditure-reducing policy for balance-of-payments purposes.[18]

Conclusion

We presented in this chapter a formal analysis of devaluation that incorporated both variations in relative prices and changes in the level of output. It was shown under fairly restrictive assumptions, especially with regard to the constancy of domestic and foreign prices and the constancy of the marginal propensities with respect to changes in the terms of trade, that the Marshall-Lerner condition for an improvement of the trade balance had to be modified to include terms for the marginal propensity to import. If prices were permitted to vary, the condition for improvement in the trade balance remains the same, but the amount of such improvement would be smaller than if prices were constant. Although interest rates were not introduced formally into the model, their importance for trade-balance stability was shown by contrasting the potentially explosive effects at full employment of continuous monetary expansion as in the standard Keynesian model with the stabilizing effects of interest-rate variation as in the orthodox model. It was concluded finally that the analysis of a devaluation should be based on a comprehensive model that permitted incomes, prices, and output to change. This meant that the analysis could not be broken down neatly into an elasticities solution and an income-absorption solution.

Although subject to much criticism, Alexander's development of the absorption approach was of fundamental importance because it focused attention upon balance-of-payments problems as essentially monetary phenomena. This meant that policies dealing with the balance of payments had to take monetary considerations explicitly into account. The kinds of

18. Nurkse (1961, p. 193–94) has suggested with regard to a policy of expenditure reduction that the measures taken should be thought of in terms of shifting the export-supply (or import-demand) schedule. He pointed out that it might be inappropriate, therefore, to talk, strictly speaking, in terms of elasticities since they cannot be defined to take policy changes into account.

policies to be followed were treated in terms of Johnson's distinction between stock and flow decisions leading to a balance-of-payments deficit, and the need for policies to accomplish expenditure reduction and/or expenditure switching in correcting the deficit. Since many of the factors at work in evaluating the effects of these policies were of a monetary nature and involved aggregate expenditure considerations, it was concluded that the absorption and elasticities approaches to balance-of-payments analysis and policy had to go hand in hand.

Appendix: The Analysis of a Devaluation with Variations in Domestic and Foreign Prices[1]

Our purpose here will be to analyze the effects of a devaluation on the trade balance when prices are permitted to vary at home and abroad. The authorities are assumed to hold interest rates constant in what amounts to a "Keynesian-neutral" monetary policy.[2] The model is the one referring to the two-country case, with foreign repercussions, examined earlier:

$$B \equiv pX - rp_2M \tag{7.A.1}$$

$$Y = D + B \tag{7.A.2}$$

$$\frac{D}{p^i} = D\left(\overset{+}{\frac{Y}{p^i}}\right) \tag{7.A.3}$$

$$p^i \equiv arp_2 + (1 - a)p \tag{7.A.4}$$

$$M = M(\overset{+}{Y}, \overset{+}{p}, \overset{-}{rp_2}) \tag{7.A.5}$$

$$X = X\left(\overset{+}{Y_2}, \overset{-}{\frac{p}{r}}, \overset{+}{p_2}\right) \tag{7.A.6}$$

$$Y_2 = D_2 - \frac{B}{r} \tag{7.A.7}$$

$$\frac{D_2}{p_2^i} = D_2\left(\overset{+}{\frac{Y_2}{p_2^i}}\right) \tag{7.A.8}$$

$$p_2^i \equiv a_2\left(\frac{p}{r}\right) + (1 - a_2)p_2 \tag{7.A.9}$$

$$T \equiv \frac{p}{rp_2} \tag{7.A.10}$$

1. This appendix was prepared in the main by J. David Richardson. It was adapted from Richardson (1971a).
2. See Richardson (1971a) for an analysis that incorporates an "orthodox-neutral" monetary policy that holds the money supply constant.

with the addition of (7.A.10) that defines the terms of trade as seen by the home country.

The exchange rate and the interest rate are taken as exogenous variables in the model. If prices were also assumed fixed, as in our treatment in the text, the model is fully determined and we can reach the results already noted. But if prices are not fixed, the model is underdetermined. As will be explained in greater detail below, we would have to add at least two equations to explain prices to get a complete solution. Some interesting conclusions nevertheless follow from the underdetermined model that we may now examine. In proceeding, let us assume with regard to price movement that devaluation will tend to raise domestic prices in the devaluing country and lower them in the other country, that is, $dp/dr \geq 0$ and $dp_2/dr \leq 0$. This simply expresses the intent of devaluation, which is to shift both home and foreign expenditure away from foreign and onto home goods. We shall assume, as before, that quantity units for each country's goods are defined so that $p = p_2 = 1$ initially and that currency units are defined so that $r = 1$ initially. The full differentiated form of the model is as follows:

$$dB = dX + X\,dp - dM - M(dr + dp_2) \qquad (7.A.1')$$

$$dY = dD + dB \qquad (7.A.2')$$

$$dD = (1 - s)\,dY + \left[D - (1 - s)Y\right]dp^i \qquad (7.A.3')$$

$$dp^i = a(dp_2 + dr) + (1 - a)\,dp \qquad (7.A.4')$$

$$dM = m\,dY + M\eta_m(dr + dp_2) + M\xi_m\,dp \qquad (7.A.5')$$

$$dX = m_2\,dY_2 + X\eta_x(dp - dr) + X\xi_x\,dp_2 \qquad (7.A.6')$$

$$dY_2 = dD_2 - dB + B \qquad (7.A.7')$$

$$dD_2 = (1 - s_2)\,dY_2 + \left[D_2 - (1 - s_2)Y_2\right]dp_2^i \qquad (7.A.8')$$

$$dp_2^i = a_2(dp - dr) + (1 - a_2)\,dp_2 \qquad (7.A.9')$$

$$dT = dp - dr - dp_2 \qquad (7.A.10')$$

where ξ_m represents the cross-elasticity of demand for imports with respect to the price of the home good and ξ_x the cross-elasticity of demand for exports with respect to the price of the foreign good.

Our objective is to analyze the sign and size of dB/dr, which will be positive for a successful devaluation. Thus, substituting (7.A.5') and (7.A.6') into (7.A.1'), we obtain:

$$\frac{dB}{dr} = \left[m_2\frac{dY_2}{dr} + X\eta_x\left(\frac{dp}{dr} - 1\right) + X\xi_x\frac{dp_2}{dr}\right]$$
$$- \left[m\frac{dY}{dr} + M\xi_m\frac{dp}{dr} + M\eta_m\left(\frac{dp_2}{dr} + 1\right)\right]$$
$$+ X\frac{dp}{dr} - M\frac{dp_2}{dr} - M. \qquad (7.A.11)$$

Equation (7.A.11) can be simplified by assuming initial current-account balance, that is, $B = 0$, $Y = D$, and $Y_2 = D_2$, and by substituting (7.A.3′) and (7.A.8′), (7.A.4′) and (7.A.9′), and (7.A.10′) into (7.A.2′) and (7.A.7′) to obtain:[3]

$$\frac{dY}{dr} = -M\frac{dT}{dr} + D\frac{dp}{dr} + \left(\frac{1}{s}\right)\frac{dB}{dr} \tag{7.A.12}$$

$$\frac{dY_2}{dr} = X\frac{dT}{dr} + D_2\frac{dp_2}{dr} - \left(\frac{1}{s_2}\right)\frac{dB}{dr}. \tag{7.A.13}$$

Making use of the homogeneity-of-degree-zero-assumption that is attached to the import and export functions, the following relationships are implied between the cross- and own-price elasticities:[4]

$$M\xi_m = -M\eta_m - mY \tag{7.A.14}$$

$$X\xi_x = -X\eta_x - m_2 Y_2. \tag{7.A.15}$$

3. Note that differentiating (7.A.2) with respect to r, we have:

$$\frac{dY}{dr} = \frac{dD}{dr} + \frac{dB}{dr}$$

or from (7.A.3′)

$$\frac{dY}{dr} = (1 - s)\frac{dY}{dr} + [D - (1 - s)Y]\frac{dp^i}{dr} + \frac{dB}{dr}.$$

If trade is balanced initially $Y = D$, and

$$\frac{dp^i}{dr} = a\left(\frac{dp_2}{dr} + 1\right) + (1 - a)\frac{dp}{dr}$$

$$\frac{dp^i}{dr} = -a\left(\frac{dp}{dr} - \frac{dp_2}{dr} - 1\right) + \frac{dp}{dr} = -a\frac{dT}{dr} + \frac{dp}{dr}.$$

But $a = rp_2 M/D = M/D$ by definition. Therefore

$$\frac{dY}{dr} = (1 - s)\frac{dY}{dr} + D[1 - (1 - s)]\left(-\frac{M}{D}\frac{dT}{dr} + \frac{dp}{dr}\right) + \frac{dB}{dr}$$

$$\frac{dY}{dr} = (1 - s)\frac{dY}{dr} + s\left(-M\frac{dT}{dr} + D\frac{dp}{dr}\right) + \frac{dB}{dr}$$

from which we get (7.A.12). Equation (7.A.13) is obtained analogously.

4. Write equation (7.A.5) in the form of relatives as:

$$\frac{dM}{M} = \left(m\frac{Y}{M}\right)\frac{dY}{Y} + \eta_m\left(\frac{dr + dp_2}{rp_2}\right) + \xi_m\left(\frac{dp}{p}\right).$$

Homogeneity of degree zero, that is, absence of money illusion, means that if we change money income and all prices by the same proportion, δ, the quantity imported will not change. Thus, when

$$\frac{dY}{Y} = \frac{(dr + dp_2)}{rp_2} = \frac{dp}{p} = \delta$$

If we now substitute (7.A.14) and (7.A.15) and (7.A.12) and (7.A.13) into the expression for dB/dr in (7.A.11), the expressions in dp/dr and dp_2/dr alone subtract out and we are left only with expressions in dT/dr. We thus have:[5]

$$\frac{dB}{dr} = -M \left(\frac{s}{s + m + m_2(s/s_2)} \right) (\eta_x - \eta_m - 1 - m - m_2) \left(\frac{dT}{dr} \right).$$

$$(7.A.16)$$

The first term in equation (7.A.16) will be recognized as the multiplier for dB/dX that was derived in Table 6.4, Chapter 6. The second term represents the more stringent elasticities condition derived earlier in this chapter. This second term will be positive only if the sum of the elasticities of import demand exceeds the sum of one plus the marginal propensities to import. What is noteworthy is that the expression for the change in the terms of trade (dT/dr) enters multiplicatively into the expression for dB/dr. If the terms of trade improve, dT/dr will be positive, and if the terms of trade deteriorate, dT/dr will be negative. Thus, taken by itself, the elasticities condition is neither necessary nor sufficient for an improvement in the trade (current-account) balance when prices are permitted to vary. If, for example, the elasticities condition were satisfied and the terms of trade were to improve with a devaluation, the trade (current-account) balance would deteriorate. The necessary and sufficient conditions for improvement of the trade balance are therefore either satisfaction of the elasticities condition and deterioration of the terms of trade or failure of the elasticities condition to hold and improvement of the terms of trade.

It is also evident from (7.A.16) that if the elasticities condition is satisfied, price variation in each country reduces the power of a successful devaluation. When prices are assumed unchanged, as in equation (7.16) above, the terms of trade deteriorate in the same proportion as the devaluation, that is, $dT/dr = -1$. But when price variation is allowed, the terms of trade must have deteriorated, although by less than when prices are unchanged, that is, $-1 < dT/dr < 0$. The size of dB/dr is thus reduced in (7.A.16) as compared to (7.16).

---

then $dM/M = 0$ so that

$$0 = \left(m \frac{Y}{M} \right) \delta + \eta_m \delta + \xi_m \delta$$

and we obtain (7.A.14). Equation (7.A.15) is obtained in the same way.

5. If we were abstracting from foreign repercussions, the expression for the change in the trade (current-account) balance would be:

$$\frac{dB}{dr} = -M \left(\frac{1}{s + m} \right) (\eta_x - \eta_m - 1 - m) \frac{dT}{dr}$$

where $dT/dr = (dp/dr) - 1$.

It is of interest, finally, to close the model by introducing two supply equations that are inverted so that they solve for price:[6]

$$p = p\left(\overset{+}{\frac{Y}{p}}\right) \tag{7.A.17}$$

$$p_2 = p_2\left(\overset{+}{\frac{Y_2}{p_2}}\right). \tag{7.A.18}$$

When these equations are differentiated with respect to the exchange rate, $dp/dr > 0$ and $dp_2/dr < 0$. It is entirely possible that $dp/dr - dp_2/dr > 1$ so that there is nothing to suggest that the terms-of-trade change,

$$\frac{dT}{dr} = \frac{dp}{dr} - \frac{dp_2}{dr} - 1,$$

would necessarily be negative. It is conceivable therefore that if the price response is so great as to make the terms of trade improve and the elasticities condition is satisfied, the devaluation will be unsuccessful.

6. This is the way the model is closed in the appendix in Chapter 10 when we analyze monetary and fiscal policies under alternative exchange-rate systems. An alternative way to close the model is to assume that trade unions bargain in such a way that money wages rise to the extent of the rise in the price index so that real wages are kept constant:

$$\frac{W}{p^i} = k$$

$$\frac{W_2}{p_2^i} = k_2$$

where W and W_2 refer to money wages and k and k_2 are constants. Prices will then respond to the rise in money wages. But if the prices of nonlabor factors do not rise as money wages rise and if units of labor time are defined so that $W = W_2 = 1$ initially, we could probably claim that

$$p = p(W) \qquad , \qquad \frac{\partial p}{\partial W} < 1$$

$$p_2 = p_2(W_2) \qquad , \qquad \frac{\partial p_2}{\partial W_2} < 1.$$

If this assumption holds, the terms of trade will deteriorate with a devaluation, and price variation does not affect the chances of success of a devaluation, although such variation, as already noted, does reduce the size of dB/dr.

8

International Long-Term Capital Movements

Thus far, our treatment of international long-term capital movements has been tangential. Accordingly, the present chapter will deal explicitly with the three major forms that such movements take and with the theoretical mechanism of the process of capital transfer. Our final concern will be with the efficiency and welfare implications of capital transfer.

Portfolio Foreign Investment

Portfolio foreign investment refers to international transactions involving the purchase and sale of securities, chiefly bonds and equities, and to the extension of long- and medium-term bank loans. Some indication of the importance of these types of investments for private U.S. investors abroad is given in Table 8.1. It is evident that these private long-term investments in foreign securities and other claims were in total only about one-third as large as direct foreign investment in 1970. U.S. liabilities to foreigners are shown in Table 8.2. Interestingly enough, foreign portfolio investments were about $2\frac{1}{2}$ times as large as direct foreign investment in the U.S. in 1970.

It is common to consider portfolio investment as long term in view of the nature of the instruments being bought and sold. This is so even when the investor is motivated by short-term influences, as, for example, may occur when there is trading of outstanding securities. However, since we rarely have direct information on investor motivations, there is usually little choice but to treat all observed portfolio-capital movements as long term and trust that not too much violence will be done to reality. We shall go one step further and confine our attention to transactions in bonds, leaving it to the reader to make the necessary emendations in what follows with regard to equity investments and bank lending.

It is a matter of common observation that capital by no means moves freely across national boundaries. If it did, long-term borrowers and lenders

225

TABLE 8.1

U.S. Assets Abroad at Yearend, by Area, 1970[a]

(Billions of Dollars)

Type of Investment	Western Europe	Canada	Japan	Latin America	Other Countries	Int'l. Org. & Unalloc.	Total
Total assets	$41.4	$37.0	$7.2	$28.5	$32.0	$20.4	$166.6
Nonliquid assets	40.0	35.9	7.1	28.3	31.8	6.6	149.7
U.S. Government	8.0	—	0.7	6.3	15.8	1.4	32.2
Long-term credits	7.7	—	0.7	6.3	13.6	1.4	29.7
Short-term assets	0.3	—	—	—	2.2	—	2.5
Private long-term	29.6	35.1	2.3	18.1	14.4	5.2	104.7
Direct investments	24.5	22.8	1.5	14.7	11.1	3.6	78.1
Foreign securities	3.1	11.1	0.6	1.2	2.0	1.6	19.6
Other claims	2.0	1.2	0.3	2.2	1.3	—	7.0
Private short-term	2.4	0.8	4.0	3.8	1.7	—	12.8
Liquid assets	1.4	1.0	0.2	0.2	0.1	13.9	16.9
Private	0.8	1.0	0.2	0.2	0.1	—	2.4
U.S. monetary reserve assets	0.6	—	—	—	—	13.9	14.5

[a] Preliminary.

SOURCE: U.S. Department of Commerce, Survey of Current Business (October 1971), p. 21.

TABLE 8.2

U.S. Liabilities to Foreigners at Yearend, by Area, 1970[a]
(Billions of Dollars)

Type of Investment	Western Europe	Canada	Japan	Latin America	Other Countries	Int'l. Org. & Unalloc.	Total
Total liabilities	$60.4	$13.2	$6.1	$8.9	$6.0	$3.0	$97.5
Nonliquid liabilities to other than official agencies	36.1	6.7	0.8	3.8	1.9	1.8	51.2
U.S. Government	1.8	—	—	—	—	0.1	2.0
Private long-term	31.6	6.5	0.7	3.4	1.5	1.8	45.5
Direct investments	9.5	3.1	0.2	0.2	0.1	—	13.2
U.S. securities	17.8	3.2	—	2.3	1.0	1.3	25.6
Other	4.3	0.2	0.4	0.8	0.5	0.5	6.7
Private short-term	2.7	0.2	0.1	0.4	0.3	—	3.7
Liquid liabilities to private foreigners	10.6	3.5	n.a.	3.5	n.a.	0.6	22.6
Liabilities to foreign official agencies	13.7	3.0	n.a.	1.5	n.a.	0.6	24.4
Nonliquid	0.6	2.3	n.a.	—	n.a.	—	3.8
Liquid	13.1	0.7	n.a.	1.5	n.a.	0.6	20.6

[a] Preliminary; n.a.—not available.

SOURCE: U.S. Department of Commerce, Survey of Current Business (October 1971), p. 21.

would operate in each other's capital market, taking advantage of differences in the costs of borrowing and rates of return and in the process reducing or even removing such differences altogether. In actuality, we have to make explicit allowance for various impediments to capital movements, which, aside from risk-related factors, involve such things as monopolistic influences, imperfect information, and government restrictions of different kinds. As a means of understanding the factors involved in the purchase and sale of bonds and other financial assets, it may be useful to proceed within a somewhat formal framework. Let us for this purpose draw upon a portfolio model of investor behavior. Such a model focuses our attention on the stock demand for financial assets in relation to returns and risk subject to the overall wealth constraint of the investor. Thus, the decision to borrow or lend and to buy or sell outstanding issues is more than a matter of comparing domestic and foreign rates or yields.

STATIC PORTFOLIO ANALYSIS

Suppose that we have an investor whose portfolio consists of domestic and foreign financial assets. We can then write:

$$A_k = A_k(\mu_k, \sigma_k, \mu_c, \sigma_c, W) \qquad (8.1)$$

to indicate that investment in the stock holdings of asset K will depend upon the expected return to K, μ_k; the risk associated with K, σ_k; the return μ_c and risk σ_c of the alternative asset; and the investor's wealth or net worth, W. This formulation can also be used to characterize the borrowing decision. That is, we can interpret the supply of security K as depending upon expected interest payment and the variability of that payment, similar variables for a substitute credit source, and the borrower's wealth or net worth. Equation (8.1) can thus be taken to describe the desired stock of assets or of liabilities. The flow of portfolio investment that we would observe in any given period would correspond to a change in the stock of these assets/liabilities that is induced by a change in the explanatory variables on either the supply or demand side. If investors (borrowers) behave according to portfolio-model precepts, they would balance off expected returns and risk for different combinations in which the asset may be held.[1]

PORTFOLIO ANALYSIS WITH GROWING WEALTH

We are interested not only in how an investor allocates a given amount of wealth among alternative assets, but also how increments to wealth are allocated. This is a question that is important for the understanding of investment behavior over time. It is also one that has important implications for a country's balance of payments. Thus, suppose that we have a home country, h, and foreign country, f, in which financial wealth, W, can be held in the

1. For an elaboration of details and the determination of the optimum combination of domestic and foreign assets, see Miller and Whitman (1970, pp. 177–79).

form of bonds with infinite maturity that are issued by the home, B, or foreign, F, governments.[2] The prices of these bonds are assumed equal to unity and they carry rates of return, r_h and r_f, that are constant over time. The rate of foreign exchange is assumed to be fixed and equal to unity. At a given moment in time, we have:

$$W_t^h = B_t^h + F_t^h \quad \text{and} \quad W_t^f = B_t^f + F_t^f, \tag{8.2}$$

where superscripts refer to the country of ownership. From the standpoint of the home country, F^h is the stock of international investment and B^f is the stock of international liabilities. The desired composition of total financial wealth in the individual countries will be determined according to portfolio-balance precepts by:[3]

$$\frac{F_t^h}{W_t^h} = \lambda_h(r_f - r_h) \quad \text{and} \quad \frac{B_t^f}{W_t^f} = \lambda_f(r_h - r_f). \tag{8.3}$$

Thus, investors in the two countries will hold higher proportions of foreign relative to domestic bonds in their portfolios depending upon the difference in rates of return.

Assume that wealth grows exponentially at rates g_h and g_f, that is, $W_t^h = W_o^h e^{g_h t}$ and $W_t^f = W_o^f e^{g_f t}$. Holding the current account constant, the balance of payments of the home country, defined in terms of the changes in its foreign exchange reserves, R, will be increasing at a given moment in time at a rate equal to:

$$\dot{R}_t = \dot{B}_t^f - \dot{F}_t^h + r_f F_t^h - r_h B_t^f, \tag{8.4}$$

where the dots over the variables indicate derivatives with respect to time. Equation (8.4) thus states that the rate of change in the home country's foreign exchange reserves will be equal to the algebraic sum of the rates of change in the home country's international borrowing, $\dot{B}_t^f$, and investment, $\dot{F}_t^h$, and its interest inflow, $r_f F_t^h$, and outflow, $r_h B_t^f$. Since in equilibrium all components of wealth grow at the same rate, we can write equation (8.4) as:[4]

$$\dot{R}_t = B_t^f(g_f - r_h) + F_t^h(r_f - g_h). \tag{8.5}$$

---

2. The discussion that follows is based upon Morton (1970, esp. pp. 38–46). As he points out, bonds with infinite maturity (i.e., consols) are used to avoid the complications of debt refunding and amortization. The results are not materially different, however, when these complications are taken into account.

3. Writing the equations in the form of (8.3) assumes that the demand for all assets is homogeneous of degree one in wealth. This is a common assumption in long-run analysis. The symbols λ_h and λ_f refer to the wealth allocation functions for investors in the two countries. That is, no matter how great wealth becomes, the proportion of it held in foreign consols depends upon the interest-rate differential. Thus,

$$\frac{d(F_t^h/W_t^h)}{d(r_f - r_h)} \quad \text{and} \quad \frac{d(B_t^f/W_t^f)}{d(r_h - r_f)} > 0.$$

4. Note that g_f is defined as the rate of growth of B^f, that is, $\dot{B}^f/B^f$, and g_h is defined similarly. If these definitions are substituted in equation (8.5), we get (8.4).

Whether $\dot{R}_t$ will be positive or negative will evidently depend on the magnitudes of the growth and interest rates. Thus, for example, if the rate of flow of foreign borrowing (i.e., the capital inflow) exceeds the interest outflow and the interest inflow exceeds the rate-of-flow purchase of foreign bonds (i.e., the capital outflow), the home country's foreign exchange reserves will increase, and conversely.

Equation (8.5) suggests some implications for policy with respect to interest and growth rates that are worth examining. Suppose that the authorities in the home country wish to increase the rate of interest, r_h, for balance-of-payments purposes. In our discussion of internal-external balance in Chapter 10, we shall consider combinations of monetary and fiscal policies that are designed to achieve certain specified targets in the short run. We shall abstract then from considerations of portfolio balance and interest payments over time. These longer-run factors can be taken into account, however, with the aid of the present model. Let us for this purpose abstract from the policy effects on domestic income and focus solely on the home country's capital account. It is important here to distinguish the short-run and intermediate-run effects from the long-run effects of the increase in the rate of interest.

Thus, in the static case with $g_h = g_f = 0$ and with a fixed stock of wealth, when r_h is raised, there will be a once-and-for-all adjustment of existing wealth portfolios in both the home country and the foreign country away from foreign into home-country securities. This will result in an increase in home-country reserves as the stock adjustment takes place. Let us indicate the stock of reserves at time t as $\bar{R}_t$. The stock adjustment effect will then be $d\bar{R}_t/dr_h$. Note that this is not meant to indicate a change over time. Rather it is simply the *difference* in reserves at time t under the alternative assumptions: (1) the interest rate is r_h; and (2) the interest rate is $r_h + dr_h$, with immediate full adjustment of stocks taking place. Noting from equation (8.3) that $B_o^f = W_o^f \lambda_f$ and $F_o^h = W_o^h \lambda_h$, the short-run stock effect will be:[5]

$$\frac{d\bar{R}_t}{dr_h} = W_o^h \lambda_h' + W_o^f \lambda_f' > 0. \tag{8.6}$$

5. The stock adjustments are:

$$\frac{d\bar{R}_t}{dr_h} = \frac{dB_t^f}{dr_h} - \frac{dF_t^h}{dr_h}.$$

Note that if we assume a constant level of wealth, equation (8.3) is:

$$F_t^h = W_o^h \lambda_h(r_f - r_h)$$

and

$$B_t^f = W_o^f (r_h - r_f).$$

Differentiating with respect to r_h, we have:

$$\frac{dF_t^h}{dr_h} = W_o^h \lambda_h' \frac{d(r_f - r_h)}{dr_h} = -W_o^h \lambda_h'$$

But changing r_h also alters the rate of growth of reserves as well as the level of reserves due to the adjusted portfolios and changed interest rate. There will be a continuing negative effect on reserves because the home country will experience higher interest payments and lower interest income as a consequence of the initial stock adjustment. This negative effect will be equal to:[6]

$$\frac{d\dot{R}_t}{dr_h} = -W_o^h \lambda_h' r_f - W_o^f \lambda_f' r_h - W_o^f \lambda_f < 0. \tag{8.7}$$

Combining the impact effect in (8.6) with the continuing (steady-state) effect in (8.7), we have:[7]

$$\left[\frac{d\bar{R}_t}{dr_h} + \frac{d\dot{R}_t}{dr_h}\right] = W_o^h \lambda_h'(1 - r_f) + W_o^f \lambda_f'(1 - r_h) - W_o^f \lambda_f. \tag{8.8}$$

If we were to insert reasonably realistic parameter values into (8.8), it is likely that the expression would be positive. That is, it is likely that the positive impact effect of the stock adjustment on reserves due to an increase in the home country's rate of interest would in this case be larger than the negative continuing effect of higher interest payments and lower receipts. This is by no means the whole story, however, because once we permit wealth to increase, that is $g_h > 0$ and $g_f > 0$, we cannot determine a priori whether in the long run an increase in r_h will improve or worsen the home country's reserve position. The result according to equation (8.5) will depend on the growth and interest rates and, in addition, upon the substitutability of domestic and foreign securities with respect to the interest rate.[8]

---

and

$$\frac{dB_t^f}{dr_h} = W_o^f \lambda_f' \frac{d(r_h - r_f)}{dr_h} = W_o^f \lambda_f'.$$

If r_h is altered in period t and if adjustment is immediate, the immediate impact on reserve levels is as indicated in equation (8.6).

6. From equation (8.5), with $g_h = g_f = 0$, we have:

$$\dot{R}_t = -B_t^f r_h + F_t^h r_f.$$

Differentiating with respect to r_h, we obtain:

$$\frac{d\dot{R}_t}{dr_h} = -B_t^f - \frac{dB_t^f}{dr_h} r_h + \frac{dF_t^h}{dr_h} r_f.$$

In light of the preceding footnote, we get equation (8.7).

7. Note that the stock of reserves at time $t + 1$ is:

$$\bar{R}_{t+1} = \bar{R}_t + \dot{R}_t$$

so that

$$\frac{d\bar{R}_{t+1}}{dr_h} = \frac{d\bar{R}_t}{dr_h} + \frac{d\dot{R}_t}{dr_h}.$$

8. The long-run effect of a change in r_h, with growing wealth, will be:

$$\frac{d\dot{R}_t}{dr_h} = W_t^h \lambda_h' (g_h - r_f) + W_t^f [\lambda_f' (g_f - r_h) - \lambda_f],$$

which may be either positive or negative. See Morton (1970, pp. 41–42) for further details.

It may also be of interest to consider the foreign reserve implications of changes in g_h, the home country's growth-rate of financial wealth. This can be seen by differentiating equation (8.5):[9]

$$\frac{d\dot{R}}{dg_h} = W_t^h \lambda_h [t(r_f - g_h) - 1].\tag{8.9}$$

The reserve effect will depend here upon the relative magnitudes of r_f and g_h. It will be noted that a change in g_h will not have any effect upon the return variables, but there will be an effect on the rate of purchase of foreign bonds. If new purchases continuously exceed interest income, that is if $g_h > r_f$, there will be a net loss of reserves. This loss could be reduced by lowering g_h, and conversely. As will be noted below, this result may have some bearing upon the question of sustaining given levels of foreign lending and borrowing.

The model presented in the foregoing paragraphs would of course have to be articulated more fully in order to adapt it for empirical application and policy-making purposes. Empirical specification would require information on expected returns and risks of the assets or liabilities involved, the wealth constraint that affects the lenders and borrowers, and empirical counterparts of the different impediments affecting lending and borrowing.[10] The intermediate and long-run effects of interest rate and other policy changes upon both the home country and the rest of the world must also be spelled out more precisely in theoretical terms. Such effects involve the impact of policy changes upon the current as well as the capital accounts and the associated impacts upon income at home and abroad.[11]

9. Rewriting equation (8.5):

$$\dot{R}_t = (W_t^f \lambda_f)(g_f - r_h) + (W_t^h \lambda_h)(r_f - g_h)$$

and differentiating with respect to g_h, we have

$$\frac{d\dot{R}_t}{dg_h} = W_t^h \lambda_h(-1) + \lambda_h(r_f - g_h)\frac{dW_t^h}{dg_h}.$$

Since

$$W_t^h = W_o^h e^{g_h t} \quad \text{and} \quad \frac{dW_t^h}{dg_h} = tW_o e^{g_h t} = tW_t^h,$$

we have

$$\frac{d\dot{R}_t}{dg_h} = -W_t^h \lambda_h + \lambda_h(r_f - g_h)tW_t^h$$

which simplifies to equation (8.9).

10. See Branson (1968; 1970) and Miller and Whitman (1970) for an empirical analysis of U.S. portfolio investment using a stock-adjustment model; Lee (1969) and Freedman (1970) develop and estimate a model for portfolio investment and borrowing between the U.S. and Canada. See Leamer and Stern (1970, esp. pp. 92–105; 1972) for a discussion of measurement problems and a brief review of the empirical literature.

11. Morton's work (1970) represents an important beginning along these lines, especially for long-run analysis. What is needed now is analysis of medium-run periods and the ways in which balance-of-payments disequilibria can be removed in such circumstances.

Direct Foreign Investment

The difference between portfolio and direct foreign investment is chiefly one of management control of the foreign assets in question. In a perfectly competitive world with certainty, free access to knowledge, no government restrictions, and barring externalities and dynamic considerations, firms will invest abroad so long as the foreign rate of return exceeds what could be earned on alternative investment at home. That is, the existence of differential profit rates, which are indicative of differences in the marginal productivity of capital, will create an inducement for foreign investment. But why direct rather than portfolio investment? A major reason is that the returns to direct investment may include a return for entrepreneurial decision-making as well as a normal return for capital. Without such returns to entrepreneurship, foreign investment would more likely take the form of purchases of bonds or equities, and domestic firms would sell or rent any patents that the firms abroad might need in addition to the capital funds. The existence of disequilibrium profits is, of course, only one possible reason why direct foreign investment may occur. If we take into account the existence of imperfections in competition and in the availability and implementation of knowledge, government policies of various kinds, and dynamic factors, there may be ample scope for firms to expand their profit horizons by means of direct investment in other countries.

Before exploring more fully the various forces motivating direct investment, it might be useful to look briefly at the pattern of U.S. investments abroad and foreign investments in the U.S. The reason for focusing on the U.S. is that this nation's investments are by far the largest of any of the industrialized countries. U.S. investments are also documented in much greater detail than other countries. We might recall that, as shown in Table 8.1, U.S. direct investments abroad in 1970 were $78.1 billion. This was nearly three times greater than portfolio investments, although these latter investments have risen rapidly during the 1960's. Direct investments have not always been so prominent, however, for during the 1920's U.S. portfolio investments were greater, except for 1929.[12]

12. According to data reproduced in Mikesell (1962, p. 53), net U.S. private capital outflows during the 1920's were as follows (in millions of dollars):

	1920	1921	1922	1923	1924
Portfolio	400	477	669	235	703
Direct	154	111	153	148	182
Total	554	588	822	383	885

	1925	1926	1927	1928	1929
Portfolio	603	470	636	752	34
Direct	268	351	351	558	602
Total	871	821	987	1,310	636

TABLE 8.3

Book Value of U.S. Direct Investments Abroad at Yearend, by Area and Industry, 1970[a]
(Millions of Dollars)

Area	Mining and Smelting	Petroleum	Manufacturing	Other	Total	Percent
Canada	$3,014	$4,809	$10,050	$4,927	$22,801	29%
United Kingdom	1	1,852	4,988	1,174	8,015	10
EEC	15	2,525	7,126	2,029	11,695	15
Other W. Europe	55	1,110	1,590	2,005	4,761	6
Japan	—	540	753	198	1,491	2
Australia, New Zealand, and S. Africa	572	909	2,241	627	4,348	6
Latin America and Other W. Hemisphere	2,037	3,929	4,604	4,115	14,683	19
Other Africa	350	1,916	100	245	2,612	3
Middle East	3	1,466	86	90	1,645	2
Other Asia and Pacific	91	1,066	692	628	2,477	3
Int'l, unalloc.	—	1,667	—	1,896	3,563	5
Total	$6,137	$21,790	$32,231	$17,932	$78,090	100%
Percent	8%	28%	41%	23%		100%

a Preliminary.

SOURCE: U.S. Department of Commerce, *Survey of Current Business* (October, 1971), p. 32.

U.S. direct investments abroad by areas and industry are recorded for 1970 in Table 8.3. Evident from this table is the emphasis upon extractive industries—mining and smelting and petroleum—that produce primarily for the U.S. market and markets in the other advanced industrial countries. Investments in these industries accounted for 36 percent of total direct investment. The percentage is still larger if we take into account the separate recording of international shipping, which includes substantial investment in oil tankers, and trade, which includes the retail distribution of petroleum products. It can also be seen in Table 8.3 that the bulk of U.S. direct investment in manufacturing is located in the advanced countries: Canada, Europe, Japan, Australia, New Zealand, and South Africa accounted for 83 percent of the manufacturing total in 1970. The remaining manufacturing investments in the less developed countries reflect of course the relatively small markets in these countries.

Foreign direct investments in the U.S. are recorded in Table 8.4 for 1970. These investments were only about one-sixth as large as U.S. investments abroad. As would be expected, the largest investors in the U.S. are the other industrialized countries, in particular, Canada, the United Kingdom, the Netherlands, and Switzerland. The investments are concentrated mainly in manufacturing and to a somewhat lesser extent in petroleum and insurance and other finance.

If one contemplates the kinds of firms that engage in direct foreign investment, the picture that emerges is more the prototype of the relatively large enterprise that is part of an oligopolistic market structure rather than the

TABLE 8.4

Book Value of Foreign Direct Investments in the U.S. at Yearend, by Area and Industry, 1970[a]
(Millions of Dollars)

By Area		By Industry	
Canada	$3,112	Petroleum	$2,981
United Kingdom	4,110	Manufacturing	6,105
EEC	3,528	Trade	1,002
Other W. Europe	1,877	Insurance and other finance	2,250
Japan	233	Other industries	871
Latin America and Other		Total	$13,209
W. Hemisphere	228		
Other	121		
Total	$13,209		

[a] Preliminary.
SOURCE: U.S. Department of Commerce, *Survey of Current Business* (October, 1971), p. 38.

atomistic member of a highly competitive market structure.[13] In cases where relative market dominance is less pronounced, the firms engaging in direct investment are likely to have some specialized managerial, technical, or other expertise that may afford them a leadership position. What this suggests is that it may be more fruitful in analyzing the motivations for direct investment to proceed within a framework in which disequilibrium factors and market imperfections of various kinds play a central role. Let us proceed now to examine these motivations in greater detail.

THE INITIAL FOREIGN INVESTMENT DECISION[14]

In considering the motivations for direct investment, a distinction must be drawn between the firm's initial decision to invest abroad and the investment decisions with regard to already established foreign affiliates. The initial decision is, in principle at least, a discrete one whereas ongoing investment is undertaken in a context in which resources have been previously committed. This makes the initial investment decision inherently more risky. But completely apart from risk, firms may also be viewed as having subjective horizons and rates of discount with respect to space that are analogous to those with respect to time.[15] Imperfections in competition and information will lead to both risk and such subjective "spatial preference."

As a result of these subjective influences, a firm may prefer to invest in markets where it already operates unless the pecuniary rewards from venture investments are sufficiently great to offset risk and other subjective impediments. Thus, a premium may be required for initial investment and there may be certain factors that are much more important for this kind of decision than for ongoing investment. Among these factors are: (1) adequacy of information about opportunities in foreign markets; (2) foreign experience via exporting; (3) political and other influences affecting the "investment climate"; (4) expected foreign growth opportunities; and (5) actions of competitors regarding foreign investment.

What limited evidence is available suggests that the initial investment decision may in fact be susceptible to the kinds of influences described. For example, in the case of domestic manufacturing industries in the less developed countries especially, where subjective deterrents would be relatively strong, policies designed to encourage inward investment have not met with much success. This is in sharp contrast with extractive investment where the stakes are frequently more clearly defined and the major markets already established in the advanced industrialized countries. We observed earlier that

13. See U.S. Department of Commerce, Office of Business Economics, *Survey of Current Business* (May 1969), pp. 34–51, for some details on the export and size characteristics of U.S. firms and their foreign affiliates.

14. This section is based mainly on Richardson (1971b). His paper contains detailed references. I am indebted to Richardson and to W. E. Alexander for additional clarifying comments.

15. For details, see Richardson (1971b).

the bulk of U.S. direct foreign investment in manufacturing was concentrated in the advanced countries. This is not surprising, for in the case of firms with previous exporting experience in these markets, the relative merits of foreign investment might be assessed more readily at any given time.

It may be noted, finally, that the calculation of pecuniary reward is perhaps more subtle for an initial investment than for ongoing investment. What may be most important is not rates of return calculated with respect to normally defined costs, but rather with respect to the cost of scarce and not easily purchasable factors. This applies in particular to trained management and suggests that the shadow price of such a factor may be a crucial variable for decision-making connected with venture investments.[16]

FACTORS INFLUENCING ONGOING FOREIGN INVESTMENT[17]

In contrast to the initial foreign investment decision, which is discrete in character, ongoing foreign investment decisions must be made periodically in the context of past commitments by the parent firms. These latter decisions appear especially complex due to the fact that the behavior of foreign affiliates will depend upon their age and maturity in combination with the degree of independence in their operations vis-à-vis the parent company.

In its early phases, a foreign affiliate is mostly concerned with such objectives as establishment of a market for its products and the development of a network for distribution. In cases where exports had been important, the foreign affiliate's concern might be with defending the market for its product that already exists. The parent company's foreign investment will thus be motivated at this stage more by strategic and competitive factors than by such short-term considerations as the foreign affiliate's liquidity, immediate profitability, and adaptability of production methods to local resource availabilities.[18]

As a foreign affiliate matures in the sense that its product line and degree of vertical integration closely parallel the parent company, the affiliate may

16. See Richardson (1971b) for a formal outline of the steps in the initial investment decision and for an extension of the analysis to cover intermediate goods and the intertemporal stages in the transition from exports to production abroad, as, for example, in Vernon's theory of the product cycle (1966).

17. This section is based mainly on Richardson (1971c). Again, see his paper for detailed references.

18. The strategic and competitive variables operative in the foreign market might include, according to Richardson (1971c, p. 92): "(1) the age (maturity) of competing firms, both domestic and foreign; (2) the number of competing firms relative perhaps to the number of competitors in similar products in the parent's home market; (3) the number of competitors relative to the total size of the expected market from foreign operations . . . ; (4) the degree of 'competitiveness' of competitors, measured by variables such as the proportion of total expenditures devoted to advertising, or the degree of price variation; (5) the breadth of the distributional or marketing network of competitors; (6) the number of crucial patents held by competitors; and (7) realized increases in the market share of the focus firm over a number of recent years."

Similar variables may be operative also in the parent company's home area and in areas adjacent to the foreign market in question.

be more concerned with defending rather than expanding its market position. By the same token, greater emphasis will be placed upon the profitability of the affiliate and more attention given to cost reduction and adaptation to local institutions. The affiliate may in this latter regard rely for expansion purposes more upon retained earnings and funds obtained from flotations of debt and equity in local capital markets than upon transfers of capital from the parent company. In other words, the investment behavior of the mature foreign affiliate may be influenced by considerations similar to the parent company operating in the home country.

Besides distinguishing the behavior of a foreign affiliate on the basis of its age and maturity, it may also be useful to draw a distinction according to the degree of independence of the affiliate vis-à-vis the parent company. An *independent* affiliate makes investment decisions primarily with regard to its objectives in the particular markets in which it operates, whereas the decisions of an *international* affiliate are made in the light of the world-wide objectives of the parent company. In analyzing direct investment behavior, the importance of particular determinants will thus depend upon whether a foreign affiliate is young and independent, young and international, mature and independent, or mature and international.

Since ongoing direct investment at a given point in time and through time will reflect a mixture of the foregoing cases, many difficulties are bound to be encountered in trying to isolate the factors determining investment for particular firms and for industries. This suggests the desirability of tailoring the analysis according to the similarities and differences that typify the operations of foreign affiliates on the basis of the considerations outlined above. Perhaps the most noteworthy of these considerations are the importance of strategic and competitive factors in the case of the young affiliate and the interdependence of decisions across the entire spectrum of operations in the case of the international affiliate. Fairly detailed information on foreign affiliates and the markets in which they operate will thus be required to gain adequate understanding of the complexities of ongoing direct investment.

Foreign Economic Assistance

We have already taken note of the relative importance of portfolio foreign investment prior to World War II and of direct investment thereafter in meeting the capital needs of borrowing countries. The bulk of these investments went traditionally either to relatively high income countries that were experiencing rapid economic growth or to countries, both rich and poor, with supplies of natural resources that could be developed with the help of foreign capital. After World War II, it became increasingly evident that many of the world's poorer countries were not able to draw upon private international capital markets to meet their capital needs. While the International Bank for

Reconstruction and Development (IBRD) had been established in anticipation of this contingency, it came to play only a limited role in the postwar period. This was because the major industrialized countries felt that their own national interests would be best served by channeling foreign assistance through their own bilateral programs rather than multilaterally through institutions such as the IBRD.

Some indication of the changes from 1960–70 in the official and private makeup of the net flow of financial resources from the rich to the poor countries is given in Table 8.5.[19] It is evident that total official flows rose by about $3.0 billion and private flows by $3.6 billion in the years shown. The chief expansion in the official flows has come in the form of loans rather than grants. The increase in private flows has been mainly in direct investment and in export credits guaranteed by the lending-country governments. The

TABLE 8.5

The Net Flow of Financial Resources from Development Assistance Committee (DAC) Member Countries, 1960–70[a]
(Millions of Dollars)

	1960	1965	1970
I. Official Development Assistance	$4,665	$5,916	$6,808
1. Bilateral grants and grant-like flows	3,692	3,714	3,298
2. Bilateral loans at concessional terms	439	1,854	2,386
3. Contributions to multilateral institutions	534	348	1,124
II. Other Official Flows	300	283	1,159
1. Bilateral	233	278	886
2. Multilateral	67	5	273
Total Official Flows (I + II)	4,965	6,199	7,967
III. Private Flows	3,150	4,121	6,735
1. Direct investment	1,767	2,468	3,408
2. Bilateral portfolio	633	655	809
3. Multilateral portfolio	204	247	343
4. Export credits	546	751	2,174
IV. Grants by Private Voluntary Agencies	n.a.	n.a.	840
Total Net Flow	8,115	10,320	15,542

[a] Gross disbursements minus amortization receipts on earlier lending.
SOURCE: OECD, *1971 Review; Development Assistance: Efforts and Policies of the Members of the Development Assistance Committee* (Paris, 1971), p. 34.

19. The totals shown refer to the countries that are members of the Development Assistance Committee of the Organization for Economic Cooperation and Development (OECD). These countries are listed in Table 8.6 below. No account is taken in what follows of the net flows emanating from other countries, chiefly Finland, New Zealand, South Africa, and the centrally planned economies.

multilateral flows through the IBRD and other specialized international institutions were clearly small in relation to the bilateral flows.

While it would take us too far afield to discuss all the issues involved in foreign economic assistance, it may nevertheless be interesting to look briefly at how donor-country aid performance is to be assessed.[20]

ASSESSING DONOR-COUNTRY AID PERFORMANCE

If we look upon aid giving as a means of redistributing income from the world's rich to the poor countries, the question arises as to how equitably the burden of transfer is being shared among the donor countries. Some information on this issue is given in Table 8.6. The members of the Development Assistance Committee (DAC) of the Organization for Economic Cooperation and Development (OECD) are listed in the order of their GNP per capita in 1970. Presumably this ranking offers some crude indication of the ability to pay, which might be taken as the criterion for a system of international burden sharing. It is of interest then to compare the GNP per capita rankings with the other rankings shown in the table. To simplify the discussion, we shall focus on the five largest donor countries as indicated in columns (9) and (10): the U.S., France, Germany, the United Kingdom, and Japan. The details are as follows:

		Rankings Based on		
			Total Official Flows (% of GNP)	
	GNP per Capita	*Total Official and Private Net Flows (% of GNP)*	*Net Flows*	*Grant Element*
United States	1	15	12–13	12–13
Germany	6	8	8	9–10
France	8	2	2–3	1
United Kingdom	12	5	9–10	7–8
Japan	14	7	5	12–13

It may be easy enough to interpret the GNP per capita rankings, but what about the other ones shown? Should official and private net flows be considered in total, or should we consider only official net flows? Should our criterion be in nominal or real terms? The answers to these questions depend upon what we mean by foreign economic *assistance*. If we mean the amount of real resources being transferred by the donor country *without any quid pro quo*, then what we want is to find a common denominator for measuring the

20. See Stern (1969) for a discussion of such other issues as: the emphasis on project rather than program financing; aid tying; and loan terms, suppliers' credits, and problems of debt servicing. The question of linking creation of new international reserves with development assistance will be discussed below in Chapter 12.

TABLE 8.6
Comparative Aid-Giving Performance in 1970

Countries Ranked in Order of Per Capita GNP	GNP per Capita		Total Official and Private Net Flows[a]		Total Official Flows				Total Net Flows	
					Net Flows[b]		Grant Element[c]		Official & Private[a]	Official
	$	Rank	% of GNP	Rank	% of GNP	Rank	% of GNP	Rank	Mill. $	Mill. $
	(1)	(2)	(3)	(4)	(5)	(6)	(7)	(8)	(9)	(10)
United States	4,770	1	0.61	15	0.33	12–13	0.29	12–13	5,971	3,050
Sweden	3,900	2	0.73	11	0.37	9–10	0.36	7–8	229	117
Canada	3,780	3	0.77	10	0.50	6	0.46	5–6	626	346
Switzerland	3,240	4	0.67	12–13	0.12	16	0.14	15	137	29
Denmark	3,170	5	0.62	14	0.36	11	0.35	9–10	97	59
Germany	3,010	6	0.80	8	0.39	8	0.35	9–10	1,487	599
Norway	2,890	7	0.59	16	0.33	12–13	0.33	11	67	37
France	2,870	8	1.24	2	0.67	2–3	0.65	1	1,808	951
Australia	2,740	9	1.12	4	0.61	4	0.59	2	385	203
Belgium	2,600	10	1.23	3	0.48	7	0.50	4	309	120
Netherlands	2,400	11	1.46	1	0.67	2–3	0.80	5–6	457	196
United Kingdom	2,170	12	1.04	5	0.37	9–10	0.36	7–8	1,259	447
Austria	1,930	13	0.67	12–13	0.14	15	0.11	16	96	19
Japan	1,900	14	0.93	7	0.59	5	0.29	12–13	1,824	458
Italy	1,700	15	0.78	9	0.19	14	0.17	14	725	147
Portugal	650	16	1.02	6	0.90	1	0.52	3	65	29
Total DAC	3,170	—	0.78	—	0.40	—	0.34	—	15,542	6,808

[a] Including grants by private voluntary agencies.
[b] Gross flows less amortization payments received.
[c] Gross disbursements less estimated present values (discounted at 10 percent) of expected future receipts of amortization and interest on loans disbursed in 1970.

SOURCE: OECD, 1971 Review; Development Assistance: Efforts and Policies of the Members of the Development Assistance Committee (Paris, 1971), pp. 144–45 and 164–65.

real resource transfers. This is what is referred to above and in Table 8.6 as the *grant element* in total official net flows. To determine the grant element, it is necessary to estimate the present value of the expected future receipts of amortization and interest payments in relation to the face value of the disbursement. Thus, a disbursement for which there is no return payment to be made has a grant element of 100 percent. One for which return payments are to be made at the going commercial rate, which is assumed to be equal to the (social) opportunity cost of capital, has a grant element equal to zero. Private net flows do not enter therefore into the calculation of the grant element since they reflect strictly commercial considerations, with a quid pro quo based on the earnings from these investments in the recipient countries.

There are of course many serious difficulties that arise in choosing a rate of discount that reflects the opportunity cost of capital in the donor countries. Moreover, it is necessary to take into account other special factors such as the valuation of aid-in-kind as, for example, in the case of surplus agricultural commodities and technical assistance, the excess costs arising from aid tying, and the beneficial effects of preferential donor-country arrangements favoring imports from particular countries. There is the further problem that the opportunity costs of capital may be different in the recipient than in the donor country.[21] Since many of these difficulties cannot be surmounted because we lack the requisite information to deal with the hypothetical circumstances, the grant element cannot be calculated with complete precision. These calculations are nevertheless interesting and important because they indicate that nominal flows of capital do not provide an accurate indication of the real resource transfers and the burdens of these transfers for individual donor countries. The comparative rankings of the five countries noted above and the details for all DAC member countries are instructive in these regards.

The Theory of International Capital Transfer

Having examined some of the important conceptual issues involved in the three main types of international long-term capital transfers, we turn next to consider the theoretical mechanism of the transfer process itself. That is, we shall look at the effects of a capital transfer on relative prices, income, and the balance of payments of the transferring and receiving countries.

Before proceeding to our theoretical analysis, it may be useful to remind the reader that when capital is transferred from one country to another, it means that there must be a net export of goods and services that matches the amount of the long-term international financial transaction that takes place. In other words, in a two-country world starting from initial balance, if

21. See Mikesell (1968, esp. pp. 227–36) for a good discussion of the many problems arising in attempting to measure the real burden of aid.

country 1 is to transfer capital to country 2, then 1 must generate a surplus on current account in the amount of the transfer that will be matched by a deficit on current account for 2. There are of course a number of ways in which country 1 can generate an export surplus: (1) increase its exports; (2) reduce its imports; and (3) a combination of increased exports and reduced imports so that there is no net change in trade.

A related point worth mentioning is that when we speak of *capital exports*, we do not mean necessarily that the transferring country be exporting *capital goods*. Thus, for example, the transferring country might export consumption goods, which enables resources in the borrowing country to be released for production in that country's capital goods industries. The point is that the transfer of goods will reflect the comparative advantages and disadvantages of the capital exporting and importing countries, respectively.[22]

As in our previous discussion of balance-of-payments adjustment, the mechanism of capital transfer can be analyzed in both classical (price approach) and Keynesian (income approach) terms. In the classical model which assumes full employment, perfectly competitive markets with flexibility of wages and prices, and some variant of the gold standard, the main issue for analysis is whether the capital transferring country can generate a sufficiently large current-account surplus to effectuate the transfer without undergoing a deterioration in its terms of trade. Alternatively, in the Keynesian model with underemployment and constant prices, the issue is how the capital transfer will affect the level of income and balance of trade in the capital exporting and importing countries and whether or not the transfer can be effectuated completely without necessitating some further change in the level of income or in the exchange rate. Let us proceed now to examine each of these models in turn.

THE CLASSICAL MODEL

As already indicated, the classical model of transfer can be analyzed in terms of our earlier treatment of the gold standard. For this purpose, we can refer back to Figure 2.7, which illustrates the adjustment process under the gold standard. The initial equilibrium is at P, where the demand and supply of pounds are equal. If a capital transfer takes place from America to England, there will be a shift in the demand for pounds from $D_£^a$ to $D_£^{a'}$. The new equilibrium point will be at C, where $D_£^{a'}$ intersects the gold-export point, S_{GX}^a. Since the dollar price of pounds has increased from OQ to OA, American imports are more costly and exports cheaper in terms of pounds. The demand for pounds for import purposes thus is reduced from OM to OG, whereas

---

22. To illustrate this point, we may note that during and after World War II when the U.S. furnished substantial assistance for relief and reconstruction to the Western European countries especially, U.S. exports consisted in large part of foodstuffs and raw materials. This enabled the Western European countries to free resources for use in the manufacturing and related sectors.

the supply of pounds arising from exports is increased from *OM* to *OH*. These changes are insufficient, however, to generate a larger supply of pounds to match the transfer of *GF*. The balancing item is of course the gold flow, which is equivalent to *HF* in pounds. The balance of payments of the two countries at point *C* is therefore:

	England (£)		America ($)	
	Credit	Debit	Credit	Debit
Exports and Imports	OG			$OADG$
Capital movement	GF	$< OH$	$OAEH >$	$GDCF$
Balancing item (gold movement)		GH	$HECF$	

If we now invoke the rules of the game of the gold standard, America, which has exported gold, will experience a reduction in its money supply and in the level of money income as prices are forced down domestically. As a consequence, the demand and supply schedules for pounds will be shifted to the left and right respectively until the gold movement ceases. In the new equilibrium, which will be below the gold-export point, the amount of pounds demanded for current-account and capital-export purposes will equal the amount of pounds supplied from current-account receipts. This further enlargement of the export surplus to match the capital transfer has evidently occurred as a consequence of worsened terms of trade for America. Thus, insofar as a capital transfer is incompletely effectuated and there is a specie flow, the presumption of the classical model is that the transferor will undergo worsened terms of trade.

The foregoing explanation of the effects of a capital transfer under the gold standard is not necessarily realistic or correct. As pointed out in Chapter 4, the international financial system did not operate prior to World War I on the basis of the rules of the game in the sense of the monetary authorities responding passively to gold inflows or outflows and international trade adjusting to the consequent changes or relative prices. But even more important is that no account is taken of the expenditure changes associated with the transfer in the transferring and receiving countries. The classical view of the transfer mechanism was nevertheless widely accepted before and after World War I. This is best illustrated by a famous article that Keynes wrote (1929) on the subject of German reparations. He argued that while Germany might be able to generate enough taxation to deal with the domestic budgetary aspects of the reparations payments, it could not effect the transfer without encountering a serious deterioration in its terms of trade. The reason was that exports especially could not be expanded significantly without a substantial reduction in their price in terms of foreign currency. It should be noted that in reaching this conclusion Keynes was abstracting from the purely monetary effects of transitional gold flows discussed above and was concerned rather with the nonmonetary or barter implications of the transfer.[23]

Keynes' view of the transfer problem and thus of the correctness of the classical presumption concerning the terms of trade came to be questioned by Ohlin (1929), who contended that Keynes had neglected the shifting of demand in terms of the "buying power" that was being transferred via reparations from the paying to the receiving country. To illustrate this, suppose that we have two countries, 1 and 2, producing A and B goods and that there are no costs of transporting these goods between countries and no tariffs or other impediments to trade. If we assume that countries 1 and 2 have identical marginal preferences, the demand schedules for goods would be shifted downward in 1, the transferring country, and upward in 2, the receiving country. Country 1 would then be able to effect the transfer completely without any impact on its terms of trade. This is illustrated in Figure 8.1a, where it can be seen that the "block of buying power" subtracted from country 1 and added on to 2 results simply in 2 consuming the exact amounts of A and B goods that country 1 gives up in the budgetary process of the reparations transfer.

Suppose alternatively that preferences differ in the two countries. Thus, in Figure 8.1b, where 1 has a relatively stronger preference for B goods than does country 2, the reparations transfer will result on balance in a reduced demand for B goods and an increased demand for A goods. As a consequence, country 1's terms of trade will be improved in this case. On the other hand, if country 1 has a stronger preference for A goods than does country 2, as in Figure 8.1c, the transfer will on balance reduce the demand for A goods and increase the demand for B goods, thus worsening country 1's terms of trade. The upshot of Figure 8.1 is therefore that, contrary to the classical view, there is no presumption for the terms of trade to be moved in one way or another. It all depends upon the relative preferences of the capital transferring and receiving countries.

Expressed more formally, following Samuelson (1952, 1954; 1968), what really matters is the relative strength of the marginal propensities of countries 1 and 2 to consume A and B goods. That is, if we designate the proportion of each country's expenditures on A and B goods as A_1 and B_1 and A_2 and B_2, assuming zero saving propensities, the terms of trade will be unchanged by the capital transfer if:

$$\frac{A_1}{A_2} = \frac{B_1}{B_2}. \tag{8.10}$$

This is the case of identical preferences in Figure 8.1a. It thus follows that country 1's terms of trade will improve if $A_1/A_2 < B_1 B_2$ (Figure 8.1b) and

23. But as Samuelson (1952; 1954; 1968, p. 117) has pointed out: "An intuitionist like Keynes . . . may really have derived his belief about the terms of trade primarily from his notions about monetary effects of international trade on gold, employment, and other aggregate magnitudes."

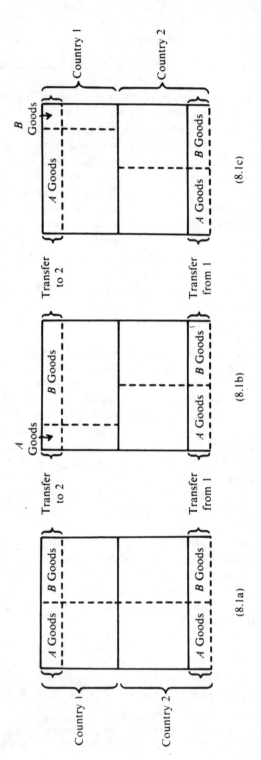

FIGURE 8.1.

Shifts of Buying Power and the Terms of Trade

In 8.1a, with identical preferences for A and B goods, a transfer from country 1 to 2 will have no effect on the terms of trade. With nonidentical preferences, the terms of trade are moved in favor of country 1 in 8.1b and against 1 in 8.1c.

worsen if $A_1/A_2 > B_1/B_2$ (Figure 8.1c). This latter criterion, which is the classical presumption, can also be stated in terms of the sum of marginal propensities to import in the two countries being less than unity. That is, if good B is imported by country 1 and good A by country 2, and $B_1 = m$ and $A_2 = m_2$ are the respective marginal propensities to import, we have:[24]

$$1 - m - m_2 > 0 \quad \text{(for } A\text{'s terms of trade to worsen).} \qquad (8.11)$$

As we shall see later, this criterion has a counterpart in the Keynesian model of capital transfers.

To determine which of the foregoing cases is the most plausible, we evidently must have information on marginal expenditure propensities in the two countries. Thus, it could be, as in Figure 8.1b, that country 1 spends relatively more on A goods than country 2. In order for this to be the case, Johnson (1956; 1968, pp. 153–54) has pointed out that it would require that tastes differ in the two countries and the countries are biased towards consumption of their exportables, which in our example correspond to A goods for country 1 and B goods for country 2. Alternatively, if tastes are identical and if the goods differ in degree of necessity, the country with the higher income per head should produce the more "luxurious" good for export. Whether or not these requirements will be satisfied is an empirical rather than a theoretical question. Matters become even more complicated when we relax the assumptions of zero transport costs and no impediments to trade.[25] We may conclude then that the effects of a capital transfer under classical assumptions will depend upon the circumstances of the particular case with regard to consumption preferences and the importance of real and artificial impediments to trade. In addition, one might want to introduce other

24. To see this, note that all the marginal propensities are assumed to be positive and that they sum to unity in countries 1 and 2.

$$A_1, B_1, A_2, B_2 > 0$$

$$A_1 + B_1 = A_2 + B_2 = 1.$$

From equation (8.10), the criterion for the terms of trade of the transferring country, 1, to worsen is:

$$\frac{A_1}{A_2} - \frac{B_1}{B_2} > 0.$$

Substituting, we have:

$$\frac{1 - B_1}{A_2} - \frac{B_1}{1 - A_2} > 0.$$

If $B_1 = m$ and $A_2 = m_2$, the foregoing expression simplifies to equation (8.11).

25. For detailed analysis, see Samuelson (1952; 1954; 1968, esp. pp. 129–47) and Johnson (1956; 1968, pp. 151–52).

realistic considerations into the model, such as nontraded goods and the expansion of the number of commodities and countries.[26]

Let us now move from a classical to a Keynesian world in which resources are underemployed to the extent that output is in perfectly elastic supply at a fixed price level domestically. The exchange rate is assumed fixed and interest rates are held constant by actions of the monetary authorities. Accommodating capital movements occur to finance trade imbalances. Other capital movements are assumed to be independent of national incomes.

It is interesting first to consider the analogue to the classical model in which the capital transfer results in equal expenditure changes in the two countries, these changes being divided between A and B goods and with zero savings. The difference now as compared to the classical model is that the capital transfer between the two countries will affect incomes rather than prices. Thus, suppose that we have a case in which country 1 makes a capital transfer to country 2 in the amount of 100. Assume that in country 1 the marginal propensity to import good B from country 2 is equal to 0.4 and that in country 2 the marginal propensity to import good A from country 1 is 0.6. As shown in Case 1 in Table 8.6, the reduction of 100 in 1's expenditure will be divided between A goods (-60) and B goods (-40) while the increase of 100 in 2's expenditure will be divided similarly. Since 1's imports fall by 40 and her exports rise by 60, 1's balance of trade will increase by 100, which is exactly the amount of the transfer. The criterion as to whether the transfer will be completely or only partly effected is thus the same as noted in equation (8.14): it will depend on whether the sum of the marginal propensities to import is less than, equal to, or greater than unity.

Two other cases are shown in Table 8.7. Case 2 refers to a situation in which the sum of the marginal propensities to import is greater than unity. A capital transfer of 100 from country 1 to 2 will thus be overeffected in this instance and there will be an increase in 1's income matched by a reduction in income in 2. These changes in income will of course have multiplier effects in the two countries and there will be induced changes in trade. We shall say more about this below. Case 2 also suggests that if marginal import propensities are relatively large in the two countries (and sum to greater than unity), the capital transferring country need not reduce its domestic

---

26. In the case of nontraded goods that substitute in production with exports, Viner (1937, pp. 348–49) has purported to show that the classical presumption will be valid. This will not be true, however, as Samuelson has noted (1952; 1954; 1968, p. 147), in the event that nontraded goods substitute with imports. For the in-between cases, the effects on the transferring country's terms of trade will depend on the circumstances in question. It is interesting in this regard that Samuelson's casual empiricism leads him to the conjecture that Viner's hypothesis and the classical presumption represent the most plausible outcome. See also Samuelson (1971).

TABLE 8.7

Impact Effect on National Income and the Balance of Trade of a Capital Transfer of 100 from Country 1 to 2 under Classical Assumptions

Case 1: Sum of marginal propensities to import equal to 1.

$$m = 0.4$$
$$m_2 = 0.6$$
$$\text{Sum} = 1.0$$

Country	Change in Expenditure on		Total Change in Expenditure
	A Goods	B Goods	
1	−60	−40	−100
2	+60	+40	+100

Change in National Income	
Country 1	—
Country 2	—

Country 1's exports rise by 60 and imports fall by 40. The balance of trade moves 100 in country 1's favor. National income is unchanged in both countries.

Case 2: Sum of the marginal propensities to import greater than 1.

$$m = 0.6$$
$$m_2 = 0.7$$
$$\text{Sum} = 1.3$$

Country	Change in Expenditure on		Total Change in Expenditure
	A Goods	B Goods	
1	−40	−60	−100
2	+70	+30	+100

Change in National Income	
Country 1	+30
Country 2	−30

Country 1's exports rise by 70 and imports fall by 60. The balance of trade moves 130 in country 1's favor. National income rises by 30 in country 1 and falls by 30 in country 2.

Case 3: Sum of the marginal propensities to import less than 1.

$$m = 0.3$$
$$m_2 = 0.2$$
$$\text{Sum} = 0.5$$

Country	Change in Expenditure on		Total Change in Expenditure
	A Goods	B Goods	
1	−70	−30	−100
2	+20	+80	+100

Change in National Income	
Country 1	−50
Country 2	+50

Country 1's exports rise by 20 and imports fall by 30. The balance of trade moves 50 in country 1's favor. National income falls by 50 in country 1 and rises by 50 in country 2.

SOURCE: Adapted from Meade (1951, pp. 90–91).

expenditure by the full amount of a given capital transfer. Thus, in this instance, country 1 could have transferred 130 to country 2 without worsening its trade balance, while reducing its domestic expenditure only by 100.

Case 3 in Table 8.6 represents the classical presumption insofar as the marginal propensities to import sum to less than one. Thus, a capital transfer of 100 from country 1 to 2 will be undereffected here since 1's balance of trade will be improved only by 50. Now since 1's reduction in expenditure has been felt most heavily on *A* goods and the increase in expenditure in country 2 concentrated on *B* goods, we see that 1's income will fall by 50 and 2's will rise by this amount. As in Case 2, there will be multiplier effects and induced changes in trade in the two countries. But assuming there is some finite limit on country 1's ability to generate accommodating finance and that 1 is not willing to deflate its income further, it will not be possible to effect the transfer without some change in prices. In the present example, this can be accomplished by country 1 devaluing its currency. Since we have assumed infinite supply elasticities and so long as the price elasticities of demand for imports sum to greater than one, we know from the Marshall-Lerner condition that country 1's terms of trade will deteriorate. We thus find that the Keynesian model gives the same results for the direction of changes in the terms of trade as the classical model when the same assumptions are made concerning expenditure changes and their division between exportables and importables.

Let us now proceed more explicitly within the framework of a simplified Keynesian model. We may note first that in contrast to the classical model there is no reason to assume that the capital transfer need be reflected in equal expenditure changes in the two countries. Thus, for example, a transfer from country 1 to 2 need not necessarily reduce expenditures in 1 if the capital transferred is generated by additional bank credit or by the dishoarding of idle balances. By the same token, part of the transfer may be generated from or absorbed in domestic saving in the respective countries. This suggests that it will be important in the Keynesian model to specify exactly the policies of the capital transferring and receiving countries with respect to the financing and disposal of the transfer. The second difference to be noted in contrast to the classical model is that we must take account of the multiplier effects that the expenditure changes will have upon income and the balance of trade between the two countries in order to assess whether the transfer will be effectuated.

For purposes of analysis, we shall utilize an adaptation of the Keynesian model set forth in Chapter 6 in connection with the foreign trade multiplier, including foreign repercussions. Following Johnson (1956; 1968, p. 155), our objective is to derive the multiplier equations for *changes* in the national incomes of our two countries and in the balance of payments in terms of the *changes* in autonomous expenditures and transfers that may take place. The model is as follows:

$$\Delta Y = \Delta I + c\,\Delta Y + \Delta M_2 + m_2\,\Delta Y \qquad (8.12)$$

$$\Delta Y_2 = \Delta I_2 + c_2\,\Delta Y_2 + \Delta M + m\,\Delta Y \qquad (8.13)$$

$$\Delta B = \Delta M_2 + m_2\,\Delta Y_2 - \Delta M - m\,\Delta Y - \Delta U \qquad (8.14)$$

where ΔY, ΔY_2, and ΔB are the *total changes* in the national incomes of country 1 (without subscript) and 2 (with subscript) and in 1's balance of payments (all measurements assumed to be made in foreign currency units with an exchange rate of unity); ΔI and ΔI_2 refer to the autonomous *changes* in the consumption and investment demands for domestically produced goods in each country; ΔM and ΔM_2 are the autonomous *changes* in each country's demand for the other country's goods; ΔU is an autonomous *change* in capital transfers from country 1 to 2; c, c_2, m, and m_2 are the marginal propensities to consume domestically produced goods and imports in the respective countries.[27] We shall confine our attention to the case of positive marginal saving propensities, s and s_2, in the two countries. This will guarantee that the system will be stable.[28]

As noted above, it is necessary in the Keynesian model for analyzing capital transfers to make explicit allowance for the changes in expenditures associated with the transfer in the transferring and receiving countries. As Johnson points out (1956; 1968, pp. 156–57), these changes can be taken into account in terms of the changes in (1) the demand for home goods, (2) the demand for imports, or (3) the accumulation of assets through saving that stem directly from the financing or disposal of the transfer. Expressing these changes as proportions of ΔU, the amount transferred, and assuming for now that, with the transfer, expenditures are reduced in country 1 and increased in 2, we have:

$$m' = -\frac{\Delta M}{\Delta U} \quad \text{and} \quad s' = -\frac{\Delta S}{\Delta U} \quad \text{since} \quad \Delta M \text{ and } \Delta S < 0$$

$$m'_2 = \frac{\Delta M_2}{\Delta U} \quad \text{and} \quad s'_2 = \frac{\Delta S_2}{\Delta U} \quad \text{since} \quad \Delta M_2 \text{ and } \Delta S_2 > 0.$$

27. This model, being expressed in terms of changes, differs from the one presented in Chapter 6 in terms of levels. Note that c and c_2 are defined here with respect to expenditures on domestic goods and are thus exclusive of imports. Johnson's notation has been changed to make it consistent with that used in preceding chapters.

28. Metzler (1942a) analyzes the cases in which the transferring country or the receiving country are unstable in isolation. As noted in Chapter 6, the system will be stable under these conditions, but not if both countries are unstable in isolation.

The resulting multiplier equations for the *changes* in incomes in countries 1 and 2 and in 1's balance of payments are therefore:[29]

$$\Delta Y = \frac{1}{s}(\Delta B + s'\,\Delta U) \tag{8.12a}$$

$$\Delta Y_2 = \frac{1}{s_2}(\Delta B + s_2'\,\Delta U) \tag{8.13a}$$

$$\Delta B = \left(m' + m_2' - \frac{m}{s}s' - \frac{m_2}{s_2}s_2' - 1\right)\frac{ss_2}{\Delta}\,\Delta U, \tag{8.14a}$$

where $\Delta = ss_2 + sm_2 + s_2 m$. It follows from equation (8.14a) that the transfer will be undereffected or overeffected, that is, $\Delta B \lessgtr 0$, depending on whether:

$$m' + m_2' \lessgtr \frac{m}{s}s' + \frac{m_2}{s_2}s_2' + 1. \tag{8.15}$$

Some numerical examples based on a capital transfer of 100 from country 1 to 2 and assumed values of the marginal propensities and proportions of the transfer in terms of changes in the demand for imports and in saving are given in Table 8.8. In Case 1, the transfer is undereffected and there is a decline in income in country 1 and an increase in 2. In Case 2, where the transfer is reflected in substantial changes in the demand for imports in the two countries, the transfer is overeffected and there is an increase in income in 1 and a decline in 2.[30] Cases 3 and 4 are familiar from Metzler's analysis (1942a) and are consistent with his results. In Case 3, there is a reduction in expenditure in country 1 equal to the amount of the transfer, but no change in country 2. The transfer is undereffected and income declines in both countries. In Case 4, there is no change in expenditure in country 1 and an increase in 2 equal to the amount of the transfer. The transfer is again undereffected, but now income rises in both countries. This is an interesting result because it shows that income need not necessarily be deflated in the transferring country.

In Case 5, it is assumed that the transfer affects imports and saving in the same manner as any other change in income so that $m' = m$ and $s' = s$.[31]

---

29. See the appendix to this chapter for details of the derivation of these multiplier equations.

30. As Johnson notes (1956; 1968, p. 157), this result is contrary to the earlier findings of Metzler (1942a) and Machlup (1943) that the transfer would be undereffected if both countries had positive marginal propensities to save. The Metzler-Machlup result corresponds to Case 5 in Table 8.8.

31. This was the assumption made in the earlier Keynesian analyses of the transfer problem, as in Metzler (1942a) and Machlup (1943), which can be seen as special cases of Johnson's analysis.

TABLE 8.8

Effects on National Income and the Balance of Trade of a Capital Transfer of 100 from Country 1 to 2 in a Simplified Keynesian Model[a]

	ΔY	ΔY_2	ΔB
Case 1: Transfer undereffected $m = 0.3 \quad s = 0.2 \quad m' = 0.3 \quad s' = 0.1$ $m_2 = 0.2 \quad s_2 = 0.3 \quad m_2' = 0.3 \quad s_2' = 0.1$	-49.0	32.6	-19.8
Case 2: Transfer overeffected $m = 0.3 \quad s = 0.2 \quad m' = 0.7 \quad s' = 0.1$ $m_2 = 0.2 \quad s_2 = 0.3 \quad m_2' = 0.8 \quad s_2' = 0.1$	95.0	-63.3	9.0
Case 3: Transfer undereffected (Change in expenditure in 1; no change in 2) $m = 0.3 \quad s = 0.2 \quad m' = 0.0 \quad s' = 0.0$ $m_2 = 0.2 \quad s_2 = 0.3 \quad m_2' = 0.0 \quad s_2' = 1.0$	-267.0	-155.2	-53.4
Case 4: Transfer undereffected (No change in expenditure in 1; change in 2) $m = 0.3 \quad s = 0.2 \quad m' = 0.0 \quad s' = 1.0$ $m_2 = 0.2 \quad s_2 = 0.3 \quad m_2' = 0.0 \quad s_2' = 0.0$	100.0	266.4	-80.0
Case 5: Transfer undereffected ($m' = m$ and $s' = s$) $m = m' = 0.3 \quad s = s' = 0.2$ $m_2 = m_2' = 0.2 \quad s_2 = s_2' = 0.3$	-60.0	6.7	-32.0
Case 6: Transfer completely effected (Sum of import propensities equals unity) $m = m' = 0.4 \quad s = 0.2 \quad s' = 0.0$ $m_2 = m_2' = 0.6 \quad s_2 = 0.3 \quad s_2' = 0.0$	0.0	0.0	0.0

[a] Results derived by substituting assumed parameter values noted in each case in equations (8.12a)–(8.14a).

The transfer must evidently be undereffected in these circumstances.[32] Case 6 corresponds to Meade's Case 1 noted in Table 8.7, in which the sum of the marginal propensities to import is equal to unity and the transfer does not change savings.[33] The transfer is exactly effected and there is no change in income in either country.

32. Thus, equation (8.14a) will reduce to:

$$B = - \frac{ss_2}{\Delta} \Delta U$$

so that the transfer will be undereffected so long as s and s_2 are positive.

33. Thus, equation (8.15) reduces to:

$$m + m_2 = 1,$$

which is the classical criterion for the transfer to be completely effected. Case 6 in Table 8.8. is not exactly comparable to Meade's Case 1 in Table 8.7 insofar as in Case 6 it will

Continued on p. 254

It would be possible of course to construct an endless number of cases by varying the parameter values in Table 8.8. Some conclusions can be drawn nevertheless from the cases we have examined: (1) the likelihood of a transfer being effected under Keynesian assumptions is greatest when the expenditure changes are concentrated on imports in the two countries; (2) the most unfavorable effects upon income occur when the receiving country does not increase its expenditure directly with the transfer; (3) conversely, income will rise in both countries when the receiving country increases its expenditure while the transferring country keeps expenditure unchanged; and (4) to the extent that the transfer is undereffected, the transferring country will have to resort to other means such as relative price changes to complete the transfer. We cannot, however, establish a priori the likelihood of the need for relative price changes since this will depend upon the parameter values in the given circumstances.

THE PRICE AND INCOME APPROACHES TO CAPITAL TRANSFER

Our interest in the classical and Keynesian models of capital transfer has been to determine what proportion of a transfer will be effected from the standpoint of the transferring country's balance of payments. We saw in particular in both models that the transfer would be more readily effected the greater the preferences of the countries for each other's goods. However, insofar as the transfer was undereffected, the transferring country's balance of payments would be in deficit and some further adjustment would be required. In the classical model, this adjustment would result in a change in relative prices either as a consequence of the impact of international monetary movements on domestic price levels or via shifts in international real demand due to the transfer. Adjustment in the Keynesian model would also necessitate a change in relative prices by means of altering the rate of exchange since domestic prices are assumed to be constant.

The question for analysis therefore is whether these changes in relative prices will serve to effect the remainder of the transfer. Put differently, we want to determine whether the transferring country's balance of payments will be improved or worsened by the change in relative prices. This is of course the same question that concerned us earlier, especially in Chapters 2 and 7, when we were investigating the conditions for stability of the foreign exchange market.

We have noted in the classical model that the transfer would be undereffected or overeffected depending upon whether the sum of the marginal propensities to import was less than or greater than unity. Johnson has

be noted that the marginal saving propensities are positive. If these propensities are equal to zero, Johnson's system noted in equations (8.12)–(8.14) is not defined. The comparability in the two cases follows from the fact that the transfer in Table 8.8 is divided in the two countries between expenditure on domestic goods and imports, with $m = m'$ and $s' = 0$.

pointed out in this regard (1956; 1968, p. 163) that a transfer can be equated with a devaluation, with the elasticities playing the same role as the marginal propensities did above.[34] The transfer will thus be effected, that is the foreign exchange market will be stable, depending upon whether the sum of these elasticities is greater or less than unity. The reader will of course recognize this as the Marshall-Lerner condition that we have discussed at length earlier.

In the Keynesian model, assuming that the transferring country is forced to devalue, the criterion for determining whether or not the transfer will be effected will depend not only upon the sum of the price elasticities of import demand being greater or less than unity, but also upon the impact that the devaluation has upon income in the two countries. Thus, we saw in Chapter 7 that, taking income effects into account, the criterion for a successful devaluation was:

$$\eta_m + \eta_x > 1 + m + m_2$$

where η_m and η_x refer to the price elasticities of import demand and m and m_2 to the marginal propensities to import in the two countries.

It will be recalled that in developing this criterion in Chapter 7 we assumed that the marginal effects on domestic consumption, imports, and saving were the same for changes in real output or in the terms of trade due to devaluation. In our presentation of Johnson's analysis of capital transfer in a Keynesian framework, it was assumed that the marginal effects just mentioned would be different for a capital transfer as compared to a change in output. Johnson's analysis can be made applicable to handle relative price changes by redefining s' to refer to the effect of a decrease in the price of imports upon saving or an increase in the price of imports upon expenditure, based on the initial income and taken as a proportion of the initial value of imports. The

---

34. As Johnson notes (1956; 1968, p. 162), a reduction in the price of country 1's exportables relative to country 2's exportables amounts to a transfer from 1 to 2 equal to the increase in the cost of 1's initial volume of imports, or equivalently, to the reduction in the cost of 2's initial volume of imports. Thus, defining M as the quantity of imports and p as the price of imports in terms of exports and assuming initial balance, for a small price change the change in import expenditure, valued at the pretransfer price, can be written:

$$p \cdot \frac{\partial M}{\partial p} \cdot dP = \left(-\frac{p}{M} \frac{\partial M}{\partial p} \right)\left(-pM \frac{dp}{p} \right).$$

Since $\eta_m = -\dfrac{p}{M} \dfrac{\partial M}{\partial p}$ and the implicit transfer is $-pM(dp/p)$, the change in expenditure on imports as a proportion of the transfer is:

$$\eta_m = \frac{p \cdot \dfrac{\partial M}{\partial p} \cdot dp}{-pM \dfrac{dp}{p}}$$

which in our earlier notation corresponds to $\dfrac{|\Delta M|}{\Delta U}$.

criterion for devaluation to improve the trade balance can thus be written as a variant of equation (8.15):

$$\eta_m + \eta_x > 1 + \frac{m}{s}\, s' + \frac{m_2}{s_2}\, s'_2,$$

with the outcome depending on the particular values of the parameters noted. Our earlier formulation in Chapter 7 is thus satisfactory only if we assume in particular that the marginal propensity to save is the same regardless of the nature of the change in income. Should these assumptions apply, $s' = s$ and the simpler criterion noted above would hold.

The classical and Keynesian models are of course extremes in view of their respective assumptions of full employment and flexible domestic prices and underemployment and constant domestic prices. In actuality, prices and incomes vary together and a truly meaningful analysis would have to take these variations into account. Some indication was given in Chapter 7 of the complexities encountered in trying to comprehend the variations occurring within and between the individual countries as a consequence of a devaluation. We shall not pursue these matters further in the present chapter since it is hoped that we have obtained many useful insights into the capital-transfer mechanism on the basis of the classical and Keynesian approaches that have been outlined above.

SOME EMPIRICAL EXAMPLES OF THE TRANSFER MECHANISM

Having treated at length certain theoretical aspects of the capital-transfer mechanism, it may be of interest to consider briefly some empirical examples of this mechanism. In both the classical and Keynesian models just presented, capital transfers were taken as autonomous in character and we asked to what extent the trade balance on goods and services adjusted to the transfer. Insofar as the transfer was not completely effected, accommodating capital movements took place in order to finance the trade imbalance. Thus, whatever secondary adjustment occurred was designed to remove the trade imbalance.

Reparations payments and other unilateral transfers are perhaps the best illustration of the sequence of events just described. However, other long-term capital movements such as portfolio and direct foreign investment need not conform to the same pattern since, as already noted, they are responsive to a variety of economic and political motivations at home and abroad. It is quite conceivable therefore that these latter types of capital movements may not be autonomous in the same sense as a reparations payment, and that they may occur in conjunction with increased flows of goods and services in response to some common economic cause. A good example of this would be when both goods and capital move from one country to another in response to a domestic boom in the receiving country.

It is difficult for the foregoing reasons to study the capital transfer mechanism in the light of the formal models discussed. That is, there may be no clear way to distinguish between the cause and effect of observed capital movements. Moreover, as our earlier discussion of balance-of-payments equilibrium in Chapter 1 revealed, it is virtually impossible to distinguish autonomous from accommodating capital movements since we have no knowledge of the underlying motivations of the transactors. It is therefore only when a capital transfer occurs and there are no other important changes that we can obtain a reasonably clear view of the workings of the transfer mechanism. Unfortunately, there are not many instances when this is the case.

It may be useful nevertheless to consider briefly a few well known historical cases of capital transfer. These are cited in Table 8.9, which shows for the years indicated the average amounts of the trade balance and the foreign transfer and the relative size of the transfer with respect to the transferring country's exports and national income.[35] The data for Great Britain refer to the substantial overseas expenditures in continental Europe especially during the Napoleonic Wars. While detailed information on Britain's balance of payments and national income is lacking, it would appear that the transfer was relatively large compared to the exports but relatively small compared to national income. It is of interest to note that during the years of the largest transfers, between 1811 and 1815, according to Imlah (1958, p. 94), Britain's net barter terms of trade deteriorated by about 30 percent.

The French data refer to the five-billion franc indemnities to be paid to Prussia by 1875, following the conclusion of the Franco-Prussian War in 1871. The bulk of these indemnities was financed by domestic bond issues in France that were purchased in large measure by foreigners and by French investors who disposed of some of their foreign investments. However, French investors replenished their portfolios with purchases of foreign securities in subsequent years and the government also made payments to service its foreign-owned debt. While it is thus not clear precisely when the real transfer took place, if we assume that it was spread over the four years, 1872–75, it appears that the transfer averaged about 30 percent of France's exports and 5.6 percent of national income.[36] It is evident in the table that France's trade balance became positive during 1872–75, although the cumulative trade surplus was equal only to about half of the transfer. The remainder of the transfer apparently took place subsequently. While the real transfer was relatively large, it apparently was made fairly smoothly. For as

35. Useful surveys of the capital transfer experiences noted in Table 8.9 are to be found in Machlup (1964; 1968), Kindleberger (1968, pp. 325–33), and Cohen (1967).

36. According to Machlup (1964, pp. 381 and 393), if one-half of the indemnity was assumed to be transferred each year in 1872–73, this would have amounted to 60.0 percent of exports and 11.2 percent of national income. If one-third had been transferred annually during 1872–74, this would have been 40.0 percent of exports and 7.5 percent of national income.

TABLE 8.9

Some Historical Examples of Foreign Transfers in Relation to Foreign Trade and National Income

	Average Trade Balance		Average Foreign Transfer		For. Transf. / Exports	For. Transf. / Nat'l Income
Great Britain						
1793–1805		n.a.	£	3.0 mill.	6.4%	1.0%
1796–1805		n.a.		2.3 mill.	4.9	n.a.
1806–1816		n.a.		10.9 mill.	20.1	n.a.
France						
1867–1871	Fr.	−119 mill.		—	—	—
1872–1875		510 mill.	Fr.	1,248 mill.[a]	30.0%	5.6%
Germany						
1925–1928	RM	−1,384 mill.	RM	1,182 mill.	10.9%	⎱2.5%[b]
1929–1932		1,406 mill.		1,498 mill.	14.7	⎰
1953–1959	$	914 mill.	$	233 mill.	2.0	0.6
1959–1965		1,275 mill.		573 mill.	3.8	0.9
Finland						
1944–1948		n.a.	OM	7,832 mill.	n.a.	4.0%
1948–1952	OM	17,200 mill.		10,446 mill.	8.7%	2.2
Italy						
1947–1956	$	− 682 mill.	$	23 mill.	0.015%	0.002%
1956–1965		−1,078 mill.		15 mill.	0.004%	0.001%
Japan						
1955–1960	$	−559 mill.	$	45 mill.	1.5%	0.002%
1960–1965		−833 mill.		63 mill.	1.1	0.001
United States						
1950–1955	$	2.4 bill.[c]	$	4.4 bill.[d]	29.0%	1.5%
1956–1961		4.4 bill.		7.0 bill.	31.1	1.8
1962–1967		5.4 bill.		8.1 bill.	25.4	1.5

[a] Assuming one-fourth of the indemnity to be transferred annually.
[b] Refers to average of 1924–32.
[c] Refers to goods and services, excluding earnings from capital and military expenditures.
[d] Sum of military expenditures abroad, remittances and pensions, net U.S. Government grants and loans, and net private U.S. capital less net earnings from capital and net foreign long-term capital.

SOURCE: Adapted from Machlup (1964; 1968, pp. 210–11), Cohen (1967), and Jensen (1966).

Kindleberger noted (1968, pp. 327–28), France and Germany deflated and inflated relative to each other, with trade being adjusted triangularly with France displacing German exports to Britain and Britain selling more to Germany than formerly to France.

The case of German reparations following World War I is next represented in Table 8.9. As mentioned earlier, Keynes and Ohlin engaged in a famous exchange over the issue of Germany's ability to effect the transfer. The issue was obscured in part because there was a substantial capital inflow into Germany from 1925–28 at the time the transfers were being made. This is reflected in the negative trade balance shown. However, after the capital inflow ceased, the German trade balance turned positive in 1929–32 in an amount that corresponded roughly with the amount of the transfer. It is interesting to note that the transfers were a relatively small proportion of German exports and national income. However, with the onset of the Great Depression, the receiving countries were not in a position to increase expenditure. Germany thus bore the brunt of the transfer by domestic deflation, this being a factor that led to the moratorium on further transfers in mid-1931. In retrospect, it thus appears that neither Keynes nor Ohlin was correct in their views of German reparations since, on the one hand, German export prices were not reduced drastically and, on the other hand, the receiving countries did not expand their domestic expenditure significantly to help effect the transfer. German reparations following World War II are also shown in Table 8.9. It is evident that the transfers involved were easily covered by the German trade surpluses and that they were small in relation to exports and national income. The fact that more substantial reparations were not imposed on Germany after World War II no doubt reflects the unfavorable experiences two decades earlier.

The case of Finland's reparations to the Soviet Union is next shown. Insofar as these reparations were to be paid in kind, there was no transfer problem of the usual sort. The Finnish economy was nevertheless subjected to some strain especially prior to 1948, since its manufacturing sector had to be expanded and larger quantities of imported raw materials were needed. By 1952, however, Finland's economy had expanded to the point where the indemnities were not particularly burdensome.[37] Italian and Japanese reparations following World War II were clearly a tiny fraction of the exports and national incomes of these countries.

The final case shown in Table 8.9 refers to the U.S., which since World War II has made large absolute amounts of foreign transfers for foreign aid, overseas military spending, and foreign investments. It is evident that these transfers have on average been substantially in excess of the trade balance. The difference has been absorbed primarily by the increased dollar holdings of foreign central banks for official reserve purposes. Should the foreign central banks become less willing to keep accumulating additional dollar reserves, the U.S. would be obliged to reduce its foreign transfers and/or to reduce its domestic expenditure so as to free more real goods and services for transfer purposes.

While the data in Table 8.9 convey but a small part of the capital-transfer experiences of the countries noted, the comparisons are nevertheless interesting. The French indemnities of the 1870's were certainly substantial in

37. For further details, consult Jensen (1966).

relation to France's foreign trade and national income, much more so than was the case for Germany during 1925–32. The deflationary pressure exerted on Germany by the real transfer following the cessation of the capital inflow had serious consequences for the level of German employment. This experience was influential in part in the decisions following World War II to forego the imposition of sizable reparations for fear that they would be difficult to transfer. Thus, while Germany, Italy, and Japan have made some reparations transfers, they have been small in relation to the levels of their foreign trade and national incomes. Finally, the case of the U.S. is a special one insofar as the capital transfer has been financed by the dollar accumulations of foreign central banks for official reserve purposes.

Having focused our remarks thus far on the capital transferring country, it is of some interest to cite two well known cases of capital-transfer receipts. The first is that of the U.S. during 1820–1913. According to a study by Williamson (1963), the sequence of events differed from what we would expect under the gold standard. That is, gold movements did not occur at the beginning of the transfer process. Rather as the American economy expanded and foreign borrowings were increased, there was both an inflow of goods and a monetary inflow. This latter inflow served as a means of satisfying the credit needs of the economy. The pattern was reversed when the growth of the American economy subsided.

The second case is that of Canada, which had very substantial inflows of capital from Britain in the years prior to World War I, rising from £29.5 million in 1904 to £375.8 million in 1913, according to Meier (1953, p. 7). The Canadian experience was first studied in detail by Viner (1924), who adapted the framework of the classical model of capital transfer to the Canadian context. He concluded that the model was borne out on the whole. Subsequent studies, especially by Meier (1953), Ingram (1957), and Stovel (1959), have questioned Viner's conclusions, however. It has been argued in particular that Viner placed too little emphasis upon the antecedents of the domestic boom that began in Canada in the late 1890's and that led to increases in domestic income and prices. Thus, the subsequent increases in imports and the capital inflow occurred in response to these antecedent changes rather than as the classical model posited. In addition, Viner had been unable to offer an adequate explanation of the substantial increase in Canadian exports during this period insofar as the classical model did not provide for any link between the capital imports, increases in productive capacity, and consequent increases in exports. The general conclusion that has emerged from these various studies is therefore that the Canadian experience is best understood by means of a combination of the classical and Keynesian models in which prices and income were interacting in the process of economic growth, with capital imports both being abetted by and aiding this process.

The instances of capital transfer reviewed above were selected mainly because they have received attention in the literature. There are many other possible cases that could be studied in their own right. In doing so, it would appear that neither the classical nor the Keynesian model is sufficient by itself for analytical purposes. This is especially the case when both prices and income are changing over time in the country or countries being studied. It may be difficult, moreover, particularly with respect to portfolio and direct foreign investment, to establish the order of causation for analytical purposes. This is because such investment may not be fully autonomous, but may occur as well in response to or coincidentally with other phenomena.

BORROWING COUNTRY REPAYMENT PROBLEMS

In our earlier treatment of portfolio investment, we abstracted from the transfer issues just discussed. There are two questions of particular interest here: (1) from the standpoint of the borrowing country, should borrowed capital be invested in export or import-competing industries in order to provide a built-in solution to potential transfer difficulties; and (2) from the standpoint of the lending country, should there be any concern over the import surplus that may develop over time as the return flow of principal and interest payments exceeds the outflow of new lending?

The answer to the first question is negative, at least in principle. That is, capital should be invested where it brings the highest (social) rate of return. This is not necessarily in export or import-competing industries, although if these industries are the most highly productive, the transfer of debt servicing will be greatly eased as foreign exchange capabilities will be directly increased. The point is, however, that if capital is invested productively with maximum yield, let us say by the public authorities, the returns can be tapped by fiscal measures so as to solve the purely budgetary aspects of the transfer. The transfer itself requires, of course, that the borrowing country develop an export surplus in foreign currency to effect the debt service, assuming that new capital inflows are insufficient for the country to maintain an import surplus. If the borrowing country has in fact invested productively and economic growth has occurred, the question is whether exports will expand more rapidly than imports. By the same token, if the investment leads to a reallocation of resources, more goods may become available for export and the domestic production of import substitutes may be greater. But there is no guarantee that this will happen since the need and demand for imports may also expand. Thus, economic growth and the adaptation of resources may or may not have favorable balance-of-payments effects.

There is a further problem arising from investment in infrastructure as compared to directly productive activities. If investment in public overhead facilities (e.g., transport, communications, power) is made substantially ahead of the demand for the output of these facilities and if foreign capital is employed in significant amounts in such investment, the borrowing country may well experience transfer difficulties. Consider, for example, Figure 8.2

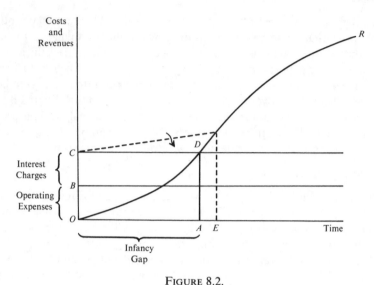

FIGURE 8.2.

The Infancy Gap in Public Overhead Investment

With a revenue growth curve of OR and operating expenses plus interest changes equal to OC per unit of time, the investment will not be self-financing until time OA. Additional financing will increase the infancy gap from OA to OE.

for some hypothetical investment in a public project that is justified on grounds of its relatively high (social) rate of return. Assume that the growth of total revenue (measured in domestic currency) follows the curve *OR* with the passage of time as the demand for the project's output grows. Assume further that the project requires operating expenses and interest charges to be paid to foreigners per unit of time in amounts equivalent to *OB* and *BC*, at some given (fixed) exchange rate. It is evident that the project will not be self-financing until time *OA*. There will be, as Nurkse put it (1961, p. 260) an "infancy gap" between the time a project is built and the time that the demand for its output has increased to the point where costs are covered. Now if during the infancy gap, the borrowing country's productive capacity has not expanded significantly and its scale of comparative advantage not been altered to speak of, it may be difficult, with a fixed exchange rate, to generate enough additional foreign exchange to effect the foreign transfer of the interest charges.

What then can be done? One possibility is that the country may undertake additional foreign borrowing to tide itself over the infancy gap. As noted in Figure 8.2, this will increase the length of this gap from *OA* to *OE*. A second possibility is that the interest charges may be financed out of increased tax revenues. The difficulty here might be that such taxation would result in cutting the use of the output of the project. In such an event, the revenue curve would be shifted to the right. This evidently would result also in a lengthening of the infancy gap. A third possibility would be to default on the interest charges in an outright manner or to seek a rescheduling of the payments. The disadvantage of outright default is that the borrower might subsequently experience difficulty in obtaining new loans. Rescheduling of the payments would depend largely upon the attitudes and generosity of the lender, subject of course to the realities of the borrower's production and foreign exchange capabilities. A final possibility is for the lender to take cognizance of the potential transfer difficulties by extending a "soft" loan, that is, a loan on concessional terms. Such a loan may carry a grace period during which no payments are required, a rate of interest below the market rate, and a longer-than-usual maturity period. Each of these possibilities has been implemented in actuality at one time or another, historically speaking.[38] The soft loan approach came to be adopted in particular in the 1960's in foreign aid and loan extensions by national governments and international agencies. The International Development Association (IDA), which is an affiliate of the International Bank for Reconstruction and Development (IBRD), was in fact created just for this purpose.

The preceding discussion suggests that while borrowing countries should invest foreign capital according to marginal productivity criteria, the expansion and diversification of the country's productive capacity cannot necessarily be relied upon to generate the foreign exchange proceeds required for repayment purposes. Transfer difficulties may arise especially if the borrowing country has invested substantially in public overhead facilities that require a comparatively long period before they become self-financing. In such instances, special arrangements may be required for servicing foreign debts.

LENDING COUNTRY REPAYMENT PROBLEMS

We know from our discussion of the transfer problem that the transfer will be eased if the receiving country expands its income and the transfer made more difficult if it is offset or if the receiving country contracts its income by an amount in excess of the transfer. This suggests in the present context that the repayment problems of the borrowing country can be eased significantly if the lending country follows a liberal commercial policy with respect to imports and if full employment is maintained over time. This will enable a rising flow of goods and services to be imported by the lending country as repayments are received from the borrower. Lending country policies will

---

38. For some illustrative nineteenth century experiences, see Nurkse (1961, pp. 261–67).

thus have an important bearing on the relative ease or difficulty with which foreign debt service is transferred.[39]

As noted earlier, there might be some concern from the standpoint of the lending country with regard to the possibly deflationary impact of running an import surplus as inflows of debt service exceeded total outflows.[40] It will be recalled from equation (8.9) that the foreign reserve effect of changes in the home country's financial wealth depended on the relative magnitudes of g_h, the growth rate of financial wealth, and r_f, the foreign country's interest rate. If the lending (home) country were in fact concerned about avoiding an inflow in excess of its outflow, it could always increase g_h, which would result in an increase in the purchase of foreign bonds. So long as $g_h > r_f$, there would be no deflationary problems associated with the return flow.[41]

Suppose, however, that $g_h < r_f$, which means that foreign interest payments exceed new lending. Is this something that really need worry the lending country? To answer this question, we may note first that insofar as interest income may be added to financial wealth, the repayments of capital may be relent, depending upon investment conditions at home and abroad. Alternatively, the receipt of interest income may lead to increased expenditure, which may have a stimulating effect on the lending country. Aside from the foregoing possibilities, any deflationary potential of the return flow could

39. This point can be illustrated by the experiences of the U.S. in the late 1920's and early 1930's. According to data reproduced in Mikesell (1962, p. 53), the U.S. virtually stopped lending abroad after 1929–30, and there was actually a reverse flow of net lending into this country from 1931–38. At the same time, with the onset of the Great Depression, there was a substantial decline in world trade in general and U.S. trade in particular. For example, according to Lary and Associates (1943, p. 216), U.S. current-account receipts dropped from \$7.1 billion in 1929 to \$2.4 billion in 1933 and payments from \$6.4 billion to \$2.3 billion in the years indicated. These declines reflect of course the drop in world income, which unfortunately was exacerbated by the erection of higher tariff and other trade barriers by the U.S. in a futile attempt to ward off further reductions in employment. With the substantial cut in foreign lending and the drying up of proceeds from trade with the U.S., the rest of the world, which was faced with dollar obligations amounting to about \$1 billion annually, was placed under tremendous strain, especially in 1931–34. It is no wonder, therefore, that there were so many defaults on obligations during these years.

40. This was perceived by some writers in the years following World War II to be a potentially serious problem that the U.S. might eventually have to face. See Domar (1950) and the references cited therein.

41. This result is analogous to the one reached by Domar (1950) and expressed in his well known formula:

$$R_L = \frac{a + i}{a + g}$$

where R_L is the ratio of inflow of debt service to outflow as time approaches infinity, a is the rate of amortization computed as a constant fraction of the net debt outstanding, i is the rate of return on foreign lending, and g is the rate of growth of new lending. Thus, Domar concluded that so long as $g > i$, there will be no import surplus. This could be attained by increasing g or by lowering i. Note that i in Domar's model corresponds to r_f in our model based upon Morton's work (1970). The effect of changes in r_f could be determined by differentiating equation (8.5) noted earlier.

always be dealt with by offsetting domestic monetary and fiscal policies designed to maintain income at the full employment level. There is no particular need therefore for the lending country to be unduly concerned about the handling of the return flow.

BALANCE-OF-PAYMENTS AND INCOME EFFECTS
OF DIRECT FOREIGN INVESTMENT

It is of some interest to note that the two-country model of capital transfer discussed earlier is relevant in assessing the impact of direct foreign investment upon national income and the balance of payments of the capital transferring and receiving countries. This is an especially pertinent subject in view of the fact that, in both the U.S. and the United Kingdom, policies for controlling direct investment outflows were implemented during the 1960's for balance-of-payments reasons. There has also been continuing discussion in many receiving countries concerning possible measures designed to restrict direct investment inflows.

Comprehensive studies of the issues have been made by Hufbauer and Adler (1968) for the U.S. and by Reddaway *et al.* (1967; 1968) for the U.K.[42] The Hufbauer-Adler (H-A) work is particularly interesting since their theoretical framework is based in part upon Johnson's two-country model of capital transfer that we discussed at length earlier. Briefly, the objectives and rationale of the H-A study were (1968, p. 2):

...to assess the balance-of-payments impact of overseas manufacturing investment in terms of "payments recoupment periods." These recoupment periods purport to tell how many years are required before a single direct investment outflow, e.g., 1967, will produce a cumulative stream of balance of payments inflows equal to itself. The method of assessment is historical. Recoupment periods for the future are based on *average* inferences from the past. The word "average" deserves special emphasis. Recoupment periods for different firms building different plants in different countries are not going to be the same. Some investments will show very much shorter recoupment periods than others. The figures reached ... represent the average behavior of a representative basket of direct investment projects....

Why are we so interested in recoupment periods? The rationale ... runs along the following lines. Direct investment and other capital flows exhibit ... abrupt increases and decreases. Whether these abrupt changes cause no real balance-of-payments dislocation ... is a matter of considerable interest. If recoupment periods ... are quite short and the dislocation merely temporary, it follows that measures designed to restrain direct investment will quickly prove counterproductive. Within a few years, the balance-of-payments advantage gained on capital account will be offset by deterioration elsewhere. But if recoupment periods are long, restraints may improve the balance of payments for a substantial period of time.

42. For earlier treatments with regard to the U.S., see Bell (1962), Krause and Dam (1964), and Polk *et al.* (1966).

The relationships used by H-A in calculating the recoupment periods were based on data for the 1950's and the first half of the 1960's. The calculations themselves pertaining to a unit of direct foreign investment were based upon parameters incorporating the following effects: (1) the estimated earnings that foreign manufacturing affiliates would remit to their parent U.S. firms; (2) estimates of the changes in U.S. exports of capital equipment and of parts and components, royalties and fees paid to the parent firm, imports into the U.S., displacement of U.S. exports by foreign affiliates and other firms producing abroad, and changes in U.S. exports and imports in response to recurrent increases in income earned abroad; and (3) changes in U.S. exports and imports due to immediate and sustained multiplier effects on income at home and abroad.

Where relevant, the calculations were made on the basis of three alternative assumptions concerning the capital transfer: (1) "classical substitution" assumptions according to which the capital outflow for direct investment reduces home investment and supplements foreign investment by the exact amount of the transfer; (2) "reverse classical" substitution assumptions according to which the transfer has no impact on investment either at home or abroad; and (3) "anticlassical substitution" assumptions according to which the transfer has no impact on investment at home but adds to investment abroad.[43]

The H-A results are summarized in Table 8.10. It is evident that these results are quite sensitive to the transfer assumptions made, and that in some instances the recoupment periods are negative, implying that direct investment outflows will have a permanently negative effect on the U.S. balance of payments. In examining the detailed results in the H-A work (1968, pp. 60–65), their calculation of the export-displacement effect turns out to be of major importance except in the reverse classical case where U.S. investment is assumed to substitute for native and/or other foreign investment. Although they made some allowance for increases in U.S. exports induced by increases in foreign income, the multiplier effect in question is much smaller than the trade-displacement effect.[44] It is noteworthy that in the reverse classical case, where it is assumed that the transfer has no effect on investment either at home or abroad, the stabilization authorities are supposed to maintain the level of investment. This means that if a U.S. firm invests in Europe, the authorities in Europe will take measures to cause European or other foreign firms to reduce their investment by a like amount. If it were supposed, alternatively, that consumption or government expenditures are reduced in Europe rather than investment, it turns out, as Branson has noted (1969a,

---

43. In terms of Johnson's model discussed earlier, the classical assumptions imply that $s' = s'_2 = 0$ (Case 6 in Table 8.8), the reverse classical assumptions that $s' = s'_2 = 1$, and the anticlassical assumptions that $s' = 1$ and $s'_2 = 0$ (Case 4 in Table 8.8).

44. This and other limitations of the H-A study are discussed in Cooper (1969b, pp. 1208–11).

TABLE 8.10

Adjusted Recoupment Periods by Regions under Alternative Transfer Assumptions of an Outflow of U.S. Direct Investment[a]

Assumptions and Regions	Hufbauer-Adler	Branson
Classical assumptions[b]		
Canada	Negative	
Latin America	Negative	
Europe	7.5	
Rest of world	22.2	
Reverse classical assumptions[c]		
Canada	10.2	3.1
Latin America	9.8	7.5
Europe	6.5	6.0
Rest of world	6.7	6.0
Anticlassical assumptions[d]		
Canada	Negative	
Latin America	Negative	
Europe	10.8	
Rest of world	Negative	

[a] The recoupment period represents the number of years required for a unit direct investment outflow to produce a cumulative balance-of-payments surplus equal to itself. A negative recoupment period means that the balance-of-payments consequence of direct investment become increasingly worse over time.

[b] Assuming a unit of direct investment causes a unit net increase in investment in the receiving country and a unit decline in the U.S.

[c] Assuming a unit of direct investment has no effect on investment in the receiving country and the U.S.

[d] Assuming a unit of direct investment causes a unit net increase in investment in the receiving country but has no effect in the U.S.

SOURCE: Adapted from Hufbauer and Adler (1968) and Branson (1969a).

pp. 84–85) and as can be seen in Table 8.10, that the recoupment periods will be reduced because the increase in investment abroad will have a favorable effect on U.S. capital-goods exports.[45]

Assuming the recoupment periods lie roughly between the H-A and Branson estimates, what are the implications for policy?[46] It might appear

45. Using a somewhat different model than H-A and with transfer assumptions that correspond to the reverse classical case, Reddaway *et al.* (1967; 1968) concluded for the U.K. that on the average for an additional £100 of direct investment abroad in mining or manufacturing, £11 would be recouped immediately via increased U.K. exports of capital goods. There would be an additional £4 recoupment per annum due to profits and secondary increases in exports. The implied recoupment period for the U.K. is thus substantially greater than for the U.S. See Hufbauer and Adler (1968, pp. 90–91) for a comparison of their methods and results with those of Reddaway. Dunning (1969) contains a useful and insightful review of both studies.

46. See Dunning (1969) for some further calculations that have the effect of reducing the length of both the H-A and Reddaway recoupment periods.

that restrictions on direct investment outflows could be justified on short-term balance-of-payments grounds. The recoupment period is per se not a satisfactory criterion for such a judgment, however, since it does not distinguish between outflows now and outflows later. This suggests furthermore in the context of the H-A study that future effects should be discounted to the present to put them on the same footing as present outflows. The appropriate discount rate to employ for this purpose is by no means obvious. It should be mentioned, finally, that the H-A calculations were made on the assumption of a single direct investment outflow. It might be just as plausible to assume that direct investment outflows will increase with time, in which case the rate of growth of the outflows would have to be weighed against the return flows.[47]

If the recoupment periods, especially for the reverse classical case, are believable, the implication follows that direct investment will have a favorable impact on the balance of payments of the receiving country. How long this will persist will vary in given circumstances. But even if the receiving country's remissions of profits and payments for other services should be in excess of the inflow of new investment, this need not be a cause for alarm. As we have noted earlier, what is important is the impact that foreign investment will have in expanding productive capacity and the level of income in the receiving country. While there is no guarantee that the favorable balance-of-payments effects of expanded productivity will remain positive, this may well turn out to be the case. Direct investment, as we have seen, is motivated in great measure by large and expanding markets in the cases of both extractive and manufacturing investments. From the receiving country's point of view, therefore, these investments may very possibly result in both an expansion of exports and import substitution.

Apart from the longer run considerations just noted, the receiving country might be concerned over the potentially prejudicial effects of foreign remissions on the balance of payments in the short run. The issue here is mainly one of timing and whether or not foreign remissions are likely to bunch together in periods of balance-of-payments difficulties. In the present-day international monetary system, we have seen that countries can draw upon the IMF and other sources of reserves to finance temporary difficulties without having necessarily to restrict foreign remissions. Moreover, since profits from direct investment may move in sympathy with the level of income in the receiving country, foreign remissions are not likely to increase when the economy slows down. Finally, given the diversity in size and character of direct investments, there may be enough offsetting tendencies to prevent a significant bunching of remissions. An important exception to all of this is if foreign investors decide to repatriate their capital on a large scale. This

---

47. Indeed, there is one school of thought that maintains that firms must continually invest overseas to maintain their market position and that the restriction of new outflows will have an adverse effect on future inflows. This view, which has been called the "organic" approach to direct investment, is expressed in Polk *et al.* (1966) and given a sympathetic hearing in Dunning's critique (1969) of the H-A and Reddaway studies.

would indeed cause difficulties for the balance of payments, although the question here is what lay behind the decision to repatriate and what measures could be taken to forestall the repatriation.

Efficiency and Welfare Implications of Long-Term Investment and Borrowing

PORTFOLIO INVESTMENT

There has been considerable discussion since the early 1960's especially of the need to control international long-term investment. The chief grounds for such control have been to correct discrepancies between private and social rates of return and the avoidance of short-run adjustment problems that might have to be faced if a country had to deflate domestically in effecting the transfer of capital. These issues have been aired extensively in the U.S. in the context of this country's resort to the Interest Equalization Tax in 1963 and subsequent "voluntary" and mandatory controls designed to restrict the outflow of long-term capital for balance-of-payments purposes.

It is most interesting that prior to the 1960's the bulk of new security flotations took place on the New York market, in recognition of the superior efficiency and breadth of this market and the central role of the dollar in the international monetary system. However, in the years since the implementation of the U.S. capital controls, there has been a remarkable upsurge in foreign bond flotations on the domestic markets in Canada and Western Europe and in the so-called Eurobond market that has developed in London and elsewhere on the Continent.[48] These recent developments are especially noteworthy since the capital markets in Western Europe have typically been relatively fragmented and subject to both private and official restrictions of various kinds.[49]

This resurgence of the international bond market is important insofar as the major national financial markets have been brought closer together with resultant efficiency gains to the participants involved. At the same time, however, problems have been created for national policy makers who have found themselves constrained in their use of monetary policy to control domestic expenditure, more exposed to sudden changes in their foreign reserves in periods of exchange-rate uncertainty, and somewhat less able to maintain and enforce their national laws with regard to income taxation and business regulation.[50]

---

48. According to data recorded in Cooper (1970, p. 2), foreign bond flotations on European and Canadian markets rose from $426 million in 1963 to $1,185 million in 1968. International issues rose from $119 million in 1963 to $3,517 million in 1968. Foreign issues floated in the U.S. averaged $1,441 million annually during this period, with a slight uptrend. Cooper has noted that these amounts compare favorably with the average annual flotations of $2.0 billion in Europe and the U.S. in 1924–28.

49. For documentation, see the references cited in Kindleberger (1967, p. 603).

50. See Cooper (1970) for an elaboration of these points.

If one takes a cosmopolitan view,[51] the increased efficiency of the international capital market can be looked upon with favor since it means an increase in world welfare. National policy makers may thus be urged to take steps to foster even greater efficiency rather than to frustrate the workings of the market. The problem may appear rather different, however, from an individual country standpoint when account is taken of the numerous imperfections and restrictions that affect the market and the difficulties that may be posed by imperfect functioning of the mechanism of balance-of-payments adjustment. Another way to describe all of this is in terms of whether our objective should be to seek first-best or second-best solutions to questions involving economic welfare. Second-best policies can be advocated only with careful analysis and factual knowledge of the situation in question. Indeed there may be many situations, particularly in the short run, when second-best considerations are overriding. Improvements in efficiency and welfare should remain paramount objectives in the long run, however, with full recognition that increased cooperation and harmonization of national policies may be required and steps taken to improve the workings of the international financial system.[52]

In addition to questions of efficiency, we must also take equity considerations into account. On the national level, there is the concern over the distribution of the world's capital resources between the advanced industrialized countries and the less developed countries. Within individual nations, the distribution of income among the major groups—say capital, labor, and landowners—may be a prime concern.

Before World War I, long-term capital was channeled via the international capital market particularly from Great Britain mainly to the "regions of recent settlement," with the bulk of these transfers being utilized for the building of infrastructure, especially railroads.[53] A comparatively small amount of capital was loaned at that time to countries that are now considered underdeveloped. This is still the case today except for a few countries that have proven creditworthy (e.g., Mexico, Venezuela, Peru, Taiwan). The capital needs of the poor countries have thus become the province of national foreign economic assistance programs, and international agencies, in particular the IBRD and IDA. Presumably as additional countries sustain higher levels and more rapid rates of growth, they will be able themselves to borrow in the international capital market. This time is probably still far in the future, however, for a substantial number of poor countries. Official lending

51. As does Kindleberger (1967).
52. We shall have more to say on this in Chapter 12.
53. For details consult Nurkse (1961, pp. 134–50) and the references cited therein. According to Nurkse, the regions of recent settlement comprise the United States, Canada, Australia, New Zealand, South Africa, Argentina, Uruguay, and the southern tip of Brazil. Bloomfield (1968) also contains some useful material on international investment prior to World War I.

and aid will thus continue to be a major source of capital movement from the rich to the poor countries.

The question of the impact of international capital movements on the distribution of income within countries can be considered in the context of the partial and general equilibrium models used commonly in international trade theory. These models abstract from the monetary considerations that are important for the balance of payments and focus rather on the real resources involved. As far as portfolio foreign investment is concerned, the most important distributional issues arise from the capital that moves in response to artificially imposed incentives due either to monopolistic influences and/or government policies of various kinds. It is conceivable that there might be grounds for interfering with the flow of capital if there was a discrepancy between the private and social rates of return, especially if this was a consequence of the factors just mentioned.[54] We shall have more to say on this matter in our treatment of direct foreign investment to which we now turn.

DIRECT FOREIGN INVESTMENT

In our earlier discussion of direct foreign investment, we were concerned mainly with motivational factors at the firm and industry level and with possible effects of such investment on the balance of payments and income in the transferring and receiving countries. Implicit in our discussion has been the notion that private and social interests are coincident with regard to direct investment. However, this coincidence of interests need not hold. Diagrammatic analysis may be useful in illustrating the main points involved.[55]

Thus, assume as in Figure 8.3 that we have two countries with given capital stocks, OO' and O^*O', that are measured horizontally. The marginal-product-of-capital (MPC) schedule for the home country, MPC $= r_h$, is drawn with respect to the origin O and that for the foreign country, MPC* $= r_f$, with respect to O^*. In isolation, equilibrium for the home country is indicated at point J; national income is equal to the area $OCJO'$ under the MPC curve, with total returns to capital of $OAJO'$ and the remainder to labor, ACJ. The corresponding equilibrium in isolation for the foreign country is at point G, national income is O^*KGO', returns to capital are O^*LGO', and returns to labor are LKG.

If the countries are now brought into contact and there are no impediments to capital transfer, investors in the home country will invest a portion of their capital stock abroad where they can earn a higher rate of return. The new

---

54. As will be noted below, there may be, in addition, possibilities for some countries to exact gains from others along optimum tariff lines with international capital movements.

55. Much of what follows is based upon Kemp (1964, esp. Ch. 13) and MacDougall (1960; 1968, pp. 172–76). I am indebted to J. David Richardson for his assistance in clarifying and simplifying the main issues involved, and for spelling out the analytical details in connection with Figures 8.3 and 8.4.

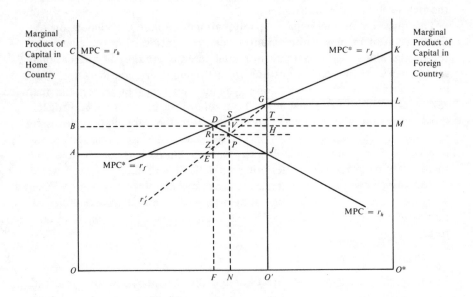

FIGURE 8.3.

Home and Foreign Investment

In isolation, equilibrium for the home country is at J and for the foreign country at G. If foreign investment now occurs, the equilibrium will be at D and world welfare will be increased by DGJ. Foreign investment of O'F will not be optimal from the home country's standpoint, however, and should be reduced to O'N.

equilibrium will be at point D, where the rates of return to capital are equated in two countries. The national incomes will then be:

Home Country Returns		*Foreign Country Returns*	
Labor	*BCD*	Labor	*MKD*
Domestic capital	*OBDF*	Domestic capital	*O*MHO'*
Foreign capital	*FDHO'*		

It is evident that, in the new equilibrium, national incomes will be higher than previously by the amount *DHJ* in the home country and *HGD* in the foreign country. World income is therefore increased by *DGJ*. It is also evident that the returns to labor in the home country have been reduced from *ACJ* to *BCD* and that the returns to capital have risen by the amount *ABHJ*. In the foreign country, the returns to labor have risen from *LKG* to *MKD* while the returns to capital have fallen by *MLGH*.

The question that now arises is whether point D in Figure 8.3 is optimal from the standpoint of maximizing the home country's income. Now it will be observed for some given level of the marginal productivity of capital (MPC) that the home country obtains both labor and capital returns on home investment, but only capital returns on foreign investment. The *national* return on foreign investment for the home country is thus lower for the same MPC. Since the home country's foreign investor considers only his own returns and not the returns to home labor, there will be a divergence between private and social returns from the home country's standpoint. In other words, the privately obtained competitive equilibrium at point D in Figure 8.3 is not socially optimal for the home country. A case can be made therefore for the home country to restrict foreign investment.

To clarify this matter, it should be noted that the returns from foreign investment in Figure 8.3 are represented by the area of inscribed rectangles such as $FDHO'$ under the $MPC^* = r_f$ curve. Since this curve measures *average* returns, it follows that the returns to foreign capital can be measured identically by the total area under a curve that is *marginal* to $MPC^* = r_f$. This marginal curve, which begins at zero foreign investment at point G in Figure 8.3, is shown as r'_f. If we were now to measure income as a result of investment at point D as the sum of the areas under the $MPC = r_h$ and r'_f curves, income would not be at a maximum for the home country. That is, by decreasing foreign investment, the home country's income could be increased by as much as ZDP. Thus, while comparing r_h, the home rate of return, with r_f, the foreign rate of return, and investing until $r_h = r_f$, the actions of the foreign investor clearly affect total foreign earnings since r_f declines as foreign investment expands. *From the national standpoint, what should be equated then is the marginal rate of return on foreign investment, r'_f, with the home rate, r_h.* Optimal foreign investment for the home country is therefore $O'N$, which is evidently less than $O'F$. With foreign investment of $O'N$, the combined area beneath the home country's $MPC = r_h$ curve and the r'_f curve is at a maximum. In this instance, the home country can therefore increase its national income by restricting foreign investment vis-à-vis the privately attained equilibrium at point D.[56]

The home country could also obtain the socially optimal level of foreign investment by taxing the earnings on foreign invested capital. As noted in Figure 8.4, the imposition of a tax by the home country will shift the $MPC^* = r_f$ curve downward to $MPC^* = r_{ft}$. This latter MPC^* curve with the tax will have a smaller intercept and a flatter slope than the MPC^* curve without

56. Thus suppose that foreign investment is restricted by the amount FN in Figure 8.3. This will increase the returns from domestically employed capital in the home country by $FNPD$. The returns from capital invested abroad will change by $VHTS - FNVD$. Since $FNVD = FNDP + PVD$, the net effect of restricting foreign investment will be: $FNPD + VHTS - FNPD - PVD$, which will be greater than zero as long as $VHTS > PVD$. Should the home country restrict foreign investment by amounts substantially in excess of FN, its national income will be lowered.

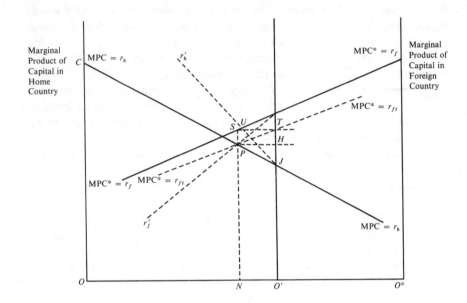

FIGURE 8.4.

Taxation of Foreign Earnings

The optimal level of foreign investment of $O'N$ from the home-country standpoint can be obtained by taxation of foreign earnings in an amount PSTH. The foreign country can also tax foreign earnings; its optimal position is indicated at U.

tax.[57] The equilibrium position shown at point P corresponds to Figure 8.3. Private earnings on foreign invested capital will be *NPHO'*, and home-country taxes on these earnings will be *PSTH*. The home country's national income will be *OCPN* from domestically employed capital plus *NSTO'* from

---

57. Since the MPC curves have been drawn as straight lines, we can write:

$$\text{MPC*} \ (= r_f) = \alpha - \beta C \qquad \alpha, \beta > 0$$

where C refers to capital. Total earnings before tax will be:

$$\text{MPC*} \cdot C = \alpha C - \beta C^2$$

and earnings after tax (t) will be:

$$(1 - t)(\text{MPC*} \cdot C) = (1 - t)(\alpha C - \beta C^2).$$

The MPC* curve with tax can then be represented as:

$$\text{MPC*} = r_{ft} = \alpha(1 - t) - \beta(1 - t)C,$$

which can be seen in Figure 8.4 to have a smaller intercept and a flatter slope than the MPC* curve without tax.

foreign investment. By the same line of reasoning, the foreign country could decide to levy a tax on earnings from foreign investment, in which case its national income would be larger by the amount *PSTH*. This suggests more generally, from the foreign country's standpoint, that since it faces rising marginal costs from reliance on foreign capital, there may be grounds for restricting foreign investment through taxation of foreign earnings.[58]

Our discussion thus far has suggested from the home country's point of view that foreign investment may be excessive because private returns will be greater than social returns under conditions of competition. The counterpart to this excessive investment will, as we have seen, redound to the benefit of the foreign country in terms of increased returns to labor. It has been suggested furthermore that the home or the foreign country can levy taxes on earnings from foreign investment so as to increase national income. Now it is common in actuality for countries to have international double taxation agreements under which the home country allows credit to investors for taxes paid to foreign governments on income earned abroad. If the foreign rate of taxation exceeded the home rate, there would be a disincentive for foreign investment based on the difference between the rates. In any event, however, so long as tax credits are granted, there is further reason to believe that there may be a discrepancy between the private and social rates of return and foreign investment may not be optimal from the home country's standpoint. The foreign country will of course stand to gain in such circumstances since it is collecting taxes that would otherwise accrue to the government of the home country.

The foregoing discussion has abstracted from a number of important considerations that may render the conclusions we have reached somewhat less exact. In particular, we have made the rather strict assumption that the MPC curves in both countries are unchanged by the foreign investment. Now it is quite plausible that foreign investment may cause the MPC curves to shift upward in one or both countries.[59] Foreign investment in extractive

58. The optimum level of foreign investment from the foreign country's standpoint, in the absence of home-country taxation, can be found by constructing the curve (r_h') that is marginal to the MPC $= r_h$ curve beginning at point J in Figure 8.4 and determining where r_h' and MPC* $= r_f$ intersect, which is at point U. Since U lies to the right of S, this implies a higher rate of taxation on foreign earnings by the foreign country and a smaller amount of foreign investment as compared to the optimal position of the home country. This result, it may be noted, is not a general one since it may vary with different locations and slopes of the curves. Note further that we have abstracted from the possible objective of maximizing world income and using transfer payments to compensate for the losses that a country suffers. For further elaboration of the issues being discussed here as well as those that arise when trade and capital movements are considered jointly with and without the existence of tariffs, see especially Kemp (1964; 1966b) and Jones (1967). Note finally that we have treated only the issue of the optimal allocation of given capital stocks. See Morton (1970) for an analysis of optimal foreign investment in a growth context embodying both real and financial considerations.

59. See Jasay (1959) for a formal analysis in which foreign investment shifts the home country's MPC upward, in which case it is not possible to reach any general presumption that foreign investment will be excessive from the home country's viewpoint.

industries might, for example, have a beneficial effect on the home country by making available larger and less costly supplies of raw materials. The foreign country might also benefit by being able to exploit hitherto untapped resources. Foreign investment in manufacturing may confer substantial benefits upon both the home and foreign countries by virtue of the extension of international specialization based on comparative advantage. In addition, there may be further gains through the realization of external economies at home and abroad.[60]

The additional potential benefits of foreign investment just mentioned may of course be muted if there are rapidly diminishing returns to increased investment and if there is only a limited degree of interdependency in the productive sectors involved.[61] It may also be the case that the gains from foreign investment may be mostly one-sided in favor of the home country because of the monopolistic power that foreign firms can exercise in markets abroad on the selling and buying sides.[62] The existence of monopolistic influences may cut both ways, however, as far as foreign investment is concerned. Thus, in countries where individual firms can exercise monopoly power, additional foreign investment might be one means to curb such power. Moreover, the existence of monopolistic firms in a given country may well reflect such government policies as tariffs and special licensing arrangements that are inimical to competition. It may not be justified in such circumstances to scorn foreign firms when it is government policy that is at fault.

In addition to the static considerations we have discussed, it should be stressed that foreign investment has important dynamic ramifications for both the home and foreign country. An important issue here is the extent to which the investing firm shares its existing stock of knowledge and additions thereto with its foreign affiliates, and vice versa. This relates both to output in terms of its efficient production and distribution and to inputs in terms of the impact of the foreign investment upon the labor and entrepreneurial resources in the foreign country. Foreign investment is frequently criticized on the grounds that the benefits of technological developments are shared unequally from the foreign country's standpoint. Such criticism frequently overlooks, however, the very substantial outlays that have been made in the home country to make the technological developments possible.

60. The potential importance of these considerations suggests the difficulties of trying to tie down the effects that are specific to particular investments. Dunning (1969) makes this point in his critique of the foreign investment studies discussed earlier.

61. It is conceivable, furthermore, contrary to our earlier analysis, that foreign investment could increase the returns to capital and lower those to labor in the foreign country. As Johnson (1970a, pp. 46–47) points out, this can happen if foreign investment increases the demand for capital in the foreign country.

62. Monopolistic influences figure prominently, for example, in the evaluation of foreign investment in Canada in the report by Watkins *et al.* (1968). See Bauer and Yamey (1968) for a treatment of monopsonistic influences especially in the case of West Africa.

A further criticism often voiced is that foreign investment may not contribute significantly to the training of the labor force and to entrepreneurial development abroad, and that in some circumstances there may even be a retarding effect on the development of these human resources. This latter criticism is difficult to evaluate because it is by no means clear what the course of events in the foreign country would have been in the absence of the foreign investment. It is conceivable that, in cases of colonial or imperialistic dominance by the home country, foreign investment might have been only marginally beneficial or maybe even harmful to the receiving country. This is an hypothesis that could be studied with respect to individual countries, although it is not likely that clear-cut conclusions would emerge because of the severe data limitations that would be encountered.

We may mention, finally, that the expansion of the multinational corporation has created potential areas of government-corporate conflict and conflict between home and foreign governments.[63] There are some difficult questions of national sovereignty that have come to the fore in recent years due to the impact that foreign firms may have upon local employment and capital markets and upon the ability and effectiveness of the government in managing its economic, political, and social affairs. On occasion the home country may adopt policies affecting firms that are heavily involved in foreign operations. Such policies may have an adverse impact on the interests of foreign countries, in which case intergovernmental tensions may be exacerbated. It has been suggested for this reason that it might be desirable to formalize a code of behavior affecting multinational corporations in the same way as there has been developed a code for international trade policy as exemplified in the General Agreement on Tariffs and Trade.[64]

Conclusion

We discussed in this chapter the three major forms of international long-term capital movements, the theoretical mechanism of the process of capital transfer, and the efficiency and welfare implications of international lending and borrowing.

The portfolio investment decision was discussed in terms of a portfolio model in which investors balance off returns and risk. This model was elaborated to take growing wealth into account, and expressions were derived for the stock-adjustment and flow effects of changes in the domestic rate of interest and rate of growth of wealth. In analyzing the motivations for direct investment, disequilibrium factors and market imperfections were

63. See Vernon (1970) and Behrman (1970) for a more extended discussion of the sources of and possible means for dealing with these conflicts.
64. Kindleberger (1969a) contains some interesting commentary concerning national and international policies with regard to the multinational corporation.

assumed to be especially important. A distinction was drawn between the initial foreign investment decision and the ongoing investment decision. The initial decision was taken to be influenced by both economic and subjective considerations, and it was shown that firms might pass up ostensibly profitable opportunities if the subjective considerations were important. The analysis of the ongoing foreign investment decision was framed according to the different objectives that might be involved depending upon the maturity of the foreign affiliate and its degree of independence vis-a-vis the parent company. In examining foreign economic assistance, we focused mainly on the comparative performance of the major donor countries, noting in particular the distinction between nominal flows and real flows based on the concept of the grant element.

As in our earlier treatment of balance-of-payments adjustment, the capital-transfer mechanism was analyzed using a classical model, a Keynesian model, and a combination of the two. Our concern was to analyze the effects of a capital transfer in a two-country model with regard to the balance of payments, terms of trade, and level of income in the transferring and receiving countries. In the classical model, the effect on the terms of trade was seen to depend upon the nature of the monetary and price-level adjustment in connection with the transfer. Abstracting from monetary considerations, the terms-of-trade effect depended on the relative preferences of the countries for each other's goods. In the Keynesian analogue to the classical model, the terms-of-trade effect was seen to depend upon whether the sum of the marginal propensities to import in the two countries was less than, equal to, or greater than unity. Making allowance for different policies and parameters for savings and imports with regard to the transfer-related expenditure changes in the two countries and taking multiplier effects into account gave results that were more complex than those just noted. Finally, we considered price adjustment via devaluation in a transfer context and reached conclusions with respect to the balance of payments that took account of the different savings parameters in the two countries. We then had occasion to examine briefly some selected historical examples illustrating the capital-transfer mechanism for individual countries, repayment problems from the standpoints of the borrowing and lending countries, and the estimated balance-of-payments and income effects of U.S. direct investment.

Questions of the efficiency of the international capital market were broached with regard chiefly to the problems faced by policy makers in connection with the balance of payments. Equity considerations were seen to be paramount in the channeling of resources from the rich to the poor countries. Our final concern was with the efficiency and welfare aspects of direct investment. We examined in particular possible sources of discrepancies between private and social returns and certain broader and more essentially dynamic issues involved in evaluating the effects of direct investment from the standpoints of the transferring and receiving countries.

Appendix

DERIVATION OF THE EQUATIONS FOR INCOME CHANGES AND THE
BALANCE OF PAYMENTS FROM EQUATIONS (8.12)–(8.14)[1]

Equations (8.12)–(8.14) for the changes in income in countries 1 and 2 and
for 1's balance of payments are as follows:

$$\Delta Y = \Delta I + c\,\Delta Y + \Delta M_2 + m_2\,\Delta Y_2 \tag{8.12}$$

$$\Delta Y_2 = \Delta I_2 + c_2\,\Delta Y_2 + \Delta M + m\,\Delta Y \tag{8.13}$$

$$\Delta B = \Delta M_2 + m_2\,\Delta Y_2 - \Delta M - m\,\Delta Y - \Delta U. \tag{8.14}$$

The solution, with details omitted, is as follows:

$$\Delta Y = \frac{1}{\Delta}\left[(\Delta I + \Delta M_2)(s_2 + m_2) + (\Delta I_2 + \Delta M)m_2\right] \tag{8.12'}$$

$$\Delta Y_2 = \frac{1}{\Delta}\left[(\Delta I + \Delta M_2)m + (\Delta I_2 + \Delta M)(s + m)\right] \tag{8.13'}$$

$$\Delta B = \Delta I\left(-\frac{s_2 m}{\Delta}\right) + \Delta M\left(\frac{s m_2}{\Delta} - 1\right) + \Delta I_2\left(\frac{s m_2}{\Delta}\right)$$

$$+ \Delta M_2\left(-\frac{s_2 m}{\Delta} + 1\right) - \Delta U \tag{8.14'}$$

where $\Delta = sm_2 + s_2 m + ss_2$.

Multiplying each of the terms in equation (8.14') by Δ/ss_2 and the entire
equation by ss_2/Δ and simplifying, we have:

$$\Delta B = \left[-\Delta M + \Delta M_2 + \frac{m}{s}\left(-\Delta U - \Delta I - \Delta M\right)\right.$$

$$\left. - \frac{m_2}{s_2}\left(\Delta U - \Delta I_2 - \Delta M_2\right) - \Delta U\right]\frac{ss_2}{\Delta}. \tag{8.14''}$$

Taking account of the fact that the capital transfer can be defined as the sum
of autonomous changes in imports, expenditure on domestic goods, and
saving, that is:

$$-\Delta U = \Delta M + \Delta I + \Delta S$$

$$\Delta U = \Delta M_2 + \Delta I_2 + \Delta S_2,$$

we can write (8.14'') as:

$$\Delta B = \left[-\Delta M + \Delta M_2 + \frac{m}{s}\Delta S - \frac{m_2}{s_2}\Delta S_2 - \Delta U\right]\frac{ss_2}{\Delta}. \tag{8.14'''}$$

1. The details of this derivation were worked out by Richard W. Kopcke. See also
Metzler (1942a; 1949, pp. 196–97).

Letting

$$m' = \frac{|\Delta M|}{\Delta U} = -\frac{\Delta M}{\Delta U} \qquad \text{assuming} \quad \Delta M < 0$$

$$s' = \frac{|\Delta S|}{\Delta U} = -\frac{\Delta S}{\Delta U} \qquad \text{assuming} \quad \Delta S < 0$$

$$m'_2 = \frac{|\Delta M_2|}{\Delta U} = \frac{\Delta M_2}{\Delta U} \qquad \text{assuming} \quad \Delta M_2 > 0$$

$$s'_2 = \frac{|\Delta S_2|}{\Delta U} = \frac{\Delta S_2}{\Delta U} \qquad \text{assuming} \quad \Delta S_2 > 0,$$

and substituting in (8.14'''), we obtain equation (8.14a) as noted in the text:

$$\Delta B = \left[m' + m'_2 - \frac{m}{s} s' - \frac{m_2}{s_2} s'_2 - 1 \right] \frac{ss_2}{\Delta} \Delta U. \qquad (8.14a)$$

Equations (8.12') and (8.13') can also be rewritten taking into account the autonomous components of the transfer and expressing them as proportions of the transfer. These revised equations, which will contain ΔB as one term as noted in equation (8.14a), will then reduce to equations (8.12a) and (8.13a) as stated in the text.

9

Restrictions on Trade and Payments for Balance-of-Payments Adjustment

Our emphasis to this point has been primarily upon the role that automatic and policy-activated changes in relative prices and incomes may play in the balance-of-payments adjustment process. We have yet to deal explicitly therefore with the use of restrictions on trade and payments for adjustment purposes. This we shall do in the present chapter.

The use of restrictions raises a number of interesting conceptual and practical issues. It will be recalled that in Chapter 1 it was suggested that balance-of-payments equilibrium might be defined subject to the attainment of such norms as full employment without inflation and without increased restrictions on trade and payments. By adopting such a definition, however, we were introducing value judgments into the concept of equilibrium. Since the norms in question might be subject to differences in interpretation and since in particular the use of restrictions for adjustment purposes appeared to be ruled out by definition, our analysis was unduly narrow. What we wish to do then is to analyze the circumstances in which the use of restrictions may be justified on balance-of-payments grounds.

Our analysis shall be undertaken in the context of the present-day international monetary system in which temporary payments imbalances are financed by the drawing down or accumulation of reserves by the authorities and in which structural imbalances are supposedly dealt with by exchange-rate variation. We shall not deal with the gold standard or freely fluctuating exchange rates since in both systems there is presumably an automatic adjustment mechanism at work which means that the need for restrictions for balance-of-payments purposes should not arise.[1]

1. It may be the case, however, as Meade (1951, esp. pp. 293–98 and 324–25) has pointed out that the adjustment mechanism does not always work effectively in correcting temporary imbalances due to sudden changes in the demand or supply of foreign traded goods or due to excessive speculation in foreign exchange. Thus, under the gold standard, an argument for restrictions could be made if there would otherwise occur a rise in domestic unemployment. Similarly with freely fluctuating exchange rates, restrictions might conceivably be defensible to avoid sudden and substantial movements in the exchange rate that could have unfavorable terms-of-trade or employment effects.

In order for the pegged-rate system to function effectively, especially with regard to the financing of deficits, a country must own or otherwise have access to reserves in sufficient amount if the need for alternative corrective measures is to be obviated. In the event that reserves are inadequate, the question we have to consider is what the hierarchy of these alternative measures should be. Thus, for example, it might be most desirable if a country in temporary surplus undertook to expand its imports by means of policy measures that raised domestic income or by unilateral reduction of import barriers. Or, if the surplus were structural, the country might be induced to appreciate its currency. While such actions by surplus countries have taken place on occasion in the postwar period,[2] they are still more the exception than the rule. This means therefore that a deficit country faced with the prospect of rapid depletion of its reserves will be under pressure to decide whether it should deflate domestically, impose restrictions on trade and payments, or perhaps devalue.

In considering these various policies, domestic deflation has the obvious drawback that it may result in increased unemployment that could be unacceptable on social and political grounds. Devaluation might be considered unwarranted if the deficit were temporary in character and if it would result in a significant deterioration in the devaluing country's terms of trade. Restrictions on trade and payments might thus represent the least undesirable of the various alternatives. Before examining the conditions when this might be the case, it may be useful to review the various forms of restrictions and their economic effects. We shall then be in a better position to evaluate the alternative policy choices in given circumstances.

Types of Restrictions

In contrast to the policy measures that affect the balance of payments through their impact generally upon the income and price mechanisms, restrictions are designed ordinarily to affect certain particular kinds of transactions in the balance of payments. Since the spectrum of restrictions is extremely broad, ranging from tax-subsidy measures that closely approximate exchange-rate changes to more narrowly defined measures with a circumscribed impact, we shall limit ourselves to a relatively brief treatment of the most important types of restrictions.[3] Following Meade (1951),[4] we shall divide restrictions into three categories: monetary, fiscal, and commercial. Monetary restrictions

2. The appreciations of the West German mark in 1961 and 1969 could be interpreted in this light.

3. See the International Monetary Fund, *Annual Report on Exchange Restrictions,* for a convenient source summarizing the measures being imposed by individual countries in given years.

4. Much of our discussion will be based upon Meade's excellent treatment of these matters.

include exchange controls, advance deposit requirements, and multiple exchange rates. Fiscal restrictions include all taxes and subsidies affecting particular balance-of-payments items. Commercial restrictions include the use of quantitative restrictions and state trading for regulating merchandise trade.[5]

MONETARY RESTRICTIONS: EXCHANGE CONTROL

The use of exchange control for balance-of-payments purposes involves the vesting of authority over all foreign exchange dealings in some government agency. By requiring legally that all foreign exchange receipts must be sold to the exchange-control authority at the official rate and that all purchases of foreign exchange be similarly made from this authority, it is possible to maintain equality between total receipts and payments. In the event that requests for purchases exceed receipts, the exchange-control authority will have to decide which requests to grant and which to deny. It is evident that complex bureaucratic arrangements will be required to oversee all of these transactions in order to make the system function effectively. Otherwise, a black market in foreign currency may be created in which transactions are carried out at depreciated rates for the domestic currency.

Thus, a system of postal control may be necessitated to prevent foreign currency dealings by mail. Limitations may have to be established and enforced with regard to the amounts of currency that tourists and other travellers may take out of and bring into the country. It may be necessary also to verify the manner in which imports and exports have been financed in order to catch barter deals that are transacted privately apart from the exchange-control network and to verify that imports are not priced unduly high and exports unduly low relative to the official rate of exchange. Moreover, in cases where a currency subject to exchange control is used extensively for the financing of international trade, it will be necessary to distinguish nonresident accounts that are freely convertible from resident accounts that are not convertible and to be sure that the transfers between such accounts are consistent with the exchange-control objectives. It should be clear therefore that the administration of exchange controls entails many problems that may be difficult to surmount.

MONETARY RESTRICTIONS: ADVANCE DEPOSIT REQUIREMENTS[6]

Under a system of advance deposit requirements, importers are forced to deposit funds usually in a commercial bank in an amount equal to some given percentage of the value of the goods involved for some specified period prior to receipt of the goods. The funds are then commonly sequestered in a special

---

5. The International Monetary Fund divides restrictive practices as follows: trade and payments restrictions; multiple currency practices; import surcharges, advance deposits, and export subsidies; bilateral payments arrangements; and measures affecting capital.

6. See Yeager (1966, p. 117).

account at the central bank. This imposes an extra cost on the importer since he must tie up his funds or else borrow the necessary amount at the going rate of interest. The importer's ability to borrow will depend importantly on the ease of access to credit that is subject to control by the monetary authority. Advance deposit requirements are thus analogous to import duties insofar as they make imports more expensive. These requirements may be easier to introduce as compared to tariffs, however, to the extent they can be implemented without cumbersome legislative procedures and without directly violating international agreements and conventions.

MONETARY RESTRICTIONS: MULTIPLE EXCHANGE RATES

Rather than buy and sell foreign exchange at the single official rate, the exchange-control authority may establish different rates depending upon the kinds of transactions involved. Thus, for example, rates in excess of the official rate might be established administratively or determined by market forces in a special exchange market for imports. Commonly, relatively high rates will be set for imports of certain specified luxury goods while relatively lower rates might be set on imports of necessities. Similar arrangements could be made for particular classes of exports. The result might be a complex system of taxes and subsidies on imports and exports, depending upon how many different rates were established. In principle at least, the rates could be varied in accordance with the relevant elasticities of demand and supply in such a way as to bring about equality in total balance-of-payments receipts and expenditures without having any effect upon the government's budgetary position. Whether or not this could be accomplished in fact is another matter, however, in view of the information on elasticities that would be required.

FISCAL DEVICES

The most prominent kinds of fiscal devices involve import duties designed to cut expenditures on imports and export subsidies intended to increase foreign exchange receipts. In both cases the impact will be greater the more highly elastic the demands in question. Since fiscal devices operate in principle identically to the taxes and subsidies involved in a system of multiple exchange rates, it is important to note some of the factors that will affect the choice of the different measures of control.

In order to operate a system of multiple exchange rates, it is necessary to have exchange control to prevent dealings in foreign exchange that seek to profit from the differences in multiple rates. Import and export taxes and subsidies can in contrast be applied to merchandise trade without reliance upon exchange control. It is much more difficult, however, to levy fiscal charges on invisible items or capital transactions without some form of exchange control. Thus, for example, in order to tax tourist expenditures abroad, it would be necessary to control the amount of funds tourists were permitted to take out of the country. In the case of capital movements, unless there were exchange controls there would be an incentive to devise methods of transferring capital to avoid taxation. It can thus be seen that fiscal devices are to be preferred for controlling merchandise trade, but that exchange control will be required for regulating invisible items and capital movements.

COMMERCIAL CONTROLS: QUANTITATIVE RESTRICTIONS

Quantitative restrictions refer to limitations established on the physical volume or value of imports or exports permitted in some specified time period. Such restrictions are most common with regard to imports, and they will usually be administered by the granting of import licenses. We should note that it is not a matter of indifference as far as the balance of payments is concerned whether imports are restricted by volume or value. If restricted by volume, in the event import demand is relatively inelastic, the price may be increased to the extent that import expenditures may rise rather than fall. This suggests furthermore an important characteristic of import restrictions, which is to drive a wedge between foreign and domestic prices, thus creating a profit margin that will accrue to someone. This is illustrated in Figure 9.1, where D_m refers to import demand and S_w to the world supply schedule of

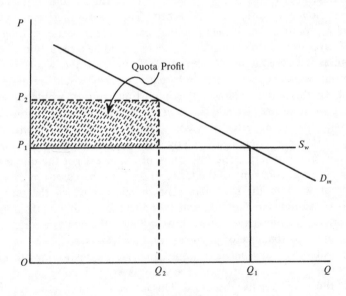

FIGURE 9.1.

Quota Profit

If imports are restricted from Q_1 to Q_2 and the supply price remains at P_1, there will be a quota profit equal to the area of the shaded rectangle.

imports, which is assumed to be infinitely elastic as would be the case for a small importing country. For simplicity there is assumed to be no domestic production.

The original equilibrium price and quantity are P_1 and Q_1. If now imports were restricted to Q_2, consumers would be willing to pay P_2. Since the supply price will remain at P_1, there is evidently a profit to be made which is indicated by the shaded area in the diagram. The question is who will get this profit. There are a number of outcomes possible in this regard. For example, if instead of the quantitative restriction on imports, the same result as in the diagram were obtained by means of a multiple exchange rate or by the imposition of an import duty, the profit would then accrue to the government. Otherwise, depending upon how the licensing system works, the profit will accrue to the private importing or exporting interests who are granted the import licenses. These interests may not get all the profit, however, since government officials may have to be bribed to get the licenses in the first place. If the government wished to keep the profit out of private hands, it could also impose price control and ration the limited supply of imports. Alternatively, it could impose a license fee or auction off the available licenses in competitive bidding.

It is important to distinguish whether the quota profit accrues to the importers or exporters as far as the balance of payments and terms of trade of the restricting country are concerned. Thus, assuming imports to be restricted by volume, even if the import demand were inelastic, so long as the importers appropriate the quota profit, there would be a reduction in import expenditures measured in foreign currency. If, however, the exporters got the quota profit, import expenditures in foreign currency would increase rather than fall. In this latter instance, the importing country would undergo a worsening in its terms of trade while in the former instance, if the foreign supply schedule were perfectly elastic, the terms of trade would remain unchanged. If imports were restricted by value, import expenditures would be reduced no matter whether the importers or exporters got the quota profit. There would be a worsening of the terms of trade in this case, however, if the quota profit went to the exporters. The manner in which the import restrictions are administered and the extent of competition among the importers and exporters will thus have a great bearing upon the effects the restrictions will have upon the balance of payments and terms of trade.[7]

It is possible, as mentioned, to apply quantitative restrictions to exports as well as imports. In such an event, the analysis would involve considerations similar to those we have just discussed. This is true also in cases where imports are restricted by tariff quotas.[8]

---

7. See Meade (1951, pp. 282–85) for a discussion of the complications of the results when differences in market organization are taken into account.
8. Under this arrangement import duties are increased as the quota is enlarged. See Meade (1951, p. 288).

COMMERCIAL CONTROLS: STATE-TRADING MONOPOLIES

A state-trading monopoly created to handle imports or exports can be operated with effects similar to those we have just described in the cases of import and export taxes and subsidies and quantitative restrictions. Thus, in the absence of bilateral monopoly, such an organization can restrict trade and appropriate whatever monopoly profits are involved. It can also expand imports or exports by means of subsidies, although it would incur losses in doing so.

CHOOSING AMONG ALTERNATIVES

It is evident from our discussion that a country contemplating the use of restrictions has a number of alternatives from which to choose. This choice will be influenced especially by the ease of administering the various alternatives and their differential impact on the balance of payments. These are considerations that will vary from country to country and will depend upon the circumstances calling for correction. The choice will be further complicated if the particular measures are designed to accomplish other objectives in addition to the attainment of external balance.[9] To discuss these matters in detail would take us too far afield. We shall proceed therefore on the assumption that a country instituting restrictions will bear in mind the administrative costs and differences in efficiency of the various alternatives.

Import Restriction and Deflation as Instruments of Balance-of-Payments Policy

Having discussed the various types of restrictions, let us now consider the factors that a deficit country with inadequate international monetary reserves should bear in mind in choosing between restrictions and domestic deflation for current-account purposes. By setting up the problem in this way, we are ruling out the possibility of devaluation. This might be justified on the grounds that the imbalance is temporary and that the country might wish in any event to avoid devaluation because of possibly unfavorable terms-of-trade effects.

In confining the choice of policies to import restriction and deflation, we shall proceed as if we can abstract from the particular means of implementing these policies. We shall also assume conditions of full employment, thus ruling out the possible use of import restrictions as a "beggar-my-neighbor" remedy in the case of domestic unemployment.[10] Furthermore, the possibility of

9. It is common in actuality to use the various measures for domestic tax and stabilization purposes as well as for the balance of payments. See de Vries (1965; 1969b) for an account of the difficulties experienced by a number of less developed countries that have relied especially upon multiple exchange rates to achieve different objectives.

10. See J. Robinson (1947a) for a classic treatment of this subject.

foreign retaliation shall be ignored. Finally, we shall abstract from capital-account considerations, leaving these for later discussion.

For purposes of simplification, let us assume for now that the distribution of income and all prices are unchanged. We can then proceed with the analysis with the aid of Figure 9.2 that has been adapted from Hemming and Corden (1958, p. 486).[11] It will be observed that imports (none of which are produced domestically) are being measured horizontally and home-produced goods, taken to comprise nontraded goods and exportables, are being measured vertically. The indifference curve shown refers to the community as a whole,

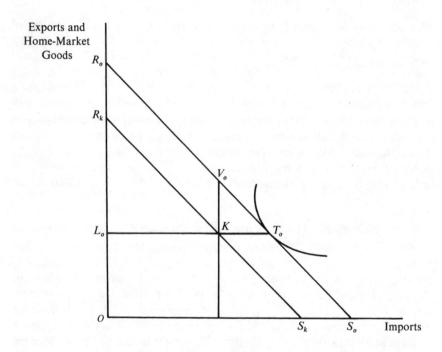

FIGURE 9.2.

Import Restriction and Deflation with Full Employment

Expenditure, R_oS_o, initially exceeds income, R_kS_k, and there is a deficit in the balance of payments of KT_o. To remove the deficit by deflation will reduce income since R_kS_k will be shifted downward. Import restriction of KT_0 will fail to remove the deficit since expenditure will be diverted to home-market goods (exports).

11. I am indebted to J. David Richardson for calling my attention to an inconsistency in Hemming and Corden's analysis of the full employment case. Much of what follows is based on Richardson's clarification (1969).

and we are ruling out intersections and other complications by holding the distribution of income constant.

The price ratio between imports and home-produced goods is given by the slope of the line R_oS_o. This line also represents the expenditure line of the economy, with the consumption point established initially at T_o, where there is a point of tangency with the community indifference curve. The income line is assumed to be R_kS_k which refers to full employment. Since expenditure evidently exceeds income, we know from the income-expenditure identity that there must be a deficit in the balance of trade. This is represented in Figure 9.2 as KT_o, measured in terms of imports.

Suppose now that we wish to introduce a policy to remove the balance-of-trade deficit. If this is accomplished by means of deflation, that is, shifting R_oS_o downward, the result will be a reduction in income, that is, a downward shift of R_kS_k. The reason for this, of course, is that a reduction in expenditure will affect both imports and home-produced goods, depending upon the marginal propensities involved. Deflation by itself will thus result in under-employment.

Suppose alternatively that the deficit was to be removed by a policy of import restriction. In this case, there will be a diversion of expenditure from imports to home-produced goods, in this case, exports. This reduction in exports is indicated in Figure 9.2 by KV_o, which is equivalent in value at the price ratio R_oS_o to KT_o. The reduction of imports by KT_o will therefore fail to remove the deficit since the consumption point after the restriction is at V_o on the expenditure line, which will still be to the right of the income line.

Let us now for a moment treat R_kS_k as a level of income below full employment, as in Figure 9.3. In such a situation, if import restriction shifts expenditure onto home-produced goods, it is possible for output to expand to meet this increased demand. With initial underemployment therefore, import restriction will have a positive effect in increasing the level of income. Thus, if imports are restricted by KT_o in Figure 9.3, R_kS_k will be shifted upward. There will be no shift in R_oS_o since import restriction simply diverts expenditure to home-produced goods. The economy might end up then on an income line such as R^*S^*. With imports restricted now to L_oK, the economy's expenditure point will be at T^*. At this point there will be a balance-of-payments deficit equal to K^*T^*, which will now be smaller than the initial deficit of KT_o.

It should now be evident that since deflation shifts R_oS_o and R_kS_k downward and since import restriction shifts R_kS_k upward, there will be some *combination* of these two policies that shifts R_oS_o downward while leaving R_kS_k unchanged. Properly selected, such policies will make R_oS_o coincident with R_kS_k, that is, expenditure will be made coincident with income so that there will be a zero trade balance. If R_kS_k represents full employment income, a properly selected combination of deflation and import restriction will thus

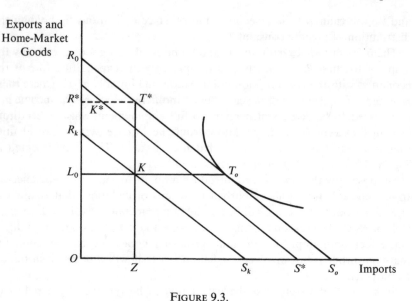

FIGURE 9.3.

Import Restriction and Deflation
with Underemployment

With underemployment and an initial imbalance of KT_o,
import restriction may increase the level of income to R^*S^*.
The new expenditure point will be at T^* with a smaller
deficit of K^*T^*. Since deflation shifts R_oS_o and R_kS_k
downward and import restriction shifts R_kS_k upward, the
policies must be used in combination so as to make ex-
penditure and income coincide.

eliminate the deficit in the balance of trade without any adverse effects on employment. Neither policy by itself could accomplish both objectives.[12]

While the use of both deflation and import restriction may spare the economy the cost of unemployment, it should be noted that there may nevertheless be some cost involved due to the distortion in demand resulting from import restriction. That is, the final point of equilibrium on the expenditure line after implementation of the tandem policy suggested above may only by chance be that point that is tangent to an indifference curve. In such an event, if the indifference curve cuts the expenditure line, there will be a cost imposed on the economy due to misallocation since the real income

12. For additional theoretical analysis of deflation and .import restriction and other policies for internal and external balance, see Corden (1960). See also Cooper (1968b, esp. pp. 234–42 and 249–54) for suggestions favoring greater reliance on controlled restraints on international trade for balance-of-payments purposes. Cooper presents (pp. 257–59) a numerical illustration to demonstrate that deflation can be far more costly than trade restriction as a method of adjustment. He shows that this will be the case particularly in a country that is relatively self-sufficient as compared to one more highly dependent on trade.

which is equivalent to money expenditure will be less than if the economy were on a higher indifference curve tangent to the expenditure line.

While the foregoing discussion of the combined use of deflation and import restriction is helpful in focusing on the relative effects and costs of these policies, the practical implications to be drawn are somewhat limited in view of the assumptions of a constant distribution of income and constant prices. On the matter of income distribution, it may be that one group is affected adversely by the misallocation due to the import restriction while another group is benefited by relative shifts in employment. Moreover, if domestic prices vary as will be likely with import restriction, the profits of importers may be increased along the lines suggested in our discussion of Figure 9.1. To handle these changes in income distribution would require some procedures for compensating those who were adversely affected by the change in policy.[13]

It is also possible that import restriction may improve the terms of trade. This may occur as foreign prices fall due to the reduction in import demand and export prices rise as the domestic price of imports is increased. The importance of these terms-of-trade effects may thus make import restriction somewhat more desirable than deflation. It is conceivable, however, that deflation might exert a downward pressure on domestic prices that would be beneficial to the balance of payments. This would depend upon how flexible the domestic price level was on the downward side.

It should be mentioned finally that the foregoing analysis has been predicated on the assumption that devaluation was either not desirable or practicable to cope with the country's balance-of-payments deficit. If we drop this assumption, we must then evaluate the desirability of devaluation vis-à-vis deflation and import restriction. It seems obvious in light of our discussion of absorption considerations that the combination of devaluation and deflation is preferable on employment grounds to reliance on deflation alone. Devaluation has the further advantage that it avoids the distortion of demand that results from import restriction. Devaluation may, however, worsen the terms of trade whereas import restriction may improve the terms of trade. The question for analysis then with regard to devaluation and import restriction is which of the foregoing effects will predominate.

Import Restriction and Devaluation as Instruments of Balance-of-Payments Policy[14]

In analyzing the choice between import restriction and devaluation for balance-of-payments purposes, we shall carry forward the assumptions of the previous section. That is, we shall continue to focus on the current account,

13. For a modern treatment of this problem, see, for example, Samuelson (1962).

14. The analysis that follows draws heavily upon Alexander's treatment of the problem (1951). I am indebted to John E. Morton for his clarification of the verbal argument and of the formal details presented in the appendix to this chapter.

abstract from the details of particular policies, assume full employment, rule out foreign retaliation, and ignore effects upon the capital account. In view of the full employment assumption, we must assume further in light of the income-absorption relationship that a policy of expenditure reduction will be implemented together with whichever expenditure-switching device is adopted.

There are two factors involved in choosing between import restriction and devaluation: (1) the relative valuation attached to consumption of importables and exportables; and (2) the terms-of-trade effect. We may note with regard to the first factor that import restriction works entirely through reducing the domestic consumption of importables whereas an "equivalent" devaluation reduces (by a lesser amount) the consumption of importables and also the consumption of exportables. Choosing import restriction instead of de-valuation therefore means less domestic consumption of importables and more of exportables. Which policy is preferable for balance-of-payments purposes will depend then upon the relative valuation attached to importables and exportables. Denoting this relative valuation as c, it may be defined as:

$$c = \frac{MU_m/p_{fm}}{MU_x/p_{fx}}, \tag{9.1}$$

where MU_m and MU_x are the marginal utilities with respect to importables and exportables as reflected in the slope of a community indifference curve and p_{fm} and p_{fx} are the prices of importables and exportables in foreign currency. If $c = 1$, it means that a dollar's worth of importables is equal in welfare terms to a dollar's worth of exportables. If $c > 1$, meaning that due to the existence of some constraint importables are relatively more highly valued than exportables, devaluation may be preferable to import restriction. The converse would apply if $c < 1$.

In considering the terms-of-trade effect, import restriction will have a positive effect in the case of a rising supply curve of imports. The reason is that restriction will cause the foreign currency price of imports to fall. Devaluation will have this effect also, but it will be smaller in magnitude since imports will be reduced less than would be the case with restriction. However, devaluation will at the same time affect the terms of trade adversely because there will be a reduction in the foreign currency price of the devaluing country's exports. Import restriction will thus always have a positive terms-of-trade effect relative to devaluation. As shown in the appendix to this chapter, the differential terms-of-trade effect can be expressed as:

$$\frac{1}{e} = \frac{1 + 1/e_m}{1 - 1/\eta_x}, \tag{9.2}$$

where e represents the relation between a dollar's worth of imports (measured in foreign prices) and the dollar value of exports that must be exchanged for the imports when price changes are taken into account; e_m is the foreign elasticity of supply of imports; and η_x is the foreign elasticity of demand for exports. This expression amounts to the elasticity of the country's offer curve and is equal to the average divided by the marginal terms of trade. It is evident from (9.2) that the terms-of-trade effect will be larger the smaller are e_m and η_x.[15] Thus, whether devaluation or import restriction is preferable will depend upon the relative valuation, c, of importables and exportables and the terms-of-trade effect, $1/e$.

To illustrate, consider an extreme case. If $e_m = \eta_x = \infty$, the terms-of-trade effect approaches zero. This means that in going from import restriction to devaluation, the only effect is a decrease in exportables and an increase in importables. This would be an improvement if importables were more highly valued than exportables. That is, if $e_m = \eta_x = \infty$, $1/e = 1$, and a devaluation will be preferred if $c > 1$. Notice also that if e_m and η_x are less than infinite, so that there is a terms-of-trade effect favoring restriction, $1/e > 1$. In this case if $c = 1$ (all goods are equally "valuable"), $c < 1/e$ and import restriction would be preferred. Put alternatively, if e_m and η_x are less than infinite, devaluation will be preferred only if $c > 1$. That is, the gained importables must enjoy a premium to compensate for the negative terms-of-trade effect. Thus, for $c > 1/e$, c must, *ceteris paribus*, be larger the smaller are e_m and η_x and the larger is $1/e$.

What is interesting about the foregoing is its exact connection with the well known optimum tariff argument. That is, devaluation will be better or worse than restriction depending on whether the existing degree of restriction is already at or above the optimal level. Thus, assume initial balance-of-payments equilibrium, and imagine that a country restricts its imports and simultaneously appreciates its exchange rate by an amount sufficient to maintain equilibrium. Whether or not the country's welfare position will be improved will depend upon the factors we have discussed. For example, if restriction is preferable to devaluation ($c < 1/e$), the action taken will yield a net welfare gain. But note that this action involves a reduction in imports and exports, which is equivalent to moving down the foreign country's offer curve. Such a movement could also be achieved by imposing a tariff. Thus, apart from balance-of-payments considerations, so long as $c < 1/e$, the country can improve its welfare position along optimum-tariff lines since the actual trade restrictions are less than optimum. In the case where $c > 1/e$, implying that actual restrictions are more than optimum, and where the trade balance is in need of correction, devaluation would be preferable to further import restriction.

While the foregoing discussion has some attraction on theoretical grounds, we should nevertheless be cognizant of its limitations. Thus, as mentioned above, import restrictions may reduce economic welfare, particularly if there

15. In what follows, we shall assume $\eta_x > 1$. See the appendix to this chapter for the case in which $\eta_x < 1$.

is retaliation. Also, the argument is usually framed in terms of a constant distribution of income. As we have already noted, import restrictions may change the distribution of income, in which case it will be necessary to devise a method of compensating those harmed by the imposition of restrictions. It may well be, furthermore, that in actuality many countries already have highly restrictive import policies and there may be little or no leeway remaining for additional restrictions to improve welfare. Finally, since countries typically trade many kinds of goods, general tariff restrictions may be too crude a device to increase welfare.

The main point we have tried here to make is that while import restriction may improve the terms of trade, it also reduces the quantity of trade. These two factors must be weighed against each other in exactly the same way as in the optimum-tariff argument, and the choice between restriction and devaluation will be made accordingly.[16]

The Control of International Capital Movements

We have dealt in the two preceding sections with alternative policies for correcting current-account imbalances. While these policies may also affect international capital movements insofar as the level of income and interest rates were changed, we abstracted from such considerations. We propose now to concentrate explicitly on policies for controlling international capital movements, recognizing but not examining in detail the impact of such policies upon current-account transactions.[17]

Under a pegged exchange-rate system, a situation may easily arise in which speculative and interest-arbitrage considerations are combined to put great pressure on a nation's spot exchange rate and force the authorities to draw heavily upon or add to their international monetary reserves in order to maintain the rate within its support limits. This will be the case particularly when the belief becomes widespread that the existing exchange rate is overvalued or undervalued.

---

16. This may oversimplify the issue, however, for as Alexander (1951, p. 380) has stated:

> When an improvement in the foreign balance is required, the final choice between import restriction and devaluation must . . . depend on many factors in addition to the trading advantage the country can gain. Such factors as international agreements to avoid restrictions, the desire to maintain stable exchange rates, the political power of groups with special interests, the greater difficulty of making necessary readjustments when one instrument is used rather than the other, the different impact on domestic prices and income, all affect the choice.

17. See Cooper (1968a) for a discussion with reference to the United Kingdom of the estimated effects of alternative policy actions embracing both the current and capital accounts. The policy actions considered were: deflation; imposition of an import surcharge on manufactures; reduction in overseas military expenditures; reduction in private capital outflow; reduction in foreign aid; and devaluation.

In the present-day system, if a country's currency comes under pressure because of a capital outflow in circumstances when the underlying domestic conditions are in fact economically sound and consistent with the existing exchange parity, the use of exchange reserves to finance the payments imbalance is the most appropriate policy to follow. This policy is facilitated in the present system by supplementing nationally-owned reserves with drawings upon the IMF, including the resources of the General Arrangements to Borrow (GAB) that are intended for use by the industrialized countries. In addition, the industrialized countries have developed among themselves since the early 1960's a very substantial network of currency swaps that are to be used for exchange-stabilization purposes. The point of the internationally supervised drawings and the currency swaps is to obviate the need for countries with insufficient national reserves to resort to more drastic measures for dealing with balance-of-payments difficulties. That is, in the absence of these supplemental financial resources, a country in difficulty might be forced to institute a policy of domestic deflation, exchange control, import restriction, or devaluation.

Of course, if the underlying domestic conditions were not economically sound and the exchange rate were in fact overvalued, exchange-market intervention by the authorities designed to maintain the rate could turn out to be a costly undertaking if devaluation were carried out subsequently. In such an event, it would be necessary for the authorities to replenish nationally-owned reserves and to repay foreign currency obligations at the new exchange rate which would be unfavorable to them. The loss that the authorities would bear under such circumstances would have its counterpart in the gains that speculators had realized from covering their open positions at the more favorable rate of exchange. The authorities will have to decide therefore whether a given situation warrants financing a payments imbalance or the introduction of corrective measures intended to remove the imbalance. In the latter event, the choice has to be made among the various alternative instruments we have described. Provided that the relevant foreign trade elasticities are reasonably large and terms-of-trade effects not important, devaluation coupled with expenditure reduction would be the most suitable policies to follow.

DIVERGENCE OF PRIVATE AND SOCIAL RETURNS

We discussed in the preceding chapter a possibly important situation in which a policy for controlling capital movements may be contemplated. This is when there is a discrepancy between the private and social rate of return on capital. Meade (1951, p. 301) has discussed in this regard a case in which the real return on capital is assumed to be higher in country B than in A, but because of heavy income or wealth taxes in B, the nominal return to private investors appears to be higher in A and capital therefore moves from B to

A.[18] Such a movement might be considered uneconomic from the world standpoint because capital was being invested in the relatively less productive location. B might be justified therefore to adopt measures to restrict the capital outflow. But what kind of measures?

If exchange control were instituted, it would be necessary as we have already noted to oversee all foreign exchange receipts and payments, including both current- and capital-account transactions, if the system were to function effectively. It would be necessary, moreover, to formulate some rules for identifying different kinds of transactions, which may in fact be difficult to do.[19] An alternative to exchange control would be to levy a tax on capital outflows of sufficient magnitude to offset the differences in nominal returns. This would require administrative procedures to identify the capital movements and enforce the imposition and collection of the tax.

It is interesting to note that in attempting to deal with its balance-of-payments difficulties, the U.S. has had occasion since the early 1960's to impose various kinds of controls on capital movements.[20] These actions have been criticized on the grounds that they are antithetical to a policy of free international movement of capital and to the efficiency gains that are realized by permitting capital to be used where it is most highly productive. It is argued, moreover, that the capital controls take no cognizance of the special role the U.S. plays in the international monetary system by supplying the rest of the world with dollar balances for private and official purposes. In view of the fact that the U.S. acts as a financial intermediary that lends long and borrows short, the U.S. balance-of-payments position should not be judged in the traditional sense of being in deficit or surplus. Rather, this position must be judged in terms of the provision of liquidity by the U.S. to the rest of the world.[21]

In evaluating the foregoing propositions, we may recall from our dis-

18. Meade has also discussed (1951, pp. 299–300) the case for controlling capital movements to counteract the effect of such movements on the terms of trade. This case is not particularly compelling, as he has noted, when account is taken of two-way capital flows, the effect of future return flows of principal and interest, and the higher real rate of return on investment abroad.

19. But assuming this identification could be achieved, it might be possible, as Meade has pointed out (1951, p. 303), to turn over the responsibilities for handling current-account transactions to specially licensed foreign exchange dealers and thus establish a reasonably competitive exchange market while at the same time keeping capital transactions in check.

20. In 1963, the U.S. imposed the Interest Equalization Tax to discourage foreign flotations in this country and the purchase of securities abroad by American residents. Exemption was made, however, for Canadian flotations in recognition of the great dependence of Canada on U.S. financial markets. Flotations by less developed countries were also exempted in light of the special capital needs of these countries. The tax per se was not sufficiently comprehensive to restrain capital outflows, however, since it did not apply initially to bank lending and direct investment. The U.S. authorities took steps subsequently to restrict these latter capital outflows by means of a "voluntary control" program that established ceilings on permissible outflows based on past years' experiences. The "voluntary" program was made mandatory in 1968.

21. See Kindleberger (1969c) and McKinnon (1969b) for an expression of these views. See also our earlier discussion in Chapter 1.

cussion in the preceding chapter that to the extent that differences exist between private and net social returns to capital, the argument in favor of free international movement of capital on efficiency grounds must be qualified.[22] Secondly, there is some question about the ease with which real resources can be transferred internationally with movements of private capital under present-day circumstances. That is, the countries transferring or receiving capital may be unwilling to take the necessary steps domestically to affect money income and prices in such a way that the real resource transfer can be fulfilled. To do so might mean sacrificing domestic objectives of full employment and price stability.

The logic of the free capital-movements position is that the transferring country should adapt its domestic monetary and fiscal policies to accommodate whatever capital movements take place. In doing so, however, the country may expose itself to a reduction in economic welfare since the domestic policies may have undesirable effects on the composition of output, particularly in the case of investment goods.[23] Selective tax measures might be preferable in such an event since they could be implemented without adverse effects on the composition of output.

But even if we were to suppose that the capital movement were justified on efficiency grounds, there might still be some question concerning the adjustment process. That is, although the transfer could be effected by a deflationary domestic policy in the transferring country, unemployment might occur in view of the downward inflexibility of prices and wages In such circumstances it might be preferable to devalue in order to complete the transfer of real resources so long as the terms-of-trade effects were less costly than the unemployment effects of deflation.

While the proponents of freedom of international capital movements would probably grant in general the points just made, they would nevertheless take issue with them as not being applicable to the U.S. They would consider the efficiency and breadth of the U.S. capital markets as prima

22. Modigliani (1966, p. 4) has noted in this connection:

. . . in a world in which net yields to private investors are affected in very large measure and in very complex ways by the entire fiscal system of the country as well as by direct controls, and in which the structure of capital markets and the intermediaries operating therein exhibit vast differences, there is not even a prima facie case for the proposition that differences in private yields can be taken as meaningful indicators of differences in social returns. On the contrary, the relation between private and social yields could be estimated only by a painstaking comparative analysis of fiscal and capital market structures, country by country. Thus, until such time as fiscal and capital market structures have been made reasonably uniform, there is no sound basis for arguing that freedom of capital to move where the private yield is greatest contributes to an improved allocation of world resources.

See also Johnson (1967, pp. 9–10).

23. See Johnson (1967, pp. 11–13) for a diagrammatic analysis and discussion of an instance in which domestic policy was used to increase the interest rate to accommodate a given capital outflow by virtue of increased domestic saving and reduce investment. Since the counterpart of increased saving represented the purchase of government debt, the economy would be deprived of future income because of the reduction in investment.

facie support of this nation's role as world banker in the efficient allocation of capital to meet the borrowing and liquidity needs of the rest of the world. Moreover, in view of the special role of the dollar as the world's intervention and reserve currency, the question of the efficacy of the adjustment mechanism would be regarded as not altogether relevant Thus, the existence of a deficit in the U.S. balance of payments as traditionally measured would not be considered meaningful, and policies to correct the deficit per se would be thought misguided. This would signify, furthermore, that since the world was on a de facto dollar standard there was no reason to contemplate the question of a possible devaluation of the dollar.[24]

It would appear in conclusion that a case can be made for selective measures for controlling capital movements when there is a discrepancy between private and social returns on capital and when the adjustment mechanism does not function smoothly in effecting capital transfers. There is some question, however, about the applicability of these points to the U.S. in view of its special position in the international monetary system. For this system to function smoothly, it is of course important that the rest of the world accepts this special position of the U.S. and that this nation is able to sustain its role within a context of domestic economic stability. In such an event the proponents of freedom of capital movements seem to have the better of the argument.[25]

Discrimination as an Instrument of Balance-of-Payments Policy[26]

Our discussion has been confined for the most part to a two-country world. While this is satisfactory for a broad range of problems, there are some special considerations that may arise in a multi-country world composed of a number of countries that may at a given time be in deficit, surplus, or balance with respect to their external accounts. The question at issue here is whether deficit countries, say, should adopt some policy measure for balance-of-payments purposes that affects their trade and payments generally with respect to all countries, both surplus and deficit, or particularly with respect only to surplus countries.

Thus, for example, suppose that countries in deficit were to impose a uniform ad valorem rate of duty on all imports, regardless of source. While such a measure would be nondiscriminatory insofar as all countries were treated

24. It does not follow that exchange rates between other currencies and vis-à-vis the dollar need remain fixed. These rates could be changed to correct structural disequilibria as in the present system or they could be freely fluctuating.

25. Fieleke (1971b) has reached a similar conclusion in his more detailed analysis of the welfare effects of the Interest Equalization Tax.

26. For a classic treatment of this subject, see especially Fleming (1951). See also Meade (1951, pp. 378–425; 1955, pp. 545–63).

alike, this might prove to be a drawback from the standpoint of the balance of payments if the mutual trade among the deficit countries were adversely affected. An argument could be made therefore for restrictions that discriminated against goods imported only from surplus countries. Such discriminatory restrictions might have the advantage of causing a smaller reduction in the volume of world trade than might be the case if restrictions affected the intra-trade of deficit countries as well. Discriminatory restrictions might be preferred therefore on welfare grounds to general nondiscriminatory restrictions.

The case for discrimination is not an unqualified one, however. Thus, for example, if imports were diverted on a substantial scale from the surplus countries to the intra-trade of the deficit countries, the ensuing welfare costs would have to be taken into account. But perhaps of greater importance, it might be asked why more general measures, such as devaluation, relying on the price mechanism would not be more effective in restoring equilibrium. The benefits of such measures would accrue in terms of the welfare gains arising from an expansion of world trade along the lines of comparative advantage.

It is of interest to note that the case for discrimination grew out of the situation existing after World War II in which there was one dominant country in surplus, the U.S., and a sizable number of countries in deficit, particularly those in Western Europe. This state of affairs was recognized by the inclusion of the "scarce-currency" provisions in the Articles of Agreement of the IMF, according to which member countries were authorized in consultation with the Fund "temporarily to impose limitations on the freedom of exchange operations in the scarce currency."[27]

While the U.S. dollar was never in fact declared by the IMF to be a scarce currency, many of the European countries nevertheless introduced special measures designed to discriminate against dollar imports and to foster intra-European trade. These measures were condoned at that time by the U.S. in view of its special position and also as a means to encourage reconstruction in Europe. In retrospect, this was probably a desirable policy to have followed. It may, of course, be true that similar results could have been obtained via devaluation or freely fluctuating exchange rates, and that the dollar restrictions remained in force in some instances longer than was perhaps justified. There was no guarantee, however, that exchange-rate variations in themselves would have worked smoothly in view of the scarcities and physical bottlenecks to increasing production that were prevalent following World War II.[28]

27. See Article VII, Sec. 3, in the IMF Articles of Agreement.
28. The aforementioned exemption of Canada and the less developed countries from U.S. capital controls might be considered as an example of the use of discrimination in the sense that these countries were spared the welfare reduction that general capital controls might have entailed. See Cooper (1968b, pp. 254–55) for additional comment along these lines.

Conclusion

A nation in balance-of-payments deficit with inadequate international monetary reserves may face the prospect of deflating, devaluing, or imposing restrictions on trade and payments. This latter alternative may be the least undesirable to follow if deflation meant increased unemployment and devaluation was deemed unsuitable because of the temporary nature of the deficit or because of possible worsening of the terms of trade.

Restrictions range from broad tax-subsidy measures that resemble exchange-rate changes to more narrowly conceived measures designed for a limited effect. The various types of restrictions involve particular problems of administration and they may have different impacts upon the balance of payments depending upon the country and the nature of the balance-of-payments difficulties. On the basis of some fairly strict assumptions, we saw that the decision to deflate or impose import restrictions could be analyzed in terms of the tradeoff between unemployment and the loss of welfare due to the distortion caused by the restrictions. The issue in comparing devaluation with import restriction was one of balancing the welfare cost of the changes in imports and exports against the changes in the terms of trade. The chief grounds for controlling international capital movements was when there was a discrepancy between the private and net social return on capital. The main question posed here with regard especially to U.S. policy was whether selective tax measures should be used to control capital movements or whether a policy of free capital movements should be followed and domestic monetary and fiscal policies adapted to permit the financing of the capital movements. We had occasion finally to consider the use of discrimination for balance-of-payments purposes in a multi-country world. Since general balance-of-payments policies would affect surplus as well as deficit countries, we saw that by discriminating against surplus countries, there might result a smaller reduction in welfare than might otherwise be the case.

Appendix: Choosing Import Restriction or Devaluation[1]

It will be recalled from equation (2.A.27) that the change in a country's trade balance expressed in foreign currency, ΔB_f, can be written as:

$$\Delta B_f = k \left[V_{fx} \frac{e_x(\eta_x - 1)}{e_x + \eta_x} + V_{fm} \frac{\eta_m(e_m + 1)}{\eta_m + e_m} \right] \qquad (9.A.1)$$

1. This appendix is based upon Alexander (1951, pp. 393–96). I am indebted to J. David Richardson and especially to John E. Morton for assistance in clarifying the details of what follows.

where k is the devaluation proportion, V_{fx} and V_{fm} are the foreign currency values of exports and imports, e_x and η_x are the home export-supply and foreign export-demand elasticities, and e_m and η_m are the foreign import-supply and home import-demand elasticities. It will be noted that the second-order terms have been dropped in the denominators of the above expression. This will be the case also in what follows.

Assume now that an import restriction of proportion j is imposed so that the foreign currency expenditure on imports becomes $V_{fm}(1 - j)$. Let the value of j be chosen so that the reduction in import expenditure equals the improvement of the trade balance as a consequence of devaluation:

$$jV_{fm} = \Delta B_f. \tag{9.A.2}$$

If we denote the changes in quantities and prices resulting from the import restriction by subscript 2, the value of imports after the restriction can be expressed in terms of the new quantity and price of imports:

$$V_{fm}(1 - j) = (M + \Delta M_2)(p_{fm} + \Delta p_{fm_2}). \tag{9.A.3}$$

Noting that $V_{fm} = p_{fm} M$ and ignoring $(\Delta M_2 \, \Delta p_{fm_2})$, we have:

$$-j = \frac{\Delta p_{fm_2}}{p_{fm}} + \frac{\Delta M_2}{M}. \tag{9.A.4}$$

Recalling the definition of the foreign import-supply elasticity from equation (2.A.17), we can write (9.A.3) as:

$$\Delta M_2 = -jM \frac{e_m}{1 + e_m}. \tag{9.A.5}$$

Given that j has been selected to obtain the same improvement in the foreign balance that would result from a devaluation in the proportion k, equations (9.A.2) and (9.A.5) can be combined to obtain:

$$-p_{fm} \Delta M_2 = \Delta B_f \frac{e_m}{1 + e_m}. \tag{9.A.6}$$

Equation (9.A.6) thus says that to improve the foreign balance by ΔB_f, imports of $\Delta B_f[e_m/(1 + e_m)]$ must be given up as a consequence of the import restriction.

Let us now denote the changes in quantities and prices resulting from a devaluation of proportion k by subscript 1. If devaluation is undertaken, imports of $-p_{fm} \Delta M_1$ and exports of $p_{fx} \Delta X_1$ must be given up. Using the definitions in equations (2.A.25) and (2.A.23), we can write:

$$-p_{fm} \Delta M_1 = kV_{fm} \frac{e_m \eta_m}{e_m + \eta_m} \tag{9.A.7}$$

$$p_{fx} \Delta X_1 = kV_{fx} \frac{e_x \eta_x}{e_x + \eta_x}. \tag{9.A.8}$$

Assume now that a dollar's worth of imports is equal in welfare terms to c times a dollar's worth of exports. If C_1 refers to the cost of the devaluation in welfare terms and C_2 to the cost of import restriction, we can then write on the basis of equations (9.A.6)–(9.A.8):

$$C_1 = p_{fx}\,\Delta X_1 - cp_{fm}\,\Delta M_1 = kV_{fx}\frac{e_x\eta_x}{e_x + \eta_x} + ckV_{fm}\frac{e_m\eta_m}{e_m + \eta_m} \qquad (9.A.9)$$

$$C_2 = -cp_{fm}\,\Delta M_2 = c\,\Delta B_f\,\frac{e_m}{1 + e_m}. \qquad (9.A.10)$$

If we substitute in (9.A.10) the value of ΔB_f from (9.A.1), we have:

$$C_2 = ck\left[V_{fx}\frac{e_x(\eta_x - 1)}{e_x + \eta_m} + V_{fm}\frac{\eta_m(e_m + 1)}{\eta_m + e_m}\right]\frac{e_m}{1 + e_m}. \qquad (9.A.11)$$

It thus follows that:

$$C_1 - C_2 = kV_{fx}\left(\frac{e_x}{e_x + \eta_x}\right)\left[\eta_x - \frac{ce_m(\eta_x - 1)}{1 + e_m}\right]. \qquad (9.A.12)$$

Since the elasticities in equation (9.A.12) are defined to be positive, whether the cost of devaluation (C_1) will be less or greater than the cost of import restriction (C_2) will depend on the sign of the bracketed term. If we assume that the foreign export-demand elasticity (η_x) is greater than one, the sign of the bracketed term will be negative so long as:[2]

$$c < \frac{1 + 1/e_m}{1 - 1/\eta_x}. \qquad (9.A.13)$$

2. It should be noted that the sign of this inequality would be reversed in the event that $\eta_x < 1$. This can be seen by noting that the condition for the bracketed term in equation (9.A.12),

$$\left[\eta_x - \frac{ce_m(\eta_x - 1)}{1 + e_m}\right] > 0,$$

reduces to, by multiplying by $1 + e_m$,

$$\eta_x(1 + e_m) - ce_m(\eta_x - 1) > 0$$

$$\eta_x(1 + e_m) > ce_m(\eta_x - 1).$$

If we divide both sides by $e_m(\eta_x - 1)$, the sign $>$ will remain the same as long as $\eta_x > 1$ since we are dividing by positive numbers. If $\eta_x < 1$, the sign will become $<$. We then have

$$\frac{\eta_x(1 + e_m)}{e_m(\eta_x - 1)} \gtrless c$$

$$\frac{\eta_x + \eta_x e_m}{\eta_x e_m - e_m} \gtrless c$$

and, dividing by $\eta_x e_m$,

$$\frac{1 + 1/e_m}{1 - 1/\eta_x} \gtrless c,$$

depending on whether $\eta_x \gtrless 1$.

Suppose then that $c > 1$, which means that importables are more highly valued in welfare terms than exportables. If $\eta_x > 1$, (9.A.13) will hold so that the cost of devaluation in welfare terms will be less than the cost of import restriction. The reason for this is that devaluation involves a smaller reduction in the consumption of importables than does restriction, for an equal improvement in the trade balance.

The expression involving the elasticities in (9.A.13) is interesting since it represents the elasticity of the country's offer curve, that is, the relation between a dollar's worth of imports and the dollar value of exports that must be exchanged for the imports when price changes are taken into account. Let us then define this elasticity as:

$$e = \frac{\Delta M}{\Delta X} \bigg/ \frac{p_{fx}}{p_{fm}} \qquad (9.A.14)$$

where ΔM and ΔX are subject to the constraint that changes in the value of imports equal changes in the value of exports:

$$p_{fx}\,\Delta X + X\,\Delta p_{fx} = p_{fm}\,\Delta M + M\,\Delta p_{fm}. \qquad (9.A.15)$$

Rewriting (9.A.15), we have:

$$\Delta X \left(p_{fx} + X\,\frac{\Delta p_{fx}}{\Delta X} \right) = \Delta M \left(p_{fm} + M\,\frac{\Delta p_{fm}}{\Delta M} \right). \qquad (9.A.16)$$

It follows that:

$$e = \frac{1 + (X/p_{fx})\,(\Delta p_{fx}/\Delta X)}{1 + (M/p_{fm})\,(\Delta p_{fm}/\Delta M)} = \frac{1 - 1/\eta_x}{1 + 1/e_m}. \qquad (9.A.17)$$

It will be evident that the expression in (9.A.17) is the reciprocal of what appears in (9.A.13). Thus, a devaluation would cost less in welfare terms than import restriction if $c > 1/e$, and conversely if $c < 1/e$.

It is of further interest to connect the foregoing discussion with optimum-tariff considerations. To see this, recall the definition of c:

$$c = \frac{MU_m/p_{fm}}{MU_x/p_{fx}} \qquad (9.A.18)$$

where MU_m and MU_x refer to the marginal utilities with respect to importables and exportables. Rewriting (9.A.18):

$$c = \frac{MU_m/MU_x}{p_{fx}/p_{fm}},$$

we may note that the same relationship should hold in domestic prices in the sense of a community indifference curve being tangent to the domestic price line:

$$c = \frac{MU_m/MU_x}{p_{hm}/p_{hx}}.$$

It thus follows that:

$$c = \left(\frac{p_{hm}}{p_{hx}}\right)\left(\frac{p_{fx}}{p_{fm}}\right) = \frac{p_{hm}/p_{hx}}{p_{fm}/p_{fx}} \qquad (9.A.19)$$

which is the ratio of relative prices in domestic and foreign currency. Suppose now that a tariff of t percent is imposed on imports. By definition.

$$t = \frac{p_{hm} - p_{fm}}{p_{fm}} = \frac{p_{hm}}{p_{fm}} - 1. \qquad (9.A.20)$$

Assuming the exchange rate equal to unity, we have:

$$t + 1 = \frac{p_{hm}/p_{hx}}{p_{fm}/p_{fx}}. \qquad (9.A.21)$$

Combining (9.A.19) and (9.A.21), we have:

$$c = t + 1. \qquad (9.A.22)$$

As Alexander has noted (1951, p. 389), the optimum tariff (t^*) on an ad valorem basis can be expressed as:

$$t^* = \frac{1}{e} - 1. \qquad (9.A.23)$$

The tariff is less than optimum if:

$$t < t^*,$$

or

$$(1 + t) < (1 + t^*),$$

or from (9.A.23)

$$(1 + t) < \frac{1}{e},$$

or from (9.A.22)

$$c < \frac{1}{e}.$$

The conclusion is therefore that if $c < 1/e$, meaning that the cost of import restriction in welfare terms is less than the cost of devaluation, the tariff is less than optimum, and conversely. The principle involved is thus very simple: a country should impose the optimum tariff.

10

Monetary and Fiscal Policies for Internal and External Balance

Our discussion has been predicated thus far on the assumption that monetary and fiscal policies could be lumped together insofar as the attainment of internal balance was concerned while exchange-rate adjustment or restrictions on trade and payments have been considered the chief ways of attaining external balance. Suppose, however, that there are constraints on the use of exchange-rate adjustment or restrictions. Does this mean that a country in balance-of-payments difficulty will be rendered helpless? According to Meade (1951), who developed much of this analysis in his pioneering work, the answer to this question was sometimes yes, depending upon the economic circumstances at home and abroad. In other words, a country could find itself faced with a conflict in policies designed to attain both internal and external balance.

This was the prevalent view until the early 1960's when Mundell in particular (1968, pp. 152–76 and 217–71) investigated in a series of articles the significance of treating monetary and fiscal policies separately according to the different impacts they will have upon the level of income on the one hand and the balance of payments on the other. In such a case, a country faced with a Meade-type conflict might be able to resolve it by a proper combination of monetary and fiscal policies that could be distinguished for purposes of internal and external balance according to their sensitivity to interest-rate changes. External balance was presumed to be the more sensitive insofar as international capital movements were responsive to such changes. The recognition that monetary and fiscal policies might have differential impacts upon internal and external balance has served to focus attention on the conditions under which the particular policies might be assigned to achieve the particular goals. The question of the relative strength of these policies under alternative exchange-rate systems has also been raised.

The purpose of the present chapter will be to elucidate the foregoing considerations. Thus, we begin with a discussion of Meade's analysis of policy conflicts, and then broaden his analysis to consider tradeoffs between inflation and unemployment in conjunction with an imbalance of payments. We next indicate how the analysis may be altered when the differential effects of monetary and fiscal policies are taken into account. Thereafter, we examine the use of monetary and fiscal policies in an open economy under conditions of fixed and freely fluctuating exchange rates. We shall develop a formal model for this purpose in order that policies under the two-exchange-rate systems can be compared. Graphic techniques will be used in our discussion insofar as possible. The mathematical details and extensions of and qualifications to the model will be found chiefly in footnotes and in the appendix to this chapter. Our final concern will be whether the monetary-fiscal mix is capable under conditions of fixed exchange rates of achieving any more than a temporary improvement in the balance of payments.

Conflicts Between Internal and External Balance[1]

According to Meade's analysis, a conflict between internal and external balance might arise in certain circumstances when there were constraints on the policies that could be used for external balance. Thus, suppose we have a world consisting of two countries in which domestic economic conditions are either deflationary or inflationary (with zero unemployment), and the balance of payments is in deficit or surplus for one or the other country. The various possible combinations of conditions and the policies called for in the two countries to obtain internal and external balance are indicated in Table 10.1.

In row (1), for example, when both countries are in recession, an increase in domestic expenditure in the surplus country, $S+$, by means of expansionary financial (i.e., monetary and fiscal) policy will work to restore internal and external balance in both countries. The deficit country is faced with a policy conflict, however. It should increase domestic expenditure, $D+$, for internal balance, but reduce expenditure $D-$ for external balance. If it increases expenditure, its balance-of-payments deficit may be worsened. In the case of worldwide recession, it is especially important therefore for the surplus country to increase domestic expenditure.

There is no guarantee, however, that action by the surplus country alone will suffice to restore equilibrium in both countries. This will depend upon the seriousness of the respective imbalances. Thus, for example, if the

---

1. The following discussion is based upon Meade (1951, esp. pp. 114–24). It is being assumed that the marginal propensities to import are positive and their sum is less than one in order to avoid the complications of inferior goods and to assure that the countries are stable in isolation. We shall abstract from growth considerations, which will be treated in the next chapter.

TABLE 10.1

Policies for Internal and External Balance

		To Obtain			
Surplus Country (S)	*Deficit Country (D)*	*External Balance*	*Internal Balance in S*	*Internal Balance in D*	
Recession	Recession	$S+$ $D-$	$S+$ $D+$	$S+$ $D+$	(1)
	Inflationary pressure	$S+$ $D-$	$S+$ $D+$	$S-$ $D-$	(2)
Inflationary pressure	Recession	$S+$ $D-$	$S-$ $D-$	$S+$ $D+$	(3)
	Inflationary pressure	$S+$ $D-$	$S-$ $D-$	$S-$ $D-$	(4)

SOURCE: Adapted from Meade (1951, p. 117).

external imbalance were relatively small, its removal might still leave both countries in recession. Or it could be that the internal imbalance was removed in one country and not in the other and that the external imbalance remained. In such circumstances, it is possible that the countries might merely change positions in row (1) or that there will be a shift to row (2) or (3) depending upon which country's internal imbalance was the first to disappear.

In row (4) when both countries are experiencing inflationary pressure, there is a clear mandate for the deficit country to reduce domestic expenditure, $D-$, on all accounts. The surplus country will face a conflict, however, since a reduction of expenditure, $S-$, is needed to obtain internal balance and an increase, $S+$, to obtain external balance. The responsibility of the deficit country in this case of worldwide inflationary pressure is nevertheless clear. As in the row (1) case, action by the deficit country alone may not suffice to restore equilibrium all around and the situation may be changed analogously as outlined above.

Should it happen in the row (1) or (4) situation that the surplus or deficit country fails to act, the other country could take steps on its own to increase or reduce expenditure, as the case might be. This would be beneficial to internal balance in the other country, but it would result in an otherwise larger external imbalance. This could be sustained, of course, if the means were available for financing a larger imbalance. It would also be possible for the deficit country in row (1) to reduce domestic expenditure, $D-$, for external balance and the surplus country in row (4) to increase domestic expenditure, $S+$, for external balance. These would be unlikely occurrences, however, for the result would be to exacerbate the recession or inflationary pressure in the respective instances.

In row (2) with recession in the surplus country and inflationary pressure in the deficit country, it is evident that an increase in domestic expenditure, $S+$, is called for in the former and a reduction, $D-$, in the latter country in order to obtain balance all round. There is a definite advantage in the countries acting together in this case and it is a matter of degree as to the changes in expenditures that will be required in each of them. In the event that the surplus country failed to act, a reduction in expenditure by the deficit country would help to achieve its internal and external balance objectives. But the consequence would be to worsen the recession in the surplus country. Each country is best advised in this instance therefore to adopt policies to suit their respective interests.

Row (3) in which there is inflationary pressure in the surplus country and recession in the deficit country represents the most difficult of all the situations to cope with that are depicted in Table 10.1. This is because there is no combination of domestic policies in the two countries that will work to restore balance. If domestic expenditure were reduced in the surplus country, $S-$, and increased in the deficit country, $D+$, to obtain internal balance, there will be a worsening in the external imbalance as the surplus country's imports fell and the deficit country's imports rose. By the same token, if the surplus country increased expenditure, $S+$, and the deficit country reduced expenditure, $D-$, to obtain external balance, the inflationary pressure and recession would be made worse in the respective countries.

Row (3) thus stands in marked contrast to all the other possible cases in which the countries acting on their own will be able either to remove the existing imbalances completely or reduce them to a smaller magnitude of the row (3) type. So long as an increased external imbalance cannot be financed due to a lack of international monetary reserves, countries are reluctant to expose themselves to added inflationary pressure or deflation, and there is a constraint on the use of exchange-rate adjustment or restrictions on trade and payments, row (3) is apparently a policymaker's nightmare.

INFLATION, UNEMPLOYMENT, AND EXTERNAL BALANCE[2]

We have already mentioned that it may be an oversimplification to treat the attainment of internal balance in terms of zero unemployment and perfect price stability. Rather, the situation, especially in the advanced industrialized countries, is one in which price inflation and unemployment may coexist. The policy problem is therefore one of seeking a tradeoff between socially

2. I am indebted to J. D. Richardson and especially to W. L. Smith for assistance in clarifying the content of this section. An excellent treatment of the issues involved in the analysis of the Phillips curve is to be found in Smith (1970, esp. pp. 350–71, 381–83, and 480–82). See also Fleming (1971a, esp. pp. 486–88).

acceptable levels of inflation and unemployment that are in turn consistent with the objective of external balance.

To elucidate, consider Figure 10.1 in which we depict a Phillips curve, *PP*, that shows the tradeoff assumed to exist between the rate of inflation (measured vertically) and the unemployment rate (measured horizontally). Also shown are curves I_0, I_1, and I_2 that reflect the preferences of the policymakers with regard to inflation and unemployment. These latter curves are indifference curves. That is, each curve represents the combinations of inflation and unemployment that are equally acceptable to the authorities. Curves that lie closer to the origin are preferred to those lying further out. Thus, for example, each unemployment rate is associated with a lower rate of inflation along I_0 than along I_1. The preferences depicted in these indifference curves presumably reflect the social desires of the population that the authorities represent in the process of policymaking.

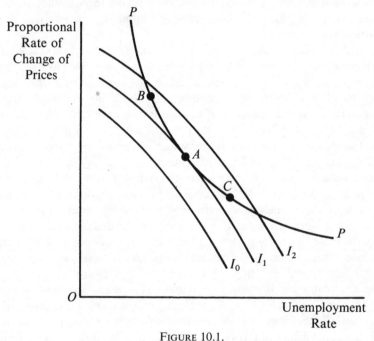

FIGURE 10.1.

Tradeoff Between Inflation
and Unemployment

The tradeoff assumed to exist between inflation and unemployment is given by the Phillips curve, PP. The indifference curves, I_0, I_1, and I_2, each represent the combination of inflation and unemployment equally acceptable to the policymakers. Point A is the optimal inflation-unemployment mix. Point B is a situation of excessive inflation and C is one of excessive unemployment.

In choosing the appropriate target for inflation and unemployment, the authorities should attempt to select the point on the Phillips curve that is tangent to the lowest indifference curve. This is indicated at point *A* in Figure 10.1. In this instance, "full employment" might be defined in terms of the rates of inflation and unemployment at *A* since this is the optimal position, given the existing tradeoff relation and the preferences of the authorities depicted along *PP* and I_1.

Let us now interpret Figure 10.1 subject to the additional policy objective of external balance. Assume for this purpose in our two-country world that both countries have the same Phillips curve and that their policymakers have the same preference function. Two additional points, *B* and *C*, are indicated along the Phillips curve. Point *B* is assumed to reflect "excessive inflation" and point *C* to reflect "excessive unemployment." Suppose further that point *A* represents the attainment of both internal and external balance for the two countries. Points *B* and *C* can then be interpreted subject to an assumed balance-of-payments deficit or surplus that is to be removed as the authorities seek to move to *A*.

The problem then looks very much the same as set forth in Table 10.1. Thus, if both countries are at point *C*, where there is excessive unemployment as in row (1) of Table 10.1, it will be especially important for the surplus country to increase domestic expenditure for both internal and external balance to be attained at point *A*. If both countries were at *B*, with excessive inflation as in row (4) of Table 10.1, the deficit country should reduce domestic expenditure for internal and external balance. Suppose the surplus country was at *C* and the deficit country at *B*, as in row (2) of Table 10.1. Each country should then act in its own interest in reducing inflation or unemployment and at the same time seeking external balance. It is interesting to note, however, that should neither or only one country fail to act, the problem may get worse since prices tend to rise more in the deficit country. If there are lags in policy formation and implementation, a dilemma of a different sort may emerge insofar as the problem may take a relatively long time to work itself out and things may get worse before they get better.

Suppose, finally that the surplus country was at *B* and the deficit country at *C*, as in row (3) of Table 10.1. We evidently have a conflict, as noted earlier, since if the deficit country increases domestic expenditure for internal balance, its balance of payments will worsen. By the same token, if the surplus country reduces domestic expenditure for internal balance, its surplus will become even larger. The conflict is less serious than before, however, in the event that neither or only one country does nothing since prices tend to rise more in the surplus country. Here then the problem will tend to work itself out in contrast to the case just examined when the positions were reversed.

It should be noted that the cases discussed in connection with Figure 10.1 and Table 10.1 do not correspond exactly with those implied by our analysis in preceding chapters since there is a different adjustment mechanism at work in each instance. In our earlier discussion, it was changes in *levels* of prices and real incomes that made for balance-of-payments adjustments, whereas here it is the proportional *rate of change* in prices that is important for adjustment. The static theory of balance-of-payments adjustment, which deals with the effects of changes in price and income levels, may therefore not be suitable, except in a very gross way, to a dynamic situation in which responses to deviations in rates of change are at issue.

A further point of importance is that countries may differ in their inflation-unemployment tradeoff. That is, the shape and position of national Phillips curves may differ. It is also possible that the authorities of the two countries have different welfare functions and thus attach different weights to the inflation-unemployment objectives. For example, in Figure 10.1, suppose *PP* is the Phillips curve for both countries, but because the authorities have different preferences as expressed in their indifference curves, the point of tangency for one country is at *A*, while in the other it is at *B*. What is noteworthy is that there is a conflict in the fundamental long-run sense that even when the countries have achieved their internal policy targets, the price level in one will rise more rapidly than in the other. This is, in time, bound to lead to balance-of-payments difficulties with fixed exchange rates.

In what follows, we shall abstract from the inflation-unemployment tradeoffs and the dynamic character of the adjustment mechanism. Thus, we shall proceed within the usual comparative-static framework and work with changes in income and price levels, as we have done previously for the most part. Our analysis is therefore limited in an important way, but we may nevertheless be afforded with some useful insights in the process.

MONETARY AND FISCAL POLICIES AS INDEPENDENT INSTRUMENTS

The dilemmas posed in our preceding discussion may be more apparent than real, at least for short-period analysis, when it is recognized that monetary and fiscal policies may be treated as two independent instruments of policy rather than a single instrument as Meade did.[3] What distinguishes these two policies is their differential impact on the balance of payments. In our discussion thus far of balance-of-payments adjustment, we have been concerned primarily with changes in the balance on current account due to variations in the level of national income and domestic prices. This is only one aspect

---

3. It will be noted that we are using here the terminology derived from Tinbergen's writings (1952) on the theory of economic policy. The famous rule propounded by Tinbergen is that to achieve any given number of independent targets, there must be at least the same number of independent instruments that are effective. Thus, in Meade's analysis, the two targets are internal and external balance and the two instruments are financial (i.e., fiscal and monetary) policy and relative price adjustment through exchange-rate changes especially. Row (3) in Table 10.1 is evidently a problem in this regard because of the assumed constraint on the policy for external balance. In other words, we have only one instrument to achieve two targets. For an exposition of the nature of policy choices, including the mathematical aspects of the theory of policy, see Mundell (1968, esp. pp. 201–16).

of the balance of payments, however. The other aspect concerns the capital account in which we record changes in international capital movements. We know, for example, that capital flows are affected by changes in the domestic as compared to the foreign rate of interest. Since the rate of interest will depend upon the "mix" of monetary and fiscal policies adopted to achieve internal balance, it may thus be possible to adjust the current and capital accounts and at the same time attain internal balance by a proper mix of these policies.

The use of monetary and fiscal policies as independent instruments of policy for the purpose of obtaining internal and external balance raises a number of interesting and important analytical questions that we shall now examine. One important point deserves emphasis before we proceed, however. This concerns the fact that a country gets into balance-of-payments difficulties often because its domestic cost and price structure is out of line with the rest of the world. It is for this reason that such great importance has been attached especially to changes in the exchange rate to help bring about adjustment in the balance of payments. The use of monetary and fiscal policies may enable a nation temporarily to attain its objectives of internal and external balance while at the same time keeping its exchange rate fixed. But these policies in themselves may do nothing to bring about adjustment and in some circumstances they may be inimical to adjustment. This distinction between financing and adjustment should thus be borne in mind in the course of the discussion that follows. We shall recur to it at a later point.

Monetary and Fiscal Policies in an Open Economy[4]

We shall approach the study of monetary and fiscal policies in an open economy by means of a traditional short-run Keynesian model similar to the one used earlier in Chapters 6 and 7. The present model, which will be developed below for a single country, will contain an explicit monetary sector and the foreign sector will include both trade and capital flows. After laying out the model, we shall reduce it to equations for the real, monetary, and foreign sectors in terms of income and the rate of interest. This will enable us to represent algebraically and graphically the traditional *IS* and *LM* curves and a *B* curve with reference to the balance of payments.[5] We shall then

4. This section was drafted in large part by J. David Richardson. It follows closely Richardson and Stern (1970).
5. See Wrightsman (1970) and Levin (1970b) for an *IS-LM* construction similar to the one below for the case of fixed exchange rates. Wrightsman does not spell out his model mathematically, however, thus obscuring several critical issues. Neither Wrightsman nor Levin treats the case of freely fluctuating exchange rates. Takayama (1969) and Dernburg (1970) also have brief graphic presentations that parallel ours in certain respects, but they are concerned mainly with questions different from the ones we consider. See Roper (1972) for a graphic exposition of the *IS-LM* model in the context of a two-country analysis.

analyze monetary and fiscal policies under conditions of fixed and freely fluctuating exchange rates.

We shall also have occasion to discuss the assignment problem made familiar by Mundell (1968, esp. pp. 233–39) according to which policies should be assigned to the objectives they influence the most. In his context, this would mean assigning monetary policy to external balance and fiscal policy to internal balance. Finally, we shall indicate some possible extensions of and qualifications to the analysis.

THE MODEL

The model to be used for purposes of analysis is basically the same as in Chapter 7. It is shown below, with the signs of the partial derivatives indicated as + or −:

The real sector.

(Equilibrium condition) $\quad Y = D + (pX - rp_2M) + G \quad$ (10.1)

(Behavioral equation) $\quad \dfrac{D}{p^i} = D\left(\overset{+}{\dfrac{Y}{p^i}}, \overset{-}{i}\right) \quad$ (10.2)

(Definition) $\quad p^i = arp_2 + (1 - a)p \quad$ (10.2a)

(Behavioral equations) $\quad \begin{cases} X = X\left(\overset{-}{\dfrac{p}{r}}, \overset{+}{p_2}\right) & (10.3) \\[3mm] M = M(\overset{+}{Y}, r\overset{-}{p_2}, \overset{+}{p}) & (10.4) \end{cases}$

(Policy equation) $\quad G = G^* \quad$ (10.5)

The monetary sector.

(Equilibrium condition) $\quad L = M^\$ \quad$ (10.6)

(Behavioral equation) $\quad \dfrac{L}{p^i} = L\left(\overset{+}{\dfrac{Y}{p^i}}, \overset{-}{i}\right) \quad$ (10.7)

(Policy equation) $\quad M^\$ = M^* \quad$ (10.8)

The foreign sector.

(Definition) $\quad B = pX - rp_2M + F \quad$ (10.9)

(Behavioral equations) $\quad \begin{cases} X = X\left(\overset{-}{\dfrac{p}{r}}, \overset{+}{p_2}\right) & (10.10) \\[3mm] M = M(\overset{+}{Y}, r\overset{-}{p_2}, \overset{+}{p}) & (10.11) \\[3mm] F = F(\overset{+}{i}) & (10.12) \end{cases}$

where

Y = Gross national product

D = Private national and recurring government expenditure

X = Export volume

M = Import volume

G = Government expenditure for reasons of fiscal policy

L = Nominal demand for money

$M^{\$}$ = Supply of Money

B = Surplus (or deficit, if negative) in the balance of payments measured in domestic currency

F = Capital inflow (or outflow if negative) in nominal terms

i = Rate of interest

r = Rate of exchange (in units of domestic currency per unit of foreign currency)

p = Price of country 1's output

p_2 = Price of country 2's output

p^i = Price index in country 1

$a = rp_2M/D$ = Proportion of private national and recurring government expenditure in country 1 spent on imports.

In the real sector, equation (10.1) states the equilibrium condition between gross national product and the sum of private national and recurring government expenditure (including expenditure on imports), the current-account balance, and government expenditure for reasons of fiscal policy. When $G = 0$, this means that there is no conscious fiscal policy. Equation (10.2) states that real national expenditure depends upon real income and the rate of interest. Real variables are represented as nominal variables divided by the price index, which is defined in (10.2a) as a weighted average of foreign and domestic prices. The weights are the proportion of national expenditure spent on foreign and domestic goods, respectively. Equation (10.3) assumes that the volume of exports depends upon domestic and foreign prices; foreign income is not included here since we are abstracting from foreign repercussions. The volume of imports in (10.4) is assumed to depend upon national income and prices. Both (10.3) and (10.4) will be homogeneous of degree zero if there is no money illusion. Equation (10.5) represents the fiscal policy instrument, there being no taxes in the present model. G^* is assumed initially equal to zero. In the monetary sector, equation (10.6) states the equilibrium condition with respect to the demand and supply of money. The demand for real money balances in equation (10.7) depends upon real income and the rate of interest, and the supply of money in (10.8) represents the monetary policy instrument. In the foreign sector, equation (10.9) defines the balance of payments as the sum of the current-account balance and net positive or negative (nominal) capital flows. Equations (10.10) and (10.11) are the same as (10.3) and (10.4). Capital flows in equation (10.12) are assumed to depend on the rate of interest.[6]

In each of the three sectors, we can derive a single equation by substituting the behavioral and policy equations into the equilibrium and definition equations. We thus have:

$$Y = p^i D\left(\frac{Y}{p^i}, i\right) + pX\left(\frac{p}{r}, p_2\right) - rp_2 M(Y, rp_2, p) + G^* \qquad (10.13)$$

$$M^* = p^i L\left(\frac{Y}{p^i}, i\right) \qquad (10.14)$$

$$B = pX\left(\frac{p}{r}, p_2\right) - rp_2 M(Y, rp_2, p) + F(i). \qquad (10.15)$$

The only endogenous variables in equations (10.13)–(10.15) are Y, i, and r. G^* and M^* are to be interpreted as instrumental variables and B as a target variable in the eyes of policymakers. We will assume henceforth that prices are constant,[7] and that quantity and currency units are chosen so as to make $p = p_2 = r = 1$ initially.

If we now consider a fixed exchange-rate system $(r = r^o)$ and assume given values for G^*, M^*, and B, each of the foregoing equations can be expressed as a function of Y and i alone. These equations are depicted graphically, in linear form (for convenience), in Figures 10.2 and 10.3. Equations (10.13) and (10.14) represent the familiar *IS* and *LM* curves, respectively, while the B curve stems from equation (10.15), and is the locus of all points generating the same balance-of-payments surplus or deficit (the chosen B).

The slopes of these curves can be obtained by differentiating each equation and calculating the respective di/dY, assuming the given G^*, M^*, B, and r ($r = 1$ by assumption). The results are:

$$\text{Slope of } IS \text{ curve} \quad = \frac{s + m}{\partial D/\partial i} < 0$$

$$\text{Slope of } LM \text{ curve} = -\frac{k}{\partial L/\partial i} > 0$$

$$\text{Slope of } B \text{ curve} \quad = -\frac{m}{\partial F/\partial i} > 0,$$

where s is the marginal propensity to hoard as in Chapter 7 and $\partial D/\partial(Y/p^i) = 1 - s$; $m = \partial M/\partial Y$, the marginal propensity to import; and $k = \partial L/\partial(Y/p^i)$, the marginal propensity to hold real cash balances. All the parameters

---

6. Capital movements can also be assumed to depend on the level of income. See part 2 of the appendix to this chapter for further details.

7. This assumption is relaxed in part 4 of the appendix to this chapter, although unfortunately still in a comparative static framework. As will be noted, our results for the fluctuating exchange-rate case differ from those obtained by Krueger (1965), whose price equation was similar to the one we used.

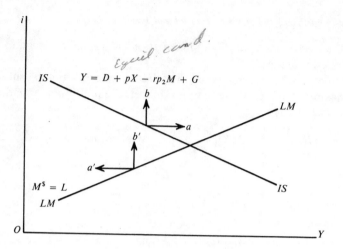

FIGURE 10.2.

IS and LM Curves

The IS and LM curves are drawn initially under the assumption that the exchange rate, r, is given. If r increases, the IS and LM curves will shift in the directions indicated by arrows a and b and a' and b', respectively.

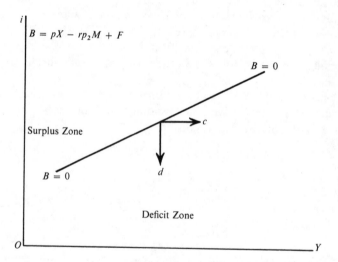

FIGURE 10.3.

The B Curve

The B curve is drawn initially to represent balance-of-payments equilibrium, B = 0, when the exchange rate, r, is given. Surpluses and deficits are represented by parallel lines above and below B = 0, respectively. If r increases, the B curve will shift in the direction indicated by arrows c and d.

are assumed to be positive except $\partial D/\partial i$ and $\partial L/\partial i$, which take account of the interest-rate effects on national expenditures and the demand for money. The term, $s + m$, that relates to the sum of the marginal propensities to hoard and import is taken here to be positive and is simply the assumption of "stability in isolation." The *IS* curve will thus have a negative slope.[8] The *LM* curve will have a positive slope, and the system will be stable.[9] The slope of the *B* curve will also be positive here.[10] It will be of concern to us below whether or not the *B* curve is steeper than the *LM* curve.[11]

It should be emphasized that the *B* curve is not an equilibrium curve in the same sense as the *IS* and *LM* curves since we have to select a target level of *B* to generate the *B* curve. Thus, for example, if we assume the policy goal for external balance were $B = 0$, we can say that all along the *B* curve the economy will be "satisfied" with its foreign sector position.[12] For values of $B > 0$, which would be indicative of a balance-of-payments surplus, we would get a series of parallel curves lying above $B = 0$. Differing balance-of-payments deficits ($B < 0$) would generate a parallel series of curves below $B = 0$.[13]

Now let us consider a freely fluctuating exchange-rate system in which the exchange rate varies so as always to clear the demand and supply of foreign exchange, i.e., $B = 0$. From equations (10.13)–(10.15) the *IS*, *LM*, and *B* curves will depend not only upon *Y* and *i*, but upon *r* as well. In the case of

8. It is conceivable that the total propensity to spend could be greater than unity, particularly if account were taken of income-induced changes in investment. The *IS* curve would be upward sloping in such an event. We shall not deal with the possibility, demonstrated by Levin (1970b), that the *LM* curve may be negatively sloped, as would occur when imports are additionally related to the interest rate and the demand for money is made a function of expenditure, *D*, rather than income, *Y*.

9. The condition for stability is:

$$\text{Slope of } IS < \text{Slope of } LM.$$

This will hold even with an upward sloping *IS* curve so long as this slope is less than that of the *LM* curve.

10. The *B* curve has a positive slope since increases in income that lead to increases in imports must be accompanied by increases in the interest rate, thus leading to capital inflows which maintain the same balance-of-payments position. In the extreme cases, the *B* curve will be horizontal when capital is perfectly mobile, that is, when $\partial F/\partial i$ is infinite, and vertical when capital is immobile, that is, when $\partial F/\partial i$ is zero. If capital movements respond to changes in the level of income, the *B* curve will have a negative slope if $\partial F/\partial Y > m$.

11. See part 2 of the appendix to this chapter for analysis of a downward sloping *B* curve that is steeper than the *IS* curve.

12. The distinction being made here is especially important under a system of fixed exchange rates since the economy need not necessarily be "satisfied" with its balance-of-payments position even when it is in equilibrium in the *IS-LM* sense. This is of course what will lead to further changes in the policy instruments, G^* and M^*, as will be noted below.

13. To illustrate, assume some particular values of *Y* and *i* on $B = 0$. Holding *Y* constant, an increase in *i* will generate an inflow of capital, thus leading to a balance-of-payments surplus. By the same line of reasoning, a reduction in *i* will generate an outflow of capital and a balance-of-payments deficit.

the *LM* curve, in particular, the exchange rate is included in the definition of the price index, p^i. Equation (10.15) for the *B* curve is no longer a definition in this regime, but an equilibrium condition. To determine how the three curves will shift when the exchange rate is changed, differentiate equations (10.13)–(10.15), assuming $dG* = dM* = 0$, remembering that $p = p_2 = r = 1$, and assuming an initially balanced current account, that is, $pX = rp_2M$ or $Y = D + G = D$ (because there is assumed to be no conscious fiscal policy initially):

$$dY = \left(\frac{1}{s+m}\right)\left[(X\eta_x - M\eta_m - M + sM)\,dr + \frac{\partial D}{\partial i}\,di\right] \qquad (10.13')$$

$$0 = k\,dY + \frac{\partial L}{\partial i}\,di + \left(1 - k\frac{Y}{L}\right)aL\,dr \qquad (10.14')$$

$$0 = (X\eta_x - M\eta_m - M)\,dr - m\,dY + \frac{\partial F}{\partial i}\,di \qquad (10.15')$$

where $\eta_x = (r/X)(\partial X/\partial r)$ and $\eta_m = (r/M)(\partial M/\partial r)$.

The slopes of the *IS*, *LM*, and *B* curves in Figures 10.2 and 10.3 will remain unchanged since di/dY (for $dr = 0$) has not changed. Then to determine how each of the curves *shifts* with changes in *r*, we must know the sign of $[1 - k(Y/L)]$ in (10.14') and the sign of $(X\eta_x - M\eta_m - M)$ in (10.15'). The signs of both terms will be taken here to be positive.[14, 15]

How then do the *IS*, *LM*, and *B* curves shift when *r* is changed? It follows from equation (10.13') that for the *IS* curve:

$$\frac{\partial Y}{\partial r} \qquad \text{for} \quad di = 0 \quad \text{is} \quad > 0$$

$$\frac{\partial i}{\partial r} \qquad \text{for} \quad dY = 0 \quad \text{is} \quad > 0.$$

Either of these inequalities implies that the *IS* curve shifts upward to the right, as indicated by arrows *a* and *b* in Figure 10.2, the higher the rate of exchange (as measured in units of domestic currency per unit of foreign currency).[16] That is, as the exchange rates goes up, so does expenditure,

14. With respect to the term $[1 - k(Y/L)]$, which amounts to one minus the income elasticity of demand for money, there is some a priori expectation on theoretical grounds that it should be nonnegative, but no certainty. The quantity theory of money constrains the income elasticity of demand for money to be unity, making the foregoing term equal to zero. The inventory-theoretic approach to the demand for money, however, as represented in Baumol (1952) and Tobin (1956), constrains this elasticity to be less than one. Many empirical studies—see, for example, Goldfeld (1966) and the literature and evidence cited in Goodhart (1970)—also have found this elasticity to be less than one.

15. With regard to the term $(X\eta_x - M\eta_m - M)$, we shall assume that the Marshall-Lerner condition holds so that this expression is positive. If so, then the term $(X\eta_x - M\eta_m - M + sM)$ in (10.13') must also be positive.

16. If the exchange rate is expressed, for example, in terms of the dollar price (domestic currency) of pounds (foreign currency), a rise in the exchange rate will be indicative of a depreciation of the dollar and conversely for a fall in the exchange rate.

because of the favorable impact on exports. Likewise we can conclude from equation (10.14′) that for the *LM* curve:

$$\frac{\partial Y}{\partial r} \quad \text{for} \quad di = 0 \quad \text{is} \quad < 0$$

$$\frac{\partial i}{\partial r} \quad \text{for} \quad di = 0 \quad \text{is} \quad > 0.$$

Either of these inequalities implies that the *LM* curve shifts upward and to the left, as indicated by arrows *a′* and *b′* in Figure 10.2, the higher the rate of exchange.[17]

Finally, we can conclude from equation (10.15′) that for the *B* curve.

$$\frac{dY}{dr} \quad \text{for} \quad di = 0 \quad \text{is} \quad > 0$$

$$\frac{di}{dr} \quad \text{for} \quad dY = 0 \quad \text{is} \quad < 0.$$

Either of these inequalities implies that a rise in the exchange rate will shift the *B* curve downward and to the right, as indicated by arrows *c* and *d* in Figure 10.3. This simply reflects the fact that as the exchange rates rises, exports rise and imports fall, enabling equilibrium to take place at a lower interest rate (with smaller capital inflow).

So much for the model and its graphic representation. We are now in a position to discuss how the various curves will shift with changes in monetary and fiscal policies. We must be clear on the definitions of these policies.[18] By fiscal policy, we shall mean simply an increase in government expenditure, G^*, with no effects on the money supply. Presumably, if fiscal policy results in the issuance of new money, this would immediately be offset by open market operations on the part of the central bank to keep the money supply unchanged. By monetary policy, we shall mean simply an increase in the stock of money, M^*, assuming government expenditure unchanged. In the case of both monetary and fiscal policy, the interest rate must change to equilibrate the system. Expansionary fiscal policy can thus be represented diagrammatically by an upward shift of the *IS* curve and expansionary monetary policy by a downward shift of the *LM* curve. Neither policy instrument operates directly on the *B* curve, although as just noted, this curve, as well as the *IS* and *LM* curves, will shift if the exchange rate is altered as a result of policy changes.

17. The explanation is that a rise in r for constant Y and i has two effects: (1) it lowers real income because it raises the price index (p^i) and thus reduces the *demand* for real cash balances; and (2) it reduces the real value of the given money supply ($M^\$/p^i$), thus reducing actual *holdings* of real balances. If holdings are reduced more than demand [$k(Y/L) < 1$], there will be an excess demand for real balances. This can be offset only by a decrease in income, an increase in the interest rate, or some combination of the two.

18. The literature on this subject is frequently confusing because of the lack of uniformity in the definition of policy. A useful comparison of the different models and results obtained based on different assumptions concerning policy is to be found in Helliwell (1969).

MONETARY AND FISCAL POLICIES UNDER FIXED EXCHANGE RATES

Suppose now that the exchange rate, r, is fixed, and a stabilization authority with official reserves buys and sells foreign exchange to maintain that rate in cases of balance-of-payments surplus and deficit. In addition to the general assumptions made so far—including the assumption of no foreign repercussions—let us assume initially that changes in official foreign exchange reserves are not allowed to affect the money supply. Such changes are sterilized, which is to say that if the stabilization authority is absorbing foreign exchange in return for domestic currency, the monetary authority is engaging in open market sales at the same rate. The converse is assumed to be the case when foreign exchange is being sold by the stabilization authority.

In Figure 10.4, the *IS*, *LM*, and *B* curves (for $B = 0$) are depicted with a mutual intersection at P. At this point, the economy will be in internal balance, although not necessarily at full employment, and in external balance, since $B = 0$. If the authorities now engage in expansionary monetary policy, which shifts the *LM* curve to LM_1, it can be seen that this will always increase income, lower the interest rate, and create a deficit in the balance of payments (the new equilibrium at Q lies below $B = 0$).

Expansionary fiscal policy, which shifts *IS* to IS_1, will always increase income and the interest rate, but it will not necessarily result in a balance-of-payments deficit. Expansionary fiscal policy will lead to a surplus (as depicted in Figure 10.4 at R) as long as the slope of the *LM* curve is steeper than the slope of the *B* curve. On examining the parameters of the two curves (m, $\partial F/\partial i$, k, and $\partial L/\partial i$), we can show that an expansionary fiscal policy will be more likely to lead to balance-of-payments improvement the larger are $\partial F/\partial i$ and k and the smaller m and $\partial L/\partial i$.[19, 20]

If the assumption of sterilization is now removed, balance-of-payments

---

19. To obtain this result, capital inflows, as determined by $\partial F/\partial i$, must outweigh the increase in imports as determined by m. Note that the larger the interest-rate increase as a result of expansionary fiscal policy, the more likely that the capital inflows will outweigh the import change. The size of this interest-rate change will depend on k and $\partial L/\partial i$ in the following manner. Additional monetary transactions balances must be made available to finance the fiscal expansion. Since by assumption the money supply is constant, privately held bonds are sold in an attempt to increase transactions balances. Such sales raise the interest rate, and as a result do in fact attract the additional transactions balances from speculative holdings. Since the interest-rate effect must be relatively strong to get a positive effect on the balance of payments, we want both the pressure for transactions balances to be large (i.e., k large) and the effects of any increase in the demand for money to have a strong effect on the interest rate (i.e., $\partial L/\partial i$ small).

Baggott and Flanders (1969) have discussed at length the foregoing and other important relationships with regard to the policy changes and various parameters. Wrightsman (1970, p. 205) asserts without evidence that expansionary fiscal policy will "normally" lead to a balance-of-payments deficit. Rhomberg (1964, p. 3), however, found the opposite for the Canadian economy.

20. If the *B* curve had a negative slope, expansionary fiscal policy would always increase income and the interest rate and create a surplus in the balance of payments. Expansionary monetary policy would always increase income and decrease the interest rate, but would create a balance-of-payments surplus only if the *B* curve were steeper (i.e., more nearly vertical) than the *IS* curve. See part 2 of the appendix to this chapter for additional details.

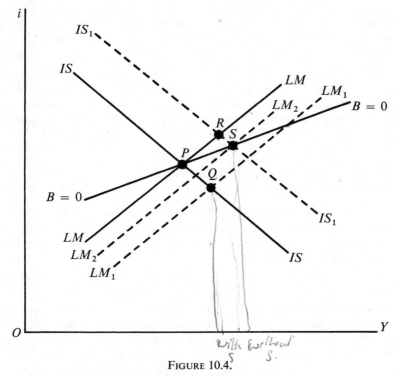

FIGURE 10.4.

The Effects of Expansionary Fiscal and Monetary
Policy under Fixed Exchange Rates

At P, the economy is in internal-external balance. Assuming steriliza-
tion, expansionary monetary policy, which shifts LM to LM_1, will
increase Y, lower i, and create a deficit in the balance of payments at Q.
Expansionary fiscal policy, which shifts IS to IS_1, will increase Y and i
and create a surplus in the balance of payments at R so long as the slope
of LM > B. With nonsterilization, expansionary monetary policy will
cause the LM curve to shift upward until the deficit was eliminated
at the original position at P. With expansionary fiscal policy, the LM
curve will shift downward until the surplus was eliminated at S.

deficits will lead to decreases in the money supply, which will shift the *LM*
curve up. Balance-of-payments surpluses will lead to increases in the money
supply, which will shift the *LM* curve down. The process would continue
until the deficit or surplus was eliminated. Thus, in the absence of sterilization,
surpluses and deficits would be eventually self-correcting, as under the gold
standard.[21] In Figure 10.4, the deficit caused by expansionary monetary

21. Note that since sterilization implies that the monetary authorities alone control the
money supply (position of the *LM* curve) and hence the interest rate, this assumption is
inconsistent with that of perfect international capital mobility (flat *B* curve), which implies
that the interest rate, and hence the money supply, is given by world capital markets. See
Mundell (1968, pp. 256–57).

policy (shift of *LM* to *LM₁*) would cause the *LM* curve to shift up from *LM₁* until the deficit was eliminated at the original position, point *P*. On the other hand, the surplus caused by expansionary fiscal policy (shift of *IS* to *IS₁*) would cause the *LM* curve to shift down to *LM₂*, and the surplus would be eliminated at point *S*. Neither fiscal nor monetary policy affects the balance of payments in the long run. In addition, monetary policy has no power over either the level of income or the interest rate. It is completely ineffective, except insofar as the level of official reserves falls under the deficits caused by expansionary monetary policy and rises under the surpluses caused by contractionary monetary policy.[22]

MONETARY AND FISCAL POLICIES UNDER FREELY FLUCTUATING EXCHANGE RATES

Suppose now the exchange rate is allowed to vary and is assumed to clear the foreign exchange market without intervention. In addition, assume that capital flows, *F*, are not affected by the exchange rate. We are thus abstracting from exchange-rate speculation.

The *IS*, *LM*, and *B* curves are depicted in Figure 10.5, although as we have seen, any movement in the exchange rate, *r*, will shift the *IS*, *LM*, and *B* curves. Figure 10.5 differs from Figure 10.4, however, in that under fixed exchange rates, point *Q* was a potential point of short-run equilibrium, even though it implied a balance-of-payments deficit and hence a steady loss of official reserves. Under freely fluctuating exchange rates, *Q* cannot be considered a point of equilibrium. Rather, since it implies an incipient deficit in the balance of payments, the foreign exchange rate (domestic price of foreign currency) will be bid up. As *r* rises, we have seen that the *IS* and *LM* curves are shifted upward and the *B* curve downward. At point *P*, the process stops since equilibrium in the real and monetary sectors (intersection of *IS₁* and *LM₁*) is established along *B₁*, the new locus of equilibria in the foreign exchange market. At point *P*, there is no further pressure on the exchange rate.

Expansionary monetary and fiscal policy are considered in Figures 10.6 and 10.7, where the slope of the *B* curve has been drawn flatter than the *LM* curve.[23] In Figure 10.6, initial equilibrium is at *P*, and the monetary authority is assumed to increase the money supply, shifting the *LM* curve to *LM₁*. Since point *Q* represents an incipient foreign exchange deficit, there is pressure on the exchange rate to rise. As it does, exports increase, imports decline, and there is an upward movement in the *IS* curve (to *IS₁*) and a downward movement of the *B* curve (to *B₁*). The real value of the money supply also

22. As Takayama (1969) and Roper (1971, p. 125) point out, the ineffectiveness of monetary policy that Mundell (1968, pp. 254–55) demonstrated is due to the assumption of no sterilization, and that this ineffectiveness will hold for cases of perfect and imperfect capital mobility when sterilization is not pursued.

23. The reader will find it instructive to work through the analysis for the case in which the *B* curve is steeper than the *LM* curve.

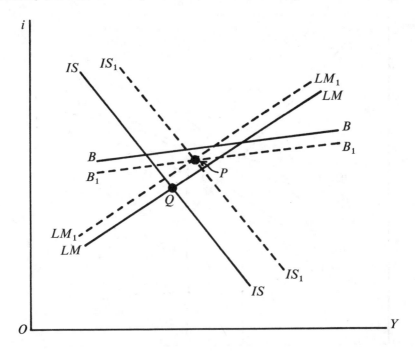

FIGURE 10.5.

Effect of Exchange-Rate Changes on the
IS, LM, and B Curves

At Q, there is an incipient deficit in the balance of payments, causing
r to rise. The curves are then shifted to IS_1, LM_1, and B_1. At P, there
will be no pressure on the exchange rate.

shrinks somewhat, creating some excess demand, and generating a partially offsetting upward movement of the *LM* curve to LM_2. Equilibrium is restored at *R*, a point of higher income but not necessarily lower interest rate. In Figure 10.7, initial equilibrium is again at *P*, and the fiscal authorities are assumed to increase expenditures, shifting the *IS* curve to IS_1. The resultant downward pressure on the exchange rate shifts the *IS* curve *back* to IS_2, the *LM* curve down to LM_1, and raises the *B* curve to B_1. Equilibrium is restored at *R*, a point of higher income and interest rate.

COMPARISON OF MONETARY AND FISCAL POLICIES UNDER
FIXED AND FREELY FLUCTUATING EXCHANGE RATES

The question is sometimes asked under which exchange-rate system monetary or fiscal policy is the more powerful. In this context, "powerfulness" refers usually to the size of dY/dG^* and dY/dM^* (the policy "multipliers") under the two systems. We will also consider fixed exchange rates with and without

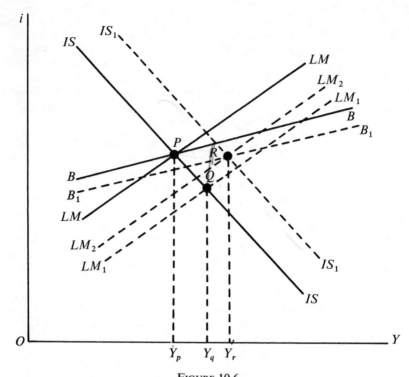

FIGURE 10.6.
*Expansionary Monetary Policy under Fixed and
Freely Fluctuating Exchange Rates*

*With initial equilibrium at P with freely fluctuating exchange rates, a
shift in the LM curve will result in an incipient balance-of-payments
deficit at Q. The exchange rate will then rise, causing the IS, LM, and
B curves to shift to IS_1, LM_2, and B_1, with final equilibrium at R.
Income will rise from Y_p to Y_r. Under fixed exchange rates, expansionary
monetary policy will increase income from Y_p to Y_q, with sterilization;
without sterilization, there is no ultimate effect on income. Monetary
policy is therefore more powerful under fluctuating exchange rates* in
this case.

sterilization of the money-supply effects of balance-of-payments surpluses
and deficits. The multipliers involved can be read directly from Figures
10.6 and 10.7.[24]

24. See part 1 of the appendix to this chapter for a numerical illustration of the effects
of monetary and fiscal policies under fixed rates based upon an hypothetical model. The
various multipliers are calculated there in obtaining the numerical results of the assumed
changes in policy. See Caves and Reuber (1971) for some empirical estimates of the impact
and cumulative effects on GNP, the long-term interest rate, foreign exchange reserves, and
the exchange rate of changes in fiscal, monetary, and debt-management policies in Canada
based upon the period, 1951–62.

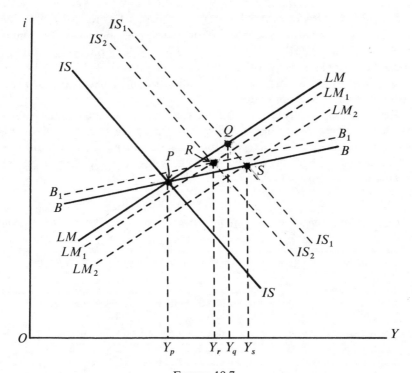

FIGURE 10.7.

Expansionary Fiscal Policy under Fixed and
Freely Fluctuating Exchange Rates

With initial equilibrium at P with freely fluctuating exchange rates,
a shift in the IS curve to IS_1 will result in an incipient balance-of-
payments surplus at Q. The exchange rate will then fall, causing a
shift from IS to IS_2, LM to LM_1, and B to B_1, with final equilibrium
at R. Income will rise from Y_p to Y_r. Under fixed exchange rates,
expansionary fiscal policy will increase income from Y_p to Y_q, with
sterilization, and to Y_s, without sterilization. Fiscal policy is therefore
more powerful under fixed exchange rates in this case.

Thus, expansionary monetary policy indicated in Figure 10.6 would lead
to an increase in income under freely fluctuating rates of $Y_p Y_r$. Under fixed
exchange rates with sterilization, however, the increase in income would be
only $Y_p Y_q$, accompanied by a continuing decline in international monetary
reserves due to the balance-of-payments deficit. Under fixed exchange rates
without sterilization, we have seen that monetary policy has *no* ultimate
effect on income, although there is a "one-shot" decline in international
monetary reserves due to the temporary balance-of-payments deficit. Since
$Y_p Y_r > Y_p Y_q > 0$, it would appear that monetary policy is most powerful
under freely fluctuating exchange rates *in this case.*

A similar analysis of expansionary fiscal policy in Figure 10.7 reveals that the same fiscal expansion would generate a change in income of $Y_p Y_r$ under freely fluctuating rates, $Y_p Y_q$ under fixed rates with sterilization, and $Y_p Y_s$ under fixed exchange rates without sterilization. Since $Y_p Y_s > Y_p Y_q > Y_p Y_r$, fiscal policy would appear to be most powerful under fixed exchange rates without sterilization *in this case.*

The foregoing results are by no means general as the italics are meant to indicate. Suppose, for example, that the *B* curve were steeper than the *LM* curve. Under these circumstances, both monetary *and* fiscal policy are most powerful under freely fluctuating exchange rates. The different results are summarized in Table 10.2.[25]

TABLE 10.2

Ranking of Exchange-Rate Systems by "Power" (Size) of the Policy Multiplier on Income

Condition	Rank	Monetary Policy	Fiscal Policy
B curve flatter than	1	Fluctuating	Fixed without sterilization
LM curve	2	Fixed with sterilization	Fixed with sterilization
	3	Fixed without sterilization*	Fluctuating
B curve steeper than	1	Fluctuating	Fluctuating
LM curve	2	Fixed with sterilization	Fixed with sterilization
	3	Fixed without sterilization*	Fixed without sterilization

* The monetary policy multiplier on income is zero in this case.

ADJUSTMENT AND THE ASSIGNMENT PROBLEM

Our discussion in the sections preceding has concentrated on the *use* of monetary and fiscal policy as instruments rather than the *purpose* of these policies, which is to achieve various economic goals of the policymaker. Prominent among these are full (but not overfull) employment, growth, equitable income distribution, and a given balance of payments under fixed exchange rates. In this section, we consider a fixed exchange-rate system with only two of these goals: (1) full employment defined as zero unemployment with perfect price stability; and (2) a given balance-of-payments position.[26]

25. Morton (1970, pp. 15–18) and Roper (1970, pp. 14–17) demonstrate these conclusions in algebraic fashion. It is interesting to note, as they do, that the income multipliers under freely fluctuating exchange rates and fixed exchange rates without sterilization always bracket the income multiplier under fixed exchange rates with sterilization. For additional formal analysis, see Caves and Reuber (1971, esp. pp. 361–96).

26. The system is restricted to two goals because of the generally applicable rule that the number of instruments or tools must be at least as great as the number of goals to satisfy them (Tinbergen (1952)). It would perhaps be more realistic if we treated internal balance in terms of the inflation-unemployment tradeoff discussed earlier. In order to do this, we would need an additional instrument such as an incomes policy to deal with the inflation.

We will consider three cases, of increasing degrees of realism: (1) policy authorities have full knowledge of the economy at every point in time and carry out policy changes smoothly; (2) authorities have incomplete knowledge, but carry out policy changes smoothly; and (3) authorities have incomplete knowledge and carry out policy changes discontinuously.

The full knowledge-smooth adjustment case is depicted in Figure 10.8. Policy authorities are assumed to desire full employment (internal balance), as represented by the line Y_F, and no balance-of-payments surplus or deficit. In addition, they are assumed to have full knowledge of the slopes and positions of the *IS*, *LM*, and *B* curves and of their response to changes in the money supply, M^*, and government expenditure, G^*. Thus, if the economy is initially at point Q, a point of underemployment (Q is to the left of the Y_F line) and balance-of-payments deficit (Q is below the $B = 0$ line), policy authorities would simply expand government expenditure, shifting IS_1 to IS_3 and expand the money supply, lowering LM_1 to LM_3. Full employment with external balance, $B = 0$, is achieved at P. If the economy were initially at R instead of Q, expansionary fiscal policy along with *contractionary*

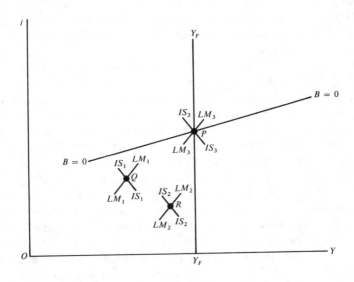

FIGURE 10.8.

*Attaining Internal and External Balance under
Complete Knowledge and Smooth Adjustment*

*To, attain full employment and external balance at P,
movement from initial points Q or R, both representing
underemployment and balance-of-payments deficits, requires
expansionary fiscal policy and expansionary (from Q) or
contractionary (from R) monetary policy.*

monetary policy would be required to obtain both internal and external balance. (LM_2 would have to be *raised* to LM_3.)[27]

It is much more realistic to assume that policy authorities do not have full knowledge of the system. That is, they are unsure of the underlying parameters and responses. This can be visualized by assuming the authorities do not know the exact position, slope, or response of the *IS*, *LM*, *B*, and Y_F curves. If, however, we retain the assumption of smooth adjustment of policy instruments, several adjustment strategies could be worked out. The most famous, although somewhat unrealistic, strategy is the "assignment" of a given policy goal to a given instrument. That is, for example, the fiscal authority might be invested with the responsibility of attaining internal balance and the monetary authority external balance.

Consider point Q in Figure 10.9. We shall assume that the policy authorities at least recognize it as a point of underemployment and balance-of-payments deficit, and that the fiscal authorities are aware that fiscal expansion leads to a balance-of-payments surplus (the *B* curve is flatter than the *LM* curve). Under the assumed assignment rule, expansionary fiscal policy would take place in order to increase employment and contractionary monetary policy to raise the interest rate and stimulate capital inflow. The *IS* curve would be smoothly shifted outward and the *LM* curve smoothly shifted up. The assignment rule would lead the economy toward internal and external balance at point P, as indicated by arrow a.[28]

Now if the assignment rule were reversed, expansionary fiscal policy would still be in order since this leads by assumption to balance-of-payments surplus. Monetary policy, however, would become expansionary in order to stimulate employment. Thus, the *IS* curve would be smoothly shifted outward and the *LM* curve smoothly shifted downward. But this assignment rule would *also* lead to internal-external balance at P, as indicated by arrow b.

The assignment of fiscal policy to external balance and monetary policy to internal balance does not, however, lead to internal and external balance if the *B* curve is steeper than the *LM* curve, that is, if autonomous increases in expenditures lead to balance-of-payments deficits. Consider point R. Fiscal policy would have to be contractionary to attain a balance-of-payments surplus, and monetary policy expansionary to attain full employment. The requisite movements in the *IS* and *LM* curves would move the economy in the direction indicated by arrow c, away from internal-external balance.

By contrast, it can be shown that the original assignment rule of fiscal policy to internal balance and monetary policy to external balance moves the economy toward P. Since application of this rule always leads to internal

27. See Roper (1970a) for a formal analysis of the policy-response equations when there is full knowledge of the parameters.

28. It is possible that the approach to equilibrium via the assignment rule takes the economy in a cobweb-like pattern around point P. But the path is necessarily convergent. See Levin (1972).

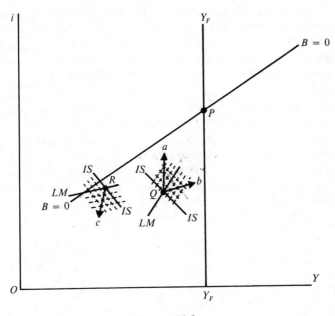

FIGURE 10.9.

Attaining Internal and External Balance
under Incomplete Knowledge and Smooth Adjustment
Using Assignment Rules

The policy authorities do not know how much they need to change G^* and M^* to obtain Y_F and $B = 0$, but do know that Q and R are points of underemployment and balance-of-payments deficit. At Q, where the B curve is flatter than the LM curve, arrows a and b show that P is attained when either policy is assigned to either goal. At R, where the B curve is steeper than the LM curve, arrow c shows that assigning fiscal policy to external balance and monetary policy to internal balance will lead the economy away from P.

and external balance, its use has been recommended in all cases where there is incomplete knowledge of important economic parameters and responses (Mundell (1968, pp. 233–39)). It is interesting to note, however, as shown in part 5 of the appendix to this chapter, that if the B curve is negatively sloped due to income-sensitive capital movements, then there is an equally strong case for what we might call the "inverse" assignment rule (monetary-internal, fiscal-external).[29]

When we add the assumption of the third case, however, that policy adjustments do not take place in a smooth, continuous manner, even the

29. Ablin (1968) also comes to this conclusion.

generality of the assignment rule breaks down.[30] Discontinuous policy adjustment comes about because there are lags in the recognition of an adverse state of the economy, lags in the implementation of policy, lags in the effects on the economy, and again, lags in recognition of such effects. There is neither continuous adjustment nor continuous monitoring of adjustment-induced changes.

For example, suppose the economy is depicted again at a position of underemployment and balance-of-payments deficit, as at Q in Figure 10.10. Being a situation of incomplete knowledge on the part of policy authorities, suppose the traditional assignment rule (fiscal-internal, monetary-external) is adopted. Assume, however, that the authorities make a series of once-for-all changes in policy rather than smooth, continuous adjustments. In addition, suppose the monetary and fiscal authorities act simultaneously, but in a

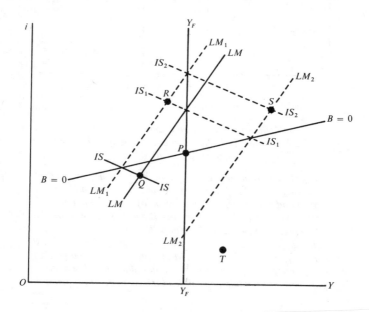

FIGURE 10.10.

Failure to Attain Internal-External Balance under Discontinuous Policy Adjustment Using the Traditional Assignment Rule (Fiscal-Internal, Monetary-External)

If the policy authorities act independently and do not adjust policy in a smooth, continuous manner, divergence from internal-external balance at P is possible even under the traditional assignment rule. Starting at Q, the policy adjustments may move the economy on a diverging path indicated by R, S, T, etc.

30. This conclusion is shown formally by Patrick (1968, pp. 273–75).

noncoordinated manner. The monetary authorities would then contract the money supply, shifting the *LM* curve to a position around LM_1, which would achieve external balance, assuming *IS* was unchanged. (LM_1 would not be likely to be attained exactly, however, since the authorities do not know the location of the *B* curve.) The fiscal authorities would expand expenditures, shifting the *IS* curve to a position around IS_1, which would achieve internal balance, assuming *LM* was unchanged. The economy would eventually end up at a position such as *R*, a point of underemployment and balance-of-payments surplus, which when recognized by the authorities, would set off a new round of adjustments according to the assignment rule. LM_1 would shift via monetary expansion to a position around IS_2. The economy might end up at *S*. The next round of adjustments could bring it to *T*, and so on in what is in this case a path diverging from internal-external balance.

It can be seen that the assignment rule no longer *guarantees* the attainment of internal-external balance at *P* (although it does in cases where the *B* curve is steeper than the *LM* curve).[31] Thus, its usefulness is reduced in the case of discontinuous adjustment unless the authorities have knowledge of the relevant slopes and positions of the curves. But what is important is that if the authorities do in fact have such knowledge, the assignment rule is useless since they should then go directly to equilibrium as in Figure 10.8. A summary of assignment rules is given in Table 10.3.

Although the discussion of policy adjustment under conditions of incomplete knowledge has focused on the assignment problem, this is due primarily to the historical emphasis placed on the "proper" assignment. Yet assignment is not the only adjustment strategy it is possible to adopt under the circumstances. Nor is it likely to be the most efficient strategy, eschewing coordinated policy action as it does (coordinated policy is still possible under

TABLE 10.3

Assignment Rules to Attain Internal and External Balance under Certain Conditions

	Policy Assignment	
Condition	Smooth Adjustment	Discontinuous Adjustment
B curve flatter than *LM* curve	Monetary-external and fiscal-internal, *or* vice versa	Impossible to determine without further knowledge of parameters
B curve steeper than *LM* curve	Monetary-external and fiscal-internal	Monetary-external and fiscal-internal

31. Mundell's original demonstration of the assignment rule (1968, pp. 233–39) assumed a discontinuous adjustment mechanism, and yet *did* guarantee internal-external balance. The difference between his conclusion and ours arises from the fact that he defined the monetary policy instrument as the interest rate rather than the money supply as we have done. The correspondence between his approach and ours is demonstrated in part 5 of the appendix to this chapter.

incomplete knowledge). For example, another alternative strategy to adopt in the case of unemployment and balance-of-payments deficit is as follows: even under incomplete knowledge, the authorities *know* fiscal policy should be expansionary. The reason is that if they had perfect knowledge as in Figure 10.8, fiscal policy would always be expansionary. They cannot be sure about monetary policy. Therefore, fiscal expansion (outward shifts of the *IS* curve) should be carried out alone until the economy reaches either external balance, $B = 0$, or internal balance, Y_F. If external balance is reached before internal balance, a coordinated policy of continued fiscal expansion and monetary expansion is called for. If internal balance is reached before external balance, a coordinated policy of continued fiscal expansion and monetary contraction is called for. The general strategy rule suggested might be called a "two-stage" rule: first employ only the policy tool whose required adjustment is unambiguous, until one goal is reached; the direction of adjustment of the second tool will then also be unambiguous, and both should be applied in a coordinated fashion.[32]

Other strategic adjustment rules could be devised in addition to this "two-stage" rule,[33] of which all would be alternatives to the assignment rule. It is an interesting question as to which of the possible adjustment rules would be superior with respect to convergence, speed of adjustment, and practical implementation. But it must be emphasized that a full analysis of the very practical problem of policy adjustment would be extremely complex. It could only be dealt with, if at all, by means of an explicitly dynamic model that took into account the lags for different kinds of policies and for the response of different targets to the same policy instrument.

EXTENSIONS OF THE ANALYSIS

The model used in the preceding sections was relatively simple in structure. Three possible extensions are considered in parts 2–4 of the appendix to this chapter. First, the model is adapted to make capital flows dependent on both

32. In a situation of underemployment with a balance-of-payments surplus, when the *B* curve is flatter than the *LM* curve, the required adjustment of monetary policy is unambiguously expansionary. Thus, it should be used in the first stage alone. If external balance is reached first, then both monetary and fiscal policy should become expansionary in the second stage; if internal balance is reached first, fiscal policy should be contractionary. It can be shown, however, that if the *B* curve is steeper than the *LM* curve in conditions of underemployment and balance-of-payments surplus, the authorities cannot be sure under incomplete knowledge of the movement of *either* monetary or fiscal policy. An acceptable rule in this case, however, might be to pursue coordinated expansionary monetary and fiscal policy as the first stage. Then if external balance is reached first, monetary policy should become contractionary in the second stage; if internal balance is reached first, fiscal policy should become contractionary. The other policy in each case would remain the same in the second stage.

33. D. E. Roper has suggested a generalization of the "two-stage" rule to the effect that policymakers place relatively more weight on those policies about which we have greater knowledge of their impact. What is not clear is whether this formulation would require less information than alternative rules in order to obtain convergence.

the rate of interest and level of income. This introduces the possibility of a negatively sloping B curve and makes for further complications of the effects of monetary and fiscal policies and the use of assignment rules. Next, the model is expanded to take two countries explicitly into account and the effects of monetary and fiscal policies are then examined under a system of fixed exchange rates. The final extension involves the introduction of a price equation into the single-country model in order to analyze policies under the alternative exchange-rate systems.

Other extensions besides the foregoing ones are possible. For example, we could intoduce varying import propensities with regard to consumption, investment, and government expenditure and taxation.[34]

QUALIFICATIONS[35]

Although the model presented in this chapter is at least to some degree a familiar one, there are a number of fundamental criticisms to which it is subject.

First the model is restricted to short-run situations. The facts that there is a limit to any continued loss (or gain) of official foreign exchange reserves, that domestic investment and international capital movements affect capital formation, and that a change in interest rates generates only a transitory international capital flow in a static model have all been ignored.

This last point is an exceptionally important one. Because changes in rates of return generate only an adjustment of existing *stocks* of assets in a static model, there can be no long-run effect of a change in the money supply or interest rates on the capital account. That is, in terms of our model, F is not a function of i so that $\partial F / \partial i = 0$. To see the effects of taking stock equilibrium into account, it is necessary only to apply the concept somewhat loosely and examine a single equation. Thus, suppose that "stock equilibrium" is taken to mean that the economy's total wealth must be constant, although its distribution may be changing. Then since the government budget deficit pumps assets into the economy, and balance-of-payments deficits remove them, using equations (10.3)–(10.5), we have:

$$G^* = rp_2 M(Y, rp_2, p) - pX \left(\frac{p}{r}, p_2 \right). \qquad (10.16)$$

The only endogenous variable in equation (10.16) is income, which is therefore completely determined by the exogenous variables in the equation. Hence,

---

34. The effects of multiple import propensities on the conclusions of the model are examined by Ott and Ott (1968), Jones (1968), and Levin (1970b). One straightforward effect is that tax policy can be distinguished from government expenditure as a separate instrument. Levin also shows that multiple import propensities can lead to a negatively sloped B curve, although it is necessarily more vertical than the IS curve.

35. An excellent, extended summary of qualifications to the model of this chapter is found in Whitman (1970). See also Smith (1970, pp. 507–09).

fiscal policy (G^*) can influence income; monetary policy cannot, since neither the money supply nor the interest rate appears in equation (10.16).[36]

It should be pointed out, however, that even in stock-equilibrium models, monetary policy does have an effect on the *level* of official foreign exchange reserves and may therefore not be completely eliminated as a policy tool. Secondly, if growth is allowed into the system, a change in interest rates *can* lead to an enduring capital flow.[37] Finally, it is possible to take account of servicing charges on the stock of domestic assets held by foreigners. Equation (10.16) must be altered to read:

$$G^* = rp_2 M(Y, rp_2, p) - pX\left(\frac{p}{r}, p_2\right) + iS(i), \qquad (10.16')$$

where $S(i)$ equals the stock of foreign holdings of domestic assets. The effect of monetary policy on income and the balance of payments is restored since the interest rate enters equation (10.16'), although now the effect of contractionary monetary policy on the balance of payments (with income held constant) is negative rather than positive.[38] As might be expected, it can be shown that if assignment rules are to be followed in such an economy, the proper assignment rule is the "inverse" (monetary-internal, fiscal-external) rule, not the traditional one.[39]

Another important drawback of our model concerns the specification of "fixed targets" such as full employment.[40] It can be argued, for example, that if with two policy instruments we can satisfy two goals, one of which is some specified level of real income, why not set this level infinitely high? That is, assuming there is excess capacity in the economy, a policymaker need not be satisfied with a particular level of income when he can obtain some higher level simply by changing the policy mix while at the same time remaining on the given balance-of-payments curve. The model we have used thus fails to take into account the constraints of the economic system in which the policymaker must act.[41] It has been suggested therefore that instead of a fixed-

36. An example of this type of model is given in part 6 of the appendix to this chapter. Additional details can be found in Levin (1970a), McKinnon (1969a), McKinnon and Oates (1966), Whitman (1970), and Harkness (1970). For a critique, see Morton (1970, pp. 18–29).

37. See Willett and Forte (1969, p. 248) and Grubel (1968). Morton (1970) has constructed a stock-equilibrium model that takes growth explicitly into account. His work also contains a critique of another growth-stock equilibrium model, that of Floyd (1969).

38. See Levin (1972) and Willett and Forte (1969). Levin also analyzes the possible adverse effects of increased interest rates on the trade account.

39. Levin (1972) also analyzes the assignment problem in a hybrid model, where interest-rate changes generate both a flow of capital and a change in interest servicing cost. Nothing can be said about the proper assignment rule unless the parameters of the system are known, in which case assignment rules become senseless. See Roper (1972) for an argument that the deficiency of the capital-flow function does not affect the Mundell assignment rule.

40. This is apart from the statistical and philosophical problems that arise in attempting to define these targets to begin with.

41. For an elaboration of this line of thinking, see in particular Krueger (1965, p. 201) and (1968), Niehans (1968, pp. 896 seq.), Fleming (1968b), and Arndt (1971).

targets approach, one should use an "optimizing" approach in which a social welfare function is to be maximized, subject to the constraints imposed by the system. A great advantage of the optimizing approach is that it is not required to assume that all the parameters of the system (e.g., m, $\partial F/\partial i$, etc.) are constants. They too can be functions, say, of the interest rate.[42] Moreover, this approach enables one to consider cases in which the number of goals exceeds the number of instruments, as may be true in actuality.[43] The significance of this last point is enhanced especially when we take Phillips-curve considerations into account in view of the tradeoff that may be sought between inflation and unemployment. By the same token, this is not to say of course that the fixed-targets approach is entirely without merit, especially since policies may in fact often be made in this light.

There are a number of other qualifications that can be made with respect to our model. We have already mentioned that the conclusions may be subject to change, depending upon how monetary and fiscal policies are defined.[44] It may also be the case that we have insufficient knowledge of the orders of magnitude and time lags of adjustment to policy changes, and that there exist limitations on the values that variables can assume. Thus, for example, a country following a high interest-rate policy for balance-of-payments purposes might underestimate the long-run impact on investment, pro-ductivity, and the rate of growth. Or it could be the case that government expenditure or taxes cannot be changed in relatively large amounts or the rate of interest permitted to rise to relatively high levels.[45] Moreover, there are many other possible goals of economic policy that we have not considered, among which may be mentioned the rate of economic growth, an equitable distribution of income, and the composition of the balance of payments as between the balances on current and capital accounts.[46]

It will be recalled furthermore that we have abstracted from foreign exchange-market considerations. This is an important omission. For example,

42. This would certainly represent a step towards reality. For example, do we really expect the same capital flow when the interest rate rises from 1 to 2 percent as when it rises from 6 to 7 percent? This is what a constant $\partial F/\partial i$ implies.

43. The fixed targets approach can deal with such cases only by adopting the welfare function of the optimizing approach. See Mundell (1968, p. 210).

44. This is the case, for example, with regard to the question of neutralizing the monetary effects of changes in fiscal policy and the balance of payments. See Takayama (1969) for an analysis of the effects of different degrees of neutralization.

45. Ott and Ott (1968) present some illustrative examples of the changes in government expenditure, tax rates, and interest rates that would be required to maintain GNP in the United States at its 1966 level and reduce the balance-of-payments deficit, measured on the gross liquidity basis, to zero. Their examples suggest that the relatively substantial changes in policies required might be unattainable in present-day political circumstances. See also the numerical examples presented in part 1 of the appendix to this chapter.

46. Helliwell (1969) has also suggested that policymakers may establish a target level of reserves in a fixed rate system or a target range of permissible movement of the exchange rate in a fluctuating rate system. The effects of policies in such an event will differ from those we have shown.

in a system of freely fluctuating exchange rates, stabilizing speculative flows might well offset policy-induced changes in the exchange rate, thus negating any employment effects of such changes. It is possible to add another policy instrument by considering that the authorities may engage in forward market transactions in order to counteract the forward-exchange differentials created by domestic interest-rate changes or changes in speculative positions.[47]

Finally, we need to know more about how other countries may respond to changes in policies in a given country and the conditions under which policy coordination may be desirable. The importance of this point was demonstrated in our discussion of policy conflicts in connection with Table 10.1 and Figure 10.1, where the effects of changes in policies were seen to depend upon economic conditions at home and abroad. It is obvious that if a foreign country alters its policies to ward off effects transmitted from changes in policy in a given country, the given country will be frustrated somewhat in attaining its domestic goals. This may be especially the case in a multicountry world where there are inconsistencies in national targets with respect to desired levels of international monetary reserves.[48] It may also happen that countries may adopt similar policies for different objectives without fully considering the overall impact. Thus, for example, one country might attempt to raise domestic interest rates for external reasons and another in turn might do the same thing for internal reasons. A worldwide escalation of interest rates might then occur, with undesired effects on capital formation and rates of economic growth.

Finance versus Adjustment in the Balance of Payments

In the first part of this chapter, we examined the possible conflicts between internal and external balance that might arise in the context of a two-country world when there are constraints on the use of exchange-rate adjustment or restrictions on trade and payments. So long as monetary and fiscal policies were treated as a single policy and the aforementioned constraints held, we would have a situation in which there was available but one policy instrument to achieve two goals. This situation was by no means hopeless, however, once it was recognized that monetary and fiscal policies might be regarded as separate instruments of policy, being differentiated according to the effects they had on the current and capital accounts, respectively. It was shown to be possible in such an event to attain internal and external balance under conditions of fixed exchange rates by a proper mix of the two policies. The question that arises here, however, is whether this mix is capable of achieving

47. See Levin (1970a) for a formal analysis of the use of forward-exchange policy in the attainment of internal-external balance. See also Grubel (1966).
48. See Bryant (1968) for additional discussion of this point.

any more than a short-run or temporary improvement in the balance of payments.

The answer would appear to depend upon the nature of the balance-of-payments disequilibrium. It is fruitful here to recall the distinction made in Chapter 7, due to Johnson (1958b), between a stock deficit and a flow deficit in the balance of payments. A stock deficit that involved a once-for-all change in a given aggregate portfolio would be temporary in character. A flow deficit, in contrast, would not be temporary and might be indicative of a worsening of the country's international competitive position.

In the event that a country in stock deficit had insufficient international monetary reserves to cope with this deficit, it could conceivably design a mix of monetary and fiscal policies that would render relief to the balance of payments at least in the short run. However, as we pointed out, there is a distinct possibility that such improvement might be negated in the long run particularly on account of rising interest payments to foreigners and adverse effects on the trade accounts. The important point though, growth considerations aside, is that the stock deficit will disappear once the adjustment of portfolios has been completed.

Matters may be different with a flow deficit since there is no self-correcting mechanism at work. What the authorities should do in such an event will be determined largely by the domestic economic conditions accompanying the balance-of-payments deficit. For example, in the case of inflation and deficit, the solution appears straightforward since monetary and fiscal policies can be employed to reduce domestic expenditure and therefore imports and to have a favorable effect on the capital account. The question that arises, however, is whether this short-term expedient will be sufficient to remove the basic cause of the flow deficit. If the country's cost and price structure were out of line with the rest of the world, it is likely that the deficit in the balance-of-payments would re-emerge as income and expenditure were expanded. There may, in other words, be a need to undertake a policy of expenditure-switching by means of a change in the exchange rate in order to effect a lasting improvement in the balance of payments. Looked at in this way, the use of monetary and fiscal policies may be a chimera insofar as there is failure to deal with the roots of the flow deficit.[49]

Conclusion

The main purpose of this chapter has been to review the use of monetary and fiscal policies in an open economy. We have shown how these policies can be used as separate instruments under a system of fixed exchange rates and freely fluctuating exchange rates to attain internal and external balance.

---

49. For further elaboration of these issues, see Ablin (1966) and Johnson (1967).

Using the standard *IS-LM* curve macroeconomic framework supplemented by a balance-of-payments relation, the effects of changes in policy were examined with regard to the rate of interest and level of income and conclusions were drawn concerning the powerfulness of the two policies in the two exchange-rate systems (Table 10.2).

We also had occasion to examine the adjustment of policy to attain internal balance (full employment) and external balance (a desired balance-of-payments surplus) under fixed exchange rates. Various adjustment strategies, among them the "assignment" of monetary policy to one goal and fiscal policy to another, were discussed. Possible or desirable adjustment strategies were seen to vary with how well known the economy was, whether policy adjustment was smooth or discontinuous, and some general parametric characteristics of the system (Figure 10.8 and Table 10.3).

Finally, a number of criticisms of and qualifications to the model were discussed, including considerations of stock equilibrium and portfolio balance, the interest cost of servicing international capital stocks, the use of a fixed-targets approach, possible limitations on the values that the variables could assume, other goals of economic policy besides internal-external balance, the abstraction from foreign exchange market considerations, and the issue of financing as contrasted to adjustment. It was necessary at several points to re-emphasize the basically short-run nature of our model and the conclusions derived from it.

Appendix

1. NUMERICAL EXAMPLES OF THE EFFECTS OF MONETARY AND FISCAL POLICIES UNDER FIXED EXCHANGE RATES[1]

Some numerical examples may be useful to supplement our discussion in the text of the effects of monetary and fiscal policies under fixed exchange rates. We shall employ for this purpose a model that is basically similar to the one given in the text, except that prices are assumed constant and hence are excluded from the expenditure functions and the demand for money. There is a one-to-one correspondence between money and real variables if prices are assumed equal to unity. Since we assume prices (and the exchange rate) equal to unity, they are not shown explicitly in the model. There are separate equations for consumption, C, as a function of disposable income, Y_d, taxes, T, as a function of the level of income, Y, and investment, I, as a function of the interest rate, i. The fiscal policy variables now include both taxes and government expenditure. We shall assume that capital movements respond only to the rate of interest for purposes of simplicity. The authorities are

---

1. This section is based on Nobel (1967).

assumed to <u>sterilize changes in official reserves</u>. The model in linear form with hypothetical values indicated is as follows:

Real sector

$$Y = C + I + G + X - M \tag{10.A.1}$$

$$C = 35 + 0.75Y_d \tag{10.A.2}$$

$$Y_d = Y - T \tag{10.A.3}$$

$$T = -20 + 0.2Y \tag{10.A.4}$$

$$I = 85 - 2i \tag{10.A.5}$$

$$G = 110 \tag{10.A.6}$$

$$X = 35 \tag{10.A.7}$$

$$M = -30 + 0.1Y \tag{10.A.8}$$

Monetary sector

$$L = M^\$ \tag{10.A.9}$$

$$L = 0.25Y - 7i \tag{10.A.10}$$

$$M^\$ = 115 \tag{10.A.11}$$

Foreign sector

$$B \equiv X - M + F \tag{10.A.12}$$

$$X = 35 \tag{10.A.13}$$

$$M = -30 + 0.1Y \tag{10.A.14}$$

$$F = -32 + 4.4i \tag{10.A.15}$$

With appropriate substitutions, we can reduce the model to three equations showing the equilibrium conditions in terms of i and Y for the three sectors, as follows:

$$i = 155 - 0.25Y \qquad \text{(Real)}$$

$$i = -16.45 + 0.036Y \quad \text{(Monetary)}$$

$$B = 33 - 0.1Y + 4.4i \quad \text{(Foreign)}$$

We can then solve the foregoing equations for the equilibrium values of Y, i, and B. The equilibrium value of B is understood to be the value that is consistent with equilibrium of Y and i. The results are:

$$Y = 323.75 + 1.75G - 1.3125T_o + 0.5M^\$ = 600$$

$$i = 11.5625 + 0.0625G - 0.046875T_o - 0.125M^\$ = 5\%$$

$$B = 51.5 + 0.1G - 0.075T_o - 0.6M^\$ = -5$$

The equilibrium values of all the variables are given in the first column of Table 10.A.1.

The multipliers can be calculated by differentiating the equations for the equilibrium Y, i, and B with respect to the policy variables, G, T_o, and $M^\$$, as follows:

$$\frac{dY}{dG} = 1.75 \qquad \frac{di}{dG} = 0.0625 \qquad \frac{dB}{dG} = 0.1$$

$$\frac{dY}{dT_0} = -1.3125 \qquad \frac{di}{dT_0} = -0.046875 \qquad \frac{dB}{dT_0} = -0.075$$

$$\frac{dY}{dM^\$} = 0.5 \qquad \frac{di}{dM^\$} = -0.125 \qquad \frac{dB}{dM^\$} = -0.6$$

Now suppose there is an increase of $20 billion in government expenditures. With a multiplier of 1.75 for dY/dG and a multiplier of 0.1 for dB/dG, this will raise income by $35 billion and decrease the balance-of-payments deficit by $2 billion. The new values of all the variables are given in the second column of Table 10.A.1.

The government deficit increases by only $13 billion, since tax collections increase by $7 billion due to the increase in income. The increase in income increases the demand for money for transactions purposes, and, with an

TABLE 10.A.1

Numerical Example of Multiplier for Government Expenditures
(Dollar Amounts in Billions)

	Original Equilibrium	New Equilibrium[a]	Change
Gross National Product (Y)	600.0	635.0	+35.0
Consumption (C)	410.0	431.0	+21.0
Investment (I)	75.0	72.5	− 2.5
Government Purchases (G)	110.0	130.0	+20.0
Exports (X)	35.0	35.0	0
Imports (M)	30.0	33.5	+ 3.5
Taxes (T)	100.0	107.0	+ 7.0
Disposable Income (Y_d)	500.0	528.0	+28.0
Money Stock ($M^\$$)	115.0	115.0	0
Capital Imports (F)	−10.0	−4.5	+ 5.5
Balance-of-Payments Surplus (B)	− 5.0	− 3.0	+ 2.0
Saving ($Y_d − C$)	90.0	97.0	+ 7.0
Government Deficit ($G − T$)	10.0	23.0	+13.0
Trade Balance ($X − M$)	5.0	1.5	− 3.5
Interest Rate (i)	5%	6.25%	+ 1.25%

[a] After an increase of $20 billion in the rate of government purchases.

unchanged money stock, raises the interest rate. The rise in the interest rate in turn reduces domestic investment. As far as the balance of payments is concerned, however, the higher interest rate decreases the capital outflow, and the improvement in the capital account is more than enough to offset the deterioration in the trade balance resulting from the income-induced increase in imports. Thus the balance of payments as a whole improves by $2 billion.

Suppose alternatively that there has been no increase in government expenditures, but that the money supply is increased by $20 billion. With a multiplier of 0.5 for $dY/dM^\$$, income will increase by $10 billion from the original level of $600 billion to $610 billion. The interest rate, however, will fall by 2.5 percent from its original level of 5 percent to 2.5 percent, causing an increase of $11 billion in the capital outflow. Since the trade balance also deteriorates by $1 billion, due to the income-induced increase in imports, the balance-of-payments deficit increases by a total of $12 billion. The new values of all the variables are shown in the second column of Table 10.A.2.

Suppose now that we are again in the original equilibrium situation and that we wish to raise income to the full employment level of $640 billion, while at the same time balancing the external accounts. We want to find the combination of fiscal and monetary policy that will accomplish this double task. For the sake of simplicity we will not allow any changes in the tax level (T_o). Let the required change in government expenditures be ΔG and let the required change in the money supply be $\Delta M^\$$.

TABLE 10.A.2
Numerical Example of Multiplier for the Money Supply
(Dollar Amounts in Billions)

	Original Equilibrium	New Equilibrium[a]	Change
Gross National Product (Y)	600.0	610.0	+10.0
Consumption (C)	410.0	416.0	+ 6.0
Investment (I)	75.0	80.0	+ 5.0
Government Purchases (G)	110.0	110.0	0
Exports (X)	35.0	35.0	0
Imports (M)	30.0	31.0	+ 1.0
Taxes (T)	100.0	102.0	+ 2.0
Disposable Income (Y_d)	500.0	508.0	+ 8.0
Money Stock ($M^\$$)	115.0	135.0	+20.0
Capital Imports (F)	−10.0	−21.0	−11.0
Balance-of-Payments Surplus (B)	− 5.0	−17.0	−12.0
Saving ($Y_d − C$)	90.0	92.0	+ 2.0
Government Deficit ($G − T$)	10.0	8.0	− 2.0
Trade Balance ($X − M$)	5.0	4.0	− 1.0
Interest Rate (i)	5%	2.5%	− 2.5%

[a] After an increase of $20 billion in the money stock.

Then we have one equation for the change in income,

$$\frac{dY}{dG} \Delta G + \frac{dY}{dM^\$} \Delta M^\$ = \Delta Y$$

and one equation for the change in the balance of payments,

$$\frac{dB}{dG} \Delta G + \frac{dB}{dM^\$} \Delta M^\$ = \Delta B.$$

Inserting the values for the multipliers and for ΔY and ΔB, we have the following two equations in two unknowns,

$$1.75 \, \Delta G + 0.5 \, \Delta M^\$ = 40$$

$$0.1 \, \Delta G - 0.6 \, \Delta M^\$ = 5.$$

The solution is:

$$\Delta G = 24.1$$

$$\Delta M^\$ = -4.3.$$

Thus government expenditures will have to increase by \$24.1 billion and the money supply must simultaneously be reduced by \$4.3 billion.

The new values of all the variables are shown in the second column of Table 10.A.3. A greater demand for money due to the rise in income must

TABLE 10.A.3

*Numerical Example of Multipliers for Government Expenditures and the Money Supply
(Dollar Amounts in Billions)*

	Original Equilibrium	New Equilibrium[a]	Change
Gross National Product (Y)	600.0	640.0	+40.0
Consumption (C)	410.0	434.0	+24.0
Investment (I)	75.0	70.9	− 4.1
Government Purchases (G)	110.0	134.1	+24.1
Exports (X)	35.0	35.0	0
Imports (M)	30.0	34.0	+ 4.0
Taxes (T)	100.0	108.0	+ 8.0
Disposable Income (Y_d)	500.0	532.0	+32.0
Money Stock ($M^\$$)	115.0	110.7	− 4.3
Capital Imports (F)	−10.0	−1.0	+ 9.0
Balance-of-Payments Surplus (B)	− 5.0	0	+ 5.0
Saving ($Y_d - C$)	90.0	98.0	+ 8.0
Government Deficit ($G - T$)	10.0	26.1	+16.1
Trade Balance ($X - M$)	5.0	1.0	− 4.0
Interest Rate (i)	5%	7.05%	+ 2.05%

[a] After an increase of \$24.1 billion in the rate of government expenditures and a decrease of \$4.3 billion in the money supply.

now be satisfied with a reduced money supply, and the interest rate consequently rises even more than in our first example (see Table 10.A.1). The high interest rate is instrumental, however, in reducing the capital outflow by \$9 billion. Although imports rise by \$4 billion, the balance of trade is now equal to the balance on capital account, and the balance of payments is thus in equilibrium.

2. INCORPORATION OF INCOME-SENSITIVE CAPITAL MOVEMENTS INTO THE MODEL[2]

Income-sensitive capital movements can be incorporated into the model for a single country by rewriting equation (10.12) as:

$$F = F(\overset{+}{Y}, \overset{+}{i}), \tag{10.12'}$$

where F refers to the capital inflow in nominal terms, Y is GNP, and i is the rate of interest. The treatment of capital flows as responding to income levels is due to Johnson (1966a), with amendment by Baggott and Flanders (1969), who defended it as representing the positive stimulus given to direct investment and other long-term capital flows by a high income economy. Sohmen (1967, p. 516) has argued, however, that any such stimulus should be fully reflected in interest rates, and Ablin (1968) has also expressed doubts about the relationship. While Sohmen's criticism may be correct in principle, it may not apply to the large numbers of countries with shallow domestic capital markets. Borrowers (demanders of capital) may turn to foreign capital markets early under the pressure of a high income economy. Nor is it clear that interest rates in such countries have any close relation to the profitability of direct investment. Moreover, international direct investment reflects capital flows for both net investment and replacement purposes. The latter may reasonably be related to the level of income as a scale variable. Empirically, Rhomberg (1964) and Caves and Reuber (1971) have found support for income-sensitive capital movements in their studies dealing with Canada, as have Miller and Whitman (1970) for the U.S. and Arndt (1970) for France.

The equation (10.15) for the balance of payments now becomes:

$$B = pX\left(\frac{p}{r}, p_2\right) - rp_2M(Y, rp_2, p) + F(Y, i). \tag{10.15'}$$

With a fixed exchange rate and given values for G^*, M^*, and B, we can express (10.15') as a function of Y and i as before. It now appears that the B curve can assume a positive slope, as in Figure 10.3, or a negative slope. That is, differentiating (10.15') and calculating di/dY, we have:

$$\text{Slope of } B \text{ curve} = \frac{(\partial F/\partial Y) - m}{\partial F/\partial i} \lessgtr 0.$$

2. This and the following four sections were prepared by J. David Richardson.

TABLE 10.A.4

Ranking of Exchange-Rate Systems by "Power" (Size) of the Policy Multiplier on Income with a Negatively Sloped B Curve

	Rank	Monetary Policy	Fiscal Policy
B curve less vertical than *IS* curve	1	Fluctuating	Fixed without sterilization
	2	Fixed with sterilization	Fixed with sterilization
	3	Fixed without sterilization*	Fluctuating
B curve more vertical than *IS* curve	1	Fixed with sterilization	Fixed without sterilization
	2	Fluctuating	Fixed with sterilization
	3	**	Fluctuating

* The monetary policy multiplier on income is zero in this case.
** The assumption of nonsterilization under fixed exchange rates is incompatible with the stability of the system in this case.

Thus, if the income-induced inflow of capital, $\partial F/\partial Y$, is high enough, the *B* curve will have a negative slope. The reason is that since the *B* curve is a locus of all points generating the same balance-of-payments results, increases in income generate such large inflows of capital that they outweigh imports. In order to maintain the same balance of payments, the interest rate must go down to discourage further inflows. If the exchange rate is permitted to vary and the *B* curve has a negative slope, the curve will shift downward and to the left when *r* increases. In this case, exports will increase and imports will fall, thus enabling equilibrium to take place at a lower interest rate.

The analysis of monetary and fiscal policies under fixed and freely fluctuating exchange rates can be adapted to take into account a negatively sloped B curve that is less or more steep than the *IS* curve. The results are given in Table 10.A.4, which is analogous to Table 10.2.[3] The analysis of the assignment problem can also be adapted in this light. The results are given in Table 10.A.5, which is analogous to Table 10.3. It is of interest to note that when the *B* curve is more nearly vertical than the *IS* curve, the assignment rule is just the reverse of the traditional monetary-external and fiscal-internal rule.

3. A TWO-COUNTRY MODEL WITH FIXED EXCHANGE RATES

In extending our model to two countries, we could analyze the cases of both fixed and freely fluctuating exchange rates. We shall deal, however, only with

3. It will be noted in Table 10.A.4 that the assumption of nonsterilization is inconsistent with the stability of the model when the *B* curve is more nearly vertical than the *IS* curve. Expansionary monetary policy in this case leads to a balance-of-payments surplus and in turn to further monetary expansion, which leads to a larger surplus, and so on.

TABLE 10.A.5

Assignment Rules to Attain Internal and External Balance with a Negatively Sloped B Curve

	Policy Assignment	
Condition	Smooth Adjustment	Discontinuous Adjustment
B curve less vertical than *IS* curve	Monetary-external and fiscal-internal, *or* vice versa	Impossible to determine without further knowledge of parameters
B curve more vertical than *IS* curve	Monetary-internal and fiscal-external	Monetary-internal and fiscal-external

the case of fixed rates.[4] The equivalent of the system (10.13–(10.15) in the text is shown below for the two-country setting. For simplicity, capital movements are assumed to respond only to the rate of interest. This model is very similar to the one used by Cooper (1969a), except that he does not assume complete neutralization of balance-of-payments effects on the money supply. It will be noted that equation (10.A.18), which refers to the balance of payments, holds in both country 1 and country 2 since all trade and capital flows are confined to these countries. The variables have the same definitions as in the text, with country 2's variables indicated by a subscript 2.

$$Y = p^i D\left(\frac{Y}{p^i}, i\right) + pX\left(Y_2, \frac{p}{r}, p_2\right) - rp_2 M(Y, rp_2, p) + G^*$$

$$\text{(10.A.16)}$$

$$M^* = p^i L\left(\frac{Y}{p_i}, i\right) \tag{10.A.17}$$

$$B = pX\left(Y_2, \frac{p}{r}, p_2\right) - rp_2 M(Y, rp_2, p) + F(i, i_2) \tag{10.A.18}$$

$$M_2^* = p_2^i L_2\left(\frac{Y_2}{p_2^i}, i_2\right) \tag{10.A.19}$$

$$Y_2 = p_2^i D_2\left(\frac{Y_2}{p_2^i}, i_2\right) + p_2 M(Y, rp_2, p) - \frac{p}{r} X\left(Y_2, \frac{p}{r}, p_2\right) + G_2^*$$

$$\text{(10.A.20)}$$

If this system is now differentiated, it can be written in matrix form as follows, where the *s*, *m*, and *k*'s refer to the marginal propensities to hoard,

---

4. For treatment of fluctuating rates in a two-country model, see Krueger (1965) and Mundell (1968, esp. pp. 262–69). For an empirical study of Canadian experience in the postwar period with freely fluctuating and fixed exchange rates, including some analysis of the speed of adjustment to policy changes, see Rhomberg (1964).

import, and hold real cash balances in the two countries:

$$
\begin{bmatrix}
(s+m) & -\dfrac{\partial D}{\partial i} & 0 & 0 & -m_2 \\[2ex]
k & \dfrac{\partial L}{\partial i} & 0 & 0 & 0 \\[2ex]
m & -\dfrac{\partial F}{\partial i} & 1 & -\dfrac{\partial F}{\partial i_2} & -m_2 \\[2ex]
0 & 0 & 0 & \dfrac{\partial L_2}{\partial i_2} & k_2 \\[2ex]
-m & 0 & 0 & -\dfrac{\partial D_2}{\partial i_2} & (s_2+m_2)
\end{bmatrix}
\begin{bmatrix}
dY \\[2ex] di \\[2ex] dB \\[2ex] di_2 \\[2ex] dY_2
\end{bmatrix}
=
\begin{bmatrix}
dG^* \\[2ex] dM^* \\[2ex] 0 \\[2ex] dM_2^* \\[2ex] dG_2^*
\end{bmatrix}
$$

To find the monetary and fiscal policy multipliers for this system, we could either go through tedious substitutions or use a shortcut for solving a system of this type known as Cramer's Rule.[5] Cramer's Rule simply states that in a system of equations

$$
n \times m \text{ matrix } \leftarrow A \begin{pmatrix} x_1 \\ \vdots \\ x_i \\ \vdots \\ x_n \end{pmatrix} = y \rightarrow n \times 1 \text{ vector}
$$

the solution for x_i in terms of the parameters in A and in terms of y is:

$$
x_i = \frac{|A_i^*|}{|A|}
$$

where the vertical slashes indicate the determinant of the matrix and A_i^* is an artificial matrix made up of exactly the same columns as A, except for the ith column, for which is substituted the vector y. For example, in the two-country system, if the 5×5 matrix is A, the solution for di in terms of the parameters and all the policy changes is:

$$
di = \frac{1}{|A|}
\begin{vmatrix}
(s+m) & dG^* & 0 & 0 & -m_2 \\[2ex]
k & dM^* & 0 & 0 & 0 \\[2ex]
m & 0 & 1 & -\dfrac{\partial F}{\partial i_2} & -m_2 \\[2ex]
0 & dM_2^* & 0 & \dfrac{\partial L_2}{\partial i_2} & k_2 \\[2ex]
-m & dG_2^* & 0 & -\dfrac{\partial D_2}{\partial i_2} & (s_2+m_2)
\end{vmatrix}
$$

5. For a discussion of Cramer's Rule, see, for example, Chiang (1967, pp. 113–15).

Working out all the necessary determinants for this system is tedious, but less so than other methods of solution. Here only the results will be given. The determinant of the entire system (Δ) is:

$$\Delta = \left[(s + m) \frac{\partial L}{\partial i} + k \frac{\partial D}{\partial i} \right] \left[(s_2 + m_2) \frac{\partial L_2}{\partial i_2} + k_2 \frac{\partial D_2}{\partial i_2} \right] - mm_2 \frac{\partial L}{\partial i} \frac{\partial L_2}{\partial i_2}$$

The product of the bracketed terms is unambiguously positive. To show that the unbracketed term can never make Δ negative, consider that one of the terms in the bracketed product will be:

$$(s + m)(s_2 + m_2) \frac{\partial L}{\partial i} \frac{\partial L_2}{\partial i_2}$$

and it is always true that

$$(s + m)(s_2 + m_2) \frac{\partial L}{\partial i} \frac{\partial L_2}{\partial i_2} - mm_2 \frac{\partial L}{\partial i} \frac{\partial L_2}{\partial i_2} > 0.$$

Hence the determinant Δ will always be positive.

The income multipliers for country 1 can all be derived from

$$\Delta \cdot dY = \left[(s_2 + m_2) \frac{\partial L_2}{\partial i_2} + k_2 \frac{\partial D_2}{\partial i_2} \right] \left[\frac{\partial L}{\partial i} dG_2^* + \frac{\partial D}{\partial i} dM^* \right]$$

$$+ m_2 \left(\frac{\partial L}{\partial i} \right) \left[\frac{\partial L_2}{\partial i_2} dG_2^* + \frac{\partial D_2}{\partial i_2} dM_2^* \right].$$

The income multipliers for country 2 would be exactly symmetric to these only with country 1 parameters replacing country 2's. Notice that an increase in government expenditure or in the money supply in either country unambiguously increases income in both countries.

The interest rate multipliers for country 1 (or, symmetrically, for country 2) can be derived from:

$$\Delta \cdot di = \left\{ k \left[(s_2 + m_2) \frac{\partial L_2}{\partial i_2} - k_2 \frac{\partial D_2}{\partial i_2} \right] \right\} dG^*$$

$$- \left\{ - \frac{\partial L_2}{\partial i_2} [(s + m)(s_2 + m_2) - mm_2] - k_2(s + m) \frac{\partial D_2}{\partial i_2} \right\} dM^*$$

$$+ km_2 \left(- \frac{\partial L_2}{\partial i_2} dG_2^* - \frac{\partial D_2}{\partial i_2} dM_2^* \right).$$

As we might expect, we can show from the above that the interest rate at home always responds positively to an increase in home or foreign government expenditure and to an increase in the foreign money stock. It responds negatively to an increase in the home-money stock. We can also derive the balance-of-payments multipliers for this system. However, the results are complicated and do not yield unambiguous signs.

In addition to the effects of one country's monetary or fiscal policies upon income and interest rates in the rest of the world, it is also interesting to ask how policy authorities in a large country should alter their responses to domestic disequilibrium when there is unemployment or inflation in the rest of the world. Using a two-country model similar to the one employed above, Cooper (1969a) has shown that the need for the international coordination of policies increases as economic interdependence rises among countries. In particular, he demonstrated that when there are strong economic linkages between countries, the time it takes policymakers to attain their economic targets following a macroeconomic disturbance is substantially decreased when policies are coordinated between countries. Using the same two-country model, Roper (1971) showed that the ingredient of Cooper's coordination proposal that is most responsible for the faster attainment of economic targets is the international or joint elimination of sterilization policies. However, Roper pointed out that the case for reducing sterilization policies also depends upon how much the rates of change of interest rates as compared to interest-rate levels affect capital flows.

4. INCORPORATION OF A PRICE EQUATION INTO THE MODEL

Returning now to our model of a single country, let us introduce the following price equation:

$$p = p\left(\frac{Y}{p}\right) = p(Q) \qquad \frac{\partial p}{\partial Q} > 0 \qquad (10.A.21)$$

where Q refers here to the level of output.[6] This equation suggests on more than that increases in income shift the aggregate demand curve outward relative to the aggregate supply curve, which in a short-run Keynesian model is assumed to be fixed. The outward shift raises price. It is not an equation to describe the rate of inflation, which might better depend on the gap between the actual and full employment level of income, Y_f, that is, $dp/dt = f(Y - Y_f)$. This formulation would capture some of the Phillips curve considerations, but it would unfortunately be unworkable in our present model.

Our model can be represented in terms of equations (10.13)–(10.15) in the text above:

$$Y = p^i D\left(\frac{Y}{p^i}, i\right) + pX\left(\frac{p}{r}, p_2\right) - rp_2 M(Y, rp_2, p) + G^* \qquad (10.13)$$

$$M^* = p^i L\left(\frac{Y}{p^i}, i\right) \qquad (10.14)$$

$$B = pX\left(\frac{p}{r}, p_2\right) - rp_2 M(Y, rp_2, p) + F(i). \qquad (10.15)$$

6. Note that if Y is money income, in a one-good Keynesian world:

$$\frac{Y}{p} = \frac{pQ}{p} = Q = \text{output.}$$

In our earlier treatment, p was held constant whereas now it becomes another unknown. Since we add one unknown and one equation (10.A.21), the system is still determinate.

If we differentiate the foregoing system, and adopt the following conventions:[7]

$$U = \eta_x - \eta_m - 1 > 0$$

$$V = \frac{\partial p/\partial Q}{1 + Y(\partial p/\partial Q)} > 0$$

$$W = 1 - k\frac{Y}{L} > 0,$$

then we have the following two systems in matrix form, where s, m, and k are the marginal propensities to hoard, import, and hold real cash balances, and a is the proportion of expenditure spent on imports:[8]

Fixed exchange rates:

$$
\begin{bmatrix}
(s + m)(1 - VY) + aVY(U + s) & -\dfrac{\partial D}{\partial i} & 0 \\[2ex]
[k + VW(1 - a)] & \dfrac{\partial L}{\partial i} & 0 \\[2ex]
[m(1 - VY) + aVYU] & -\dfrac{\partial F}{\partial i} & 1
\end{bmatrix}
\begin{bmatrix}
dY \\[2ex] di \\[2ex] dB
\end{bmatrix}
=
\begin{bmatrix}
dG^* \\[2ex] dM^* \\[2ex] 0
\end{bmatrix}
$$

Freely fluctuating exchange rates:

$$
\begin{bmatrix}
\begin{aligned} &(s + m)(1 - VY) \\ &\quad + aVY(U + s) \end{aligned} & -\dfrac{\partial D}{\partial i} & -M(U + s) \\[3ex]
[k + VW(1 - a)] & \dfrac{\partial L}{\partial i} & aW \\[2ex]
[m(1 - VY) + aVYU] & -\dfrac{\partial F}{\partial i} & -MU
\end{bmatrix}
\begin{bmatrix}
dY \\[2ex] di \\[2ex] dr
\end{bmatrix}
=
\begin{bmatrix}
dG^* \\[2ex] dM^* \\[2ex] 0
\end{bmatrix}
$$

We can in principle solve each system for its multipliers, with the aid of Cramer's Rule outlined earlier. It is noteworthy that the sign of the income

7. The expression for V is the proportional factor relating changes in price to changes in money income. It comes from differentiating (10.A.21). See our earlier discussion in the text regarding $[1 - k(Y/L)] > 0$.

8. To get these results, we had to make use of the assumption that the import function was homogeneous of degree zero. Thus, as in Chapter 7 above:

$$M\xi_m = -M\eta_m - mY$$

where the cross-price elasticity $\xi_m = (p/M)(\partial M/\partial p)$.

multipliers will be determinate in both cases so long as $\eta_x - \eta_m > 1 + m$, which is the elasticities condition derived earlier in Chapter 7. Thus, the determinant of the fixed exchange-rate system is:

$$\Delta_1 = \frac{\partial L}{\partial i}\left[(s + m)(1 - VY) + aVY(U + s)\right] + \frac{\partial D}{\partial i}\left[k + VW(1 - a)\right],$$

which is always negative.[9] The multipliers on income can be derived from:

$$dY = \frac{1}{\Delta_1}\left[\frac{\partial L}{\partial i} dG^* + \frac{\partial D}{\partial i} dM^*\right],$$

both of which will be positive.

The determinant of the fluctuating exchange-rate system is more complicated:

$$\Delta_2 = A_{11}\left[-MU\frac{\partial L}{\partial i} + aW\frac{\partial F}{\partial i}\right] + A_{21}\left[-MU\frac{\partial D}{\partial i} + M(U + s)\frac{\partial F}{\partial i}\right]$$
$$+ A_{31}\left[M(U + s)\frac{\partial L}{\partial i} - aW\frac{\partial D}{\partial i}\right],$$

where A_{11}, A_{21}, and A_{31} refer, respectively, to the first, second, and third elements in the first column of the freely fluctuating-system matrix. The expression can be simplified somewhat by combining the first and third terms, in order to show that Δ_2 is unambiguously positive, as long as $(U - m) > 0$ (this is the elasticities condition mentioned above):

$$\Delta_2 = -sM(1 - VY)(U - m)\frac{\partial L}{\partial i} + saW[1 - (1 - a)VY]\left(\frac{\partial F}{\partial i} - \frac{\partial D}{\partial i}\right)$$
$$+ A_{21}\left[-MU\frac{\partial D}{\partial i} + M(U + s)\frac{\partial F}{\partial i}\right].$$

Each term in this expression is positive, making the whole determinant positive. The multipliers on income can then be derived from:

$$dY = \frac{1}{\Delta_1}\left\{\left[-MU\frac{\partial L}{\partial i} + aW\frac{\partial F}{\partial i}\right]dG^* + \left[-MU\frac{\partial D}{\partial i} + M(U + s)\frac{\partial F}{\partial i}\right]dM^*\right\},$$

both of which will be positive.[10]

9. Note that $(1 - VY)$ is positive because

$$1 - VY = 1 - \left[\frac{\partial p/\partial Q}{1 + (\partial p/\partial Q)Y}\right] Y = \frac{1}{1 + (\partial p/\partial Q)Y}.$$

10. Our results for the fluctuating exchange-rate case differ from those obtained by Krueger (1965) who developed a model similar to the one presented here. These differences stem from the fact that Krueger left out the exchange rate and the price level in her

The income multipliers in the two systems can be compared as follows:

$$\left(\frac{dY}{dG^*}\right)_{\text{fixed}} = \frac{1}{\Delta_1}\left(\frac{\partial L}{\partial i}\right)$$

$$\left(\frac{dY}{dG^*}\right)_{\text{fluctuating}} = \frac{1}{\Delta_2}\left[-MU\frac{\partial L}{\partial i} + aW\frac{\partial F}{\partial i}\right]$$

$$\left(\frac{dY}{dM^*}\right)_{\text{fixed}} = \frac{1}{\Delta_1}\left(\frac{\partial D}{\partial i}\right)$$

$$\left(\frac{dY}{dM^*}\right)_{\text{fluctuating}} = \frac{1}{\Delta_2}\left[-MU\frac{\partial D}{\partial i} + M(U + s)\frac{\partial F}{\partial i}\right].$$

We would have to know the actual parameter values in order to evaluate these multipliers.

5. CORRESPONDENCE BETWEEN ALTERNATIVE APPROACHES TO THE ASSIGNMENT PROBLEM

Since Mundell's approach to the assignment problem (1968, pp. 233–39) is perhaps more familiar than the one used in the text, it may be useful to show how the two approaches correspond. Mundell's basic diagram had a fiscal policy variable on the vertical axis and a monetary policy variable on the horizontal axis, similar to what is shown in Figure 10.A.1. If both policies were directed towards a single goal, there is an infinite number of combinations of these policies that could achieve the goal. For example, if the economy is at full employment (i.e., in internal balance), we could maintain that state of full employment by raising government expenditure and lowering the money supply just enough to offset the expansionary fiscal effect. Similarly, if our payments balance were presently zero, and fiscal expansion increases imports to a greater extent than it induces capital flows (for either interest rate or income reasons), then any fiscal expansion must be offset by monetary expansion (to raise the interest rate still further) if payments balance is to be maintained.[11] Thus, in Figure 10.A.1, there is a locus of policy combinations that defines internal balance and a locus that defines external balance. The area of the figure can evidently be broken down into the four quadrants

---

equations for the balance of payments and private domestic expenditure, D. The exchange rate and price level must appear in the balance-of-payments equation in order to express the balance of payments in monetary rather than real terms. See Sohmen (1967).

The exchange rate and the price level must appear in the D equation, moreover, since D here is the sum of expenditure on domestic goods and imports. Unless there is a one-to-one substitution between these types of expenditure when prices or exchange rates change, the equation for D must include both. A further difference between Krueger's model and ours is that she defines monetary policy as changes in the interest rate rather than changes in the money supply.

11. We are assuming here that fiscal expansion, *ceteris paribus*, leads to a balance-of-payments deficit, that is, the LM curve is flatter than the B curve.

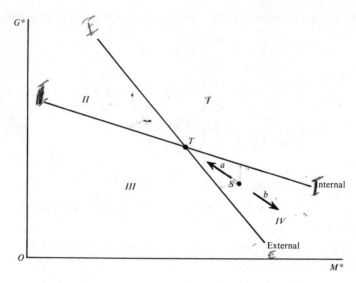

FIGURE 10.A.1.

*Assignment of Fiscal and Monetary Policies for
Internal and External Balance, with Smooth
Policy Adjustment*

I: *Overemployment (balance-of-payments) Deficit*
II: *Overemployment, Surplus*
III: *Underemployment, Surplus*
IV: *Underemployment, Deficit*

*Starting at S, the economy will move toward T with a fiscal-
internal and monetary-external assignment. With the inverse
assignment, the economy would move away from T.*

shown, indicating the conditions of the level of income and the balance of payments.

Suppose we start in quadrant IV at S, and "assign" internal balance to an independent fiscal authority and external balance to an independent monetary authority. Assume that the authorities carry out policy changes smoothly, as in the text above. The fiscal authorities will then be moving smoothly north away from S, reassessing their position after an infinitesimal movement, and the monetary authorities will be moving smoothly west in the same manner. The result will be that the economy will move in the direction of the arrow a, converging toward T. If the inverse rule were followed, the fiscal authorities would move south and the monetary authorities east, thus making the economy move in the direction indicated by arrow b, *away* from equilibrium.

If we suppose now that the external balance line in Mundell's diagram has a positive slope, the analysis becomes more complex. This will occur if we

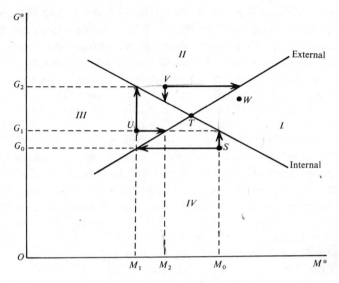

FIGURE 10.A.2.

Policy Assignment, with Discontinuous Adjustment,
Leading to Divergence from Equilibrium

Starting at S, the actions of the fiscal and monetary authori-
ties lead to points U, V, and W, etc. The system will diverge
away from T.

consider the case in which an expansionary fiscal policy *improves* the balance of payments. Let us also assume discontinuous rather than smooth policy adjustment. Therefore, the quadrants in Figure 10.A.2 are labelled so that the area above the external balance line represents balance-of-payments *surplus*. (I, II, III, and IV stand for the same conditions as before.) Suppose we start at S, a point of underemployment and balance-of-payments deficit and follow the traditional rule. The fiscal authorities will increase G^* from G_0 to a position near G_1, if they accurately forecast the parameters associated with the economy; the monetary authorities will decrease M^* from M_0 to a position near M_1, again assuming accurate guessing. The economy will end up at U, a point of underemployment and balance-of-payments surplus. Now the fiscal authorities will increase G^* from G_1 to near G_2; the monetary authorities will increase M^* from M_1 to near M_2. The economy will end up at V, a point of overemployment and balance-of-payments surplus. The reader will find it instructive to carry the analysis one step further (to point W), in order to conclude that the system will diverge away from T, even though we are following the traditional rule. This was the conclusion derived in the text from Figure 10.10, where the LM curve was steeper than the B curve.

The correspondence between the diagrams in the text and Mundell-type diagrams is summarized in Table 10.A.6, where the quadrants are labelled as defined earlier. It will be noted that this table incorporates both Tables 10.3 and 10.A.5 above, where the *B* curve was positively or negatively sloped.

In order to prove rigorously the foregoing assertions, we can derive the properties of the internal and external balance schedules from equations (10.13), (10.14), and (10.15') above. We shall merely outline the main considerations involved so that the reader can work it out for himself. The system of equations in question depends on five unknowns in its most general form: Y, i, B, G^*, and M^*. G^* and M^*, being policy parameters, are usually specified so that we can solve the system for Y, i, and B. Instead, in order to derive an internal balance line, we choose Y to be full employment income, Y_f. Then, the system of three equations in four unknowns can be reduced to one equation in two unknowns, namely G^* and M^*, to get the internal balance line. Similarly, the equation for the external balance line comes from setting B equal to zero and reducing the three equations to one equation in G^* and M^*.

In each case, we can examine the slope of the internal balance line by determining the sign of dG^*/dM^* in the one remaining equation. This slope will always be negative. With regard to the external balance line, the sign of dG^*/dM^* will depend on

$$\left(\frac{\partial F}{\partial Y} - m - \frac{k \, (\partial F/\partial i)}{\partial L/\partial i} \right).$$

If this is less than zero, the *B* curve has a positive slope and is steeper than the *LM* curve, and the external balance line has a negative slope, as in the second case of Table 10.A.6. If the expression is greater than zero, we shall have a positively sloped external balance line, as in the first case of Table 10.A.6.

6. A PORTFOLIO-BALANCE MODEL OF INTERNAL-EXTERNAL BALANCE

The model in the text was presented as if it were a complete model of an economy. Implicit in it, however, was a "bonds" sector since open market operations were carried out by means of exchanging bonds for privately held money and the international capital flow was at least in part a flow of bonds. Explicit treatment of this bonds sector was ignored, as it has been traditionally in discussion of internal-external balance, by resorting to Walras' Law. That is, if we know that a whole economy is in equilibrium and that every market save one is also in equilibrium, then we can be sure that that particular market is also in equilibrium.

Recent "portfolio-balance" approaches to internal-external balance—see, for example, McKinnon and Oates (1966), McKinnon (1969a), and Levin (1970a)—have criticized this relegation of the bond market to a residual role. These approaches point out that any given intersection of *IS* and *LM* (and *B*) curves may not be a true static equilibrium since the supply of "outside"

TABLE 10.A.6

Correspondence Between Alternative Approaches to the Assignment Problem

Condition	Policy Assignment		Mundell Diagram[a]
	Smooth Adjustment	Discontinuous Adjustment	
B curve of positive slope — Flatter than LM curve	Monetary-external and fiscal-internal, or vice versa	Impossible to determine without further knowledge of parameters	
B curve of positive slope — Steeper than LM curve	Monetary-external and fiscal-internal	Monetary-external and fiscal-internal	
B curve of negative slope — Less vertical than IS curve	Monetary-external and fiscal-internal, or vice versa	Impossible to determine without further knowledge of parameters	
B curve of negative slope — More vertical than IS curve	Monetary-internal and fiscal-external	Monetary-internal and fiscal-external	

[a] I: overemployment—deficit; II: overemployment—surplus; III: underemployment—surplus; IV: underemployment—deficit.

bonds (bonds not issued by the private sector) may be rising or falling continuously. The reasons for this will be discussed below.

The typical portfolio-balance approach to internal-external balance employs Walras' Law in a different way. Instead of making the bonds sector the residual sector, it makes the real sector residual and focuses primarily on the financial sectors. The fact that different answers to internal-external balance questions emerge from the portfolio-balance approach is a demonstration of the pitfalls of employing Walras' Law. We cannot therefore ignore any sector about which we have behavioral ideas. Neither the bonds nor the real sector can be properly ignored.

We shall not develop a model which incorporates these two sectors, however. Rather, our objective will be to outline a very simple portfolio-balance model in order to provide a flavor of this approach and to demonstrate the conclusions that follow from it. Several notions are crucial to our presentation.

The first is the fact that there can be no government budget deficit or surplus without some change in the privately held stock of assets in the economy. A budget deficit must be financed either by the issue of bonds to the public in return for private money balances or by the creation of new money either by printing it or by selling bonds to the central bank in return for deposits there. In the first case, after the government has spent the money balances obtained, the private money stock is unchanged while the private bond stock is increased. In the second case, the private money stock is increased while the private bond stock is unchanged.

The second important notion is that current-account surpluses or deficits have exactly analogous effects on the stock of privately held assets in the economy. For example, a balance-of-payments deficit implies that the stabilization fund is supplying foreign exchange to the economy in return for money balances. Thus, a balance-of-payments deficit implies that the domestic money stock is decreasing, unless such a decrease is offset (neutralized) by the central bank. But in order to neutralize the effects of a balance-of-payments deficit on the money stock, the central bank must, by open market operations, buy privately held bonds in exchange for money. Consequently, if there is to be no change in the privately held money stock, there must be a decrease in the privately held stock of bonds. The principle just described will hold analogously for balance-of-payments or government budget surpluses.

Finally, of crucial importance in portfolio-balance analysis is that a change in the interest rate may generate a change in desired stocks of different assets. Thus, a change in the interest rate may generate some international capital inflow or outflow initially. But at the new equilibrium, flow asset changes will be zero.

With the foregoing points in mind, we shall proceed to construct a portfolio-balance model of internal-external balance for a single country. The model is again comparative static in character. Therefore, equilibrium is defined as that point at which the stocks of all assets are constant and there is no change in income or the interest rate. In addition, any changes in the government budget surplus or in the balance-of-payments surplus are assumed to affect the stock of money in the economy, not the stock of bonds. This assumption is made for expositional convenience only, and it is assumed that this was not always true for this economy.[12]

The following notation is to be used in addition to what has appeared previously:

V^d = Demand for the stock of domestic bonds

V_s = Supply of bonds

V_o = Exogenous stock of bonds used to finance past government deficits

E = All past effects of government budget surpluses and balance-of-payments surpluses on the money supply

T = Taxes (exogenous)

V^f = Demand for the stock of foreign bonds

t = Time.

The model is as follows:

1. *The bonds sector*

(Identity)	$V^d \equiv V^s$	(10.A.22)
(Behavioral equation)	$V^d = V^d(Y, i)$	(10.A.23)
(Policy equation)	$V^s = -M^* + V_o$	(10.A.24)

2. *The monetary sector*

(Identity)	$M^\$ \equiv L$	(10.A.25)
	$L = L(Y, i)$	(10.A.26)
	$M^\$ = M^* + E$	(10.A.27)
(Behavioral equations)	$\dfrac{dE}{dt} = B + (G - T)$	(10.A.28)
	$T = T_o$	(10.A.29)
(Policy equation)	$G = G^*$	(10.A.30)

12. This is exactly the opposite assumption of the one made in our discussion in the text, where any effects of the balance of payments or government expenditures on the money supply were assumed to be neutralized. That is, the central bank offset them by open market operations, with the result that the balance of payments and government expenditures affected the stock of bonds in the economy but not the stock of money.

3. *The foreign sector*

$$\text{(Identity)} \qquad\qquad B \equiv X - M + \frac{dV^f}{dt} \qquad\qquad (10.\text{A}.31)$$

$$\text{(Behavioral equations)} \quad \begin{cases} X = X_o & (10.\text{A}.32) \\[2mm] M = M(Y) & (10.\text{A}.33) \\[2mm] V^f = V^f(Y, i) & (10.\text{A}.34) \end{cases}$$

This model is very similar to the one in the text, except that the bonds sector has now replaced the real sector. The demand for money is in nominal terms. Prices and the exchange rate are assumed fixed and equal to unity and are thus not shown explicitly. This again insures a one-to-one correspondence between nominal and real variables. The stock demand for bonds in (10.A.23) is assumed to depend on income and the interest rate. A more sophisticated model might include wealth as a third argument. The supply of bonds in (10.A.24) is assumed to be equal to net open market operations since the beginning of the central bank, $-M^*$, and an exogenous variable, V_o, that represents the stock of bonds placed other than by the central bank, for example those bonds used to finance government deficits in the past.

In the monetary sector, the money supply in (10.A.27) is assumed to depend both upon cumulative net open market operations, M^*, and the past effects of government budget surpluses and balance-of-payments surpluses on the money stock, E. Moreover, any present balance-of-payments surplus, B, or government deficit, $G - T$, is assumed in (10.A.28) to have a positive influence on E. That is to say, the mere existence of a balance-of-payments surplus and a budget deficit means the money supply is expanding ($dE > 0$). Taxes in (10.A.29) are considered exogenous.

In the foreign sector, the stock demand for foreign bonds (V^f) in (10.A.34) depends on domestic income and the rate of interest. It is assumed that $\partial V^f/\partial Y > 0$, reflecting the fact that total portfolio size increases with rising income. It should be noted, however, that dV^f is an increased demand for foreign bonds and represents therefore a capital *outflow* in the balance-of-payments identity (10.A.31).[13] This is in contrast to our earlier model where F, the capital *inflow*, increased with rising income.

---

13. In defining V^f as the stock demand for foreign bonds and dV^f as sales or purchases of these bonds by domestic citizens, we are ignoring the fact that capital inflows and outflows could also be due to sales or purchases of domestic bonds by foreign citizens. In other words, it is being assumed that no foreigners hold domestic bonds. Otherwise, the supply of domestic bonds would depend not only on the actions of the monetary and fiscal authorities, but also on whether a capital outflow was due to foreigners selling their domestic bonds (increased domestic bond supply) or domestic citizens buying foreign bonds (no change in domestic bond supply).

Since in equilibrium, it is assumed that stocks of assets are constant, we have two equilibrium conditions:

$$\frac{dE}{dt} = 0$$

$$\frac{dV^f}{dt} = 0.$$

The model can be condensed into three equations, as follows:

$$-M^* + V_o = V^d(Y, i) \tag{10.A.35}$$

$$M^* + E = L(Y, i) \tag{10.A.36}$$

$$T_o - G^* = X_o - M(Y) \tag{10.A.37}$$

Equation (10.A.35) refers to the bonds sector, (10.A.36) to the monetary sector, and (10.A.37) to the remaining equations, including the equilibrium conditions.

Equation (10.A.37) is the crucial equation in a portfolio-balance model. It says that in order for there to be static equilibrium (constant M and i and unchanging stocks of assets), the budget surplus or deficit must equal the balance-of-payments surplus or deficit. If this is not so, then the supply of money in the economy will be continually changing. What makes (10.A.37) interesting is that for the exogenous values of T and X and for a given value of G^*, there is only one value of Y that satisfies this equation. That is, the equilibrium value of Y is completely determined by equation (10.A.37) that contains only the fiscal policy variable. We can already see therefore that monetary policy has no effect on the equilibrium level of income in a static portfolio-balance model. Moreover, by differentiating (10.A.37), we find that the fiscal policy multiplier is simply

$$\frac{dY}{dG^*} = \frac{1}{m},$$

or the reciprocal of the marginal propensity to import.

It may be fruitful to pursue the portfolio-balance analysis graphically, as in Figure 10.A.3. Equation (10.A.35) determines what we shall call a VV line in $Y - i$ space, which will be negative in slope, assuming $\partial V^d/\partial Y$ and $\partial V^d/\partial i$ are > 0. Equation (10.A.36) determines the LM curve; (10.A.37)

The foreign bond market is supposed always to be in equilibrium. That is, supplies of foreign bonds are always forthcoming to meet the demand (V^f). The foreign market is linked to the domestic market, however, insofar as an increase in the interest rate decreases the demand for foreign bonds ($\partial V^f/\partial i < 0$) and increases the demand for domestic bonds ($\partial V^D/\partial i > 0$).

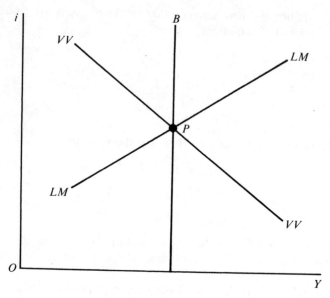

FIGURE 10.A.3.

Portfolio Balance

Portfolio balance is obtained at point P.

determines a vertical line that is the equivalent of the B line in our previous analysis. Since to the right of this vertical line, income is higher, imports will also be higher and

$$T_o - G^* > X_o - M(Y).$$

The money stock will be decreasing in this case because of the excess of the budget surplus over the trade balance. Similarly to the left of the vertical line, the money stock will be increasing.

Let us now look at the effects of an attempted expansionary monetary policy by open market purchases, as in Figure 10.A.4. Since M^* goes up, the supply of money is increased and the supply of privately held bonds is decreased. LM shifts to the right and downwards to LM_1. VV shifts to the left and downwards to VV_1. The resulting point of intersection of LM_1 and VV_1 could be either to the left or to the right of B, depending on the parameters of the money and bond-demand function. It has been indicated here at R to the right of the B line, suggesting that this attempt at expansionary monetary policy *temporarily* increases income and hence imports, thus leading to a drain on the money stock. But as the money stock decreases, the LM curve undergoes a second shift upward and to the left. The decrease in the stock of money is halted only when the LM curve shifts to LM_2, at which time the

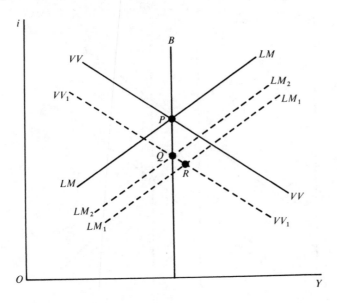

FIGURE 10.A.4.

Expansionary Monetary Policy and Portfolio Balance

With initial portfolio balance at P, monetary expansion (shift of LM to LM_1) results in a decrease of privately held bonds (shift from VV to VV_1). Income and imports are temporarily increased at R, leading to a drain on the money supply. The decrease in the money supply will cease at Q. Expansionary monetary policy thus lowers the interest rate, but has no effect on income.

economy is in equilibrium again at Q. The equilibrium effects of the attempt at expansionary monetary policy are to lower the interest rate and to cause no change in income. Monetary policy for income adjustment is therefore ineffective.

Fiscal policy, however, does work, since it changes the position of the *B* curve. For example in Figure 10.A.5, an expansionary fiscal policy shifts the *B* curve to the right. Thus if the economy starts at *P* and government expenditure increases, the *B* curve will shift from *B* to B_1. *P* is now a point to the left of the *B* curve, and as such, the money supply must be increasing. That is, the increased government deficit or reduced surplus must be financed by pumping money into the economy. The increasing money surplus shifts the *LM* curve downward and to the right until it intersects the *B* curve at *Q*, at which point equilibrium is attained and there is no further change in the money stock. The effect of expansionary fiscal policy is to raise income and now to *lower* the interest rate.

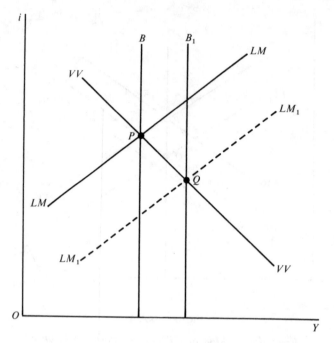

FIGURE 10.A.5.

Expansionary Fiscal Policy and
Portfolio Balance

With initial portfolio balance at P, fiscal policy, financed by
an increase in the money supply, shifts the B curve to B_1.
Any further increases (or decreases) in the money supply
caused by balance-of-payments disequilibrium will cease at
Q. Expansionary fiscal policy thus raises income and lowers
the interest rate.

The foregoing model and results are designed primarily to demonstrate a
different approach to internal-external balance. Although the model is over-
simplified, the framework and results are nevertheless typical of the portfolio-
balance approach.[14]

14. A critical evaluation of static portfolio-balance models is to be found in Morton
(1970, esp. pp. 18–29).

11

Economic Growth and the
Balance of Payments

Having proceeded thus far mainly within a comparative static framework, we shall now take growth considerations explicitly into account. We shall first develop a simplified Harrod-Domar model of economic growth in the context of an open economy. This model, which is purely formal in character, builds upon our earlier discussion in Chapters 6 and 7. We shall then present a simplified neoclassical growth model with a foreign sector, and compare thereafter the results of this model with the Harrod-Domar one.

We know from our earlier discussion that an increase in income due to some exogenous change domestically will ordinarily lead to a worsening of the trade balance because of the induced effects upon imports and the possible deflection of exports to home consumption. Yet, observation of real world experiences since World War II has disclosed some important instances among the industrialized countries—Italy, Japan, and West Germany in particular—in which rapid economic growth has been associated with an improvement rather than a worsening in the balance of payments. Given the importance of foreign trade in many industrialized countries, a number of writers have attempted to analyze the various experiences within the framework of models of "export-led" growth. We shall examine the salient features of these models in the third section of the chapter. Attention has become focused more recently in this same context upon the role of monetary influences in the growth and balance-of-payments processes. We shall outline these influences in the fourth section of the chapter and contrast them with the nonmonetary influences emphasized in the export-led models. We shall have occasion, finally, to discuss the implications of the alternative approaches to growth and the balance of payments for the formulation of policies designed to attain full employment and external balance and to effectuate growth objectives.

A Simplified Harrod-Domar Model of Growth in an Open Economy[1]

We shall first approach the study of growth in an open economy as an extension of the Harrod-Domar model of growth in a closed economy. It is important to note that the Harrod-Domar model is built on the assumption that the saving and output-capital ratios are given. While this may be reasonable in the short run, it is much less so in the long run. Indeed, it was in recognition of the rigidity of the Harrod-Domar model, particularly with regard to the constancy of the output-capital ratio, that the neoclassical model of growth was developed. Despite its limitations, the Harrod-Domar model has some interesting analytical properties that are worth pursuing. Following Johnson (1953b), we begin by examining growth from the standpoint of a single country in a two-country world in which foreign repercussions are assumed to be absent. We then introduce the second country explicitly in order to take foreign repercussions into account and to determine the requirements for equilibrium growth in the two countries. In both of these cases, we assume the exchange rate to be fixed and that accommodating capital movements occur when there is a trade imbalance. We alter this particular assumption in our final case in which the exchange rate is permitted to vary in response to an imbalance of trade.

The following notation will be used:

I = Real investment, taken in this case to be the required amount of investment to keep the existing stock of capital fully utilized

Y = Real output corresponding to full capacity use of the capital stock

s = Saving ratio (fraction of output devoted to saving)

a = Output-capital ratio

R = Equilibrium rate of growth

X = Volume of exports

x = Rate of growth of exports

M = Volume of imports

m = Import ratio (fraction of output devoted to imports).

The foregoing notation refers to country 1; country 2 is to be designated by a subscript.

FOREIGN REPERCUSSIONS ABSENT

We assume domestic prices are constant and equal to unity in country 1 and that country 1's exports are given exogenously by world demand. The exchange rate is assumed fixed and initially equal to unity, and trade imbalances are financed automatically by accommodating capital movements.

---

1. This and the following section were written in large part by Johan A. Lybeck.

The import content of investment and of domestic production is assumed to be zero, and international interest payments arising from settlement of trade imbalances are to be ignored.[2] We abstract, finally, from autonomous capital movements and assume that accommodating capital movements are neutralized by the monetary authority. The assumption of continuous accommodation, which is admittedly unrealistic in a growth context, will be relaxed below when we permit the exchange rate to vary.

In the Harrod-Domar growth model, there are two basic relations:

$$I = s Y \qquad\qquad (11.1)$$

$$\frac{dY}{dt} = aI. \qquad\qquad (11.2)$$

According to equation (11.1), investment in any period must equal saving, that is, the fraction of income (output) saved multiplied by capacity output in order to utilize fully the existing capital stock. Equation (11.2) states that the growth in capacity output equals the amount of investment, I, multiplied by the (marginal) output-capital ratio, where I is assumed to adjust in such a way as to maintain total demand equal to the available supply. Substituting (11.1) into (11.2) and dividing through by Y, we obtain R, the rate of growth of capacity and investment that keeps productive capacity fully employed in all periods:

$$\frac{1}{Y}\frac{dY}{dt} = R = as. \qquad\qquad (11.3)$$

R refers here to what Harrod has called the warranted rate of growth for a closed economy. This is to be distinguished from the natural rate of growth that would maintain full employment of labour. In order for the warranted and natural rates of growth to be equal, we must assume therefore that the labor force is also growing at rate R. Alternatively, we could assume that technical progress is taking place so that the output-capital ratio is maintained and that there is no forced idleness of the capital stock because of lack of labor.

If we now introduce a foreign sector, imports will constitute a leakage additional to saving, and exports as well as investment may fill the gap between domestic demand for home production and the existing supply at full capacity. Assuming a constant linear relationship between imports and output, equation (11.1) becomes:

$$I + X = (s + m)Y, \qquad\qquad (11.4)$$

which will be recognized from Chapter 6 as an alternative way of expressing equilibrium between output and expenditure.

---

2. Johnson's analysis (1953b) takes these factors explicitly into account.

Rearranging (11.4), substituting it into (11.2), and dividing through by Y, we obtain the equilibrium rate of growth in an open economy:

$$R = a\left(s + m - \frac{X}{Y}\right) = a\left(s - \frac{I_f}{Y}\right), \qquad (11.5)$$

where $I_f(= X - M)$ is net foreign investment. What this says is that a deficit in the trade balance is associated with higher growth because there is investment from abroad, and conversely.

If we now wish to determine the effect of trade on the rate of growth, we can differentiate (11.5) with respect to time, which gives:[3]

$$\frac{dR}{dt} = a\frac{X}{Y}(R - x). \qquad (11.6)$$

Equation (11.5) indicates that the equilibrium rate of growth is higher the higher the output-capital ratio, the saving ratio, the import ratio, and the level of capacity output, and the lower the level of exports.[4] For R to be a long-run equilibrium rate, however, exports, X, and output, Y, must grow at the same rates in order to keep their ratio, X/Y, constant. This can be seen more clearly in equation (11.6), which shows that as the growth rate of output, R, exceeds that of exports, x, R itself will rise. Thus, if from an initial position of $R_o = x_o$, x were to rise, dR/dt would become negative and bring about a change in R in (11.5) via the change in X/Y. Alternatively, if R_o were to rise, R will rise in (11.5) until it reaches a limiting value, $R = a(s + m)$. It cannot surpass this level since this would mean from (11.5) that $X/Y = 0$, that is, exports would have completely vanished. Since consumption is determined by a constant saving ratio, the implication is that all available resources are already being devoted to investment.

3. That is:

$$\frac{dR}{dt} = -a\frac{d(X/Y)}{dt} = \frac{-a[(dX/dt)Y - (dY/dt)X]}{Y^2}.$$

Dividing numerator and denominator by XY, we have:

$$\frac{dR}{dt} = \frac{-a[(dX/dt)\,1/X - (dY/dt)\,1/Y]}{Y/X}.$$

Noting that the numerator of this expression refers to the rates of growth, respectively, of exports and output, with some rearrangement we obtain (11.6).

4. See Johnson (1953b, esp. pp. 123–24) for a rigorous demonstration of these conclusions based on the solution of a differential equation in Y.

If we relax the assumption that the import content of investment is zero and posit that the creation of new capacity requires a certain proportion of imports, equation (11.5) would have to be adjusted upward according to Johnson (1953b). This would be the case also if domestic production involved some import content. In a long-run growth context, it is not really legitimate to abstract from international interest payments. The inclusion of such payments complicates the analysis, however, and, as Johnson notes, makes it difficult to reach straightforward conclusions regarding the equilibrium growth rate. Some simplifications regarding interest payments and their relation to long-term capital movements are treated in Massell (1964).

The economic meaning of the foregoing is that if R_o were to rise in excess of x, the country must grow at an increasing rate to keep its productive capacity fully utilized. Since imports constitute a fixed fraction of income (output), they will rise at the same rate as income. In these circumstances, the country's trade balance will deteriorate over time. If x rises in excess of R_o, the country must grow at a decreasing rate to make room for an even larger share of export demand in its capacity output, fewer resources being available for investment. Indeed, at some stage, exports will be maintained by dis-investing domestically. The balance of trade will improve continually, implying that resources are moved from domestic to foreign investment. The balance of trade will of course remain unchanged when $R_o = x$, if trade was balanced initially. If the trade balance were initially in deficit or surplus, this will be maintained in relation to income, that is, it will grow at the same rate as the economy.

A TWO-COUNTRY MODEL WITH FOREIGN REPERCUSSIONS

We have assumed thus far that country 1's exports and their rate of growth are given exogenously by world demand, irrespective of the growth of the country's output and imports. We shall now treat the rest of world, country 2, explicitly in order to determine the requirements for equilibrium growth in both countries. Thus, let us assume that we have a closed system of two countries trading exclusively with each other, and that all the other assumptions hold that were stated earlier.

Noting that country 1's exports are by definition the imports of country 2 and vice versa:

$$X = m_2 Y_2 \quad \text{and} \quad X_2 = mY,$$

we can then derive equations (11.7a) and (11.7b) as obvious extensions of (11.5):

$$R = a\left(s + m - m_2 \frac{Y_2}{Y}\right) \tag{11.7a}$$

$$R_2 = a_2\left(s_2 + m_2 - m \frac{Y}{Y_2}\right). \tag{11.7b}$$

Differentiating these equations with respect to time, the equations analogous to (11.6) are:[5]

$$\frac{dR}{dt} = am_2 \frac{Y_2}{Y}(R - R_2), \tag{11.8a}$$

$$\frac{dR_2}{dt} = a_2 m \frac{Y}{Y_2}(R_2 - R). \tag{11.8b}$$

5. See footnote 3 above for details.

Thus, if the equilibrium rate of growth is higher in country 1 than in 2, that is, if $R > R_2$, R will rise over time and R_2 will fall continuously. The economic meaning of $R > R_2$ is that country 1's imports and thus country 2's exports are rising at the higher rate. This would imply that country 2's growth rate has to fall to make room for additional exports at the expense of a lower increase in investment. By the same token, country 1's growth rate must rise since its exports will absorb a falling share of output and thus an increasing proportion of output will go to investment. The conclusion is, therefore, that if growth rates are different initially, these rates will tend to diverge further. The country with the more rapidly rising rate of growth will experience a deterioration in its balance of trade, matched by a corresponding improvement in the other country.

EXCHANGE-RATE VARIATIONS IN A TWO-COUNTRY MODEL

Suppose now that instead of keeping the exchange rate fixed and having trade imbalances being settled by accommodating capital movements, we permit the exchange rate to vary for balance-of-payments adjustment purposes. Assume that trade is balanced initially and that the rate of exchange, r, defined in units of domestic currency per unit of foreign currency, is to begin with equal to unity. The question is then what adjustment in the exchange rate must occur to keep trade in balance as the two countries grow. To maintain balance, we have the condition that:

$$m \frac{dY}{dt} = m_2 \frac{dY_2}{dt} . \tag{11.9}$$

The foregoing condition is simplified by stating it in terms of equilibrium growth rates and income elasticities of demand for imports. Now if we assume constant proportions of imports in relation to output and income, the income elasticities will be equal to unity and will drop out so that the condition for trade to balance reduces to:[6]

$$R = R_2. \tag{11.10}$$

Equation (11.10) implies that for trade to remain balanced when the two countries have equal income elasticities, the countries have to grow at the same equilibrium growth rates.[7] This condition would of course not be satisfied except by coincidence. What is of interest therefore is to derive the change in the exchange rate that is necessary to maintain balance under conditions when the countries grow at different equilibrium rates. Let us proceed by defining B, the balance of trade, in terms of domestic currency

6. The income elasticities of demand for imports for the two countries are: $m(Y/M)$ and $m_2(Y_2/M_2)$. Thus, with constant proportions of imports in relation to output, the marginal and average propensities will be equal and the income elasticities will be unity.

7. If income elasticities are permitted to differ, the equilibrium growth rates will have to vary inversely with the income elasticities to maintain trade in balance with the exchange rate constant.

(country 1), remembering that domestic and foreign prices are constant and assumed equal to unity. The initial condition is then:

$$B = M_2 - rM = 0. \tag{11.11}$$

To this we add two equations defining the determinants of imports:

$$M = M(\overset{+}{Y}, \overset{-}{r}) \tag{11.12}$$

$$M_2 = M_2(\overset{+}{Y_2}, \overset{+}{r}). \tag{11.13}$$

Differentiating this system with respect to time gives us:

$$\frac{dB}{dt} = \frac{\partial M_2}{\partial r}\frac{dr}{dt} + m_2\frac{dY_2}{dt} - M\frac{dr}{dt} - r\frac{\partial M}{\partial r}\frac{dr}{dt} - rm\frac{dY}{dt}. \tag{11.14}$$

Setting (11.14) equal to zero, we obtain the necessary change in the exchange rate to keep trade in balance:

$$\frac{dr}{dt} = \frac{rm\,(dY/dt) - m_2\,(dY_2/dt)}{\partial M_2/\partial r - r\,(\partial M/\partial r) - M}. \tag{11.15}$$

Taking note of the definitions of the price elasticities of demand for imports (η_m) and exports (η_x) for country 1:

$$\eta_m = -\frac{r}{M}\frac{\partial M}{\partial r}$$

$$\eta_x = \frac{r}{M_2}\frac{\partial M_2}{\partial r},$$

transforming (11.15) into the required proportional change in the exchange rate, observing the possible substitutions from (11.11), and recalling that we have assumed income elasticities equal to unity, we have:[8]

$$\frac{1}{r}\frac{dr}{dt} = \frac{(R - R_2)}{\eta_x + \eta_m - 1}. \tag{11.16}$$

8. Dividing equation (11.15) through by r and noting from (11.11) that $r = M_2/M$, we have:

$$\frac{1}{r}\frac{dr}{dt} = \frac{(M_2/M)m\,(dY/dt) - m_2(dY_2/dt)}{r(\partial M_2/\partial r) - r^2(\partial M/\partial r) - rM}.$$

Multiplying the first term of the numerator by Y/Y and the second term by Y_2/Y_2, dividing both numerator and denominator by M_2, and transposing, we have

$$\frac{1}{r}\frac{dr}{dt} = \frac{m(Y/M)(dY/dt)(1/Y) - m_2(Y_2/M_2)(dY_2/dt)(1/Y_2)}{(r/M_2)(\partial M_2/\partial r) - (r^2/M_2)(\partial M/\partial r) - (rM/M_2)}.$$

Since the income elasticities, $m(Y/M)$ and $m_2(Y_2/M_2)$ are assumed to be unity, the numerator of the above expression reduces to $R - R_2$. The first term of the denominator is η_x. Noting again that $r = M_2/M$, the second and third terms reduce respectively to η_m and -1. Hence the result shown in equation (11.16).

We recognize in the denominator of (11.16) the critical value of the Marshall-Lerner condition, which says that the balance of trade will be improved by a devaluation provided that the sum of the demand elasticities is greater than one. If this condition is fulfilled, the denominator of (11.16) will be positive and the foreign exchange market will be stable. It follows therefore that if country 1's rate of growth in equilibrium exceeds country 2's rate, that is, if $R > R_2$, r must rise. In other words, country 1's currency must be depreciated in order to maintain trade in balance. If exchange rates adjust to keep trade balanced, then exports will always equal imports, and saving must equal investment as in a closed model. Thus, since as in equation (11.3), $R = as$, the trading economy with flexible exchange rates is just like a closed economy.

The preceding discussion assumed that the equilibrium rates of growth were constant in both countries even when the exchange rate was altered. We have seen that the equilibrium rate of growth equals the product of the output-capital ratio and the saving ratio. While the output-capital ratio may be assumed unchanged for present purposes,[9] the saving ratio is not likely to remain constant when the exchange rate and the purchasing power of money are varied, unless we make allowance for money illusion.[10] Suppose money illusion were not allowed and country 1 experiences a higher rate of growth and its currency depreciates. Then if country 1's residents attempt to maintain the real value of consumption, this will cause the saving ratio to fall. The saving ratio may rise in country 2 for similar reasons. This would imply in turn that if the exchange market is stable, a difference in growth rates leading to exchange-rate changes would cause the growth rates to converge. At some point the condition expressed in equation (11.10) would be fulfilled, making further exchange-rate changes unnecessary.

A Simplified Neoclassical Growth Model with a Foreign Sector[11]

The Harrod-Domar growth model for a closed economy that formed the basis of our discussion in the preceding section states that the rate of growth is determined essentially by two constants, the output-capital ratio and the saving ratio. To assure this result, we had to assume a fixed rate of growth in the labor force that amounted at least to the rate of growth of output. As already noted, this model is subject to the obvious criticism of being rigid insofar as it lacks an adequate mechanism to correct inconsistencies. Thus,

9. In developing a neoclassical growth model in the following section, we shall take variations in the output-capital ratio explicitly into account, while assuming the saving ratio constant.

10. See our earlier discussion in Chapters 7 and 8 pertaining to changes in consumption and saving in the context of exchange-rate variations.

11. This section has benefited materially from the model analyzed in Deardorff (1971).

for example, if the rate of growth of the labor force, that is, in Harrod's terminology the natural rate of growth, exceeded the warranted rate, there would be unemployment. If the opposite were the case, inflation would occur. It was to avoid problems such as these that we assumed the natural and warranted rates of growth to be equal.

It was in the light of the rigidity of the Harrod-Domar model that the neoclassical model of growth came to be developed. The point of the neoclassical model is that, given stable prices, while it might be reasonable to assume that the saving and import ratios are fairly constant in the long run, it seems much less reasonable to assume that production takes place under fixed proportions. Abstracting from technical change, the rate of growth of capital, labor, and output will have to be equal in equilibrium. But in the process of adjustment, after say a shift in the saving or import function, variable proportions in the utilization of factors would seem logical. Let us turn then to the development of a neoclassical growth model for an open economy that involves the foregoing considerations. We shall be interested in particular in how this model behaves when there is unbalanced trade.

We assume as before that the saving ratio, import ratio, the rate of growth of the labor force, and the rate of growth of exports are exogenously determined, and investment adjusts automatically to exhaust demand for full employment output. Now, however, the capital-output ratio, instead of being a constant, becomes a variable. To achieve consistency, we must make the further assumption that there exists only one good, which can be used in consumption, investment, and foreign trade. We shall confine our discussion for the most part to a single country, thus abstracting from foreign repercussions. A fixed exchange rate is assumed throughout.

The following notation will be used:

Y = Real output
C = Real consumption
I = Real investment
X = Volume of exports
M = Volume of imports
s = Saving ratio
m = Import ratio
K = Stock of capital
L = Labor force
k = Capital-labor ratio
R = Rate of growth of output.

Dots over variables indicate derivative with respect to time.

We start with the familiar equilibrium equation:

$$Y = C + I + X - M, \tag{11.17}$$

where C and M are assumed to be constant fractions of output:

$$C = (1 - s)Y \tag{11.18}$$

$$M = mY. \tag{11.19}$$

Combining these three equations and assuming that there is no depreciation, that is, all investment goes to increase capacity, we obtain:

$$\dot{K} = I = (s + m)Y - X. \tag{11.20}$$

Dividing through by K, we get the rate of growth of capital:

$$\frac{\dot{K}}{K} = (s + m)\frac{Y}{K} - \frac{X}{K} = \frac{L}{K}\left[(s + m)\frac{Y}{L} - \frac{X}{L}\right]. \tag{11.21}$$

The rates of growth of the labor force, n, and of exports, x, are exogenously given:

$$\frac{\dot{L}}{L} = n, \tag{11.22}$$

$$\frac{\dot{X}}{X} = x. \tag{11.23}$$

To simplify the discussion, we introduce a production function of the Cobb-Douglas variety. This assumes that production takes place under conditions of constant returns to scale, which is consistent with the assumption made in previous chapters of infinite supply elasticities, but that there is diminishing marginal productivity to both factors. We thus have:

$$Y = K^\alpha L^{1-\alpha} \tag{11.24}$$

where α is a parameter referring to the elasticity of output with respect to the particular input and representing also the particular factor share.

Utilizing the production function in equation (11.24), output per unit of labor (i.e., per capita output) can be written as:

$$\frac{Y}{L} = \left(\frac{K}{L}\right)^\alpha = k^\alpha. \tag{11.25}$$

Since the rate of growth of a ratio is equal to the difference between the growth rates of the numerator and denominator, we can state the rate of growth of the capital-labor ratio, k, making use of equations (11.21), (11.22), and (11.25), as follows:

$$\frac{\dot{k}}{k} = \frac{L}{K}\left[(s + m)k^\alpha - \frac{X}{L}\right] - n. \tag{11.26}$$

Multiplying through by $k(= K/L)$ gives:

$$\dot{k} = (s + m)k^\alpha - \left(\frac{X}{L} + nk\right). \tag{11.27}$$

The two terms in equation (11.27) are graphed in Figure 11.1. The first term is drawn on the assumption that the marginal product of capital approaches infinity and zero as k approaches zero and infinity, respectively. The second term is a straight line with intercept X/L and slope n. The vertical distance between the two curves is equal to $\dot{k}$ so that k can be momentarily stationary only where the curves intersect. If $(s + m)k^{\alpha}$ is higher than $(X/L + nk)$, k will be increasing, and conversely.

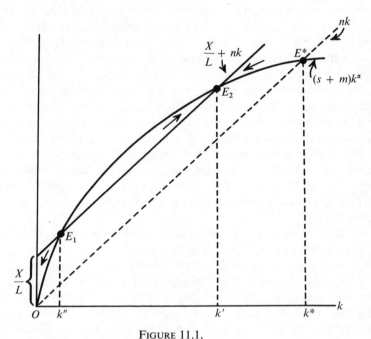

FIGURE 11.1.

*Neoclassical Growth Equilibrium with
a Foreign Sector*

*The intersection at E_2 is a stable steady state and at E_1,
unstable. Since in steady state equilibrium, the rate of growth
of output is equal to n, international trade will not change
the steady-state growth rate. If exports grow at a slower
rate than labor, the equilibrium will lie at E^*; since imports
will grow at the same rate as output, the trade balance will
deteriorate continually.*

It will be recalled that exports are an exogenous function of time so that if they grow at a rate different from labor, the ratio X/L will change over time, thus changing the curve in Figure 11.1 that depends on X/L. But if X and L grow at the same rate, the curves will be stationary and can be used to analyze the growth process. Note that if X/L is positive, the curves will intersect twice, if at all. At the intersections shown, $\dot{k} = 0$. The intersection at E_2 will be a stable steady state and the one at E_1 unstable. This is because k is falling above k' and below k'' since labor is growing faster than capital, but rising between k'' and k' since capital is growing faster than labor. Note further that if X/L is sufficiently large, the curves may not intersect, in which case there will be no steady state and k will decline continually.

If a steady state equilibrium is attained, as we have stated, $\dot{k} = 0$. This means that per capita output (Y/L) will remain constant. This rate of growth of output will be equal to n, irrespective of whatever the values are of any other parameters in the model. Thus, in contrast to the Harrod-Domar model, the introduction of international trade does not have the power to change the steady-state growth rate of the economy.[12] The inclusion of a foreign sector may be important nonetheless because it may affect the *level* of the growth path or the rate of growth in the adjustment period. As to the first point, it will be noted from equation (11.25) that income per capita (Y/L) is a direct function of the capital-labor ratio, k. Thus, anything that increases the steady state value of k will also raise the growth path. Looking at Figure 11.1, it is evident that increases in the propensities to save and import will shift E_2 to the right, raising k and therefore steady-state per capita output. By the same token, increases in the level of per capita exports (X/L) or the rate of growth of labor, n, will shift E_2 to the left and will lower per capita output.[13]

As already noted, X and L must grow at the same rates in order to arrive at a steady-state growth. But since the rate of growth of X is exogenous, it may not be equal to the growth rate of labor so that X/L may change. Figure 11.1 can nevertheless be used to depict the result of maintaining X/L at any particular level, which we may refer to as a momentary equilibrium situation. Thus, if exports were to grow at a slower rate than labor, X/L would fall continually and the economy will then move towards a situation where X/L is zero and only the equilibrium at E^* exists. This lies obviously to the right of E_2 and involves a higher level of per capita output than in the

---

12. If we set equation (11.21) above equal to n, in equilibrium we have:

$$n = \frac{Y}{K}\left(s + m - \frac{X}{Y}\right).$$

We can compare this with the Harrod-Domar result in equation (11.5):

$$R = a\left(s + m - \frac{X}{Y}\right).$$

While these two equations look identical, it must be noted that they imply completely different adjustment mechanisms. In the neoclassical mechanism, Y/K will adjust until capital grows at a rate equal to that of labor. In the Harrod-Domar model, labor *must* grow at a certain rate to be consistent with the parameters of the model.

13. As Deardorff (1971) points out, anything that decreases the stable steady state also increases the unstable steady state and enhances the likelihood of continued decline in both k and Y/L.

case of a positive X/L.[14] Since imports will grow at the same rate as output, which will be intermediate to the growth rates of capital and labor, the trade balance will deteriorate continually.

Thus, we see that, in the Harrod-Domar and neoclassical models, a negative balance of trade (i.e., imports growing faster than exports) will result in a faster rate of growth of capital. In the Harrod-Domar model, this leads to a higher warranted rate of growth since the output-capital ratio is fixed. In the neoclassical model, the equilibrium rate of growth is unchanged since it is fixed by the growth of the labor force. What happens is that the output-capital ratio falls (i.e., k rises), causing a rise in the level of the growth path and in per capita income.[15]

The preceding discussion is limited in at least two important ways. First, we have assumed exports to be exogenously determined, and, secondly, we have perhaps placed undue emphasis on the steady-state growth rate. These limitations can be met by developing an explicit two-country model in which foreign repercussions are treated and examining the various growth paths. This has been attempted by Deardorff (1971) whose results indicate that the greater the interdependence of the economies, or the more they trade, the greater appears the likelihood of unstable growth paths. These results stem in particular from the assumptions built into the model that investment adjusts automatically to yield full employment and that, whatever the level of exports demanded of a country, they will be supplied by the country. The consequence of these two assumptions is that an excess of imports over exports will stimulate growth since investment can then exceed domestic saving, and conversely if exports exceed imports.

A trade imbalance then stimulates growth in the net importing country and retards it in the net exporting country. But when growth is stimulated, the net importing country will import even more while the other country whose growth is being retarded increases its imports less rapidly. An unequal trade balance tends therefore to become even more unequal through its effects on growth rates. Pushed to an extreme, exports from the net exporting country may eventually exceed that country's output and may be possible only if there is disinvestment. While such an outcome is interesting theoretically, the likelihood of it actually occurring is probably not very great because no country would voluntarily finance its own self destruction. The model may nevertheless contain an important grain of truth insofar as it suggests that a country may grow faster if it can augment its domestic saving by means of inward foreign investment via an excess of imports over exports.

14. Note that if exports grow faster than labor, Y/L will rise and there will be no equilibrium point, with the consequence that k will continue to decline forever and so will per capita income. See Deardorff (1971) for a phase diagrammatic analysis of possible growth paths with changing X/L.

15. For a further elaboration of the effects of trade on growth in a neoclassical model, see Corden (1971) and Lybeck (1970).

This will be the case particularly if we continue to assume that the country is spared the interest costs of servicing the foreign investment. But this may not be completely realistic either.

It should be evident from our discussion that the formal analysis of growth with unbalanced trade yields results that are sensitive to the assumptions being made in the particular models. As such, the analysis is mainly of heuristic interest. More remains to be done, particularly in the neoclassical model, to introduce international capital movements that are endogenous and to allow for forces that will work to correct disequilibria in the balance of payments.

"Export-Led" Growth

Our preceding discussion has suggested that net importing countries are likely to experience a higher rate of growth or greater per capita output, depending upon the model employed. This conclusion runs counter to observation, however, for in the 1950's and 1960's, some of the most rapidly growing industrialized countries, such as Italy, Japan, and West Germany, have exhibited substantial strength on trade account. In contrast, slowly growing countries such as the U.K. and U.S. had much less favorable trade experiences. These empirical observations suggest that the traditional models may fail to capture some elements arising from the foreign sector that in actuality may be rather important. Two such elements have figured prominently in recent theoretical discussions. The first of these concerns the impact of increased exports upon investment, productivity, and relative prices so that a country with rapidly expanding exports will find that its economic growth will be reinforced. The second element derives from monetary and capital-account considerations involved in the demand and supply relationships for money and securities.

Historically speaking, foreign trade served apparently as an important engine of growth in the rapid expansion of world production and trade particularly in the decades preceding World War I.[16] These developments were integrated into theoretical models of the international economy only with a lag, however, since traditionally these models were concerned primarily with efficiency in the use of the existing stock of resources. The inclusion of a foreign sector in Keynesian models represented an important theoretical advance insofar as changes in foreign trade and national income were linked together via the foreign trade multiplier. In these models, as presented earlier in Chapters 6 and 7, the income generating effects of autonomous changes in exports and imports were looked upon in the same light as other autonomous changes in expenditures. It was only incidentally that we had occasion to consider the interrelation between, say, exports and investment as a consequence of induced or accelerator effects of changes in income.

16. See, for example, Nurkse (1961, esp. pp. 283–90). But for a dissenting view, see Kravis (1970).

In the simplified Harrod-Domar growth model presented earlier in this chapter, growth was stimulated the *higher* the output-capital ratio, the saving ratio, the import ratio, and the level of capacity output, and the *lower* the level of exports. In our neoclassical growth model, foreign trade was seen to have no effect at all on the steady-state rate of growth, which was found to depend on the growth of the labor force, although a *negative* trade balance (or rather, imports growing faster than exports) was associated with a higher per capita income. These particular conclusions may seem a bit strange when juxtaposed against the foreign-trade-multiplier effects of an autonomous change in exports and the possible interactions between exports and investment.

It may be helpful in analyzing the foregoing considerations to proceed in terms of some explicit models that have been developed for the purpose of analyzing export-led growth. We shall examine two such models. It will be convenient in this regard to abstract from the domestic monetary and capital-account relationships mentioned earlier.

THE LAMFALUSSY MODEL

The first model we shall discuss was propounded originally by Lamfalussy (1963a, b).[17] It was elaborated subsequently by Caves (1970), whose version we shall rely on for the most part. The notation is as follows:

I = Real investment
Y = Real output (income)
S = Real savings
X = Volume of exports
M = Volume of imports
α, β, and μ refer to autonomous components.

17. In formulating his model, Lamfalussy assumed explicitly that in the postwar period all the countries concerned had either finished or were actively in the process of liberalizing their import controls and tariffs, and that the goals of government policy were to promote full employment and stimulate growth without inflation and external imbalance. He observed that the pursuit of full employment and growth objectives would of course increase income and, in turn, imports. Exports would have to be sufficiently expanded, therefore, in order at least to maintain external balance. Otherwise, external disequilibrium would necessitate government policies to restrict home demand, with the result that the level of employment and the rate of growth might be adversely affected.

The achievement of equilibrium, or better yet a surplus, in the balance of payments was of great importance according to Lamfalussy because it thereby enabled the government to follow expansionist policies that encouraged domestic investment. Moreover, he maintained that the increase in exports would itself stimulate investment because of accelerator effects. These increases in investment would have the consequence of increasing internal demand and, at the same time, would expand productive capacity and productivity. If money wages were then assumed to be increasing at the same rate in all of the relevant countries, the increase in productivity in the given country would result in a relatively less rapid increase or in greater stability of its domestic prices and an improvement in its international competitive position. So long as exports kept rising, it was concluded that there would thus be a self-reinforcing tendency for a country to maintain its competitive position and to continue its rapid rate of economic growth.

See Stern (1967, esp. pp. 57–62) for additional details and a critique of Lamfalussy's model.

The model is as follows:

$$\frac{I}{Y} = v\left(\frac{X}{Y}\right) + \alpha \qquad v > 0, \alpha > 0 \qquad (11.28)$$

$$\frac{S}{Y} = b\left(\frac{\Delta Y}{Y}\right) + \beta \qquad b > 0, \beta > 0 \qquad (11.29)$$

$$\frac{M}{Y} = m\left(\frac{\Delta Y}{Y}\right) + \mu \qquad m > 0, \mu > 0 \qquad (11.30)$$

$$\frac{S}{Y} = \frac{I + X - M}{Y}. \qquad (11.31)$$

The export-led nature of the model is represented in equation (11.28), which links exports to investment in terms of their respective proportions of total income.[18] The saving equation (11.29) is somewhat unusual insofar as the saving ratio is related to the proportional rate of growth of income rather than being independent of such change as in the usual formulation. This kind of saving behavior assumes that as income grows there will be changes in the distribution of income in favor of higher profits and taxes without corresponding increases in expenditure. The import equation (11.30) also embodies a marginal effect for growth in income. Equation (11.31) states the familiar equilibrium condition between savings and investment and the trade balance, $X - M$.

Substituting (11.28)–(11.30) into (11.31) and solving for the proportional rate of growth of income, we obtain:

$$\frac{\Delta Y}{Y} = \frac{v + 1}{b + m} \cdot \frac{X}{Y} + \frac{\alpha - \mu - \beta}{b + m}. \qquad (11.32)$$

According to (11.32), the rate of growth will be higher the higher the co-efficient of the export ratio and the autonomous component of the export ratio and the lower the coefficients and autonomous components in the saving and import equations. While it is evident from (11.32) that the X/Y term has a positive influence on the rate of growth, the second term may be negative so that the sign of (11.32) will not necessarily be positive. By the same line of reasoning if we were to express the growth-rate determinants in (11.32) in terms of the relation between the trade balance and the growth of income, we would not be able to discern unambiguously if a positive rate of growth improved or worsened the trade balance.[19]

The preceding model is thus ambiguous with respect to the relation

18. The model is presented here in ratio form in keeping with Lamfalussy's formulation. It could of course be written in terms of levels and first differences by multiplying through by Y. This would change the interpretation of the individual equations to some extent, but the solution noted below would not be affected.

19. This is evident from the following expression relating the trade balance to the growth of income:

$$\frac{X - M}{Y} = \frac{b - vm}{v + 1} \cdot \frac{\Delta Y}{Y} + \frac{\beta - \alpha - v\mu}{v + 1}$$

between the development of exports and the rate of growth of income and the balance of trade. It is also conceivable, as Caves (1970) has noted, that models of this kind may result in unstable growth paths in the sense of Harrod's mechanism of output adjustment. Thus, for example, if the economy were displaced upward from the warranted rate of growth, the creation of excess demand might well lead to greater imports and a worsening of the trade balance. Moreover, if the warranted rate of growth exceeded the natural rate of growth, there would be an upward pressure on wages and prices at full employment and a consequent deterioration of the trade balance.

THE BECKERMAN MODEL

The model we shall consider now differs from the one just presented insofar as it focuses more directly on relationships involving exports, productivity, wages, prices, and unemployment. The model was developed initially by Beckerman (1962) to explain the divergent rates of growth of the industrialized countries in the years following World War II.[20] As we shall see in a moment, while the model offers some useful insights into the nature of export-led growth, it is not altogether complete since, as Caves (1970) has noted, it lacks an equilibrium condition and asserts some relationships that may or may not be true.

The following notation is to be used:

X = Volume of exports
O = Labour productivity
W = Money wages
P = Domestic prices
P_f = Foreign prices
U = Rate of unemployment

x, o, w, and p represent the proportionate rates of change per unit of time for a given country.

α, γ, and θ are constants; β, δ, and λ are coefficients. The model is as follows:

$$x = \alpha + \beta(1 - P/P_f) \quad \beta > 0 \tag{11.33}$$

$$o = \gamma + \delta x \quad \delta > 0 \tag{11.34}$$

$$w = \theta + \lambda o \quad 1 > \lambda > 0 \tag{11.35}$$

$$p = w - o. \tag{11.36}$$

20. Beckerman's interpretation of this experience was that rapid growth depended upon confident expectations concerning future demand prospects both domestically and in foreign markets. Entrepreneurs were thus motivated to increase their investment rates and take other steps to expand their rates of productivity increase per unit of input. A favorable initial position of international price competitiveness that permitted rapid growth would tend, consequently, to be perpetuated or maybe even accentuated by the increases in investment and productivity. Some countries would therefore experience significantly more rapid growth as compared to other countries in which foreign trade prices especially were uncompetitive and might become increasingly so.

For additional details and a critique of Beckerman's model, see Stern (1967, esp. pp. 62–67).

The export equation (11.33) states that the rate of increase in a country's exports, x, will exceed or fall short of the rate of increase in world trade, α, depending upon the country's relative prices. It is assumed in the productivity equation (11.34) that the rate of increase in labor productivity, o, is positively correlated with the rate of increase in output, which is in turn correlated with the rate of increase in exports x.[21] That the relation between o and x may not be proportional can be allowed for in the size of δ in (11.34). Wages in equation (11.35) are assumed to increase at a rate, w, which is less than the rate of increase in productivity, o. As we shall note below, the wage equation is a bone of contention in the model since it does not take unemployment conditions explicitly into account. The rate of change of prices, p, in equation (11.36) depends on the rates of change of wages, w, and productivity, o; this equation is designed to measure the "wage drift" on the (implicit) assumption of constant distributive shares since it is written without a coefficient for $w - o$.

From (11.35) and (11.36) it follows that:

$$p = \theta + o(\lambda - 1) \tag{11.37}$$

and from (11.33) and (11.34) for a given country:

$$o = (\gamma + \alpha\delta) + \beta\delta(1 - P/P_f). \tag{11.38}$$

Thus, if a given country has a competitive advantage in trade ($P/P_f < 1$), its rate of productivity growth, o, will exceed the average, $\gamma + \alpha\delta$, by

$$\beta\delta(1 - P/P_f).$$

Since by assumption in (11.37), $\lambda < 1$, p will rise less (fall more), the greater is o. It follows therefore that an initial disparity in relative prices will tend to become accentuated and will bring about a growing disparity in growth rates.

As mentioned above, Beckerman's model lacks an equilibrium condition and the factors determining the constant terms in his equations are not altogether clear. The wage equation (11.35) in particular is open to objection, for as Balassa has noted (1963, p. 782), it apparently disregards "the possible impact of inter-country and intertemporal differences in the elasticity of labour supply on wage changes." According to "Phillips curve" reasoning therefore, Balassa suggested that equation (11.35) be written as $w = \theta - \lambda U$, where U refers to unemployment as a percentage of the labor force. This is an important consideration from the growth standpoint, of course, since the growth of the labor force is of key importance in the determination of equilibrium conditions and departures therefrom. Thus, while the Beckerman

---

21. As Beckerman (1962, p. 921) put it, borrowing Kaldor's terminology, it is being assumed "that technical dynamism may be heavily influenced by export growth and favourable foreign balance conditions. . . ."

model offers some useful insights, the basic relationships need to be formulated more completely and rigorously.[22]

FURTHER IMPLICATIONS OF EXPORT-LED GROWTH

It is evident from the foregoing discussion that there are a number of problems still to be resolved in integrating export-led growth into the usual growth-model framework. These difficulties arise in part because the framework either posits certain constants as in the Harrod-Domar model, or because the role of foreign trade is not vitally important for steady state growth in the neoclassical model. Moreover, being exploratory in character, the export-led models have abstracted from a number of realistic complications particularly with regard to firm behavior.[23] It is not altogether surprising, therefore, that what little empirical work exists in this area has on the whole been inconclusive.[24] Aside from the points just noted, the models described above are incomplete insofar as they have abstracted from domestic and international monetary and capital movements considerations. Since these considerations are interesting and important in their own right and may provide further insights into the growth experiences and policy problems of individual countries, they are worthy of separate attention.

Money, Growth, and the Balance of Payments

We have already seen in our discussion of balance-of-payments adjustment and policies the important role that monetary considerations play. It is not unexpected therefore that this is true also of the relationships involving

---

22. Gordon (1965), in an unpublished paper, has amended the Beckerman model to introduce unemployment endogenously and to relate the growth rate of exports to the rate of change in domestic prices. He also discusses in the context of his model ways in which the economy can attain given objectives with respect to unemployment, external balance, and the rate of growth.

23. See Costa (1970) for the beginnings of a theoretical model that seeks to avoid the rigidity of the Harrod-Domar model by permitting the degree of capacity utilization and the rate of growth of output to respond to expected profit considerations and thus to be independent of the rate of population expansion. Costa permits the equilibrium rate of growth to be changed under different assumptions about the behavior of the monetary authority and the Phillips curve relating to labor-supply conditions.

24. In his study of Italy's postwar growth experience, the present author (Stern, (1967)) did not find too much empirical support for the particular relationships suggested by the Lamfalussy and Beckerman models of export-led growth. Using a more disaggregated approach by industry, it was found that a flexible accelerator model did reasonably well in explaining investment expenditures in those industries that had contributed most importantly to Italy's rapid export expansion. This suggests that a better understanding of export-led growth might be obtained by concentrating on the firm and industry behavior that underlies the relationships specified in the formal models we have discussed.

Caves (1970) has tested some of the individual export-led relationships using cross-section data for the industrialized countries in the postwar period. His results were also inconclusive on the whole.

growth and the balance of payments. In order to clarify some of these relationships, we shall utilize a model developed by Laffer (1971) with reference to a "small country." We thus eschew the complications that arise in the two-country case and in the attempt to incorporate a monetary sector into a full-blown model of economic growth.[25]

The most important assumptions in Laffer's model are that the money supply is determined by the country's reserve position, and that the authorities not only refrain from sterilizing reserve changes but as well undertake no domestic policy action that has any effect on the money supply. The price level, exchange rate, and rate of interest are fixed. The following notation will be used:

Y = Real income (output)

A = Real absorption (expenditures)

L_d = Demand for money

L_s = Supply of money

F = Capital inflow (or outflow, if negative)

B = Surplus (or deficit, if negative) in the balance of payments.

Dots over variables indicate derivative with respect to time.
The model in linear form is as follows:[26]

$$\dot{L}_d = k\,\dot{Y} \qquad\qquad (11.39)$$

$$\dot{L}_d = \dot{L}_s \qquad\qquad (11.40)$$

$$\dot{L}_s = B. \qquad\qquad (11.41)$$

Income is assumed to be exogenously determined. Equation (11.39) is thus a version of the quantity theory of money used here in an inverse sense since $\dot{Y}$ rather than $\dot{L}_s$ is exogenous. Thus, given an increase in $\dot{Y}$, the demand for money ($\dot{L}_d$) must increase. But since by definition, as in equation (11.41), the supply of money ($\dot{L}_s$) can only increase through a balance-of-payments surplus, B must increase. Thus, by substitution in the above equations, we have:

$$B = k\,\dot{Y}. \qquad\qquad (11.42)$$

25. See Mundell (1968, pp. 134–39) and Komiya (1969) for models that reach conclusions for the small-country case that are similar to those to be presented using Laffer's framework. Both Laffer and Komiya also examine a two-country model, with results that parallel broadly the small-country case. See Morton (1970) for a monetary growth model that incorporates a foreign sector. Johnson (1971b) has developed an explicit monetary framework for balance-of-payments analysis that attempts to go beyond the short-run orientation of models involving considerations of elasticities, absorption, and the policy mix that were discussed in preceding chapters.

26. Laffer's model is more detailed than what follows. I am indebted to John E. Morton for boiling this model down to its essentials.

The division of this change in the balance of payments between the current and capital accounts is simply derived. Recall the income-absorption identity:

$$Y - A \equiv X - M. \tag{11.43}$$

Since Y is exogenous and expenditure (absorption) increases with $\dot{Y}$, it follows that the trade balance worsens with increases in $\dot{Y}$. Therefore $dB/d\dot{Y} > 0$ and $d(X - M)/d\dot{Y} < 0$. Since

$$B = (X - M) + F, \tag{11.44}$$

it follows immediately that

$$\frac{dF}{d\dot{Y}} > \frac{dB}{d\dot{Y}} > 0.$$

Capital movements in this model are entirely passive. Equation (11.44) determines what they must be in order to maintain monetary equilibrium, and the "correct" movement is then just assumed to occur.

What Laffer is attempting to show in his model is that when absolute growth in income occurs, an excess demand for both goods and money is created.[27] The excess demand for goods is satisfied via the current-account adjustment noted. The capital account more than compensates for the current-account worsening, however, as the excess demand for money is satisfied.[28]

As we have noted, the most noteworthy characteristic of this model is its simplicity with regard to the mechanism of money creation. If we were to introduce a monetary authority that was able to expand or contract the money supply by means of open market operations as well as by changes in international reserves, we would have then to determine how these changes operated domestically and affected the balance of payments.[29] For example, we might expect with full employment that an increase in the money supply would result in a deterioration of the balance of payments via the capital account. This would occur insofar as the private sector purchased foreign securities in order to replenish their security holdings with the money proceeds obtained as a result of the open market transactions of the monetary

27. The excess demand for goods arises from Laffer's assumption that investment is a function of the change in income while saving is a function of the level of income. Thus, the higher the proportionate change in income, the higher is investment relative to saving, with the consequence that an excess demand for goods occurs.

28. Komiya (1969) demonstrates this mechanism more clearly since his model is constructed in terms of excess demand functions for goods, money, and bonds. Assuming a constant money supply, an increase in income increases the demand for money. Since this will be a factor restricting expenditure, the balance of payments will be improved.

29. Komiya (1969) suggests a way in which his model can be used to analyze the effects of changes in the money supply, subject to a constant domestic price level and comparability of total and partial differentials in deriving his marginal propensities to hold securities and money.

authority. By the same line of reasoning if a government sector were introduced into the model and an increase in government expenditure were
financed by borrowing from the banking sector, there would be a simultaneous increase in both expenditure for goods and services and the money
supply. As a consequence, the balance of payments would deteriorate, with
the changes now occurring in the current account. Finally, if we were to
permit domestic prices and the rate of interest to vary, it would then be
necessary to include these effects in the adjustments of the excess demands in
the different markets. This would of course be an undertaking of great
theoretical complexity, particularly if we were to proceed in terms of an
explicit growth model for the two-country case.[30]

Despite its simplicity, the model we have presented serves a useful purpose
in focusing on monetary considerations that were lacking in the export-led
models outlined in the previous section. It seems clear accordingly that any
model that purports to offer a reasonably realistic explanation of the growth
and balance-of-payments experiences of the industrialized countries must
incorporate both real and monetary relationships.

Policy Implications

Although the models we have discussed are in some respects tentative and
incomplete and have different points of departure and emphasis, they
suggest nevertheless some implications for policy that are worth discussing.
It is useful to distinguish in this regard policies that are designed for short-run
purposes to achieve the full employment of resources from longer-run policies
that are designed for full employment growth.[31]

Short-run policies intended to raise the level of aggregate demand may
have a favorable once-and-for-all effect on growth as the economy is moved
towards its long-run growth path. In addition, it is possible, as our discussion
particularly of Beckerman's export-led model revealed, for growth to be
stimulated further as the private sector expands its investment and undertakes to improve its efficiency in response to favorable demand prospects. As
we have seen, these latter responses may be favorable rather than detrimental
to the country's balance of payments.

Growth may be affected, moreover, by the mix of monetary and fiscal
policies adopted in attaining internal-external equilibrium in the short run.
Thus, for example, if the country were faced with a recession and balance-of-
payments deficit, a mix involving tight monetary policy with relatively high
interest rates might result in a temporary improvement in the balance of
payments, but at the same time might affect domestic investment adversely,

30. See Morton (1970) for an exemplary work along these lines.
31. See Smith (1970, Ch. 20) for an excellent discussion of growth policy in the context
of a closed economy, with the U.S. serving as an obvious reference point.

depending upon the interest elasticity of investment.[32] This effect would have to be set against the effect that expansive fiscal policy would have upon national income and therefore upon productive capacity and investment. If the latter effect predominated, the tight monetary and expansive fiscal policies would appear to have been justified.

In order to increase growth under conditions of full employment, policy measures can be undertaken to raise efficiency and/or reallocate resources from consumption to investment. Both types of measure will increase productive capacity at full employment, perhaps necessitating as well policies designed to expand aggregate demand. Improvements in efficiency can be considered primarily as once-and-for-all gains that may stem from more effective functioning of both factor and product markets as imperfections in information and barriers to entry are overcome.[33] Such measures would have a favorable effect on the balance of payments.

The reallocation of resources from consumption to investment involves difficult problems of social choice and the determination of the social rates of return from alternative directions of investment. Thus, the government must decide whether and how its policies should affect the growth decisions evolving from the private sector. This necessitates the equalizing of marginal social productivities from alternative programs that involve such things as private fixed investment, investment in human resources, expenditures on research and development, and public investment. It is unfortunate that our present knowledge of the growth and balance-of-payments impacts of these programs is incomplete.

A conscious growth policy must also take into account the question of the proper rate of monetary expansion that will promote domestic price stability and maintain equilibrium in the balance of payments. This is a very difficult matter in a multi-country world in which countries may experience differential rates of price inflation and growth in real incomes. We saw earlier that it was possible in a simple growth model to make allowances for exchange-rate variations in response to differential income changes. Exchange-rate flexibility might therefore be considered a desideratum in a growth context in order to provide the authorities with an additional tool to enable them to attain their short- and long-run economic objectives. By the same token, fixed exchange rates can contribute to more rapid growth or higher per capita income if trade is unbalanced. However, this assumes that it will be possible to finance continuing imbalances over a long period of time, which may not be the case.

32. If investment were highly responsive to the rate of interest, an expansive monetary policy and tight fiscal policy might be good for growth, but not necessarily for the balance of payments.

33. Policies to increase efficiency might involve, for example, improving labor-market information, providing subsidies to expedite labor mobility, and enforcing antitrust measures designed to promote competition. As pointed out in Chapter 5, it is also conceivable that devaluation might increase efficiency if controls are removed that formerly led to resource misallocation.

Conclusion

Our purpose in this chapter has been to review alternative approaches to the relationship between economic growth and the balance of payments. While at times confusing because of a somewhat different point of departure and focus, each of the approaches discussed nevertheless offers some contribution to our understanding. Thus, although they are far removed from reality, the Harrod-Domar and neoclassical models of growth in the setting of an open economy call attention to the role of investment and the assumed constancy or variability of certain key parameters in attaining growth and balance-of-payments equilibrium. The export-led models and those incorporating monetary relationships are in contrast more concerned with short-run, disequilibrium characteristics of the growth and balance-of-payments adjustment processes. These different approaches bear witness to the fact that the subject is still in a state of flux and much remains therefore to be done.

12

Problems of the International Monetary System

We have emphasized in our previous discussion the lack of an effective mechanism of balance-of-payments adjustment in the system of pegged exchange rates. The inadequacy of the adjustment mechanism has been reflected in the difficulties many countries have had in maintaining their exchange rates within the official limits. In order to keep their rates pegged, as we have seen, deficit countries need international monetary reserves in sufficiently large amount so that they are not forced to institute controls over trade and payments or to adopt policies that interfere materially with domestic economic stability. Surplus countries have to be able to absorb reserves for these same reasons.

In the pegged-rate system, nationally-owned reserves consist mainly of gold, official foreign exchange holdings (largely U.S. dollars), Special Drawing Rights (SDR's) issued to member countries by the IMF (since January 1970), and reserve positions in the IMF.[1] In addition, there are supplementary facilities designed particularly for advanced industrialized countries in the form of the General Arrangements to Borrow (GAB) and special swap arrangements that can be made between central banks.[2] This reliance on

---

1. Quarterly information on country holdings and world and area official reserve totals is published monthly in IMF, *International Financial Statistics*. World reserves at the end of April 1972, in billions of U.S. dollars, consisted of:

Gold	$ 38.1
SDR's	9.1
Reserve positions in Fund	6.8
Foreign exchange	84.4
Total	$138.4

2. Information on the General Arrangements to Borrow, which is a $6.0 billion pool of currencies created in 1962 to forestall international financial difficulties, is also published every month in IMF, *International Financial Statistics*. Semiannual reports on U.S. Treasury and Federal Reserve foreign exchange operations are published in the March and September issues of the *Federal Reserve Bulletin*.

nationally owned and internationally accessible reserves has raised two important questions concerning: (1) the adequacy of the overall level of reserves in meeting the needs of an expanding world economy; and (2) the possible instability that may arise due to shifts in confidence or in the relative attractiveness of different assets held for official reserve purposes.

These issues of *adjustment, liquidity,* and *reserve composition* will constitute the subject matter of this chapter. Before proceeding further, it is important to point out that the problems of the international monetary system are closely intertwined with those of the international trading system. If our objective is the enhancement of economic welfare for individual countries and the world as a whole, then what we should seek is to implement measures that will bring about freer trade and greater domestic expansion in both advanced and less developed countries. It is in this context that solutions to international financial problems should be sought.

The Adjustment Mechanism

We have remarked earlier, especially in Chapter 5, that the pegged exchange-rate system can be characterized as a disequilibrium system in contrast to freely fluctuating exchange rates and the gold standard. In their idealized version at least, these latter systems embody automatic adjustment mechanisms that function by means of variations in relative prices, whereas, in the pegged-rate system, adjustment depends greatly upon the policy decisions and responses of the authorities. As we have seen, the authorities today must reconcile their domestic objectives of full employment, price stability, and a satisfactory rate of economic growth with their external objective regarding the balance of payments. To the extent that different nations' objectives are incompatible and result in differential rates of change in prices and income, external pressures are bound to be felt on both the current and capital accounts. With pegged exchange rates, payments imbalances are presumably to be dealt with by the drawing down or accumulation of official reserves. The former policy is no doubt the more difficult since there may be finite limits on a country's own reserves and those it can borrow. A surplus country may, in contrast, be able to sterilize reserve accumulations by offsetting domestic policies.

Given the reliance on the U.S. dollar for reserve purposes, the U.S. balance of payments has to be looked upon differently than that of other countries. That is, there will be a counterpart to the U.S. official settlements deficits in the form of additional accumulations of dollar balances by foreign official institutions. This reliance on dollar holdings for reserve purposes has given rise to the contention that the U.S. may realize seigniorage at the expense of other countries to the extent that the U.S. is able to acquire real resources in exchange for the claims created. There is the further issue that official preferences for dollars as compared to other kinds of reserve assets may vary among countries. Finally, as pointed out earlier, the dollar is used widely as a vehicle currency for private transactions in international trade and investment, and its use would most likely continue even if an alternative system of exchange rates were devised.

If a pegged exchange-rate system is to remain viable, there is an evident need for substantial reserves. How much is required will be influenced importantly by the degree of parallelism and harmonization of the economic policies implemented in individual countries. Judging from the series of international financial crises witnessed among the industrial countries since the mid-1960's, policy parallelism and harmonization have evidently been difficult to achieve. This may not be surprising given that such an objective implies adaptations of national goals in ways that sovereign nations are at times unwilling to contemplate.

What has been happening during this same period is a closer integration of the capital markets of the major industrialized countries. This has been accomplished in particular due to the growth of the Eurodollar market, which has served to narrow the interest-rate differences between the U.S. and other countries. These differences have been due, on the one hand, to statutory limitations on interest payments on bank deposits in the U.S. and, on the other hand, to restricted access to capital markets elsewhere. Since it has been difficult for the policy authorities to control lending and borrowing by commercial banks and corporations in the Eurodollar market, countries have become less able to act independently in seeking national objectives.

The contradictions of independent national policies can be dealt with in one of two ways. Policy independence can give way to greater harmonization with reliance on official reserves to preserve pegged exchange rates. Alternatively, greater flexibility in exchange rates can be introduced. If the optimum currency area embraced the world as a whole and policy harmonization achieved a unified currency on a world basis, this could be highly beneficial to economic welfare. But the optimum currency area may not embrace the entire world. Moreover, in cases where exchange rates are pegged-but-adjustable, we have seen that countries may be compelled to introduce various kinds of trade and capital controls in seeking to attain their national objectives and at the same time maintain given exchange rates. Looked at in this light, economic welfare may be diminished rather than enhanced in comparison to a system in which exchange rates were market determined or fixed once and for all.

It must of course be recognized that policymaking is not guided by economic logic alone. Moreover, there may be an understandable reluctance to depart basically from an international financial system that some might argue to have performed exceptionally well, judging from the historically high rates of expansion of world trade and income since World War II. The international financial system may thus evolve in ways that are not radically different than in the past, provided, of course, that the system is not exposed to relatively large and unexpected shocks that make it difficult for exchange rates to remain pegged. The possible options for changing the international financial system have been widened as a consequence of the decision by the U.S. on August 15, 1971 to suspend dollar convertibility and the experiences that countries have had with floating rates since that time. But since it is not possible at present (August 1972) to foresee exactly how the system will be changed, it will be assumed that exchange-rate pegging will continue in some form, thus necessitating an expansion of international liquidity for reserve purposes. It will also be assumed that instability in the system due to shifts in reserve-asset preferences is to be avoided. Let us turn then to examine in greater detail these issues of reserve creation and composition.

International Reserve Creation

We have seen that international reserves will be needed as long as exchange rates are to be pegged. If we abstract from the composition of reserves, which is considered below, the question then is how large reserves should be from the standpoint of an individual nation and the world as a whole. It will become evident, as we proceed, that this is difficult to answer.

CRITERIA OF RESERVE ADEQUACY FOR A SINGLE COUNTRY[3]

From the standpoint of an individual country, the determination of reserve adequacy involves interrelated objective and subjective factors. Objectively speaking, the "need" for reserves depends upon the magnitude, duration, and distribution of expected future deficits in the balance of payments. These imbalances are dependent, in turn, on the underlying forces affecting the current and capital accounts and the speed and effectiveness with which the adjustment mechanism functions in correcting imbalances. With pegged exchange rates that are meant to be changed at only infrequent intervals when there exists a "fundamental disequilibrium" as discussed earlier, the dispersion of the expected deficits is especially important. That is, over some given period of time if fluctuations in economic activity occur symmetrically, the mean expected deficit should be zero. If this is not the case, there exists a structural disequilibrium that should be corrected by means other than the use of reserves.

There is a definite economic cost in holding a stock of international reserves. It may be approximated by the opportunity cost in terms of the returns to capital employed in various other investment alternatives that exist in a given country. These alternatives will obviously vary as between rich and poor

---

3. These matters are discussed in greater detail especially in Grubel (1969b, esp. pp. 28–74), Niehans (1970), and in various of the official IMF position papers reprinted in IMF (1970, esp. pp. 369–490).

countries, especially in light of the differences that may exist in social preferences with regard to employment, price stability, and growth objectives. The "desire" to hold reserves will thus involve subjective determinants that will interact with the essentially precautionary motivations arising from the need to finance expected future payments imbalances.

The foregoing considerations can be viewed essentially as ex ante in character. As such, the expected and actual ex post balance-of-payments realizations may not necessarily coincide. This may be all the more true when account is taken of the internal adaptability of the economy and the particular monetary, fiscal, and exchange-rate measures instituted at home and abroad for domestic and external adjustment purposes as the authorities respond to existing pressures and seek different alternatives goals. To complicate matters even further, account must be taken of the institutional environment which can make it less or more difficult at different times for countries to supplement their national reserve holdings through the IMF, General Arrangements to Borrow, regional organizations, and by special ad hoc arrangements made with other countries.

Reserve adequacy should of course be viewed in a welfare context. Thus, abstracting from any interest returns from reserves held, the yield on reserves derived from exchange-rate stability and the minimization of domestic adjustment costs should be equated with the opportunity cost of alternative investment. It is a big step, however, to translate this into precise measurement. It will be recalled that in Chapter 1 it was argued that no unambiguous way existed of separating autonomous from accommodating transactions in the balance of payments and of taking fully into account the interactions of policies and events. The problem is made all the more difficult since we cannot readily foresee the extent to which the authorities may turn to external sources for assistance. Finally, and perhaps of greatest importance, there is the fact that the authorities have the option of altering the policy mix as between monetary-fiscal and exchange-rate measures for balance-of-payments adjustment purposes.

Despite the foregoing difficulties, there have been several attempts to develop and estimate statistically models of reserve behavior for individual nations.[4] It would take us too far afield to summarize the different assumptions made and methods utilized. In any event, it is doubtful if the results are sufficiently stable with respect to time and evolving changes in institutions and in the mix of policies that they can be easily generalized to circumstances beyond the given data periods. The question of reserve adequacy is nevertheless one that must be dealt with even though it may admit of no precise answer. For this reason, there has been a search for empirical measures, the

---

4. Among the most noteworthy of these attempts are Clark (1970a; 1970b); Courchene and Youseff (1967); Flanders (1971); Heller (1966; 1968; 1970); Kelly (1970); Kenen and Yudin (1965); Machlup (1966); Rhomberg (1966); and Thorn (1967).

ratio of reserves to imports being a prominent example, that would provide at least a clue to evaluating reserve adequacy.[5]

A possible alternative criterion for evaluating reserve adequacy, at least ex post, is to look at how the authorities have in fact behaved in given circumstances with respect to their reserve levels and policies for adjustment. It will be recalled from Chapter 1 that we defined balance-of-payments equilibrium subject to there being full employment with price stability and without any additional restrictions imposed on trade and payments. While this definition involves making value judgments about the use of controls and the choice of national objectives, it may nevertheless provide a general indication of how individual countries have viewed and acted in the past in seeking to correct imbalances with given reserve levels and existing supplemental reserve facilities. Problems would of course arise in projecting future levels of reserves from such experiences. But the margin of error might be such that a country could adapt its policy mix if it felt that its reserves were relatively too low or high. These adaptations could probably be accomplished more easily if there were a system of centralized reserve creation for the world as a whole. Let us turn then to this broader issue.

CRITERIA OF RESERVE ADEQUACY FOR THE WORLD AS A WHOLE[6]

To evaluate reserve adequacy from the world standpoint would require, ideally, knowledge of the configurations of the expected payments imbalances that would be associated with alternative policy mixes in individual countries. To determine these configurations would be especially difficult because account would have to be taken of intercountry feedback effects due to changes in real forces and in the policies of various countries. Since it is virtually impossible to implement a model that could encompass all of these complexities, there is an evident need to find simpler, albeit more crude, criteria. Here again the preferences of the authorities as revealed by their behavior might be helpful. Thus, for the world as a whole, reserve adequacy might be evaluated according to whether reserves are sufficiently large, in the major industrial countries especially, for full employment and price stability to be maintained and without the need to resort to additional restrictions on trade and payments.

On a global basis, the incidence of restrictions and departures from full employment and price stability due to external pressures are observable from past behavior in individual countries. Of course, this may not necessarily be a reliable indication of what can be expected in the future. But even though we may lack precise information on the real forces and policies affecting national reserves, some judgment about past reserve adequacy might never-

5. Salant (1970) offers numerous concrete suggestions of possible measures of reserve adequacy.
6. In addition to the references cited in the preceding footnotes, see also Fleming (1967) and the articles by Kemp and Sohmen in IMF (1970).

theless be useful in making global estimates of future reserve needs. Thus, if reserves are designed to forestall restrictions and promote maximum growth that is consistent with full employment and price stability, there might be some merit in devising rules of thumb for reserve creation and distribution that would enable these objectives to be realized nationally and therefore for the world as a whole.

It will be noted that this formulation places more emphasis on the growth rather than any particular level of reserves. It means that reserves are to be created in a sufficiently large amount and distributed in such a way that the foregoing objectives can be attained. In this regard, it may be important to err on the high side, if at all, since the pressures of a too rapid expansion of reserves can be neutralized by appropriate domestic policies more easily than if reserve expansion occurs too slowly. It may be desirable, moreover to have a well defined program that would make explicit the order of magnitude, timing, and distribution of reserves so that these factors could be built into the horizons of policymakers. The advantage here is that countries would formulate their stabilization and growth policies in a generally expansionary way since they would feel less constrained by external pressures.

In discussing global reserve adequacy, we have assumed implicitly that reserve creation and distribution would be undertaken by some international authority such as the IMF, as is presently (1972) the case regarding SDR's. This is in contrast to reserve creation by the U.S. via the buildup of dollar liabilities to foreign official institutions. Both kinds of reserve creation raise a possibly important issue, however. This has to do with the seigniorage that may accrue to the monetary authority in terms of the difference between the cost of issuance and servicing of the monetary instruments and the resources that these instruments may make available when expended. Let us look at this issue in some more detail.

THE SEIGNIORAGE PROBLEM[7]

Under the pegged-rate system, the supply to the rest of the world by the U.S. of dollar balances that are held for official reserve purposes gives the U.S. control over resources in excess of what it may cost to produce and service these balances. Expressed formally, following Grubel (1969b, p. 144), the present value of the seigniorage, S, acquired in a given year is:

$$S = \left[\frac{R - r - c}{(1 + d)} + \cdots + \frac{R - r - c}{(1 + d)^n} \right] D, \qquad (12.1)$$

where R is the marginal productivity of capital that is applicable to the resources acquired, r is the interest cost of servicing the obligations issued, c is the cost of issuance and continued maintenance, d is the social rate of

---

7. For further elaboration, see especially Grubel (1969a; 1969b), Johnson (1967; 1969), and Mundell (1971, esp. pp. 170–86).

discount, and D is the official settlements deficit that is assumed to remain constant. If the obligations have an infinite life, the seigniorage is

$$\left[\frac{R - r - c}{d}\right] D.$$

If $r = c = 0$ and $R = d$, the seigniorage equals the deficit, D.[8]

Suppose now that we contemplate a system of central reserve creation in which an organization like the IMF is empowered to create and distribute international reserves. To accomplish this would of course require the agreement and participation of all the member countries, which may not be easy to obtain. If this central reserve creation, say in the form of SDR's, is intended to substitute for a commodity reserve such as gold and we abstract from the issuance of dollar obligations by the U.S. for reserve purposes, we have here what Grubel (1969b, p. 154) has called social seigniorage, SS. This is defined as the social saving of resources made possible by the substitution of the fiat for the commodity money. If the interest payments and costs of issuance are zero and $R = d$, the social seigniorage will be equal to the face value of the fiat money issued.[9] Alternatively, if central reserve creation is to substitute for the issuance of dollar obligations, there would not be any social seigniorage to speak of, but rather a redistribution of the national seigniorage that accrues now to the U.S.

Since the seigniorage to be derived from reserve creation could be substantial, it is of interest to consider alternative ways in which it might be distributed. Grubel (1969b, pp. 156–66) has pointed out three such possibilities: (1) the central authority can distribute the seigniorage by using the reserves to purchase public goods for the benefit of all or by channeling the resources to particular income groups; (2) the distribution can take the form of interest payments to be made to the holders of the reserves equal to

8. To illustrate, at the end of 1971, foreign official dollar holdings totalled $51.1 billion according to IMF, *International Financial Statistics*. It should be clear from equation (12.1) that this amount does not represent the total seigniorage accruing to the U.S. Thus, if we were to assume that $R = d = 10$ percent and $r + c = 5$ percent, then approximately $2.4 billion in resources may have accrued to the U.S. in 1971 as a consequence of the cumulative official settlements deficits reflected in the $51.1 billion noted. Granting that we do not know precisely what the rate of return is, the foregoing calculation may nevertheless exaggerate the seigniorage that the U.S. in fact obtained in 1971. This is the case when account is taken of the extra need for the U.S. to hold gold for international reserve purposes and the special responsibility that the U.S. has for the international monetary system, which may in turn limit the range of alternative policies that the U.S. can follow with respect to attaining full employment and price stability domestically. See Grubel (1964) for some detailed calculations and further qualifications concerning the seigniorage gains to the U.S. in its role as world banker.

9. Thus, for example, if $3 billion of SDR's were to be issued in a given year in lieu of using an equivalent amount of resources to produce gold and the other assumptions held, this would be the amount of social seigniorage realized. As additional reserves were created over time in lieu of gold the realization of social seigniorage would continue. As Johnson (1967; 1969) and Mundell (1971) point out, there would also be social savings if fiat money were to replace the existing stock of commodity money.

the going rate of return, with allowance for administrative costs; and (3) the distribution of the seigniorage as such can be forestalled by allocating the reserves on the basis of individual nations' long-run average balances which would be drawn down to finance temporary deficits and increased with surpluses.

The first of these methods has been proposed as a means of combining international reserve creation with aid to poor countries by biasing the distribution of reserves in the poor countries' favor. While there is nothing in principle that would militate against this linking of reserve creation with development assistance,[10] it is important to note that this form of reserve creation and distribution is not costless from the standpoint of the developed countries in view of the resource transfers involved. It would also require agreement by the developed countries that they relinquish their national sovereignty and objectives in international aid-giving in favor of this multilateral approach. Such a change in policy might be desired in its own right, but it will no doubt be a long time in coming if the decisions regarding the initial distribution of SDR's in 1970–71 are any indication.[11]

The point of the second way of distributing seigniorage is to compensate the holders of the money balances at a rate that approximates the competitive rate of return.[12] What is envisaged here is that the central authority maintains an investment portfolio that would generate a sufficiently large return for the interest payments to be made. There are possible drawbacks, however, insofar as portfolio-management problems may be created for the central authority especially if changes in the investment portfolio had an impact on domestic financial conditions and exchange rates that was at variance with policy objectives in individual countries.

The third method mentioned has the advantage that there will be no net transfers of resources since countries will presumably balance out their use of reserves over time in offsetting external deficits and surpluses. Problems may arise, however, in determining what these long-run average reserve holdings should be since reserve adequacy is so hard to define for the reasons

10. For excellent statements and discussion of the issues involved, see the contributions of Dell, Johnson, Prebisch, Scitovsky, and Triffin in U.S. Congress, Joint Economic Committee (1969, esp. pp. 1–82). See also Cohen (1966).

11. As mentioned previously, SDR distributions are based on IMF quotas. According to Triffin—see reference in preceding footnote—only 28 percent of the distribution for 1970–72 was to be parcelled out among the 86 least developed and neediest members of the Fund. These countries will obtain some real resource benefit, however, since they are required to hold only an average SDR reserve level equal to 30 percent of their SDR allocations over a five-year period. But this is not a special provision to assist developing countries since the advanced countries receiving the bulk of the SDR's can utilize them subject to the same constraint if they wish to do so.

12. Sohmen has argued in IMF (1970) that instead of creating reserves centrally, countries seeking balance-of-payments assistance should borrow on international capital markets at competitive rates of return. The transfers involved here would thus be directly from borrowers to lenders. We shall return to this point below since it is of fundamental importance in the achievement of efficiency in the central creation of international reserves.

mentioned earlier. Some redistribution may thus occur insofar as it is difficult to devise a formula that is ethically neutral.

It is not obvious from our discussion which method of dealing with seigniorage is the best. This is the case particularly if there are alternative redistributive effects at issue. If, however, efficiency considerations are paramount, some variant of the second or third method will be chosen on the grounds that it minimizes intercountry resource transfers at subsidized rates.

EFFICIENT RESERVE CREATION AND THE WORLD PRICE LEVEL

Whatever the method chosen for creating and distributing international reserves, it is of crucial importance that the magnitude be consistent with the attainment of world price stability. With given exchange rates and commercial policies, if national authorities view prospective reserve increases to be inadequate in the light of their domestic and external objectives, deflationary pressures may be exerted on the world economy. This may occur insofar as relatively restrictive policies are implemented in important industrialized countries seeking to maintain or augment their international reserves. By the same line of reasoning, too many reserves may generate excessive expansion in countries that consequently may feel less constrained by external pressures.

Given the importance of attaining world price stability, the authorities responsible for international reserve creation and distribution must be cognizant of the distinction between the real and nominal values of existing reserve holdings and accretions thereto as well as the rates of return on real assets and real money balances. Suppose, for example, that some specified nominal amount of international reserves is distributed that is not consistent with world price stability. Assume in this regard that individual nations conceive of changes in their reserve holdings in real rather than in nominal terms, and that they vary their real reserves in strict proportion to the growth of real output. If nominal reserve creation fell short of or exceeded the desired change in real reserves, the world price level would be reduced or increased.[13]

We had occasion above to remark on the opportunity cost of international reserve holdings. Johnson (1970a) has treated this issue in the context of a competitive domestic banking system and then developed the implications for international reserve creation and distribution. Thus, as he states (1970a, p. 4):

> At the abstract level of pure theory, the costs of maintaining a system of bank accounts ... can be regarded as negligible: in theoretical terms money can be

---

13. Mundell (1971, esp. pp. 137–46) has discussed the case where there is world inflation, due presumably to excessive reserve creation, coupled with a relative shortage of reserves. This can arise, depending on the rate of inflation, if countries feel impelled to seek increased nominal reserves in an attempt to maintain their real reserve positions.

provided at zero social cost. Maximization of welfare requires that a good that can be provided at zero marginal social costs should be provided in the quantity that yields zero marginal utility, that is, that satiates demand, and this result would be ensured by the payment of competitive interest rates on chequable deposits. Similarly, the charging of competitive cost for the use of the services of the payments mechanism would induce the deposit-holding public to make optimal use of that mechanism: in other words to arrange its monetary transactions so as to use the bank account payments mechanism only for transactions that are privately worth their social cost. In short, a competitive banking system would encourage the public to hold the socially optimum quantity of money and make socially optimum use of the payments mechanism.

The conclusion is then drawn (p. 13) that for the international monetary system there should be "... some sort of international credit reserve asset, created at approximately zero social cost, which should in principle bear interest so as to encourage countries to hold as near as possible to the satiety level of demand for it, and the quantity of which should be increased by international arrangement at a rate conducive to stability of the world price level." Our preceding discussion of seigniorage suggests two possible ways in which efficient international reserve creation might be achieved.

Thus, there could be international reserve units created that were interest bearing. These reserve units could be distributed to individual countries in exchange for interest-bearing assets. The payment and receipt of interest would be self-liquidating, with allowance being made for administrative costs. The amount of reserves created and distributed could then be varied, given the goal of world price stability. This would be an efficient solution provided that the rate of interest involved reflected competitive market influences.

Alternatively, if new reserves were created and distributed and agreement reached as to their acceptability in financing payments imbalances, an arrangement could be made whereby countries would pay or receive interest on any differences between their actual reserve holdings at a given time and their shares of the newly created reserves. The rate of interest would be set at the approximate level for alternative real investment. Johnson (1970a, p. 14) likens this arrangement to that of "an individual domestic customer of a bank that charges competitive interest on overdrafts and pays competitive interest on deposits." This system would be efficient so long as the lending and borrowing rates correctly reflected the opportunity cost of investment foregone.[14]

14. E. M. Bernstein in IMF (1970, p. 46) has criticized this view on the grounds that the opportunity cost of holding reserves varies greatly, being negligible in some advanced countries and high in less developed countries. He questioned therefore whether it is appropriate to attempt to duplicate market forces in the payment of interest. In evaluating Bernstein's criticism, it should be noted that if countries can control their holdings of reserves, they will increase them up to the point where the opportunity cost equals the rate of return on the reserves. If the interest rate on reserves is the same everywhere, so will be the opportunity cost. Bernstein's criticism is thus not one against paying interest. Rather, it simply suggests that advanced countries will tend to hold more reserves than less developed countries.

Throughout this section, we have abstracted from the question of the composition of international reserves. In point of fact, reserves are held in the form of gold, foreign exchange (mainly U.S. dollars), Special Drawing Rights, and IMF positions. The interrelations among the levels and rates of change of these different reserve assets raise a number of important issues that merit separate discussion and to which we will now turn.

The Composition of International Reserves

The amount and composition of reserves held by official institutions at year-ends for selected years from 1958–71 are indicated in Table 12.1. It is evident that from 1958–68 there was practically no change in the absolute level of gold holdings and that there was a decline between 1963 and 1968. It will be recalled from our earlier discussion that, in March 1968, the official and private gold markets were separated by agreement of the major industrialized countries. The amount of gold held in official reserves was thus frozen as of that time, subject to certain subsequent qualifications regarding future official purchases from South Africa. The private market price of gold was left free to fluctuate, and at times it has been substantially in excess of the official price. The de jure convertibility of dollars held by official institutions into gold was maintained after the establishment of the two-tier market. But this convertibility was suspended by the U.S., acting unilaterally, effective August 15, 1971.

TABLE 12.1

Amount and Composition of Reserves Held by Official Institutions
(World Total at Yearend, Billions of U.S. Dollars)

	1958	1963	1968	1970	1971
Gold	$38.0	$40.2	$38.9	$37.2	$39.2
Special Drawing Rights	—	—	—	3.1	6.4
Reserve positions in Fund	2.6	3.9	6.5	7.7	6.9
Foreign currencies	17.0	22.4	31.9	44.5	77.2
Total	$57.6	$66.5	$77.3	$92.5	$129.7

SOURCE: IMF, *International Financial Statistics.*

It is also clear from Table 12.1 that from 1958–68 the increase in reserves consisted largely of increases in foreign currencies, U.S. dollars mainly, held by official institutions and to a lesser extent of reserve positions in the Fund. The increase in dollar reserves had its manifestation of course in the official settlements deficits in the U.S. balance of payments. By the mid-1960's it was generally acknowledged that the amount of gold available for reserve use was stagnant and that increases in official dollar balances were contingent upon continued U.S. deficits. Faced with such uncertain prospects for the further expansion of world reserves, international consultations took place in earnest and, as we have noted, agreement was reached regarding the creation through the IMF of Special Drawing Rights. The initial amount to be created was $9.5 billion over a three-year period, with the distribution to be made annually based on IMF quotas. The first two distributions are reflected in Table 12.1.

THE FUTURE ROLE OF GOLD IN THE INTERNATIONAL MONETARY SYSTEM

The creation of the two-tier system separating the official and private markets for gold was a remarkable step. In effect, it amounted to a near demonetization of gold and explicit creation of a world dollar standard.[15] This decision concerning gold met with widespread approval, particularly in academic circles, since the inadequacies of holding gold for reserve purposes were well known. Thus, as Triffin (1960) and later writers have pointed out, the reliance upon gold had the important disadvantage that its supply for monetary purposes lay beyond the control of national authorities and international institutions. Moreover, since the production of gold required real resources, it was socially wasteful not to substitute for gold some type of international credit instrument that could be created at zero social cost and to divert monetary gold to industrial uses. Finally, since gold was not interest-bearing, there was less incentive to hold it relative to other forms of reserves, such as dollars, that did bear interest. This would be true so long as the reserve currencies were believed to be stable in relation to gold. But when this was not the case, as occurred on some occasions prior to March 1968, the international monetary system was subject to strain as the private demand for gold for speculative purposes increased substantially in the expectation that the official price of gold might be raised.

On strictly economic grounds, there are no compelling reasons for abandoning the two-tier system and restoring gold to its previous status as an international reserve asset. It is noteworthy, however, that there are still some countries, such as France, where it is urged continually that the world should return to gold as the sole base for international reserves. This could be accomplished if, for example, the official price of gold were increased substantially and other forms of reserves were phased out. The form in which reserves are held is not the real question, however. What matters, rather, is that national stabilization authorities may not be willing to conduct their domestic policies in response to variations in reserves. A reading of the

---

15. Gold was not fully demonetized because the official floor price of $35 per ounce was guaranteed for South African gold sales in particular. If this guarantee were removed, the private market price could then fall below the official price in response to changes in private market conditions.

economic history of the past half-century should leave no doubt that priorities assigned to national employment and price-stabilization objectives greatly outweigh those with respect to the balance of payments and level of reserves.

Suppose nevertheless that the official price of gold were increased beyond the $38 level specified in the Smithsonian Agreement of late 1971. Insofar as other countries left their existing gold parities unchanged, this action would constitute a further devaluation of the U.S. dollar as against all other currencies and all operative exchange rates would have to be adjusted accordingly. The price of gold could thus be raised without there being any other changes made in the pegged-rate system. In such an event, while the nominal value of reserves would be increased, all the substantive issues that have arisen in the pegged-rate system would still remain. That is, there would still be the question of the guarantee of convertibility into gold of dollars, other reserve currencies, and SDR's. Exchange rates would remain pegged within narrow official limits. And some means would have to be found to assure sufficiently large future increases in reserves. Thus, if only the price of gold were raised further and nothing else done, it would only be a matter of time before the deficiencies of the adjustable peg system reappeared.

THE DOLLAR STANDARD

It is clear from Table 12.1 that there was a marked increase in world official reserve holdings in the period from 1968 to 1971. This came primarily in the form of increased dollar holdings and to a lesser extent via the creation and distribution of SDR's. With official gold reserves fixed more or less at their 1968 level and SDR creation still in its infancy, the international financial system had become much more obviously dependent in the late 1960's on the U.S. for major additions to official international reserves. At the same time, in principle at least, prior to August 15, 1971, the U.S. continued its policy of honoring the conversion of foreign official dollar claims into gold.

In our previous discussion of reserve creation, great stress was placed upon creating and distributing just enough reserves so that the world price level would be stabilized. In the context of the dollar standard of the late 1960's, this meant that the rest of the world should be able to satisfy its demand for official reserves via official settlements deficits in the U.S. balance of payments in amounts that were consistent with world stability. To assure this result, it was important that the U.S. maintain reasonable domestic price stability because otherwise the world would find accumulation of dollars to be unattractive, and there might be no ready way of satisfying the demand for official reserves.

Unfortunately, this proved difficult to accomplish. After 1965, with the U.S. economy approaching full employment, the increased involvement in Vietnam and the consequent rise in government expenditures began to generate inflationary pressures. Under the circumstances, it would have been desirable to institute contractionary domestic fiscal and monetary policies. But the U.S. authorities were unable to act quickly and on a large enough scale. As a consequence, inflationary pressures gathered force.

The contractionary policies that were continued and extended, following the change in national administration in 1969, succeeded in slowing down the rate of expansion of output and led to increased unemployment. But there was much less success in restraining inflation. All the while, the U.S. current-account balance deteriorated sharply and with capital transfers continuing at relatively high levels, the buildup of foreign dollar claims was accelerated significantly.

In the spring and summer of 1971, substantial short-term capital outflows from the U.S. took place, in response especially to a widening of international interest differentials. These capital flows were directed particularly towards West Germany, making it necessary for the German central bank to absorb substantial amounts of dollars in order to maintain the official exchange-rate limits and at the same time to take steps to neutralize the expansionary impact of the inflows on the domestic monetary base. When the neutralization policies proved to be only partly successful and the capital inflows picked up again in anticipation now of an upward revaluation of the mark, the authorities decided in May 1971 to cease absorbing dollar balances and thus to let the exchange rate float. They were joined in this by the Dutch while Switzerland and Austria officially revalued their currencies.

Given this buildup of foreign official dollar claims[16] and a prospective further enlargement of the official settlements deficit, the U.S. could no longer hope to honor its commitment to gold convertibility in any substantial way. As already mentioned, convertibility was suspended as of August 15, 1971 and a 10 percent surcharge was imposed on dutiable imports. The immediate purpose of these measures was to force a realignment of exchange rates with respect especially to the major industrialized countries and, at the same time, to induce movement towards further reform of the international monetary system. The reaction to the U.S. measures was that most industrialized countries let their exchange rates float upward beyond the official limits. There was some apparent management by the authorities, however, to contain the extent of the upward float (i.e., "dirty" floating) through exchange-market intervention and controls.

These actions by the U.S. changed the basis of the dollar standard since floating rates obviate the need for countries to continue accumulating dollar balances for exchange-stabilization purposes. It is worth noting that the depreciation of the dollar in terms of other currencies can occur either by floating rates, as in fact occurred, or as noted earlier, if the U.S. were to

16. As pointed out in the appendix on balance-of-payments accounting in Chapter 1, official dollar holdings may have been overstated during this period as funds were placed in the Eurodollar market and subsequently found their way again into official hands.

increase the official dollar price of gold and other countries left their gold parities unchanged and adjusted their exchange rates accordingly vis-à-vis the dollar. There could of course be some combination of these measures, as was the case in the context of the Smithsonian Agreement.

The realignment of exchange rates is mainly a technical matter, however, although it could work for some time at least to bring about adjustment of the payments imbalances of individual countries. The more important issue is what kind of international monetary system will emerge in the future, and, in this light, what the roles of the different reserve assets will be. As a means of approaching these issues, let us, for the sake of discussion, assume that there is a strong desire on the part especially of the countries in Western Europe and Japan to continue the present system of pegged exchange rates in some form, but with a discontinuance of reliance upon gold and dollars for official reserve purposes in favor of Special Drawing Rights as created by the IMF.

AN SDR STANDARD

Suppose then that the IMF member countries were to agree to turn over to the Fund their existing international reserves now held in the form of gold, dollar and other foreign currency balances, and reserve positions in the Fund. As a *quid pro quo*, the Fund could give these countries an equivalent amount of SDR's based upon the given pattern of exchange rates. From then on, each national currency could be expressed in terms of SDR units for official reserve purposes. In order to make this conversion attractive and efficient from an economic standpoint, the SDR units should bear a rate of interest that closely approximates the social opportunity costs of capital. For want of a better measure, the average long-term interest rate on new flotations in the major international capital markets could be chosen.

It would then be necessary to devise a system for the central creation and distribution of SDR's. As stated previously, the amount created should be consistent with the attainment of world price stability, given the existing structure of exchange rates and the objectives of national policies. Also, the newly created reserves should be interest bearing at a level that reflects alternative investment returns. An arrangement might be made in this regard, as mentioned earlier, for countries to pay or receive interest according to the difference between their existing holdings and original shares of the new SDR allocations. In this way, the use of reserves would reflect opportunity costs more closely. Moreover, subsidized resources transfers would not arise, as in the IMF system, due to the interest rate on the reserve unit being less than the opportunity costs of alternative investment.

The above arrangement goes far beyond the role originally conceived for SDR's as another form of reserves to exist side by side with gold and official dollar balances. Since SDR's would become the only reserve asset, gold would be demonetized once and for all. Thus, there would no longer be any need for dollar-gold convertibility and for the gold guarantee of SDR's.[17] Attaching a market-approximated interest rate to a single reserve form would also do away with problems of shifts in reserve asset preferences due to changes in the relative desirability and returns associated with different assets.[18]

The centralization of existing reserves and of new reserve creation would require an accord among nations that would be unparalleled in international monetary affairs. At the same time, agreement would have to be reached concerning the system of exchange rates to be operative under the SDR standard. At the one extreme, exchange rates could be fixed once and for all, in which case a logical next step would be a unified world currency that would displace existing national currencies. In such an event and assuming that the optimum currency areas was the world as a whole, it would be necessary to undertake the harmonization of national policies for stabilization and growth and to work out a means for income and resource transfers to forestall regional adjustment problems and perceived distributional inequities. The overriding question here is whether nations would be willing to give up the sovereignty that they have now on these matters and enter into the cooperative framework required.

Assuming that a unified world currency is not practicable, some provision would be required to insure exchange-rate flexibility for adjustment purposes. We have pointed out at great length the difficulties and drawbacks of the adjustable-peg system as it functioned from the end of World War II to the summer of 1971. Granted that this system is inadequate for the many reasons mentioned in our earlier discussion, some alternative rules for exchange-rate adjustment are necessary that would make adjustment smoother and more viable. The possibilities here involve some combination of widening the official limits for permissible exchange-rate fluctuations in the short run, and permitting these limits to change over time in response to continuing payments imbalances.

It would take us too far afield to discuss the numerous variations in moderated exchange-rate flexibility that have been devised.[19] Some

17. Prior to the creation of the two-tier market for gold in 1968, the "confidence" problem posed by dollar-gold convertibility was potentially very serious in view of the declining ratio of the U.S. gold stock to its official foreign liabilities. While the two-tier market stopped the flow of gold from official to private holdings, the confidence problem still remained so long as dollar-gold convertibility was possible. The suspension of convertibility by the U.S. on August 15, 1971 put an end to the problem, at least for the time being. For analyses of the confidence problem, see especially Triffin (1960), Kenen (1960), Johnson (1967), Officer and Willet (1969), and Makin (1971). Mundell (1968, esp. pp. 282–97) has discussed these issues in a short-term context under the rubric of what he has called the "crisis" problem.

18. See Aliber (1967b) for an application of Gresham's Law to the analysis of reserve asset preferences. See also Mundell's comments (1971, pp. 184–86) on trust as an economic variable. Further discussions of SDR's can be found in Fleming (1971b) and Hirsch (1971).

19. These proposals are reviewed briefly in Krause (1971). Various practical proposals and suggestions for implementation are treated in Halm (1970, esp. pp. 219–94) and Federal Reserve Bank of Boston (1969, esp. pp. 121–64).

comments are nevertheless in order. We may note first that while widening the official limits around parity might in itself improve the workings of the adjustment mechanism and reduce the need for reserves in the short run, the same problems would arise as in the adjustable-peg system once the authorities began experiencing difficulties in maintaining the official limits. It is for this reason that an orderly arrangement must be devised to permit the official limits to be changed without engendering the air of crisis and resort to controls so commonly witnessed during the 1960's. The degree of movement of the official limits must therefore be attainable without provoking one-way, comparatively riskless speculative options; and it must create the least possible policy conflicts between domestic and external objectives.

If some system of moderated exchange-rate flexibility is to be developed, there presumably will be a continuing need for an intervention currency. SDR's would not be well suited for this purpose since they are meant to be reserve assets held only by central banks and used to settle payments imbalances. Assuming that exchange-rate stabilization is to remain a national responsibility, countries will then seek to hold foreign currency balances for this purpose. While in principle they could hold a variety of currencies, the U.S. dollar is the most likely candidate in view of its longstanding uses as an intervention and vehicle currency.

Presumably with an SDR standard, the dollar could be permitted to fluctuate vis-à-vis other currencies. The SDR's themselves would remain stable in terms of national currencies by providing for exchange-rate guarantees. This means that transfers involving SDR's and particular national currencies would require greater or lesser amounts of these currencies to reflect whatever exchange-rate devaluations or appreciations had occurred subsequent to the initial establishment of the rates. Such an arrangement could then apply to the dollar as well as to other currencies. Official and private stocks of dollars held for intervention and commercial purposes could be protected by hedging operations in the forward exchange markets. Now if the dollar continued to serve these dual purposes, it would be desirable for its exchange value to remain fairly stable. This would require that the U.S. authorities be successful in maintaining income at full employment levels without undue price inflation. Otherwise, a relatively more stable currency other than the dollar may be sought. However, this is a matter of much less concern with an SDR standard than in the adjustable-peg system because in the latter system the dollar was both an intervention and reserve currency. Removing its function as a reserve currency in favor of SDR's would thus eliminate the role of the U.S. in creating international liquidity, although dollars would still be held as official reserves for intervention purposes. The dollar could thus continue its intervention and vehicle-currency roles without specific international design so long as the international community found such an arrangement efficient and convenient.

ECONOMIC UNION AND CURRENCY UNIFICATION

We noted in Chapter 5 that the members of the European Community instituted in 1969–70 some preliminary measures designed to achieve a common currency by the end of the 1970's. It is interesting to consider the problems that the Community is likely thereby to encounter and how the international monetary system may be affected. Let us for this purpose treat all the major European countries, including the U.K., as members of the European Community.[20]

As Johnson (1971a) has pointed out, the members of the European Community had become troubled generally by the hegemony of the U.S. in world affairs and in particular by their dependence on the dollar standard in the late 1960's. At the same time, the Community was searching for new ways to further its economic and political integration. By establishing a common currency, it was thus hoped to reduce U.S. influence and at the same time achieve broader Community goals. The issues involved in currency unification can be framed in terms of our previous discussion of alternative exchange-rate systems. It will be recalled that great emphasis was placed on the need for policy harmonization if exchange rates were to be fixed absolutely or pegged subject to certain limits. By the same token, if national autonomy was to be retained with regard to domestic objectives, exchange-rate flexibility was needed.

What the adoption of a common currency means therefore is that the members of the European Community must be prepared to limit their national sovereignty in favor of some central coordination of monetary and fiscal policies and to develop means for assisting those member countries or regions that lag behind economically.[21] If the European countries were unable or unwilling to accept these policy implications, they would have little choice but to continue their reliance upon the U.S. dollar in some form. Thus, for example, under the dollar standard they would still accumulate dollar balances for official reserve purposes. But if this proved too inflationary, they might decide to let their currencies float outside of the official limits as in fact they did in the spring and summer of 1971. What was especially noteworthy about these decisions was that each country floated its currency separately. The Community adopted a united front following the exchange-rate realignments of the Smithsonian Agreement in late 1971. But the policy

20. The original members of the Community were Belgium-Luxembourg, France, Italy, the Netherlands, and West Germany, whereas Austria, Denmark, Norway, Portugal, Sweden, Switzerland, and the U.K. comprised the European Free Trade Area (EFTA). With the U.K. and other EFTA members formally joining or working out some special relationship with the Community, EFTA will cease to exist.

21. The seminal works on balance-of-payments adjustment policies for member countries of an economic union are by Meade (1957) and Ingram (1959). For a more recent treatment, see Mintz (1970) and the references cited therein. See also Fleming (1971a).

consensus was short-lived when the U.K. decided to let the pound float in
June 1972 in response to exchange-market pressures and a drain on their
reserves.

Suppose nevertheless that the political basis for currency unification in
Europe was realized and that two major currency blocs emerged based
respectively on the U.S. dollar and a European currency. What type of
exchange-rate arrangements might then be available and what role, if any,
would there be for central reserve creation? One alternative is absolutely
fixed intra-bloc exchange rates and floating inter-bloc rates. Such an arrangement is suggested by the theory of optimum currency areas especially insofar
as foreign trade would be a relatively small part of total output in each bloc
and provided that resources could move relatively easily among the members
within a bloc. A second alternative is absolutely fixed rates both within and
between blocs. This would imply a unified world currency and a system of
adjustment among countries that would be much the same as applies to
regions within a given country. Such an arrangement seems unlikely to be
adopted, however, because it impinges so greatly upon national sovereignties.

This leaves the possibility of moderated exchange-rate flexibility between
the blocs, with international reserves being used for financing payments
imbalances. Ruling out the use of gold and continued reliance upon the
accumulation of dollar reserves, the SDR system discussed above would be a
viable alternative so long as inter-bloc exchange rates were to be pegged.
But suppose now that we relax the assumption of two blocs and permit
countries to exist that belong to neither bloc. If reserves were not centrally
created, a choice would have to be made of the currency to be held for
reserve purposes. Both currencies could be held. However, the situation
might be unstable if interest-rate differentials between the blocs changed, and
this led to large-scale shifts in official reserve asset holdings. A single reserve
standard would thus be preferable, and if there is central reserve creation,
the system could be based on SDR's.[22]

The Choices Before Us

In contemplating international monetary reform, the changes sought should
be aimed at achieving the maximum economic growth that is consistent with
the attainment of full employment and price stability in individual countries
and the world as a whole. For such growth to be efficient, international trade
and investment should be subjected to the fewest possible restrictions, except
perhaps in cases where there is a discrepancy between private and social

22. It should be pointed out that the idea of central reserve creation is by no means
new. Its ancestry can be traced back to Keynes' proposals for international monetary
reform developed in the 1940's and elaborated in the late 1950's by Triffin (1960) and
others. Excellent surveys of the various plans for reform are contained in Machlup (1964,
pp. 278–366) and Grubel (1963).

returns. As discussed especially in Chapter 10, the goals of full employment and price stability reflect social preferences that may differ from country to country in terms of what is deemed acceptable. Monetary and fiscal policies must thus be implemented in a flexible and effective manner in seeking national goals. Finally, the functioning of the international monetary system will have a direct bearing on the utilization of national resources, the distribution of income among and within countries, and the relative burdens of adjustment experienced by countries with balance-of-payments deficits or surpluses.[23]

The perhaps dominant theme of this book has been that any system of exchange rates carries with it certain presumptions about the nature and efficiency of the automatic and policy-motivated forces that operate to bring about equilibrium in a country's balance of payments. We noted earlier that the system of pegged exchange rates that evolved after World War II coincided with a remarkable expansion of world production and trade. However, this system came increasingly under strain during the 1960's due to speculative pressures quickly developing when official exchange-rate limits were in doubt, the draining of gold from official reserves into private holdings in anticipation of a possible increase in its price, and generation by the U.S. of significant domestic inflation that was transferred abroad via increases in foreign official dollar holdings. The climax came when the U.S. decided unilaterally, as of August 15, 1971, to suspend dollar-gold convertibility pending a realignment of exchange rates and the beginning of consultations on possible changes in the international monetary system.

The choices before us (in August, 1972) are essentially three in number. We could stay with the pegged-rate system with continued reliance on the dollar for reserve purposes, but perhaps with greater presumptive resort to exchange-rate flexibility than was true in the past. A second alternative would be to centralize existing reserve holdings and the creation of new reserves along the lines of the SDR standard discussed above, with a presumption of greater automaticity in exchange-rate changes by means of the widening of official limits that would be subject to change over time. A third alternative is to adopt a system of freely fluctuating exchange rates.

This last alternative may be preferable on efficiency grounds because it obviates the need for controls as in the pegged-rate system and because it would provide the greatest latitude for the pursuit of national growth and stabilization objectives. We discussed at length in Chapter 3 the possible difficulties that might arise in a system of fluctuating rates and whether such a system would be optimal for all countries. That discussion need not be repeated here. Suffice it to say that, on both theoretical and empirical grounds, many of these difficulties have been exaggerated and inappropriate conclusions have been drawn from historical experiences.

23. Krause (1971a) has elaborated on these matters at some length. See also Krause (1971b) for a proposal to reform the international monetary system.

If countries are reluctant to adopt fluctuating rates on a permanent basis and wish rather to have a system of moderated exchange-rate flexibility, the SDR standard commends itself. SDR's would be used in lieu of dollars and other reserve assets to finance payments imbalances, although the dollar could still be used for intervention purposes. The reliance on one single form of reserve held and created centrally would obviate the problems stemming from shifts in preferences when more than one type of reserve exists. Difficult technical problems would have of course to be resolved. It would be necessary in particular to determine the amount of reserve creation and distribution that was consistent with national employment and price-stabilization objectives, subject to pre-specified uses of exchange-rate changes for balance-of-payments purposes. This kind of a system requires substantial cooperation and harmonization of national policies. If the international financial system evolved further in this manner, countries would perhaps be brought closer together both economically and politically in the long run. If this served to reduce some of the antagonisms arising in the relations among sovereign nation states, the costs of economic inefficiencies in the system might be judged tolerable in a broader political and social sense.

REFERENCES

Ablin, R. 1966. "Fiscal-Monetary Mix: A Haven for the Fixed Exchange Rate?," *National Banking Review*, 4 (December), 199–204.

———. 1968. "Income, Capital Mobility and the Theory of Economic Policy," *Kyklos*, XXI (Fasc. 1), 102–07.

Alexander, S. S. 1951. "Devaluation Versus Import Restriction as a Means for Improving Foreign Trade Balance," IMF, *Staff Papers*, I (April), 379–96.

———. 1952. "Effects of a Devaluation on a Trade Balance," IMF, *Staff Papers*, II (April), 263–78. Reprinted in R. E. Caves and H. G. Johnson (eds.), *Readings in International Economics*. Homewood: Richard D. Irwin, Inc., 1968.

———. 1959. "Effects of a Devaluation: A Simplified Synthesis of Elasticities and Absorption Approaches," *American Economic Review*, XLIX (March), 22–42.

Aliber, R. Z. 1962. "Speculation in the Foreign Exchanges: The European Experience, 1919–1926," *Yale Economic Essays*, II, 171–245.

———. 1963. "More About Counter-Speculation in the Forward Exchange Market," *Journal of Political Economy*, LXXI (December), 589–90.

———. 1964. "Speculation and Price Stability Once Again," *Journal of Political Economy*, LXXII (December), 607–09.

———. 1967a. "A Note on Official Support of the Forward Exchange Rate," *Journal of Political Economy*, 75 (August, Part I), 417.

———. 1967b. "Gresham's Law, Asset Preferences, and the Demand for International Reserves," *Quarterly Journal of Economics*, LXXXI (November), 628–38.

Allen, R. G. D. 1956. *Mathematical Economics*. London: Macmillan.

Allen, W. R. 1962. "Another Balance of Payments Pitfall: 'Dollar Use' and 'Dollar Supply'," *Review of Economics and Statistics*, XLIV (November), 482–84.

Allen, W. R. and Allen, C. L. 1959. *Foreign Trade and Finance*. New York: The Macmillan Company.

Arndt, S. W. 1970. "Income and Price Adjustments and France's Basic Balance of Payments, 1961–1966," *Rivista Internazionale di Scienze Economiche e Commerciali*, 17 (May), 429–48.

———. 1971. "Policy Choices in an Open Economy: Some Dynamic Considerations," *Journal of Political Economy* (forthcoming).

Auten, J. 1963. "Forward Exchange Rates and Interest-Rate Differentials," *Journal of Finance*, XVIII (March), 11–19.

Baggott, N. and Flanders, M. J. 1969. "Economic Policy in an Open Economy: A Reader's Guide," *Economia Internazionale*, XXII (November), 3–15.

Balassa, B. 1963. "Some Observations on Mr. Beckerman's 'Export-Propelled' Growth Model," *Economic Journal*, LXXIII (December), 781–85.

———. 1964a. "Some Observations on Mr. Beckerman's Export-Propelled Growth Model: A Rejoinder," *Economic Journal*, LXXIV (March), 240–42.

———. 1964b. "Some Observations on Mr. Beckerman's Export-Propelled Growth Model: A Further Note," *Economic Journal*, LXXIV (September), 740–42.

———. 1964c. "The Purchasing-Power Parity Doctrine: A Reappraisal," *Journal of Political Economy*, LXXII (December), 584–96. Reprinted in R. N. Cooper (ed.), *International Finance: Selected Readings*. Middlesex: Penguin Books Ltd., 1969.

Bauer, P. T. and Yamey, B. S. 1968. *Markets, Market Control, and Marketing Reform*. London: Weidenfeld and Nicholson.

Baumol, W. J. 1952. "The Transactions Demand for Cash: An Inventory Theoretic Approach," *Quarterly Journal of Economics*, LXVI (November), 545–56.

——. 1957. "Speculation, Profitability, and Stability," *Review of Economics and Statistics*, XXXIX (August), 263–71.

——. 1959. "Reply" to L. G. Telser, "A Theory of Speculation Relating Profitability and Stability," *Review of Economics and Statistics*, XLI (August), 295–301.

Beckerman, W. 1962. "Projecting Europe's Growth," *Economic Journal*, LXXII (December), 912–25.

——. 1963. "Some Observations on Mr. Beckerman's 'Export-Propelled' Growth Model: A Reply," *Economic Journal*, LXXIII (December), 785–87.

——. 1964. "Professor Balassa's Comments on my 'Export-Propelled' Growth Model: A Rebuttal," *Economic Journal*, LXXIV (September), 738–40.

——. 1966. "The Determinants of Economic Growth," in P. D. Henderson (ed.), *Economic Growth in Britain*. London: Weidenfeld and Nicholson, 55–83.

Behrman, J. N. 1970. *Multinational Interests and the Multinational Enterprise: Tensions Among the North Atlantic Countries*. Englewood Cliffs: Prentice-Hall, Inc.

Bell, P. W. 1962. "Private Capital Movements and the U.S. Balance-of-Payments Position," in U.S. Congress, Joint Economic Committee, *Factors Affecting the United States Balance of Payments*. Washington: Government Printing Office.

Bernstein, E. M. 1958. "Strategic Factors in Balance of Payments Adjustment," *Review of Economics and Statistics*, XL (February, Supplement), 133–37.

Bhagwati, J. and Johnson, H. G. 1960. "Notes on Some Controversies in the Theory of International Trade," *Economic Journal*, LXX (March), 74–93.

Black, J. 1957. "A Geometrical Analysis of the Foreign Trade Multiplier," *Economic Journal*, LXVII (June), 240–43.

Bloomfield, A. I. 1949. "Induced Investment, Overcomplete International Adjustment, and Chronic Dollar Shortage," with "Rejoinder" by C. P. Kindleberger, *American Economic Review*, XXXIX (September), 970–75.

——. 1959. *Monetary Policy under the International Gold Standard: 1880–1914*. New York: Federal Reserve Bank of New York.

——. 1963. *Short-Term Capital Movements under the Pre-1914 Gold Standard*, Princeton Studies in International Finance No. 11. Princeton: International Finance Section, Princeton University.

——. 1968. *Patterns of Fluctuation in International Investment Before 1914*. Princeton Studies in International Finance No. 21. Princeton: International Finance Section, Princeton University.

Board of Governors of the Federal Reserve System. 1943. *Banking and Monetary Statistics*. Washington: Board of Governors.

Branson, W. H. 1968. *Financial Capital Flows in the United States Balance of Payments*. Amsterdam: North-Holland Publishing Company.

——. 1969a. "Review" of G. C. Hufbauer and F. M. Adler, *Overseas Manufacturing Investment and the Balance of Payments*, in *Journal of Finance*, XXIV (June), 583–85.

——. 1969b. "The Minimum Covered Interest Differential Needed for International Arbitrage Activity," *Journal of Political Economy*, 77 (November-December), 1028–35.

——. 1970. "Monetary Policy and the New View of International Capital Movements," *Brookings Paper on Economic Activity*, 2, 235–62.

Brems, H. 1956. "The Foreign Trade Accelerator and the International Transmission of Growth," *Econometrica*, 24 (July), 223–38.

Brown, A. J. 1960. "Britain in the World Economy, 1870–1914," *Yorkshire Bulletin of Economic and Social Research*, 17 (May), 46–60.

Bryant, R. C. 1968. "Balance of Payments Adjustment: National Targets and International Inconsistency," Proceedings of the Business and Economic Statistics Section of the American Statistical Association.

Canterbery, E. R. 1971. "A Theory of Foreign Exchange Speculation under Alternative Systems," *Journal of Political Economy*, 79 (May-June), 407–36.

Caves, R. E. 1970. "Export-Led Growth," in W. A. Eltis *et al.* (eds.), *Induction, Growth and Trade: Essays in Honour of Roy Harrod.* Oxford: Clarendon Press, 234–54.

Caves, R. E., Reuber, G. L., *et al.* 1971. *Capital Transfers and Economic Policy: Canada, 1951–1962.* Cambridge: Harvard University Press.

Chacholiades, M. 1971. "The Classical Theory of International Adjustment: A Restatement," *Econometrica* (forthcoming).

Chiang, A. 1967. *Fundamental Methods of Mathematical Economics.* New York: McGraw-Hill.

Clark, P. B. 1970a. "Demand for International Reserves: A Cross-Country Analysis," *Canadian Journal of Economics*, III (November), 577–94.

———. 1970b. "Optimum International Reserves and the Speed of Adjustment," *Journal of Political Economy*, 78 (March-April), 356–76.

Clendenning, E. W. 1970. *The Euro-Dollar Market.* Oxford: Clarendon Press.

Cohen, B. J. 1966. *Adjustment Costs and the Distribution of New Reserves.* Studies in International Finance No. 18. Princeton: International Finance Section, Princeton University.

———. 1967. "Reparations in the Postwar Period: A Survey," Banca Nazionale del Lavoro, *Quarterly Review*, No. 82 (September), 268–88.

Cooper, R. N. 1966. "The Balance of Payments in Review," *Journal of Political Economy*, LXXIV (August), 379–95.

———. 1968a. "The Balance of Payments," in R. E. Caves and Associates, *Britain's Economic Prospects.* Washington: The Brookings Institution.

———. 1968b. *The Economics of Interdependence: Economic Policy in the Atlantic Community.* New York: McGraw-Hill Book Company for the Council on Foreign Relations.

———. 1969a. "Macroeconomic Policy Adjustment in Interdependent Economics," *Quarterly Journal of Economics*, LXXXIII (February), 1–24.

———. 1969b. "Review" of G. C. Hufbauer and F. M. Adler, *Overseas Manufacturing Investment and the Balance of Payments*, in *Journal of Economic Literature*, VII (December), 1208–11.

———. 1970. "Vers un marché international des capitaux?," *Bulletin d'Information et de Documentation*, National Bank of Belgium, XLV (January), 1–18.

———. 1971. *Currency Devaluation in Developing Countries.* Essays in International Finance, No. 86. Princeton: International Finance Section, Princeton University.

Corden, W. M. 1960. "The Geometric Representation of Policies to Attain Internal and External Balance," *Review of Economic Studies*, XXVIII (October), 1–22. Reprinted in R. N. Cooper (ed.), *International Finance: Selected Readings.* Middlesex: Penguin Books, Ltd., 1969.

———. 1971. "The Effects of Trade on the Rate of Growth," in J. Bhagwati *et al.* (eds.), *Trade, Balance of Payments and Growth: Papers in International Economics in Honour of Charles P. Kindleberger.* Amsterdam: North-Holland Publishing Company.

Costa, G. 1970. "The Effects of a Positive Trade Balance on the Rate of Growth: A Keynesian Approach," unpublished paper, University of Michigan.

Courchene, T. J. and Youssef, G. M. 1967. "The Demand for International Reserves," *Journal of Political Economy*, 75 (August, Part I), 404–11.

Davis, T. E. 1969. "Exchange Rate Adjustment under the Par Value System 1946–68," Federal Reserve Bank of Kansas City, *Monthly Review* (September-October), 3–10.

Deardorff, A. V. 1971. "A Neoclassical Growth Model with Unbalanced Trade" (in process).

Dernburg, T. F. 1970. "Exchange Rates and Co-ordinated Stabilization Policy," *Canadian Journal of Economics*, III (February), 1–13.

Despres, E., Kindleberger, C. P., and Salant, W. S. 1966. "The Dollar and World Liquidity: A Minority View," *The Economist* (London), February 5.

de Vries, M. G. 1965. "Multiple Exchange Rates: Expectations and Experiences," IMF, *Staff Papers*, XII (July), 282–313.

———. 1969a. "Exchange Rate Adjustment," in J. K. Horsefield (ed.), *The International Monetary Fund 1945–1965. Vol. II: Analysis*. Washington: International Monetary Fund.

———. 1969b. "Multiple Exchange Rates," in J. K. Horsefield (ed.), *The International Monetary Fund 1945–1965, Vol. II: Analysis*. Washington: International Monetary Fund.

Domar, E. D. 1950. "The Effect of Foreign Investment on the Balance of Payments," *American Economic Review*, XL (December), 805–26.

Dunn, R. M., Jr. 1971. *Canada's Experience with Fixed and Flexible Exchange Rates in a North American Capital Market*. Washington: Canadian-American Committee.

Dunning, J. H. 1969. *The Reddaway and Hufbauer/Adler Reports on the Foreign Investment Controversy*. London: Waterlow and Sons, Ltd.

Einzig, P. 1961. *A Dynamic Theory of Forward Exchange*. London: Macmillan.

———. 1965. *The Euro-Dollar System*. Second Edition. New York: St. Martin's Press.

Farrell, M. J. 1966. "Profitable Speculation," *Economica, XXXIII* (May), 183–93.

Federal Reserve Bank of Boston. 1969. *The International Adjustment Mechanism*. Proceedings of the Monetary Conference (October).

Fieleke, N. S. 1971a. "Accounting for the Balance of Payments," *New England Economic Review*. Federal Reserve Bank of Boston (May-June).

———. 1971b. *The Welfare Effects of Controls over Capital Exports from the United States*. Essays in International Finance, No. 82. Princeton: International Finance Section, Princeton University.

Flanders, M. J. 1971. *The Demand for International Reserves*. Princeton Studies in International Finance, No. 27. Princeton: International Finance Section, Princeton University.

Fleming, J. M. 1951. "On Making the Best of Balance of Payments Restrictions on Imports," *Economic Journal*, LXI (March), 48–71. Reprinted in R. E. Caves and H. G. Johnson (eds.), *Readings in International Economics*, Homewood: Richard D. Irwin, 1968; reprinted in J. M. Fleming, *Essays in International Economics*, London: George Allen and Unwin Ltd., 1971.

———. 1962. "Domestic Financial Policies under Fixed and Floating Exchange Rates," IMF, *Staff Papers*, IX (November), 369–80. Reprinted in J. M. Fleming, *Essays in International Economics*, London: George Allen and Unwin, Ltd., 1971.

———. 1967. *Toward Assessing the Need for International Reserves*. Essays in International Finance, No. 58. Princeton: International Finance Section, Princeton University (February). Reprinted in J. M. Fleming, *Essays in International Economics*, London: George Allen and Unwin, Ltd., 1971.

————. 1968a. *Guidelines for Balance-of-Payments Adjustment under the Par-Value System.* Essays in International Finance, No. 67. Princeton: International Finance Section, Princeton University. Reprinted in J. M. Fleming, *Essays in International Economics,* London: George Allen and Unwin, Ltd., 1971.

————. 1968b. "Targets and Instruments," IMF, *Staff Papers,* XV (November), 387–402.

————. 1971a. "On Exchange Rate Unification," *Economic Journal,* 81 (September), 467–88.

————. 1971b. "The SDR: Some Problems and Possibilities," IMF, *Staff Papers,* XVIII (March), 25–47.

Floyd, J. E. 1969. "Monetary and Fiscal Policy in a World of Capital Mobility," *Review of Economic Studies,* XXXVI (October), 503–17.

Food Research Institute Studies. 1967. "Proceedings of a Symposium on Price Effects of Speculation in Organized Commodity Markets," Supplement to VII.

Ford, A. G. 1960. *The Gold Standard 1880–1914: Britain and Argentina.* Oxford: Clarendon Press.

————. 1964. "Bank Rate, the British Balance of Payments, and the Burdens of Adjustment, 1870–1914," *Oxford Economic Papers,* 16 (March), 24–39.

————. 1965. "Overseas Lending and Internal Fluctuations: 1870–1919," *Yorkshire Bulletin of Economic and Social Research,* 17 (May), 19–31.

Freedman, C. 1970. *Long-Term Capital Flows Between the United States and Canada,* unpublished doctoral dissertation, M.I.T.

Friedman, M. 1953. "The Case for Flexible Exchange Rates" in *Essays in Positive Economics.* Chicago: University of Chicago Press. Reprinted in R. E. Caves and H. G. Johnson (eds.), *Readings in International Economics,* Homewood: Richard D. Irwin, Inc., 1968.

Gailliot, H. J. 1970. "Purchasing Power Parity as an Explanation of Long-Term Changes in Exchange Rates," *Journal of Money, Credit, and Banking,* II (August), 348–57.

Glahe, F. R. 1966. "Professional and Nonprofessional Speculation, Profitability, and Stability," *Southern Economic Journal,* XXXIII (July), 43–48.

Goldfeld, S. M. 1966. *Commercial Bank Behavior and Economic Activity.* Amsterdam: North-Holland Publishing Company.

Goodhart, C. A. E. 1970. "The Importance of Money," Bank of England, *Quarterly Bulletin,* 10 (June), 159–98.

Gordon, R. J. 1965. "Unemployment, the Balance of Payments, and the Growth Goal," unpublished paper, M.I.T.

Grubel, H. G. 1963. *International Monetary Reform: Plans and Issues.* Stanford: Stanford University Press.

————. 1964. "The Benefits and Costs of Being the World's Banker," *National Banking Review,* 2 (December), 189–212.

————. 1966. *Forward Exchange, Speculation, and the International Flow of Capital.* Stanford: Stanford University Press.

————. 1968. "Internationally Diversified Portfolios: Welfare Gains and Capital Flows," *American Economic Review,* LVIII (December), 1299–1314.

————. 1969a. "The Distribution of Seigniorage from International Liquidity Creation," in R. A. Mundell and A. K. Swoboda (eds.), *Monetary Problems of the International Economy.* Chicago: University of Chicago Press.

————. 1969b. *The International Monetary System.* Middlesex: Penguin Books Ltd.

————. 1970. "The Theory of Optimum Currency Areas," *Canadian Journal of Economics,* III (May), 318–24.

Haberler, G. 1949. "The Market for Foreign Exchange and the Stability of the

Balance of Payments," *Kyklos*, III, 193–218. Reprinted in R. N. Cooper (ed.), *International Finance: Selected Readings*. Middlesex: Penguin Books Ltd., 1969.

Haberler, G. 1953. "Reflections on the Future of the Bretton Woods System," *American Economic Review*, LXIII (May), 84–87.

Hahn, F. 1959. "The Balance of Payments in a Monetary Economy," *Review of Economic Studies*, XXVI (February), 110–25.

Halm, G. N. (ed.). 1970. *Approaches to Greater Flexibility of Exchange Rates*. Princeton: Princeton University Press.

Harberger, A. C. 1950. "Currency Depreciation, Income, and the Balance of Trade," *Journal of Political Economy*, LVIII (February), 47–60. Reprinted in R. E. Caves and H. G. Johnson (eds.), *Readings in International Economics*. Homewood: Richard D. Irwin, Inc., 1968.

Harkness, J. P. 1970. "Monetary-Fiscal Policy and Portfolio Balance Under Fixed Exchange Rates," Discussion Paper No. 96, Harvard Institute of Economic Research.

Hause, J. C. 1966. "The Welfare Costs of Disequilibrium Exchange Rates," *Journal of Political Economy*, 74 (August), 333–52.

Hawkins, R. G. 1968. "Stabilizing Forces and Canadian Exchange-Rate Fluctuations," *The Bulletin*, No. 50–51 (July). New York University, Institute of Finance.

Heller, H. R. 1966. "Optimal International Reserves," *Economic Journal*, LXXVI (June), 296–311.

———. 1968. "The Transactions Demand for International Means of Payments," *Journal of Political Economy*, 76 (January-February), 141–45.

———. 1970. "Wealth and International Reserves," *Review of Economics and Statistics*, LII (May), 212–14.

Helliwell, J. 1969. "Monetary and Fiscal Policies for an Open Economy," *Oxford Economic Papers*, 21 (March), 35–55.

Hemming, M. F. W. and Corden, W. M. 1958. "Import Restriction as an Instrument of Balance-of-Payments Policy," *Economic Journal*, LXVIII (September), 483–510.

Hirsch, F. 1971. "SDR's and the Working of the Gold Exchange Standard," IMF, *Staff Papers*, XVIII (July), 221–53.

Hirschman, A. O. 1949. "Devaluation and the Trade Balance," *Review of Economics and Statistics*, XXXI (February), 50–53.

Holzman, F. D. and Zellner, A. 1958. "The Foreign-Trade and Balanced-Budget Multipliers," *American Economic Review*, XLVIII (March), 73–91.

Host-Madsen, P. 1962. "Asymmetries Between Balance of Payments Surpluses and Deficits," IMF, *Staff Papers*, IX (July), 182–201.

Houthakker, H. 1957. "Can Speculators Forecast Prices?" *Review of Economics and Statistics*, XXXIX (May), 153–57.

Hufbauer, G. C. and Adler, F. M. 1968. *Overseas Manufacturing Investment and the Balance of Payments*. Tax Policy Research Study Number One. Washington: U.S. Government Printing Office.

Imlah, A. H. 1958. *Economic Elements in the Pax Britannica*. Cambridge: Harvard University Press.

Ingram, J. C. 1957. "Growth in Capacity and Canada's Balance of Payments," *American Economic Review*, XLVII (March), 93–104.

———. 1959. "State and Regional Payments Mechanisms," *Quarterly Journal of Economics*, 73 (November), 619–32.

———. 1966. *International Economic Problems*. New York: John Wiley and Sons, Inc.

International Monetary Fund. 1961. *Balance of Payments Manual*. 3rd ed. Washington: International Monetary Fund.

———. 1969. *The International Monetary Fund 1945–1965, Vol. III: Documents.* Washington: International Monetary Fund.

———. 1970. *International Reserves: Need and Availability.* Washington: International Monetary Fund.

Jasay, A. E. 1959. "The Social Choice Between Home and Overseas Investment," *Economic Journal,* LXX (March), 105–13.

Jensen, B. C. 1966. *The Impact of Reparations on the Post-War Finnish Economy.* Homewood: Richard D. Irwin, Inc.

Johnson, H. G. 1951. "The Taxonomic Approach to Economic Policy," *Economic Journal,* LXI (December), 812–32.

———. 1953a. "A Diagrammatic Analysis of Income Variations and the Balance of Payments," *Quarterly Journal of Economics,* LXIV (November), 623–32.

———. 1953b. "Equilibrium Growth in an Open Economy," *Canadian Journal of Economics and Political Science,* XIX (November), 478–500. Reprinted in H. G. Johnson, *International Trade and Economic Growth,* London: George Allen and Unwin, Ltd., 1958.

———. 1956. "The Transfer Problem and Exchange Stability," *Journal of Political Economy,* LXIV (June), 212–25. Reprinted in R. E. Caves and H. G. Johnson (eds.), *Readings in International Economics,* Homewood: Richard D. Irwin, Inc., 1968.

———. 1958a. *International Trade and Economic Growth.* London: George Allen and Unwin, Ltd.

———. 1958b. "Towards a General Theory of the Balance of Payments," in *International Trade and Economic Growth,* London: George Allen and Unwin, Ltd., 1958. Reprinted in R. E. Caves and H. G. Johnson (eds.), *Readings in International Economics,* Homewood: Richard D. Irwin, Inc., 1968.

———. 1962. *Money, Trade and Economic Growth.* London: George Allen and Unwin, Ltd.

———. 1963. "Equilibrium under Fixed Exchanges," *American Economic Review,* LIII (May), 112–19.

———. 1964. "The International Competitive Position of the United States and the Balance of Payments for 1968: A Review Article," *Review of Economics and Statistics,* XLVI (February), 14–32.

———. 1966a. "Some Aspects of the Theory of Economic Policy in a World of Capital Mobility," in T. Bagiotti (ed.), *Essays in Honour of Marco Fanno.* Padua: Cedam.

———. 1966b. "The Welfare Costs of Exchange Rate Stabilization," *Journal of Political Economy,* 74 (October), 512–18.

———. 1967. "Theoretical Problems of the International Monetary System," *Pakistan Development Review,* VII (Spring), 1–28. Reprinted in R. N. Cooper (ed.), *International Finance: Selected Readings.* Middlesex: Penguin Books Ltd., 1969.

———. 1969. "Appendix: A Note on Seigniorage and the Social Saving from Substituting Credit for Commodity Money," in R. A. Mundell and A. K. Swoboda (eds.), *Monetary Problems of the International Economy.* Chicago: University of Chicago Press.

———. 1970a. *Efficiency in Domestic and International Money Supply.* University of Surrey, International Economics, Number 3 (March).

———. 1970b. "The Case for Flexible Exchange Rates, 1969," in G. N. Halm (ed.), *Approaches to Greater Flexibility of Exchange Rates.* Princeton: Princeton University Press.

———. 1970c. "The Efficiency and Welfare Implications of the International Corporation," in C. P. Kindleberger (ed.), *The International Corporation: A Symposium.* Cambridge: M.I.T. Press.

Johnson, H. G. 1971a. "Problems of European Monetary Union," *Euromoney* (April), 39–43.

———. 1971b. "The Monetary Approach to Balance-of-Payments Theory." A lecture delivered at the Graduate Institute of International Studies, Geneva, Switzerland, February 5–7, 1971.

Jones, R. W. 1960. "Depreciation and the Dampening Effect of Income Changes," *Review of Economics and Statistics*, XLII (February), 74–80.

———. 1967. "International Capital Movements and the Theory of Tariffs and Trade," *Quarterly Journal of Economics*, L (February), 1–38.

———. 1968. "Monetary and Fiscal Policy for an Economy with Fixed Exchange Rates," *Journal of Political Economy*, 76, Part II (July-August), 921–43.

Kelly, M. G. 1970. "The Demand for International Reserves," *American Economic Review*, LX (September), 655–67.

Kemp, M. C. 1963. "Speculation, Profitability, and Price Stability," *Review of Economics and Statistics*, XLV (May), 185–89.

———. 1964. *The Pure Theory of International Trade*. Englewood Cliffs: Prentice-Hall, Inc.

———. 1966a. "Monetary and Fiscal Policy under Alternative Assumptions about International Capital Mobility," *Economic Record*, 42 (December), 598–605.

———. 1966b. "The Gain from International Trade and Investment: A Neo-Heckscher-Ohlin Approach," *American Economic Review*, LVI (September), 788–809.

Kenen, P. B. 1960. "International Liquidity and the Balance of Payments of a Reserve-Currency Country," *Quarterly Journal of Economics*, LXXIV (November), 572–86.

———. 1969. "The Theory of Optimum Currency Areas: An Eclectic View," in R. A. Mundell and A. K. Swoboda (eds.), *Monetary Problems of the International Economy*. Chicago: University of Chicago Press.

Kenen, P. B. and Yudin, E. 1965. "The Demand for International Reserves," *Review of Economics and Statistics*, 47 (August), 242–50.

Keynes, J. M. 1923. *A Tract on Monetary Reform*. London: Macmillan.

———. 1929. "The German Transfer Problem," *Economic Journal*, XXXIX (March), 1–7. Reprinted in H. S. Ellis and L. A. Metzler (eds.), *Readings in the Theory of International Trade*. Philadelphia: The Blakiston Company, 1949.

Kindleberger, C. P. 1949. "The Foreign-Trade Multiplier, The Propensity to Import, and Balance-of-Payments Equilibrium," *American Economic Review*, XXXIX (March), 491–94.

———. 1965. *Balance-of-Payments Deficits and the International Market for Liquidity*. Princeton Essays in International Finance, No. 46. Princeton: International Finance Section, Princeton University.

———. 1967. "The Pros and Cons of an International Capital Market," *Zeitschrift Fur Die Gesamte Staatswissenschaft*, Band 123 (Oktober), 600–17.

———. 1968. *International Economics*. 4th Edition. Homewood: Richard D. Irwin, Inc.

———. 1969a. *American Business Abroad*. New Haven: Yale University Press.

———. 1969b. "Measuring Equilibrium in the Balance of Payments," *Journal of Political Economy*, 77 (November-December), 873–91.

———. 1969c. "The Euro-Dollar and the Internationalization of United States Monetary Policy," Banca Nazionale del Lavoro, *Quarterly Review*, No. 88 (March), 3–15.

Komiya, R. 1969. "Economic Growth and the Balance of Payments: A Monetary Approach," *Journal of Political Economy*, 77 (January-February), 35–48.

Krause, L. B. and Dam, K. W. 1964. *Federal Tax Treatment of Foreign Income.* Washington: The Brookings Institution.

Krause, L. B. 1971a. "Fixed, Flexible, and Gliding Exchange Rates," *Journal of Money, Credit, and Banking*, 3 (May), 321–38.

———. 1971b. *Sequel to Bretton Woods: A Proposal to Reform the World Monetary System.* A Staff Paper. Washington: The Brookings Institution.

Kravis, I. B. 1970. "Trade as a Handmaiden of Growth: Similarities between the Nineteenth and Twentieth Centuries," *Economic Journal*, LXXX (December), 850–72.

Krueger, A. O. 1965. "The Impact of Alternative Government Policies under Varying Exchange Systems," *Quarterly Journal of Economics*, LXXIX (May), 195–208.

———. 1968. "Reply" to M. Michaely, "The Impact of Alternative Government Policies under Varying Exchange Rate Systems: Comment," *Quarterly Journal of Economics*, LXXXII (August), 508–13.

———. 1969. "Balance-of-Payments Theory," *Journal of Economic Literature*, VII (March), 1–26.

———. 1971. "The Role of Home Goods and Money in Exchange Rate Adjustment," in W. Sellekaerts (ed.), *Essays in Honor of J. Tinbergen* (forthcoming).

Laffer, A. B. 1971. "An Anti-traditional Theory of the Balance-of-Payments under Fixed Exchange Rates," *American Economic Review* (forthcoming).

Lamfalussy, A. 1963a. "Contribution à une théorie de la croissance en economie ouverte, *Recherches Economiques de Louvain*, XXIX (December), 715–34.

———. 1963b. *The United Kingdom and the Six: An Essay on Economic Growth in Western Europe.* Homewood: Richard D. Irwin, Inc.

Lanyi, A. 1969. *The Case for Floating Exchange Rates Reconsidered.* Essays in International Finance, No. 72. Princeton: International Finance Section, Princeton University.

Lary, H. B. 1963. *Problems of the United States as World Banker and Trader.* New York: National Bureau of Economic Research.

Lary, H. B. and Associates. 1943. *The United States in the World Economy.* U.S. Department of Commerce, Bureau of Foreign and Domestic Commerce, Economic Series No. 23. Washington: Government Printing Office.

Laursen, S. and Metzler, L. A. 1950. "Flexible Exchange Rates and the Theory of Employment," *Review of Economics and Statistics*, XXXII (November), 281–99.

Leamer, E. E. 1968. "A Graphical Exposition of Spot and Forward Exchange-Market Equilibrium," Seminar Discussion Paper No. 4 (unpublished), Research Seminar in International Economics. University of Michigan, Ann Arbor: Department of Economics.

Leamer, E. E. and Stern, R. M. 1970. *Quantitative International Economics.* Boston: Allyn and Bacon, Inc.

———. 1972. "Problems in the Theory and Empirical Estimation of International Capital Movements," in F. Machlup *et al.* (eds.), *International Mobility and Movement of Capital.* New York: Columbia University Press.

Lederer, W. 1963. *The Balance on Foreign Transactions: Problems of Definition and Measurement.* Special Paper in International Economics, No. 5. Princeton: International Finance Section, Princeton University.

Lee, C. H. 1969. "A Stock-Adjustment Analysis of Capital Movements: The United States-Canadian Case," *Journal of Political Economy*, 77 (July-August), 512–23.

Leland, H. E. 1971. "Optimal Forward Exchange Positions," *Journal of Political Economy*, 79 (March-April), 257–69.

Levin, J. H. 1970a. *Forward Exchange and Internal-External Equilibrium.* Michigan International Business Studies, Number 12. University of Michigan. Ann Arbor: Bureau of Business Research, Graduate School of Business Administration.

————. 1970b. "IS, LM, and External Equilibrium: Some Extensions" (mimeographed).

————. 1972. "International Capital Mobility and the Assignment Problem," *Oxford Economic Papers*, 24 (March), 54–67.

Levy, H. and Sarnat, M. 1970. "International Diversification of Investment Portfolios," *American Economic Review*, LX (September), 668–75.

Lindert, P. H. 1969. *Key Currencies and Gold, 1900–1913.* Princeton Studies in International Finance, No. 24. Princeton: International Finance Section, Princeton University.

Little, J. S. 1969. "The Euro-dollar Market: Its Nature and Impact," *New England Economic Review.* Federal Reserve Bank of Boston (May-June).

Lybeck, J. A. 1970. "The Effects of Trade on the Rate of Growth: A Mathematical Investigation of the Corden Effects," unpublished paper, University of Michigan.

MacDougall, G. D. A. 1960. "The Benefits and Costs of Private Investment from Abroad: A Theoretical Approach," *Economic Record*, Special Issue (March). Reprinted in R. E. Caves and H. G. Johnson (eds.), *Readings in International Economics.* Homewood: Richard D. Irwin, Inc., 1968.

Machlup, F. 1939, 1940. "The Theory of Foreign Exchanges," *Economica,* VI (November and February), 375–97 and 23–49. Reprinted in F. Machlup, *International Payments, Debts, and Gold.* New York: Charles Scribner's Sons, 1964.

————. 1943. *International Trade and the National Income Multiplier.* Reprints of Economic Classics. New York: Augustus M. Kelley, Bookseller, 1965.

————. 1950. "Three Concepts of the Balance of Payments and the So-called Dollar Shortage," *Economic Journal*, LX (March), 46–68. Reprinted in F. Machlup, *International Payments, Debts, and Gold.* New York: Charles Scribner's Sons, 1964.

————. 1955. "Relative Prices and Aggregate Spending in the Analysis of Devaluation," *American Economic Review*, LXV (June), 255–78. Reprinted in F. Machlup, *International Payments, Debts, and Gold.* New York: Charles Scribner's Sons, 1964.

————. 1956. "The Terms-of-Trade Effects of Devaluation upon Real Income and the Balance of Trade," *Kyklos*, IX, 417–52. Reprinted in F. Machlup, *International Payments, Debts, and Gold.* New York: Charles Scribner's Sons, 1964.

————. 1958. "Comment: Strategic Factors in Balance of Payments Adjustment," *Review of Economics and Statistics*, XL (February, Supplement), 137–40.

————. 1964. *International Payments, Debts, and Gold.* New York: Charles Scribner's Sons.

————. 1966. "The Need for Monetary Reserves," Banca Nazionale del Lavoro, *Quarterly Review*, No. 78 (September), 175–222.

————. 1968. "The Transfer Gap of the United States," Banca Nazionale del Lavoro, *Quarterly Review*, No.86 (September), 195–238.

————. 1970. "The Forward Exchange Market: Misunderstandings Between Practitioners and Economists," in G. N. Halm (ed.), *Approaches to Greater Flexibility of Exchange Rates.* Princeton: Princeton University Press.

Makin, J. H. 1971. "Swaps and Roosa Bonds as an Index of the Cost of Cooperation in the 'Crisis Zone'," *Quarterly Journal of Economics*, LXXXV (May), 349–56.

Marsh, D. B. 1969. "Canada's Experience with a Floating Exchange Rate: A Vindication of Free Markets in Exchange," in R. Z. Aliber (ed.), *The International Market for Foreign Exchange*. New York: Praeger.

———. 1970. "Canada's Experience with a Floating Rate, 1950–62," in G. N. Halm (ed.), *Approaches to Greater Flexibility of Exchange Rates*. Princeton: Princeton University Press.

Marshall, A. 1923. *Money, Credit, and Commerce*. London: Macmillan.

Massell, B. F. 1964. "Exports, Capital Imports and Economic Growth," *Kyklos*, XVII (Fasc. 4), 627–34.

McKinnon, R. I. 1963. "Optimum Currency Areas," *American Economic Review*, LIII (September), 717–25.

———. 1969a. "Portfolio Balance and International Payments Adjustment," in R. A. Mundell and A. K. Swoboda (eds.), *Monetary Problems of the International Economy*. Chicago: University of Chicago Press.

———. 1969b. *Private and Official International Money: The Case for the Dollar*. Essays in International Finance, No. 74. Princeton: International Finance Section, Princeton University.

McKinnon, R. I. and Oates, W. R. 1966. *The Implications of International Economic Integration for Monetary, Fiscal, and Exchange-Rate Policy*. Princeton Studies in International Finance, No. 16. Princeton: International Finance Section, Princeton University.

McLeod, A. N. 1965. "A Critique of the Fluctuating-Exchange-Rate Policy in Canada," *The Bulletin*, No. 34-35 (April-June). New York: New York University, Institute of Finance.

Meade, J. E. 1951. *The Balance of Payments*. London: Oxford University Press.

———. 1955. *Trade and Welfare*. London: Oxford University Press.

———. 1957. "The Balance of Payments Problems of a European Free-Trade Area." *Economic Journal*, 67 (September), 379–96.

Meier, G. M. 1953. "Economic Development and the Transfer Mechanism: Canada, 1895–1913," *Canadian Journal of Economics and Political Science*, XIX (February), 1–19.

Mellish, G. H. 1968. "Official Intervention and the Flexible Canadian Dollar, 1950–1962," *The Bulletin*, No. 50–51 (July). New York: New York University, Institute of Finance.

Metzler, L. A. 1942a. "The Transfer Problem Reconsidered," *Journal of Political Economy*, L (June), 397–414. Reprinted in H. S. Ellis and L. A. Metzler (eds.), *Readings in the Theory of International Trade*. Philadelphia: Blakiston, 1949.

———. 1942b. "Underemployment Equilibrium in International Trade," *Econometrica*, 10 (April), 97–112.

———. 1947. "Exchange Rates and Prices," from "Exchange Rates and the International Monetary Fund," *International Monetary Policies*, Postwar Economic Studies No. 7. Washington: Board of Governors of the Federal Reserve System. Reprinted in W. R. Allen and C. L. Allen, *Foreign Trade and Finance*. New York: The Macmillan Co., 287–95.

Michaely, M. 1960. "Relative-Prices and Income-Absorption Approaches to Devaluation: A Partial Reconciliation," *American Economic Review*, L (March), 144–47.

Mikesell, R. F. (ed.). 1962. *U.S. Private and Government Investment Abroad*. Eugene: University of Oregon Press.

———. 1968. *The Economics of Foreign Aid*. Chicago: Aldine Publishing Company.

Miller, N. C. and Whitman, M. v. N. 1970. "A Mean-Variance Analysis of United States Long-Term Portfolio Foreign Investment," *Quarterly Journal of Economics*, LXXXIV (May), 175–96.

Mintz, N. N. 1970. "Monetary Union and Economic Integration," *The Bulletin*, No. 64 (April). New York: New York University, Institute of Finance.

Modigliani, F. 1966. "International Capital Movements, Fixed Parities, and Monetary and Fiscal Policies" (mimeographed, October).

Moggridge, D. E. 1969. *The Return to Gold 1925: The Formulation of Economic Policy and its Critics.* University of Cambridge, Department of Applied Economics, Occasional Papers: 19. Cambridge: Cambridge University Press.

Morton, J. E. 1970. *Portfolio Balance, Growth, and Long-Run Balance-of-Payments Adjustment.* Unpublished doctoral dissertation, University of Michigan.

Mundell, R. A. 1961. "A Theory of Optimum Currency Areas," *American Economic Review*, LI (September), 657–65. Reprinted in R. A. Mundell, *International Economics*. New York, The Macmillan Co., 1968.

————. 1968. International Economics. New York: The Macmillan Co.

————. 1971. *Monetary Theory*. Pacific Palisades: Goodyear Publishing Company, Inc.

Negishi, T. 1968. "Approaches to the Analysis of Devaluation," *International Economic Review*, 9 (June), 218–27.

Niehans, J. 1968. "Monetary and Fiscal Policies in Open Economies under Fixed Exchange Rates: An Optimizing Approach," *Journal of Political Economy*, 76, Part II (July-August), 893–920.

————. 1970. "The Need for Reserves of a Single Country," in International Monetary Fund, *International Reserves: Needs and Availability*. Washington: International Monetary Fund.

Nobel, M. M. 1967. "Fiscal and Monetary Policies in an Open Economy," University of Michigan, Ann Arbor (mimeographed).

Nurkse, R. 1944. *International Currency Experience*. Princeton: League of Nations.

————. 1945. *Conditions of International Monetary Equilibrium*. Princeton Essays in International Finance, No. 4. Princeton: International Finance Section, Princeton University. Reprinted in H. S. Ellis and L. A. Metzler (eds.), *Readings in the Theory of International Trade*. Philadelphia: The Blakiston Co., 1949.

————. 1952. "Domestic and International Equilibrium," is S. E. Harris (ed.), *The New Economics*. New York: Alfred A. Knopf.

————. 1961. *Equilibrium and Growth in the World Economy*. G. Haberler and R. M. Stern (eds.). Cambridge: Harvard University Press.

Obst, N. P. 1967. "A Connection Between Speculation and Stability in the Foreign Exchange Market," *Southern Economic Journal*, XXXIV (July), 146–49.

Officer, L. H. 1968. *An Econometric Model of Canada under the Fluctuating Rate.* Cambridge: Harvard University Press.

Officer, L. H. and Willett, T. D. 1969. "Reserve-Asset Preferences and the Confidence Problem in the Crisis Zone," *Quarterly Journal of Economics*, LXXXIII (November), 688–95.

————. 1970. "The Covered-Arbitrage Schedule: A Survey of Recent Developments," *Journal of Money, Credit, and Banking*, II (May), 247–57.

Ohlin, B. 1929. "The Reparation Problem: A Discussion," *Economic Journal*, XXXIX (June), 172–78. Reprinted in H. S. Ellis and L. A. Metzler (eds.), *Readings in the Theory of International Trade*. Philadelphia: The Blakiston Company, 1949.

Orcutt, G. H. 1950. "Measurement of Price Elasticities in International Trade," *Review of Economics and Statistics*, XXXII (May), 117–32. Reprinted in R. E. Caves and H. G. Johnson (eds.), *Readings in International Economics*. Homewood: Richard D. Irwin, Inc., 1968.

Ott, D. J. and Ott, A. F. 1968. "Monetary and Fiscal Policy: Goals and the Choice of Instruments," *Quarterly Journal of Economics*, LXXXVI (May), 313–25.

Patrick, J. 1968. "The Optimum Policy Mix: Convergence and Consistency," in P. B. Kenen and R. Lawrence (eds.), *The Open Economy: Essays on International Trade and Finance*. New York: Columbia University Press.

Pippenger, J. 1967. "The Canadian Experience with Flexible Exchange Rates," *American Economic Review*, LVII (May), 545–54.

Polak, J. J. 1947. "The Foreign Trade Multiplier," with "Comment" by G. Haberler, and "A Restatement," by J. J. Polak and G. Haberler, *American Economic Review*, XXXVII (December), 889–907.

Polk, J. *et al.* 1966. *U.S. Production Abroad and the Balance of Payments: A Survey of Corporate Investment Experience*. New York: National Industrial Conference Board.

Poole, W. 1967a. "Speculative Prices as Random Walks: An Analysis of Ten Time Series of Flexible Exchange Rates," *Southern Economic Journal*, XXXIII (April), 468–78.

———. 1967b. "The Stability of the Canadian Flexible Exchange Rate, 1950–62," *Canadian Journal of Economics and Political Science*, XXXIII (May), 205–17.

Powelson, J. 1955. *Economic Accounting*. New York: McGraw-Hill.

Reading, B. 1960. "The Forward Pound, 1951–59," *Economic Journal*, LXX (June), 309–19.

Reddaway, W. B. 1970. "Was $4.86 Inevitable in 1925?," *Lloyd's Bank Review*, No. 96 (April), 15–28.

Reddaway, W. B. *et al.* 1967. *Effects of U.K. Direct Investment Overseas: Interim Report*. University of Cambridge, Department of Applied Economics, Occasional Papers: 12. Cambridge: Cambridge University Press.

———. 1968. *Effects of U.K. Direct Investment Overseas: Final Report*. University of Cambridge, Department of Applied Economics, Occasional Papers: 15. Cambridge: Cambridge University Press.

Review Committee for Balance of Payments Statistics. 1965. *The Balance of Payments Statistics of the United States: A Review and Appraisal*. Washington: Government Printing Office.

Rhomberg, R. R. 1964. "A Model of the Canadian Economy under Fixed and Fluctuating Exchange Rates," *Journal of Political Economy*, LXII (February), 1–31.

———. 1966. "Trends in Payments Imbalances, 1962–64," IMF, *Staff Papers*, 13 (November), 371–95.

Richardson, J. D. 1969. "A Comment on Import Restriction as an Instrument of Balance-of-Payments Policy" (mimeographed, August).

———. 1971a. "Devaluation and the Terms of Trade," Social Systems Research Institute, University of Wisconsin, Workshop Series QM 7103 (mimeographed).

———. 1971b. "On 'Going Abroad': The Firm's Initial Foreign Investment Decision," *Quarterly Review of Economics and Business*, 11 (Winter), 7–22.

———. 1971c. "Theoretical Considerations in the Analysis of Foreign Direct Investment," *Western Economic Journal*, IX (March), 87–98.

Richardson, J. D. and Stern, R. M. 1970. "An IS-LM Exposition of Policies for Internal and External Balance," presented at the annual meeting of the Western Economic Association, University of California, Davis (mimeographed).

Robinson, J. 1947a. "Beggar-My-Neighbor Remedies for Unemployment," in *Essays in the Theory of Employment*. 2nd Edition. Oxford: Basil Blackwell. Reprinted in H. S. Ellis and L. A. Metzler, *Readings in the Theory of International Trade*. Philadelphia: The Blakiston Company, 1949.

———. 1947b. "The Foreign Exchanges," in *Essays in the Theory of Employment*. 2nd Edition. Oxford: Basil Blackwell. Reprinted in H. S. Ellis and L. A. Metzler (eds.) *Readings in the Theory of International Trade.* Philadelphia: The Blakiston Company, 1949.

Robinson, R. 1952. "A Geometrical Analysis of the Foreign Trade Multiplier," *Economic Journal,* LXII (September), 546–64.

Roper, D. E. 1970a. "Two Criteria for Determining Macroeconomic Policies in the World Economy," (mimeographed).

———. 1970b. *A Two-Country Analysis of the Distribution of Adjustment, Capital Flows amd Monetary Policy,* unpublished doctoral dissertation, University of Chicago.

———. 1971. "Macroeconomic Policies and the Distribution of the World Money Supply," *Quarterly Journal of Economics,* LXXXV (February), 119–46.

———. 1972. "A Note on the Mix of Policies and the Theory of Capital Movements," International Finance Discussion Paper No. 10 (March), Board of Governors of the Federal Reserve System.

Rueff, J. 1964. *The Age of Inflation.* Chicago: Henry Regnery Company.

Salant, W. S. 1969. "International Reserves and Payments Adjustment," Banca Nazionale del Lavoro, *Quarterly Review,* No. 90 (September), 281–308.

———. 1970. "Practical Techniques for Assessing the Need for World Reserves," in International Monetary Fund, *International Reserves: Needs and Availability.* Washington: International Monetary Fund.

Samuelson, P. A. 1952, 1954. "The Transfer Problem and Transport Costs," *Economic Journal,* LXII (June), 278–304 and LXIV (June), 264–89. Reprinted in abridged form in R. E. Caves and H. G. Johnson (eds.), *Readings in International Economics.* Homewood: Richard D. Irwin, Inc., 1968.

———. 1962. "The Gains From International Trade Once Again," *Economic Journal,* LXXII (December), 820–29. Reprinted in J. N. Bhagwati (ed.), *International Trade: Selected Readings.* Middlesex: Penguin Books Ltd., 1969.

———. 1964. "Theoretical Notes on Trade Problems," *Review of Economics and Statistics,* XLVI (May), 145–54.

———. 1971. "On the Trail of Conventional Beliefs About the Transfer Problem," in J. N. Bhagwati *et al.* (eds.), *Trade, Balance of Payments and Growth; Papers in International Economics in Honor of Charles P. Kindleberger,* Amsterdam: North-Holland Publishing Co.

Scitovsky, T. 1969. *Money and the Balance of Payments.* Chicago: Rand McNally and Company.

Smith, W. L. 1954. "Effects of Exchange Rate Adjustments on the Standard of Living," *American Economic Review,* XLIV (December), 808–25.

———. 1970. *Macroeconomics.* Homewood: Richard D. Irwin, Inc.

Snider, D. A. 1967. *Optimum Adjustment Processes and Currency Areas.* Essays in International Finance, No. 62. Princeton: International Finance Section, Princeton University.

Sohmen, E. 1961. *Flexible Exchange Rates.* Chicago: University of Chicago Press.

———. 1966. *The Theory of Forward Exchange.* Princeton Studies in International Finance, No. 17. Princeton: International Finance Section, Princeton University.

———. 1967. "Fiscal and Monetary Policies under Alternative Exchange Rate Systems," *Quarterly Journal of Economics,* LXXXI (August), 515–23.

———. 1969. *Flexible Exchange Rates.* 2nd Edition. Chicago: University of Chicago Press.

Sohmen, E. and Schneeweiss, H. 1969. "Fiscal and Monetary Policies under Alternative Exchange Rate Systems: A Correction," *Quarterly Journal of Economics,* LXXXIII (May), 336–40.

Spraos, J. 1959. "Speculation, Arbitrage, and Sterling," *Economic Journal,* LXIX (March), 1–21.

Stein, J. L. 1961. "Destabilizing Speculative Activity Can Be Profitable," *Review of Economics and Statistics*, XLIII (August), 301–02.

———. 1962. *The Nature and Efficiency of the Foreign Exchange Market*. Essays in International Finance, No. 40. Princeton: International Finance Section, Princeton University.

Stern, R. M. 1967. *Foreign Trade and Economic Growth in Italy*. New York: Praeger.

———. 1969. "International Financial Issues in Foreign Economic Assistance to the Less Developed Countries," in I. G. Stewart (ed.), *Economic Development and Structural Change*. Edinburgh: Edinburgh University Press.

Stolper, W. 1947. "The Volume of Foreign Trade and the Level of Income," *Quarterly Journal of Economics*, LXI (February), 285–310.

———. 1948. "Purchasing Power Parity and the Pound Sterling from 1919–1925," *Kyklos*, II, 240–69.

Stovel, J. A. 1959. *Canada in the World Economy*. Cambridge: Harvard University Press.

Takayama, A. 1969. "The Effects of Fiscal and Monetary Policies Under Flexible and Fixed Exchange Rates," *Canadian Journal of Economics*, II (May), 190–209.

Taussig, F. W. 1927. *International Trade*. New York: The Macmillan Co.

Telser, L. G. 1959. "A Theory of Speculation Relating Profitability and Stability," and "Reply" by W. J. Baumol, *Review of Economics and Statistics*, XLI (August), 295–301.

Thorn, R. S. 1967. "The Demand for International Reserves: A Note in Behalf of the Rejected Hypothesis," and Kenen and Yudin, "Demand for International Reserves: A Reply," *Review of Economics and Statistics*, 49 (November), 623–27.

Tinbergen, J. 1952. *On the Theory of Economic Policy*. Amsterdam: North-Holland Publishing Company.

Tobin, J. 1956. "The Interest-Elasticity of the Transactions Demand for Cash," *Review of Economics and Statistics*, XXXVIII (August), 241–47.

Triffin, R. 1960. *Gold and the Dollar Crisis*. New Haven: Yale University Press.

———. 1964. *The Evolution of the International Monetary System: Historical Reappraisal and Future Perspectives*. Princeton Studies in International Finance, No. 12. Princeton: International Finance Section, Princeton University.

Tsiang, S. C. 1950. "Balance of Payments and Domestic Flow of Income and Expenditures," IMF, *Staff Papers*, I (September), 254–88.

———. 1957. "An Experiment with a Flexible Exchange Rate System: The Case of Peru, 1950–54," IMF, *Staff Papers*, 5 (February), 449–76.

———. 1958. "A Theory of Foreign-Exchange Speculation under a Floating Exchange System," *Journal of Political Economy*, LXVI (October), 399–418.

———. 1959a. "Fluctuating Exchange Rates in Countries with Relatively Stable Economies: Some European Experiences After World War I," IMF, *Staff Papers*, 7 (October), 244–73.

———. 1959b. "The Theory of Forward Exchange and Effects of Government Intervention on the Forward Exchange Market," IMF, *Staff Papers*, VII (April), 75–106.

———. 1961. "The Role of Money in Trade-Balance Stability: Synthesis of the Elasticity and Absorption Approaches," *American Economic Review*, LI (December), 912–36. Reprinted in R. E. Caves and H. G. Johnson (eds.), *Readings in International Economics*. Homewood: Richard D. Irwin, Inc., 1968.

United Nations. 1949. *International Capital Movements during the Inter-War Period*. New York: United Nations.

U.S. Congress, Joint Economic Committee. 1969. *Linking Reserve Creation and Development Assistance*. Hearing Before the Subcommittee on International

Exchange and Payments, Ninety-First Congress, First Session. Washington: Government Printing Office.

Vanek, J. 1962. *International Trade: Theory and Economic Policy*. Homewood: Richard D. Irwin, Inc.

Vernon, R. 1966. "International Investment and International Trade in the Product Cycle," *Quarterly Journal of Economics*, LXXX (May), 191–207.

———. 1970. "Future of the Multinational Enterprise," in C. P. Kindleberger (ed.), *The International Corporation: A Symposium*. Cambridge: M.I.T. Press.

Viner, J. 1924. *Canada's Balance of International Indebtedness, 1900–1913*. Cambridge: Harvard University Press.

———. 1937. *Studies in the Theory of International Trade*. New York: Harper and Bros.

———. 1956. "Some International Aspects of Economic Stabilization," in L. D. White (ed.), *The State of the Social Sciences*. Chicago: University of Chicago Press.

Watkins, M. H. *et al.* 1968. *Foreign Ownership and the Structure of Canadian Industry: Report of the Task Force on the Structure of Canadian Industry*. Ottawa: Queen's Printer.

Whitman, M. v. N. 1970. *Policies for Internal and External Balance*. Special Papers in International Economics, No. 9. Princeton: International Finance Section, Princeton University.

Willett, T. D. and Forte, F. 1969. "Interest Rate Policy and External Balance," *Quarterly Journal of Economics*, LXXXIII (May), 242–62.

Willett, T. D. and Tower, E. 1970. "The Concept of Optimum Currency Areas and the Choice Between Fixed and Flexible Exchange Rates," in G. N. Halm (ed.), *Approaches to Greater Flexibility of Exchange Rates*. Princeton: Princeton University Press.

Williamson, J. G. 1963. *American Growth and the Balance of Payments, 1820–1913, A Study of the Long Swing*. Chapel Hill, N.C.: University of North Carolina Press.

Wonnacott, P. 1965. *The Canadian Dollar, 1948–1962*. Toronto: University of Toronto Press.

Wrightsman, D. 1970. "IS, LM, and External Equilibrium: A Graphical Analysis," *American Economic Review*, LX (March), 203–08.

Yamey, B. S. 1966. "Speculation and Price Stability: A Note," and "A Reply," by R. Z. Aliber, *Journal of Political Economy*, LXXIV (April), 206–08.

Yeager, L. B. 1958. "A Rehabilitation of Purchasing-Power Parity," *Journal of Political Economy*, LXVI (December), 516–30.

———. 1966. *International Monetary Relations*. New York: Harper and Row.

———. 1969. "Fluctuating Exchange Rates in the Nineteenth Century: The Experiences of Austria and Russia," in R. A. Mundell and A. K. Swoboda (eds.), *Monetary Problems of the International Economy*. Chicago: University of Chicago Press.

———. 1970. "Absorption and Elasticity: A Fuller Reconciliation," *Economica*, XXXVII (February), 68–77.

Zupnick, E. and Stern, R. M. 1964. "Devaluation in a Three-Country World," *Economia Internazionale*, XVII (November), 3–15.

Name Index

425

Subject Index